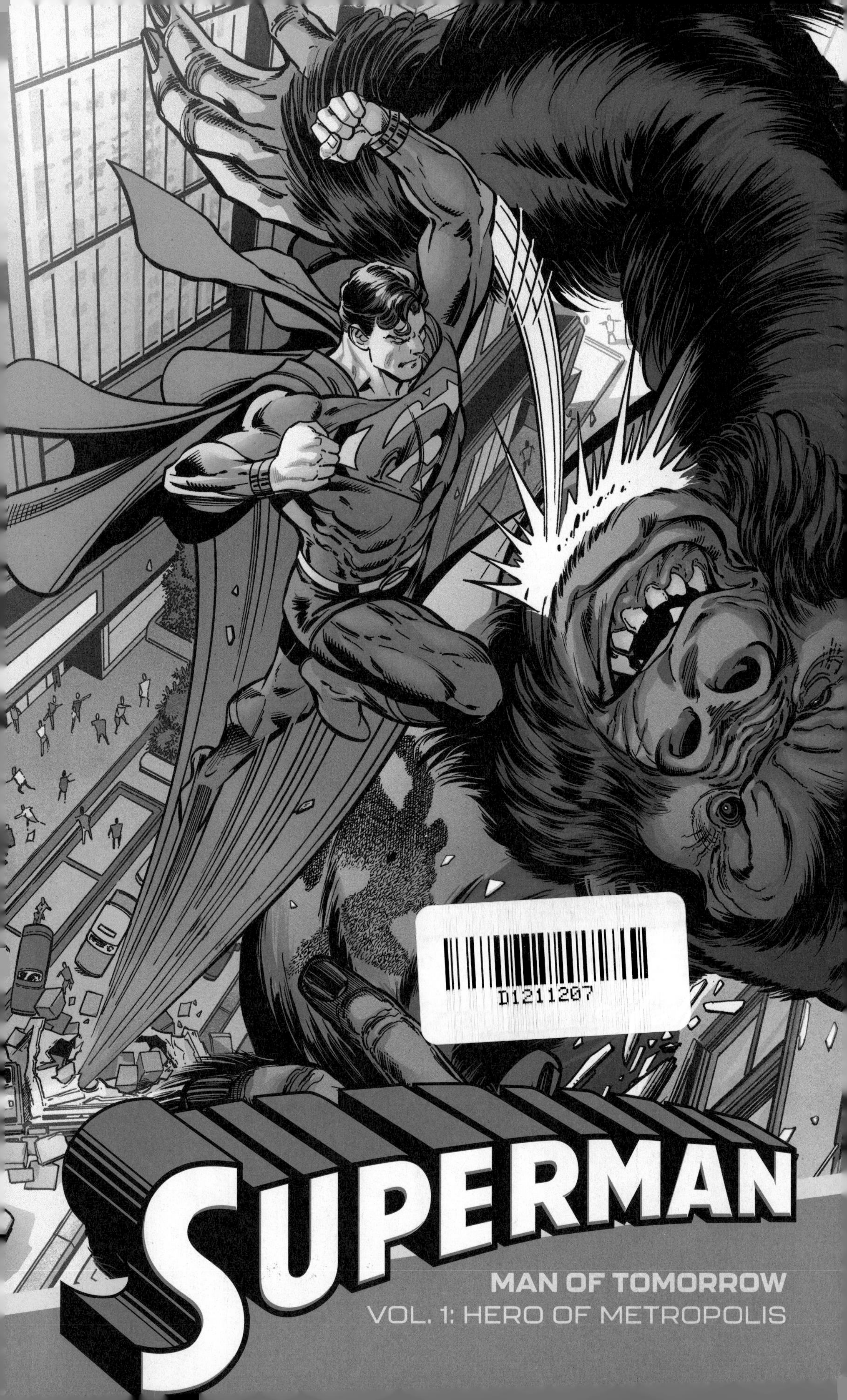

SUPERMAN

MAN OF TOMORROW

VOL. 1: HERO OF METROPOLIS

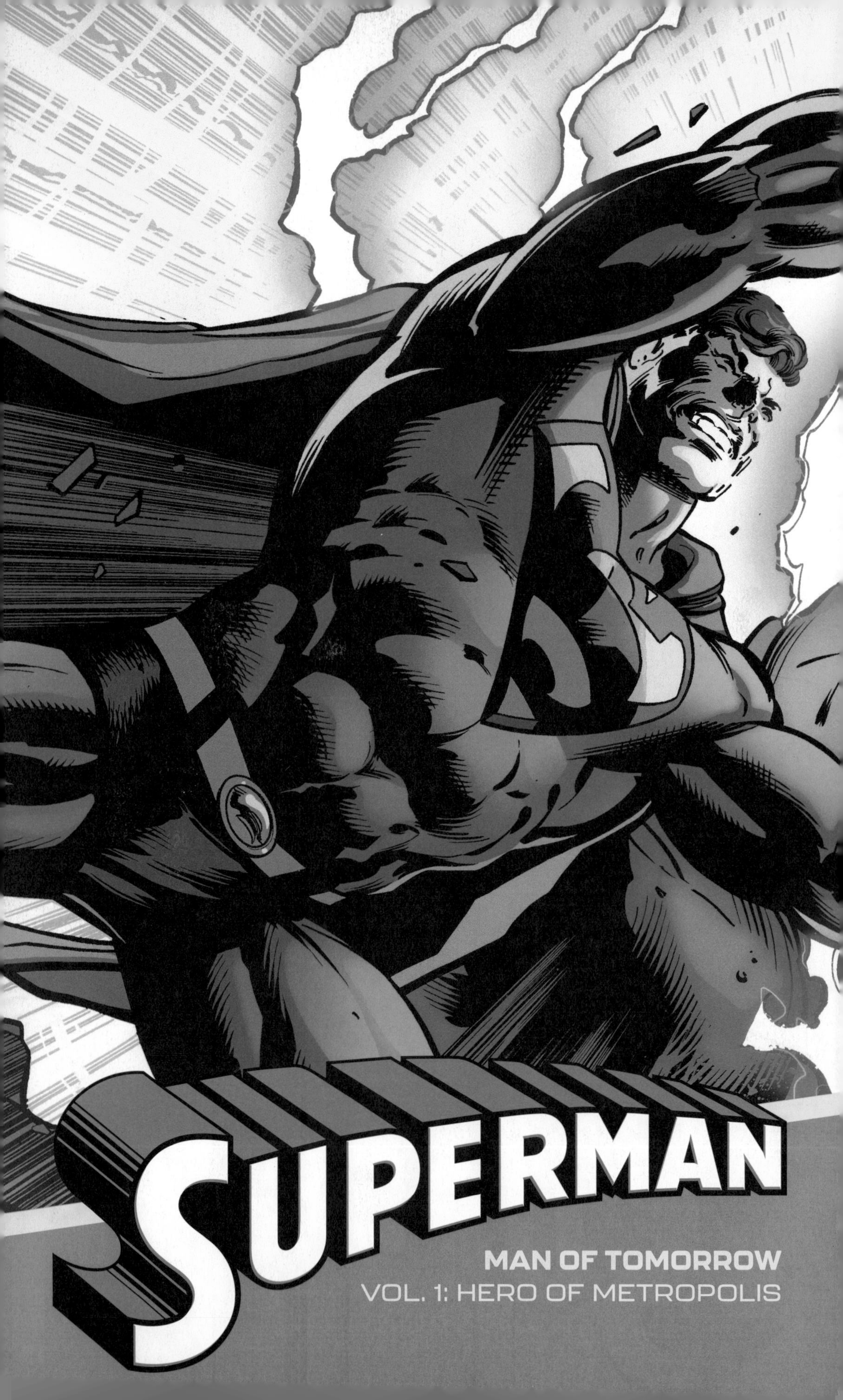

SUPERMAN

MAN OF TOMORROW

VOL. 1: HERO OF METROPOLIS

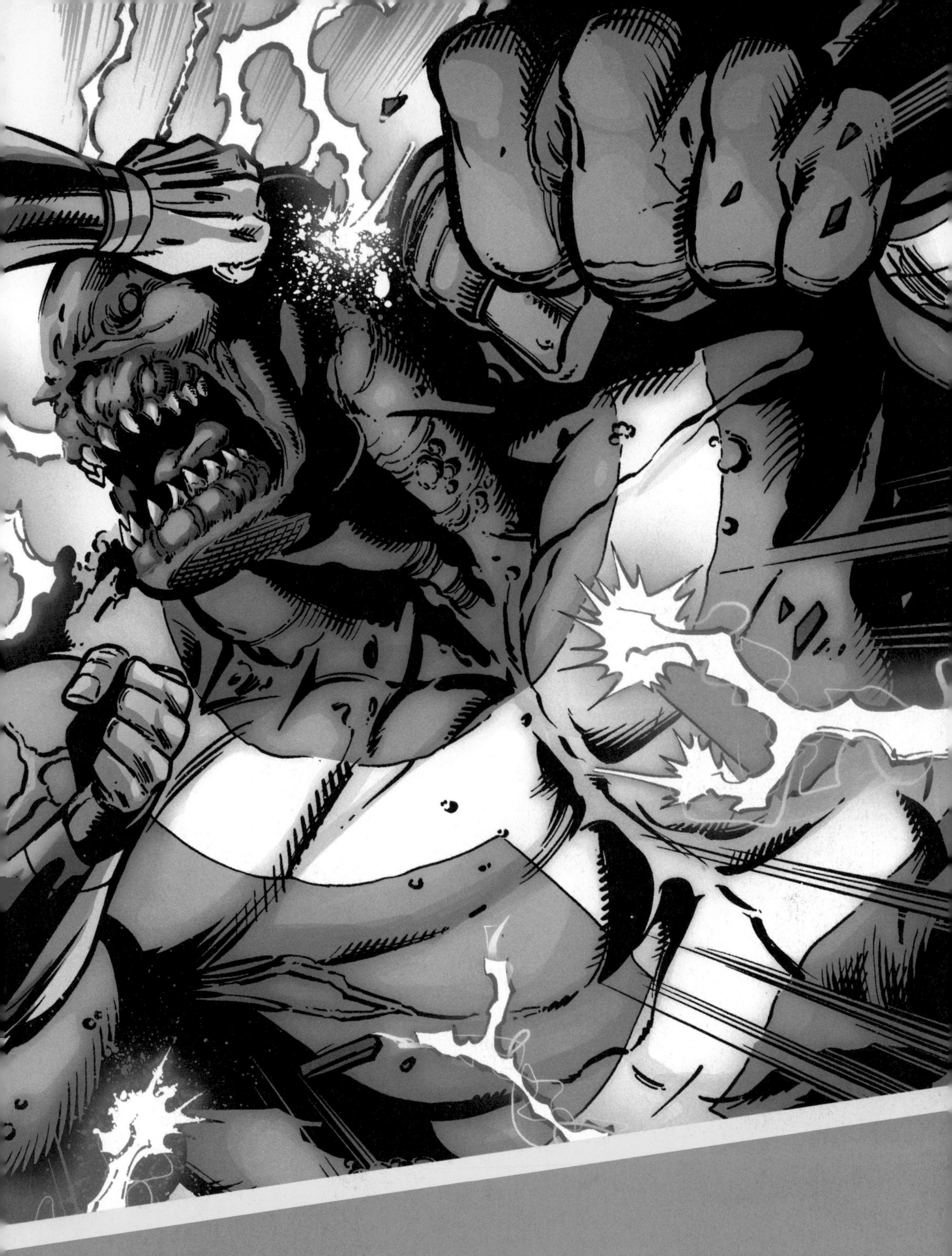

ROBERT VENDITTI
writer

PAUL PELLETIER • GLEB MELNIKOV
SCOTT HEPBURN • DAVID LAFUENTE
pencillers

DREW HENNESSY • GLEB MELNIKOV
SCOTT HEPBURN • DAVID LAFUENTE
inkers

ADRIANO LUCAS • JORDIE BELLAIRE
IAN HERRING • LUIS GUERRERO
colorists

CLAYTON COWLES
letterer

RAFA SANDOVAL • JORDI TARRAGONA
TOMEU MOREY
collection cover artists

SUPERMAN: MAN OF TOMORROW VOL. 1: HERO OF METROPOLIS

Published by DC Comics. Compilation and all new material Copyright © 2021
DC Comics. All Rights Reserved. Originally published online as *Superman: Man
of Tomorrow* Digital Chapters 1-6, 11-15. Copyright © 2020 DC Comics. All
Rights Reserved. All characters, their distinctive likenesses, and related
elements featured in this publication are trademarks of DC Comics. The
stories, characters, and incidents featured in this publication are entirely
fictional. DC Comics does not read or accept unsolicited submissions of ideas,
stories, or artwork. DC – a WarnerMedia Company.

DC Comics
2900 West Alameda Ave., Burbank, CA 91505
Printed by LSC Communications,
Owensville, MO, USA. 6/11/21.
First Printing. ISBN: 978-1-77951-130-0.
Library of Congress
Cataloging-in-Publication Data is available.

PEFC Certified
This product is from
sustainably managed
forests and controlled
sources
PEFC/29-31-337   www.pefc.org

ANDREW MARINO *Editor – Original Series & Collected Edition*
STEVE COOK *Design Director – Books*
DAMIAN RYLAND *Publication Design*
CHRISTY SAWYER *Publication Production*

MARIE JAVINS *Editor-in-Chief, DC Comics*

DANIEL CHERRY III *Senior VP – General Manager*
JIM LEE *Publisher & Chief Creative Officer*
JOEN CHOE *VP – Global Brand & Creative Services*
DON FALLETTI *VP – Manufacturing Operations & Workflow Management*
LAWRENCE GANEM *VP – Talent Services*
ALISON GILL *Senior VP – Manufacturing & Operations*
NICK J. NAPOLITANO *VP – Manufacturing Administration & Design*
NANCY SPEARS *VP – Revenue*

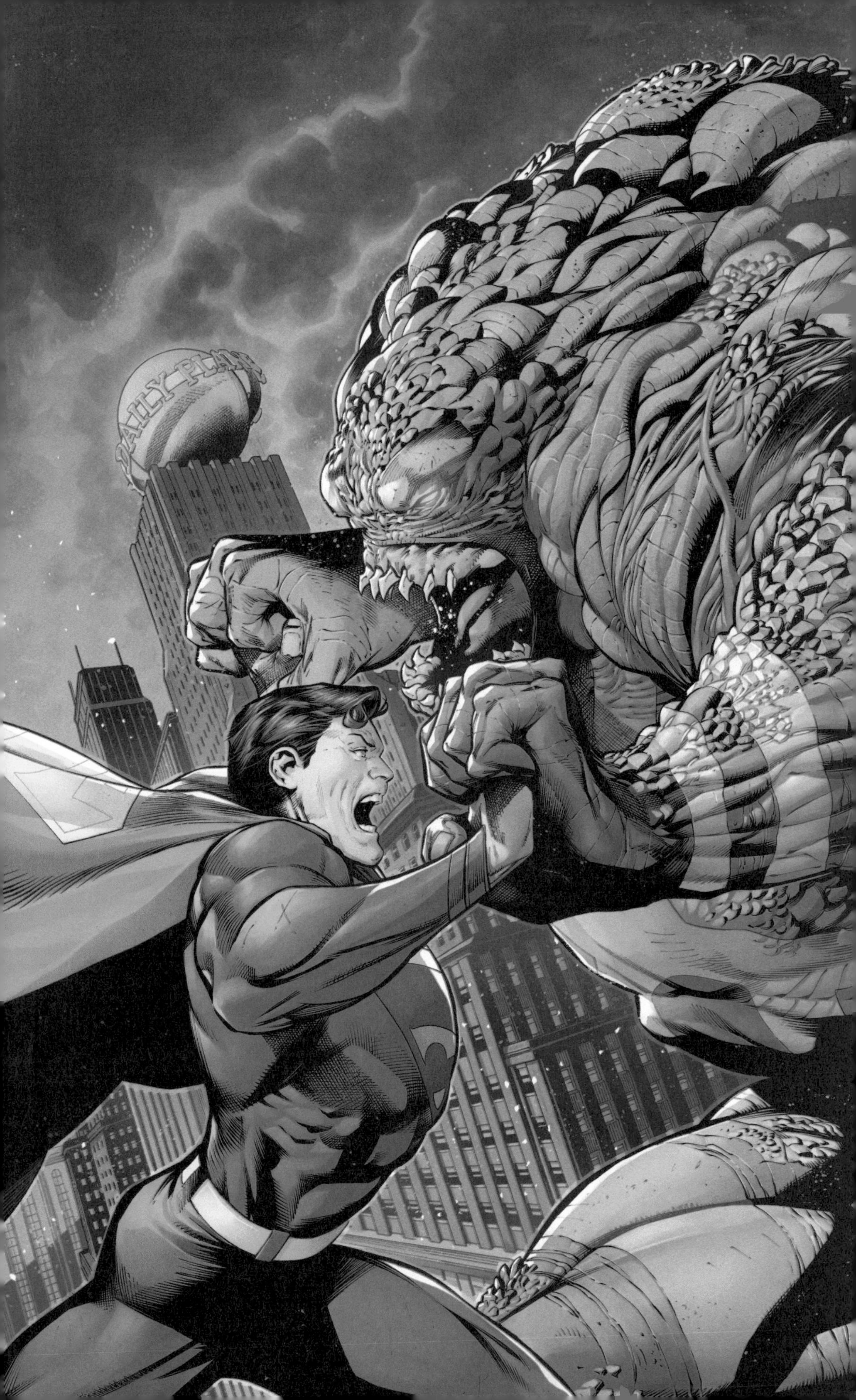

COVER ART BY
RAFA SANDOVAL, JORDI TARRAGONA,
AND **TOMEU MOREY**

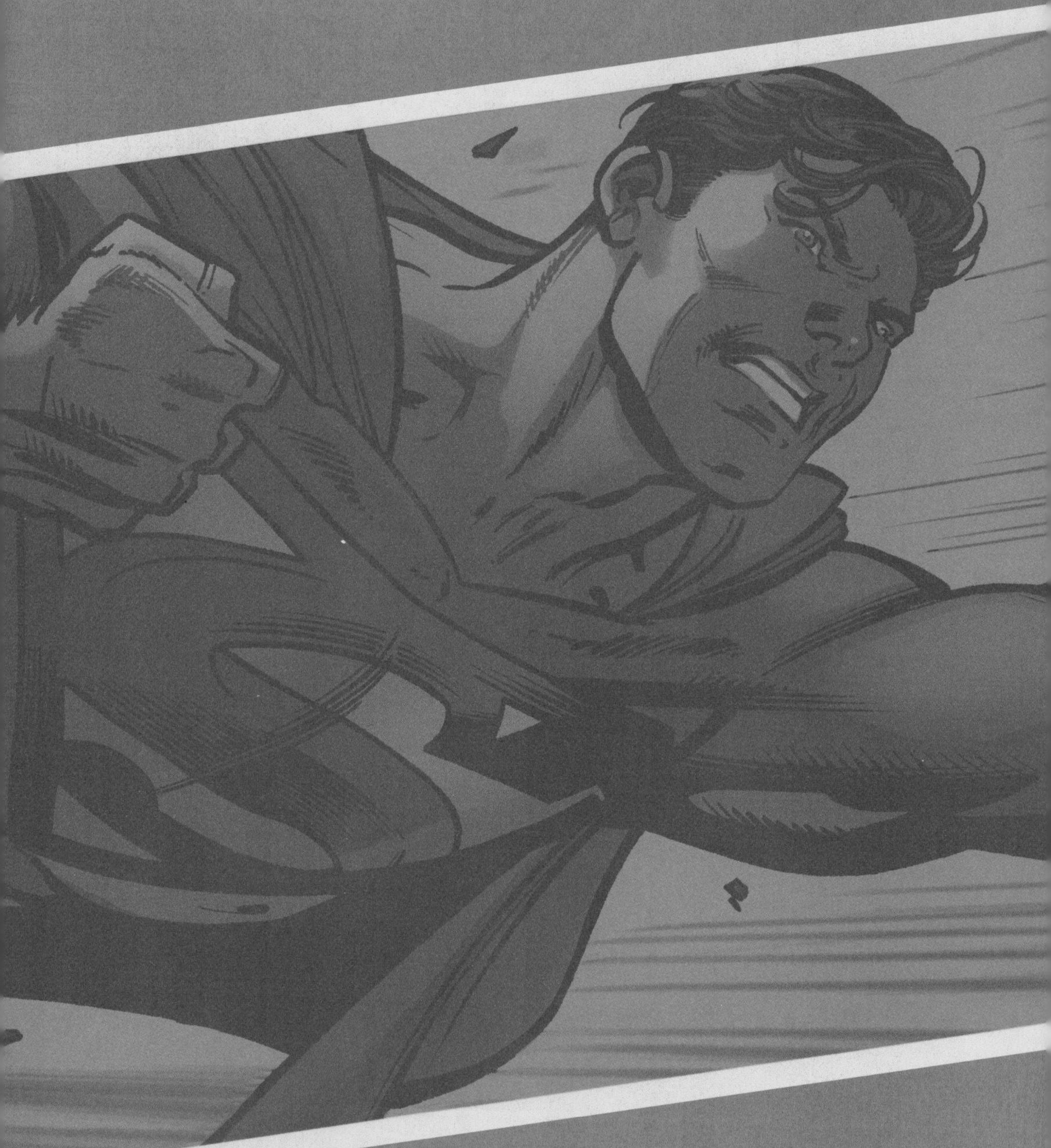

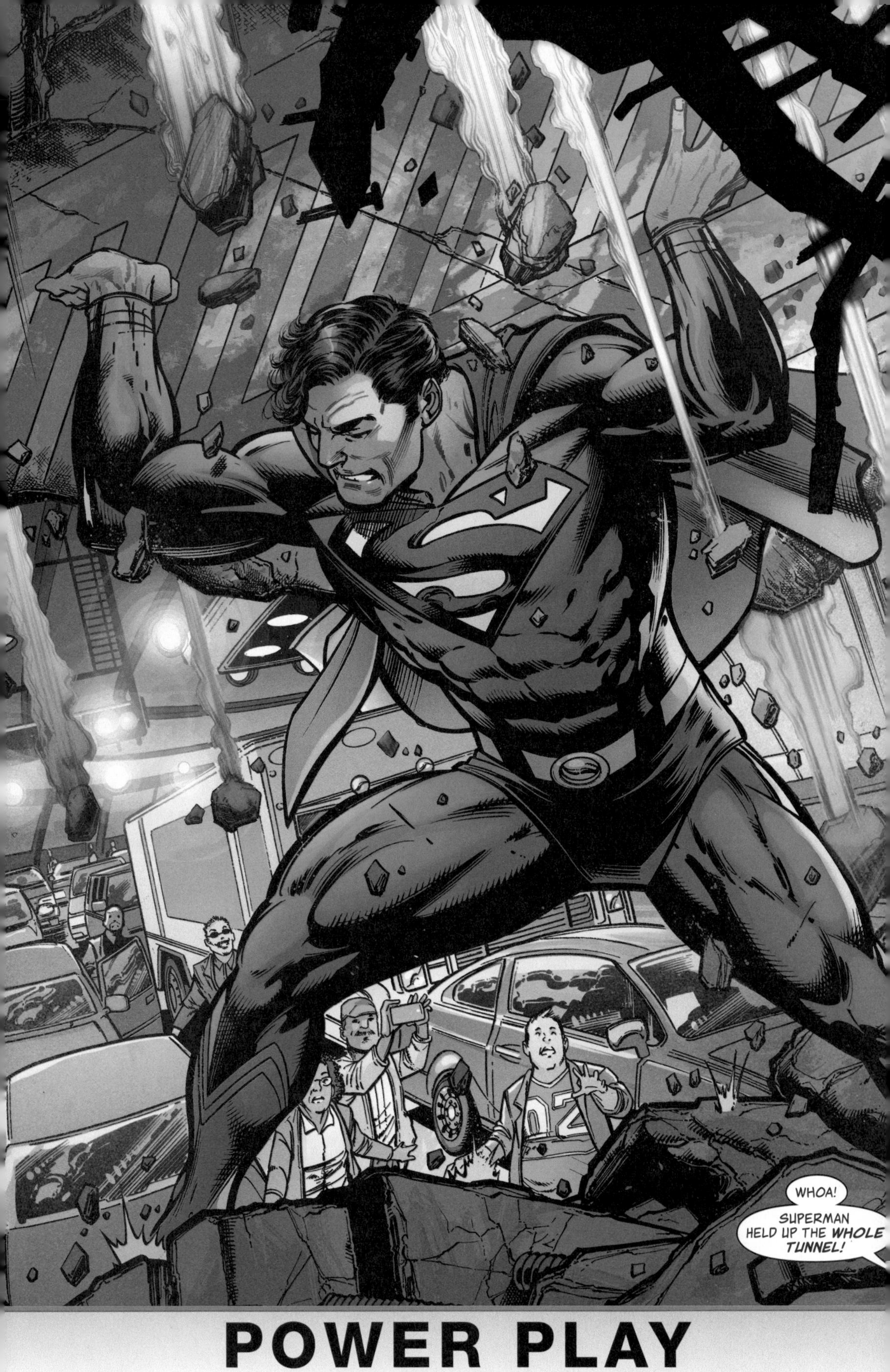
WHOA!
SUPERMAN HELD UP THE WHOLE TUNNEL!

POWER PLAY

WRITER: ROBERT VENDITTI PENCILLER: PAUL PELLETIER INKER: ANDREW HENNESSY COLORIST: ADRIANO LUCAS

LETTERER: CLAYTON COWLES COVER: RAFA SANDOVAL, JORDI TARRAGONA AND TOMEU MOREY EDITOR: ANDREW MARINO

SUPERMAN created by JERRY SIEGEL and JOE SHUSTER. By special arrangement with the JERRY SIEGEL FAMILY.

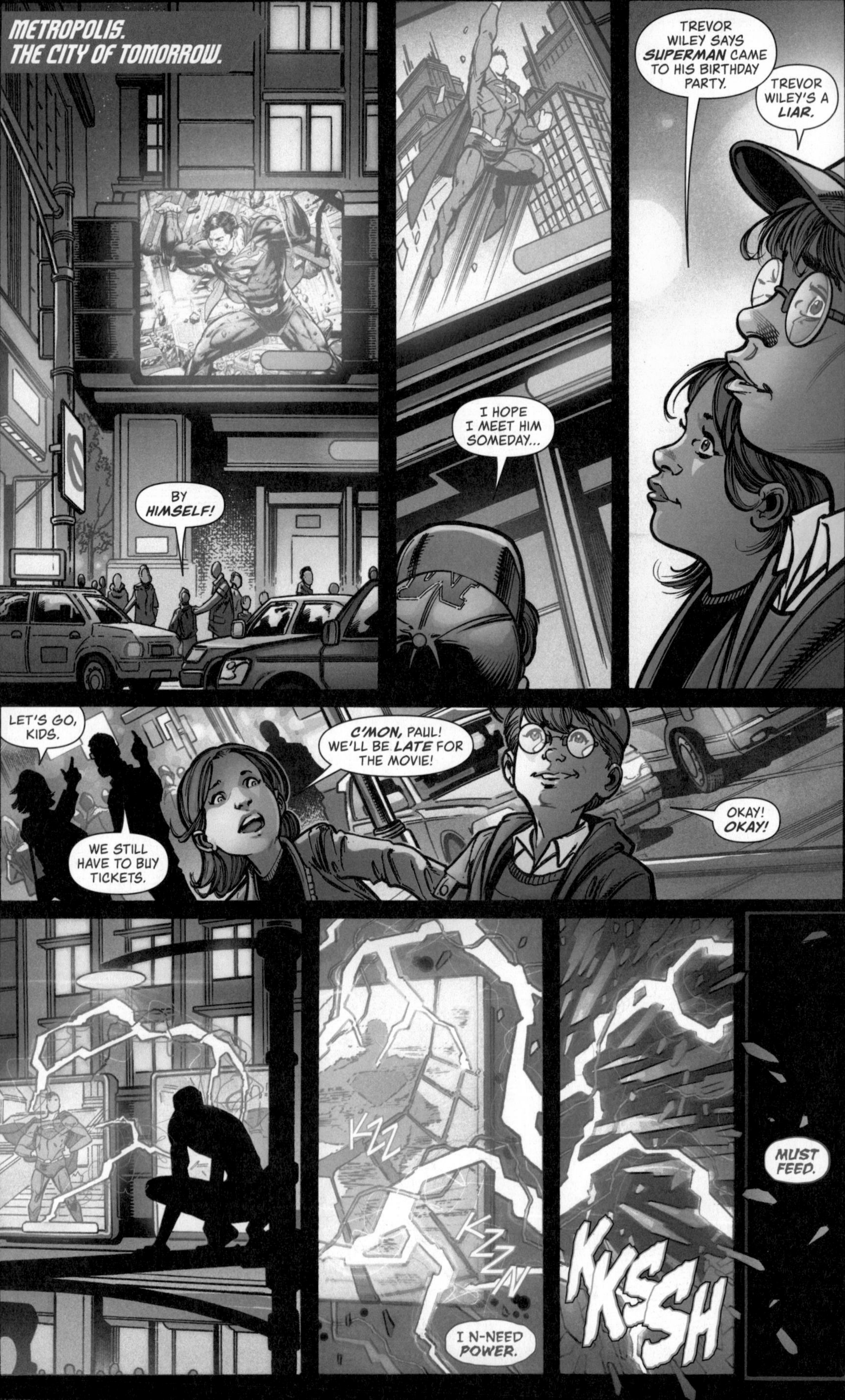
METROPOLIS.
THE CITY OF TOMORROW.
BY HIMSELF!
I HOPE I MEET HIM SOMEDAY...
TREVOR WILEY SAYS SUPERMAN CAME TO HIS BIRTHDAY PARTY.
TREVOR WILEY'S A LIAR.
LET'S GO, KIDS.
WE STILL HAVE TO BUY TICKETS.
C'MON, PAUL! WE'LL BE LATE FOR THE MOVIE!
OKAY! OKAY!
KZZ
KZZN
I N-NEED POWER.
KKSSH
MUST FEED.

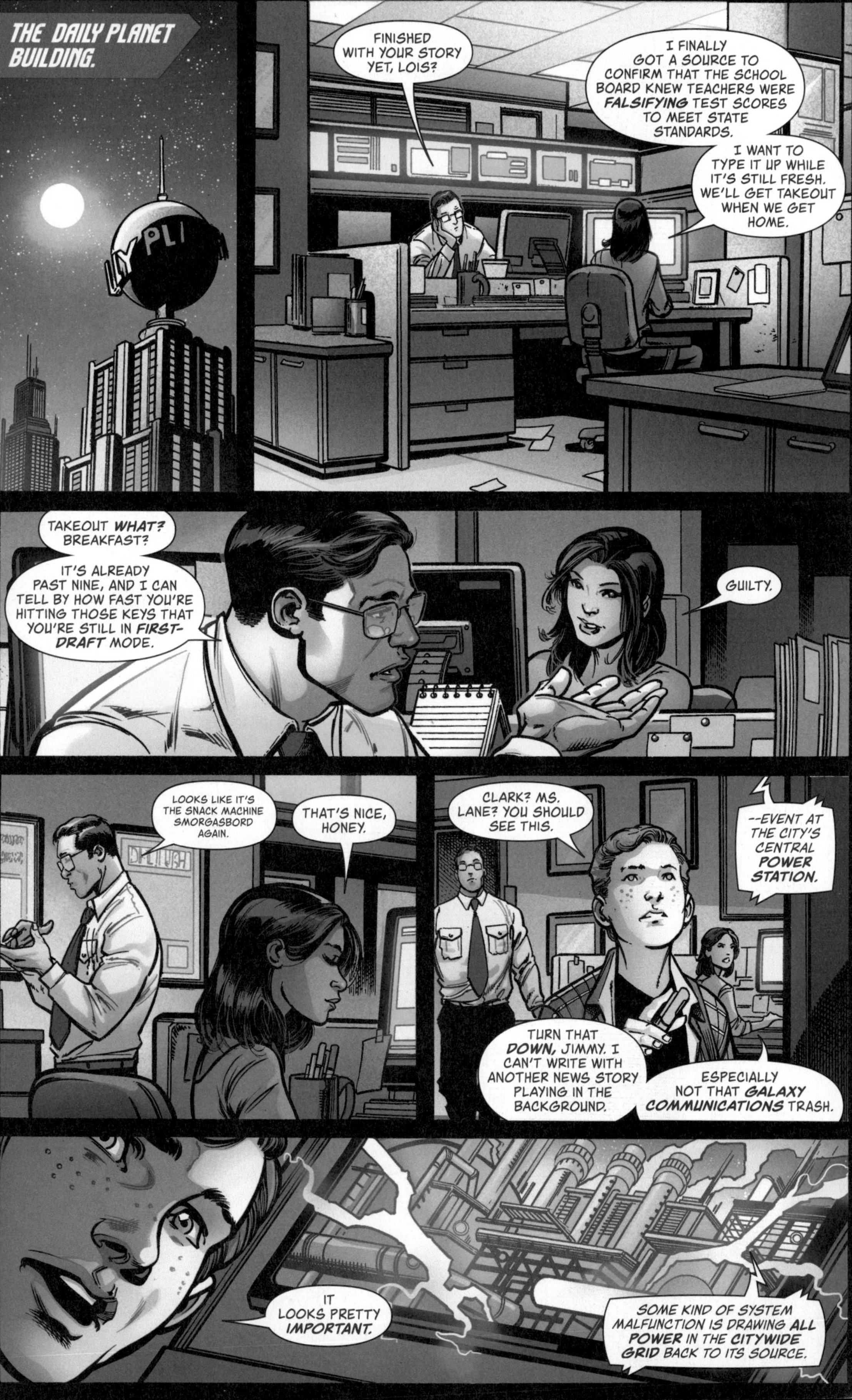
THE DAILY PLANET BUILDING.
PLI
FINISHED WITH YOUR STORY YET, LOIS?
I FINALLY GOT A SOURCE TO CONFIRM THAT THE SCHOOL BOARD KNEW TEACHERS WERE FALSIFYING TEST SCORES TO MEET STATE STANDARDS.
I WANT TO TYPE IT UP WHILE IT'S STILL FRESH. WE'LL GET TAKEOUT WHEN WE GET HOME.
TAKEOUT WHAT? BREAKFAST?
IT'S ALREADY PAST NINE, AND I CAN TELL BY HOW FAST YOU'RE HITTING THOSE KEYS THAT YOU'RE STILL IN FIRST-DRAFT MODE.
GUILTY.
LOOKS LIKE IT'S THE SNACK MACHINE SMORGASBORD AGAIN.
THAT'S NICE, HONEY.
CLARK? MS. LANE? YOU SHOULD SEE THIS.
--EVENT AT THE CITY'S CENTRAL POWER STATION.
TURN THAT DOWN, JIMMY. I CAN'T WRITE WITH ANOTHER NEWS STORY PLAYING IN THE BACKGROUND.
ESPECIALLY NOT THAT GALAXY COMMUNICATIONS TRASH.
IT LOOKS PRETTY IMPORTANT.
SOME KIND OF SYSTEM MALFUNCTION IS DRAWING ALL POWER IN THE CITYWIDE GRID BACK TO ITS SOURCE.

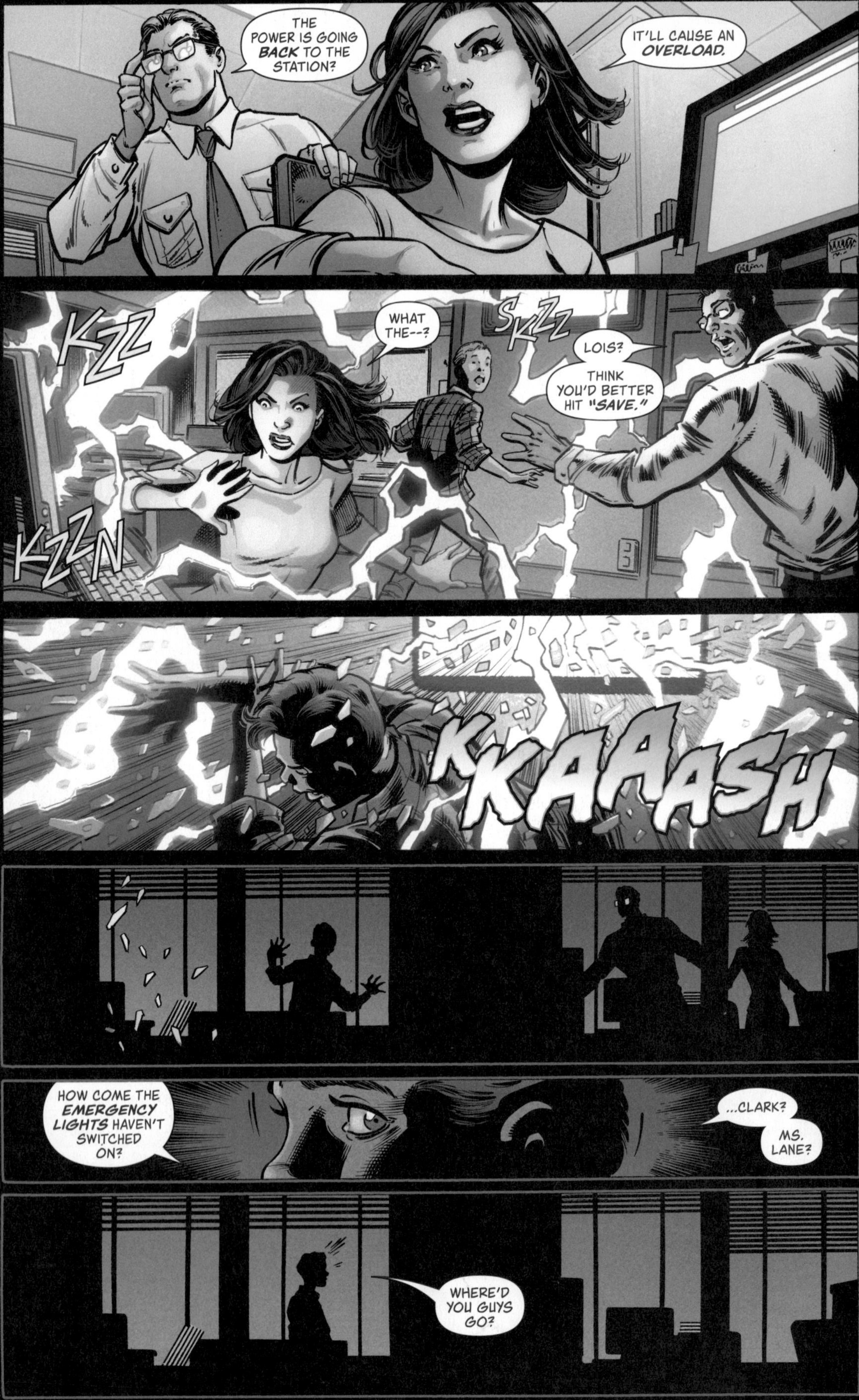
THE POWER IS GOING BACK TO THE STATION?
IT'LL CAUSE AN OVERLOAD.
KZZ
WHAT THE--?
SKZZ
LOIS?
THINK YOU'D BETTER HIT "SAVE."
KZZN
KKAAASH
HOW COME THE EMERGENCY LIGHTS HAVEN'T SWITCHED ON?
...CLARK?
MS. LANE?
WHERE'D YOU GUYS GO?

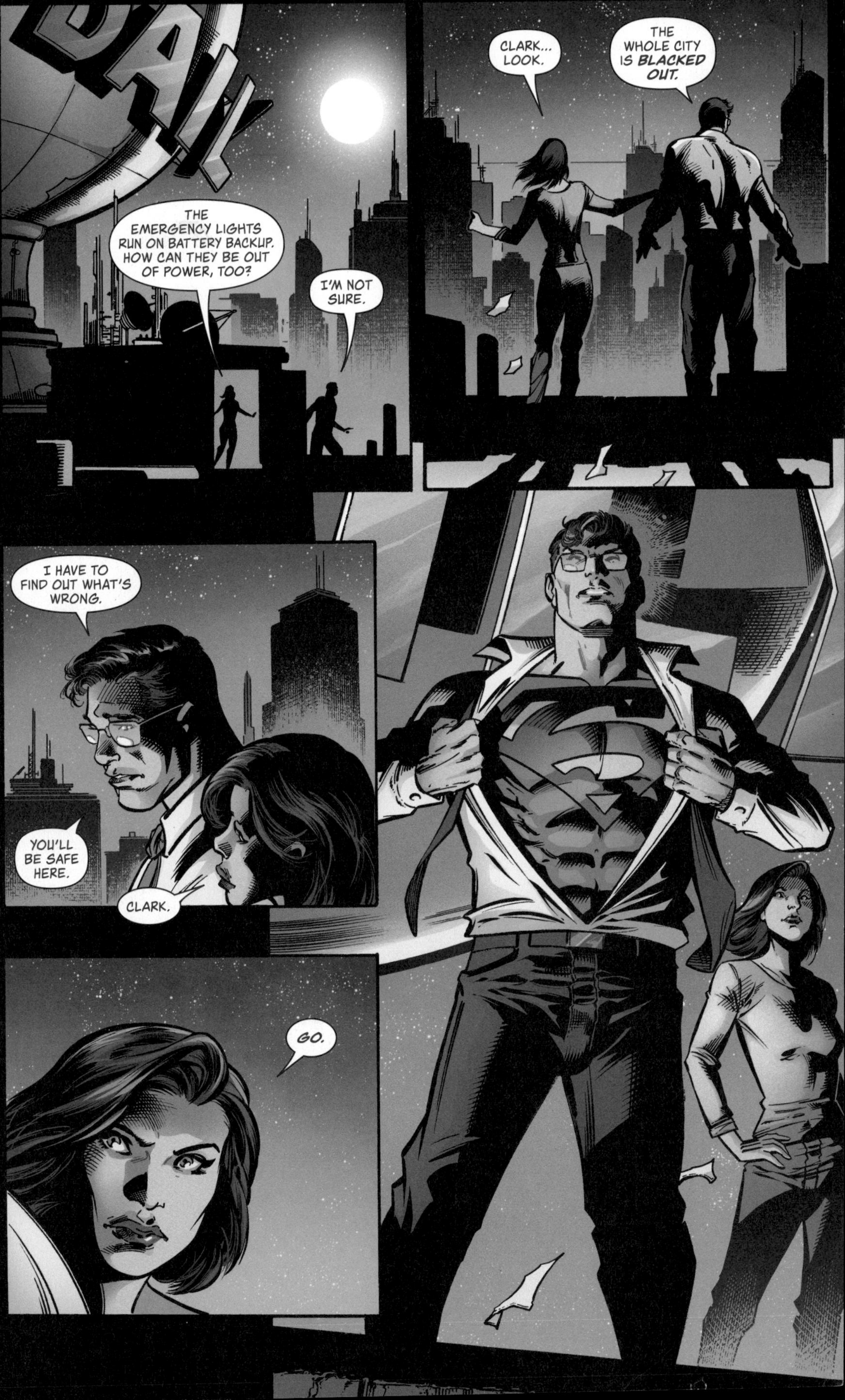
THE EMERGENCY LIGHTS RUN ON BATTERY BACKUP. HOW CAN THEY BE OUT OF POWER, TOO?
I'M NOT SURE.
CLARK... LOOK.
THE WHOLE CITY IS BLACKED OUT.
I HAVE TO FIND OUT WHAT'S WRONG.
YOU'LL BE SAFE HERE.
CLARK.
GO.

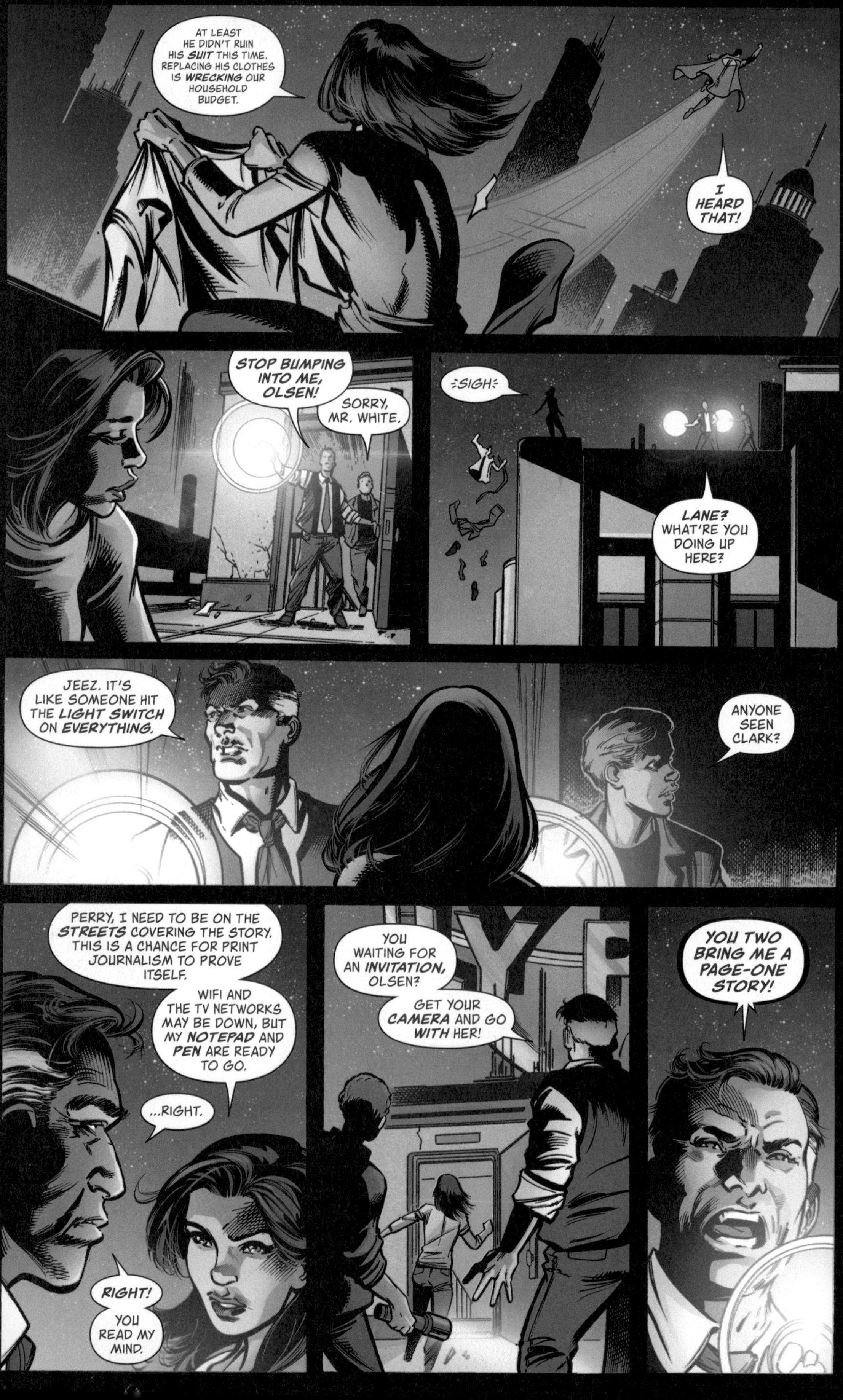
AT LEAST HE DIDN'T RUIN HIS SUIT THIS TIME. REPLACING HIS CLOTHES IS WRECKING OUR HOUSEHOLD BUDGET.
I HEARD THAT!
STOP BUMPING INTO ME, OLSEN!
SORRY, MR. WHITE.
SIGH
LANE? WHAT'RE YOU DOING UP HERE?
JEEZ. IT'S LIKE SOMEONE HIT THE LIGHT SWITCH ON EVERYTHING.
ANYONE SEEN CLARK?
PERRY, I NEED TO BE ON THE STREETS COVERING THE STORY. THIS IS A CHANCE FOR PRINT JOURNALISM TO PROVE ITSELF.
WIFI AND THE TV NETWORKS MAY BE DOWN, BUT MY NOTEPAD AND PEN ARE READY TO GO.
...RIGHT.
RIGHT!
YOU READ MY MIND.
YOU WAITING FOR AN INVITATION, OLSEN?
GET YOUR CAMERA AND GO WITH HER!
YOU TWO BRING ME A PAGE-ONE STORY!

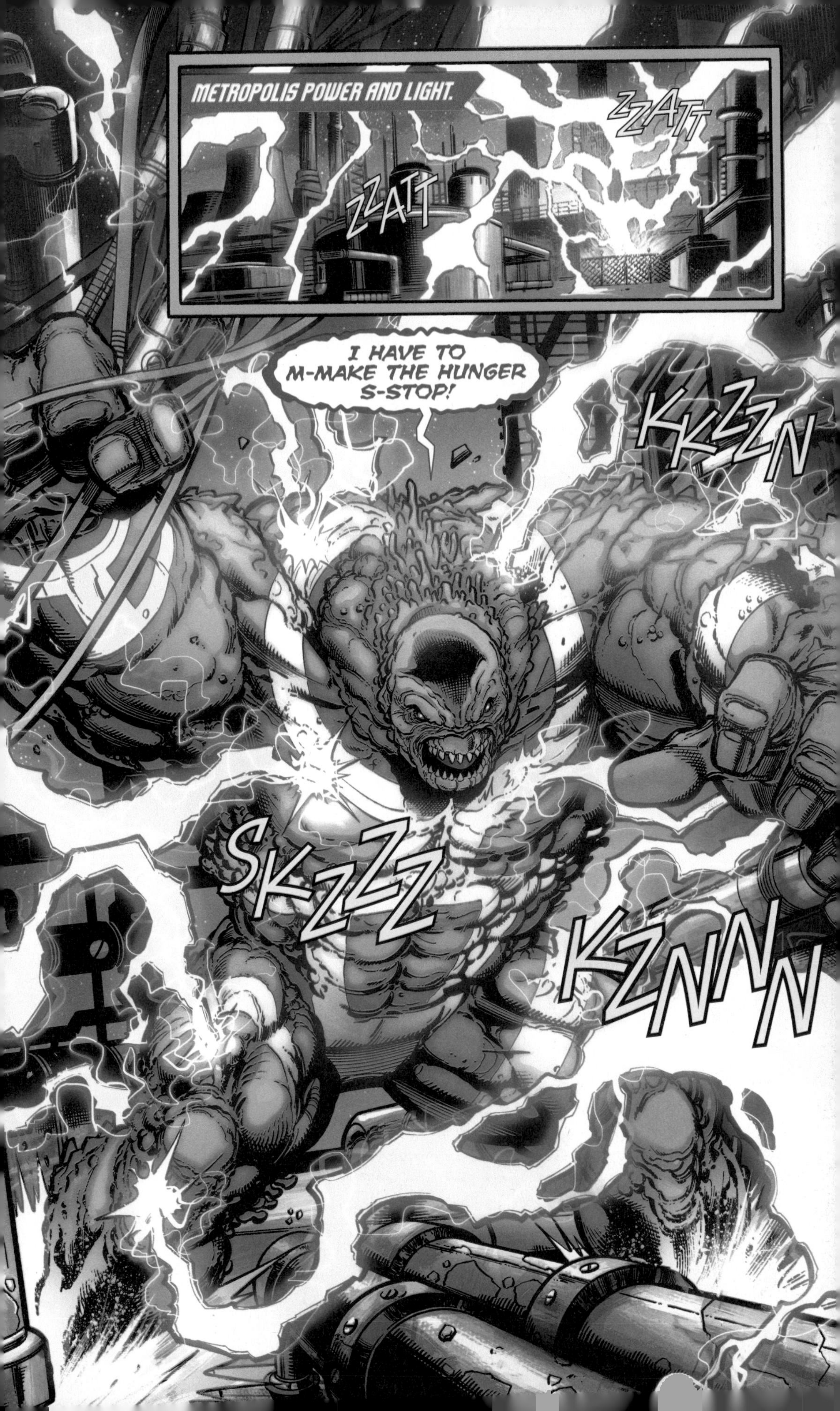
METROPOLIS POWER AND LIGHT.
ZZATT
ZZATT
I HAVE TO M-MAKE THE HUNGER S-STOP!
KKZZN
SKZZZZ
KZNNNN

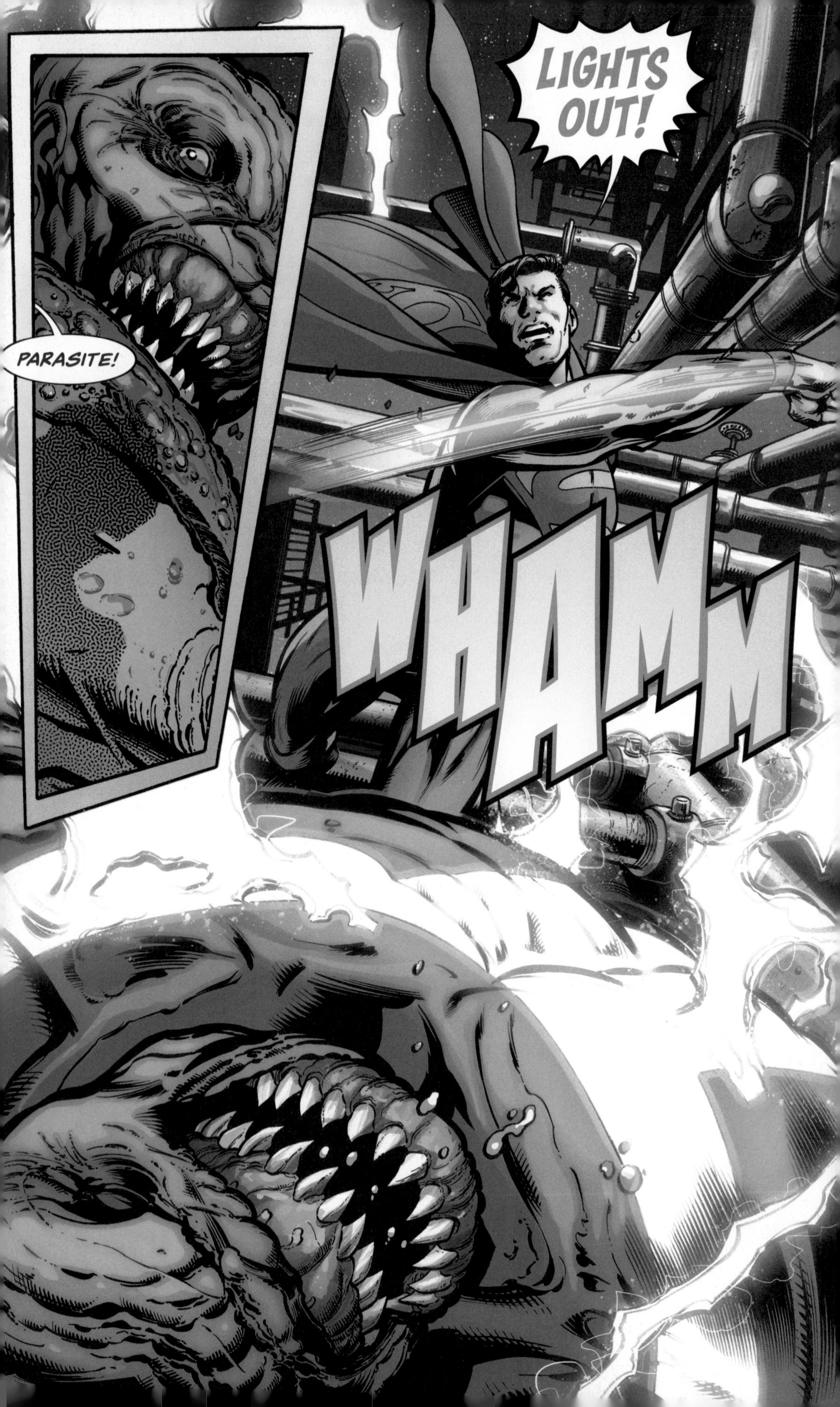
PARASITE!
LIGHTS OUT!
WHAMM

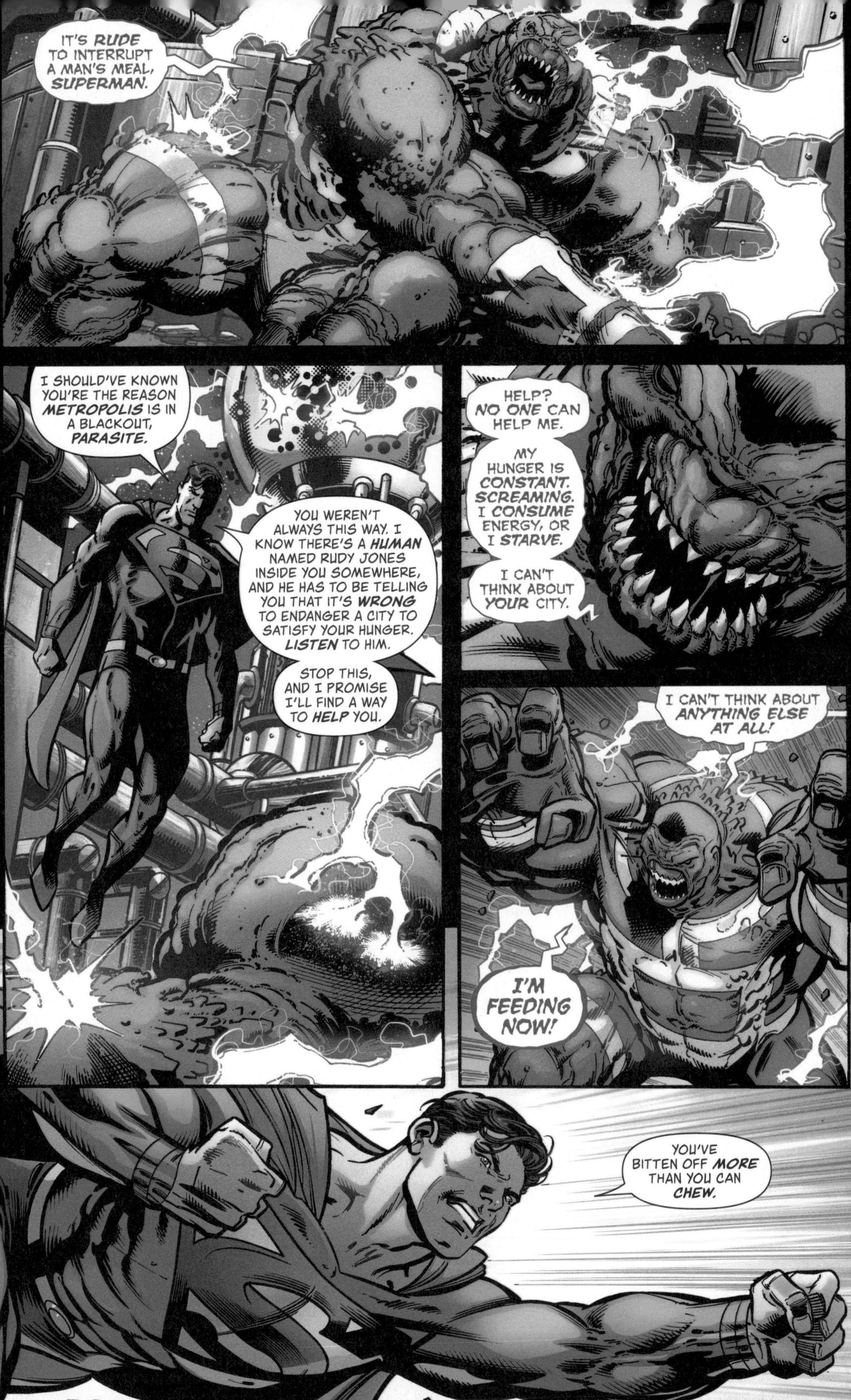
IT'S RUDE TO INTERRUPT A MAN'S MEAL, SUPERMAN.
I SHOULD'VE KNOWN YOU'RE THE REASON METROPOLIS IS IN A BLACKOUT, PARASITE.
YOU WEREN'T ALWAYS THIS WAY. I KNOW THERE'S A HUMAN NAMED RUDY JONES INSIDE YOU SOMEWHERE, AND HE HAS TO BE TELLING YOU THAT IT'S WRONG TO ENDANGER A CITY TO SATISFY YOUR HUNGER. LISTEN TO HIM.
STOP THIS, AND I PROMISE I'LL FIND A WAY TO HELP YOU.
HELP? NO ONE CAN HELP ME.
MY HUNGER IS CONSTANT. SCREAMING. I CONSUME ENERGY, OR I STARVE.
I CAN'T THINK ABOUT YOUR CITY.
I CAN'T THINK ABOUT ANYTHING ELSE AT ALL!
I'M FEEDING NOW!
YOU'VE BITTEN OFF MORE THAN YOU CAN CHEW.

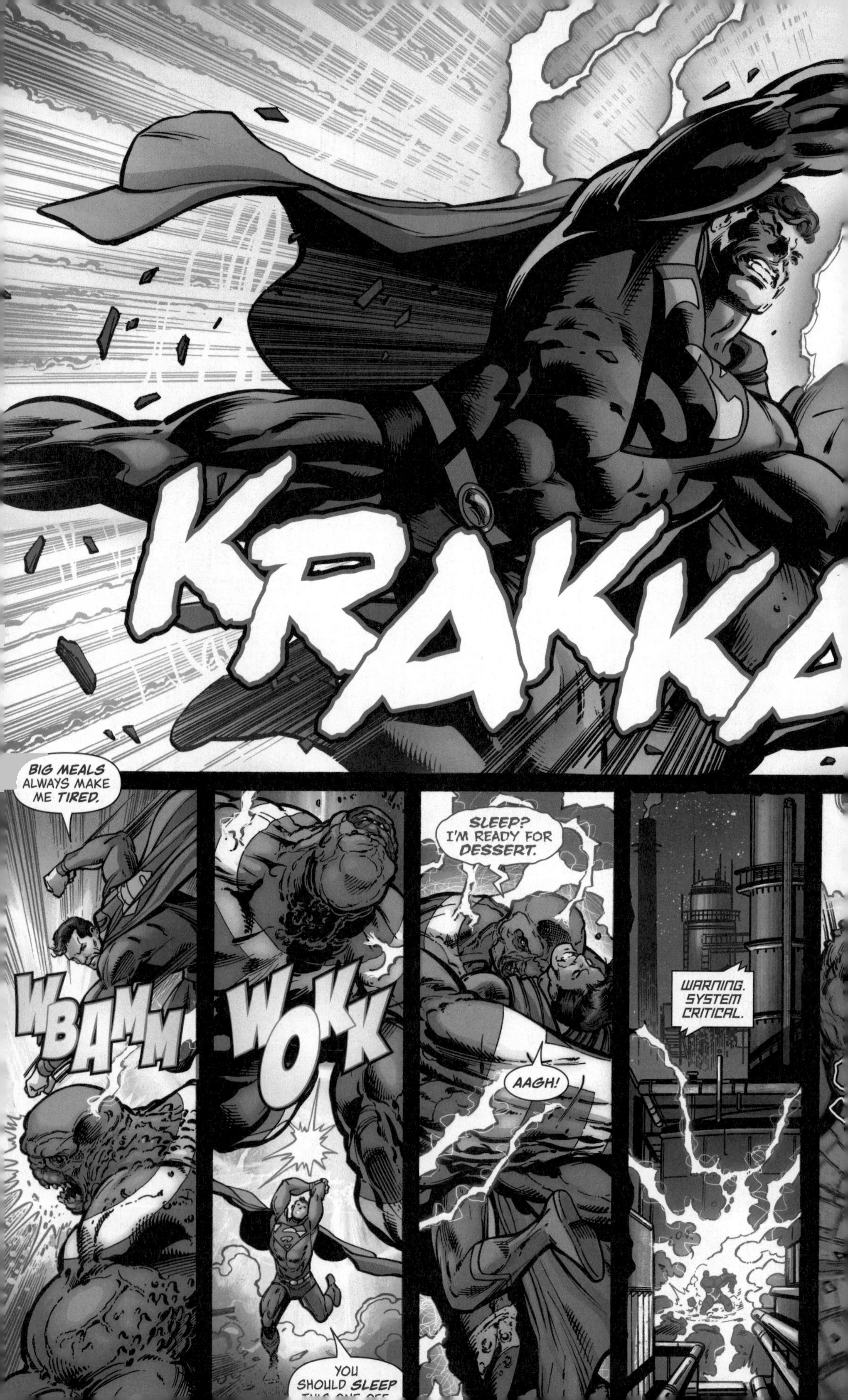
KRAKKA
BIG MEALS ALWAYS MAKE ME TIRED.
WBAMM
WOKK
YOU SHOULD SLEEP
SLEEP? I'M READY FOR DESSERT.
AAGH!
WARNING. SYSTEM CRITICAL.

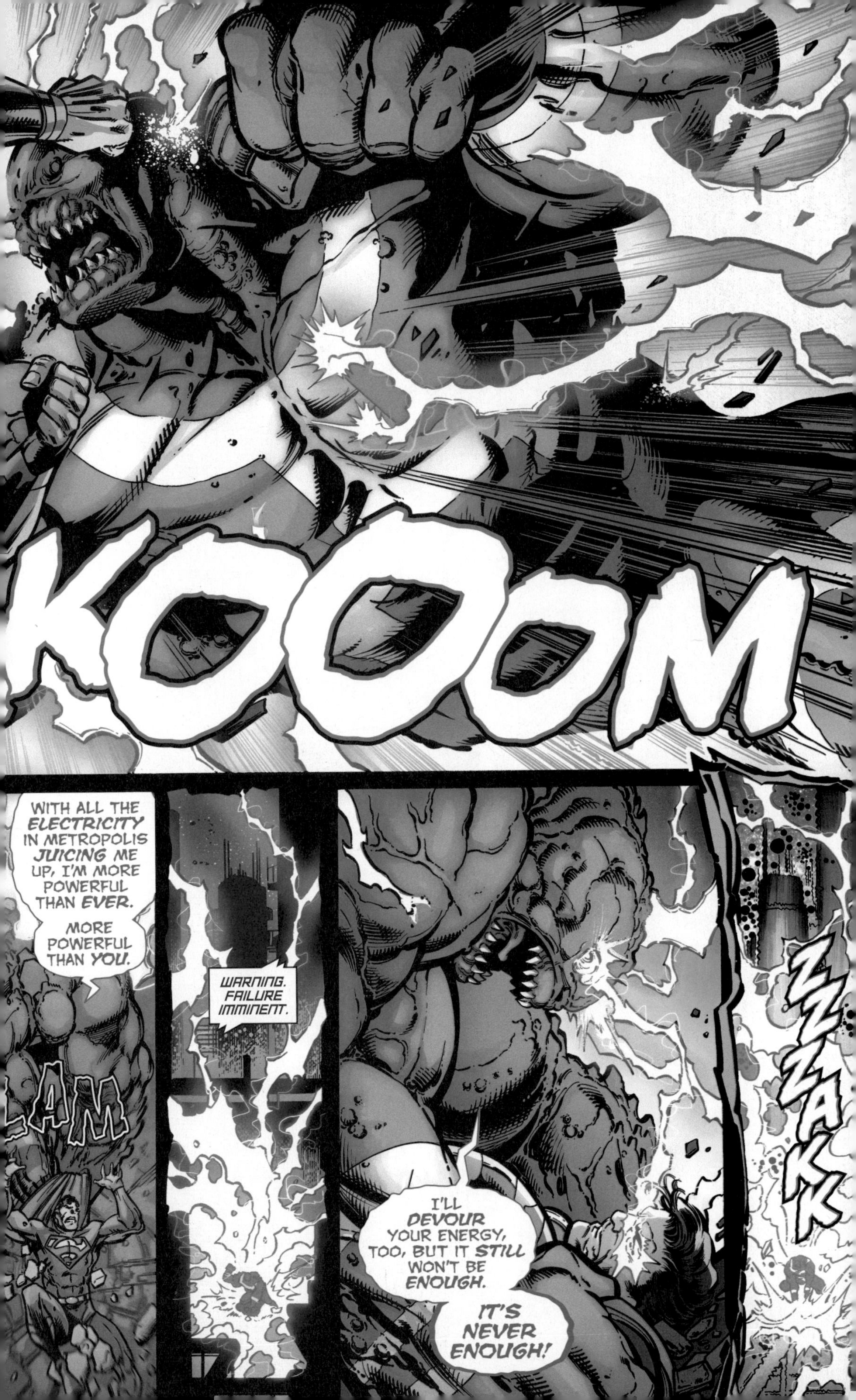
KOOOM
WITH ALL THE ELECTRICITY IN METROPOLIS JUICING ME UP, I'M MORE POWERFUL THAN EVER.
MORE POWERFUL THAN YOU.
WARNING. FAILURE IMMINENT.
I'LL DEVOUR YOUR ENERGY, TOO, BUT IT STILL WON'T BE ENOUGH.
IT'S NEVER ENOUGH!
ZZZAKK

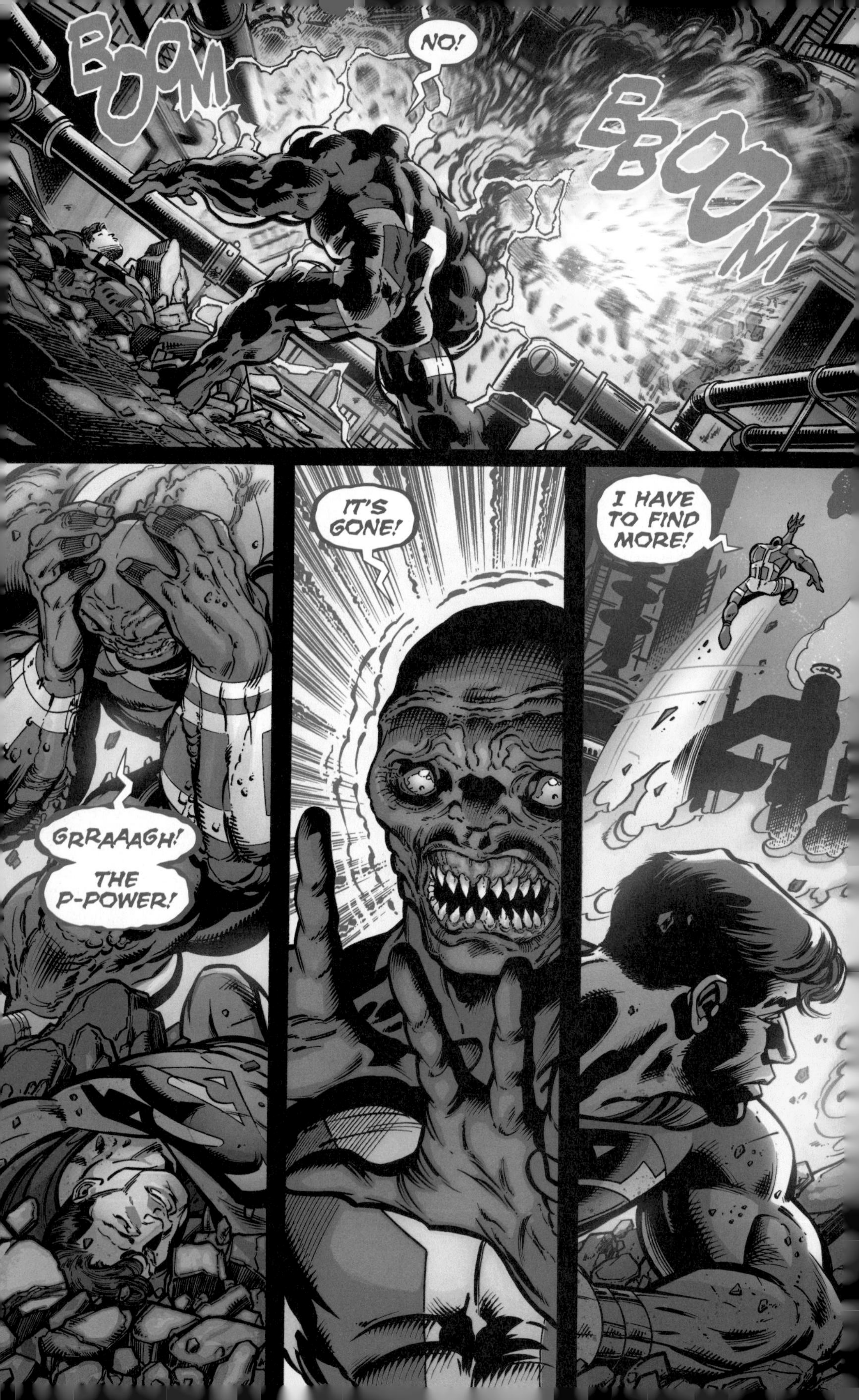
BOOM
NO!
BBOOM
GRRAAAGH! THE P-POWER!
IT'S GONE!
I HAVE TO FIND MORE!

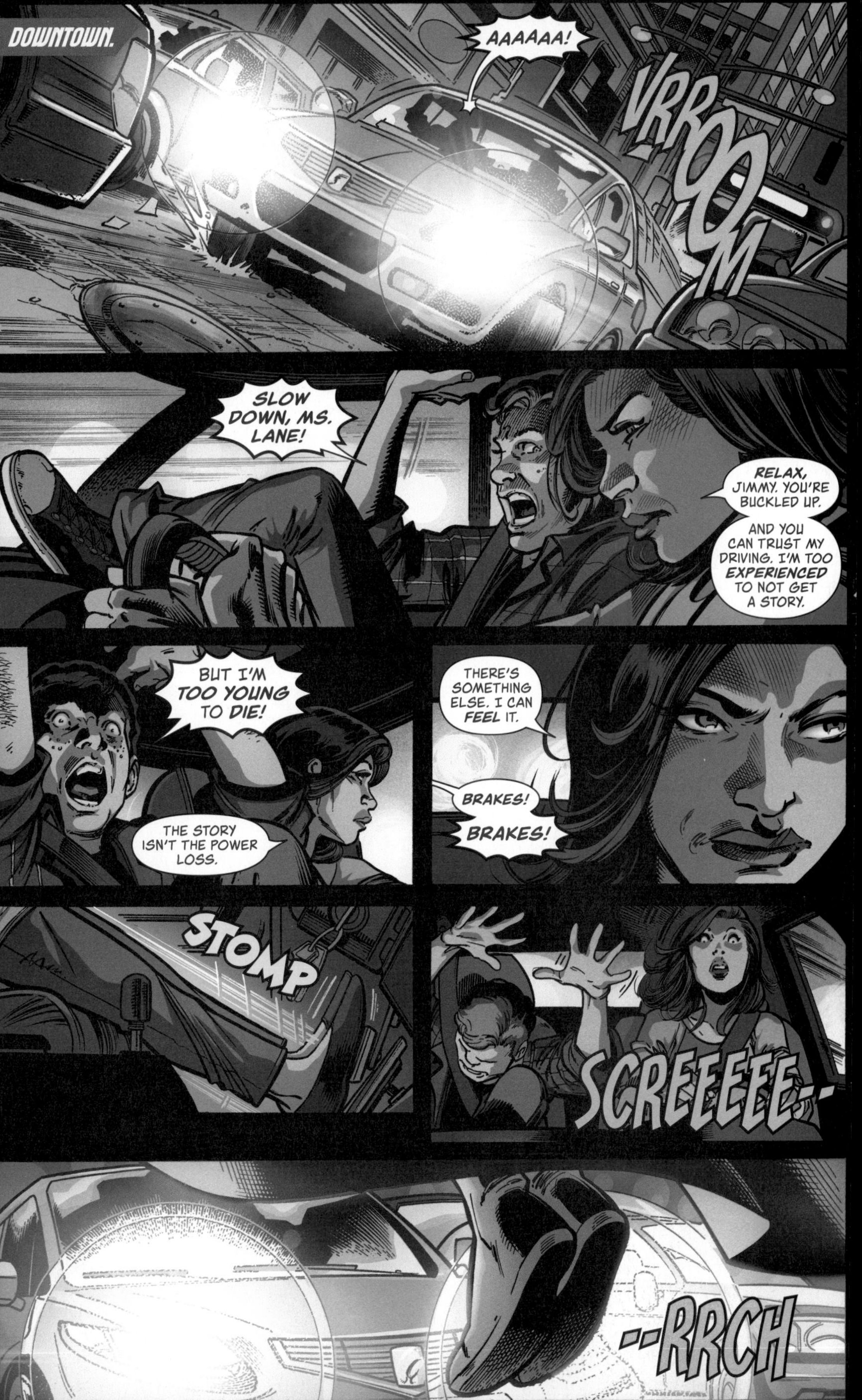
DOWNTOWN.
AAAAAA!
VRROOOM
SLOW DOWN, MS. LANE!
RELAX, JIMMY. YOU'RE BUCKLED UP.
AND YOU CAN TRUST MY DRIVING. I'M TOO EXPERIENCED TO NOT GET A STORY.
BUT I'M TOO YOUNG TO DIE!
THE STORY ISN'T THE POWER LOSS.
THERE'S SOMETHING ELSE. I CAN FEEL IT.
BRAKES!
BRAKES!
STOMP
SCREEEEE-
--RRCH

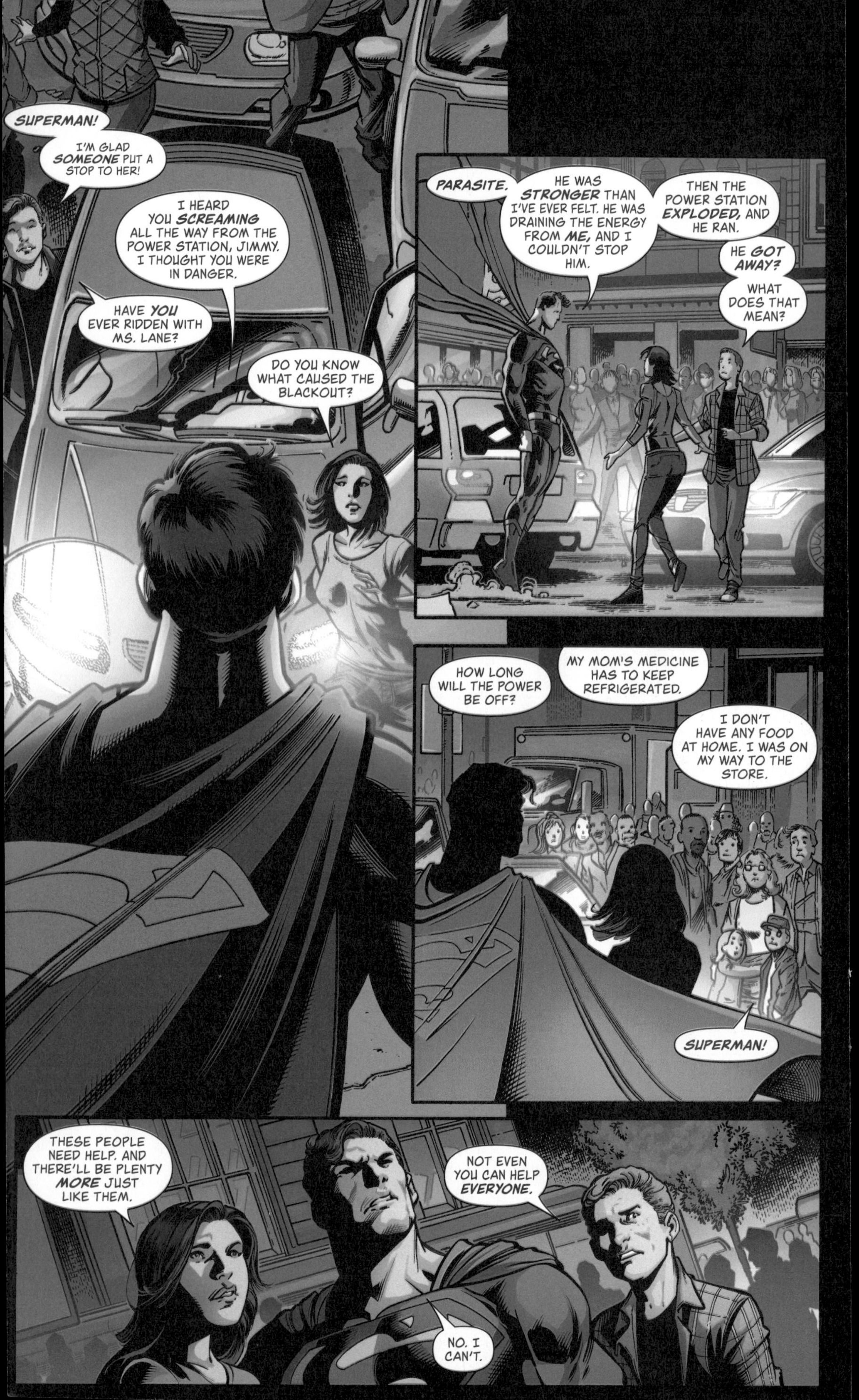
SUPERMAN!
I'M GLAD SOMEONE PUT A STOP TO HER!
I HEARD YOU SCREAMING ALL THE WAY FROM THE POWER STATION, JIMMY. I THOUGHT YOU WERE IN DANGER.
HAVE YOU EVER RIDDEN WITH MS. LANE?
DO YOU KNOW WHAT CAUSED THE BLACKOUT?
PARASITE.
HE WAS STRONGER THAN I'VE EVER FELT. HE WAS DRAINING THE ENERGY FROM ME, AND I COULDN'T STOP HIM.
THEN THE POWER STATION EXPLODED, AND HE RAN.
HE GOT AWAY?
WHAT DOES THAT MEAN?
HOW LONG WILL THE POWER BE OFF?
MY MOM'S MEDICINE HAS TO KEEP REFRIGERATED.
I DON'T HAVE ANY FOOD AT HOME. I WAS ON MY WAY TO THE STORE.
SUPERMAN!
THESE PEOPLE NEED HELP. AND THERE'LL BE PLENTY MORE JUST LIKE THEM.
NOT EVEN YOU CAN HELP EVERYONE.
NO. I CAN'T.

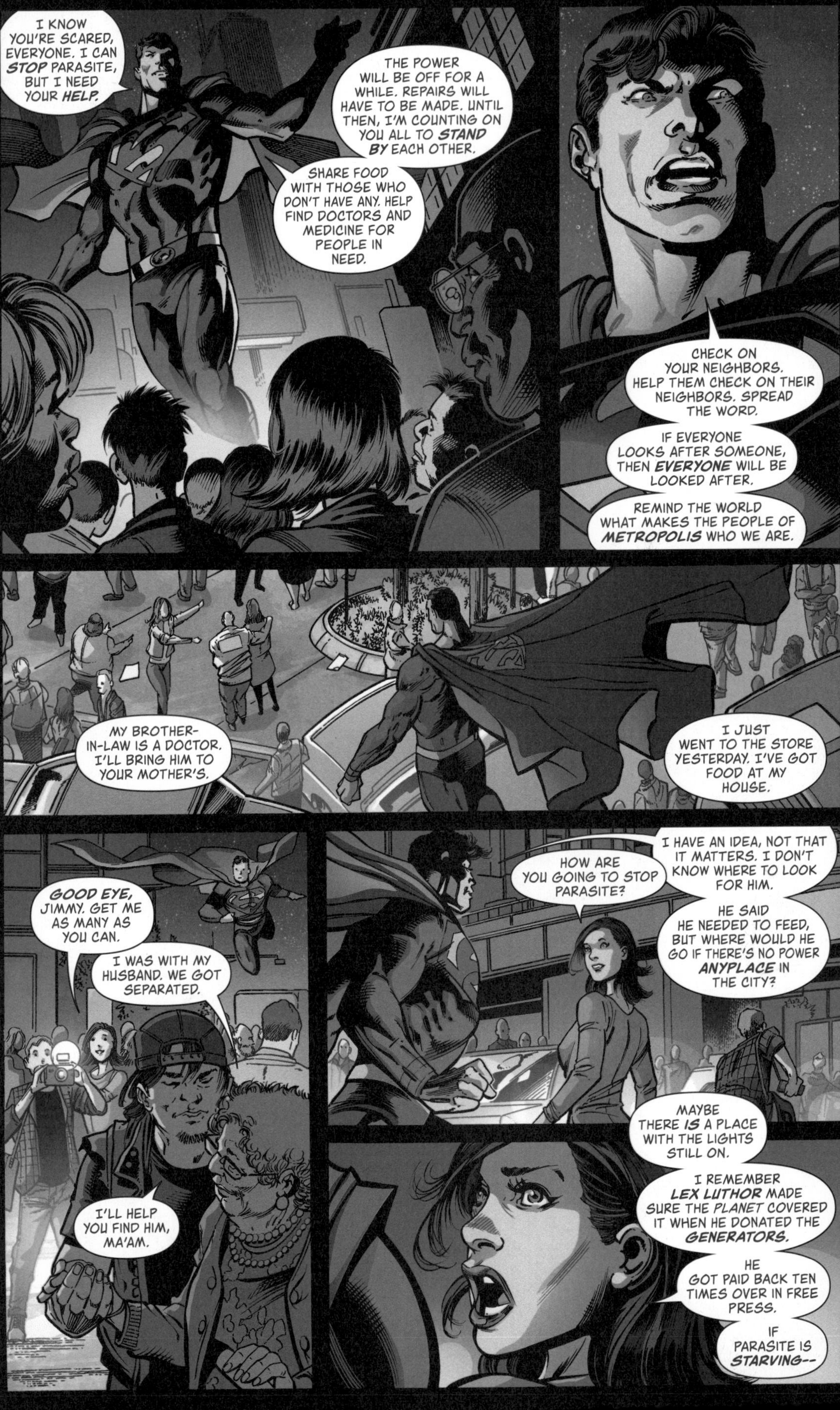
I KNOW YOU'RE SCARED, EVERYONE. I CAN *STOP* PARASITE, BUT I NEED YOUR *HELP.*
THE POWER WILL BE OFF FOR A WHILE. REPAIRS WILL HAVE TO BE MADE. UNTIL THEN, I'M COUNTING ON YOU ALL TO *STAND BY* EACH OTHER.
SHARE FOOD WITH THOSE WHO DON'T HAVE ANY. HELP FIND DOCTORS AND MEDICINE FOR PEOPLE IN NEED.
CHECK ON YOUR NEIGHBORS. HELP THEM CHECK ON THEIR NEIGHBORS. SPREAD THE WORD.
IF EVERYONE LOOKS AFTER SOMEONE, THEN *EVERYONE* WILL BE LOOKED AFTER.
REMIND THE WORLD WHAT MAKES THE PEOPLE OF *METROPOLIS* WHO WE ARE.
MY BROTHER-IN-LAW IS A DOCTOR. I'LL BRING HIM TO YOUR MOTHER'S.
I JUST WENT TO THE STORE YESTERDAY. I'VE GOT FOOD AT MY HOUSE.
GOOD EYE, JIMMY. GET ME AS MANY AS YOU CAN.
I WAS WITH MY HUSBAND. WE GOT SEPARATED.
I'LL HELP YOU FIND HIM, MA'AM.
HOW ARE YOU GOING TO STOP PARASITE?
I HAVE AN IDEA, NOT THAT IT MATTERS. I DON'T KNOW WHERE TO LOOK FOR HIM.
HE SAID HE NEEDED TO FEED, BUT WHERE WOULD HE GO IF THERE'S NO POWER *ANYPLACE* IN THE CITY?
MAYBE THERE *IS* A PLACE WITH THE LIGHTS STILL ON.
I REMEMBER *LEX LUTHOR* MADE SURE THE *PLANET* COVERED IT WHEN HE DONATED THE *GENERATORS.*
HE GOT PAID BACK TEN TIMES OVER IN FREE PRESS.
IF PARASITE IS *STARVING--*

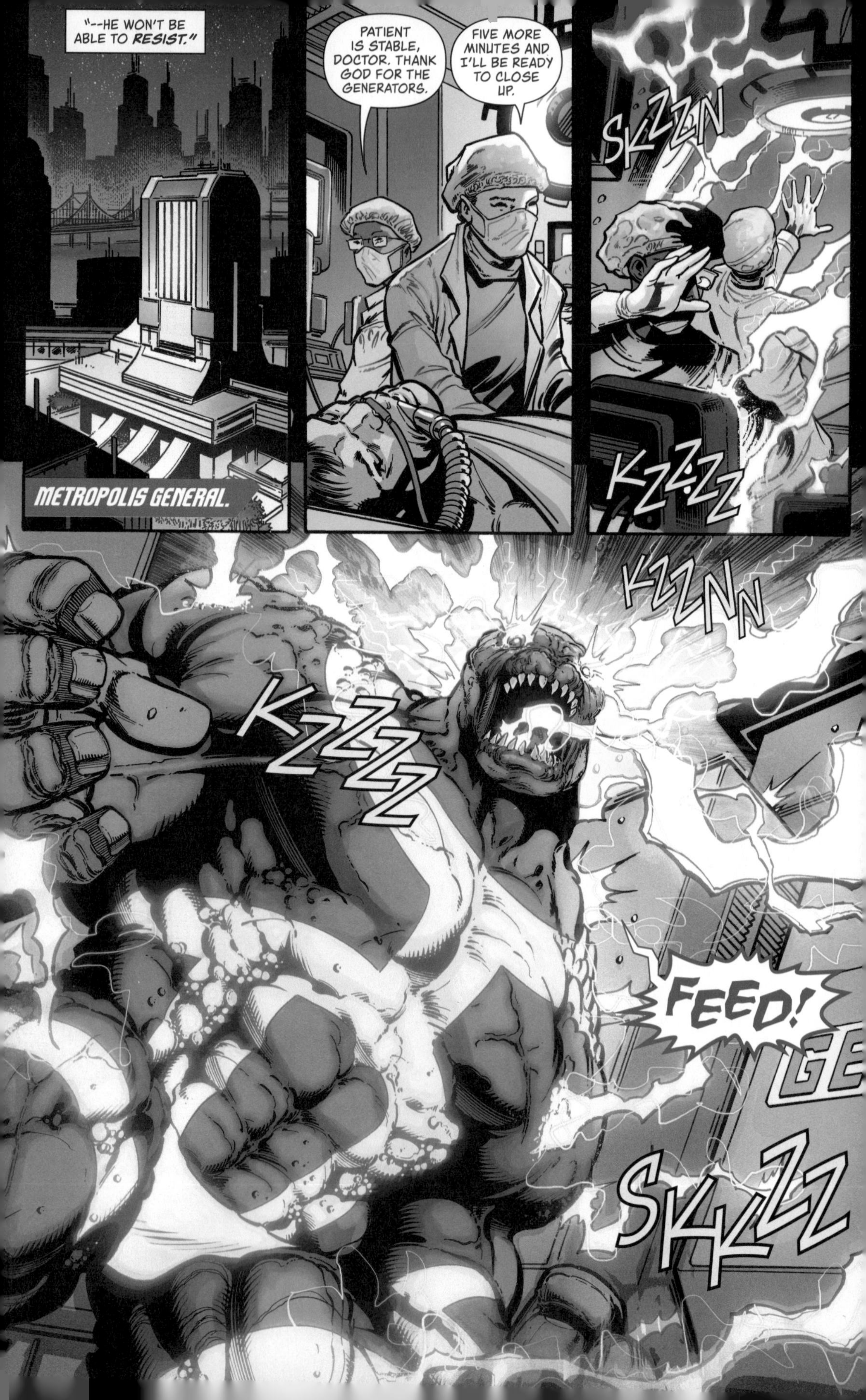
"--HE WON'T BE ABLE TO RESIST."
METROPOLIS GENERAL.
PATIENT IS STABLE, DOCTOR. THANK GOD FOR THE GENERATORS.
FIVE MORE MINUTES AND I'LL BE READY TO CLOSE UP.
SKZZZN
KZZZZ
KZZNNN
KZZZZZ
FEED!
SKKZZZ

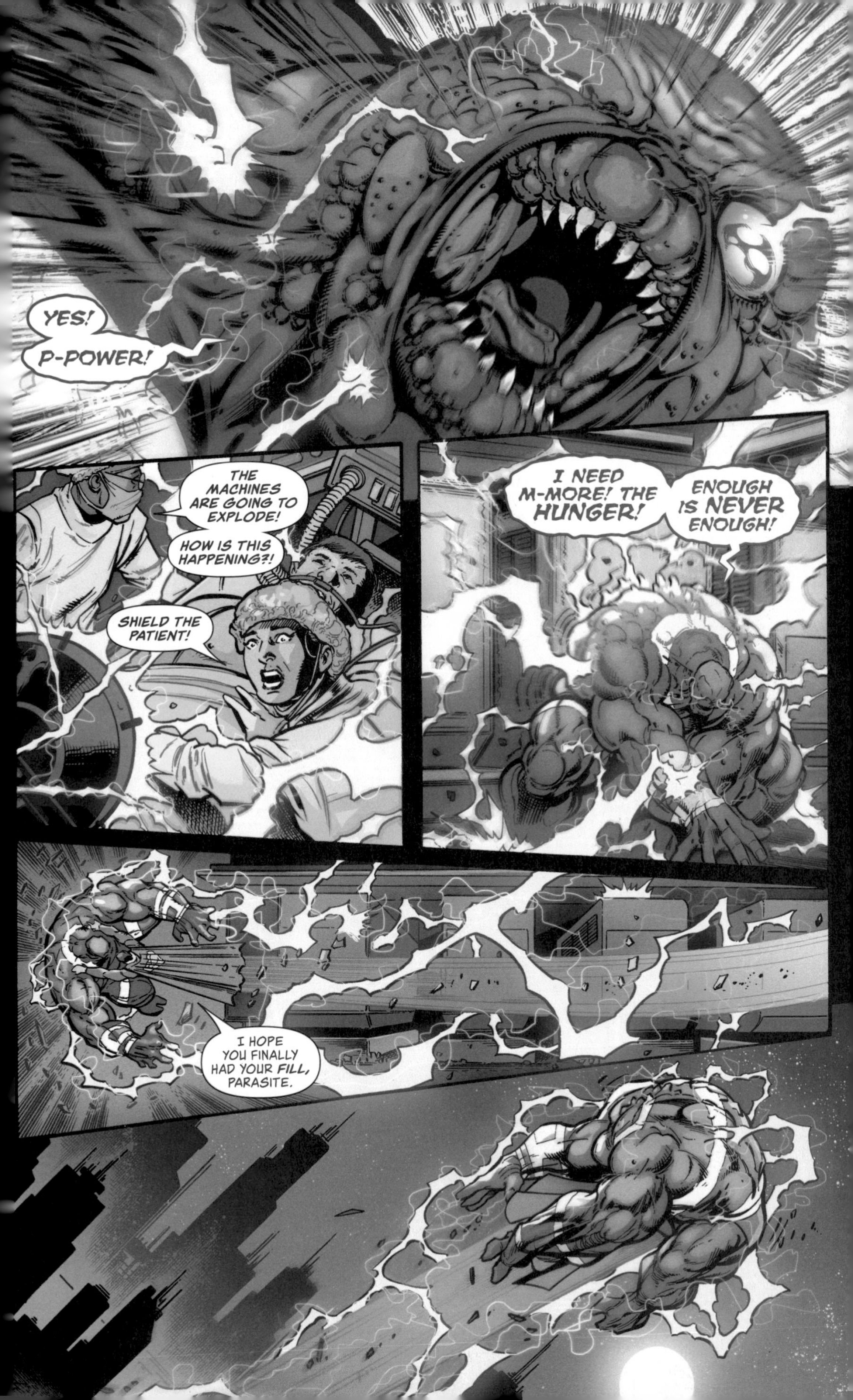
YES!
P-POWER!
THE MACHINES ARE GOING TO EXPLODE!
HOW IS THIS HAPPENING?!
SHIELD THE PATIENT!
I NEED M-MORE! THE HUNGER!
ENOUGH IS NEVER ENOUGH!
I HOPE YOU FINALLY HAD YOUR FILL, PARASITE.

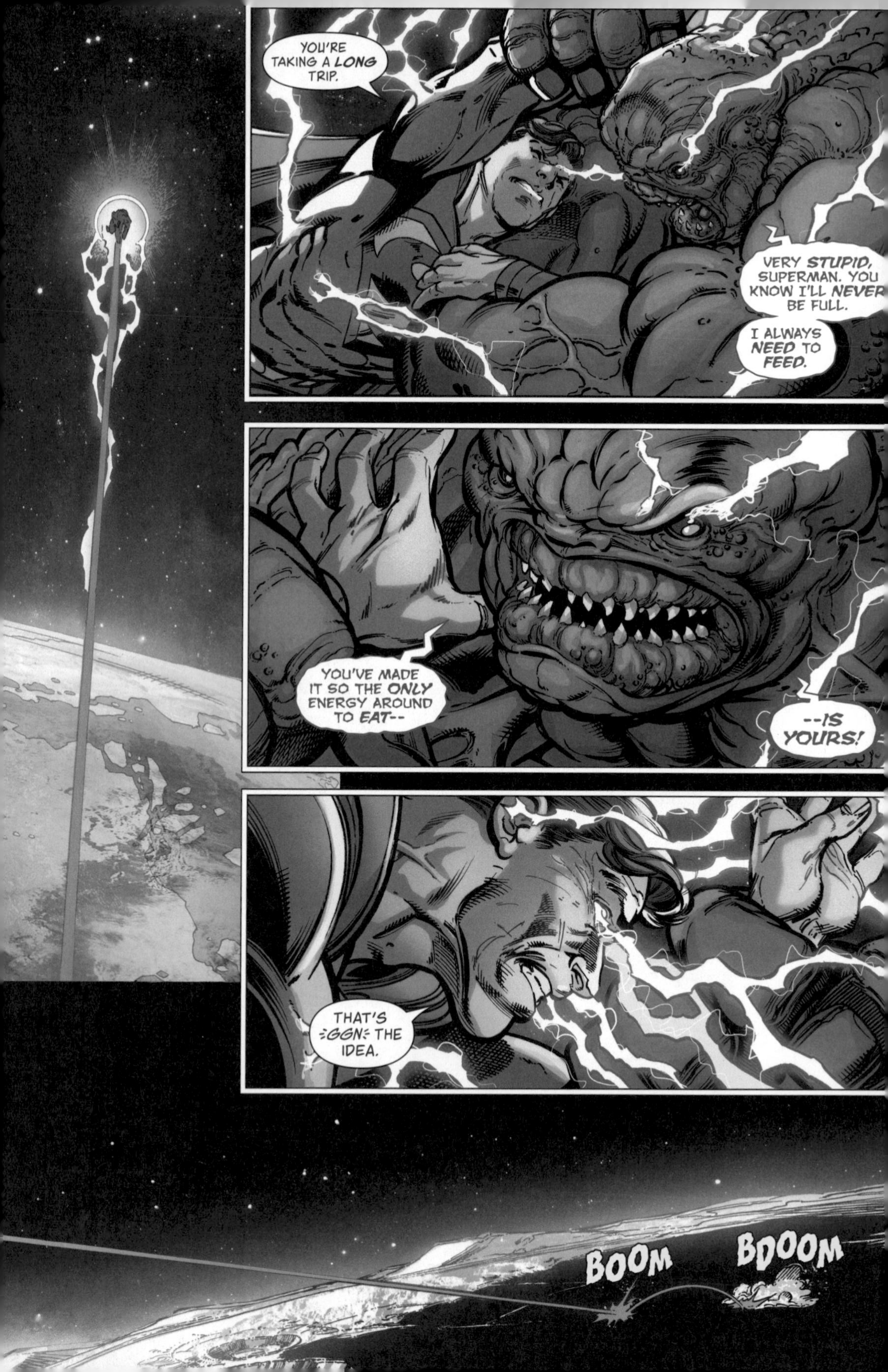

YOU'RE TAKING A LONG TRIP.
VERY STUPID, SUPERMAN. YOU KNOW I'LL NEVER BE FULL.
I ALWAYS NEED TO FEED.
YOU'VE MADE IT SO THE ONLY ENERGY AROUND TO EAT--
--IS YOURS!
THAT'S =GGN= THE IDEA.
BOOM
BDOOM

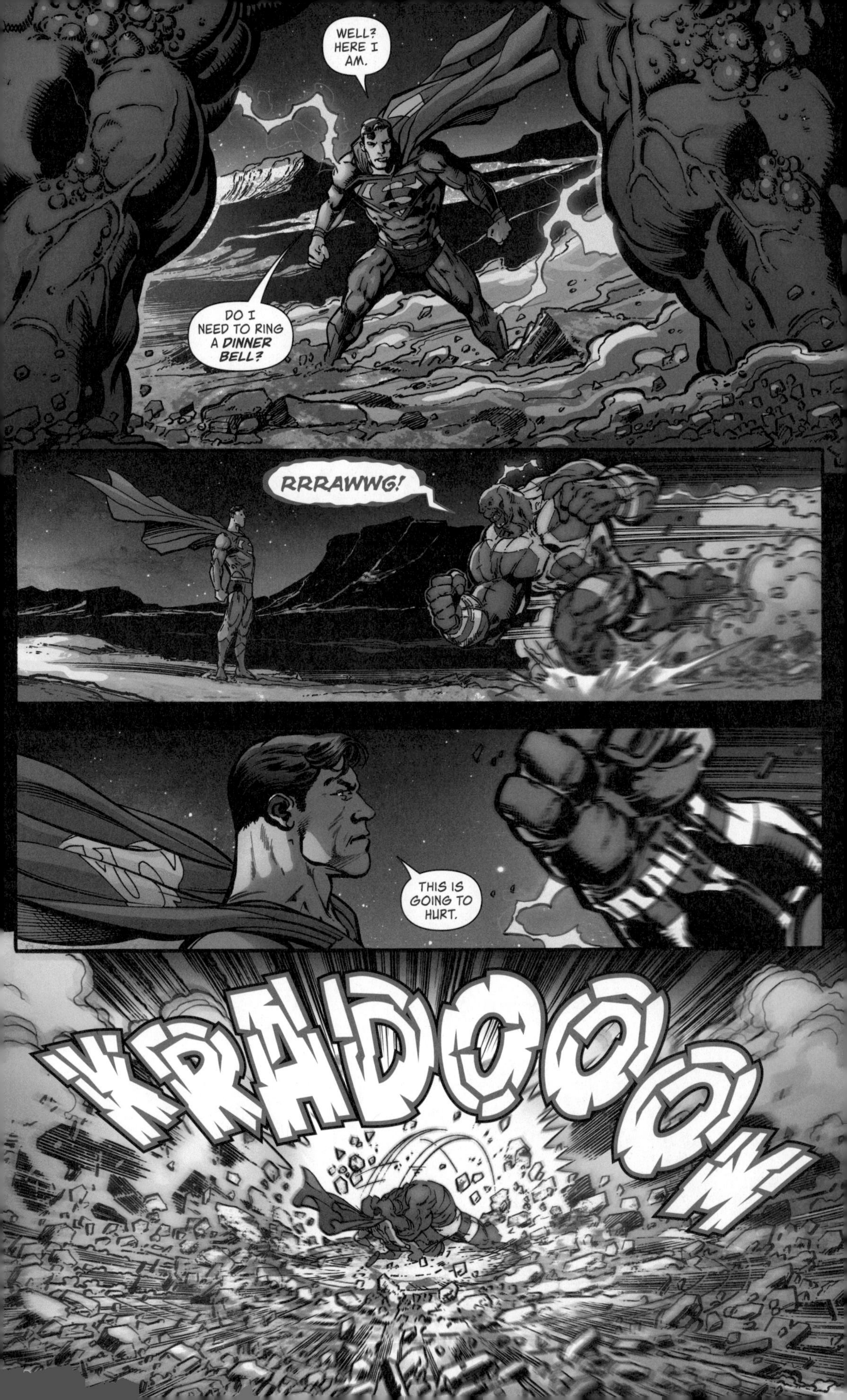
WELL? HERE I AM.
DO I NEED TO RING A DINNER BELL?
RRRAWWG!
THIS IS GOING TO HURT.
KRADOOOOM

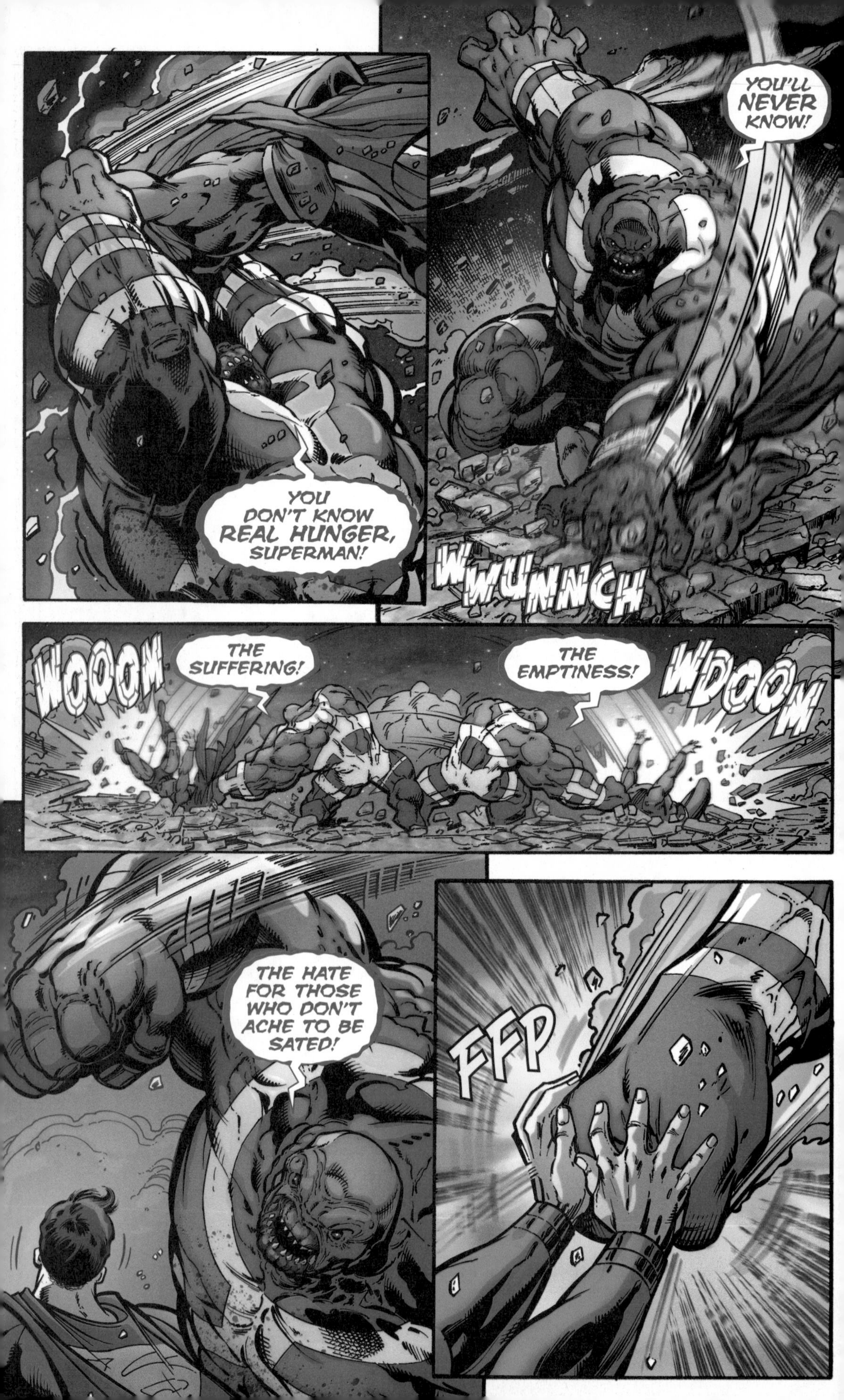
YOU DON'T KNOW REAL HUNGER, SUPERMAN!
YOU'LL NEVER KNOW!
WWUNNCH
WOOOM
THE SUFFERING!
THE EMPTINESS!
WDOOM
THE HATE FOR THOSE WHO DON'T ACHE TO BE SATED!
FFP

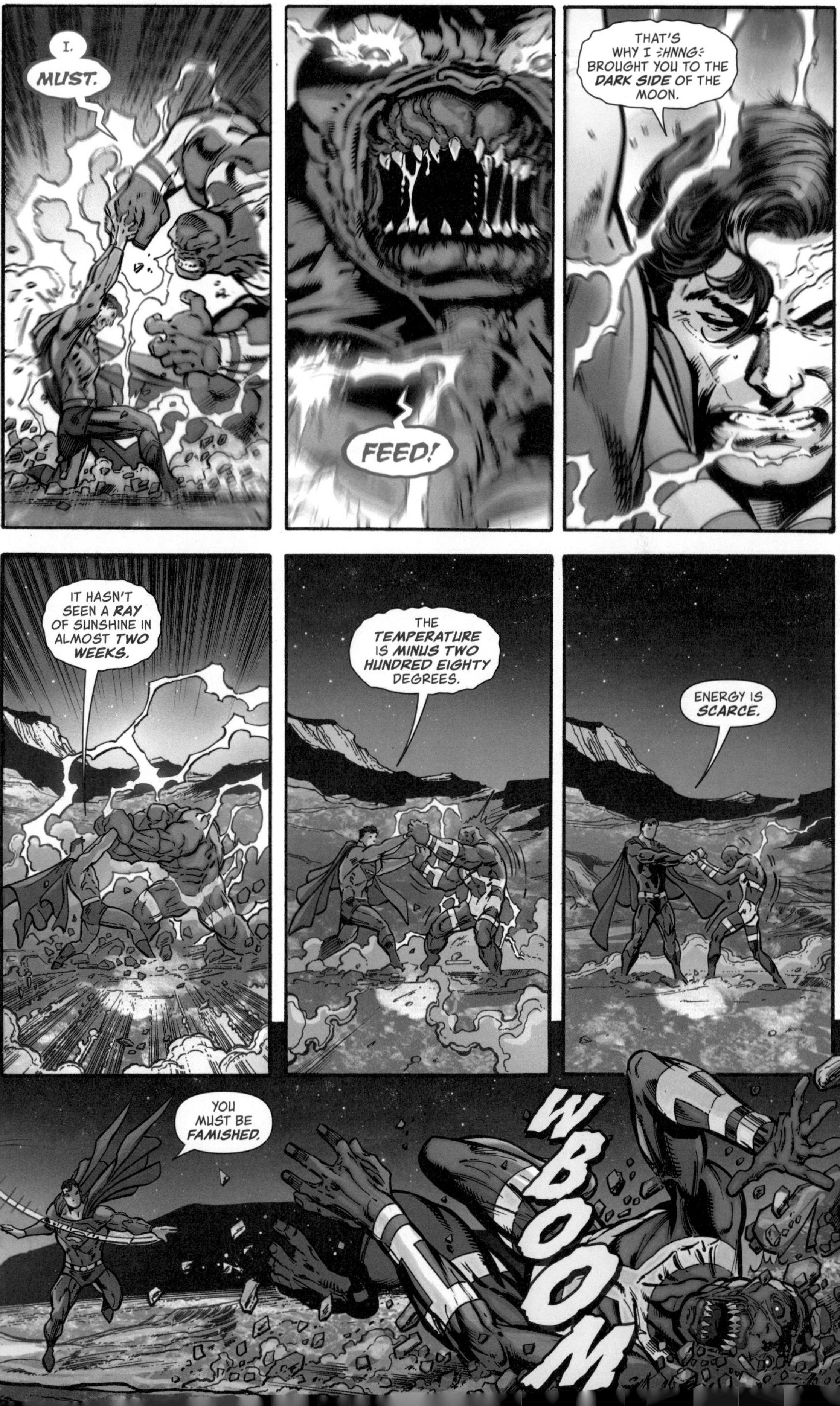
I.
MUST.
FEED!
THAT'S WHY I =HNNG= BROUGHT YOU TO THE DARK SIDE OF THE MOON.
IT HASN'T SEEN A RAY OF SUNSHINE IN ALMOST TWO WEEKS.
THE TEMPERATURE IS MINUS TWO HUNDRED EIGHTY DEGREES.
ENERGY IS SCARCE.
YOU MUST BE FAMISHED.
WBOOM

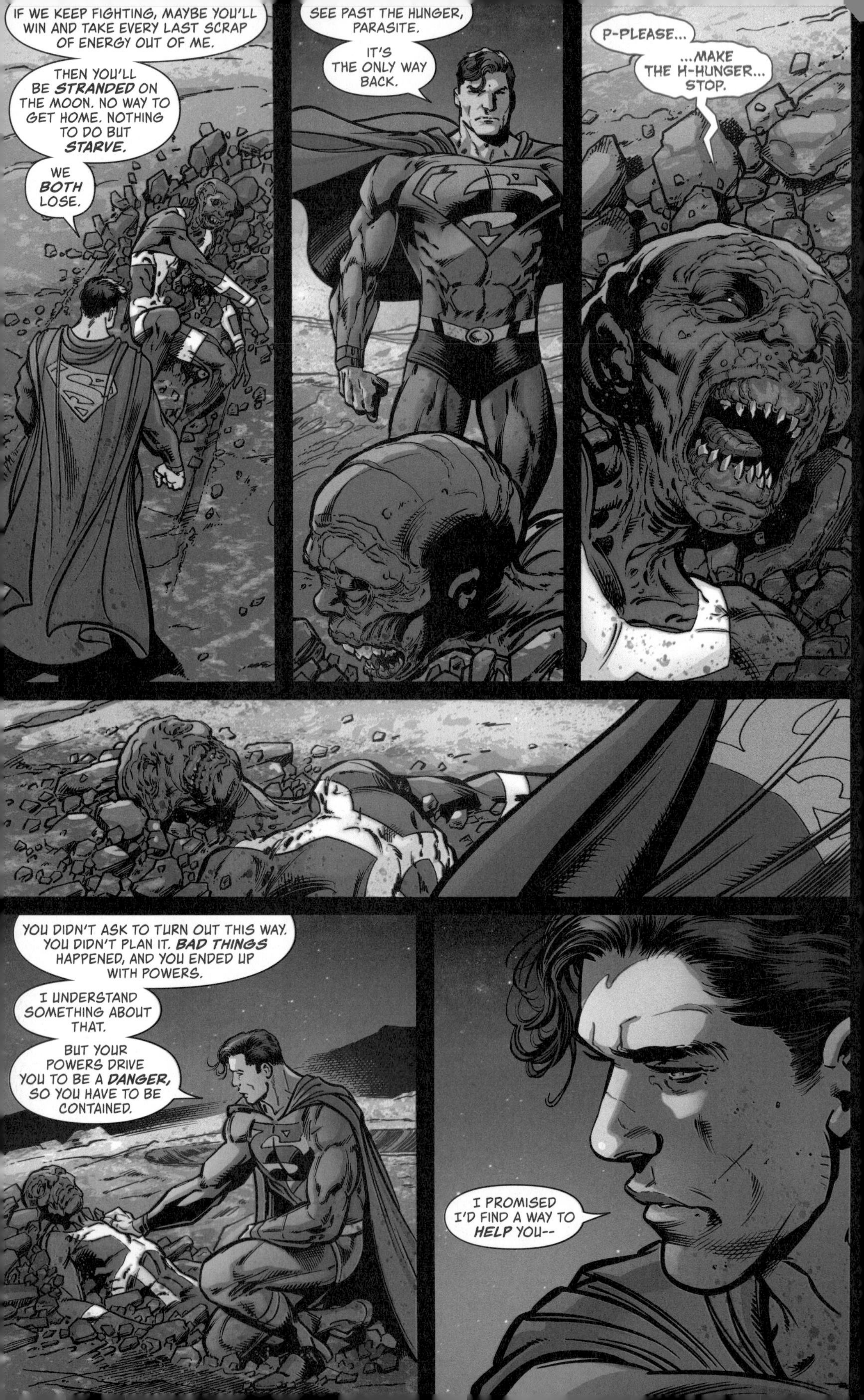
IF WE KEEP FIGHTING, MAYBE YOU'LL WIN AND TAKE EVERY LAST SCRAP OF ENERGY OUT OF ME.
THEN YOU'LL BE STRANDED ON THE MOON. NO WAY TO GET HOME. NOTHING TO DO BUT STARVE.
WE BOTH LOSE.
SEE PAST THE HUNGER, PARASITE.
IT'S THE ONLY WAY BACK.
P-PLEASE...
...MAKE THE H-HUNGER... STOP.
YOU DIDN'T ASK TO TURN OUT THIS WAY. YOU DIDN'T PLAN IT. BAD THINGS HAPPENED, AND YOU ENDED UP WITH POWERS.
I UNDERSTAND SOMETHING ABOUT THAT.
BUT YOUR POWERS DRIVE YOU TO BE A DANGER, SO YOU HAVE TO BE CONTAINED.
I PROMISED I'D FIND A WAY TO HELP YOU--

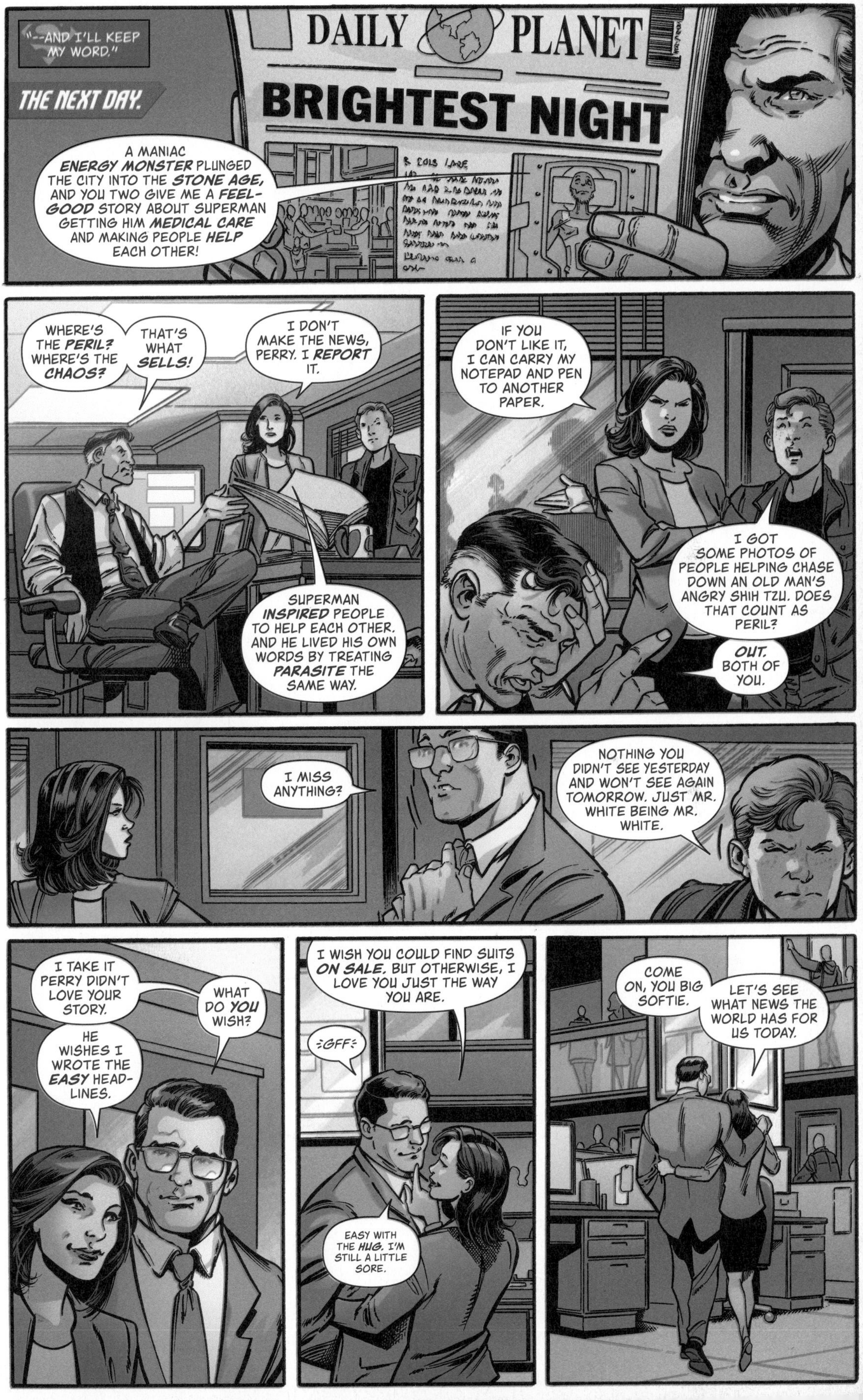
"--AND I'LL KEEP MY WORD."
THE NEXT DAY.
DAILY PLANET
BRIGHTEST NIGHT
A MANIAC ENERGY MONSTER PLUNGED THE CITY INTO THE STONE AGE, AND YOU TWO GIVE ME A FEEL-GOOD STORY ABOUT SUPERMAN GETTING HIM MEDICAL CARE AND MAKING PEOPLE HELP EACH OTHER!
WHERE'S THE PERIL? WHERE'S THE CHAOS?
THAT'S WHAT SELLS!
I DON'T MAKE THE NEWS, PERRY. I REPORT IT.
SUPERMAN INSPIRED PEOPLE TO HELP EACH OTHER. AND HE LIVED HIS OWN WORDS BY TREATING PARASITE THE SAME WAY.
IF YOU DON'T LIKE IT, I CAN CARRY MY NOTEPAD AND PEN TO ANOTHER PAPER.
I GOT SOME PHOTOS OF PEOPLE HELPING CHASE DOWN AN OLD MAN'S ANGRY SHIH TZU. DOES THAT COUNT AS PERIL?
OUT. BOTH OF YOU.
I MISS ANYTHING?
NOTHING YOU DIDN'T SEE YESTERDAY AND WON'T SEE AGAIN TOMORROW. JUST MR. WHITE BEING MR. WHITE.
I TAKE IT PERRY DIDN'T LOVE YOUR STORY.
WHAT DO YOU WISH?
HE WISHES I WROTE THE EASY HEAD-LINES.
I WISH YOU COULD FIND SUITS ON SALE. BUT OTHERWISE, I LOVE YOU JUST THE WAY YOU ARE.
GFF
EASY WITH THE HUG. I'M STILL A LITTLE SORE.
COME ON, YOU BIG SOFTIE.
LET'S SEE WHAT NEWS THE WORLD HAS FOR US TODAY.

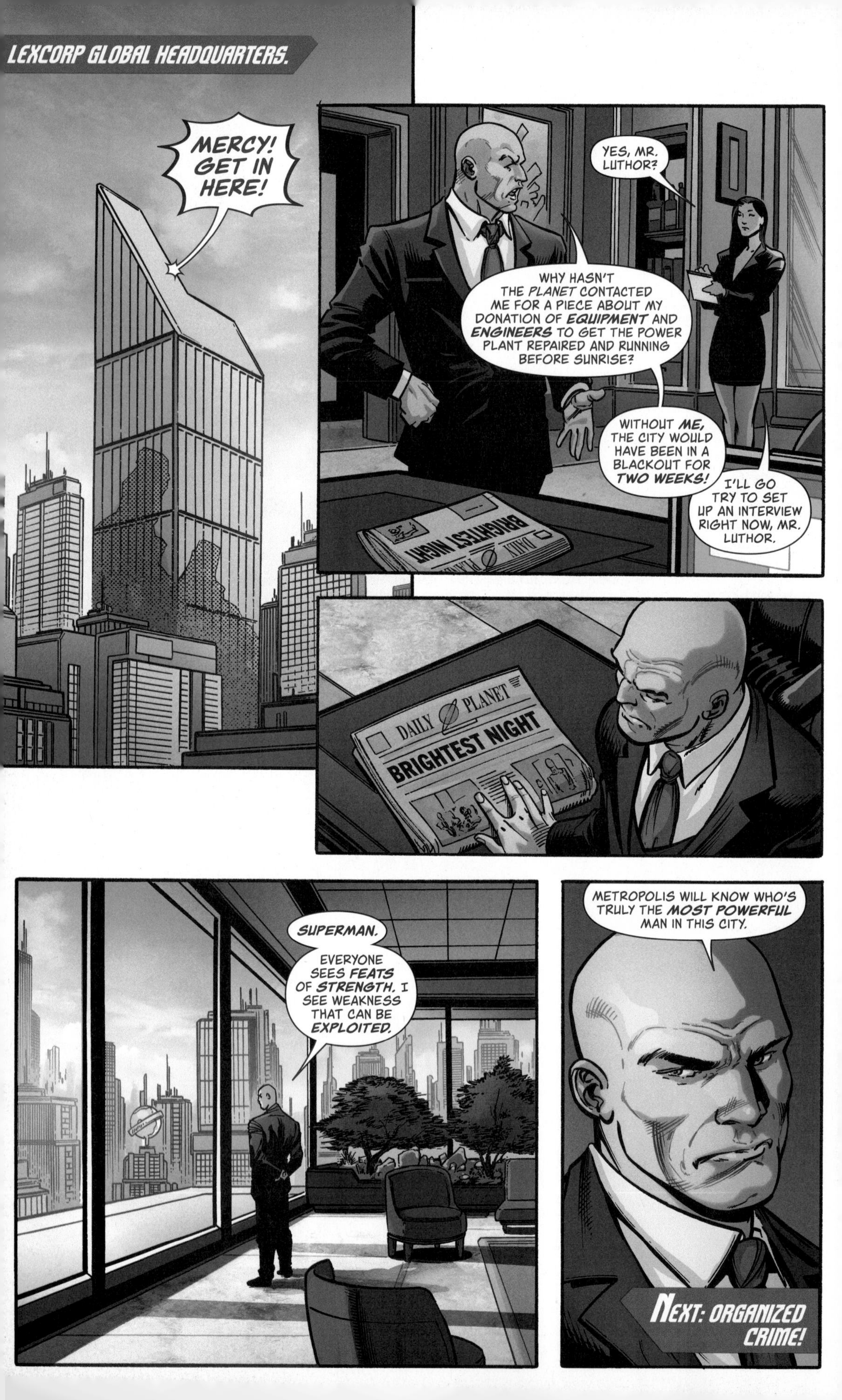
LEXCORP GLOBAL HEADQUARTERS.
MERCY! GET IN HERE!
YES, MR. LUTHOR?
WHY HASN'T THE PLANET CONTACTED ME FOR A PIECE ABOUT MY DONATION OF EQUIPMENT AND ENGINEERS TO GET THE POWER PLANT REPAIRED AND RUNNING BEFORE SUNRISE?
WITHOUT ME, THE CITY WOULD HAVE BEEN IN A BLACKOUT FOR TWO WEEKS!
I'LL GO TRY TO SET UP AN INTERVIEW RIGHT NOW, MR. LUTHOR.
DAILY PLANET
BRIGHTEST NIGHT
SUPERMAN.
EVERYONE SEES FEATS OF STRENGTH. I SEE WEAKNESS THAT CAN BE EXPLOITED.
METROPOLIS WILL KNOW WHO'S TRULY THE MOST POWERFUL MAN IN THIS CITY.
NEXT: ORGANIZED CRIME!

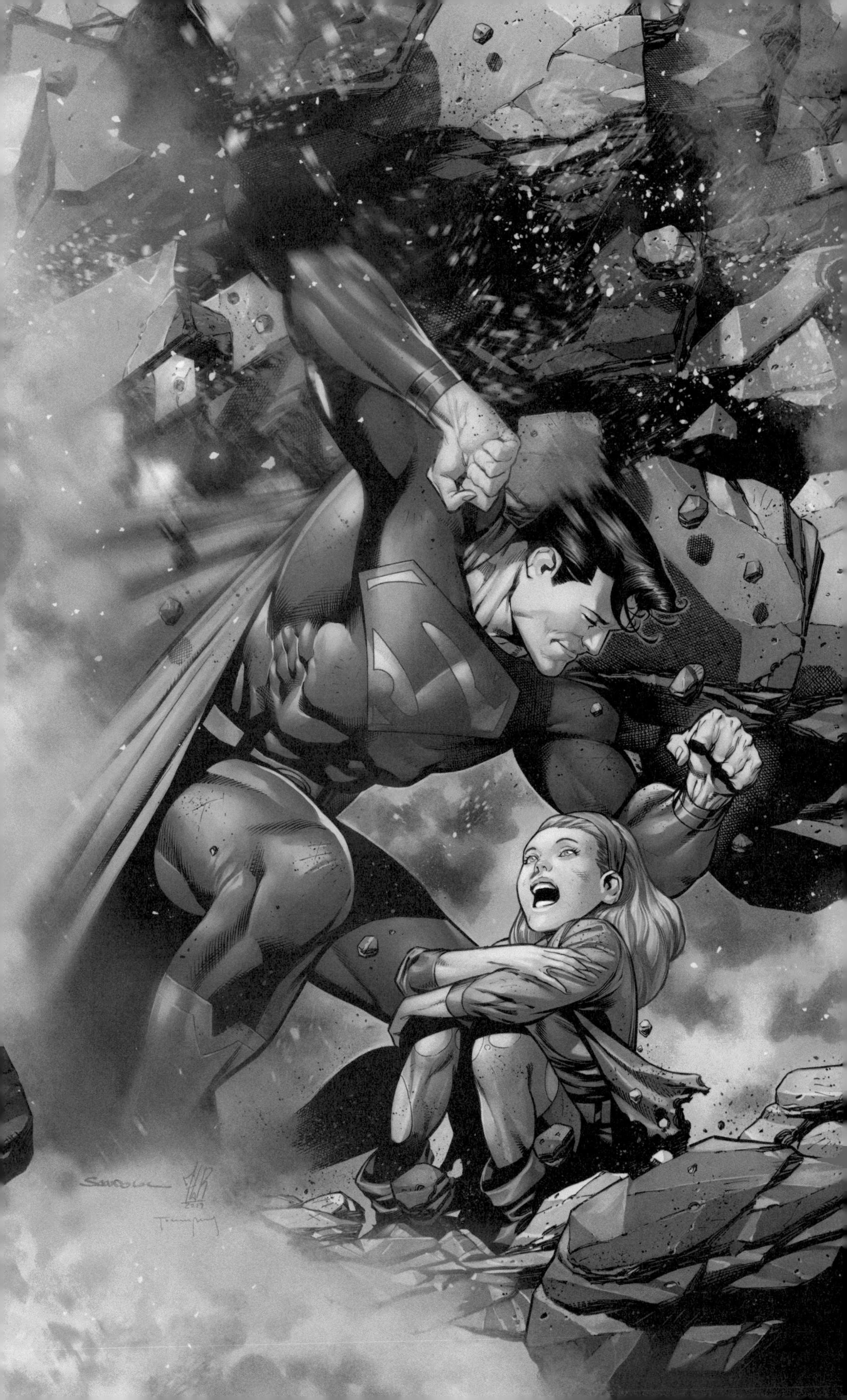

COVER ART BY
RAFA SANDOVAL, JORDI TARRAGONA,
AND **TOMEU MOREY**

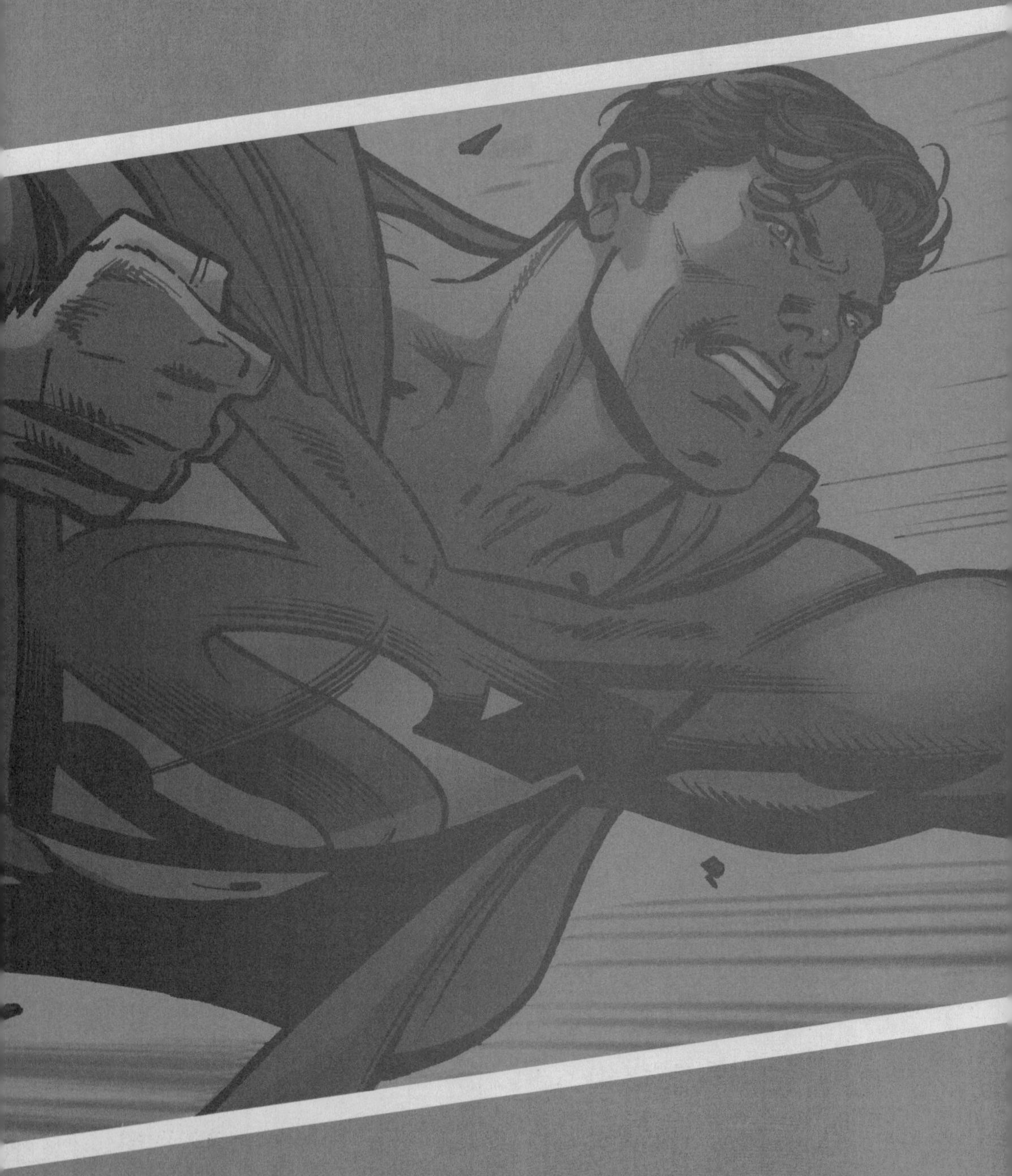

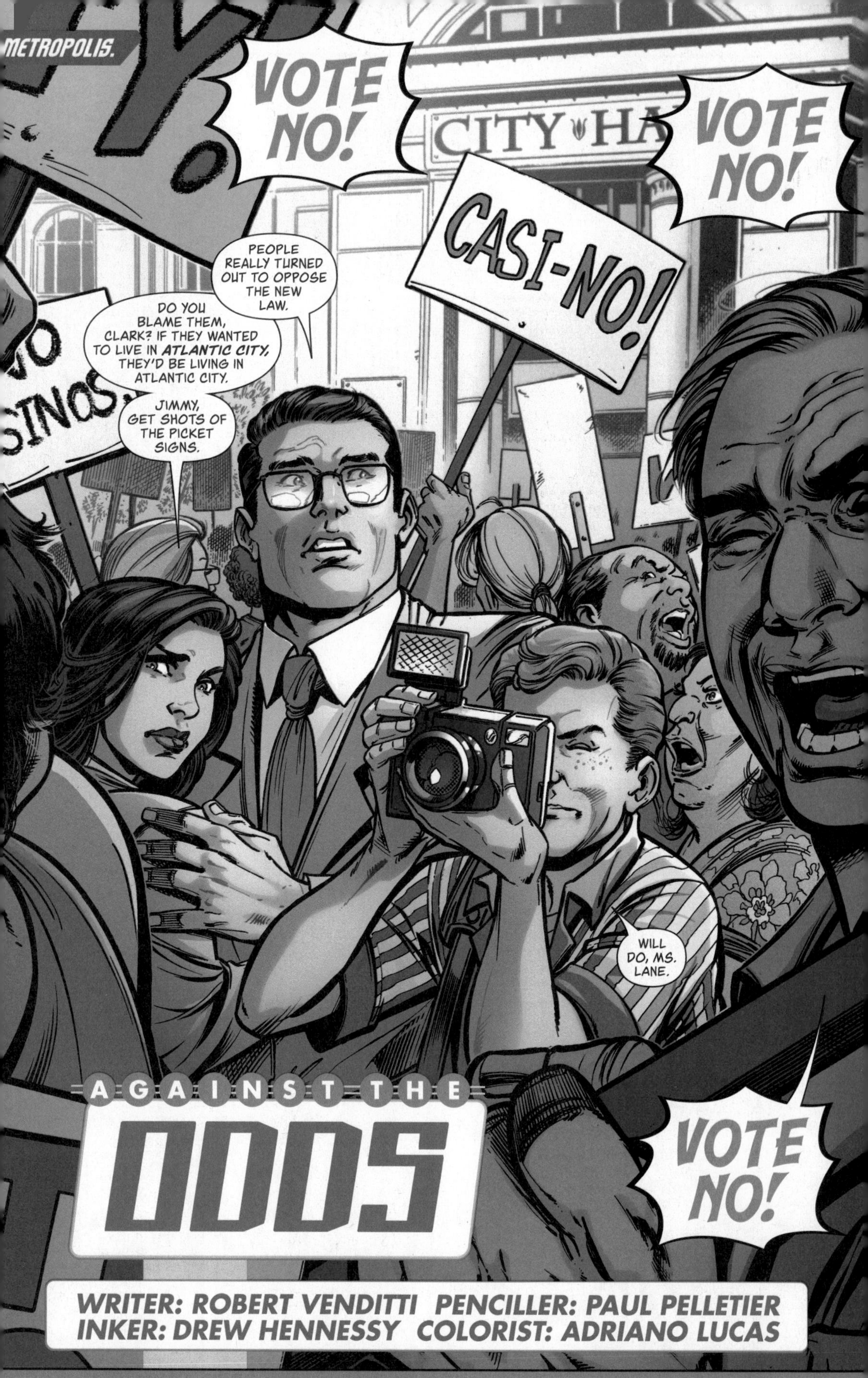
METROPOLIS.
VOTE NO!
CITY HA
VOTE NO!
CASI-NO!
PEOPLE REALLY TURNED OUT TO OPPOSE THE NEW LAW.
DO YOU BLAME THEM, CLARK? IF THEY WANTED TO LIVE IN *ATLANTIC CITY,* THEY'D BE LIVING IN ATLANTIC CITY.
JIMMY, GET SHOTS OF THE PICKET SIGNS.
WILL DO, MS. LANE.
AGAINST THE
ODDS
VOTE NO!
WRITER: ROBERT VENDITTI PENCILLER: PAUL PELLETIER
INKER: DREW HENNESSY COLORIST: ADRIANO LUCAS

LETTERER: CLAYTON COWLES COVER: RAFA SANDOVAL, JORDI TARRAGONA, TOMEU MOREY EDITOR: ANDREW MARINO
SUPERMAN created by JERRY SIEGEL and JOE SHUSTER. By special arrangement with the JERRY SIEGEL FAMILY

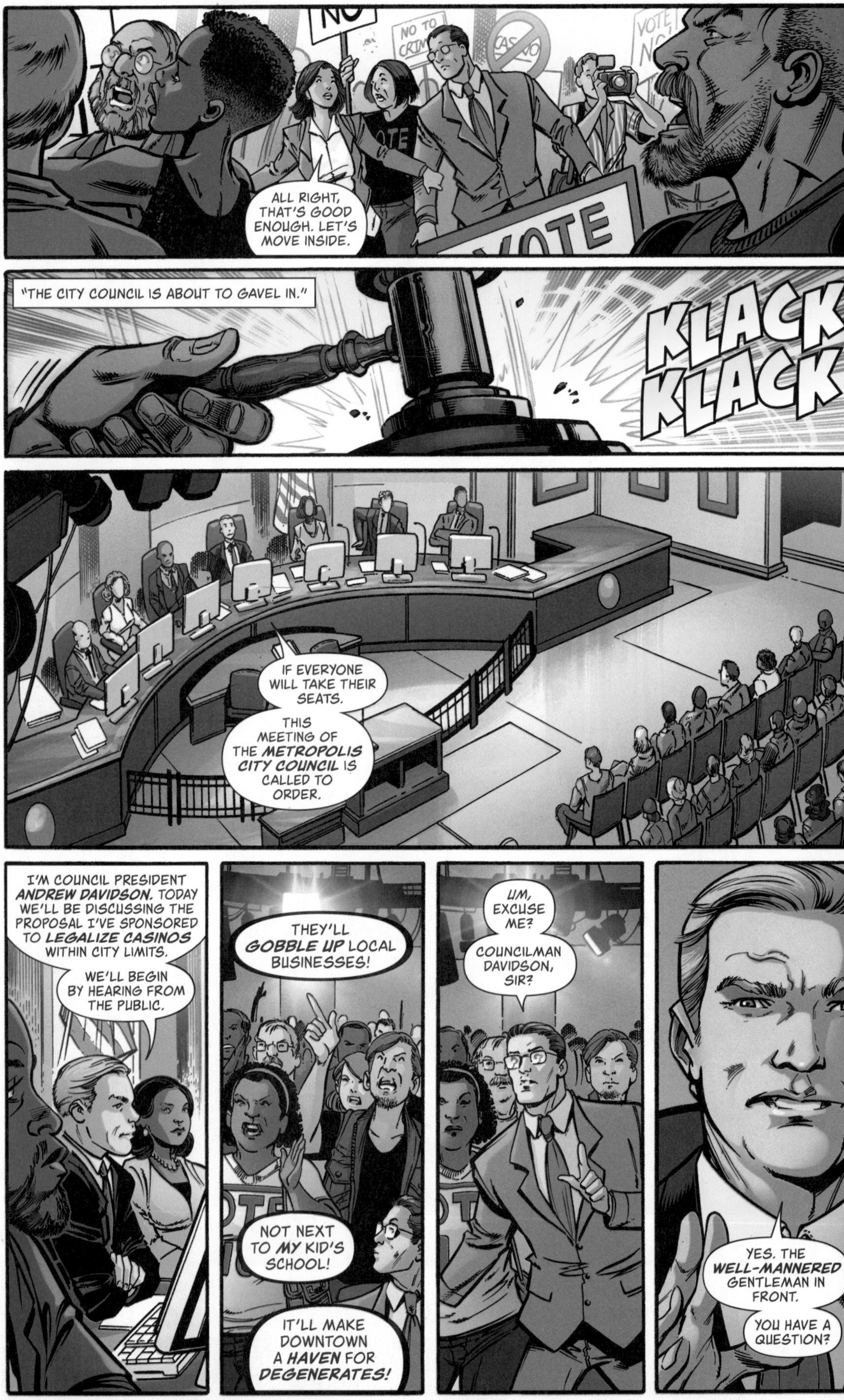
NO
VOTE
ALL RIGHT, THAT'S GOOD ENOUGH. LET'S MOVE INSIDE.
"THE CITY COUNCIL IS ABOUT TO GAVEL IN."
KLACK KLACK
IF EVERYONE WILL TAKE THEIR SEATS.
THIS MEETING OF THE *METROPOLIS CITY COUNCIL* IS CALLED TO ORDER.
I'M COUNCIL PRESIDENT *ANDREW DAVIDSON.* TODAY WE'LL BE DISCUSSING THE PROPOSAL I'VE SPONSORED TO *LEGALIZE CASINOS* WITHIN CITY LIMITS.
WE'LL BEGIN BY HEARING FROM THE PUBLIC.
THEY'LL *GOBBLE UP* LOCAL BUSINESSES!
NOT NEXT TO *MY* KID'S SCHOOL!
IT'LL MAKE DOWNTOWN A *HAVEN* FOR *DEGENERATES!*
UM, EXCUSE ME?
COUNCILMAN DAVIDSON, SIR?
YES. THE *WELL-MANNERED* GENTLEMAN IN FRONT.
YOU HAVE A QUESTION?

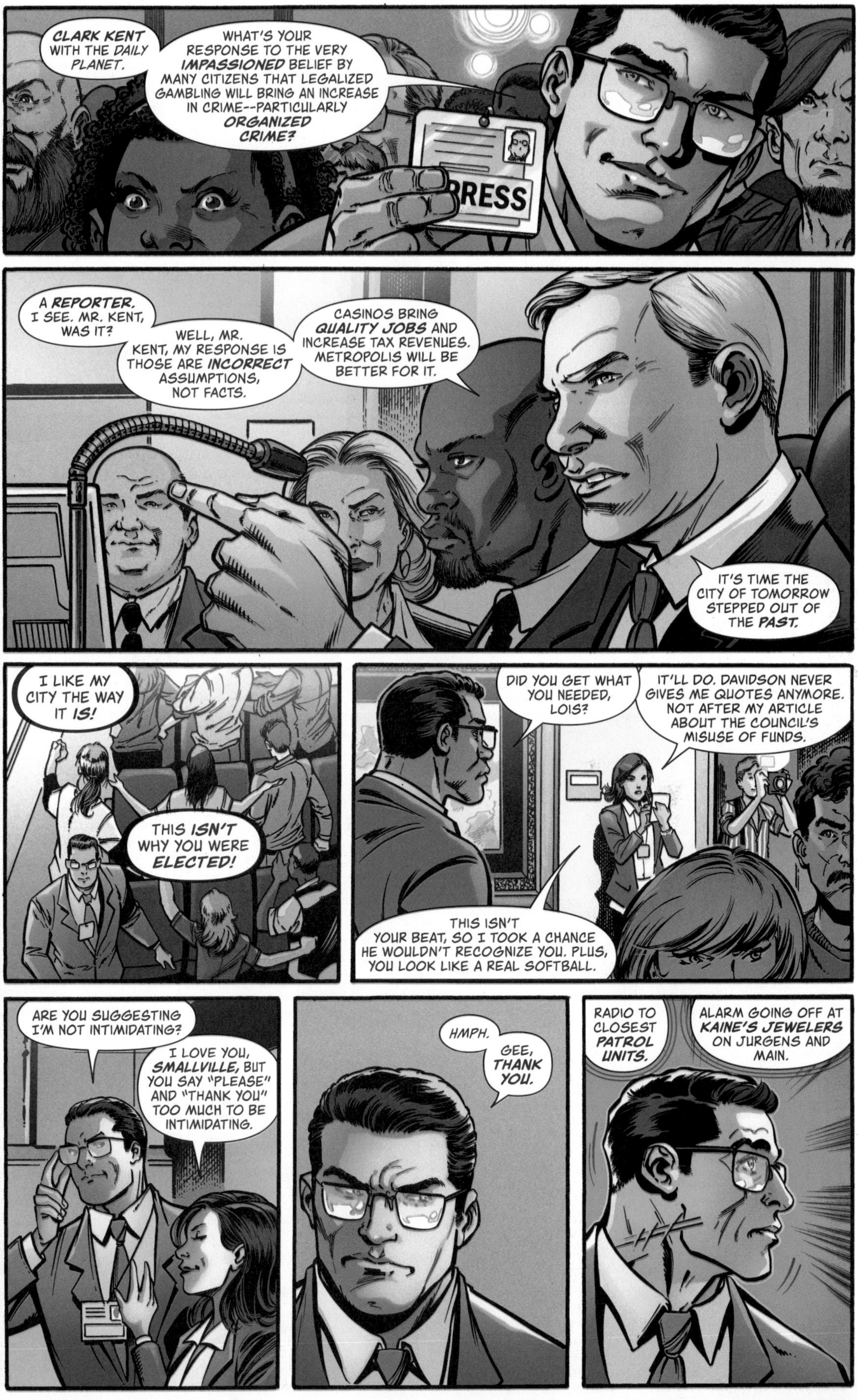
CLARK KENT WITH THE DAILY PLANET.
WHAT'S YOUR RESPONSE TO THE VERY IMPASSIONED BELIEF BY MANY CITIZENS THAT LEGALIZED GAMBLING WILL BRING AN INCREASE IN CRIME--PARTICULARLY ORGANIZED CRIME?
PRESS
A REPORTER. I SEE. MR. KENT, WAS IT?
WELL, MR. KENT, MY RESPONSE IS THOSE ARE INCORRECT ASSUMPTIONS, NOT FACTS.
CASINOS BRING QUALITY JOBS AND INCREASE TAX REVENUES. METROPOLIS WILL BE BETTER FOR IT.
IT'S TIME THE CITY OF TOMORROW STEPPED OUT OF THE PAST.
I LIKE MY CITY THE WAY IT IS!
THIS ISN'T WHY YOU WERE ELECTED!
DID YOU GET WHAT YOU NEEDED, LOIS?
IT'LL DO. DAVIDSON NEVER GIVES ME QUOTES ANYMORE. NOT AFTER MY ARTICLE ABOUT THE COUNCIL'S MISUSE OF FUNDS.
THIS ISN'T YOUR BEAT, SO I TOOK A CHANCE HE WOULDN'T RECOGNIZE YOU. PLUS, YOU LOOK LIKE A REAL SOFTBALL.
ARE YOU SUGGESTING I'M NOT INTIMIDATING?
I LOVE YOU, SMALLVILLE, BUT YOU SAY "PLEASE" AND "THANK YOU" TOO MUCH TO BE INTIMIDATING.
HMPH.
GEE, THANK YOU.
RADIO TO CLOSEST PATROL UNITS.
ALARM GOING OFF AT KAINE'S JEWELERS ON JURGENS AND MAIN.

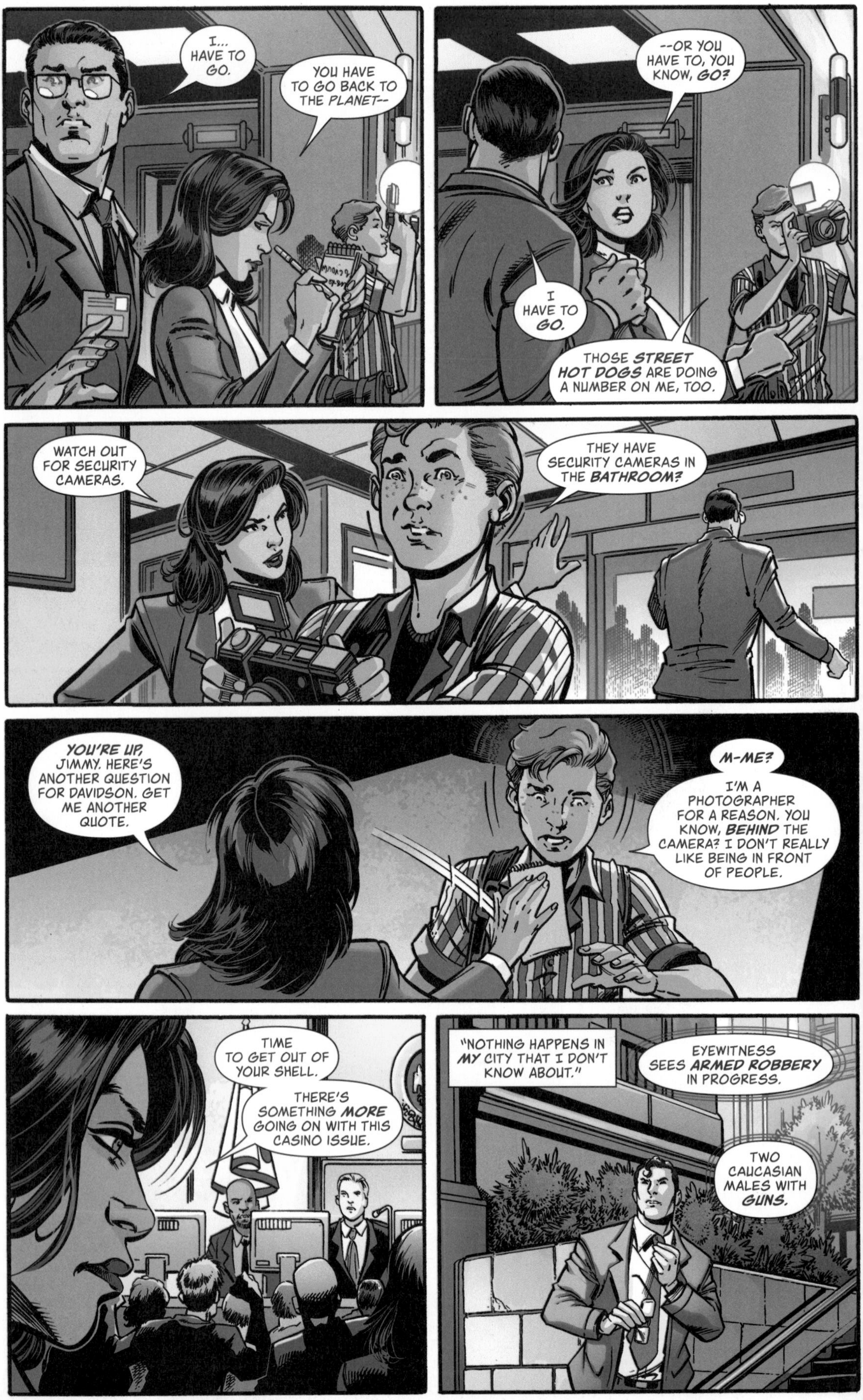
I... HAVE TO GO.
YOU HAVE TO GO BACK TO THE *PLANET*--
--OR YOU HAVE TO, YOU KNOW, *GO?*
I HAVE TO *GO.*
THOSE ***STREET HOT DOGS*** ARE DOING A NUMBER ON ME, TOO.
WATCH OUT FOR SECURITY CAMERAS.
THEY HAVE SECURITY CAMERAS IN THE ***BATHROOM?***
YOU'RE UP, JIMMY. HERE'S ANOTHER QUESTION FOR DAVIDSON. GET ME ANOTHER QUOTE.
M-ME?
I'M A PHOTOGRAPHER FOR A REASON. YOU KNOW, ***BEHIND*** THE CAMERA? I DON'T REALLY LIKE BEING IN FRONT OF PEOPLE.
TIME TO GET OUT OF YOUR SHELL.
THERE'S SOMETHING ***MORE*** GOING ON WITH THIS CASINO ISSUE.
"NOTHING HAPPENS IN ***MY*** CITY THAT I DON'T KNOW ABOUT."
EYEWITNESS SEES ***ARMED ROBBERY*** IN PROGRESS.
TWO CAUCASIAN MALES WITH ***GUNS.***

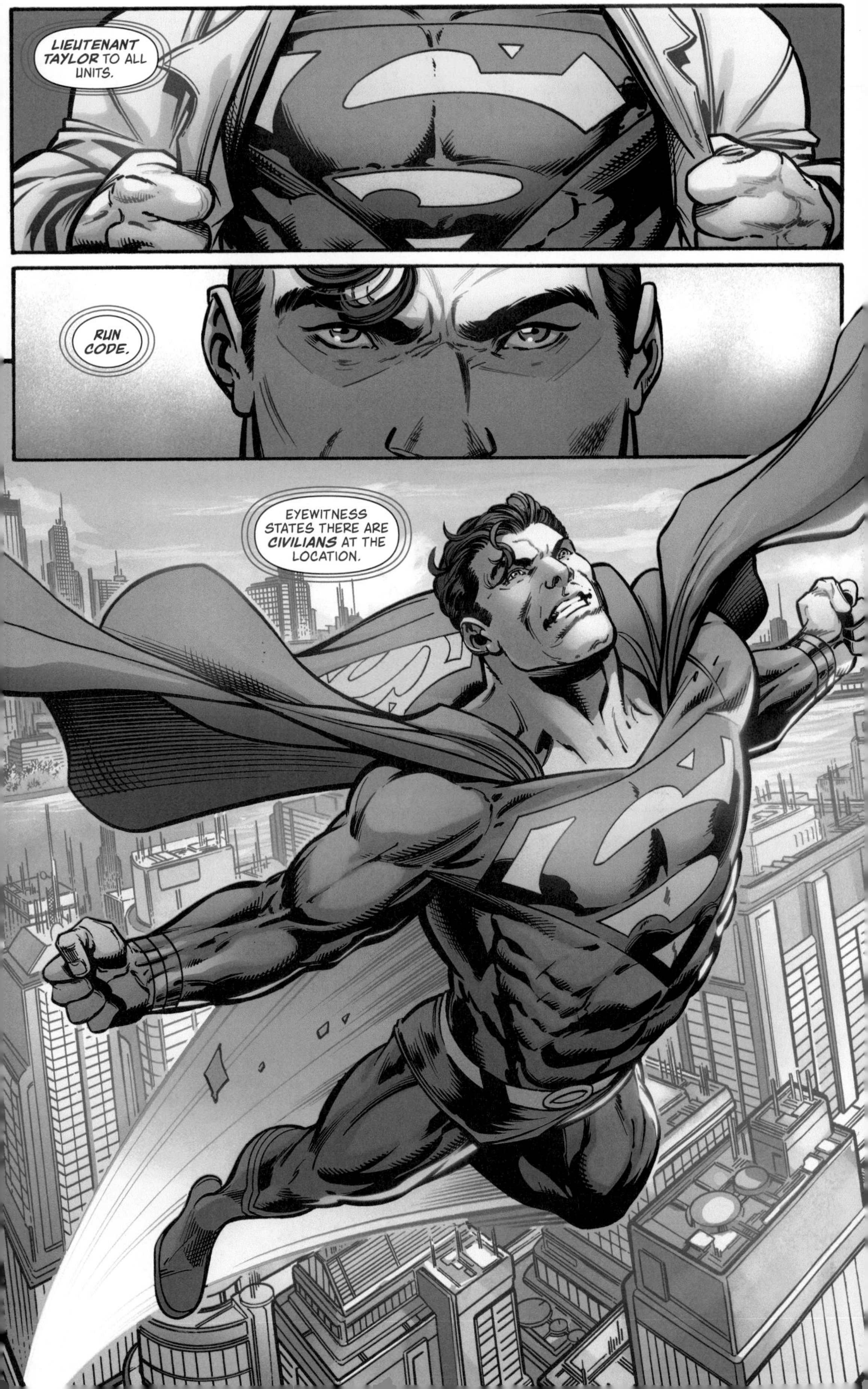
LIEUTENANT TAYLOR TO ALL UNITS.
RUN CODE.
EYEWITNESS STATES THERE ARE CIVILIANS AT THE LOCATION.

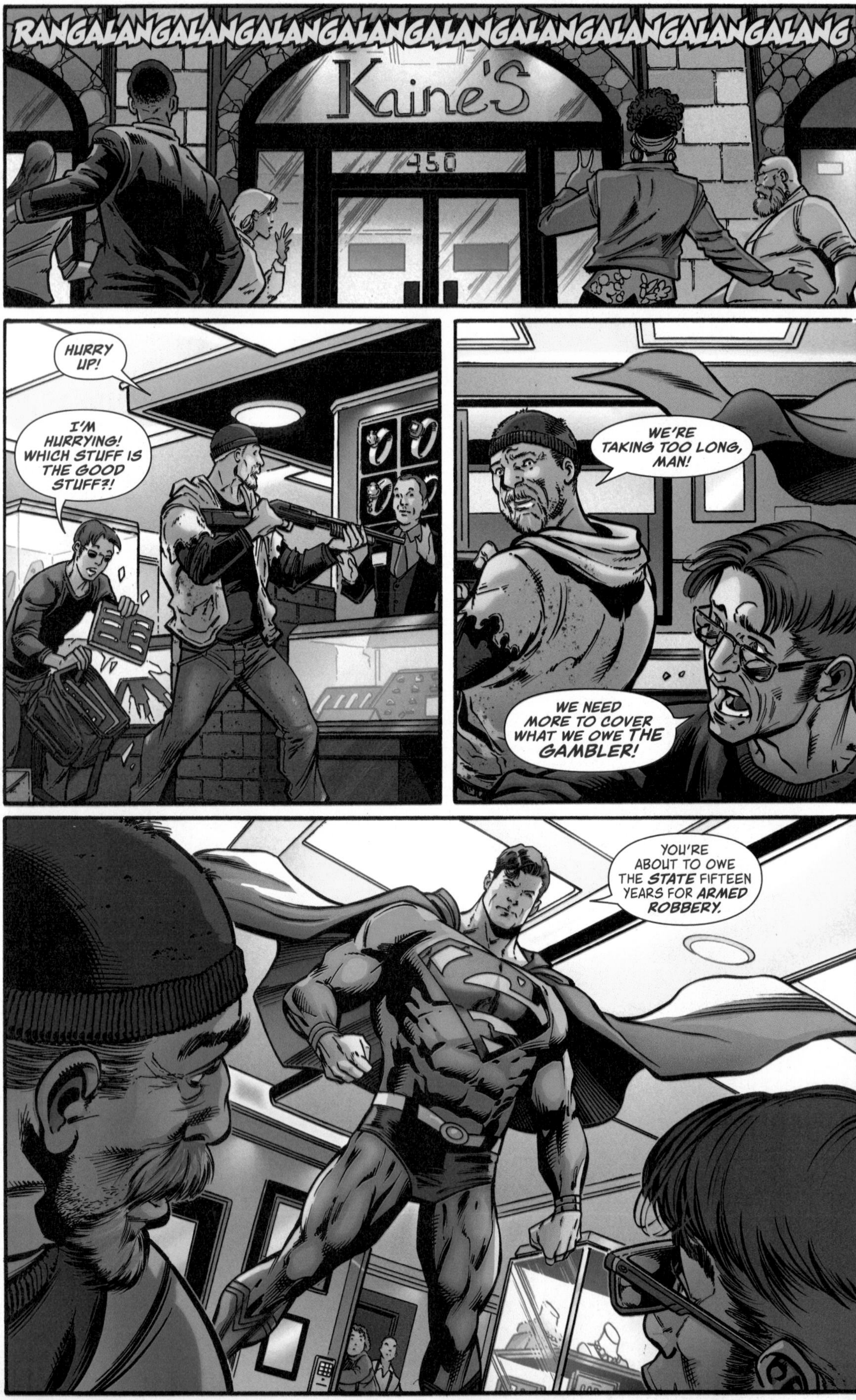
RANGALANGALANGALANGALANGALANGALANGALANGALANG
Kaine'S
450
HURRY UP!
I'M HURRYING! WHICH STUFF IS THE GOOD STUFF?!
WE'RE TAKING TOO LONG, MAN!
WE NEED MORE TO COVER WHAT WE OWE THE GAMBLER!
YOU'RE ABOUT TO OWE THE STATE FIFTEEN YEARS FOR ARMED ROBBERY.

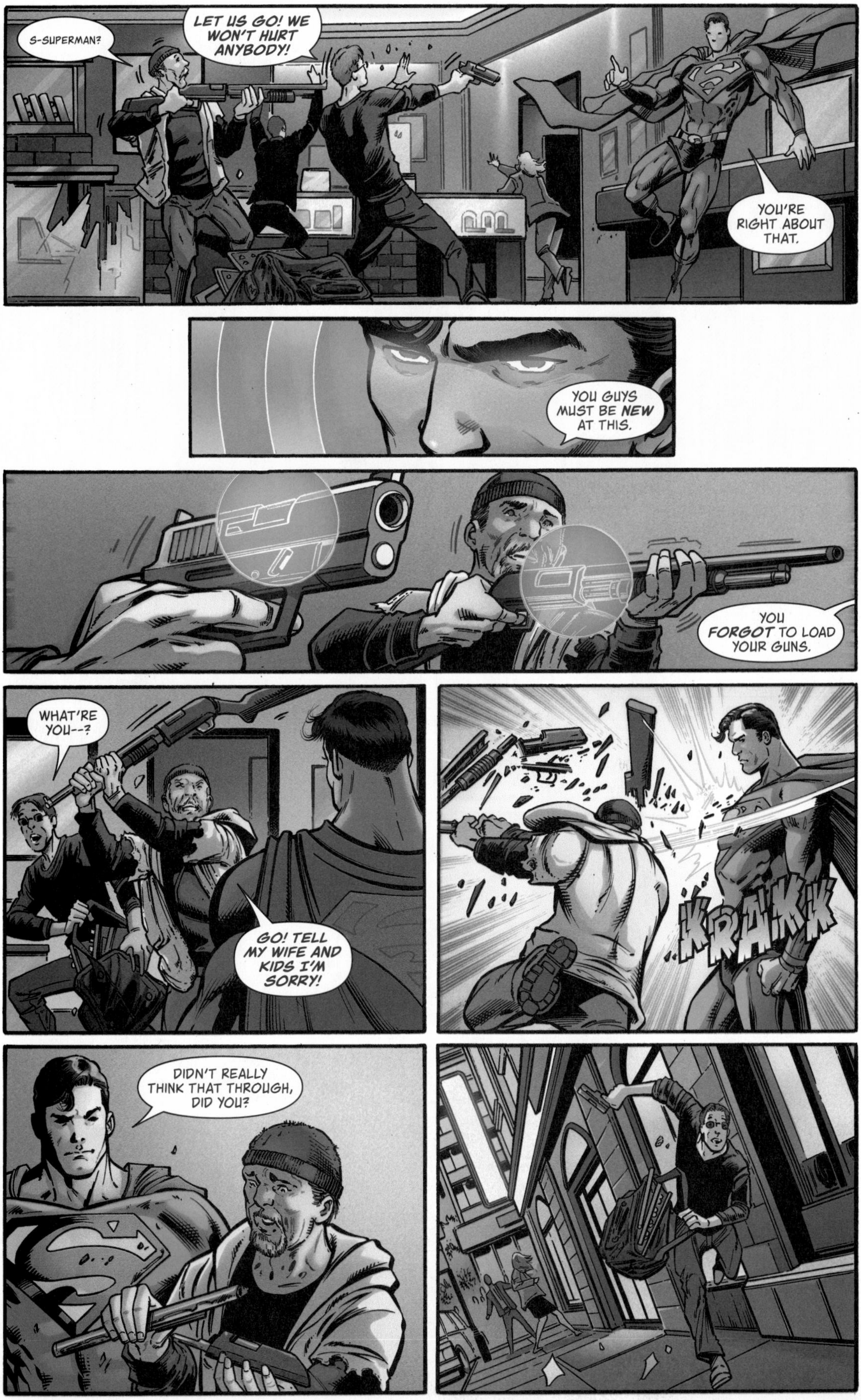
S-SUPERMAN?
LET US GO! WE WON'T HURT ANYBODY!
YOU'RE RIGHT ABOUT THAT.
YOU GUYS MUST BE NEW AT THIS.
YOU FORGOT TO LOAD YOUR GUNS.
WHAT'RE YOU--?
GO! TELL MY WIFE AND KIDS I'M SORRY!
KRAKK
DIDN'T REALLY THINK THAT THROUGH, DID YOU?

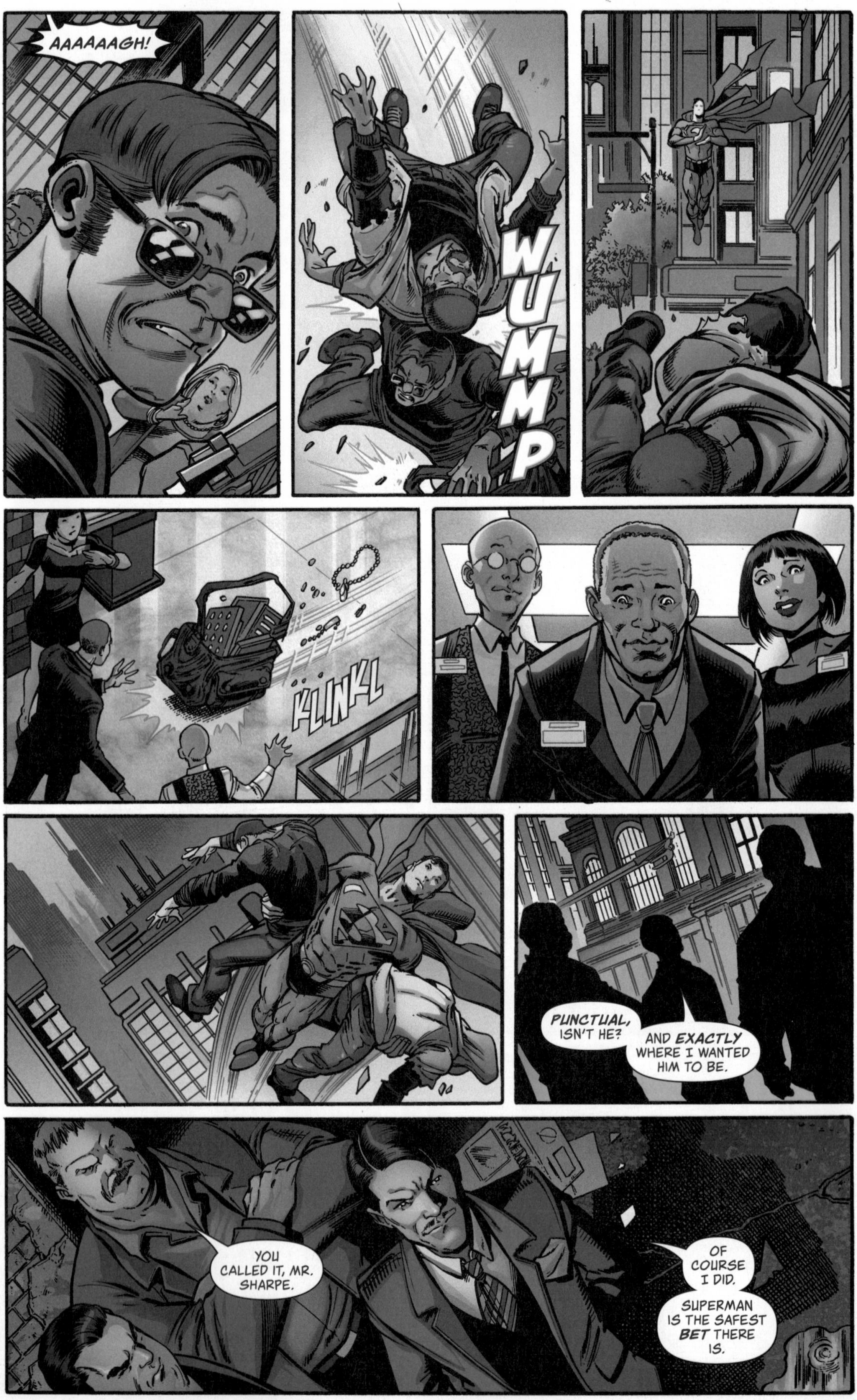
AAAAAAGH!
WUMMP
KLINKL
PUNCTUAL, ISN'T HE?
AND EXACTLY WHERE I WANTED HIM TO BE.
YOU CALLED IT, MR. SHARPE.
OF COURSE I DID.
SUPERMAN IS THE SAFEST BET THERE IS.

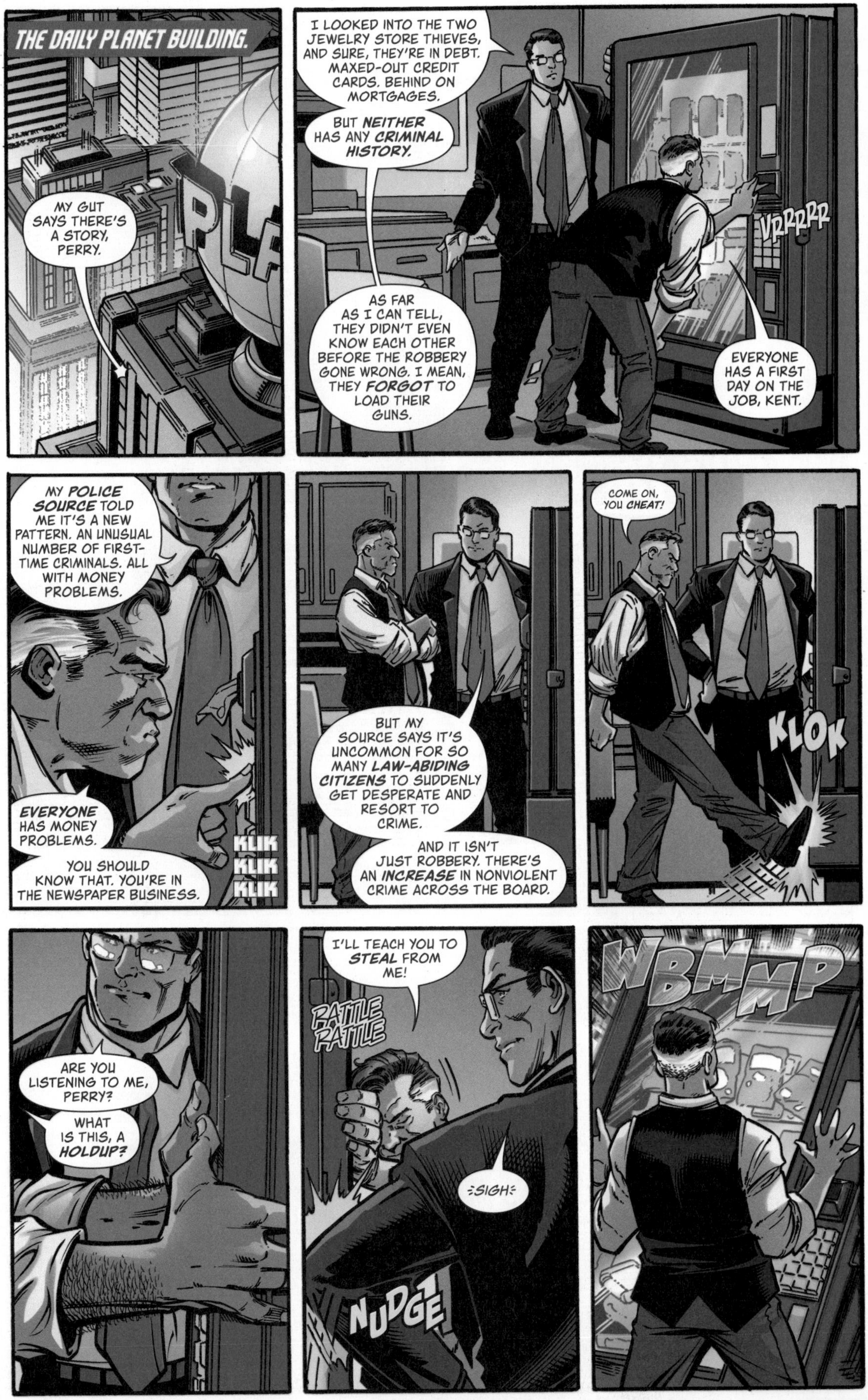
THE DAILY PLANET BUILDING.
MY GUT SAYS THERE'S A STORY, PERRY.
PLA
I LOOKED INTO THE TWO JEWELRY STORE THIEVES, AND SURE, THEY'RE IN DEBT. MAXED-OUT CREDIT CARDS. BEHIND ON MORTGAGES.
BUT NEITHER HAS ANY CRIMINAL HISTORY.
AS FAR AS I CAN TELL, THEY DIDN'T EVEN KNOW EACH OTHER BEFORE THE ROBBERY GONE WRONG. I MEAN, THEY FORGOT TO LOAD THEIR GUNS.
VRRRRR
EVERYONE HAS A FIRST DAY ON THE JOB, KENT.
MY POLICE SOURCE TOLD ME IT'S A NEW PATTERN. AN UNUSUAL NUMBER OF FIRST-TIME CRIMINALS. ALL WITH MONEY PROBLEMS.
EVERYONE HAS MONEY PROBLEMS.
YOU SHOULD KNOW THAT. YOU'RE IN THE NEWSPAPER BUSINESS.
KLIK KLIK KLIK
BUT MY SOURCE SAYS IT'S UNCOMMON FOR SO MANY LAW-ABIDING CITIZENS TO SUDDENLY GET DESPERATE AND RESORT TO CRIME.
AND IT ISN'T JUST ROBBERY. THERE'S AN INCREASE IN NONVIOLENT CRIME ACROSS THE BOARD.
COME ON, YOU CHEAT!
KLOK
ARE YOU LISTENING TO ME, PERRY?
WHAT IS THIS, A HOLDUP?
I'LL TEACH YOU TO STEAL FROM ME!
RATTLE RATTLE
SIGH
NUDGE
WBMMP

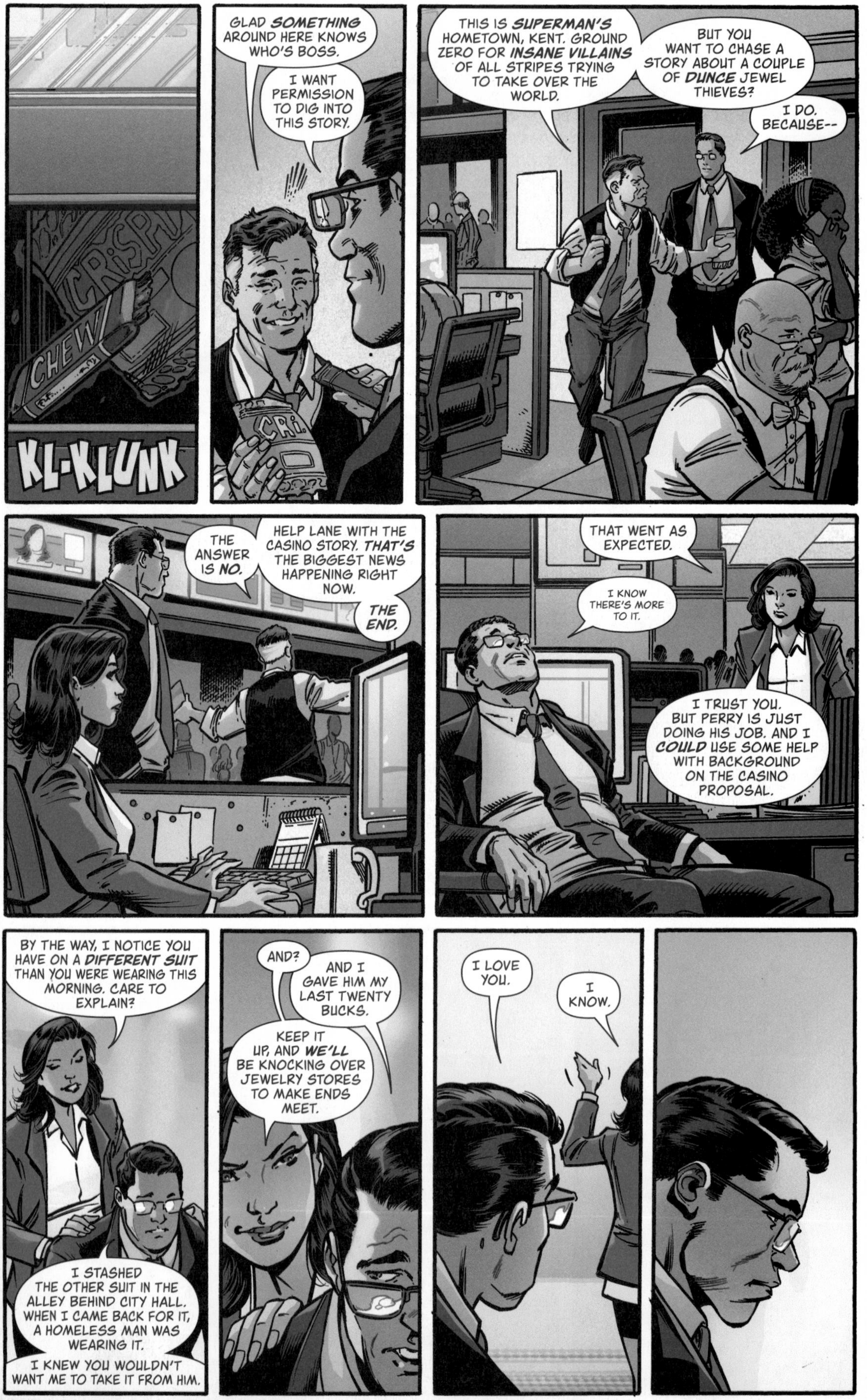
KL-KLUNK
GLAD SOMETHING AROUND HERE KNOWS WHO'S BOSS.
I WANT PERMISSION TO DIG INTO THIS STORY.
THIS IS SUPERMAN'S HOMETOWN, KENT. GROUND ZERO FOR INSANE VILLAINS OF ALL STRIPES TRYING TO TAKE OVER THE WORLD.
BUT YOU WANT TO CHASE A STORY ABOUT A COUPLE OF DUNCE JEWEL THIEVES?
I DO. BECAUSE--
THE ANSWER IS NO.
HELP LANE WITH THE CASINO STORY. THAT'S THE BIGGEST NEWS HAPPENING RIGHT NOW.
THE END.
THAT WENT AS EXPECTED.
I KNOW THERE'S MORE TO IT.
I TRUST YOU. BUT PERRY IS JUST DOING HIS JOB. AND I COULD USE SOME HELP WITH BACKGROUND ON THE CASINO PROPOSAL.
BY THE WAY, I NOTICE YOU HAVE ON A DIFFERENT SUIT THAN YOU WERE WEARING THIS MORNING. CARE TO EXPLAIN?
I STASHED THE OTHER SUIT IN THE ALLEY BEHIND CITY HALL. WHEN I CAME BACK FOR IT, A HOMELESS MAN WAS WEARING IT.
I KNEW YOU WOULDN'T WANT ME TO TAKE IT FROM HIM.
AND?
AND I GAVE HIM MY LAST TWENTY BUCKS.
KEEP IT UP, AND WE'LL BE KNOCKING OVER JEWELRY STORES TO MAKE ENDS MEET.
I LOVE YOU.
I KNOW.

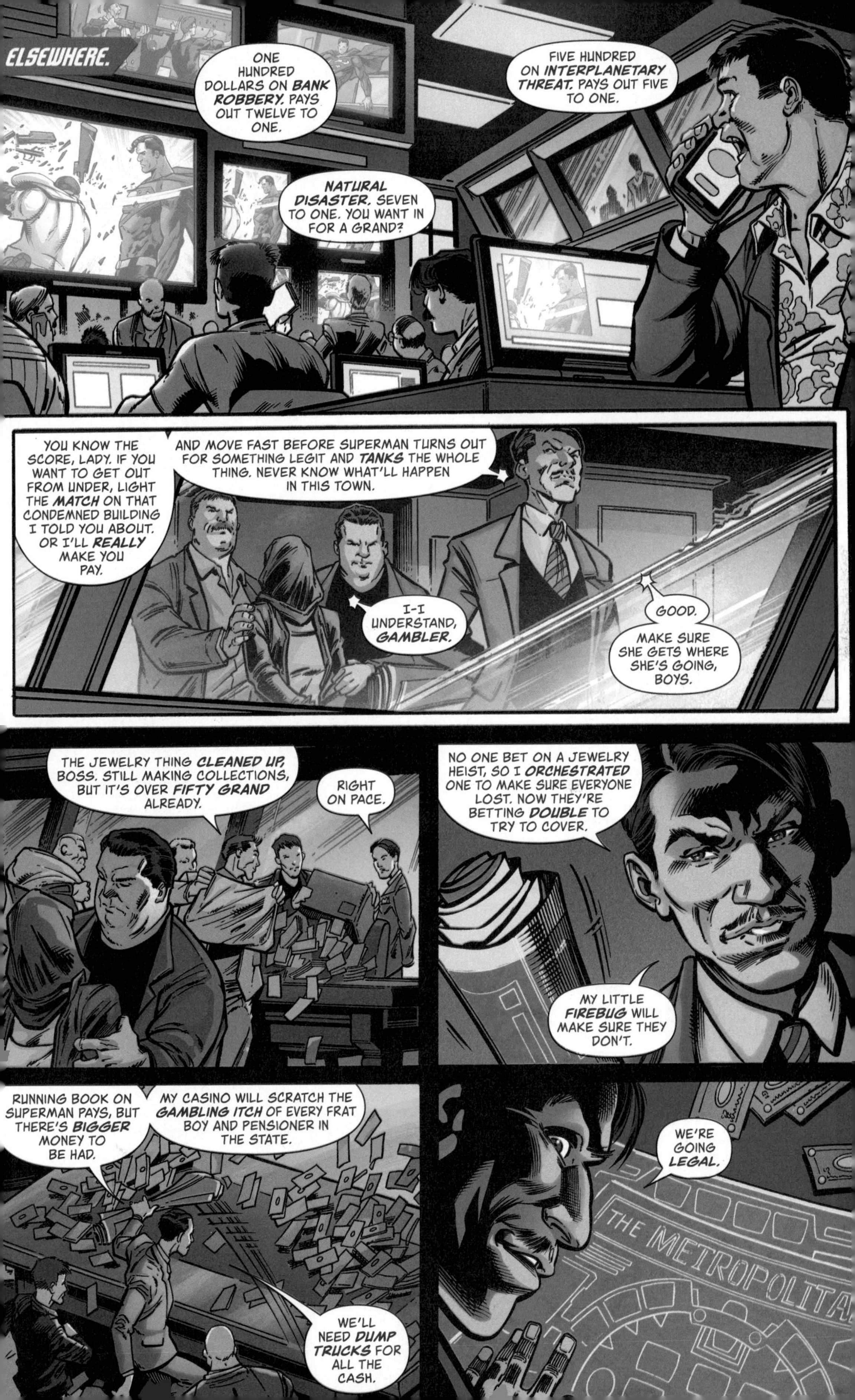
ELSEWHERE.
ONE HUNDRED DOLLARS ON BANK ROBBERY. PAYS OUT TWELVE TO ONE.
FIVE HUNDRED ON INTERPLANETARY THREAT. PAYS OUT FIVE TO ONE.
NATURAL DISASTER. SEVEN TO ONE. YOU WANT IN FOR A GRAND?
YOU KNOW THE SCORE, LADY. IF YOU WANT TO GET OUT FROM UNDER, LIGHT THE MATCH ON THAT CONDEMNED BUILDING I TOLD YOU ABOUT. OR I'LL REALLY MAKE YOU PAY.
AND MOVE FAST BEFORE SUPERMAN TURNS OUT FOR SOMETHING LEGIT AND TANKS THE WHOLE THING. NEVER KNOW WHAT'LL HAPPEN IN THIS TOWN.
I-I UNDERSTAND, GAMBLER.
GOOD.
MAKE SURE SHE GETS WHERE SHE'S GOING, BOYS.
THE JEWELRY THING CLEANED UP, BOSS. STILL MAKING COLLECTIONS, BUT IT'S OVER FIFTY GRAND ALREADY.
RIGHT ON PACE.
NO ONE BET ON A JEWELRY HEIST, SO I ORCHESTRATED ONE TO MAKE SURE EVERYONE LOST. NOW THEY'RE BETTING DOUBLE TO TRY TO COVER.
MY LITTLE FIREBUG WILL MAKE SURE THEY DON'T.
RUNNING BOOK ON SUPERMAN PAYS, BUT THERE'S BIGGER MONEY TO BE HAD.
MY CASINO WILL SCRATCH THE GAMBLING ITCH OF EVERY FRAT BOY AND PENSIONER IN THE STATE.
WE'LL NEED DUMP TRUCKS FOR ALL THE CASH.
WE'RE GOING LEGAL.
THE METROPOLITAN

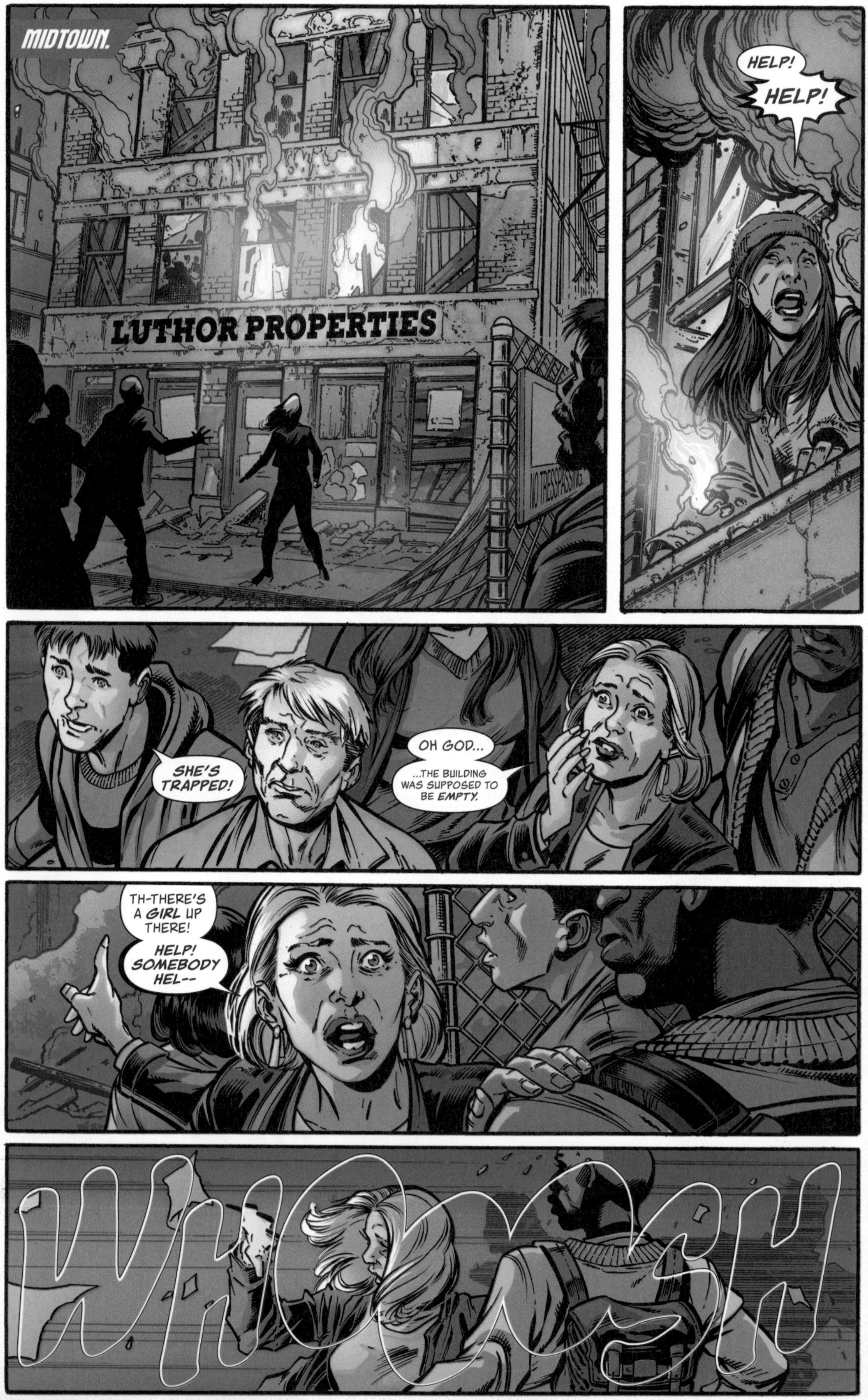
MIDTOWN.
LUTHOR PROPERTIES
NO TRESSPASSING.
HELP!
HELP!
SHE'S TRAPPED!
OH GOD...
...THE BUILDING WAS SUPPOSED TO BE EMPTY.
TH-THERE'S A GIRL UP THERE!
HELP! SOMEBODY HEL--
WHOOSH

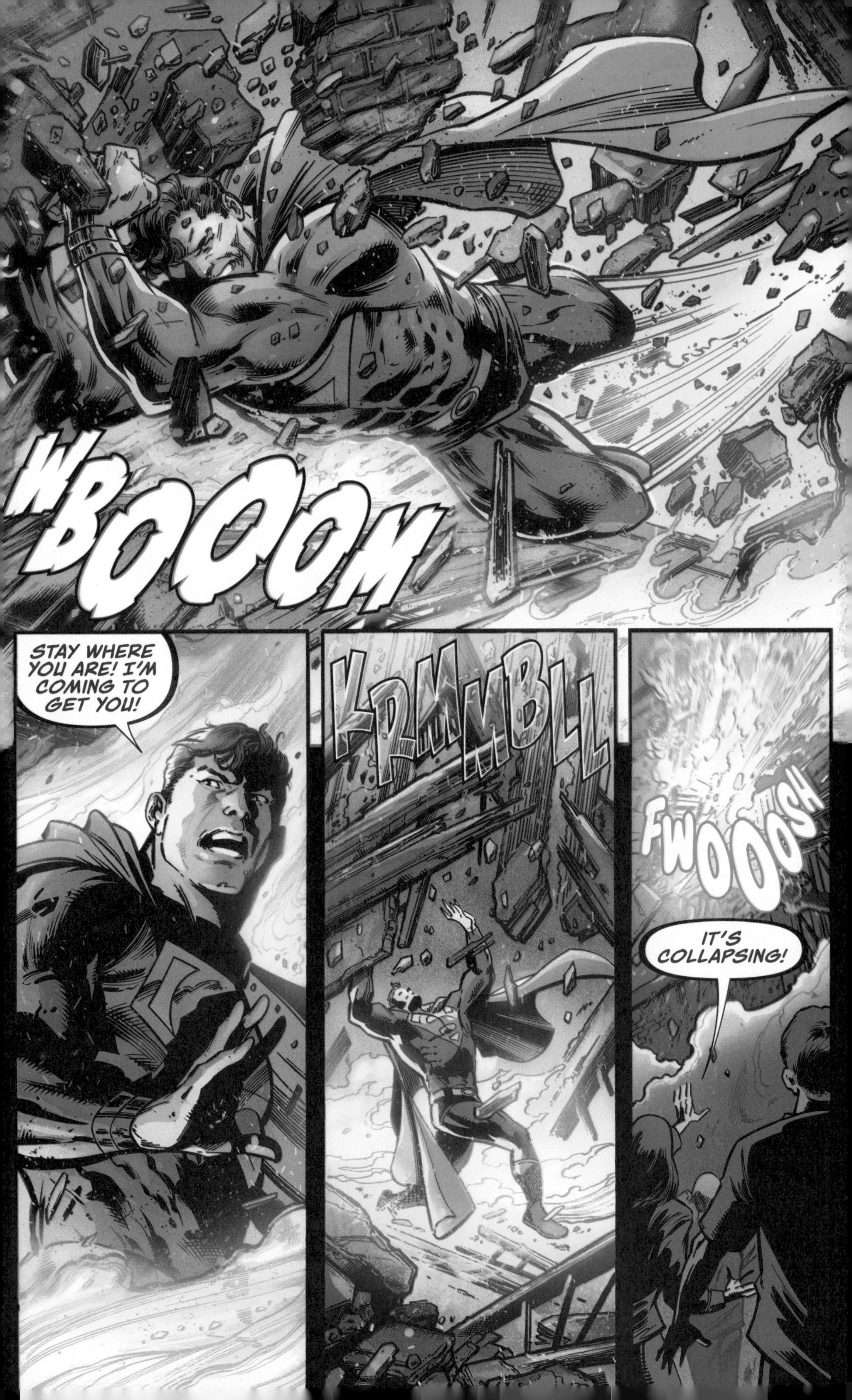
WBOOOM
STAY WHERE YOU ARE! I'M COMING TO GET YOU!
KRMMBLL
FWOOOSH
IT'S COLLAPSING!

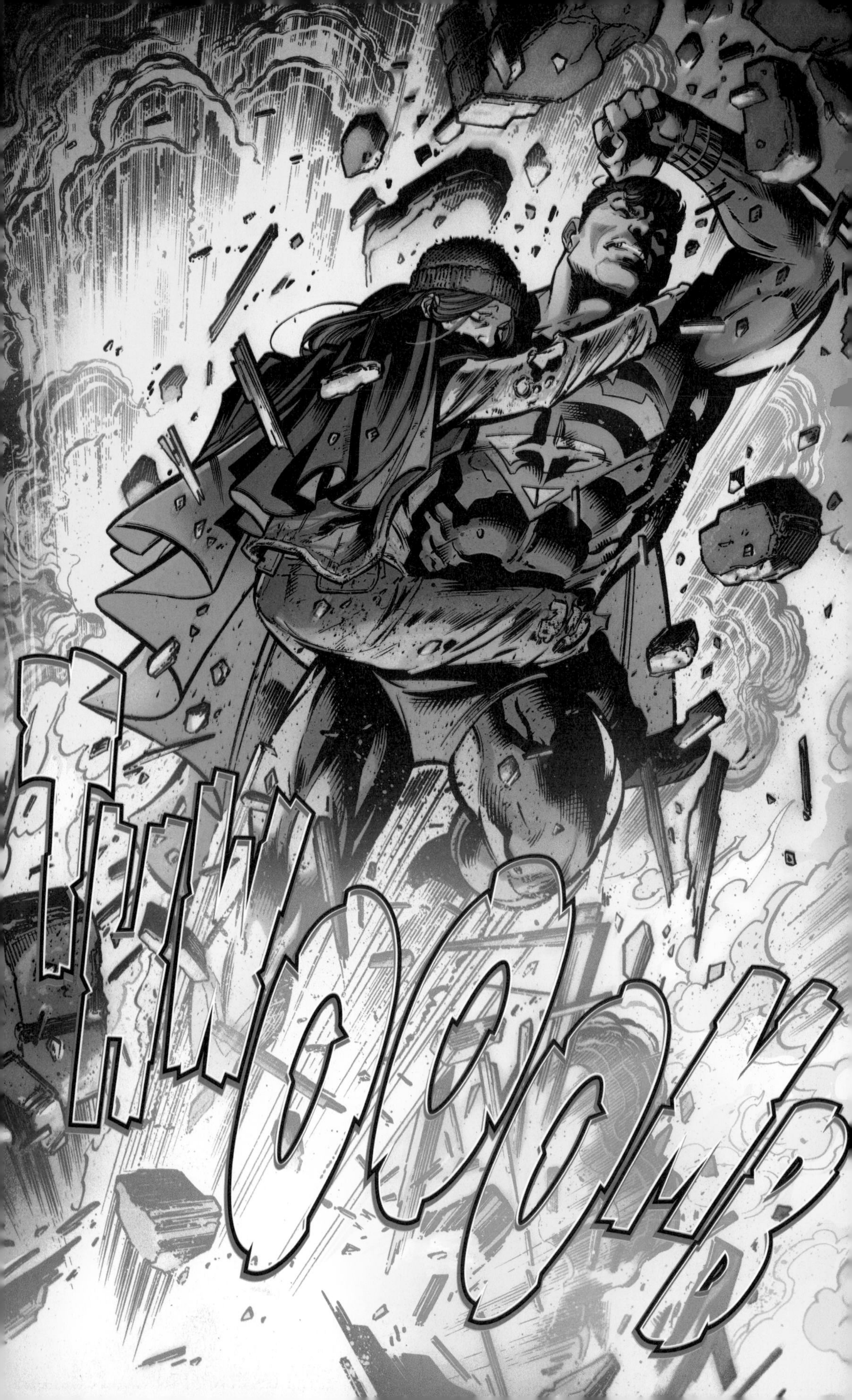
THWOOOMB

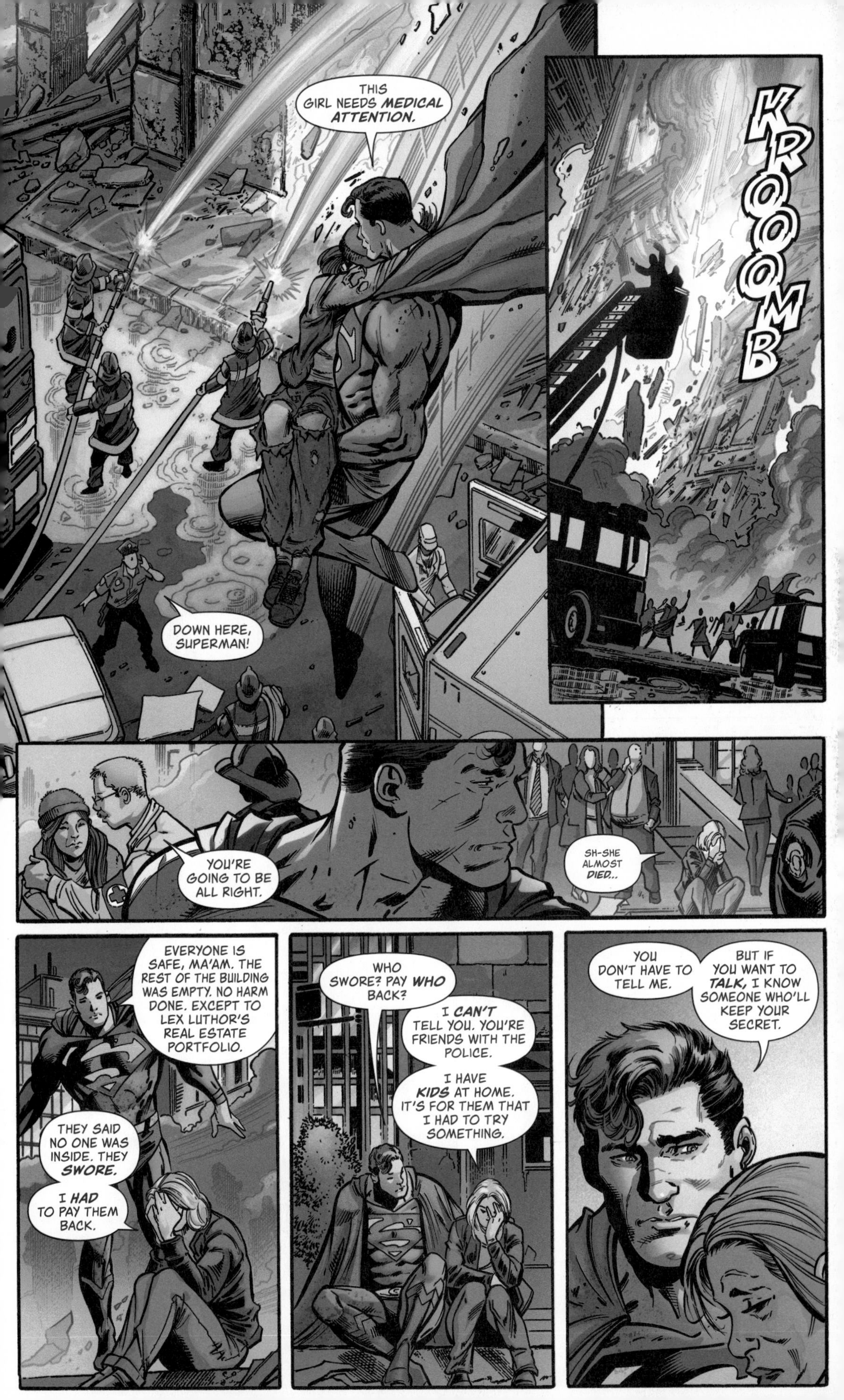

THIS GIRL NEEDS MEDICAL ATTENTION.
DOWN HERE, SUPERMAN!
KROOOMB
YOU'RE GOING TO BE ALL RIGHT.
SH-SHE ALMOST DIED...
EVERYONE IS SAFE, MA'AM. THE REST OF THE BUILDING WAS EMPTY. NO HARM DONE. EXCEPT TO LEX LUTHOR'S REAL ESTATE PORTFOLIO.
THEY SAID NO ONE WAS INSIDE. THEY SWORE.
I HAD TO PAY THEM BACK.
WHO SWORE? PAY WHO BACK?
I CAN'T TELL YOU. YOU'RE FRIENDS WITH THE POLICE.
I HAVE KIDS AT HOME. IT'S FOR THEM THAT I HAD TO TRY SOMETHING.
YOU DON'T HAVE TO TELL ME.
BUT IF YOU WANT TO TALK, I KNOW SOMEONE WHO'LL KEEP YOUR SECRET.

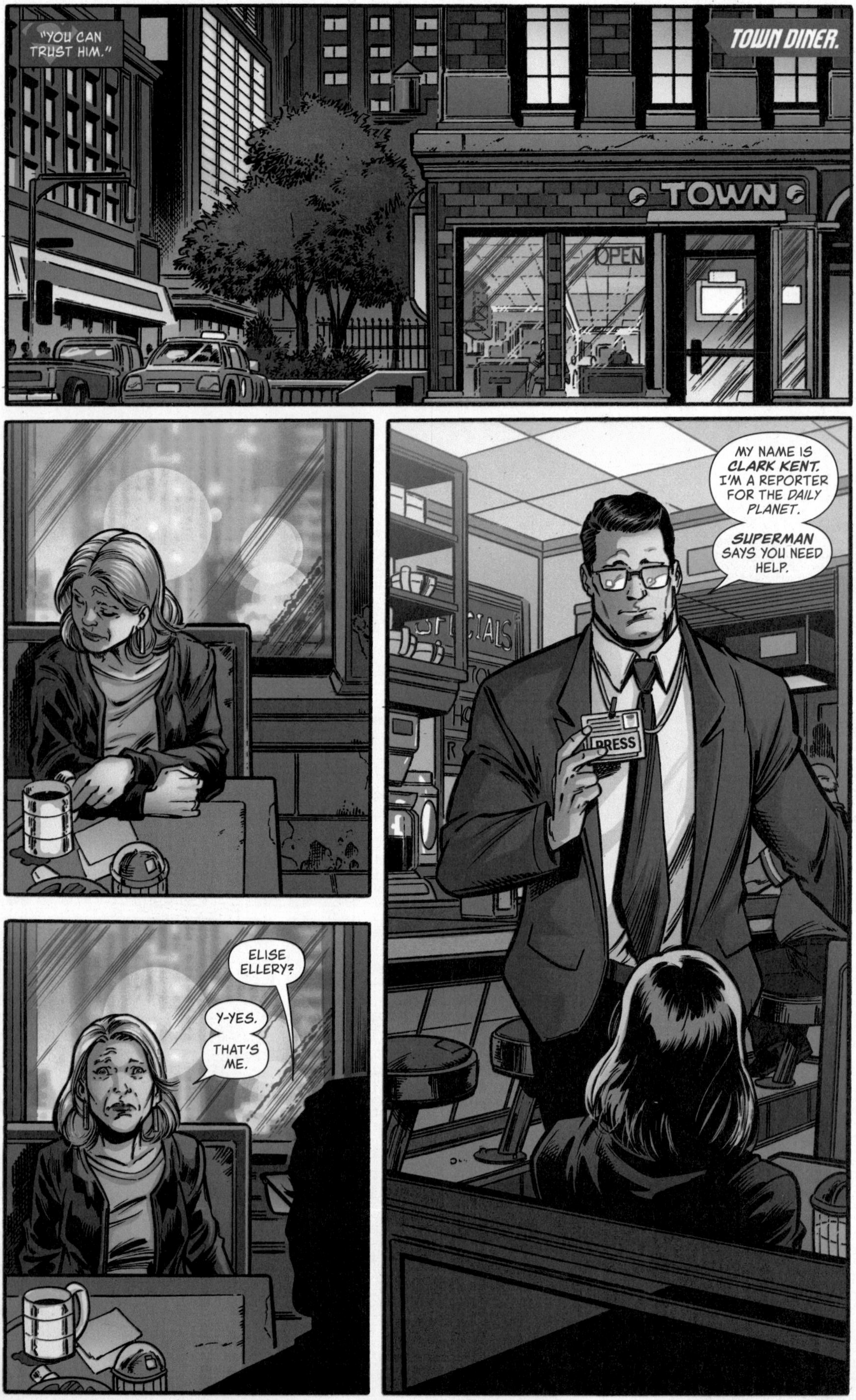
"YOU CAN TRUST HIM."
TOWN DINER.
TOWN
OPEN
MY NAME IS CLARK KENT. I'M A REPORTER FOR THE DAILY PLANET.
SUPERMAN SAYS YOU NEED HELP.
PRESS
ELISE ELLERY?
Y-YES.
THAT'S ME.

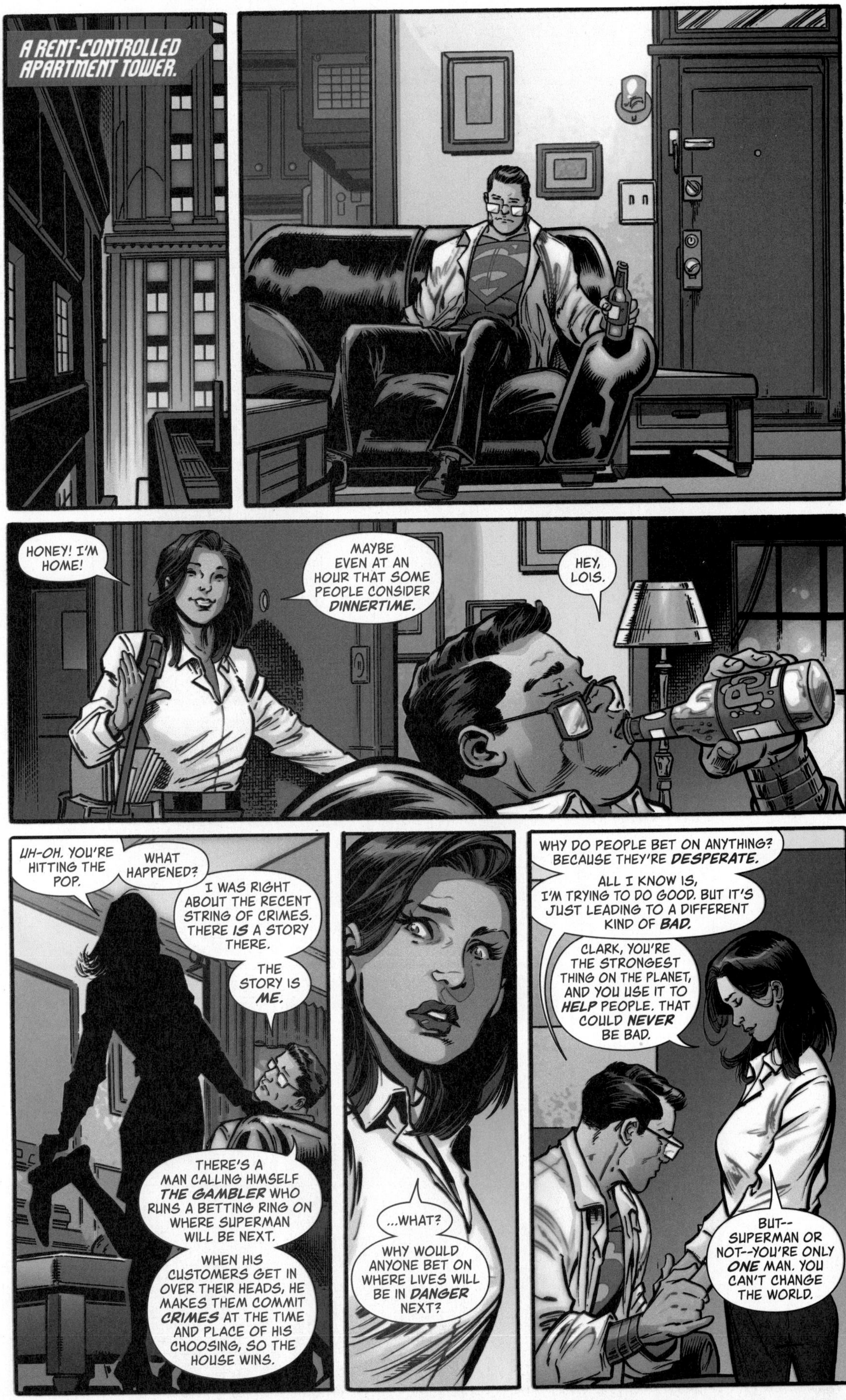
A RENT-CONTROLLED APARTMENT TOWER.
HONEY! I'M HOME!
MAYBE EVEN AT AN HOUR THAT SOME PEOPLE CONSIDER DINNERTIME.
HEY, LOIS.
UH-OH. YOU'RE HITTING THE POP.
WHAT HAPPENED?
I WAS RIGHT ABOUT THE RECENT STRING OF CRIMES. THERE IS A STORY THERE.
THE STORY IS ME.
THERE'S A MAN CALLING HIMSELF THE GAMBLER WHO RUNS A BETTING RING ON WHERE SUPERMAN WILL BE NEXT.
WHEN HIS CUSTOMERS GET IN OVER THEIR HEADS, HE MAKES THEM COMMIT CRIMES AT THE TIME AND PLACE OF HIS CHOOSING, SO THE HOUSE WINS.
...WHAT?
WHY WOULD ANYONE BET ON WHERE LIVES WILL BE IN DANGER NEXT?
WHY DO PEOPLE BET ON ANYTHING? BECAUSE THEY'RE DESPERATE.
ALL I KNOW IS, I'M TRYING TO DO GOOD. BUT IT'S JUST LEADING TO A DIFFERENT KIND OF BAD.
CLARK, YOU'RE THE STRONGEST THING ON THE PLANET, AND YOU USE IT TO HELP PEOPLE. THAT COULD NEVER BE BAD.
BUT-- SUPERMAN OR NOT--YOU'RE ONLY ONE MAN. YOU CAN'T CHANGE THE WORLD.

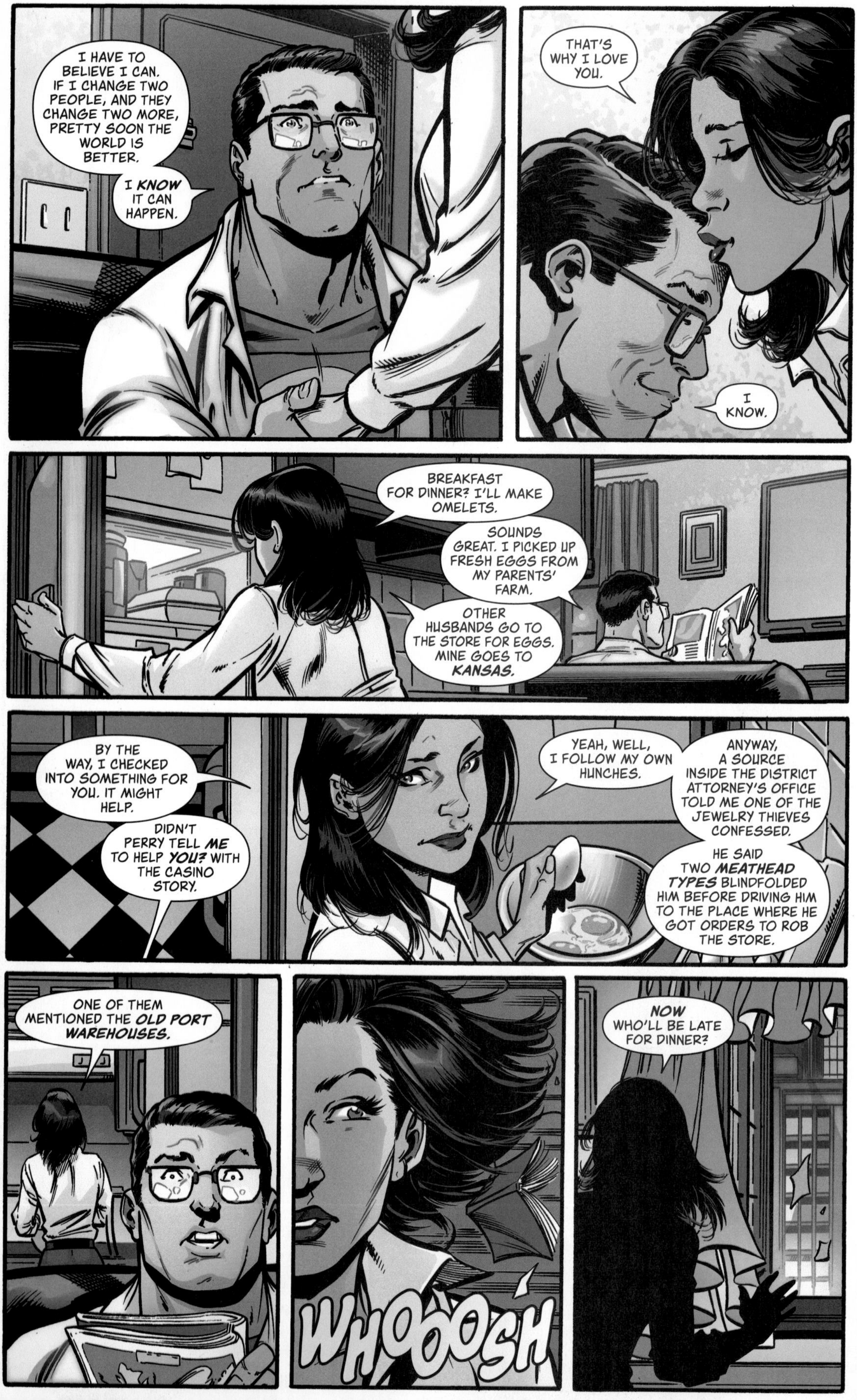

I HAVE TO BELIEVE I CAN. IF I CHANGE TWO PEOPLE, AND THEY CHANGE TWO MORE, PRETTY SOON THE WORLD IS BETTER.
I KNOW IT CAN HAPPEN.
THAT'S WHY I LOVE YOU.
I KNOW.
BREAKFAST FOR DINNER? I'LL MAKE OMELETS.
SOUNDS GREAT. I PICKED UP FRESH EGGS FROM MY PARENTS' FARM.
OTHER HUSBANDS GO TO THE STORE FOR EGGS. MINE GOES TO KANSAS.
BY THE WAY, I CHECKED INTO SOMETHING FOR YOU. IT MIGHT HELP.
DIDN'T PERRY TELL ME TO HELP YOU? WITH THE CASINO STORY.
YEAH, WELL, I FOLLOW MY OWN HUNCHES.
ANYWAY, A SOURCE INSIDE THE DISTRICT ATTORNEY'S OFFICE TOLD ME ONE OF THE JEWELRY THIEVES CONFESSED.
HE SAID TWO MEATHEAD TYPES BLINDFOLDED HIM BEFORE DRIVING HIM TO THE PLACE WHERE HE GOT ORDERS TO ROB THE STORE.
ONE OF THEM MENTIONED THE OLD PORT WAREHOUSES.
WHOOOOSH
NOW WHO'LL BE LATE FOR DINNER?

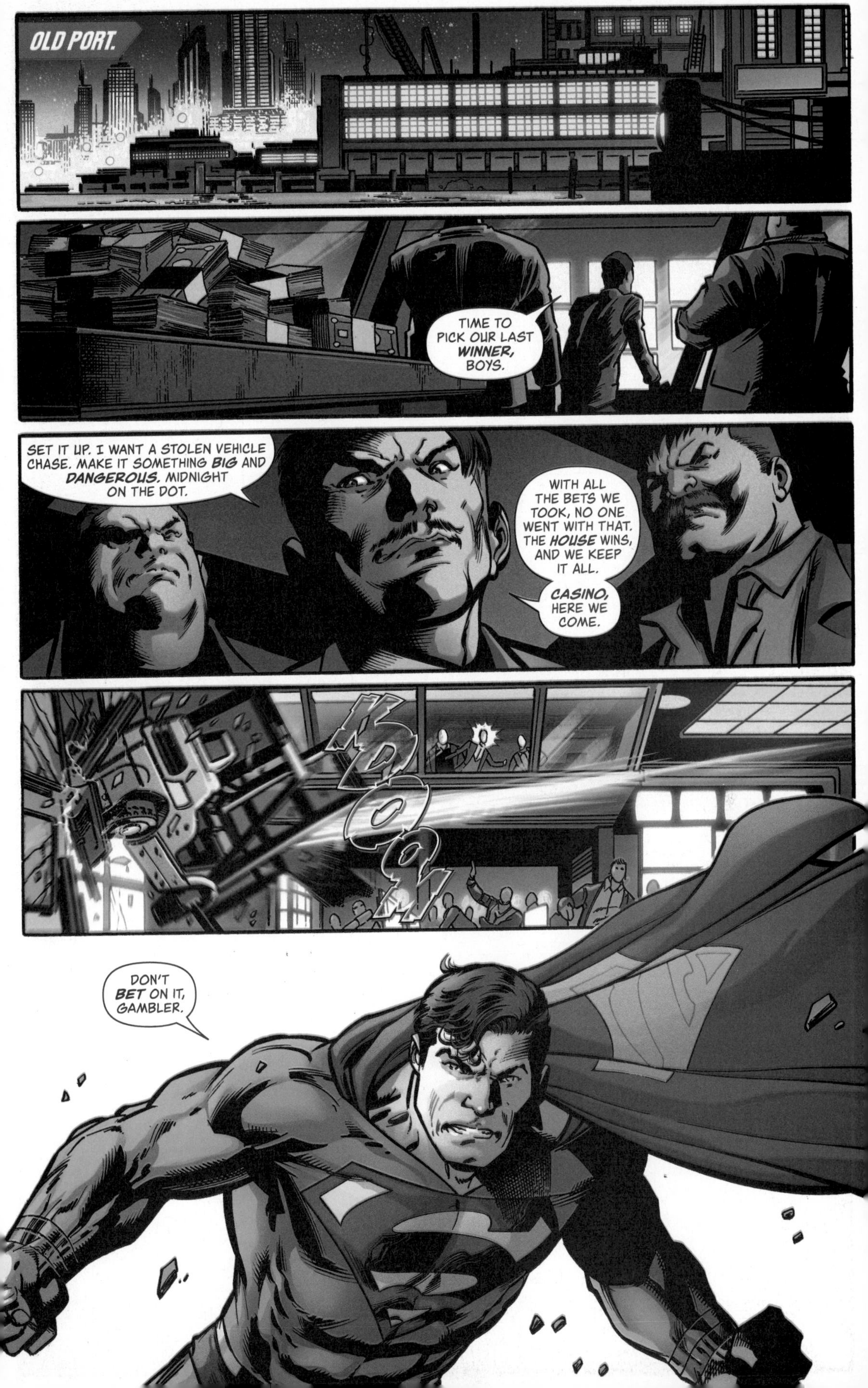
OLD PORT.
TIME TO PICK OUR LAST WINNER, BOYS.
SET IT UP. I WANT A STOLEN VEHICLE CHASE. MAKE IT SOMETHING BIG AND DANGEROUS. MIDNIGHT ON THE DOT.
WITH ALL THE BETS WE TOOK, NO ONE WENT WITH THAT. THE HOUSE WINS, AND WE KEEP IT ALL.
CASINO, HERE WE COME.
KROOOM
DON'T BET ON IT, GAMBLER.

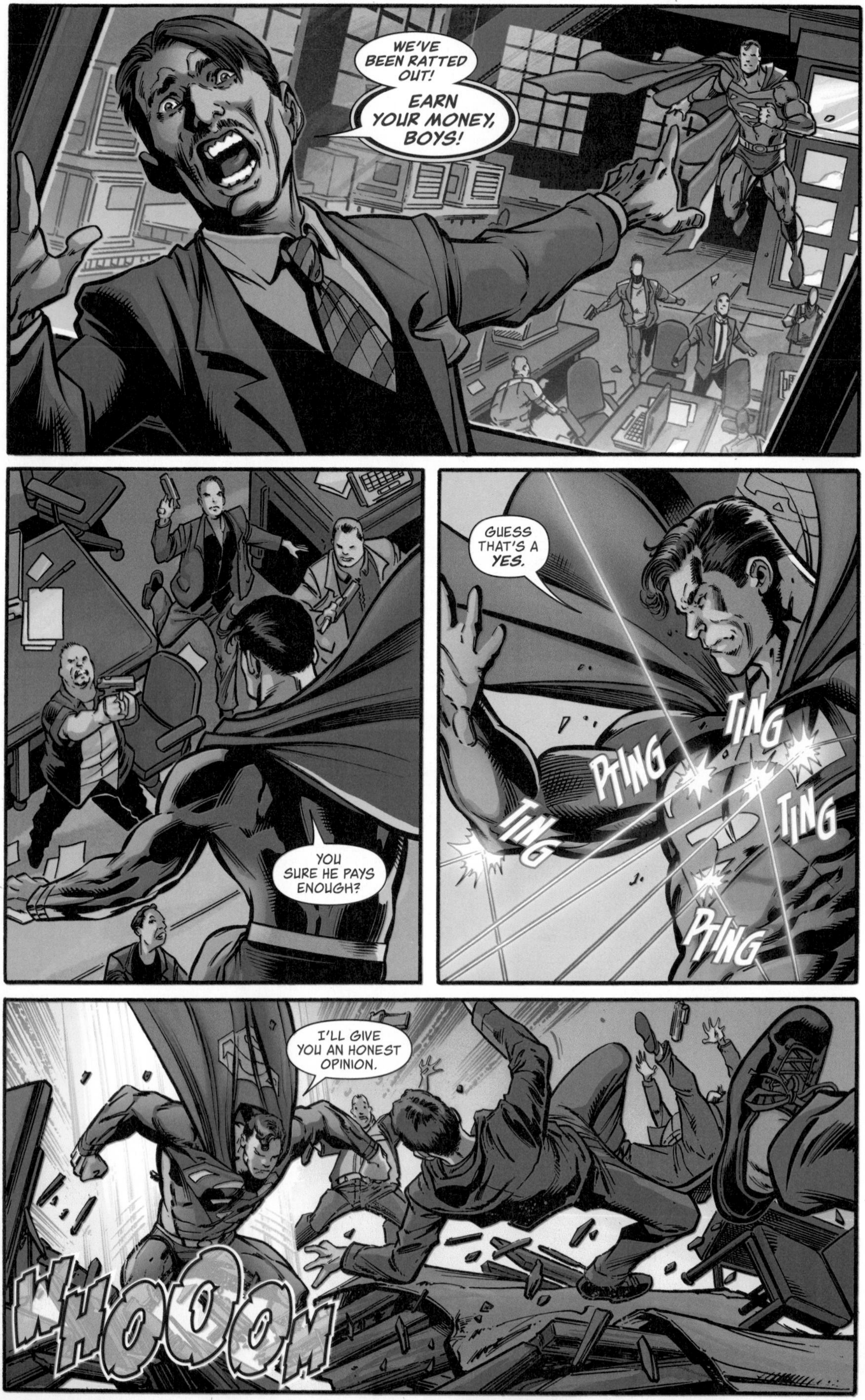
WE'VE BEEN RATTED OUT!
EARN YOUR MONEY, BOYS!
YOU SURE HE PAYS ENOUGH?
GUESS THAT'S A YES.
PTING
TING
TING
TING
PTING
I'LL GIVE YOU AN HONEST OPINION.
WHOOOOM

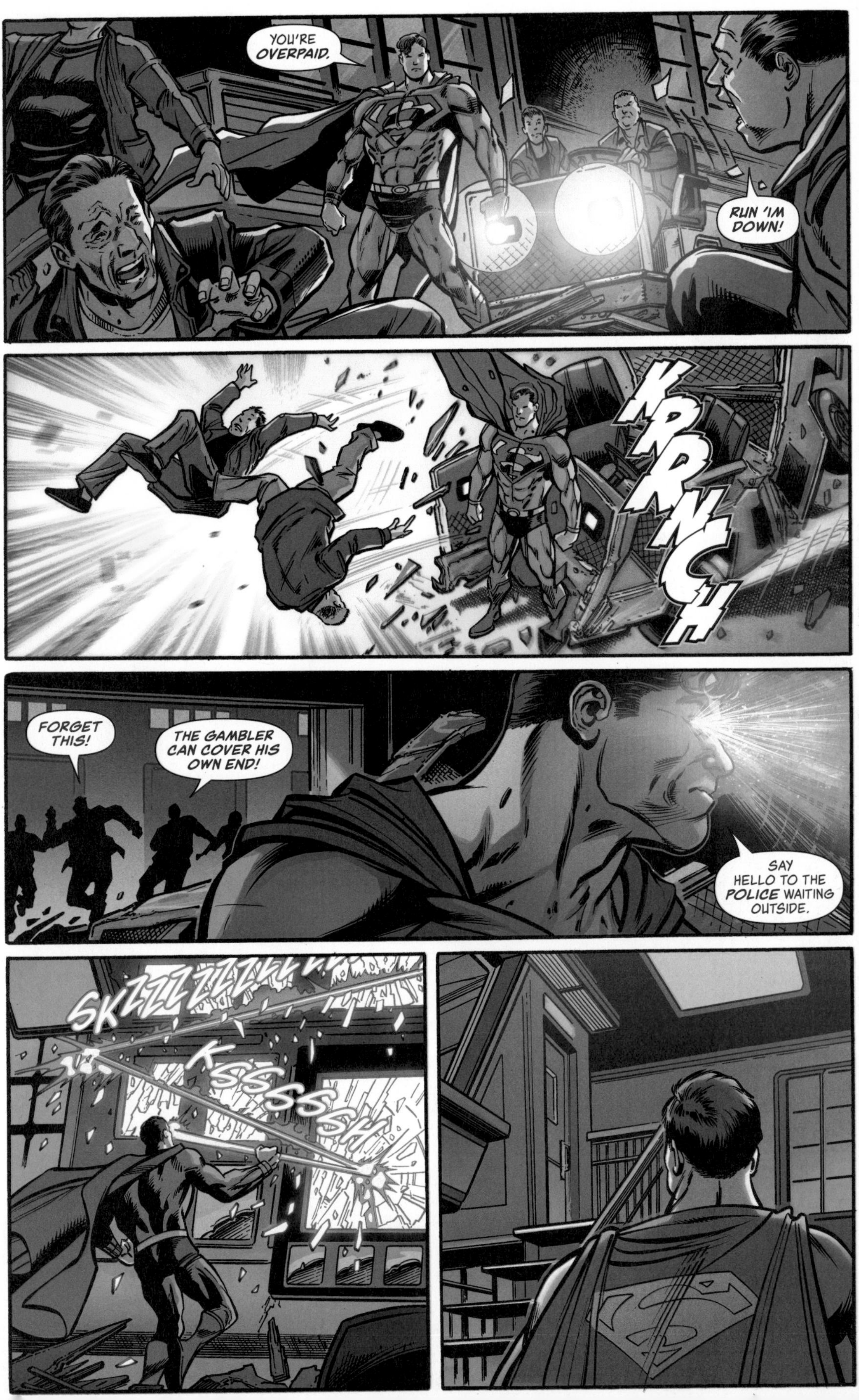
YOU'RE OVERPAID.
RUN 'IM DOWN!
KRRNCH
FORGET THIS!
THE GAMBLER CAN COVER HIS OWN END!
SAY HELLO TO THE POLICE WAITING OUTSIDE.
SKZZZZZZZZ
KSSSSSSH

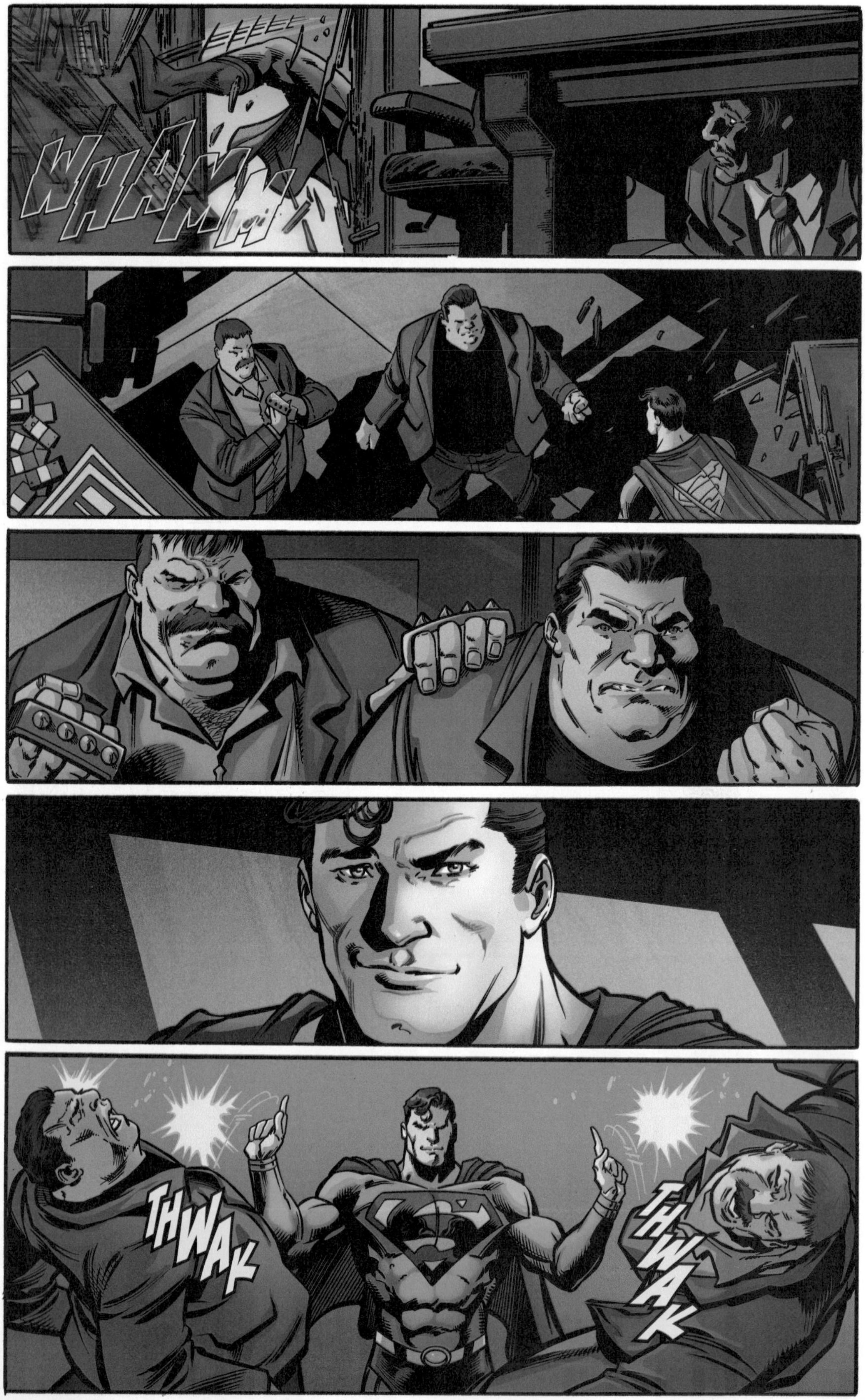
WHAMM
THWAK
THWAK

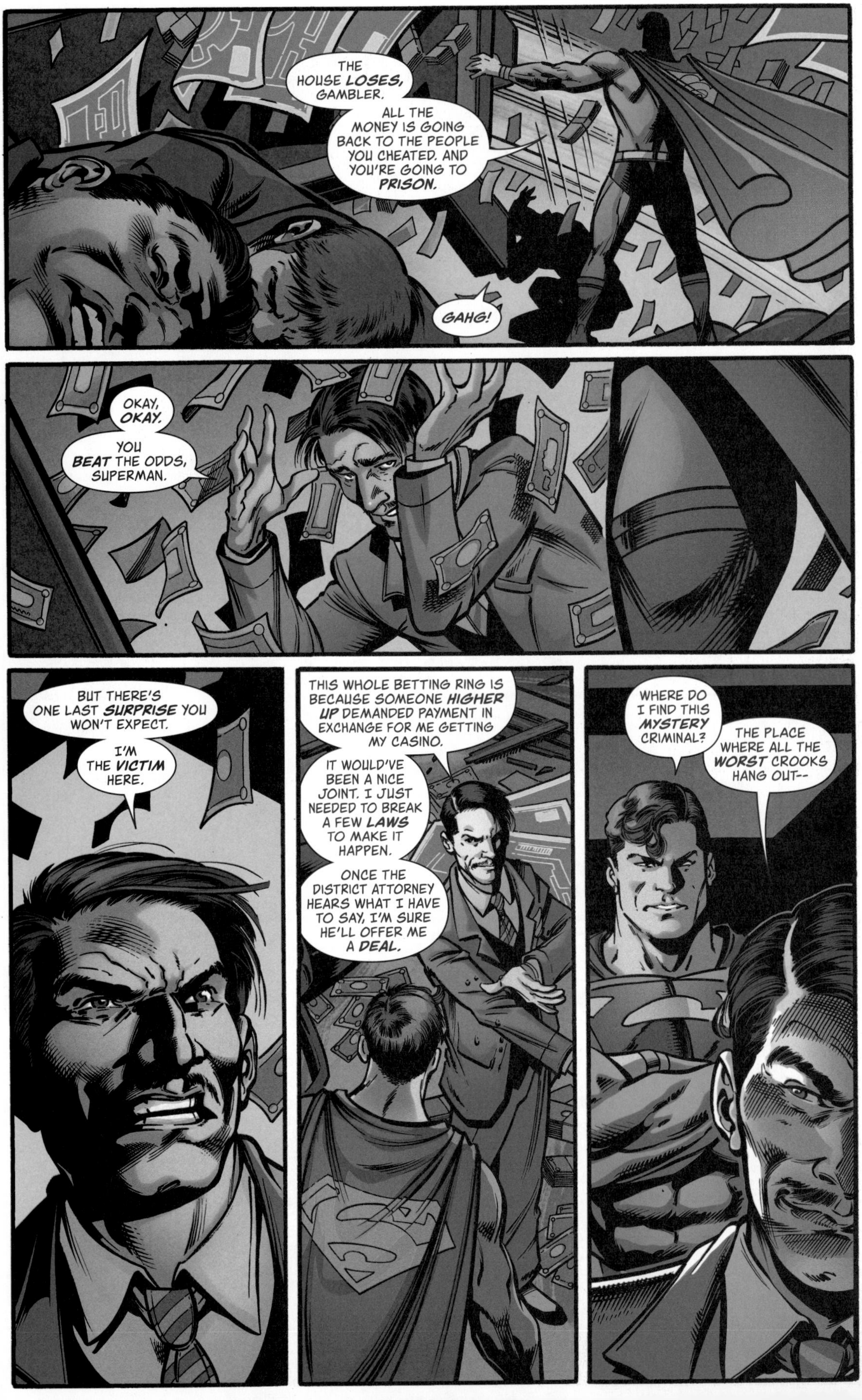
THE HOUSE LOSES, GAMBLER.
ALL THE MONEY IS GOING BACK TO THE PEOPLE YOU CHEATED. AND YOU'RE GOING TO PRISON.
GAHG!
OKAY, OKAY.
YOU BEAT THE ODDS, SUPERMAN.
BUT THERE'S ONE LAST SURPRISE YOU WON'T EXPECT.
I'M THE VICTIM HERE.
THIS WHOLE BETTING RING IS BECAUSE SOMEONE HIGHER UP DEMANDED PAYMENT IN EXCHANGE FOR ME GETTING MY CASINO.
IT WOULD'VE BEEN A NICE JOINT. I JUST NEEDED TO BREAK A FEW LAWS TO MAKE IT HAPPEN.
ONCE THE DISTRICT ATTORNEY HEARS WHAT I HAVE TO SAY, I'M SURE HE'LL OFFER ME A DEAL.
WHERE DO I FIND THIS MYSTERY CRIMINAL?
THE PLACE WHERE ALL THE WORST CROOKS HANG OUT--

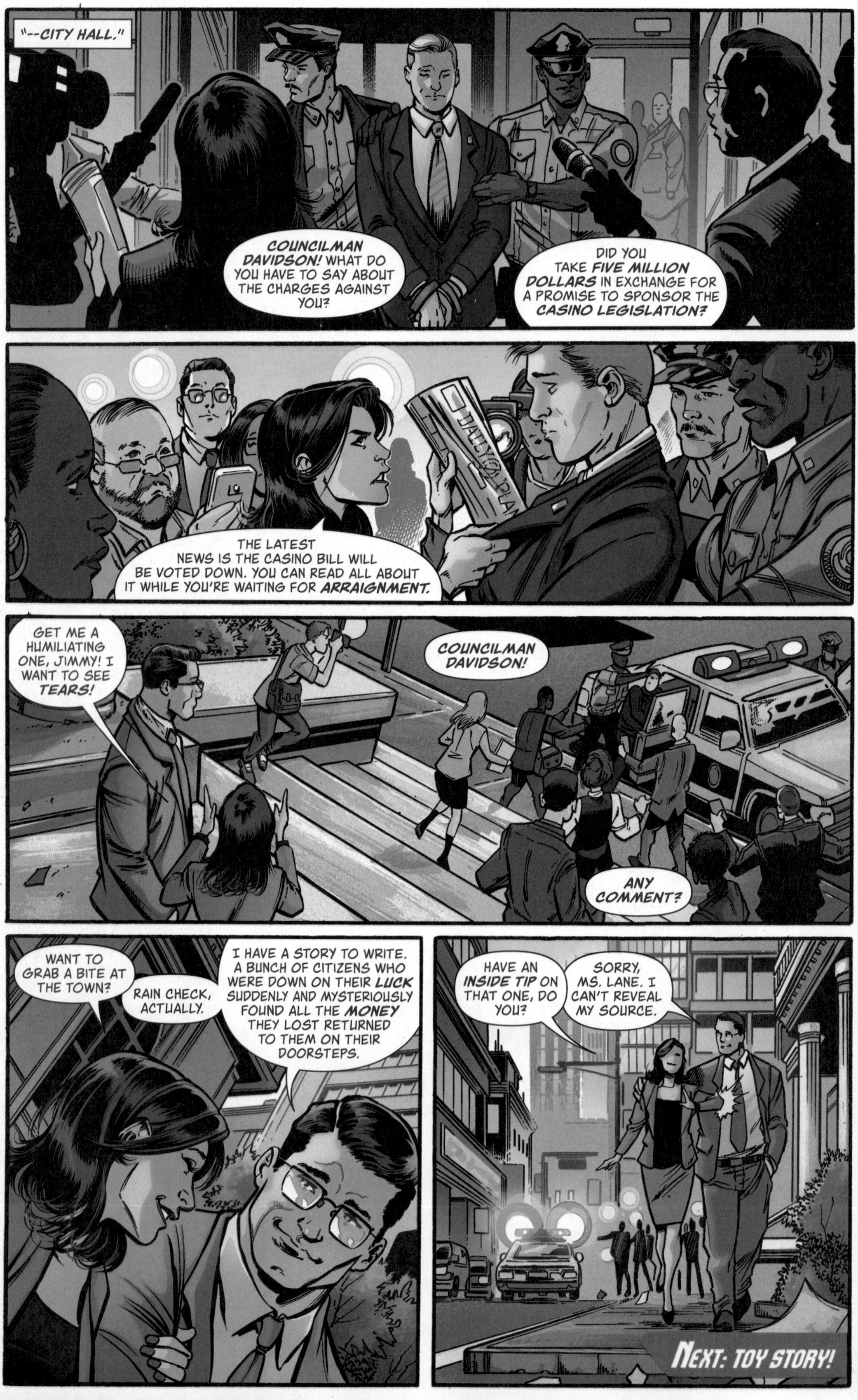
"--CITY HALL."
COUNCILMAN DAVIDSON! WHAT DO YOU HAVE TO SAY ABOUT THE CHARGES AGAINST YOU?
DID YOU TAKE FIVE MILLION DOLLARS IN EXCHANGE FOR A PROMISE TO SPONSOR THE CASINO LEGISLATION?
THE LATEST NEWS IS THE CASINO BILL WILL BE VOTED DOWN. YOU CAN READ ALL ABOUT IT WHILE YOU'RE WAITING FOR ARRAIGNMENT.
GET ME A HUMILIATING ONE, JIMMY! I WANT TO SEE TEARS!
COUNCILMAN DAVIDSON!
ANY COMMENT?
WANT TO GRAB A BITE AT THE TOWN?
RAIN CHECK, ACTUALLY.
I HAVE A STORY TO WRITE. A BUNCH OF CITIZENS WHO WERE DOWN ON THEIR LUCK SUDDENLY AND MYSTERIOUSLY FOUND ALL THE MONEY THEY LOST RETURNED TO THEM ON THEIR DOORSTEPS.
HAVE AN INSIDE TIP ON THAT ONE, DO YOU?
SORRY, MS. LANE. I CAN'T REVEAL MY SOURCE.
NEXT: TOY STORY!

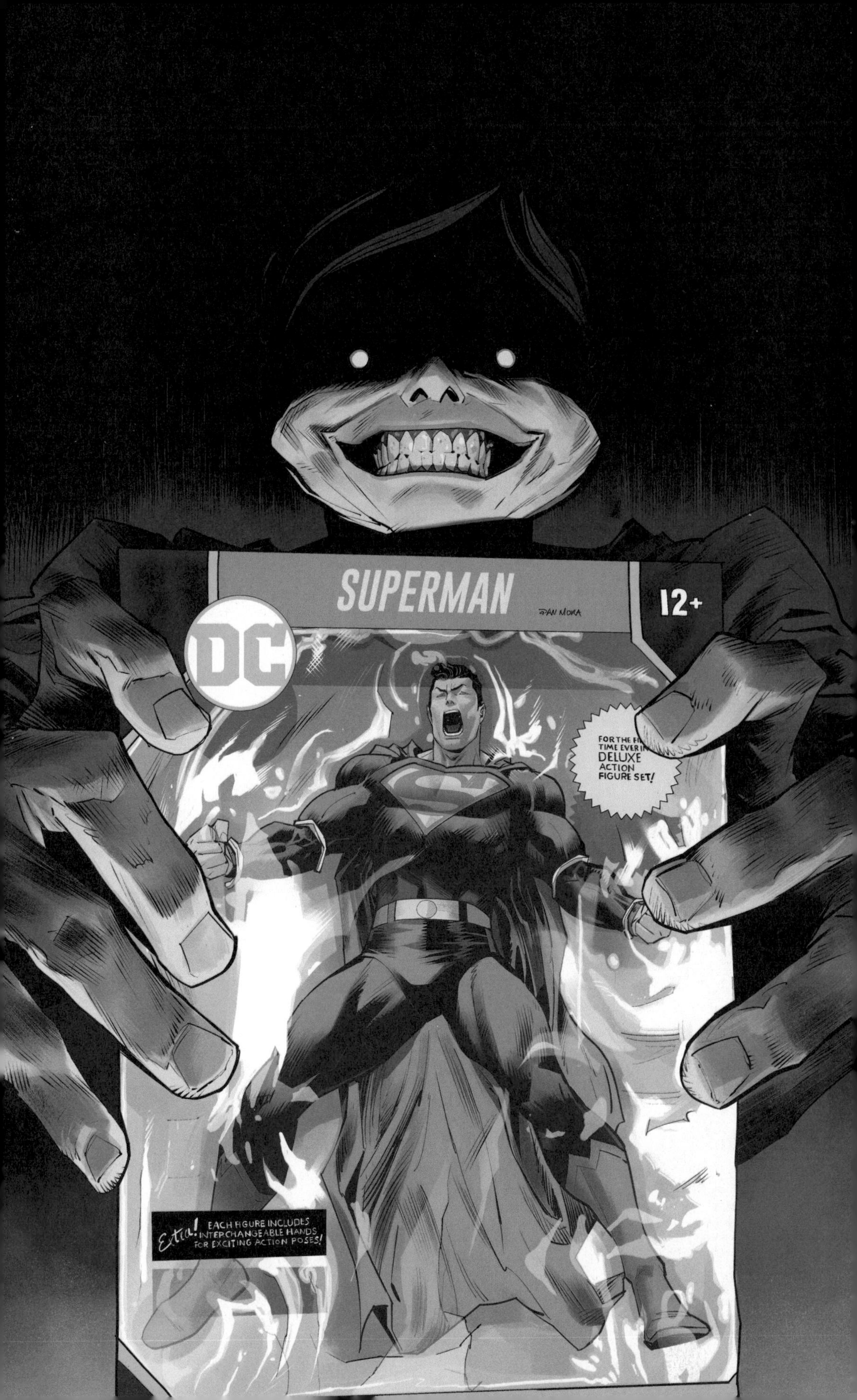
SUPERMAN
DAN MORA
12+
FOR THE FI
TIME EVER IN
DELUXE
ACTION
FIGURE SET!
Extra! EACH FIGURE INCLUDES INTERCHANGEABLE HANDS FOR EXCITING ACTION POSES!

COVER ART BY
DAN MORA

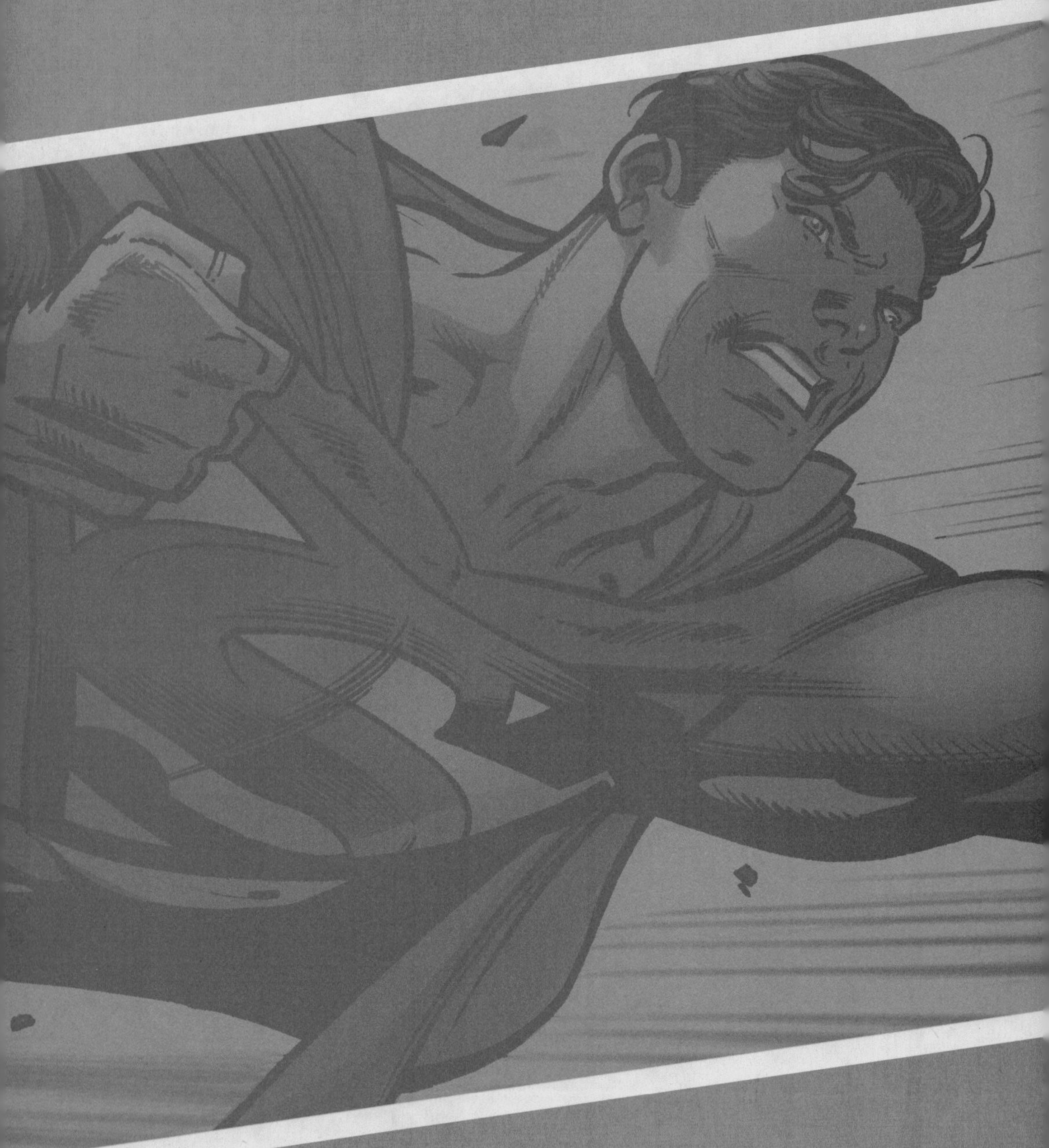

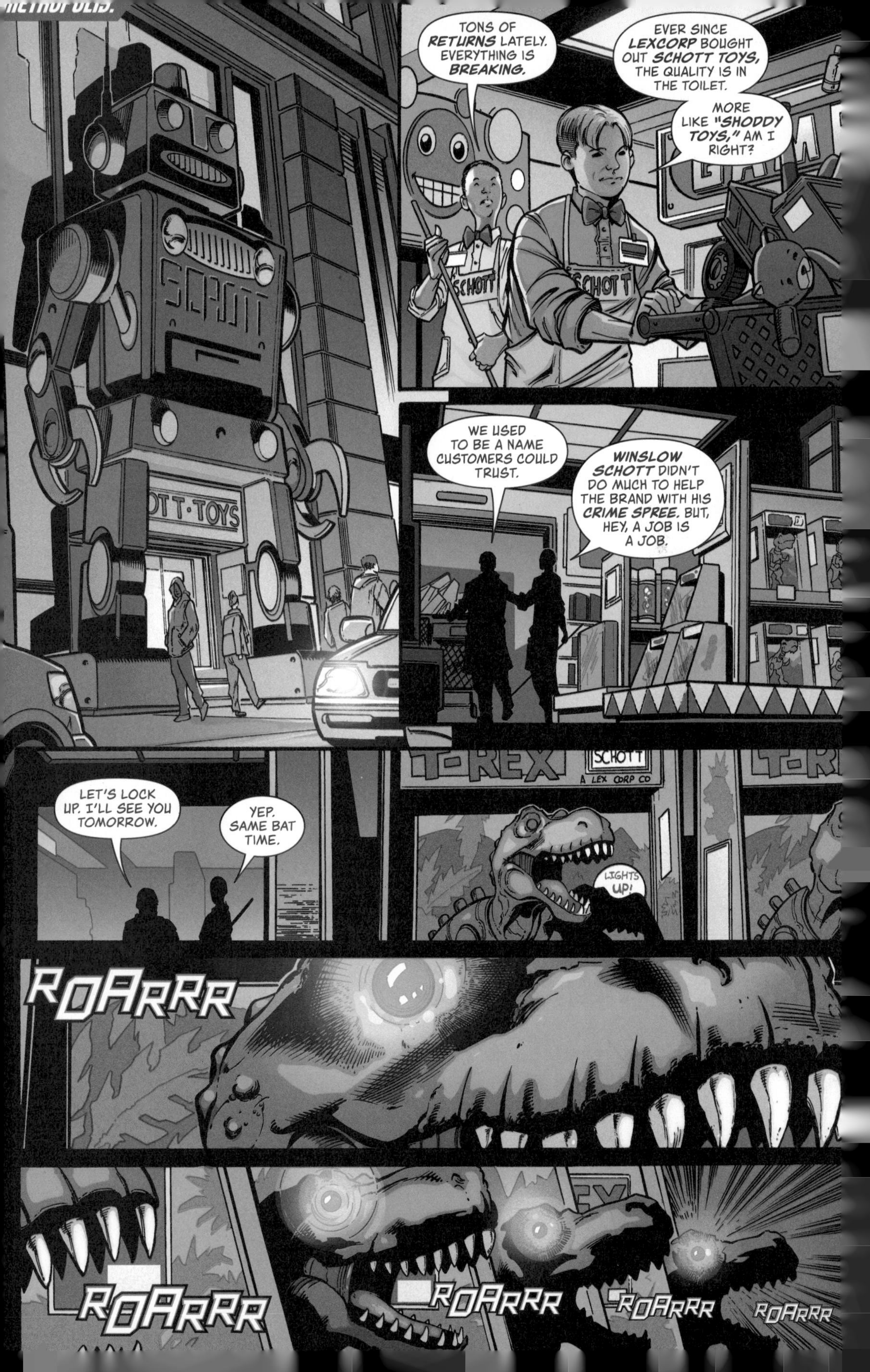

SCHOTT
OTT·TOYS
TONS OF RETURNS LATELY. EVERYTHING IS BREAKING.
EVER SINCE LEXCORP BOUGHT OUT SCHOTT TOYS, THE QUALITY IS IN THE TOILET.
MORE LIKE "SHODDY TOYS," AM I RIGHT?
SCHOTT
SCHOTT
WE USED TO BE A NAME CUSTOMERS COULD TRUST.
WINSLOW SCHOTT DIDN'T DO MUCH TO HELP THE BRAND WITH HIS CRIME SPREE. BUT, HEY, A JOB IS A JOB.
LET'S LOCK UP. I'LL SEE YOU TOMORROW.
YEP. SAME BAT TIME.
T-REX
SCHOTT
A LEX CORP CO
LIGHTS UP!
ROARRR
ROARRR
ROARRR
ROARRR
ROARRR

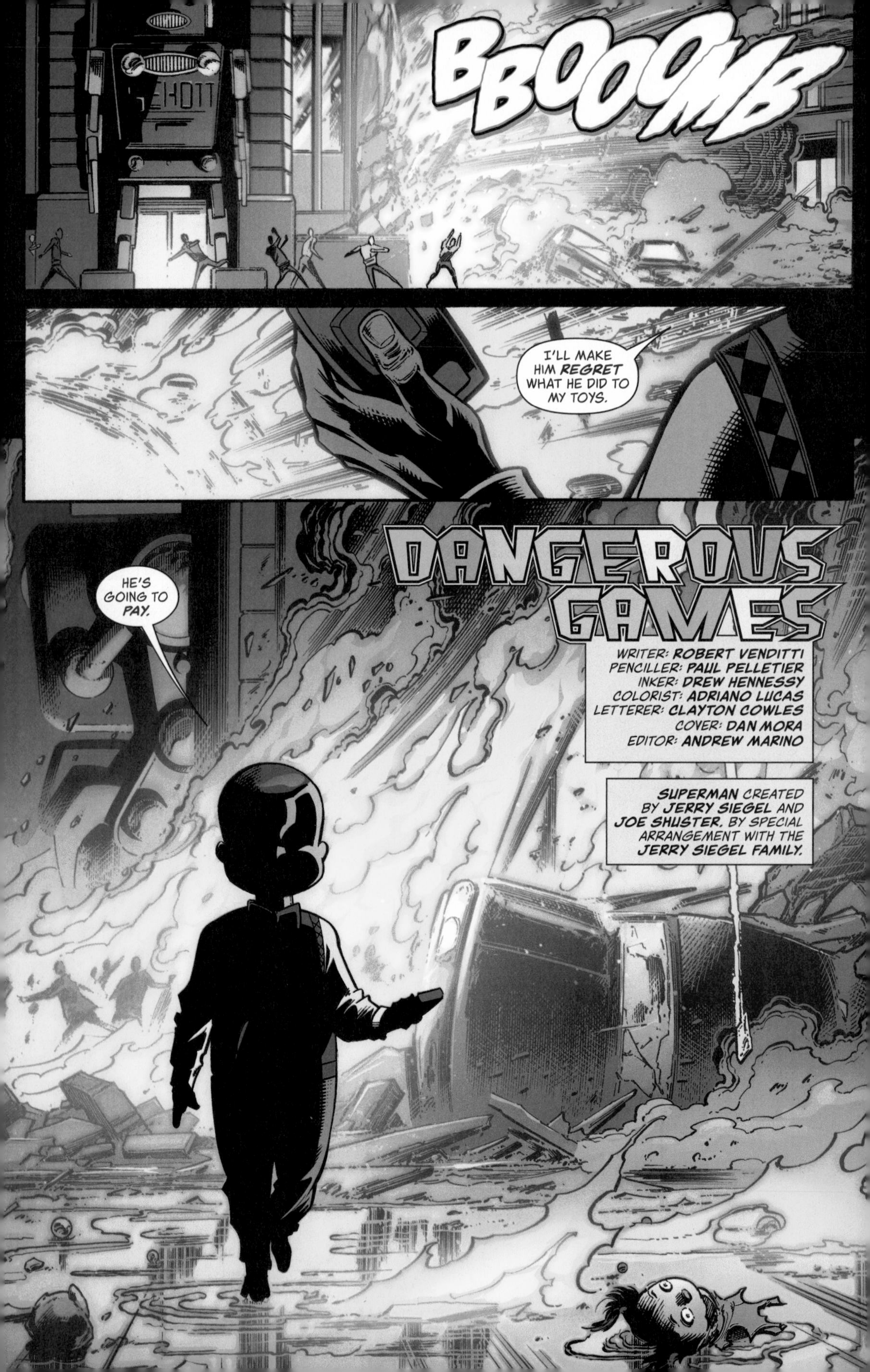
BBOOOOMB
I'LL MAKE HIM REGRET WHAT HE DID TO MY TOYS.
HE'S GOING TO PAY.
DANGEROUS GAMES
WRITER: ROBERT VENDITTI
PENCILLER: PAUL PELLETIER
INKER: DREW HENNESSY
COLORIST: ADRIANO LUCAS
LETTERER: CLAYTON COWLES
COVER: DAN MORA
EDITOR: ANDREW MARINO
SUPERMAN CREATED BY JERRY SIEGEL AND JOE SHUSTER. BY SPECIAL ARRANGEMENT WITH THE JERRY SIEGEL FAMILY.

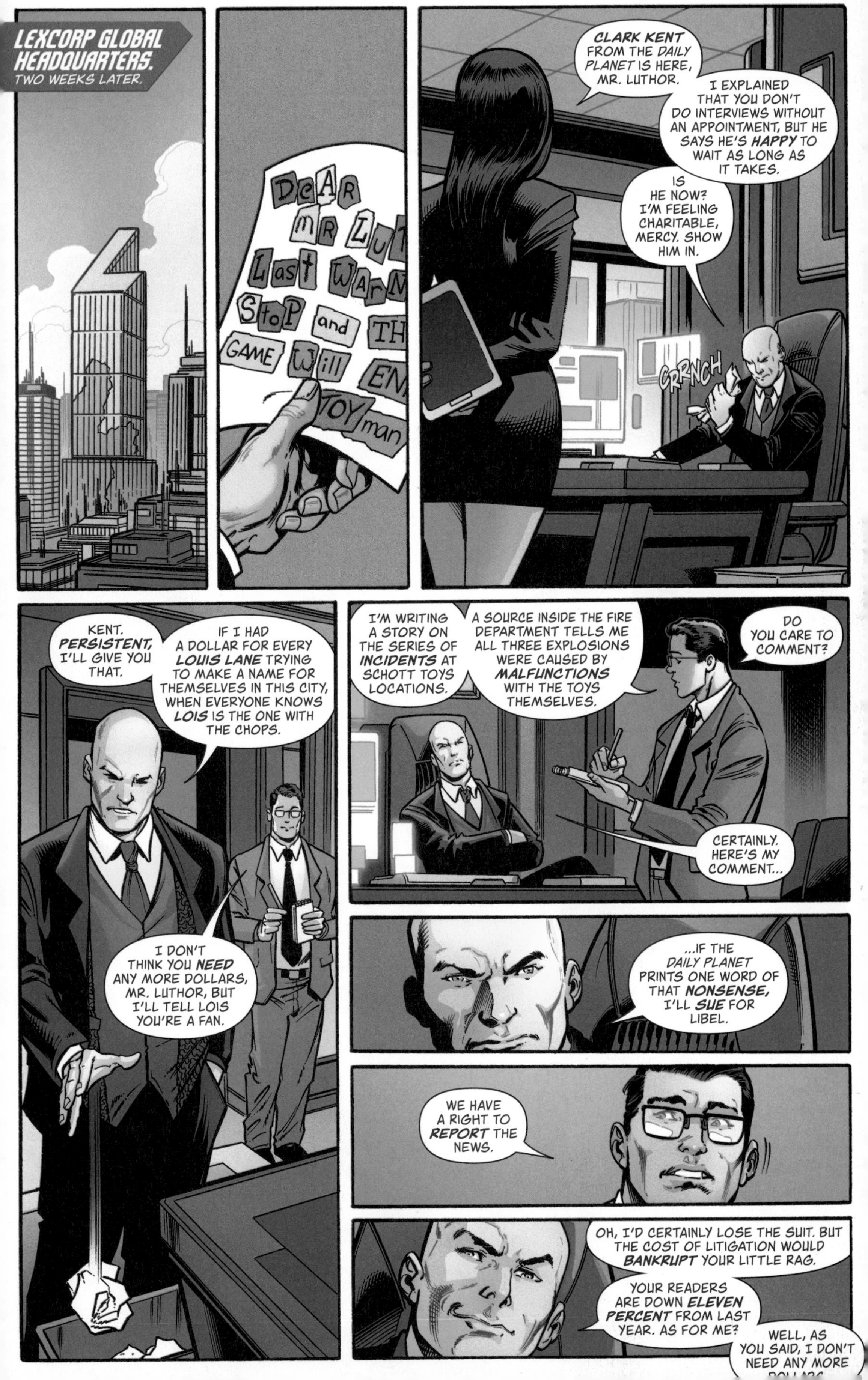
LEXCORP GLOBAL HEADQUARTERS.
TWO WEEKS LATER.
DeAR mR LUT Last WarN StoP and TH GAME Will EN TOY man
CLARK KENT FROM THE DAILY PLANET IS HERE, MR. LUTHOR.
I EXPLAINED THAT YOU DON'T DO INTERVIEWS WITHOUT AN APPOINTMENT, BUT HE SAYS HE'S HAPPY TO WAIT AS LONG AS IT TAKES.
IS HE NOW? I'M FEELING CHARITABLE, MERCY. SHOW HIM IN.
CRRNCH
KENT. PERSISTENT, I'LL GIVE YOU THAT.
IF I HAD A DOLLAR FOR EVERY LOUIS LANE TRYING TO MAKE A NAME FOR THEMSELVES IN THIS CITY, WHEN EVERYONE KNOWS LOIS IS THE ONE WITH THE CHOPS.
I DON'T THINK YOU NEED ANY MORE DOLLARS, MR. LUTHOR, BUT I'LL TELL LOIS YOU'RE A FAN.
I'M WRITING A STORY ON THE SERIES OF INCIDENTS AT SCHOTT TOYS LOCATIONS.
A SOURCE INSIDE THE FIRE DEPARTMENT TELLS ME ALL THREE EXPLOSIONS WERE CAUSED BY MALFUNCTIONS WITH THE TOYS THEMSELVES.
DO YOU CARE TO COMMENT?
CERTAINLY. HERE'S MY COMMENT...
...IF THE DAILY PLANET PRINTS ONE WORD OF THAT NONSENSE, I'LL SUE FOR LIBEL.
WE HAVE A RIGHT TO REPORT THE NEWS.
OH, I'D CERTAINLY LOSE THE SUIT. BUT THE COST OF LITIGATION WOULD BANKRUPT YOUR LITTLE RAG.
YOUR READERS ARE DOWN ELEVEN PERCENT FROM LAST YEAR. AS FOR ME?
WELL, AS YOU SAID, I DON'T NEED ANY MORE

IF THESE ATTACKS CONTINUE, SOMEONE WILL GET *HURT.*

WILL YOU AT LEAST SAY WHETHER WINSLOW SCHOTT HAS MADE ANY *THREATS* TO YOU OR YOUR COMPANY?

WINSLOW SCHOTT IS A *PSYCHOPATH* WHO COULDN'T CUT IT IN THE TOY BUSINESS, SO HE TRIED ROBBING BANKS TO PAY THE BILLS.

I'VE SPENT *VALUABLE* LEXCORP RESOURCES AND MY *CONSIDERABLY* MORE VALUABLE TIME REBUILDING THE BRAND OF A PROUD AMERICAN COMPANY THAT WOULD'VE *DIED* WITHOUT ME.

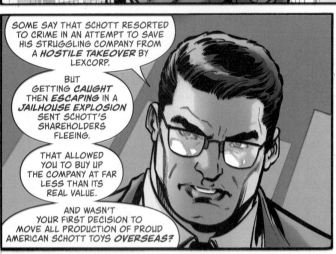

SOME SAY THAT SCHOTT RESORTED TO CRIME IN AN ATTEMPT TO SAVE HIS STRUGGLING COMPANY FROM A *HOSTILE TAKEOVER* BY LEXCORP.

BUT GETTING *CAUGHT* THEN *ESCAPING* IN A *JAILHOUSE EXPLOSION* SENT SCHOTT'S SHAREHOLDERS FLEEING.

THAT ALLOWED YOU TO BUY UP THE COMPANY AT FAR LESS THAN ITS REAL VALUE.

AND WASN'T YOUR FIRST DECISION TO MOVE ALL PRODUCTION OF PROUD AMERICAN SCHOTT TOYS *OVERSEAS?*

YOUR PAPER CONSTANTLY FAWNS OVER *SUPERMAN*--THE MOST DANGEROUS ALIEN ON THE PLANET--AND YOU'RE LECTURING *ME* ABOUT MANUFACTURING TOYS IN CHINA?

YOU DIDN'T ANSWER MY QUESTION.

NO.

NO, YOU *HAVEN'T* RECEIVED ANY THREATS FROM WINSLOW SCHOTT?

NO, I HAVEN'T ANSWERED YOUR QUESTION.

I APPRECIATE YOU WASTING YOUR CONSIDERABLY *VALUABLE* TIME, MR. LUTHOR.

KENT?

DO YOU FIND IT EMBARRASSING THAT YOUR *WIFE* IS BETTER AT YOUR JOB THAN YOU?

GEE, MR. LUTHOR--

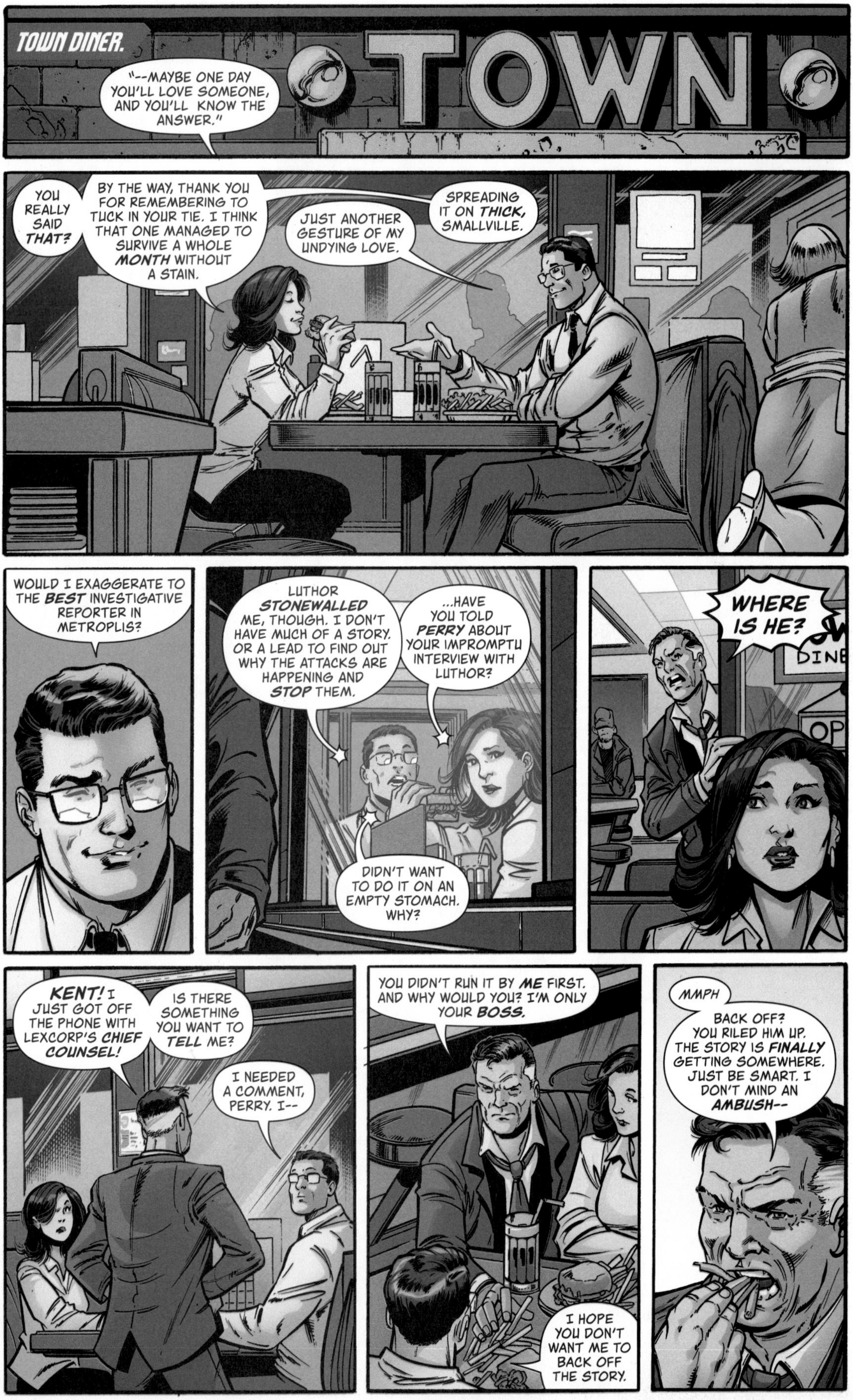

TOWN DINER.
TOWN
"--MAYBE ONE DAY YOU'LL LOVE SOMEONE, AND YOU'LL KNOW THE ANSWER."
YOU REALLY SAID THAT?
BY THE WAY, THANK YOU FOR REMEMBERING TO TUCK IN YOUR TIE. I THINK THAT ONE MANAGED TO SURVIVE A WHOLE MONTH WITHOUT A STAIN.
SPREADING IT ON THICK, SMALLVILLE.
JUST ANOTHER GESTURE OF MY UNDYING LOVE.
WOULD I EXAGGERATE TO THE BEST INVESTIGATIVE REPORTER IN METROPLIS?
LUTHOR STONEWALLED ME, THOUGH. I DON'T HAVE MUCH OF A STORY. OR A LEAD TO FIND OUT WHY THE ATTACKS ARE HAPPENING AND STOP THEM.
...HAVE YOU TOLD PERRY ABOUT YOUR IMPROMPTU INTERVIEW WITH LUTHOR?
DIDN'T WANT TO DO IT ON AN EMPTY STOMACH. WHY?
WHERE IS HE?
KENT! I JUST GOT OFF THE PHONE WITH LEXCORP'S CHIEF COUNSEL!
IS THERE SOMETHING YOU WANT TO TELL ME?
I NEEDED A COMMENT, PERRY. I--
YOU DIDN'T RUN IT BY ME FIRST. AND WHY WOULD YOU? I'M ONLY YOUR BOSS.
I HOPE YOU DON'T WANT ME TO BACK OFF THE STORY.
MMPH
BACK OFF? YOU RILED HIM UP. THE STORY IS FINALLY GETTING SOMEWHERE. JUST BE SMART. I DON'T MIND AN AMBUSH--

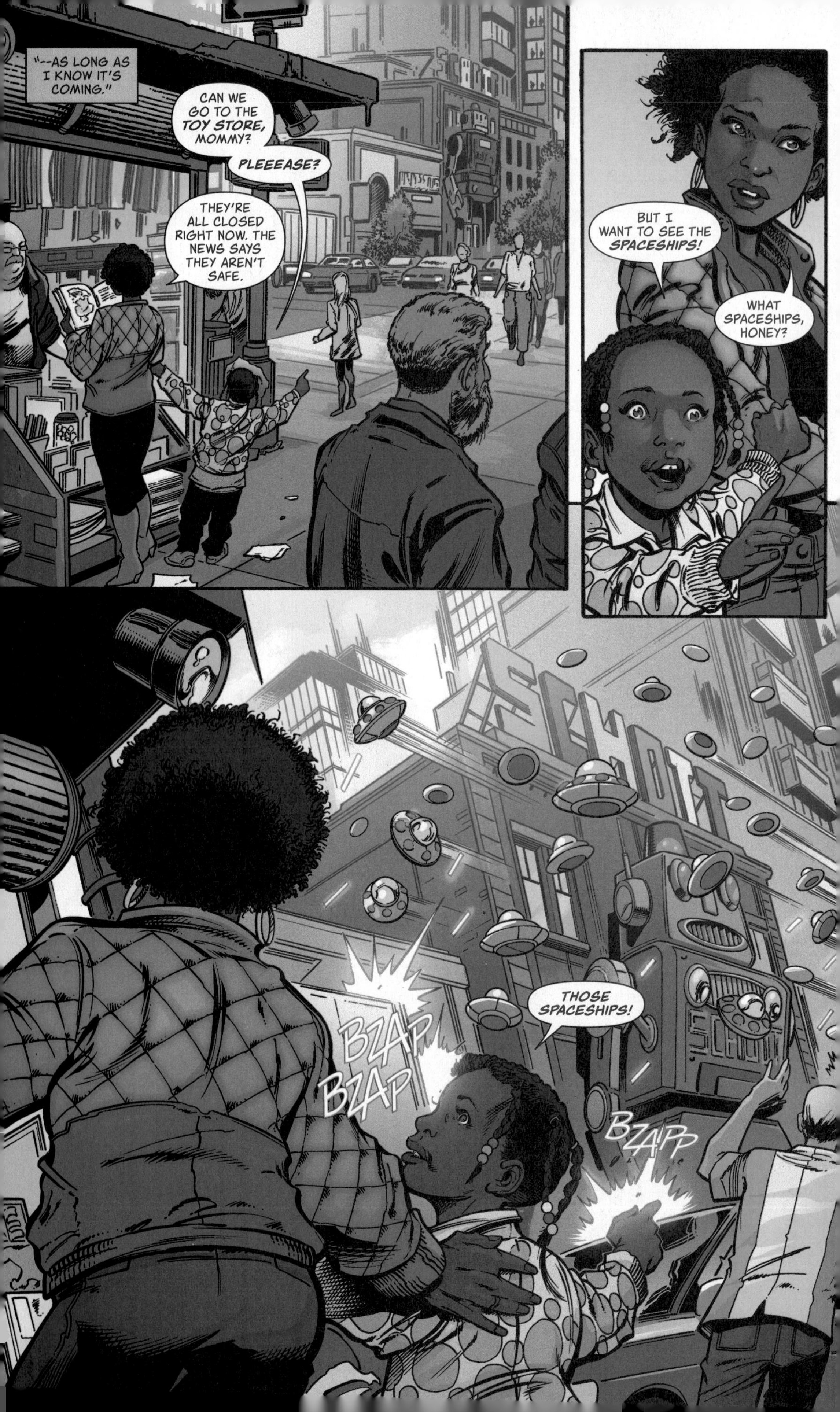
"--AS LONG AS I KNOW IT'S COMING."
CAN WE GO TO THE TOY STORE, MOMMY?
PLEEEASE?
THEY'RE ALL CLOSED RIGHT NOW. THE NEWS SAYS THEY AREN'T SAFE.
BUT I WANT TO SEE THE SPACESHIPS!
WHAT SPACESHIPS, HONEY?
THOSE SPACESHIPS!
BZAP
BZAP
BZAPP

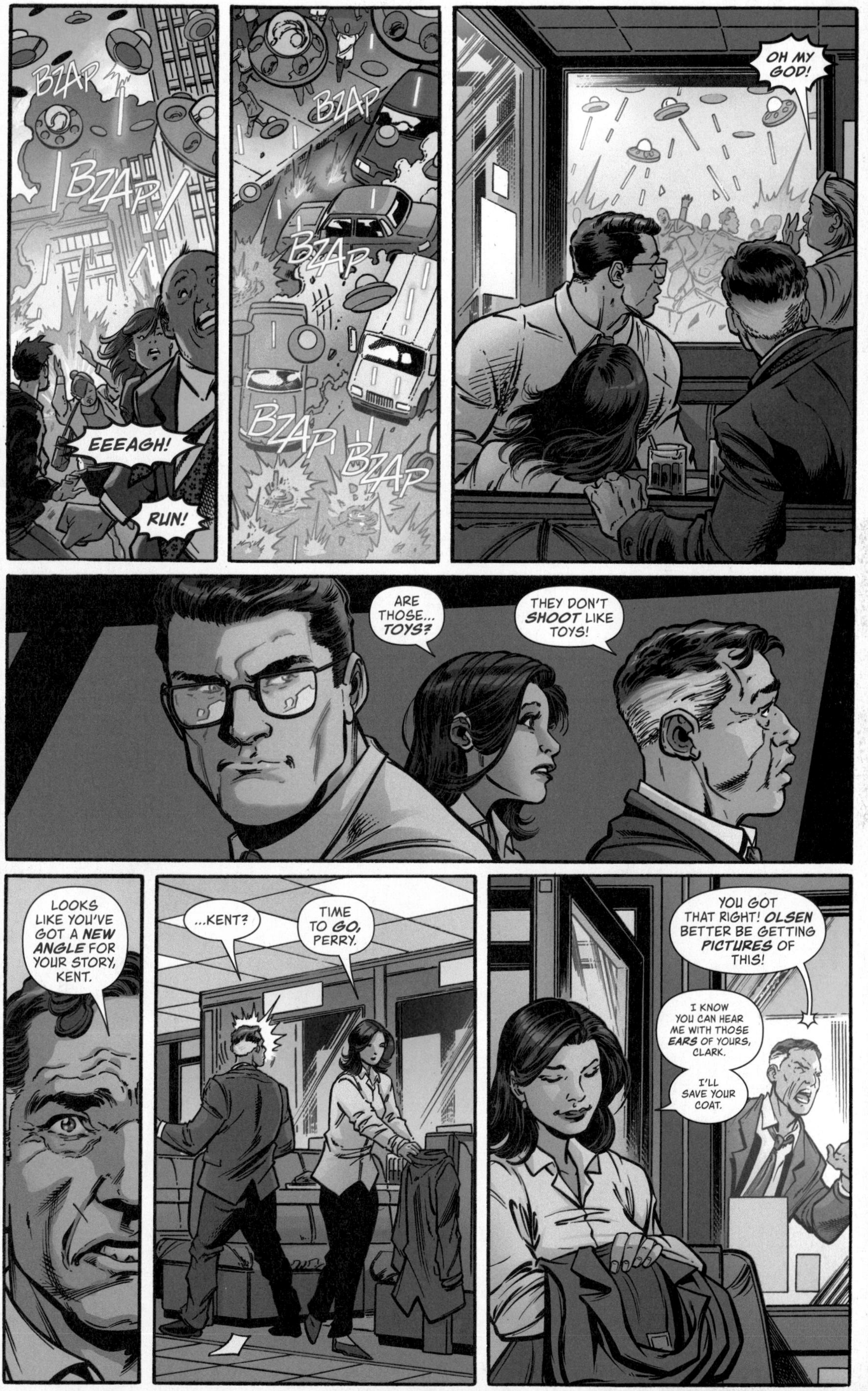
BZAP
BZAP
EEEAGH!
RUN!
BZAP
BZAP
BZAP
BZAP
OH MY GOD!
ARE THOSE... TOYS?
THEY DON'T SHOOT LIKE TOYS!
LOOKS LIKE YOU'VE GOT A NEW ANGLE FOR YOUR STORY, KENT.
...KENT?
TIME TO GO, PERRY.
YOU GOT THAT RIGHT! OLSEN BETTER BE GETTING PICTURES OF THIS!
I KNOW YOU CAN HEAR ME WITH THOSE EARS OF YOURS, CLARK.
I'LL SAVE YOUR COAT.

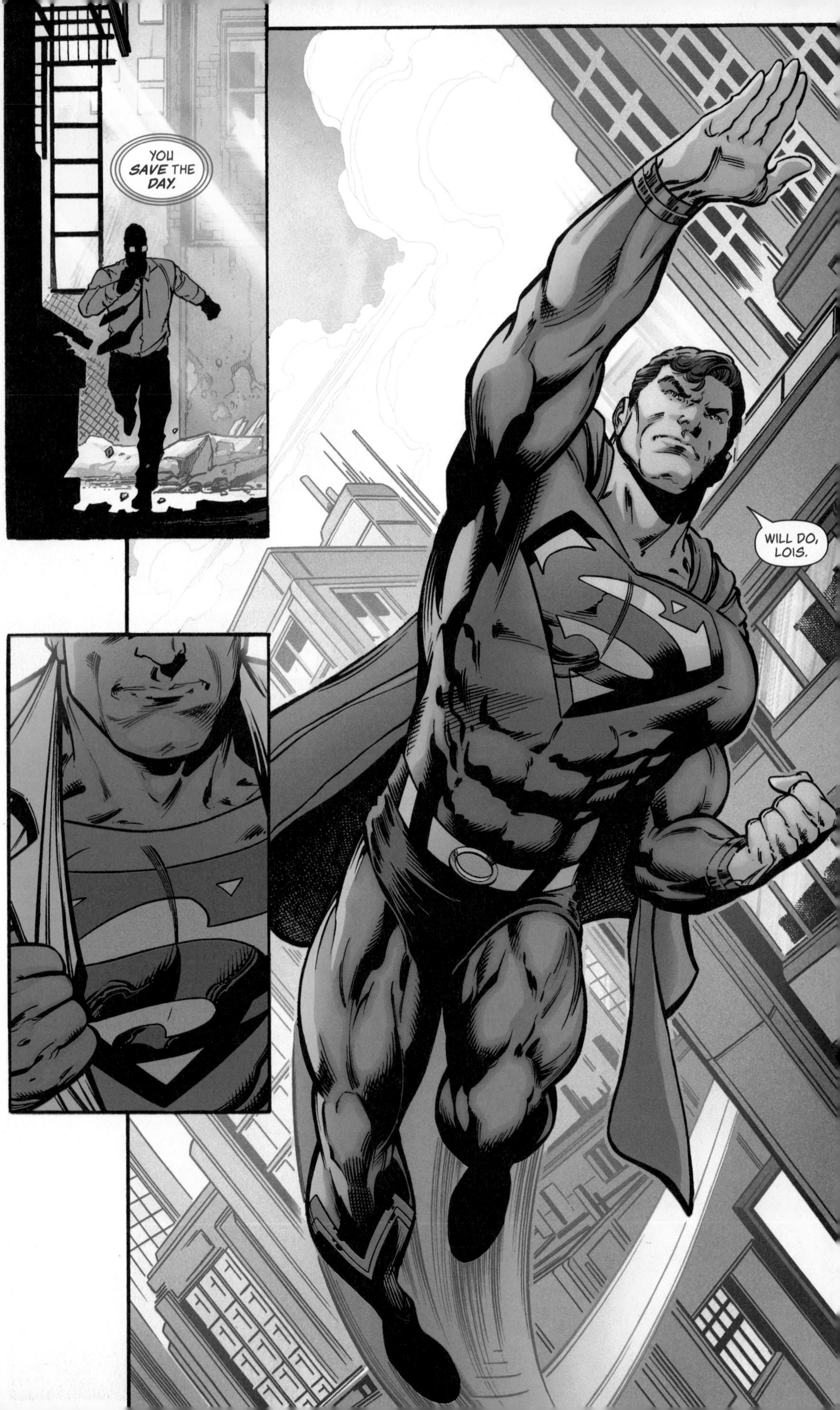
YOU SAVE THE DAY.
WILL DO, LOIS.

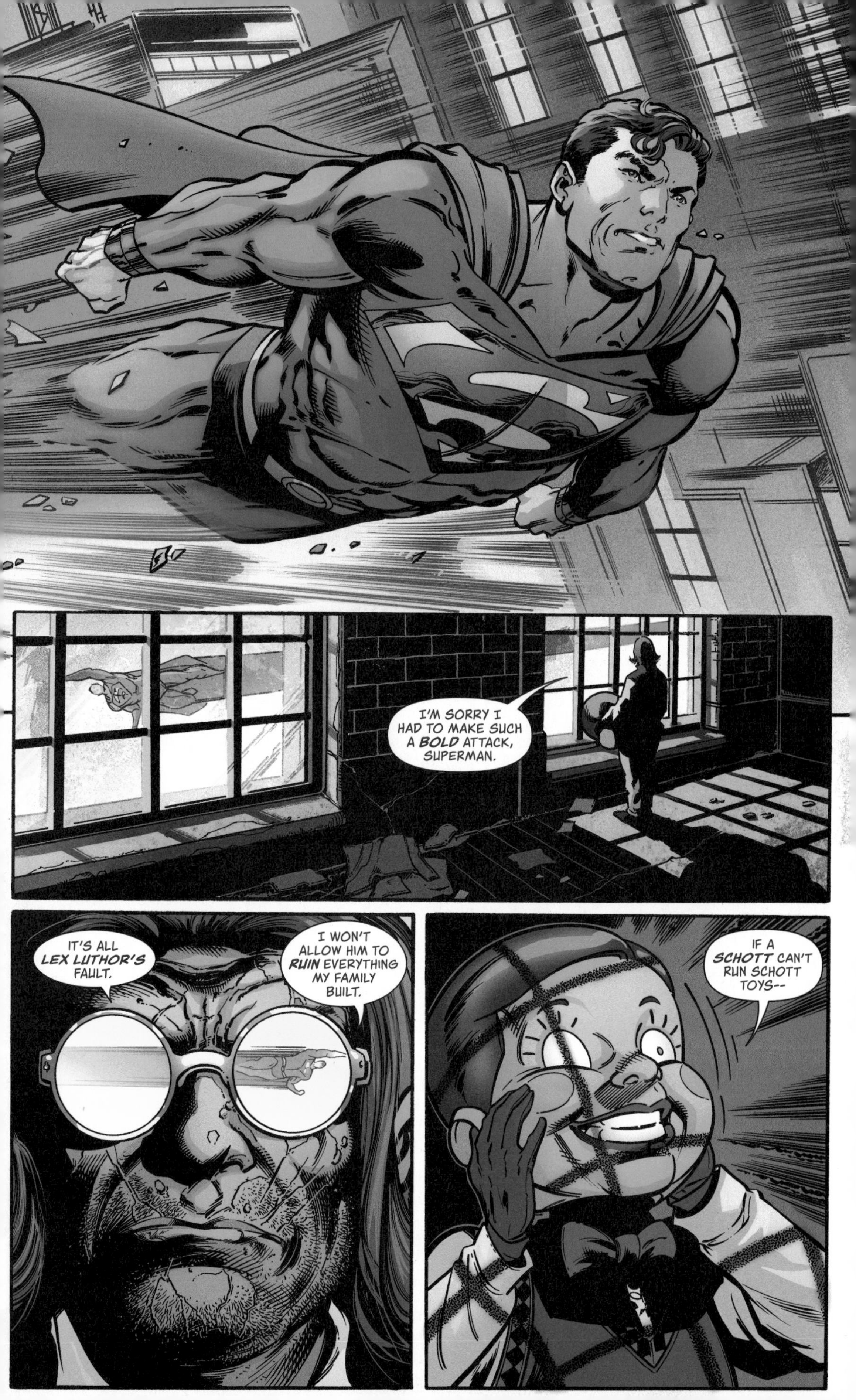
I'M SORRY I HAD TO MAKE SUCH A BOLD ATTACK, SUPERMAN.
IT'S ALL LEX LUTHOR'S FAULT.
I WON'T ALLOW HIM TO RUIN EVERYTHING MY FAMILY BUILT.
IF A SCHOTT CAN'T RUN SCHOTT TOYS--

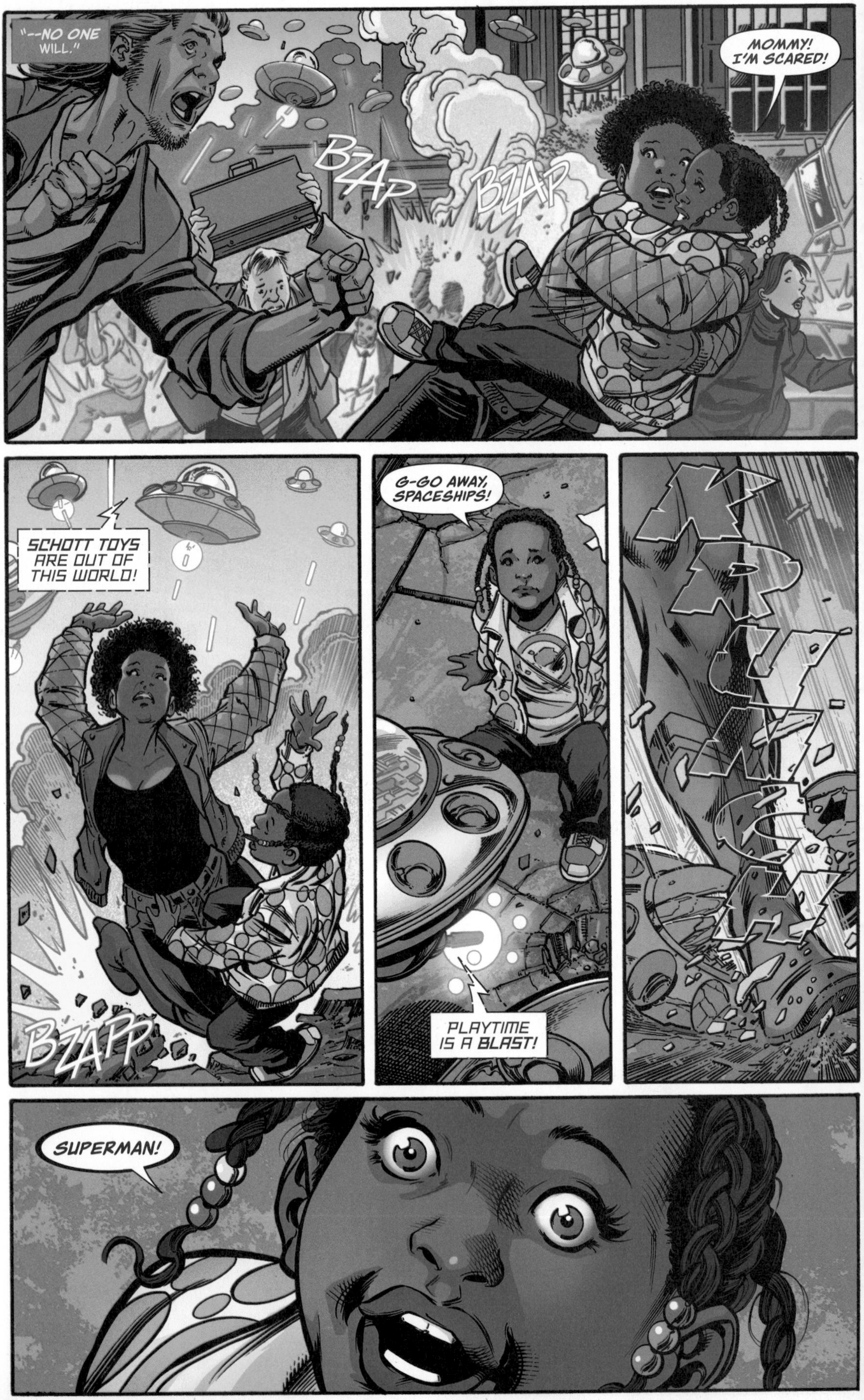
"--NO ONE WILL."
BZAP
BZAP
MOMMY! I'M SCARED!
SCHOTT TOYS ARE OUT OF THIS WORLD!
BZAPP
G-GO AWAY, SPACESHIPS!
PLAYTIME IS A BLAST!
KRUNCH
SUPERMAN!

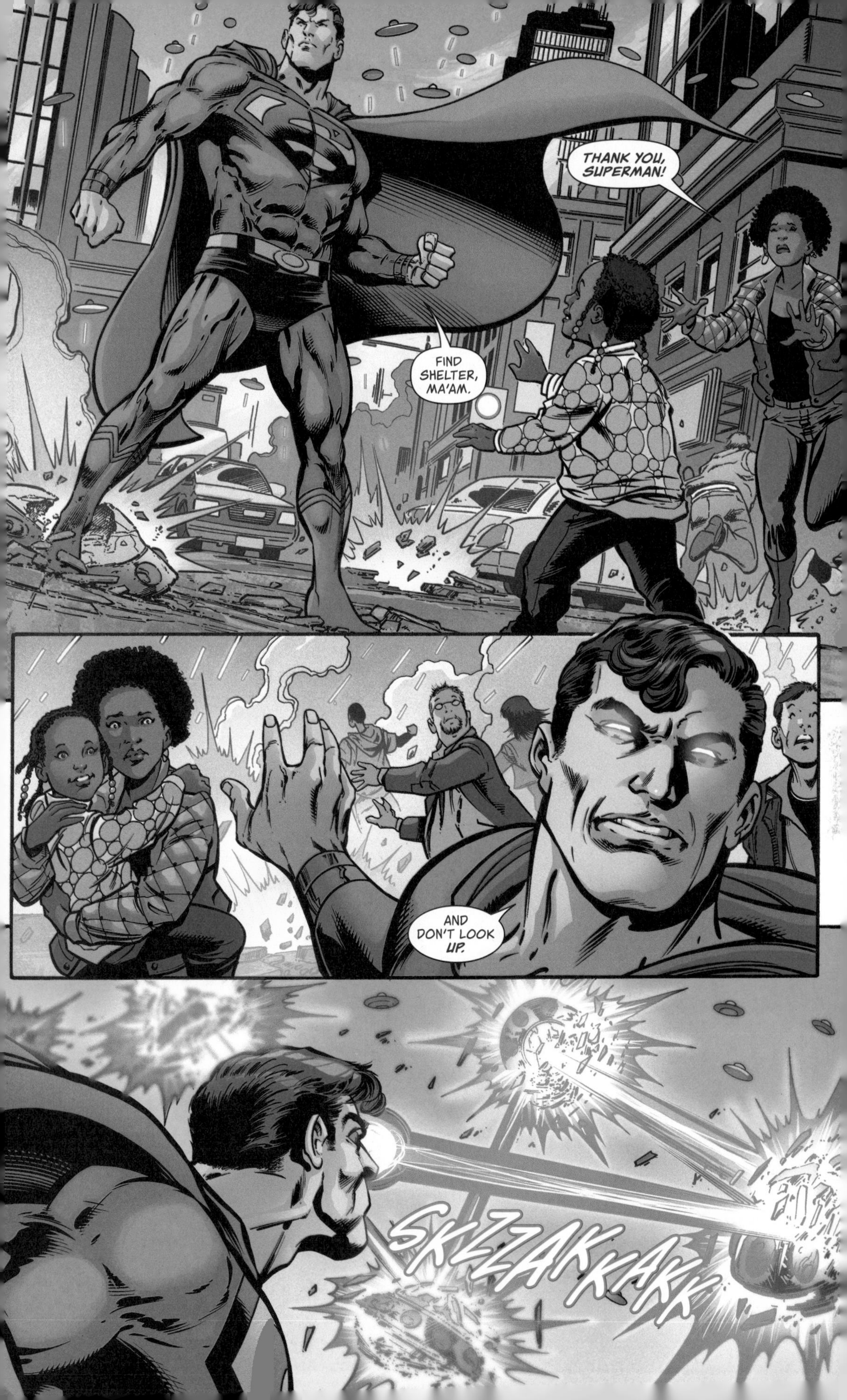
THANK YOU, SUPERMAN!
FIND SHELTER, MA'AM.
AND DON'T LOOK UP.
SKZZAKKAKK

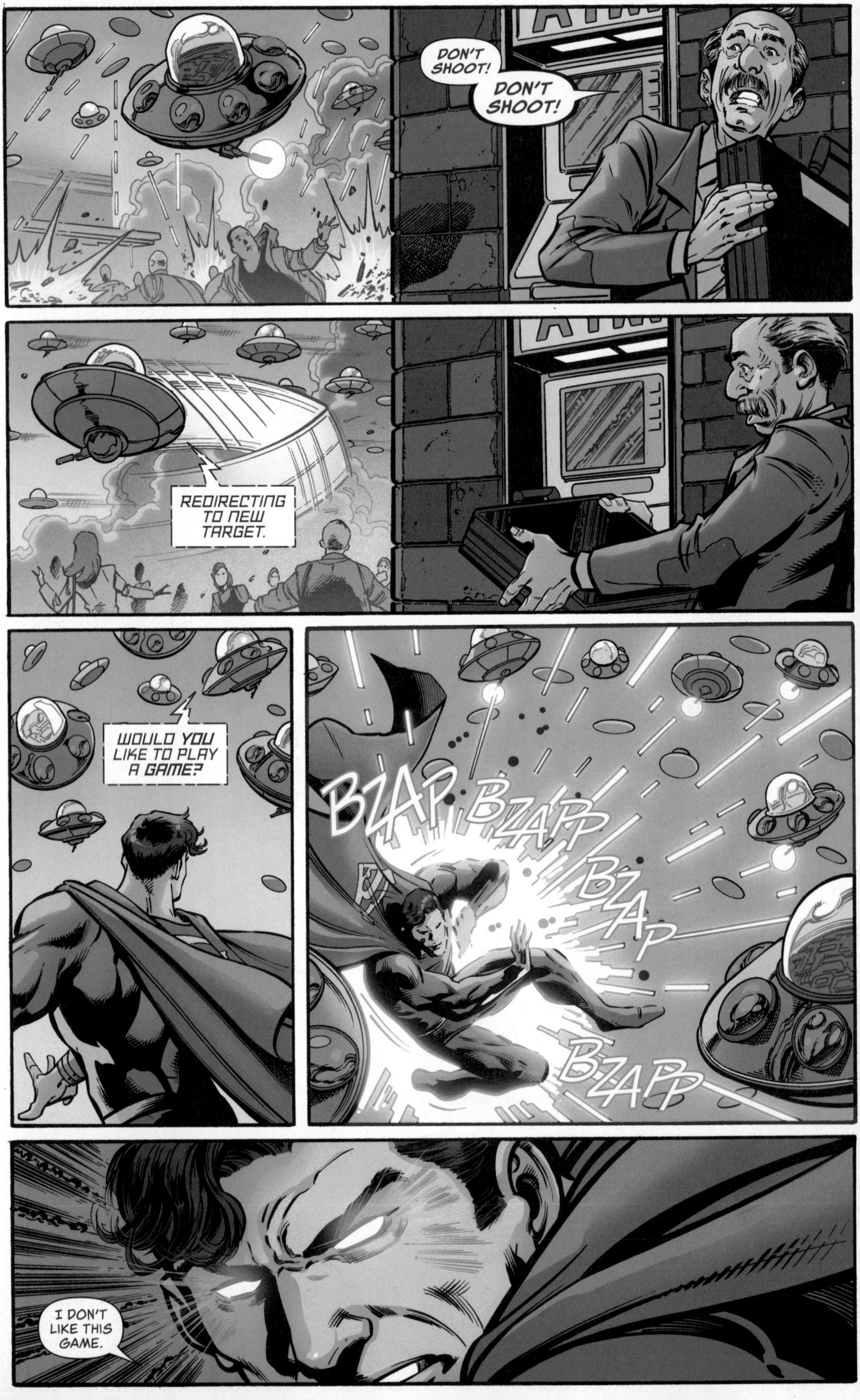
DON'T SHOOT!
DON'T SHOOT!
REDIRECTING TO NEW TARGET.
WOULD YOU LIKE TO PLAY A GAME?
BZAP BZAPP
BZAP
BZAPP
I DON'T LIKE THIS GAME.

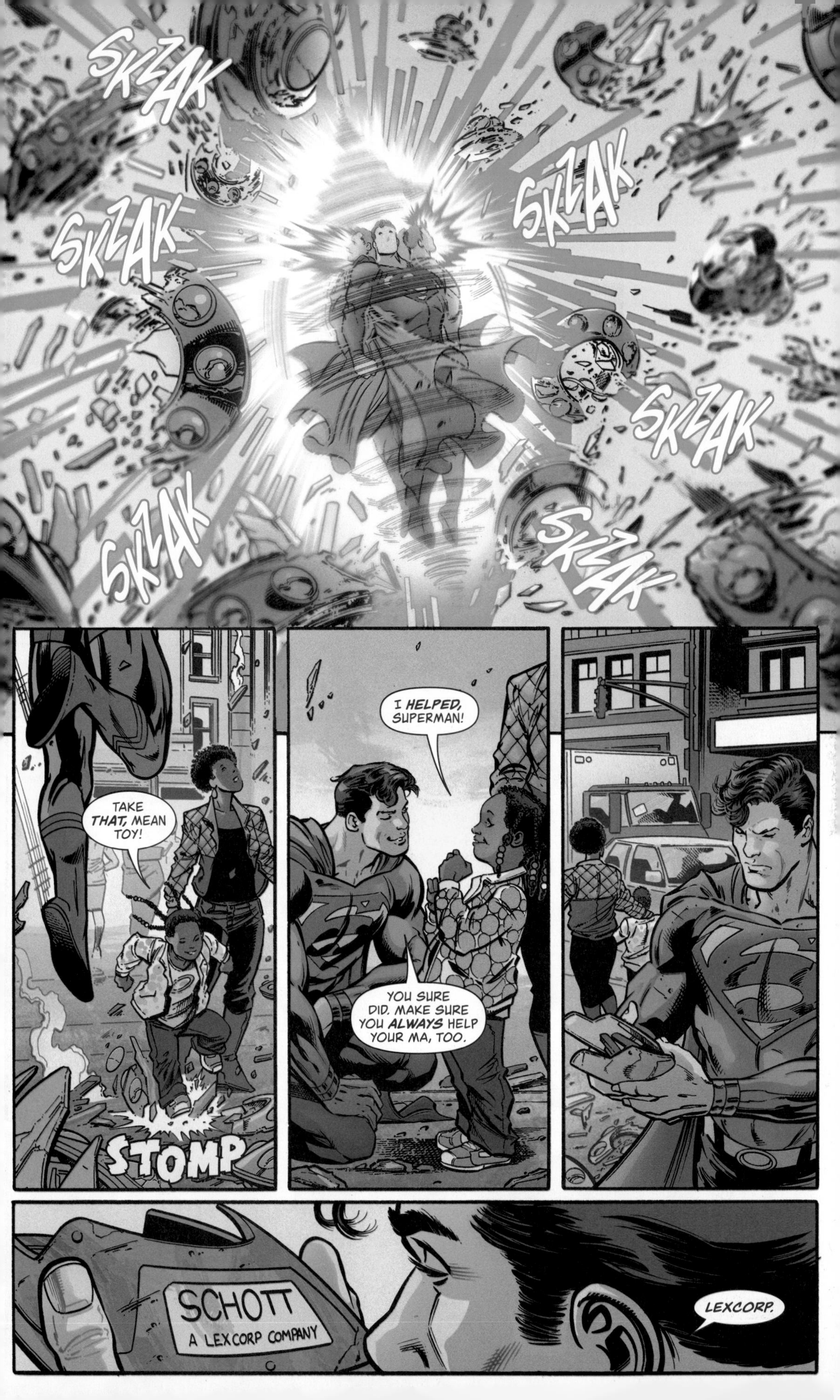
SKZAK
SKZAK
SKZAK
SKZAK
SKZAK
SKZAK
TAKE THAT, MEAN TOY!
STOMP
I HELPED, SUPERMAN!
YOU SURE DID. MAKE SURE YOU ALWAYS HELP YOUR MA, TOO.
SCHOTT
A LEXCORP COMPANY
LEXCORP.

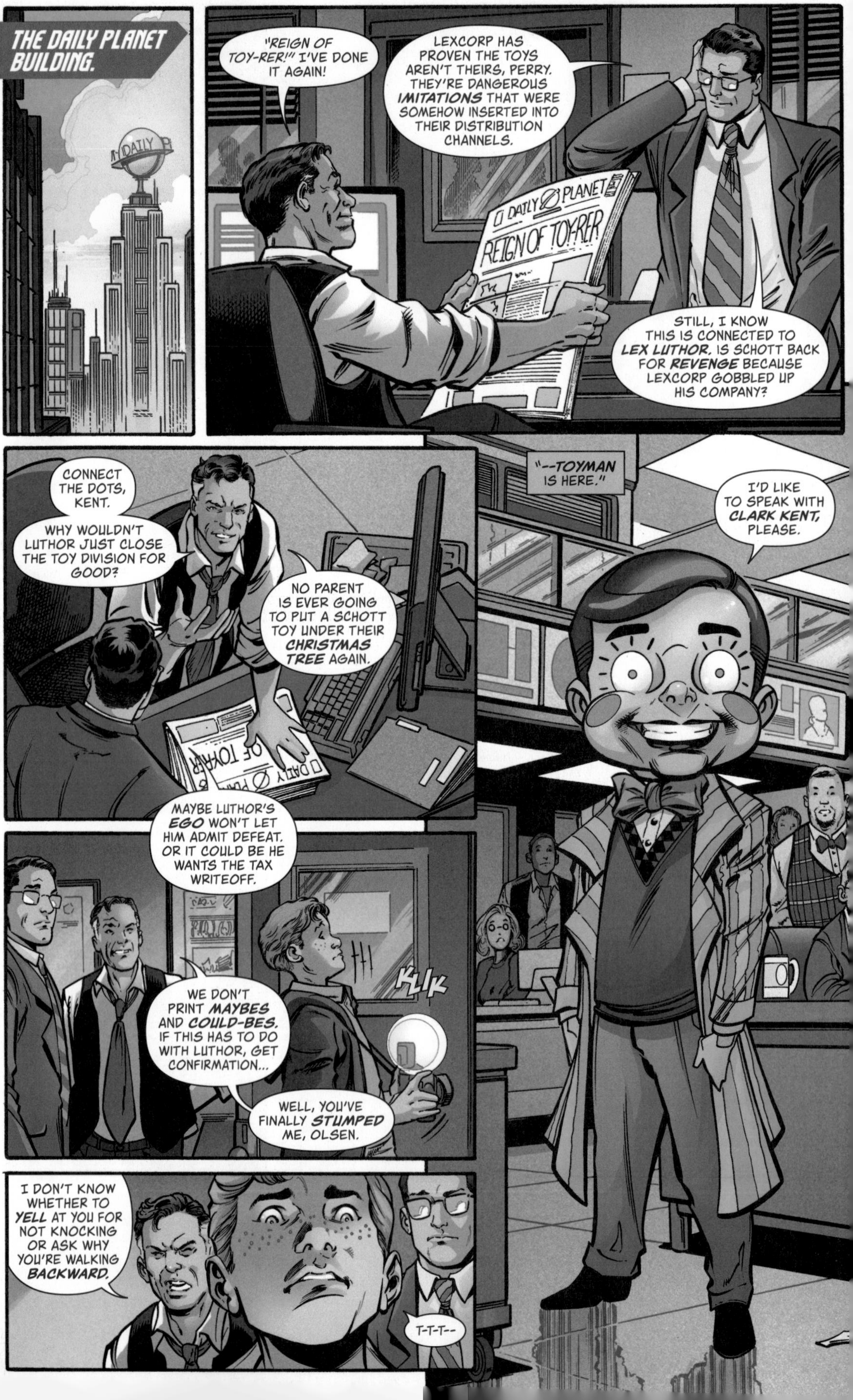
THE DAILY PLANET BUILDING.
DAILY P
"REIGN OF TOY-RER!" I'VE DONE IT AGAIN!
DAILY PLANET
REIGN OF TOY-RER
LEXCORP HAS PROVEN THE TOYS AREN'T THEIRS, PERRY. THEY'RE DANGEROUS IMITATIONS THAT WERE SOMEHOW INSERTED INTO THEIR DISTRIBUTION CHANNELS.
STILL, I KNOW THIS IS CONNECTED TO LEX LUTHOR. IS SCHOTT BACK FOR REVENGE BECAUSE LEXCORP GOBBLED UP HIS COMPANY?
CONNECT THE DOTS, KENT.
WHY WOULDN'T LUTHOR JUST CLOSE THE TOY DIVISION FOR GOOD?
NO PARENT IS EVER GOING TO PUT A SCHOTT TOY UNDER THEIR CHRISTMAS TREE AGAIN.
MAYBE LUTHOR'S EGO WON'T LET HIM ADMIT DEFEAT. OR IT COULD BE HE WANTS THE TAX WRITEOFF.
WE DON'T PRINT MAYBES AND COULD-BES. IF THIS HAS TO DO WITH LUTHOR, GET CONFIRMATION...
KLIK
WELL, YOU'VE FINALLY STUMPED ME, OLSEN.
I DON'T KNOW WHETHER TO YELL AT YOU FOR NOT KNOCKING OR ASK WHY YOU'RE WALKING BACKWARD.
T-T-T--
"--TOYMAN IS HERE."
I'D LIKE TO SPEAK WITH CLARK KENT, PLEASE.

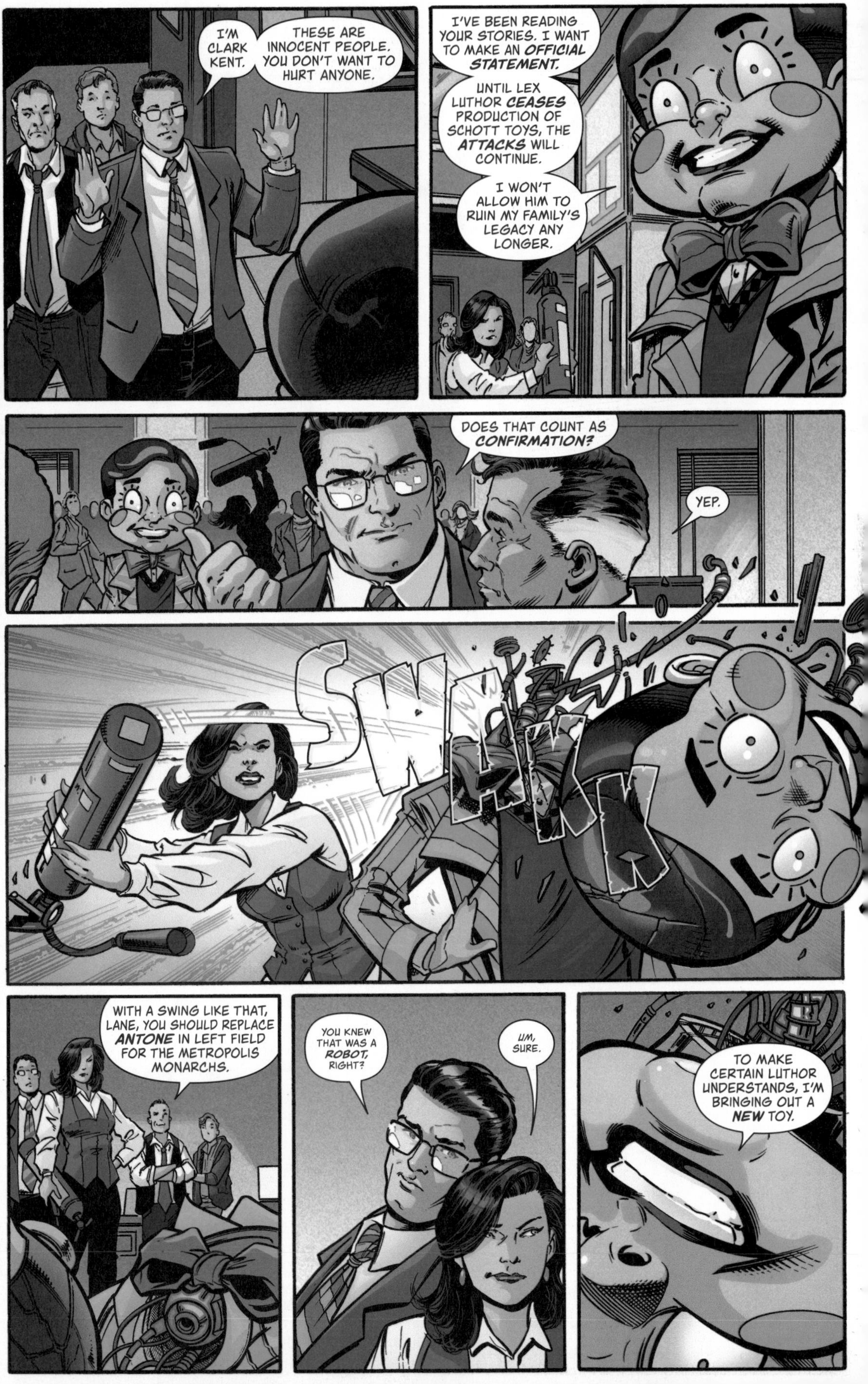

I'M CLARK KENT.
THESE ARE INNOCENT PEOPLE. YOU DON'T WANT TO HURT ANYONE.
I'VE BEEN READING YOUR STORIES. I WANT TO MAKE AN OFFICIAL STATEMENT.
UNTIL LEX LUTHOR CEASES PRODUCTION OF SCHOTT TOYS, THE ATTACKS WILL CONTINUE.
I WON'T ALLOW HIM TO RUIN MY FAMILY'S LEGACY ANY LONGER.
DOES THAT COUNT AS CONFIRMATION?
YEP.
SWAKK
WITH A SWING LIKE THAT, LANE, YOU SHOULD REPLACE ANTONE IN LEFT FIELD FOR THE METROPOLIS MONARCHS.
YOU KNEW THAT WAS A ROBOT, RIGHT?
UM, SURE.
TO MAKE CERTAIN LUTHOR UNDERSTANDS, I'M BRINGING OUT A NEW TOY.

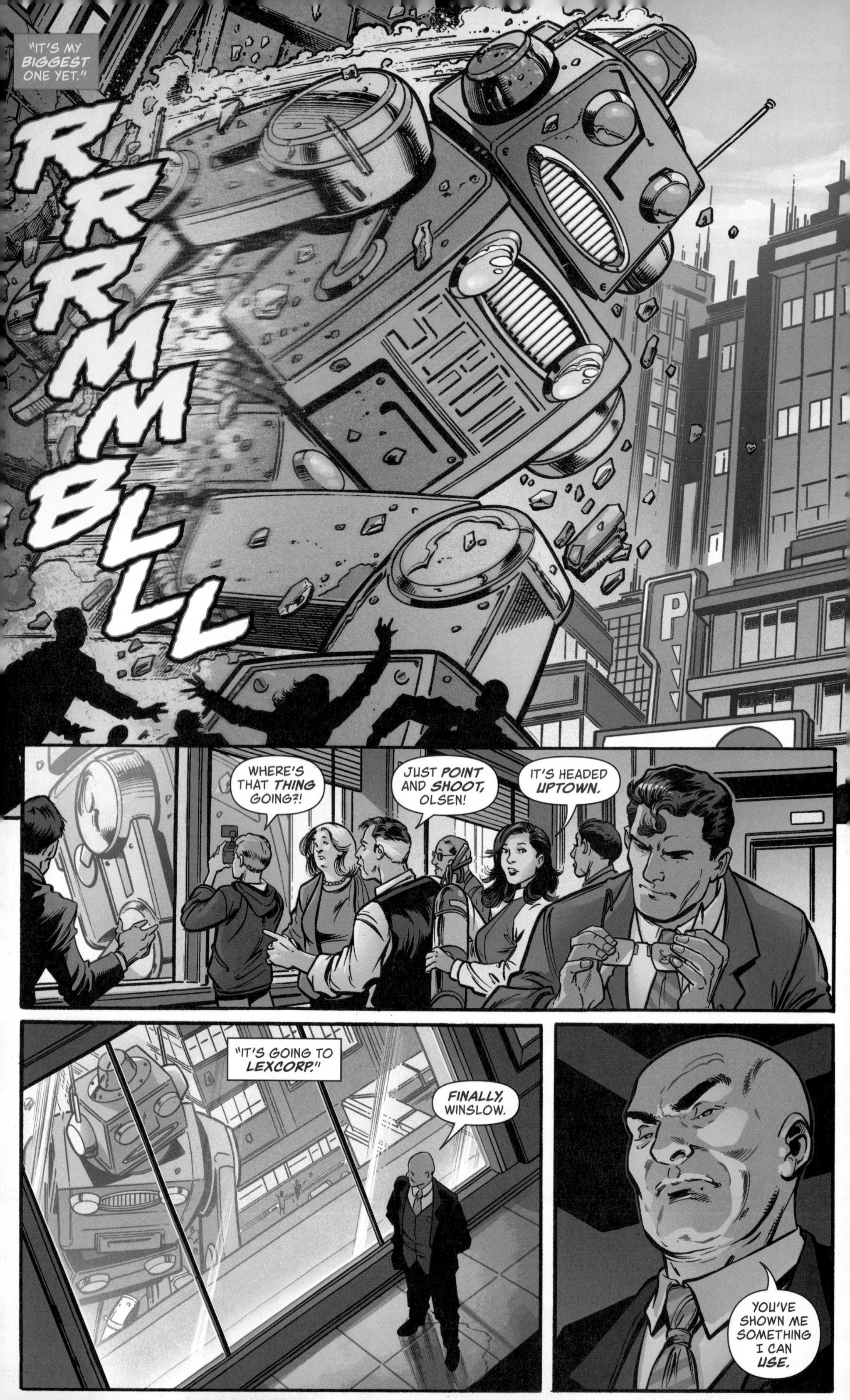

"IT'S MY BIGGEST ONE YET."
RRRMMBLLL
WHERE'S THAT THING GOING?!
JUST POINT AND SHOOT, OLSEN!
IT'S HEADED UPTOWN.
"IT'S GOING TO LEXCORP."
FINALLY, WINSLOW.
YOU'VE SHOWN ME SOMETHING I CAN USE.

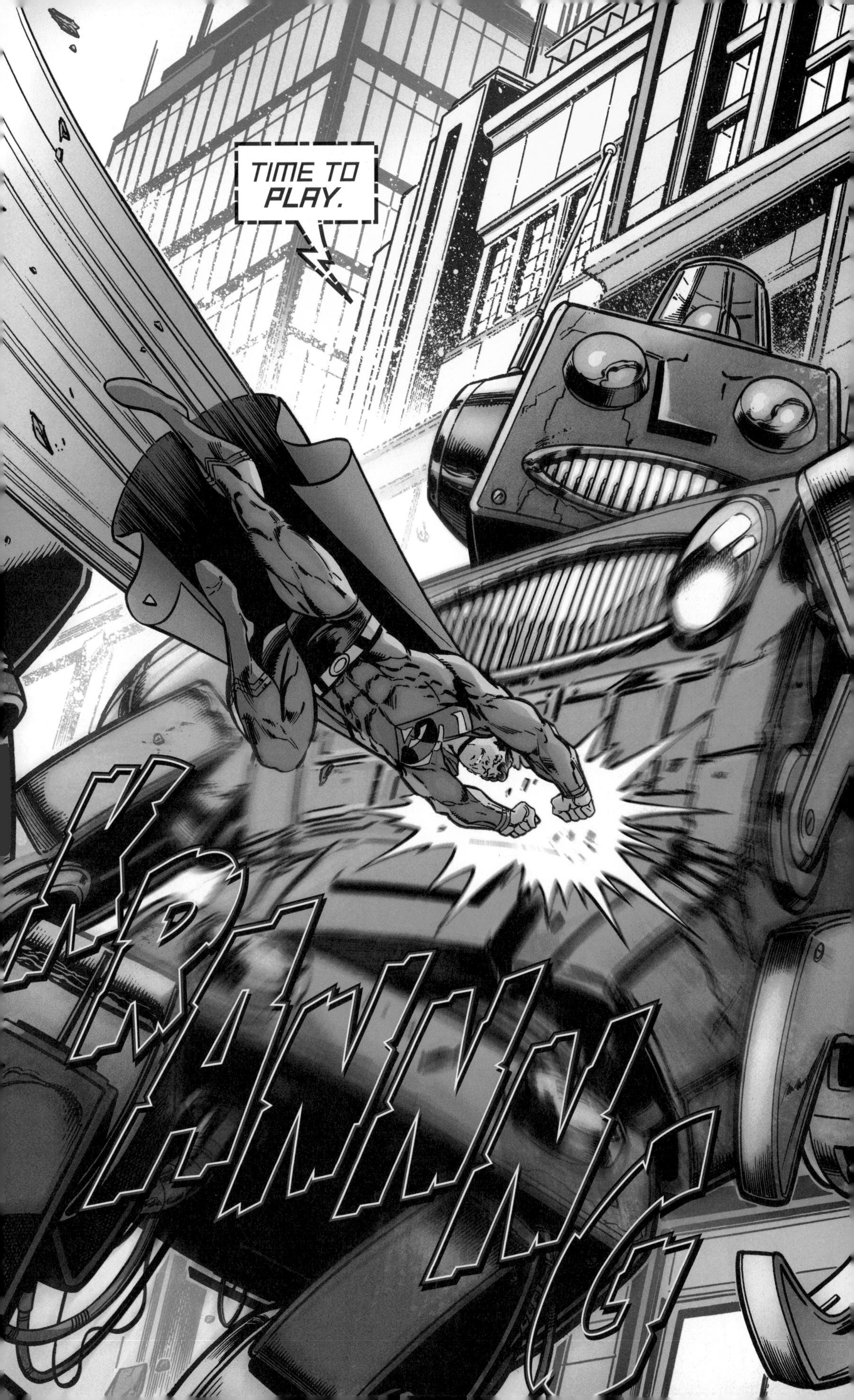
TIME TO PLAY.

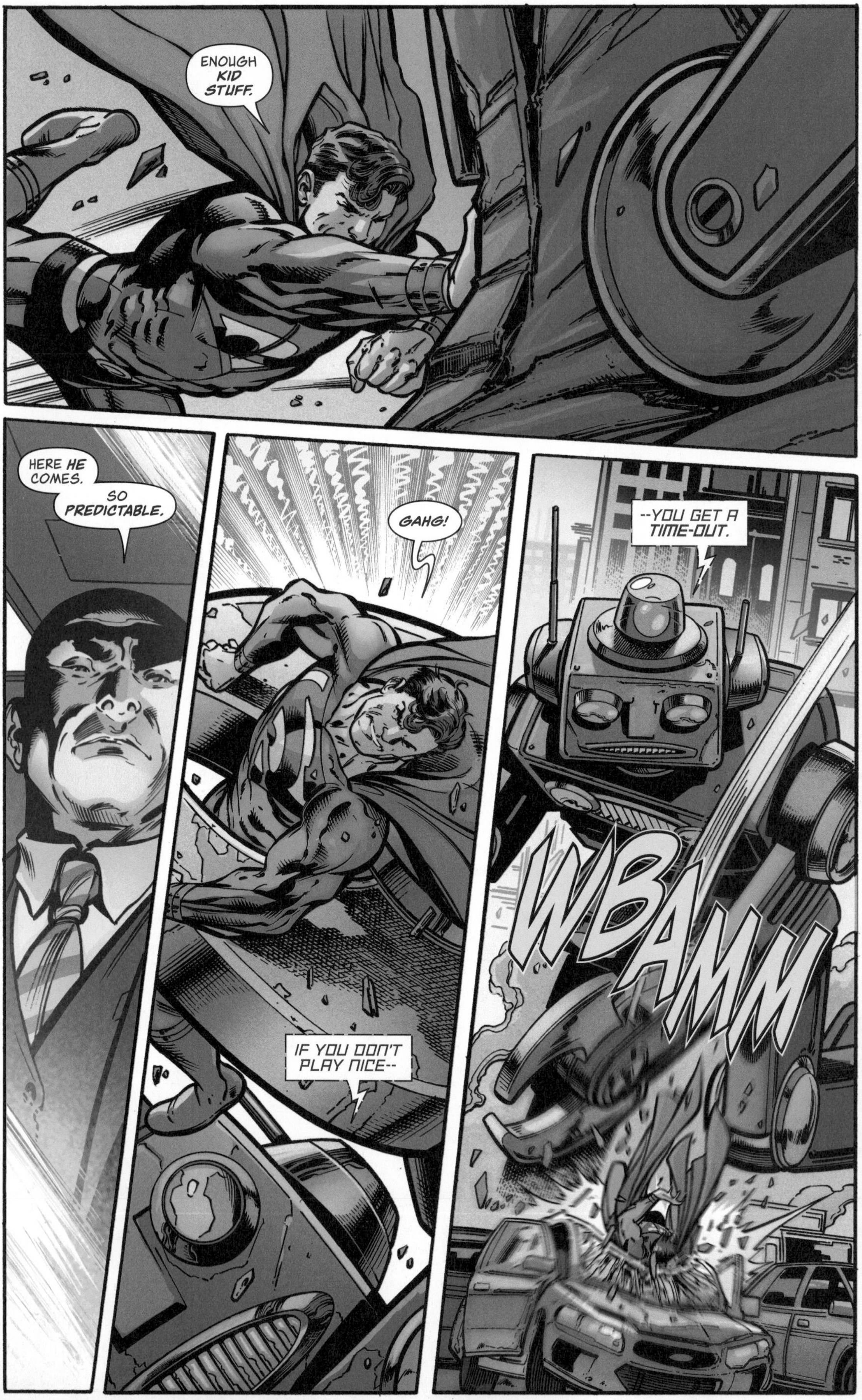
ENOUGH KID STUFF.
HERE HE COMES.
SO PREDICTABLE.
GAHG!
IF YOU DON'T PLAY NICE--
--YOU GET A TIME-OUT.
WBAMM

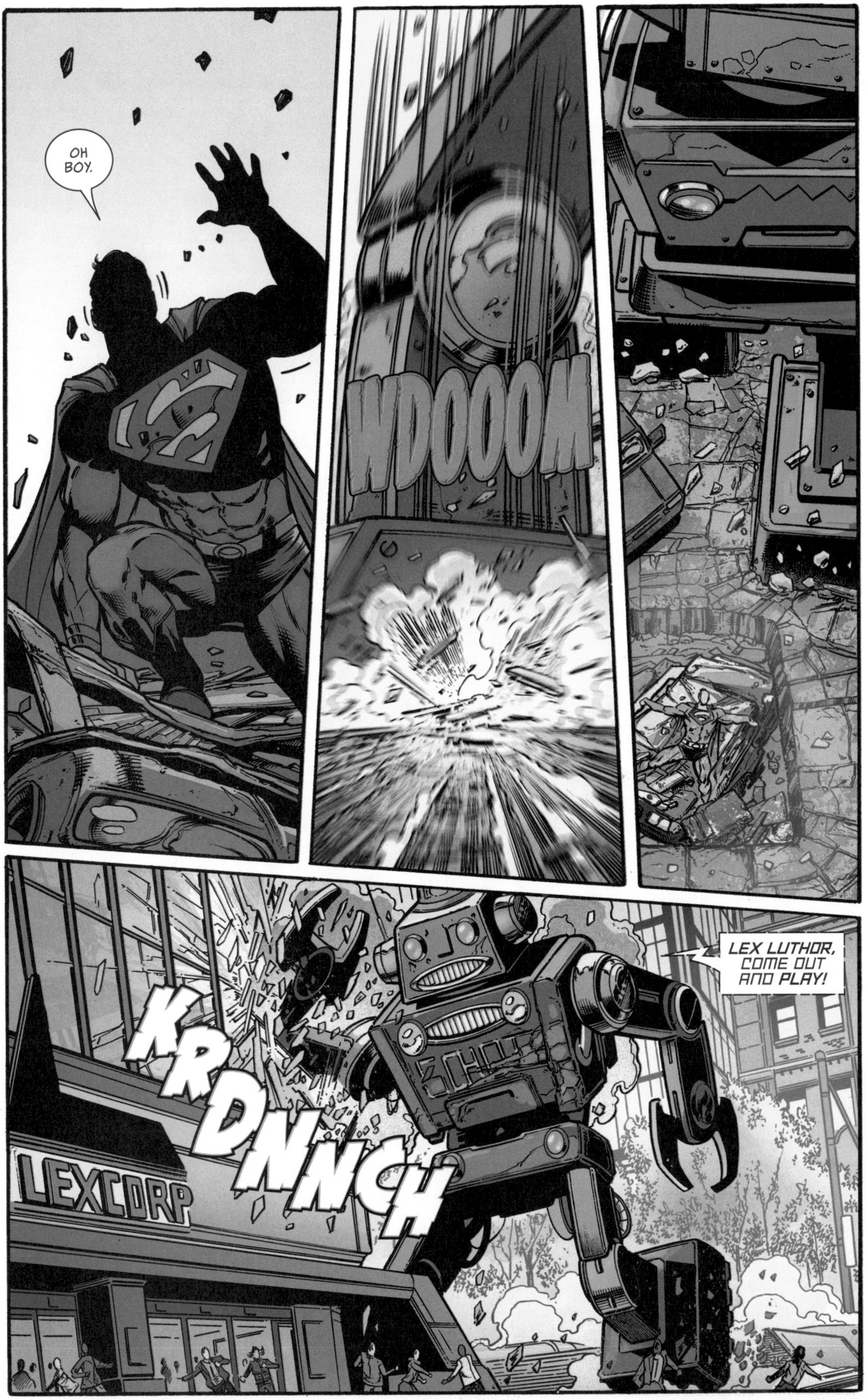
OH BOY.
WDOOOM
KRDNNCH
LEXCORP
LEX LUTHOR, COME OUT AND PLAY!

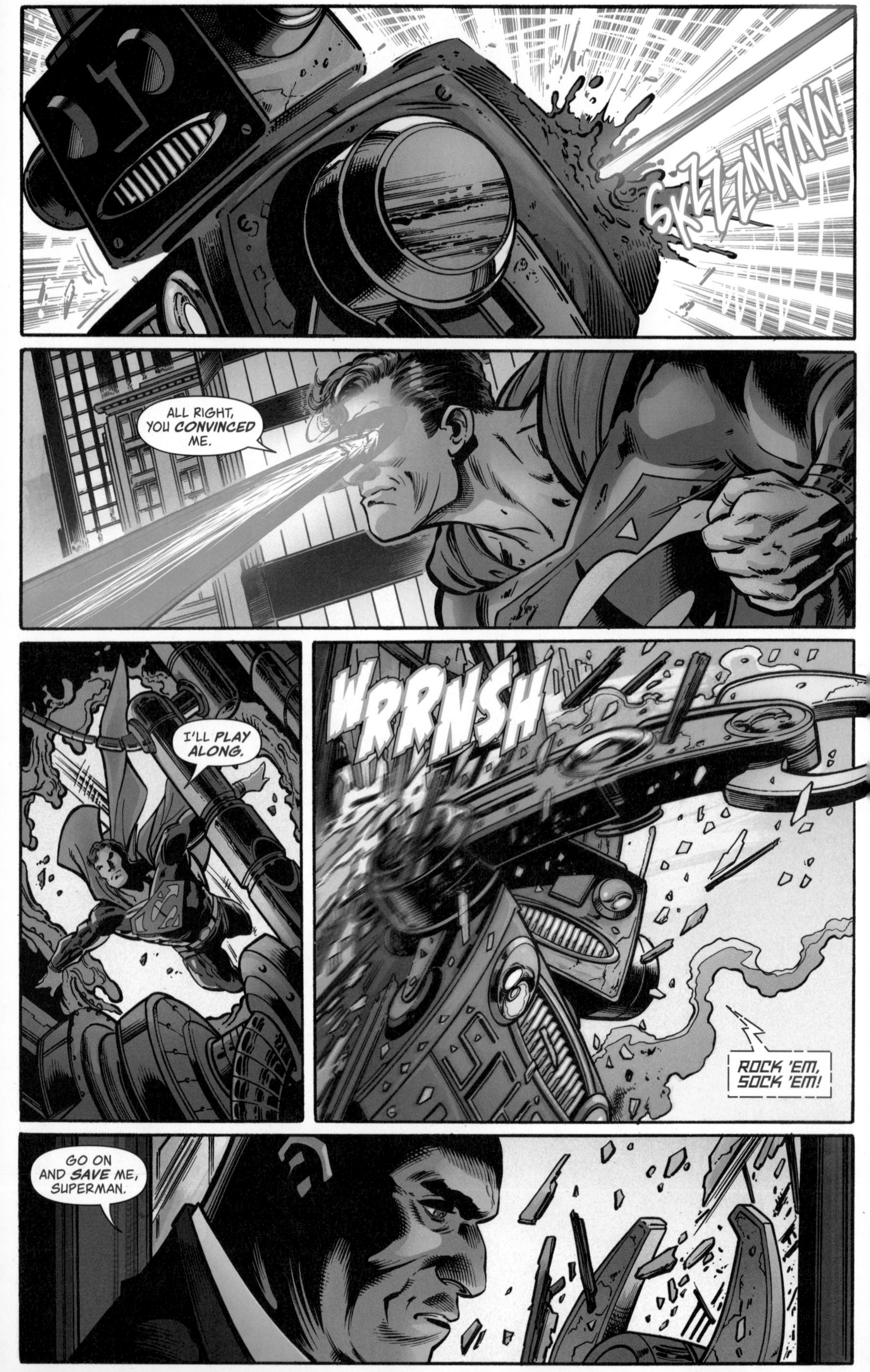
SKZZZNNNNN
ALL RIGHT, YOU CONVINCED ME.
I'LL PLAY ALONG.
WRRNSH
ROCK 'EM, SOCK 'EM!
GO ON AND SAVE ME, SUPERMAN.

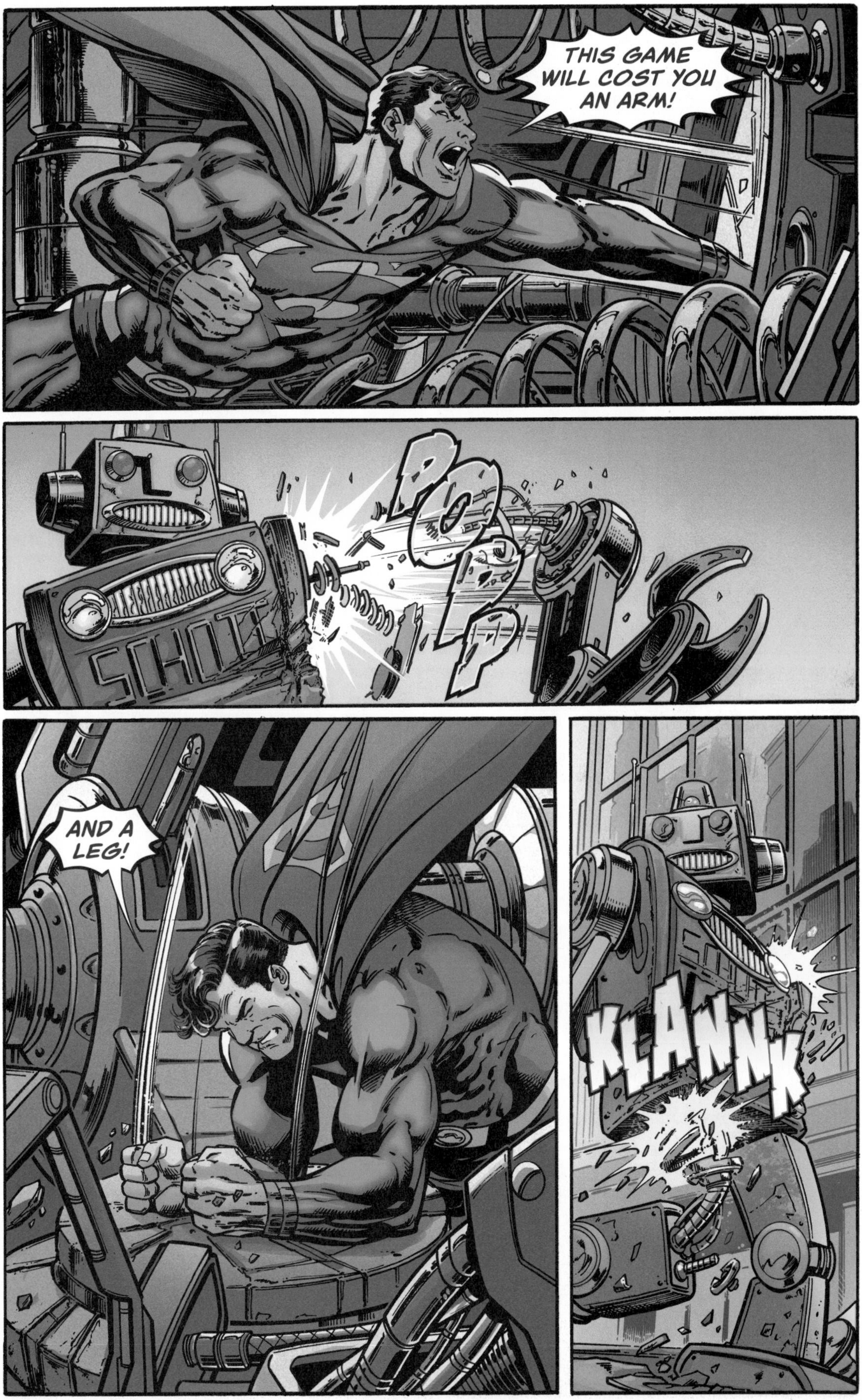
THIS GAME WILL COST YOU AN ARM!
POP
SCHOT
AND A LEG!
KLANNK

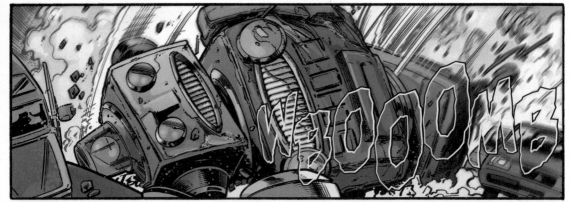
WHOOOMB

THERE'S ONE LAST GAME.

IT'S EXPLOSIVE!

MR. LUTHOR, I HAVE TO INSIST THAT YOU EVACUATE THE BUILDING--

YOU WORK FOR ME. YOU INSIST NOTHING.

THERE ARE ELEVEN SCHOTT TOYS LOCATIONS IN METROPOLIS.

THE OTHER TEN ROBOTS ARE ON THEIR WAY HERE.

THREE ≥ZZT≥ ≥KZZ≥ TWO--

RRCH

KRZZAK

PLAYTIME IS OVER.

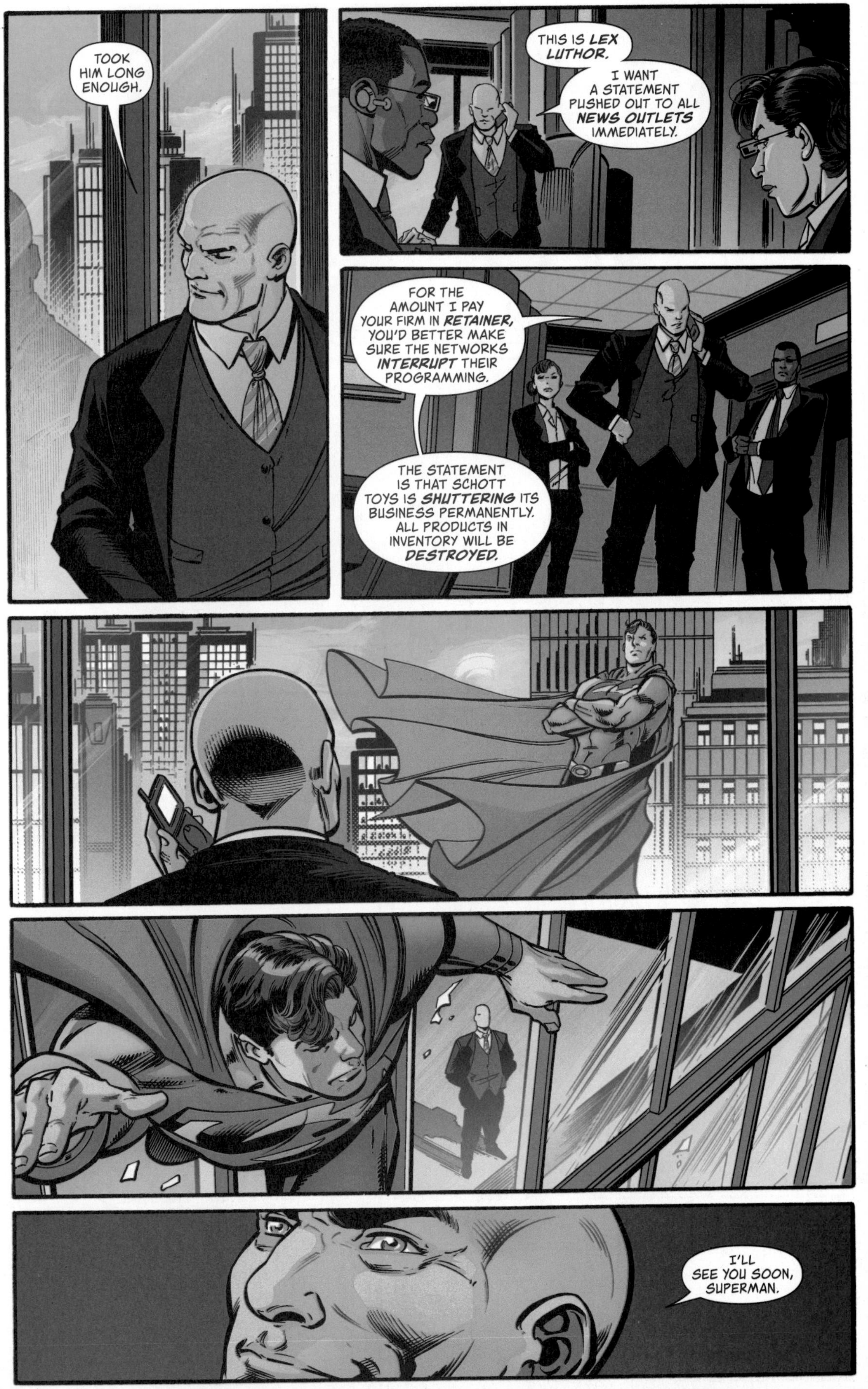
TOOK HIM LONG ENOUGH.
THIS IS LEX LUTHOR.
I WANT A STATEMENT PUSHED OUT TO ALL NEWS OUTLETS IMMEDIATELY.
FOR THE AMOUNT I PAY YOUR FIRM IN RETAINER, YOU'D BETTER MAKE SURE THE NETWORKS INTERRUPT THEIR PROGRAMMING.
THE STATEMENT IS THAT SCHOTT TOYS IS SHUTTERING ITS BUSINESS PERMANENTLY. ALL PRODUCTS IN INVENTORY WILL BE DESTROYED.
I'LL SEE YOU SOON, SUPERMAN.

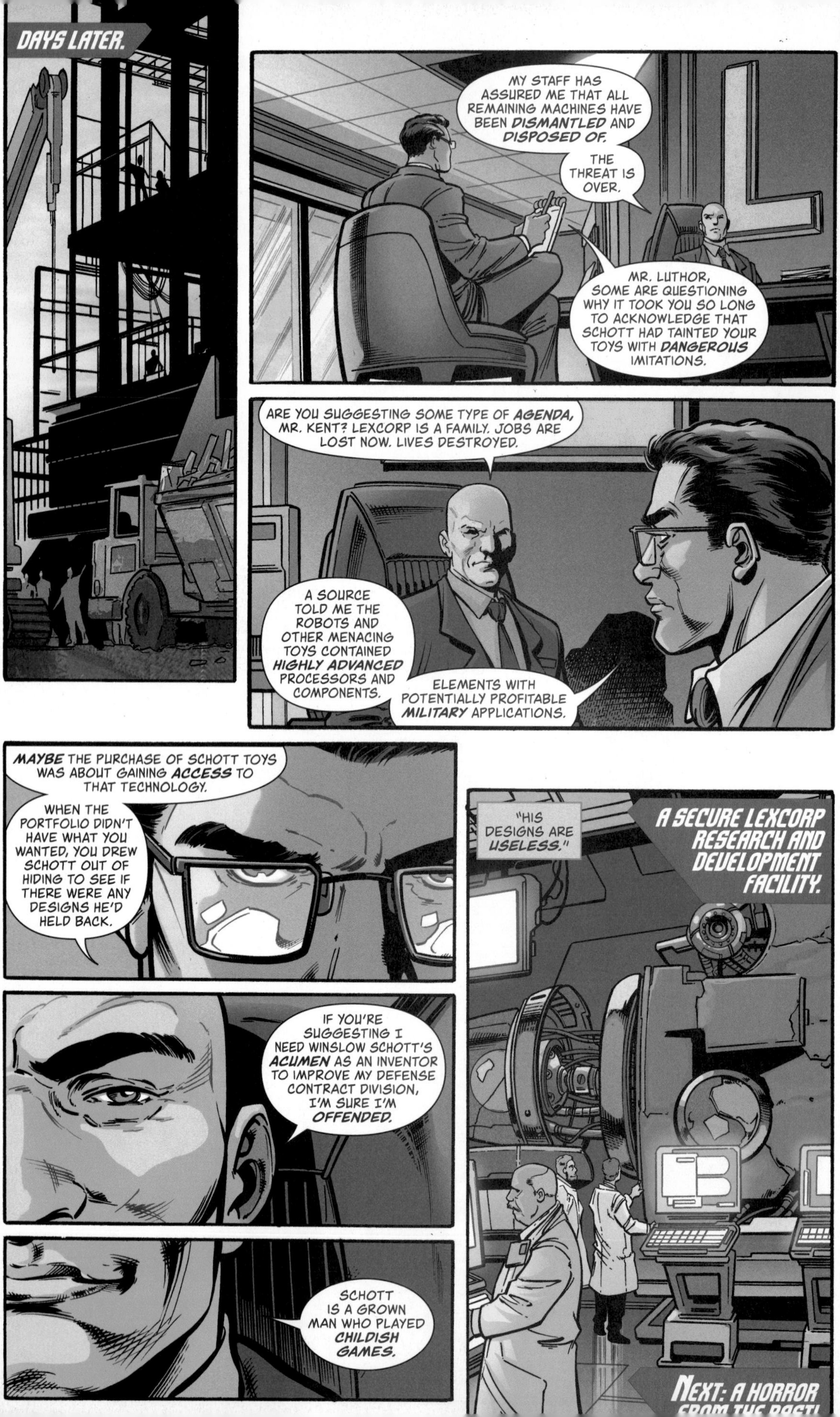
DAYS LATER.
MY STAFF HAS ASSURED ME THAT ALL REMAINING MACHINES HAVE BEEN DISMANTLED AND DISPOSED OF.
THE THREAT IS OVER.
MR. LUTHOR, SOME ARE QUESTIONING WHY IT TOOK YOU SO LONG TO ACKNOWLEDGE THAT SCHOTT HAD TAINTED YOUR TOYS WITH DANGEROUS IMITATIONS.
ARE YOU SUGGESTING SOME TYPE OF AGENDA, MR. KENT? LEXCORP IS A FAMILY. JOBS ARE LOST NOW. LIVES DESTROYED.
A SOURCE TOLD ME THE ROBOTS AND OTHER MENACING TOYS CONTAINED HIGHLY ADVANCED PROCESSORS AND COMPONENTS.
ELEMENTS WITH POTENTIALLY PROFITABLE MILITARY APPLICATIONS.
MAYBE THE PURCHASE OF SCHOTT TOYS WAS ABOUT GAINING ACCESS TO THAT TECHNOLOGY.
WHEN THE PORTFOLIO DIDN'T HAVE WHAT YOU WANTED, YOU DREW SCHOTT OUT OF HIDING TO SEE IF THERE WERE ANY DESIGNS HE'D HELD BACK.
IF YOU'RE SUGGESTING I NEED WINSLOW SCHOTT'S ACUMEN AS AN INVENTOR TO IMPROVE MY DEFENSE CONTRACT DIVISION, I'M SURE I'M OFFENDED.
SCHOTT IS A GROWN MAN WHO PLAYED CHILDISH GAMES.
A SECURE LEXCORP RESEARCH AND DEVELOPMENT FACILITY.
"HIS DESIGNS ARE USELESS."
NEXT: A HORROR

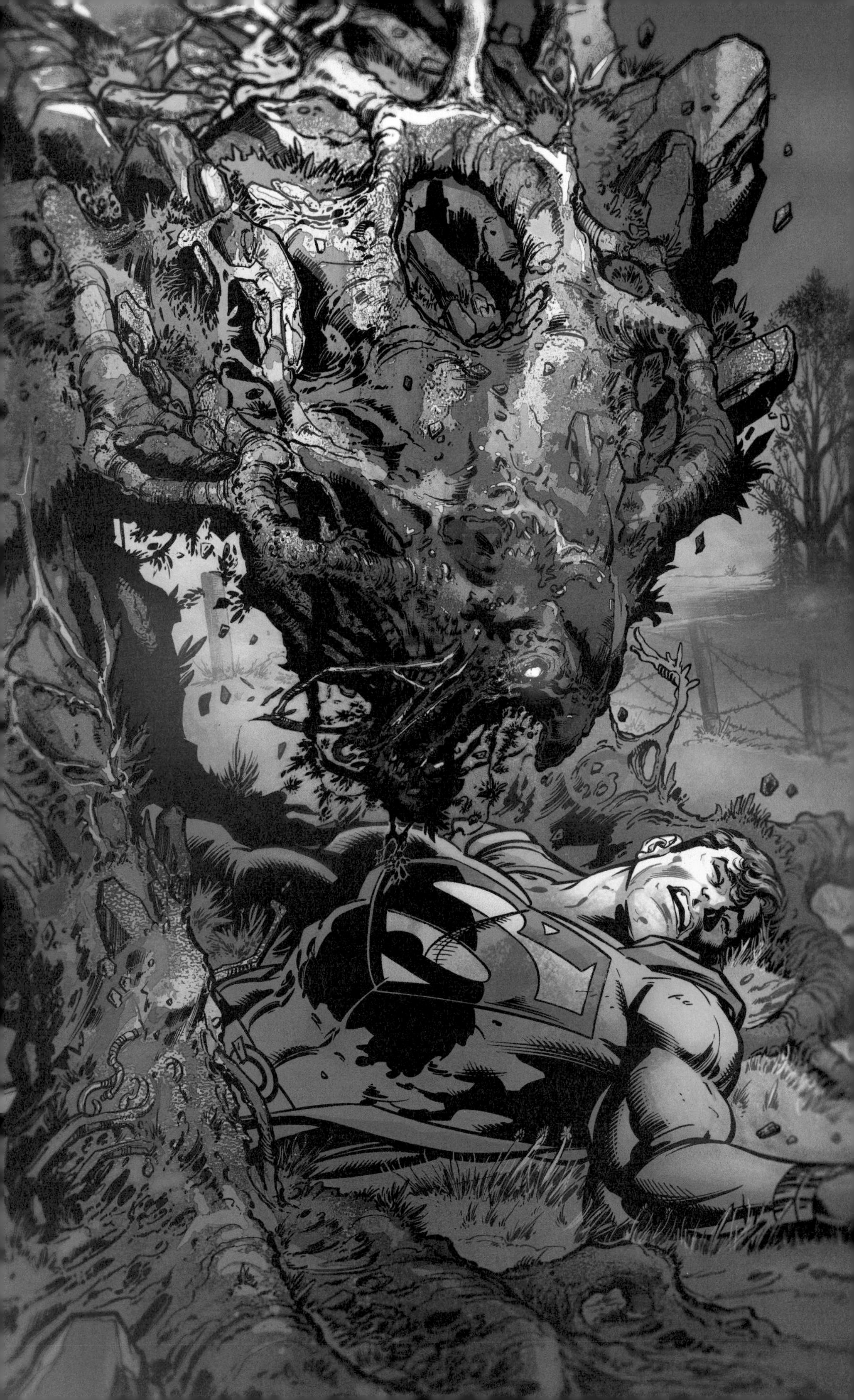

COVER ART BY
PAUL PELLETIER, DREW HENNESSY,
AND **ADRIANO LUCAS**

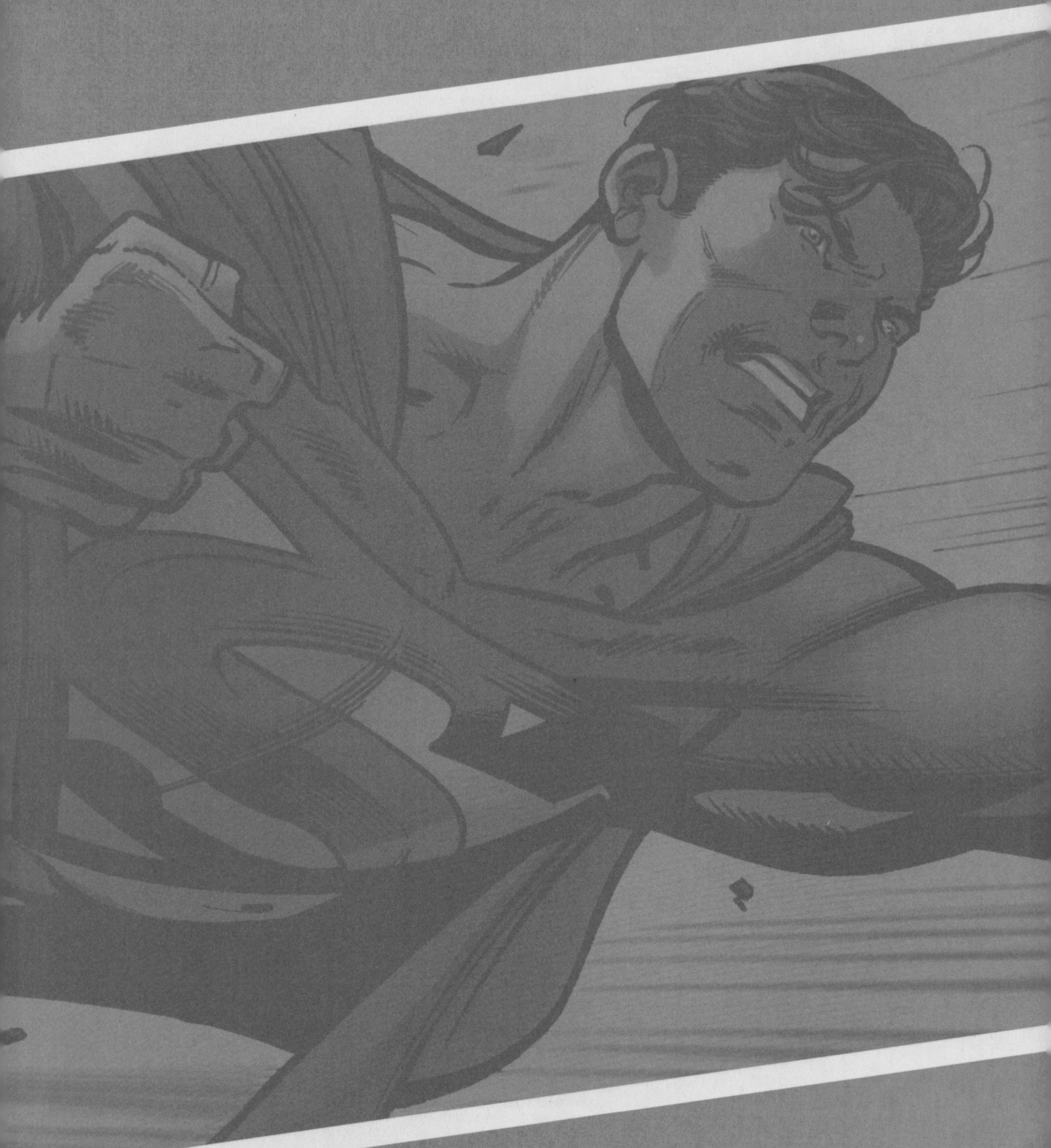

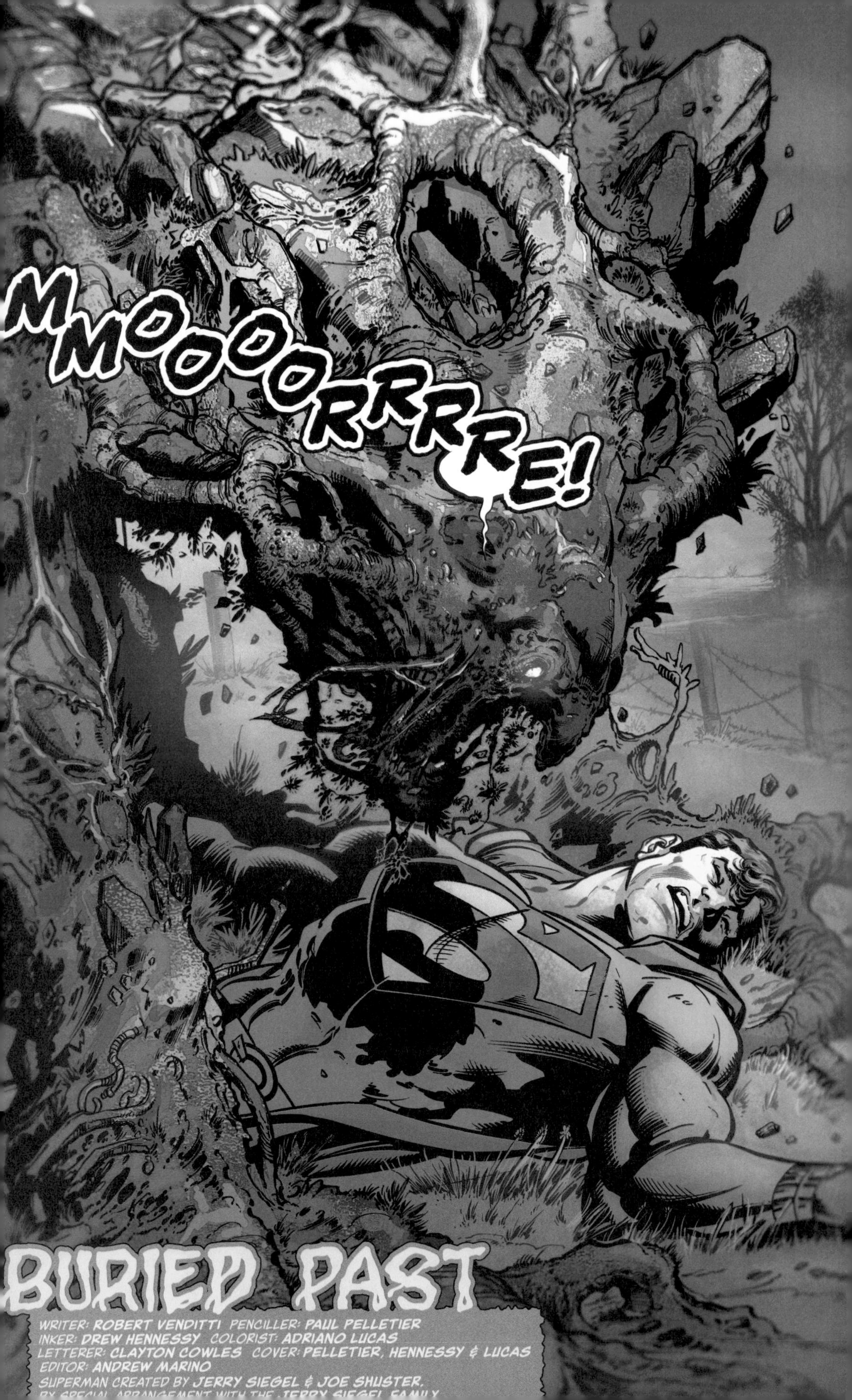
MMOOOORRRRE!
BURIED PAST
WRITER: ROBERT VENDITTI PENCILLER: PAUL PELLETIER
INKER: DREW HENNESSY COLORIST: ADRIANO LUCAS
LETTERER: CLAYTON COWLES COVER: PELLETIER, HENNESSY & LUCAS
EDITOR: ANDREW MARINO
SUPERMAN CREATED BY JERRY SIEGEL & JOE SHUSTER.

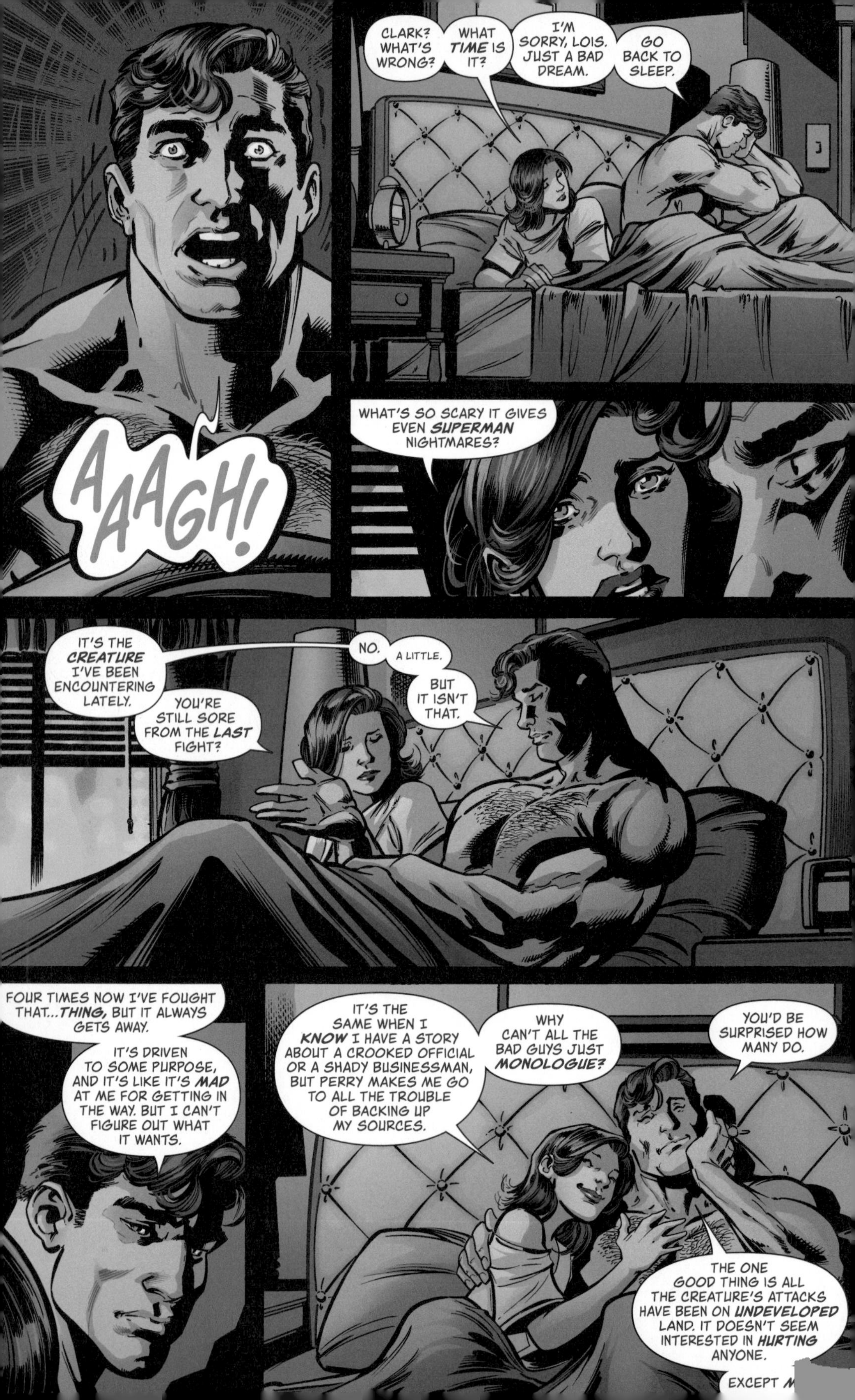

AAAGH!
CLARK? WHAT'S WRONG?
WHAT TIME IS IT?
I'M SORRY, LOIS. JUST A BAD DREAM.
GO BACK TO SLEEP.
WHAT'S SO SCARY IT GIVES EVEN SUPERMAN NIGHTMARES?
IT'S THE CREATURE I'VE BEEN ENCOUNTERING LATELY.
YOU'RE STILL SORE FROM THE LAST FIGHT?
NO.
A LITTLE.
BUT IT ISN'T THAT.
FOUR TIMES NOW I'VE FOUGHT THAT...THING, BUT IT ALWAYS GETS AWAY.
IT'S DRIVEN TO SOME PURPOSE, AND IT'S LIKE IT'S MAD AT ME FOR GETTING IN THE WAY. BUT I CAN'T FIGURE OUT WHAT IT WANTS.
IT'S THE SAME WHEN I KNOW I HAVE A STORY ABOUT A CROOKED OFFICIAL OR A SHADY BUSINESSMAN, BUT PERRY MAKES ME GO TO ALL THE TROUBLE OF BACKING UP MY SOURCES.
WHY CAN'T ALL THE BAD GUYS JUST MONOLOGUE?
YOU'D BE SURPRISED HOW MANY DO.
THE ONE GOOD THING IS ALL THE CREATURE'S ATTACKS HAVE BEEN ON UNDEVELOPED LAND. IT DOESN'T SEEM INTERESTED IN HURTING ANYONE.
EXCEPT

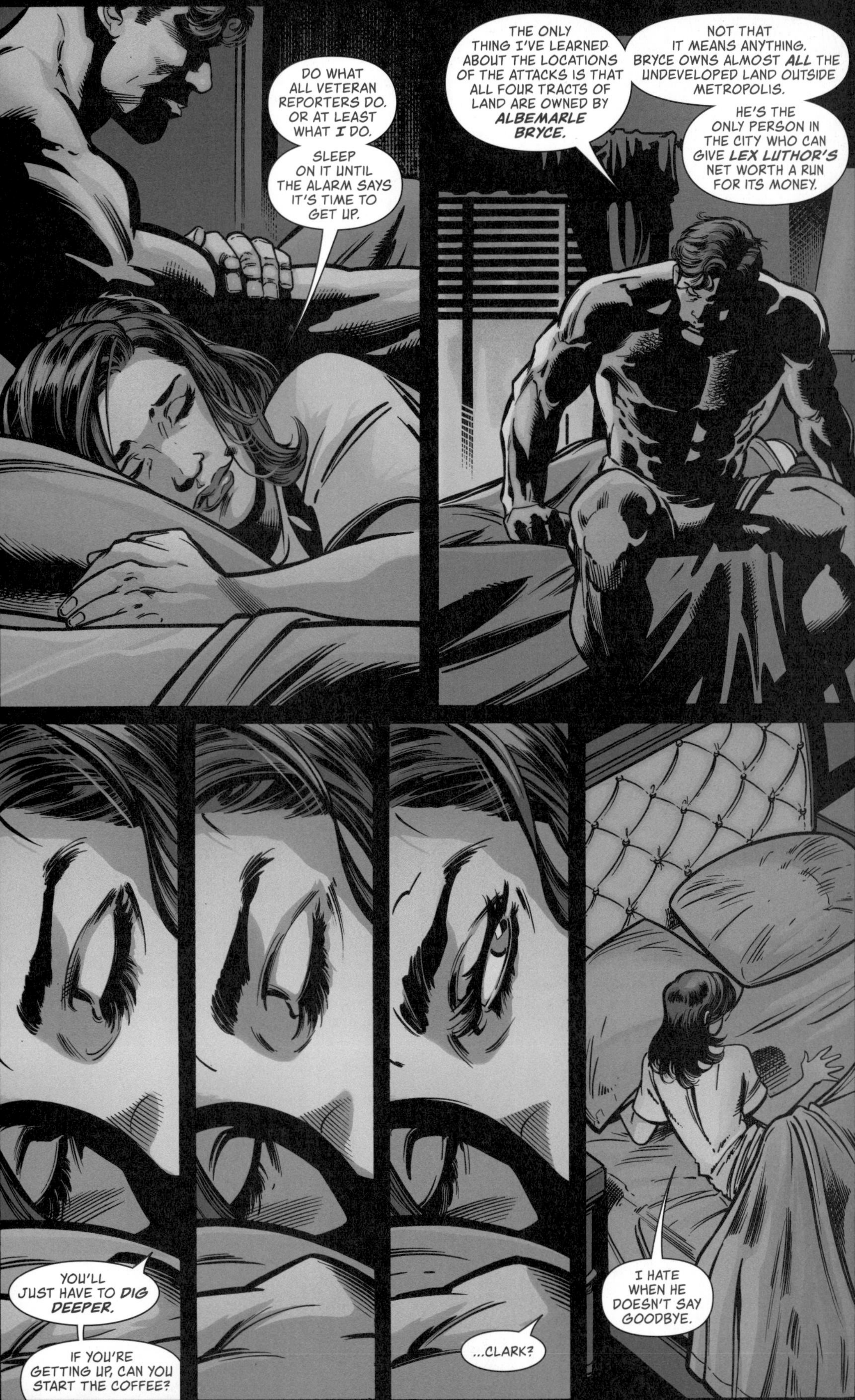
DO WHAT ALL VETERAN REPORTERS DO. OR AT LEAST WHAT *I* DO.
SLEEP ON IT UNTIL THE ALARM SAYS IT'S TIME TO GET UP.
THE ONLY THING I'VE LEARNED ABOUT THE LOCATIONS OF THE ATTACKS IS THAT ALL FOUR TRACTS OF LAND ARE OWNED BY **ALBEMARLE BRYCE.**
NOT THAT IT MEANS ANYTHING. BRYCE OWNS ALMOST **ALL** THE UNDEVELOPED LAND OUTSIDE METROPOLIS.
HE'S THE ONLY PERSON IN THE CITY WHO CAN GIVE **LEX LUTHOR'S** NET WORTH A RUN FOR ITS MONEY.
YOU'LL JUST HAVE TO **DIG DEEPER.**
IF YOU'RE GETTING UP, CAN YOU START THE COFFEE?
...CLARK?
I HATE WHEN HE DOESN'T SAY GOODBYE.

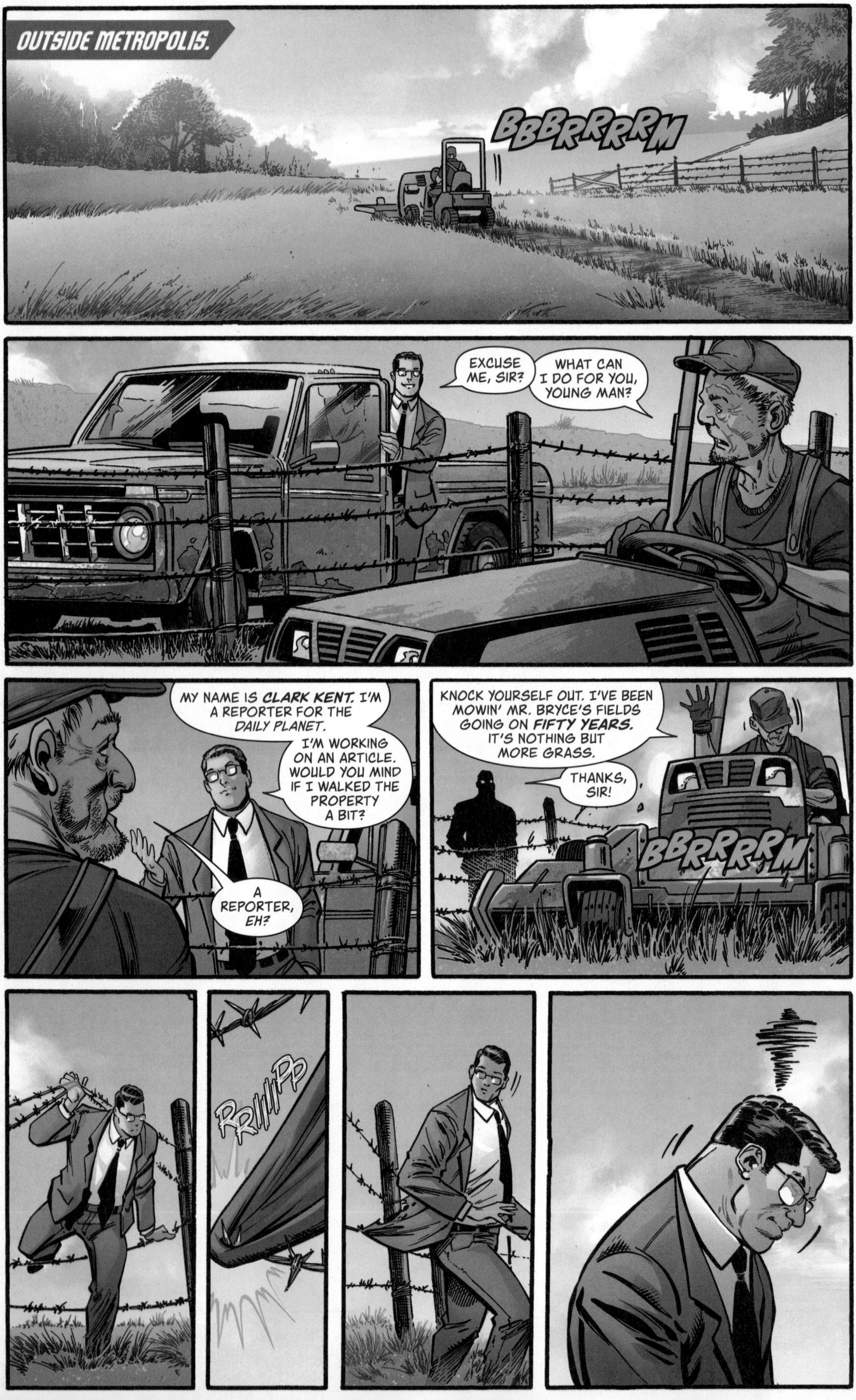
OUTSIDE METROPOLIS.
BBBRRRRM
EXCUSE ME, SIR?
WHAT CAN I DO FOR YOU, YOUNG MAN?
MY NAME IS CLARK KENT. I'M A REPORTER FOR THE DAILY PLANET.
I'M WORKING ON AN ARTICLE. WOULD YOU MIND IF I WALKED THE PROPERTY A BIT?
A REPORTER, EH?
KNOCK YOURSELF OUT. I'VE BEEN MOWIN' MR. BRYCE'S FIELDS GOING ON FIFTY YEARS. IT'S NOTHING BUT MORE GRASS.
THANKS, SIR!
BBRRRRM
RRIIIIPP

YOU WANT ME TO DIG DEEPER, LOIS?

CAN'T DO THAT WITHOUT MAKING A SCENE.

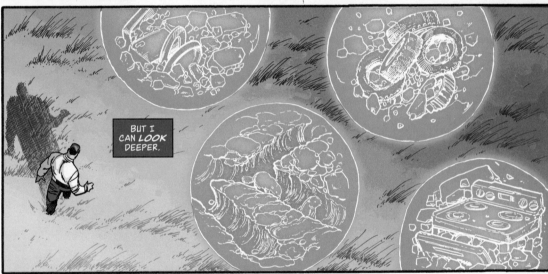

BUT I CAN *LOOK* DEEPER.

TIRES. SOME APPLIANCES.

FIELDS LIKE THESE ARE USED FOR DUMPING ALL THE TIME. NOTHING TO MAKE A *FUSS* OVER--

OH NO...

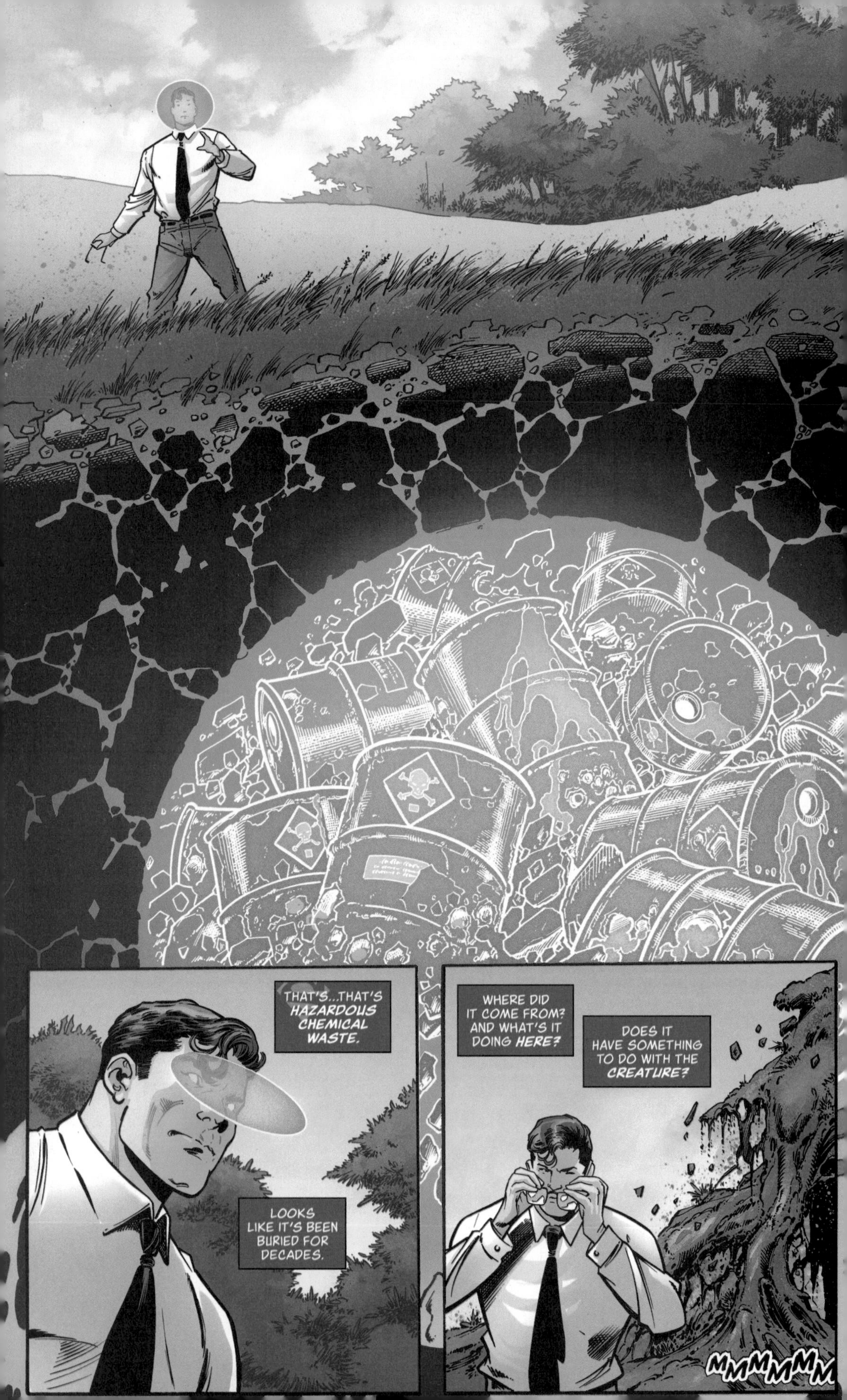
THAT'S...THAT'S *HAZARDOUS CHEMICAL WASTE.*
LOOKS LIKE IT'S BEEN BURIED FOR DECADES.
WHERE DID IT COME FROM? AND WHAT'S IT DOING *HERE?*
DOES IT HAVE SOMETHING TO DO WITH THE *CREATURE?*
MMMMMM

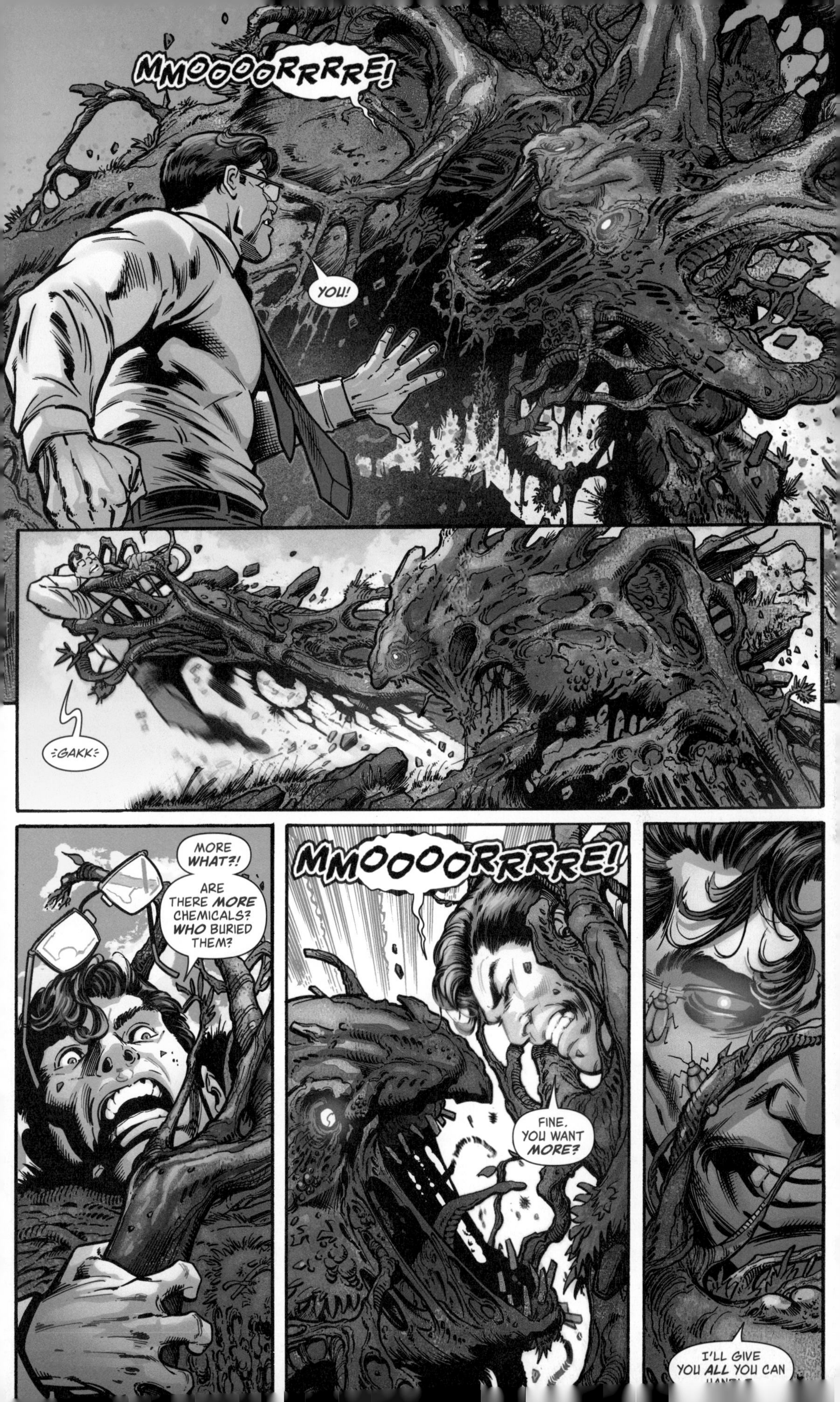
MMOOOOORRRRE!
YOU!
GAKK
MORE WHAT?!
ARE THERE MORE CHEMICALS? WHO BURIED THEM?
MMOOOOORRRRE!
FINE. YOU WANT MORE?
I'LL GIVE YOU ALL YOU CAN

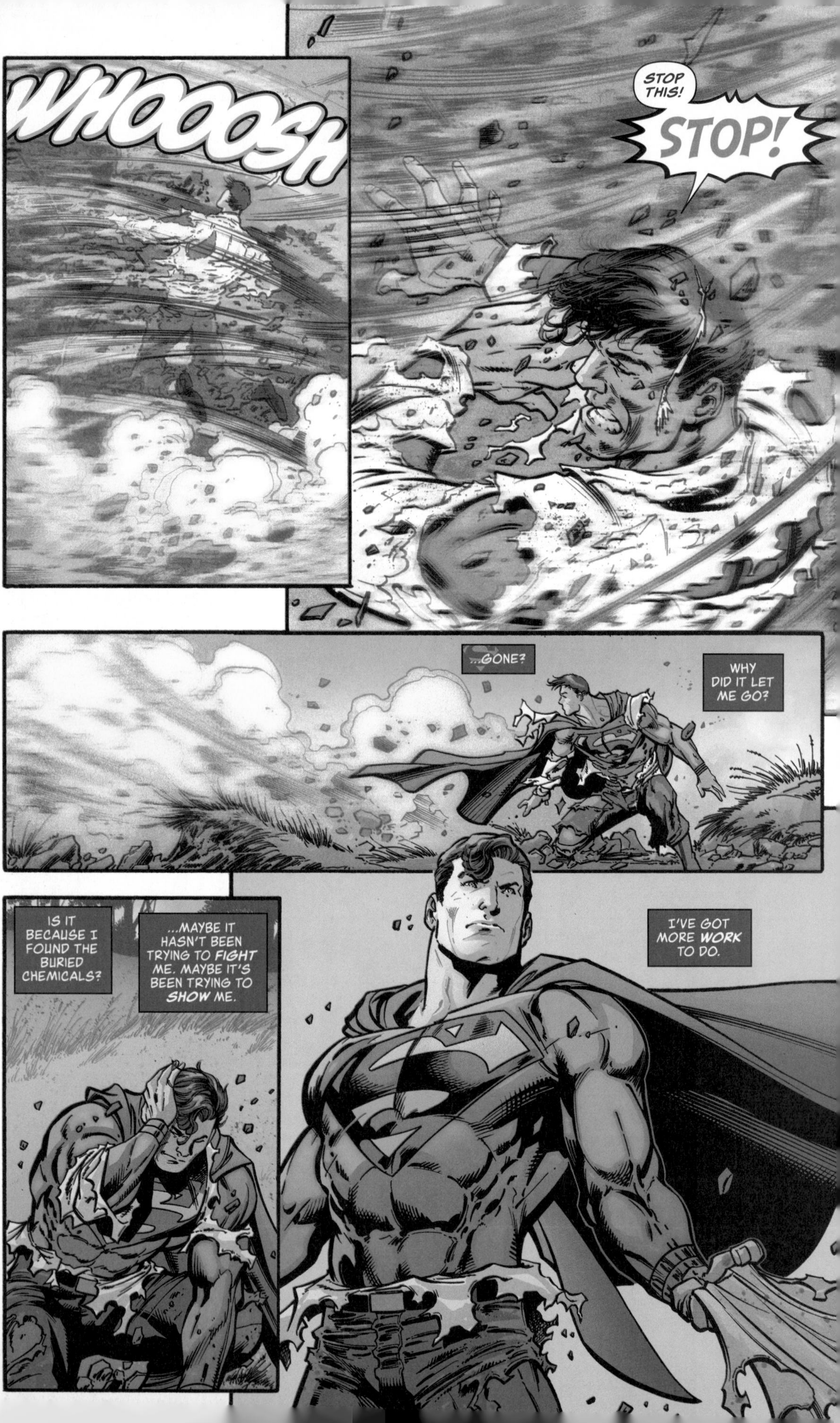
WHOOOSH
STOP THIS!
STOP!
...GONE?
WHY DID IT LET ME GO?
IS IT BECAUSE I FOUND THE BURIED CHEMICALS?
...MAYBE IT HASN'T BEEN TRYING TO FIGHT ME. MAYBE IT'S BEEN TRYING TO SHOW ME.
I'VE GOT MORE WORK TO DO.

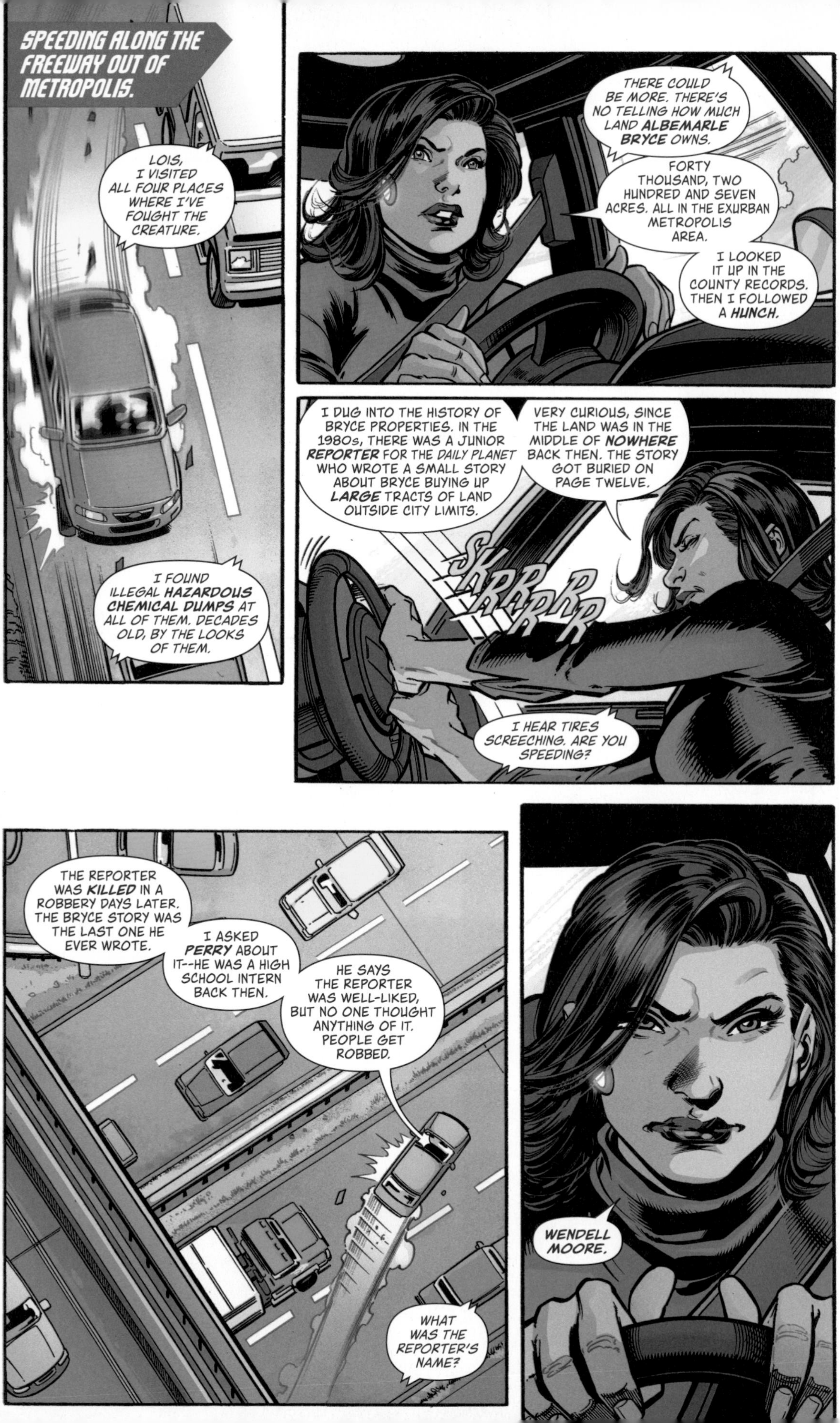
SPEEDING ALONG THE FREEWAY OUT OF METROPOLIS.
LOIS, I VISITED ALL FOUR PLACES WHERE I'VE FOUGHT THE CREATURE.
I FOUND ILLEGAL HAZARDOUS CHEMICAL DUMPS AT ALL OF THEM. DECADES OLD, BY THE LOOKS OF THEM.
THERE COULD BE MORE. THERE'S NO TELLING HOW MUCH LAND ALBEMARLE BRYCE OWNS.
FORTY THOUSAND, TWO HUNDRED AND SEVEN ACRES. ALL IN THE EXURBAN METROPOLIS AREA.
I LOOKED IT UP IN THE COUNTY RECORDS. THEN I FOLLOWED A HUNCH.
I DUG INTO THE HISTORY OF BRYCE PROPERTIES. IN THE 1980s, THERE WAS A JUNIOR REPORTER FOR THE DAILY PLANET WHO WROTE A SMALL STORY ABOUT BRYCE BUYING UP LARGE TRACTS OF LAND OUTSIDE CITY LIMITS.
VERY CURIOUS, SINCE THE LAND WAS IN THE MIDDLE OF NOWHERE BACK THEN. THE STORY GOT BURIED ON PAGE TWELVE.
SKRRRRRR
I HEAR TIRES SCREECHING. ARE YOU SPEEDING?
THE REPORTER WAS KILLED IN A ROBBERY DAYS LATER. THE BRYCE STORY WAS THE LAST ONE HE EVER WROTE.
I ASKED PERRY ABOUT IT--HE WAS A HIGH SCHOOL INTERN BACK THEN.
HE SAYS THE REPORTER WAS WELL-LIKED, BUT NO ONE THOUGHT ANYTHING OF IT. PEOPLE GET ROBBED.
WHAT WAS THE REPORTER'S NAME?
WENDELL MOORE.

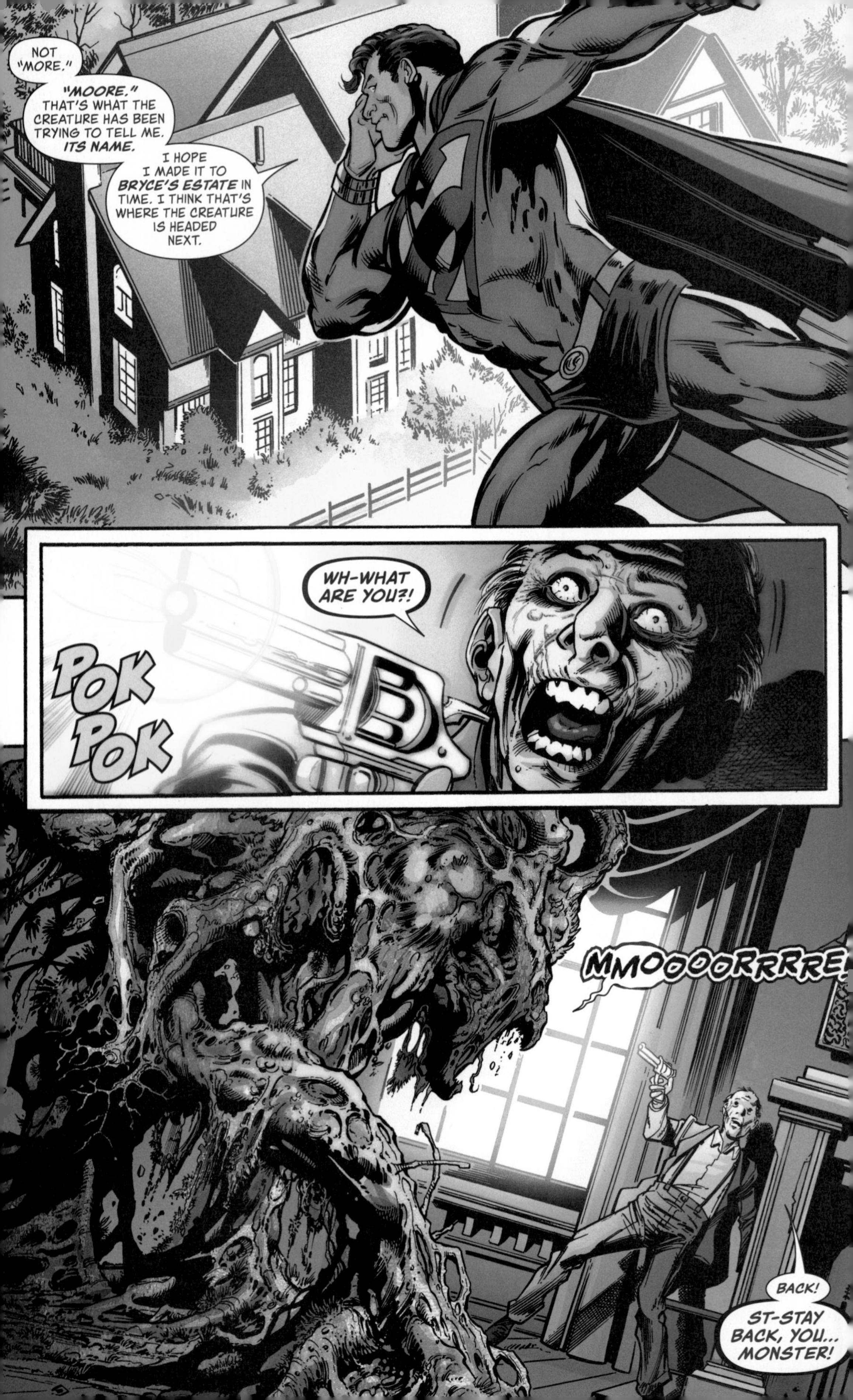
NOT "MORE."
"MOORE." THAT'S WHAT THE CREATURE HAS BEEN TRYING TO TELL ME. ITS NAME.
I HOPE I MADE IT TO BRYCE'S ESTATE IN TIME. I THINK THAT'S WHERE THE CREATURE IS HEADED NEXT.
WH-WHAT ARE YOU?!
POK POK
MMOOOORRRRE!
BACK!
ST-STAY BACK, YOU... MONSTER!

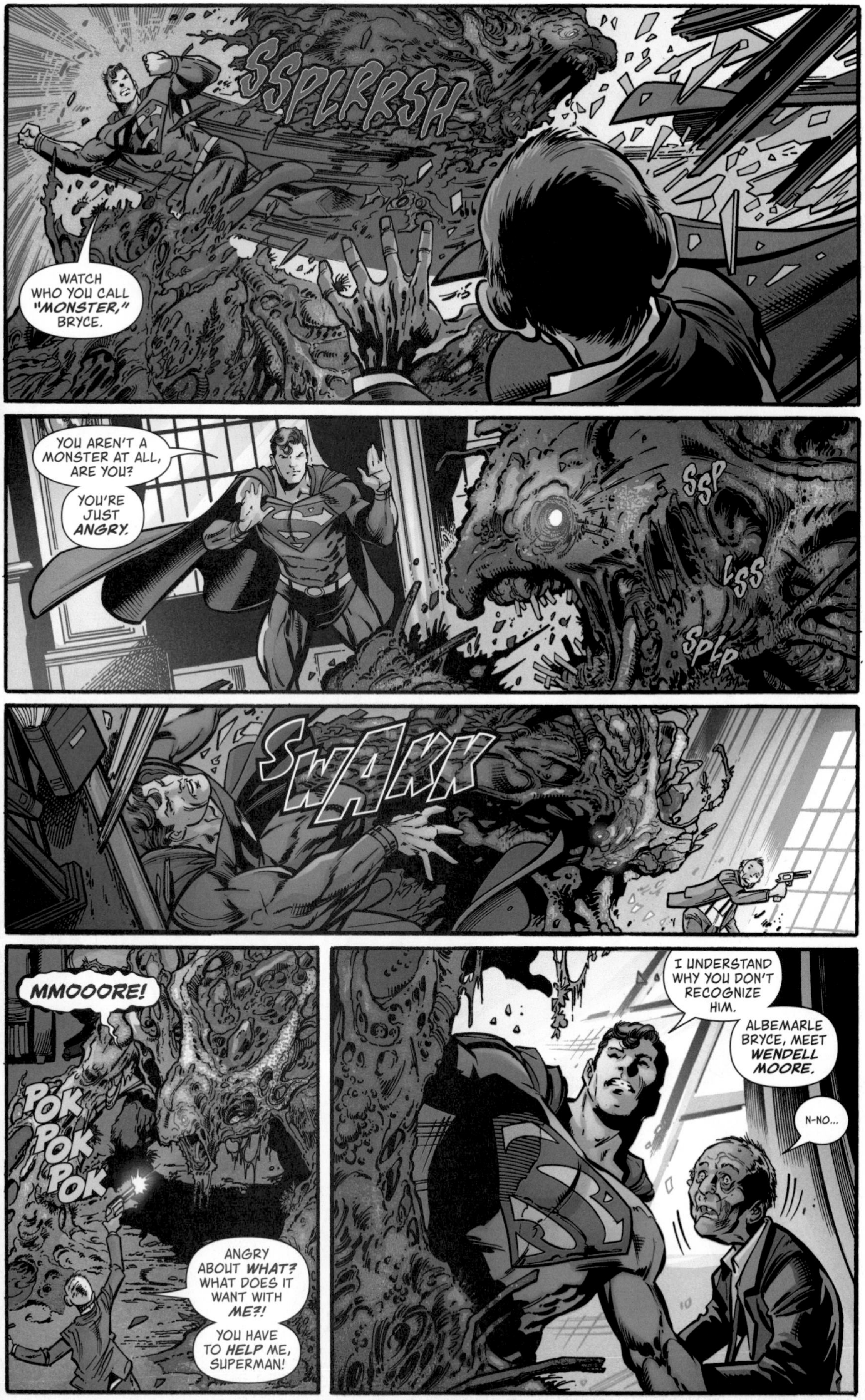
SSPLRRSH
WATCH WHO YOU CALL "MONSTER," BRYCE.
YOU AREN'T A MONSTER AT ALL, ARE YOU?
YOU'RE JUST ANGRY.
SSP
LSS
SPLP
SWAKK
MMOOORE!
POK
POK
POK
ANGRY ABOUT WHAT? WHAT DOES IT WANT WITH ME?!
YOU HAVE TO HELP ME, SUPERMAN!
I UNDERSTAND WHY YOU DON'T RECOGNIZE HIM.
ALBEMARLE BRYCE, MEET WENDELL MOORE.
N-NO...

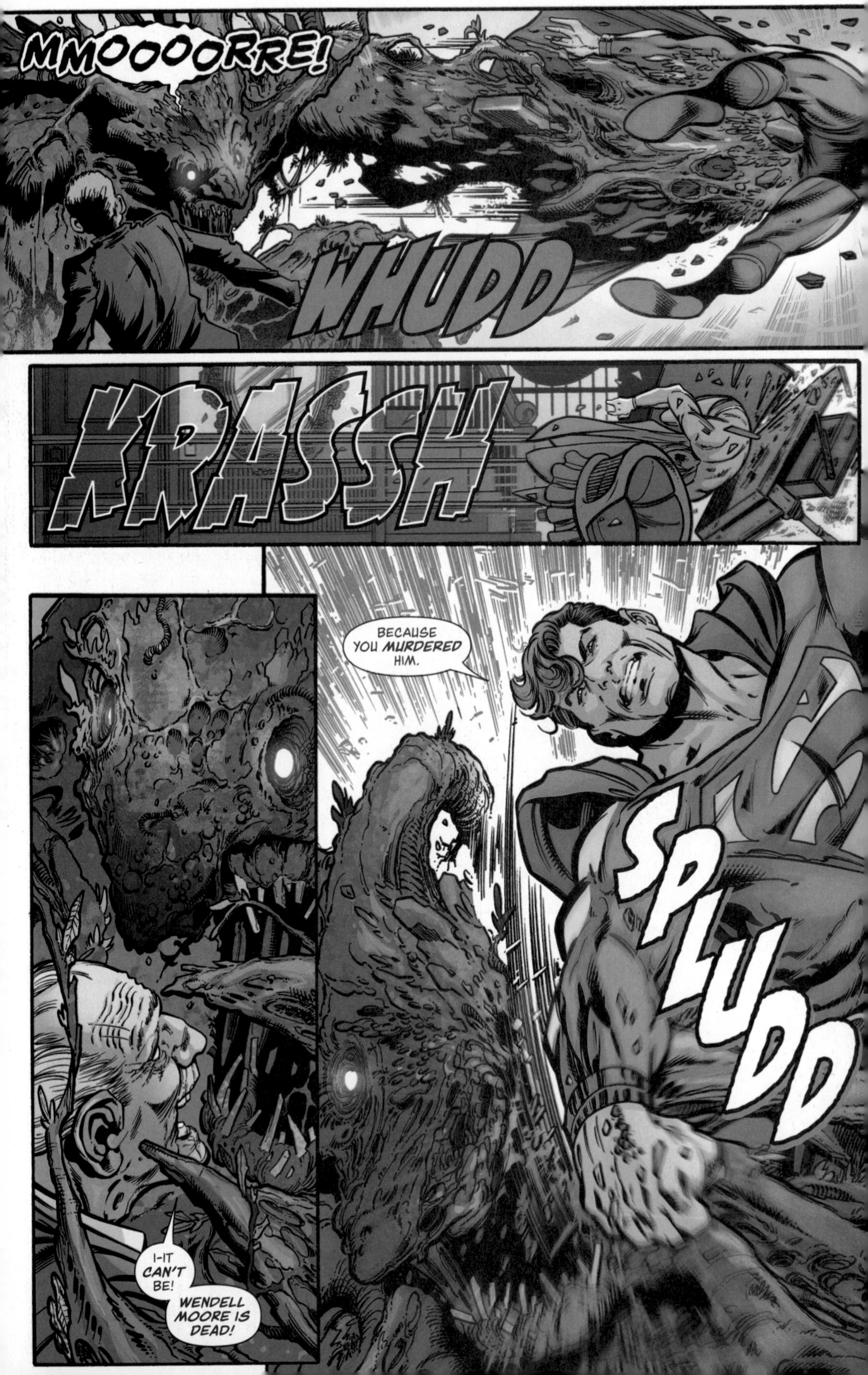
MMOOOORRE!
WHUDD
KRASSH
BECAUSE YOU MURDERED HIM.
I-IT CAN'T BE!
WENDELL MOORE IS DEAD!
SPLUDD

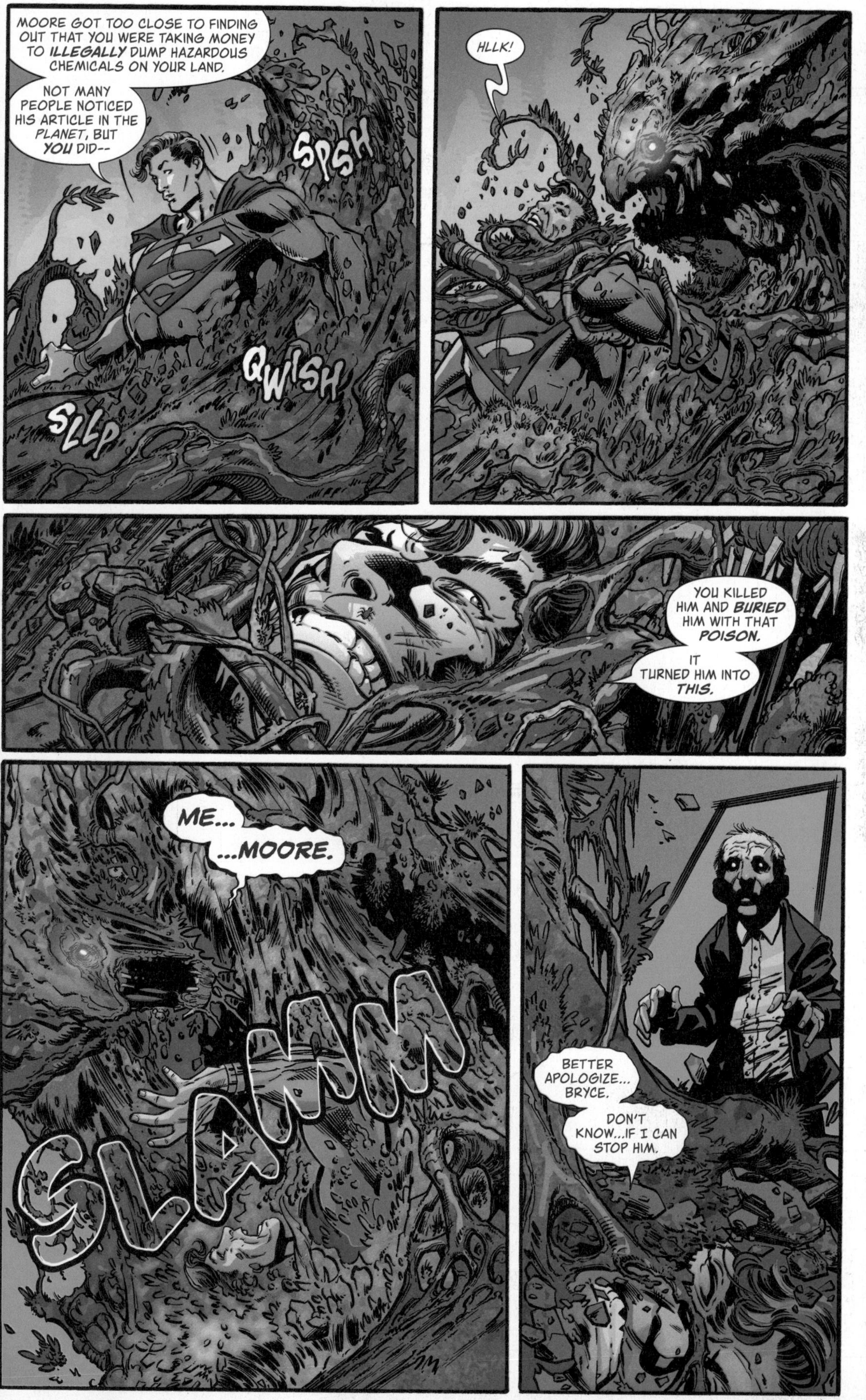

MOORE GOT TOO CLOSE TO FINDING OUT THAT YOU WERE TAKING MONEY TO ILLEGALLY DUMP HAZARDOUS CHEMICALS ON YOUR LAND.
NOT MANY PEOPLE NOTICED HIS ARTICLE IN THE PLANET, BUT YOU DID--
SPSH
QWISH
SLLP
HLLK!
YOU KILLED HIM AND BURIED HIM WITH THAT POISON.
IT TURNED HIM INTO THIS.
ME...
...MOORE.
SLAMM
BETTER APOLOGIZE... BRYCE.
DON'T KNOW...IF I CAN STOP HIM.

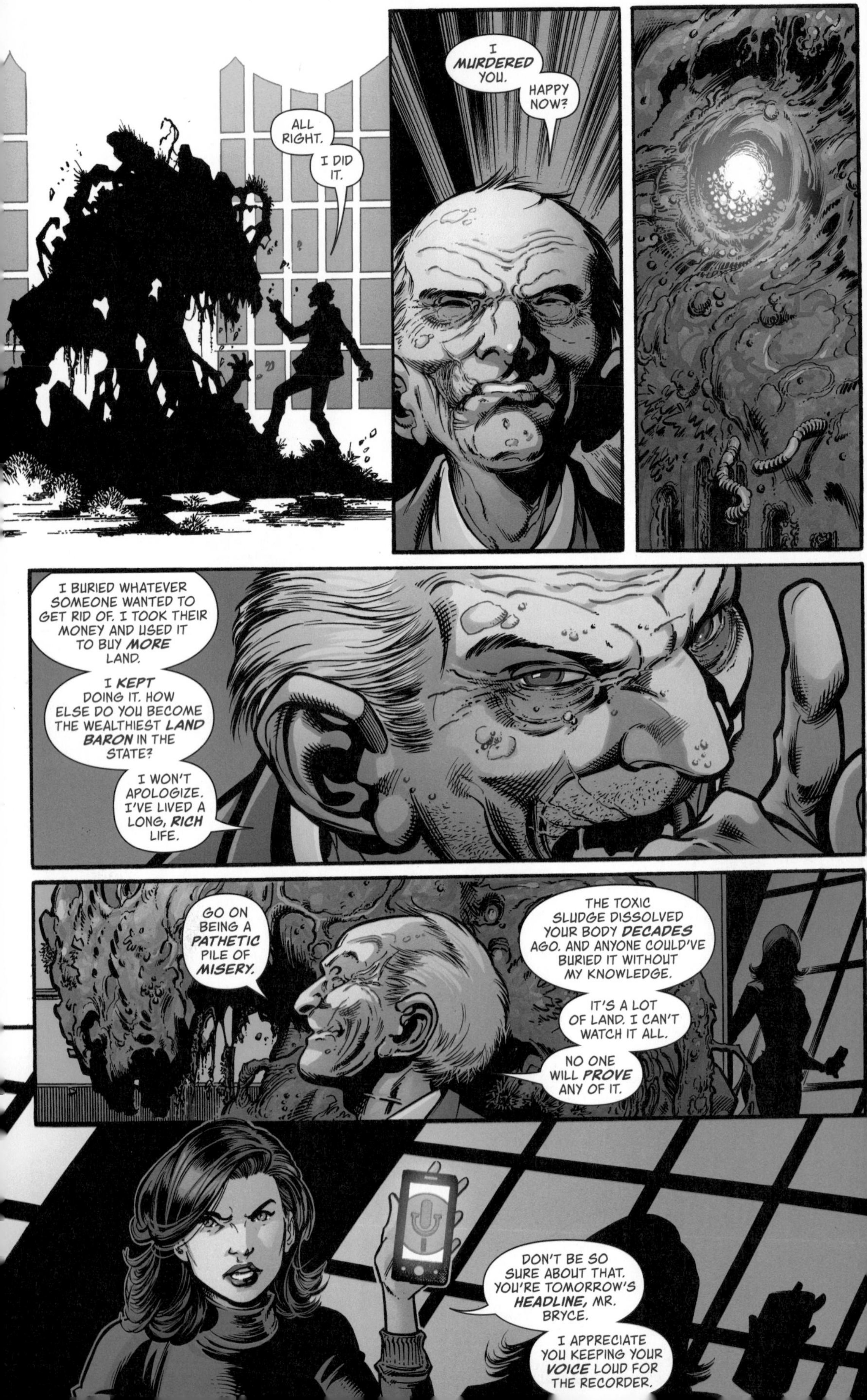

ALL RIGHT.
I DID IT.
I MURDERED YOU.
HAPPY NOW?
I BURIED WHATEVER SOMEONE WANTED TO GET RID OF. I TOOK THEIR MONEY AND USED IT TO BUY MORE LAND.
I KEPT DOING IT. HOW ELSE DO YOU BECOME THE WEALTHIEST LAND BARON IN THE STATE?
I WON'T APOLOGIZE. I'VE LIVED A LONG, RICH LIFE.
GO ON BEING A PATHETIC PILE OF MISERY.
THE TOXIC SLUDGE DISSOLVED YOUR BODY DECADES AGO. AND ANYONE COULD'VE BURIED IT WITHOUT MY KNOWLEDGE.
IT'S A LOT OF LAND. I CAN'T WATCH IT ALL.
NO ONE WILL PROVE ANY OF IT.
DON'T BE SO SURE ABOUT THAT. YOU'RE TOMORROW'S HEADLINE, MR. BRYCE.
I APPRECIATE YOU KEEPING YOUR VOICE LOUD FOR THE RECORDER.

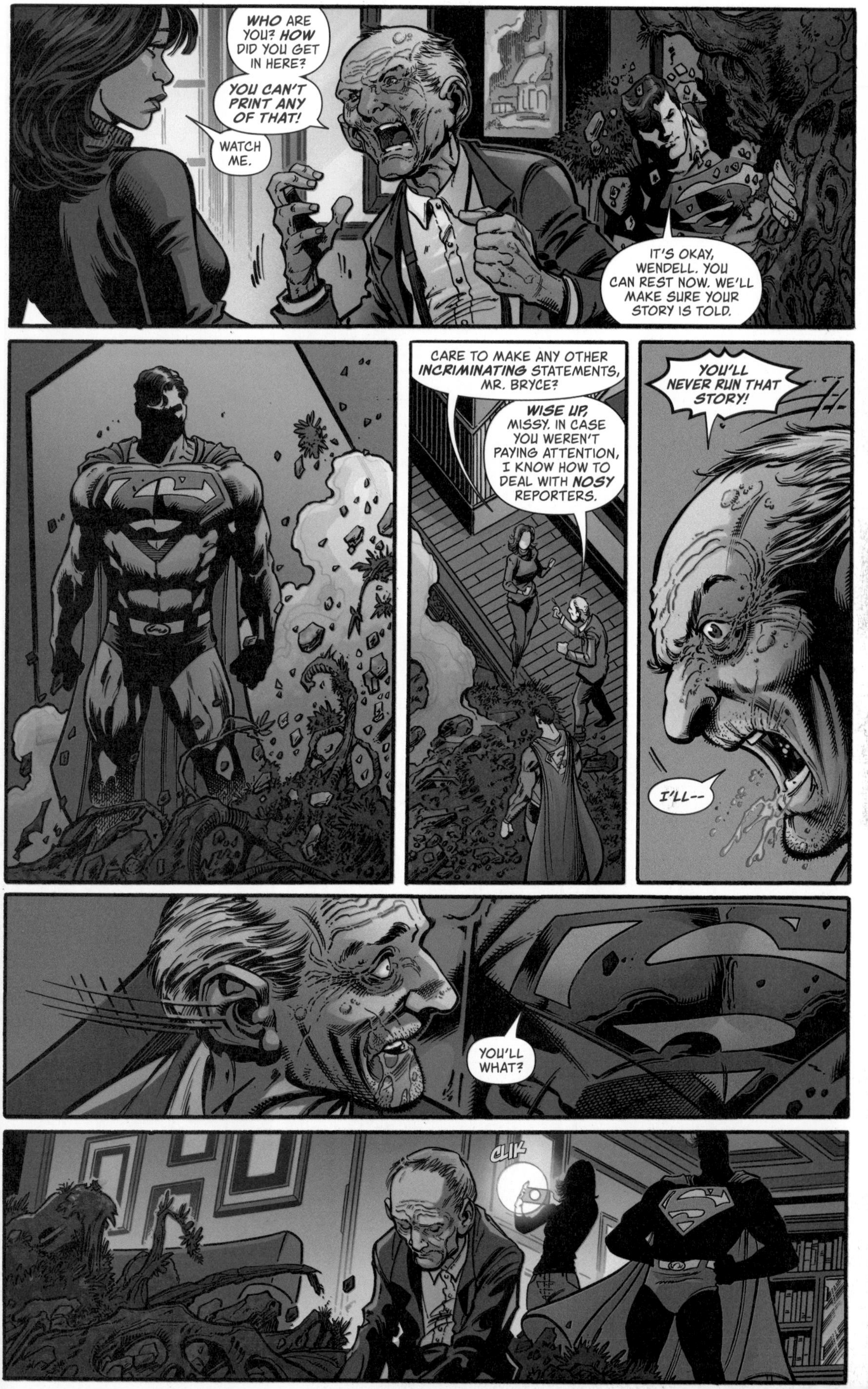
WHO ARE YOU? HOW DID YOU GET IN HERE?
YOU CAN'T PRINT ANY OF THAT!
WATCH ME.
IT'S OKAY, WENDELL. YOU CAN REST NOW. WE'LL MAKE SURE YOUR STORY IS TOLD.
CARE TO MAKE ANY OTHER INCRIMINATING STATEMENTS, MR. BRYCE?
WISE UP, MISSY. IN CASE YOU WEREN'T PAYING ATTENTION, I KNOW HOW TO DEAL WITH NOSY REPORTERS.
YOU'LL NEVER RUN THAT STORY!
I'LL--
YOU'LL WHAT?
CLIK

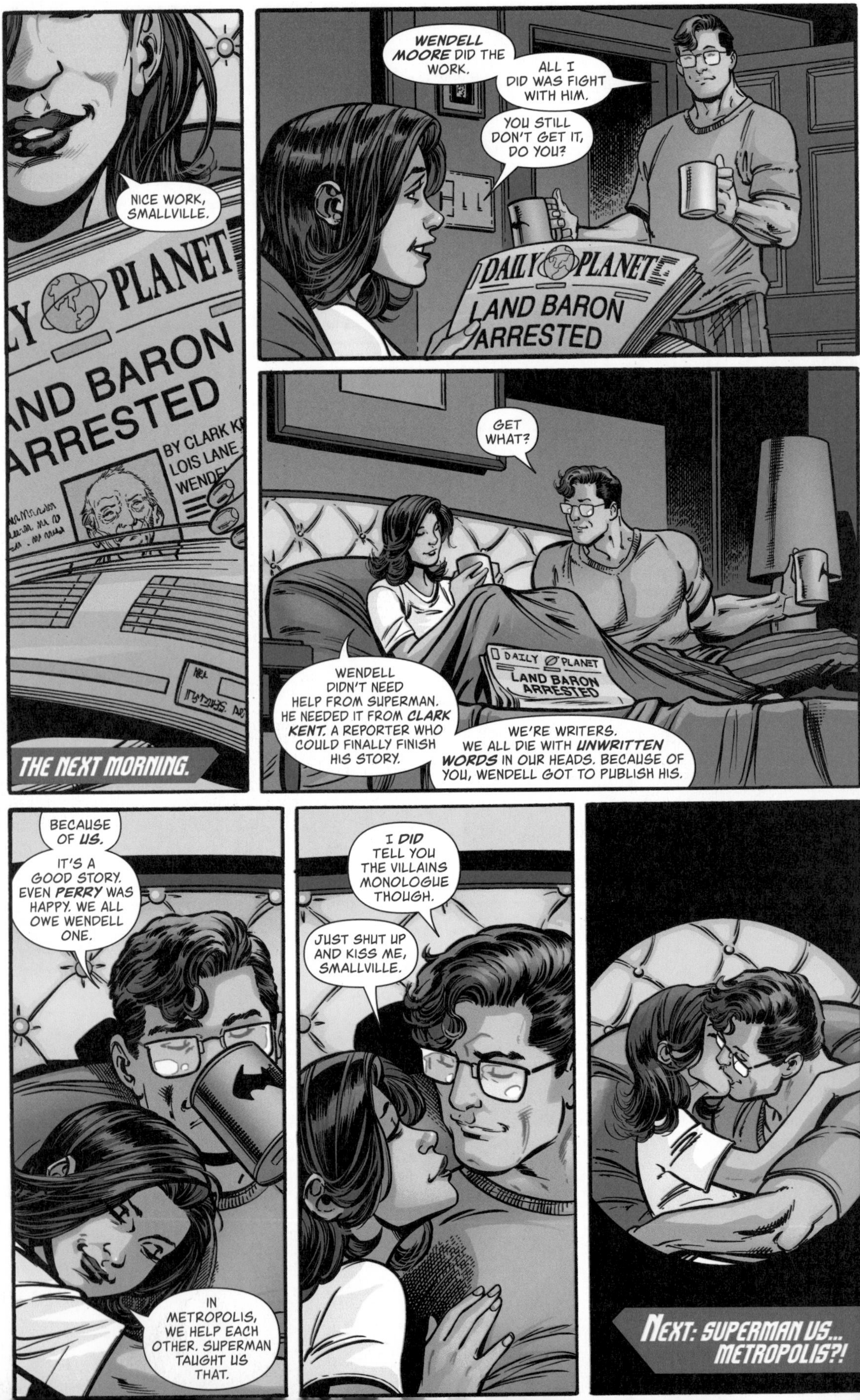
NICE WORK, SMALLVILLE.
DAILY PLANET
LAND BARON ARRESTED
BY CLARK K
LOIS LANE
WENDE
THE NEXT MORNING.
WENDELL MOORE DID THE WORK.
ALL I DID WAS FIGHT WITH HIM.
YOU STILL DON'T GET IT, DO YOU?
DAILY PLANET
LAND BARON ARRESTED
GET WHAT?
DAILY PLANET
LAND BARON ARRESTED
WENDELL DIDN'T NEED HELP FROM SUPERMAN. HE NEEDED IT FROM CLARK KENT. A REPORTER WHO COULD FINALLY FINISH HIS STORY.
WE'RE WRITERS. WE ALL DIE WITH UNWRITTEN WORDS IN OUR HEADS. BECAUSE OF YOU, WENDELL GOT TO PUBLISH HIS.
BECAUSE OF US.
IT'S A GOOD STORY. EVEN PERRY WAS HAPPY. WE ALL OWE WENDELL ONE.
IN METROPOLIS, WE HELP EACH OTHER. SUPERMAN TAUGHT US THAT.
I DID TELL YOU THE VILLAINS MONOLOGUE THOUGH.
JUST SHUT UP AND KISS ME, SMALLVILLE.
NEXT: SUPERMAN VS... METROPOLIS?!

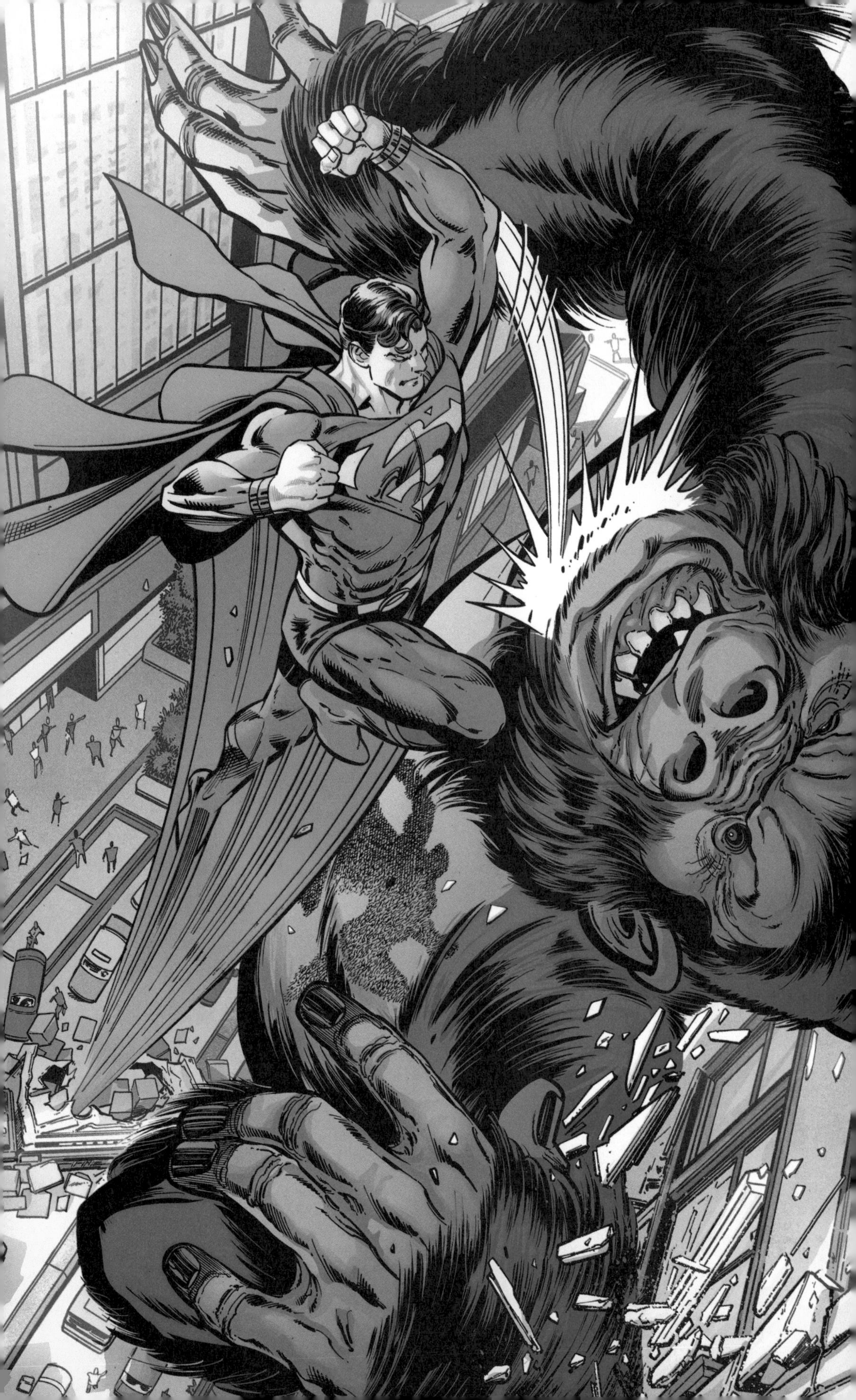

COVER ART BY
PAUL PELLETIER, DREW HENNESSY,
AND **ADRIANO LUCAS**

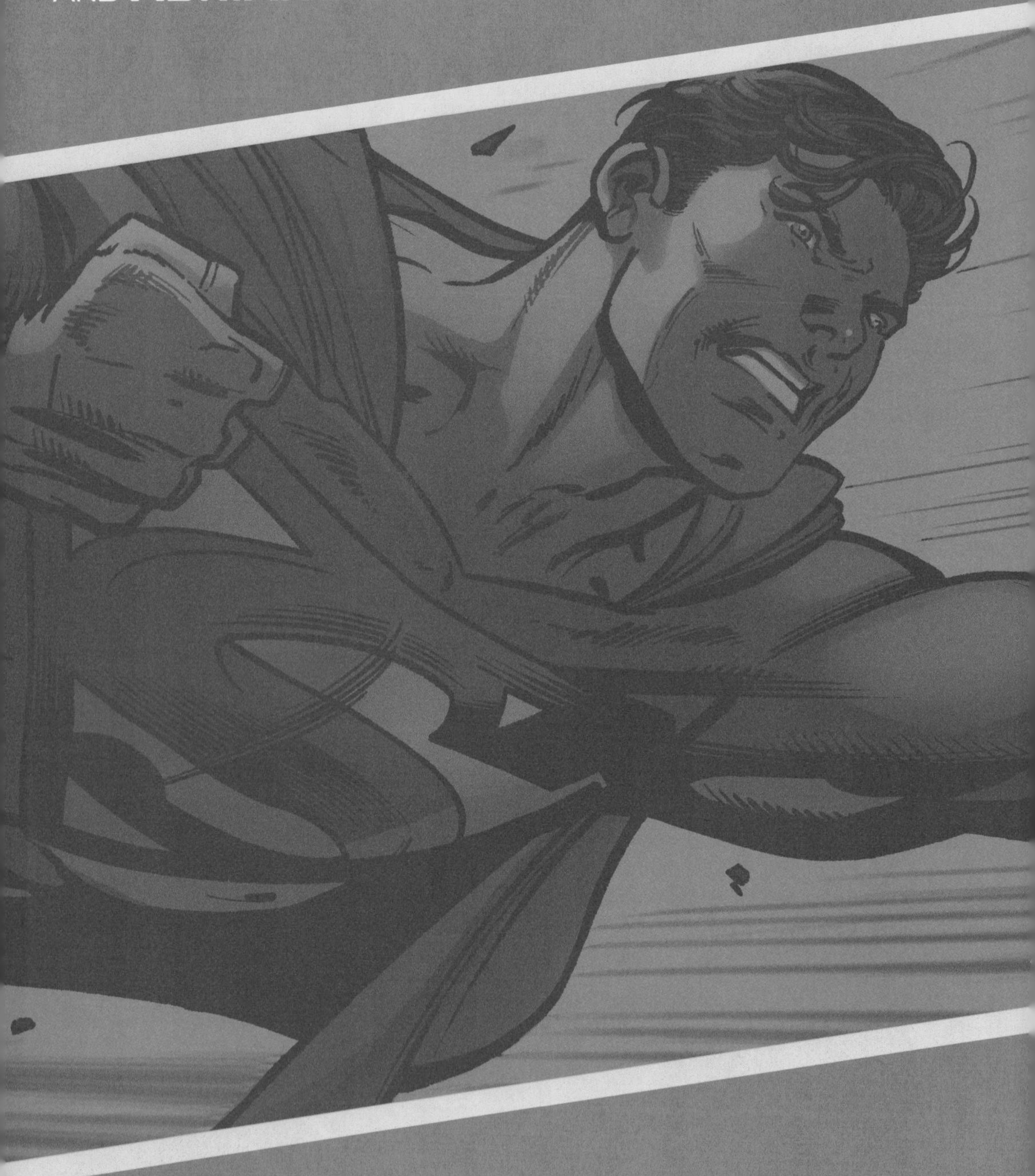

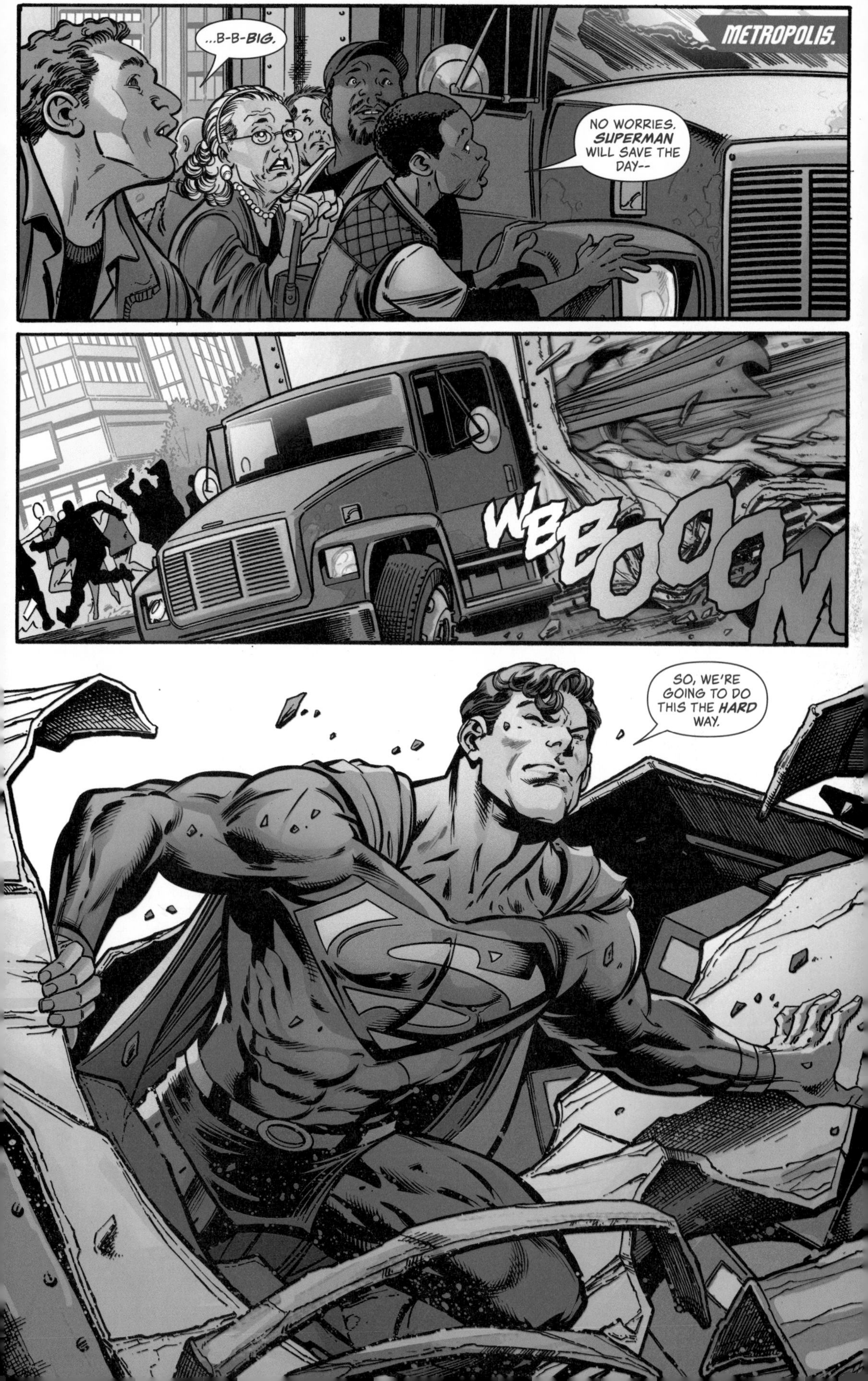
METROPOLIS.
...B-B-BIG.
NO WORRIES. SUPERMAN WILL SAVE THE DAY--
WBBOOOOM
SO, WE'RE GOING TO DO THIS THE HARD WAY.

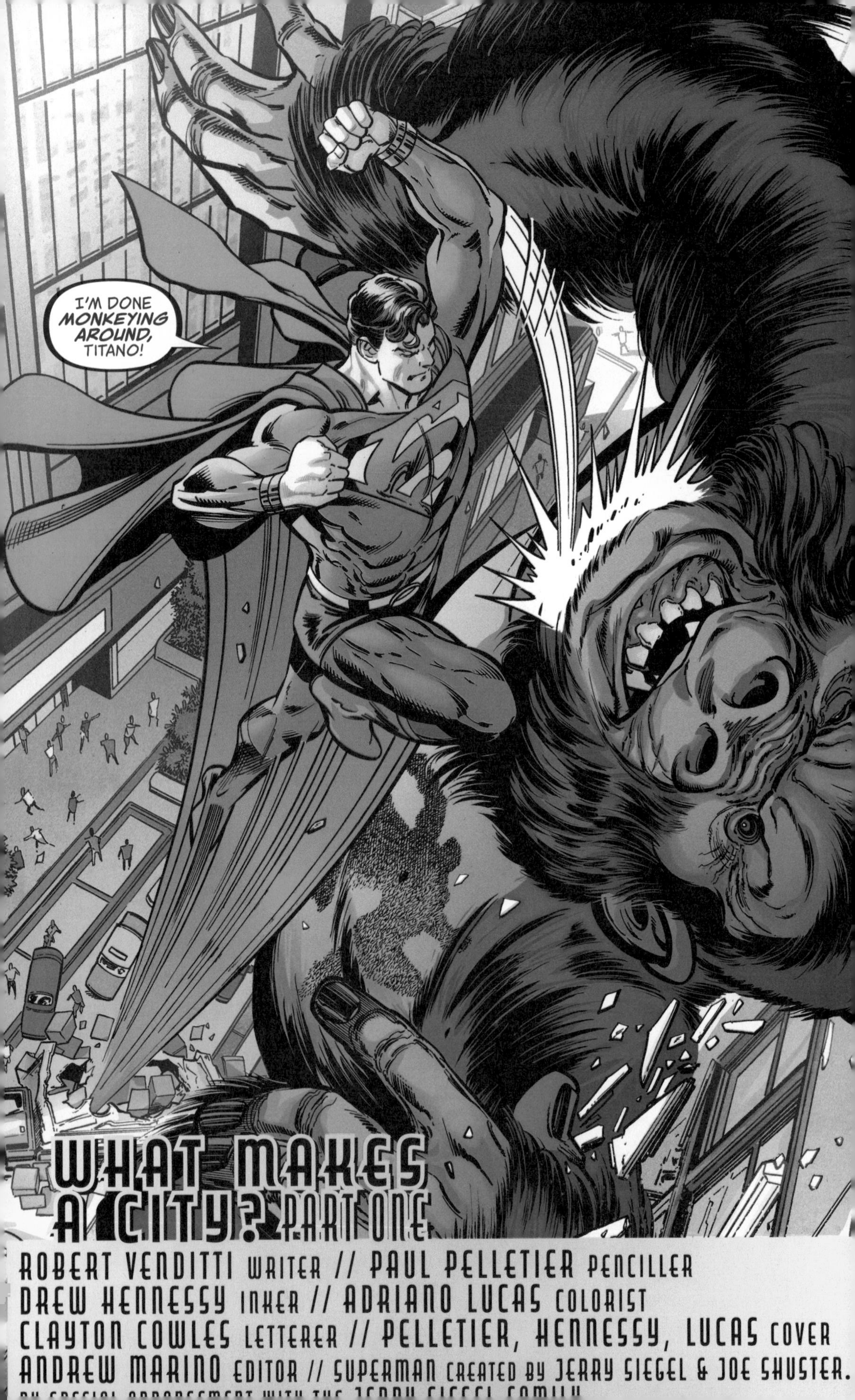
I'M DONE MONKEYING AROUND, TITANO!
WHAT MAKES A CITY? PART ONE
ROBERT VENDITTI WRITER // PAUL PELLETIER PENCILLER
DREW HENNESSY INKER // ADRIANO LUCAS COLORIST
CLAYTON COWLES LETTERER // PELLETIER, HENNESSY, LUCAS COVER
ANDREW MARINO EDITOR // SUPERMAN CREATED BY JERRY SIEGEL & JOE SHUSTER.

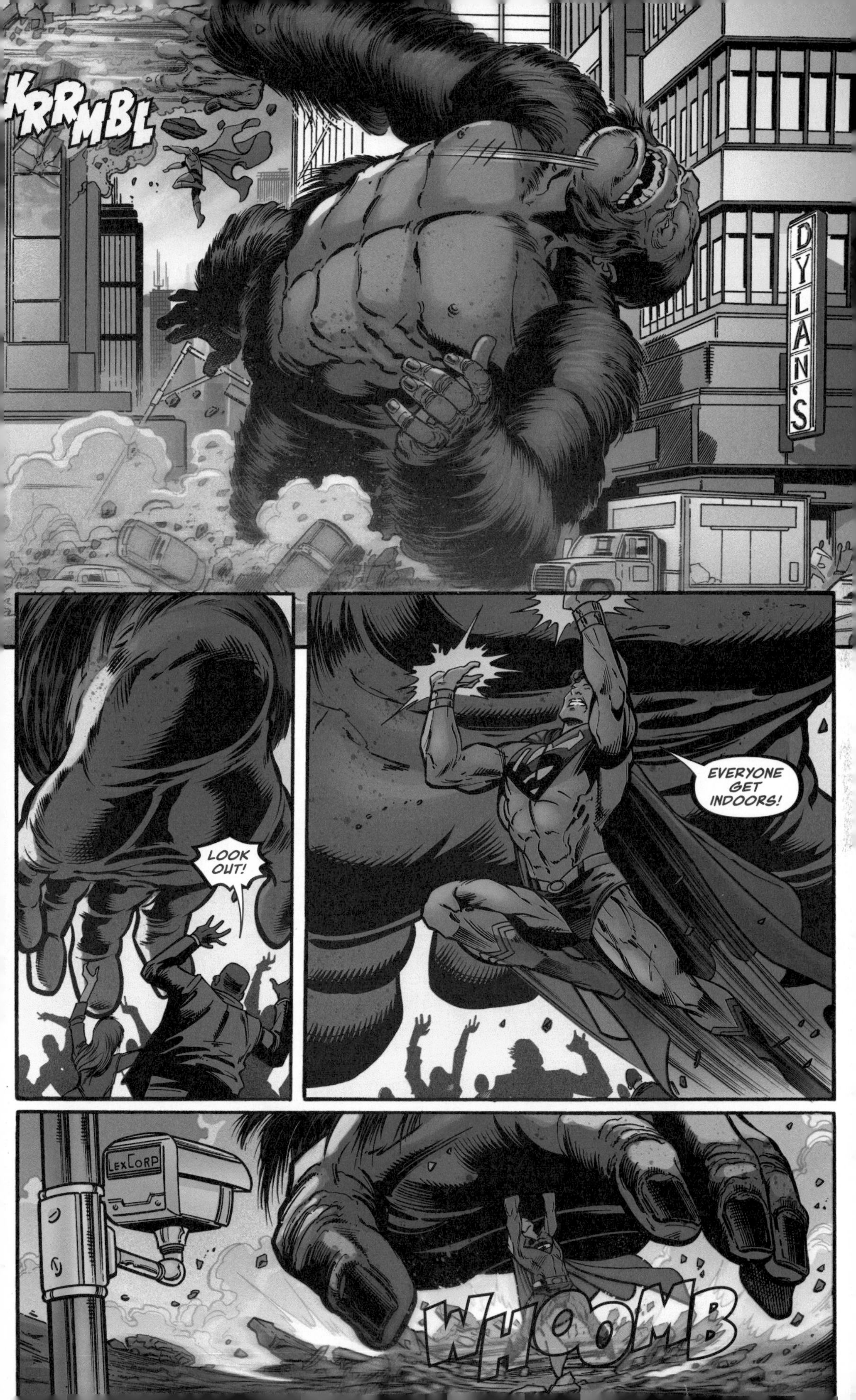
KRRMBL
DYLAN'S
LOOK OUT!
EVERYONE GET INDOORS!
LEXCORP
WHOOMB

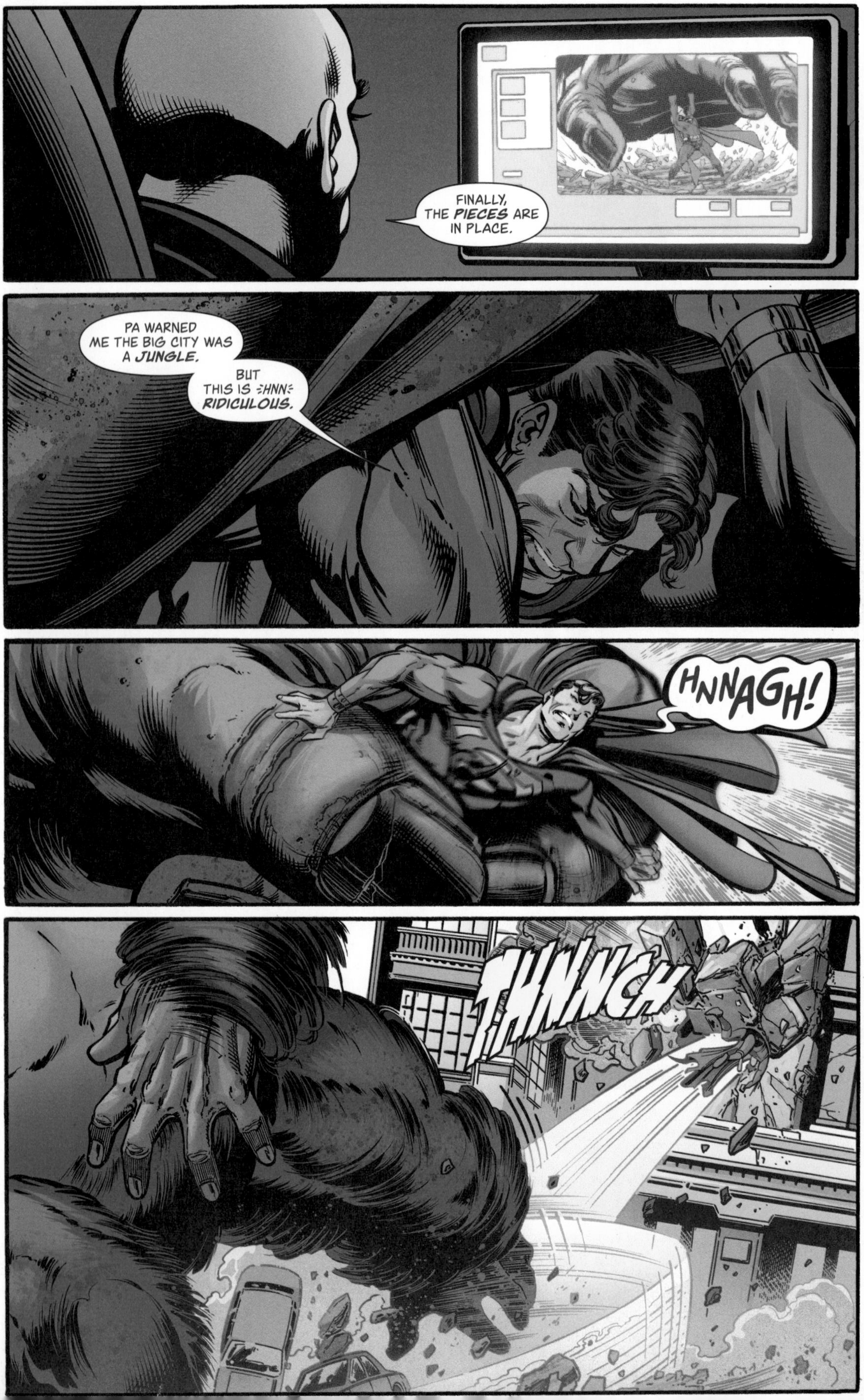
FINALLY, THE PIECES ARE IN PLACE.
PA WARNED ME THE BIG CITY WAS A JUNGLE.
BUT THIS IS =HNN= RIDICULOUS.
HNNAGH!
THNNCH

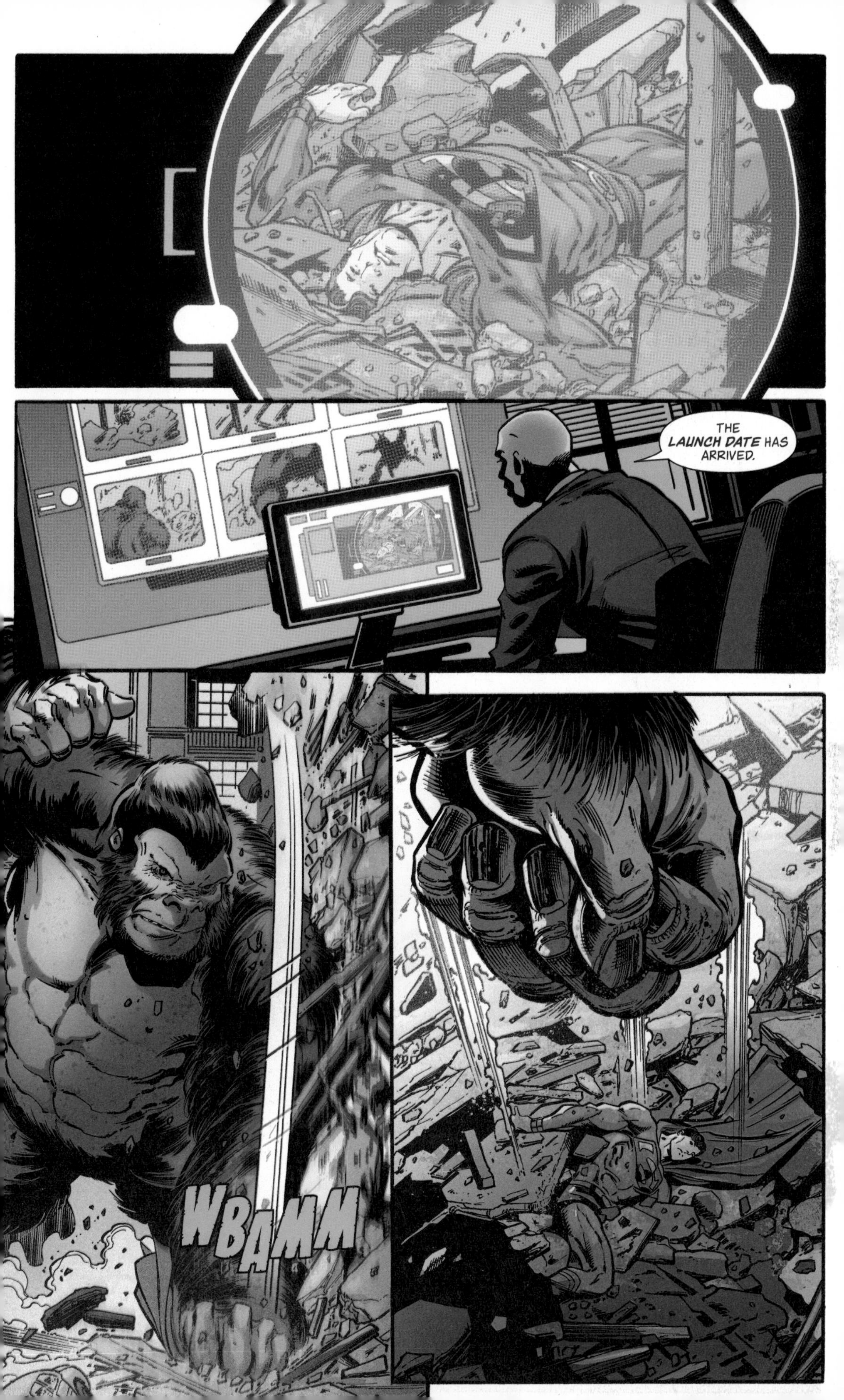
THE LAUNCH DATE HAS ARRIVED.
WBAMM

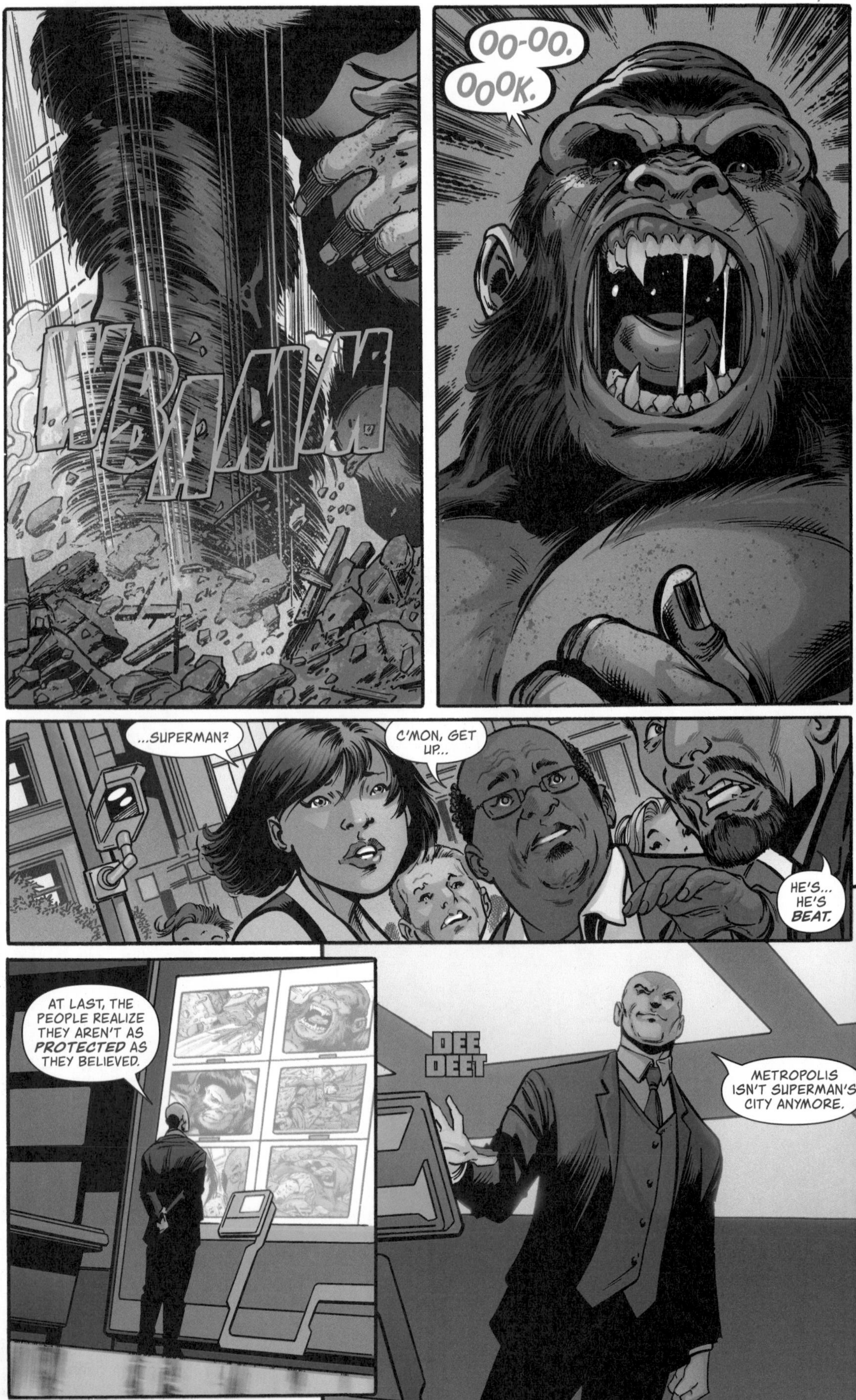
WBAMM
OO-OO. OOOK.
...SUPERMAN?
C'MON, GET UP...
HE'S... HE'S BEAT.
AT LAST, THE PEOPLE REALIZE THEY AREN'T AS PROTECTED AS THEY BELIEVED.
DEE DEET
METROPOLIS ISN'T SUPERMAN'S CITY ANYMORE.

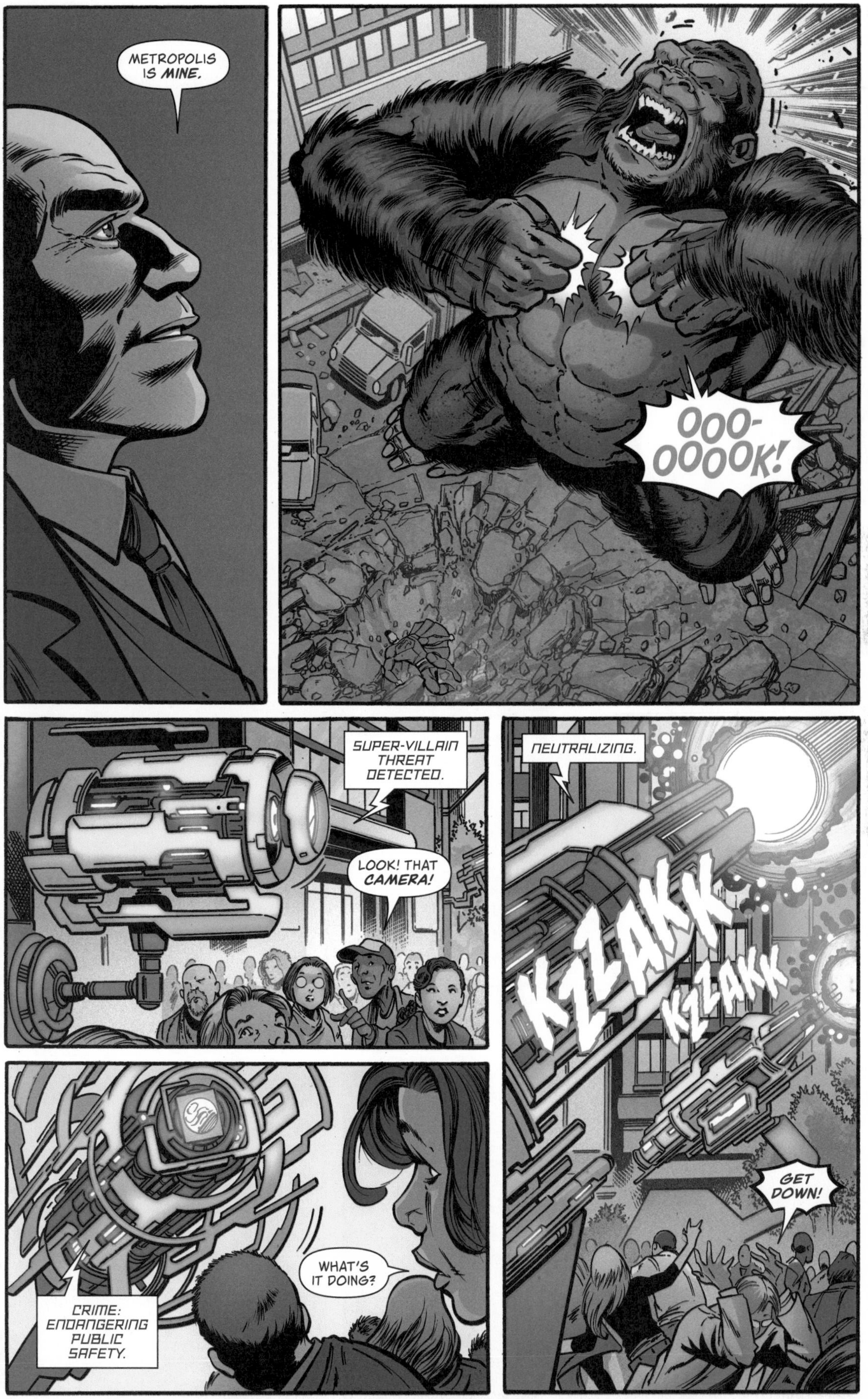
METROPOLIS IS MINE.
OOO-OOOOK!
SUPER-VILLAIN THREAT DETECTED.
LOOK! THAT CAMERA!
CRIME: ENDANGERING PUBLIC SAFETY.
WHAT'S IT DOING?
NEUTRALIZING.
KZZAKK
KZZAKK
GET DOWN!

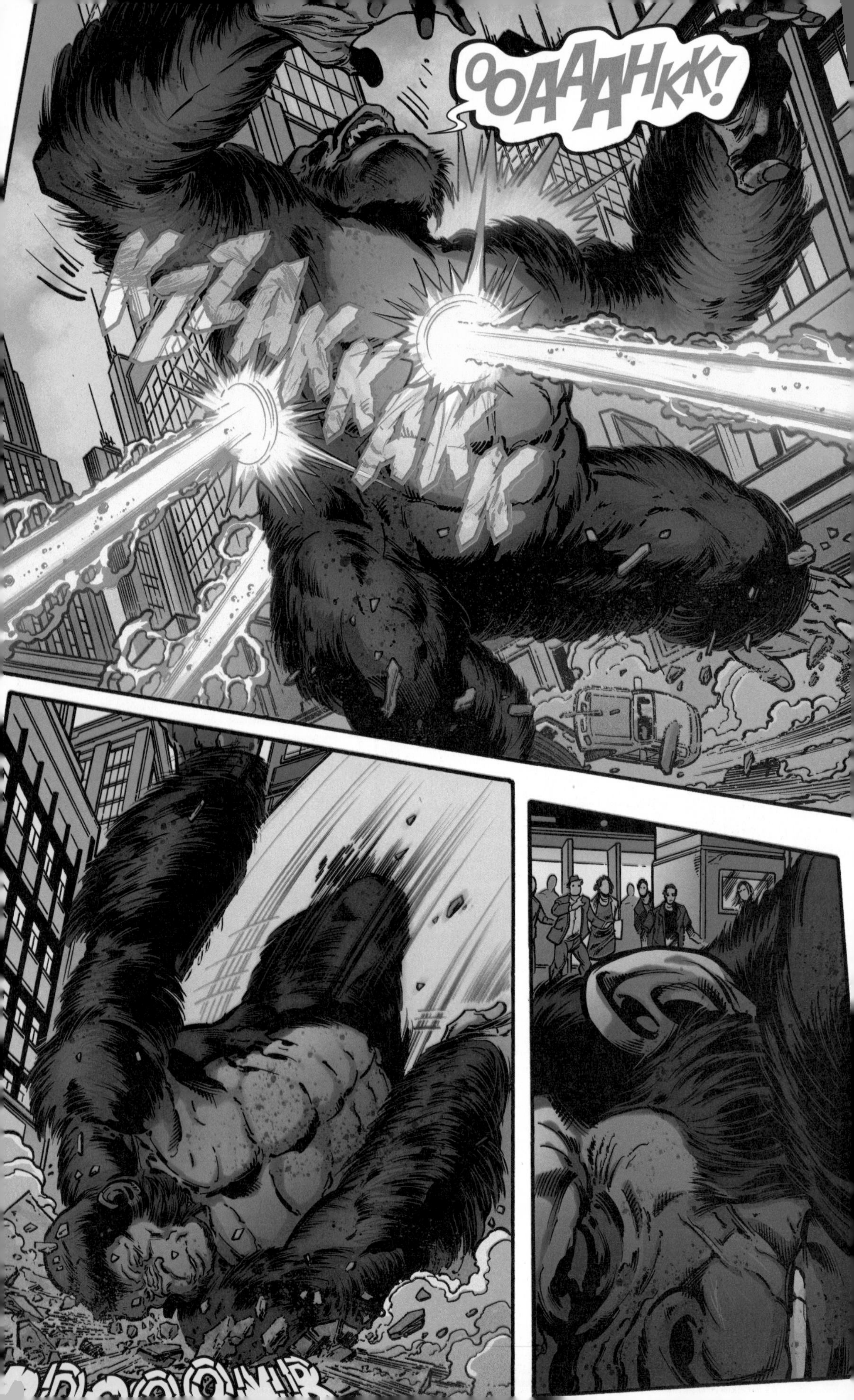
OOAAAHKK!

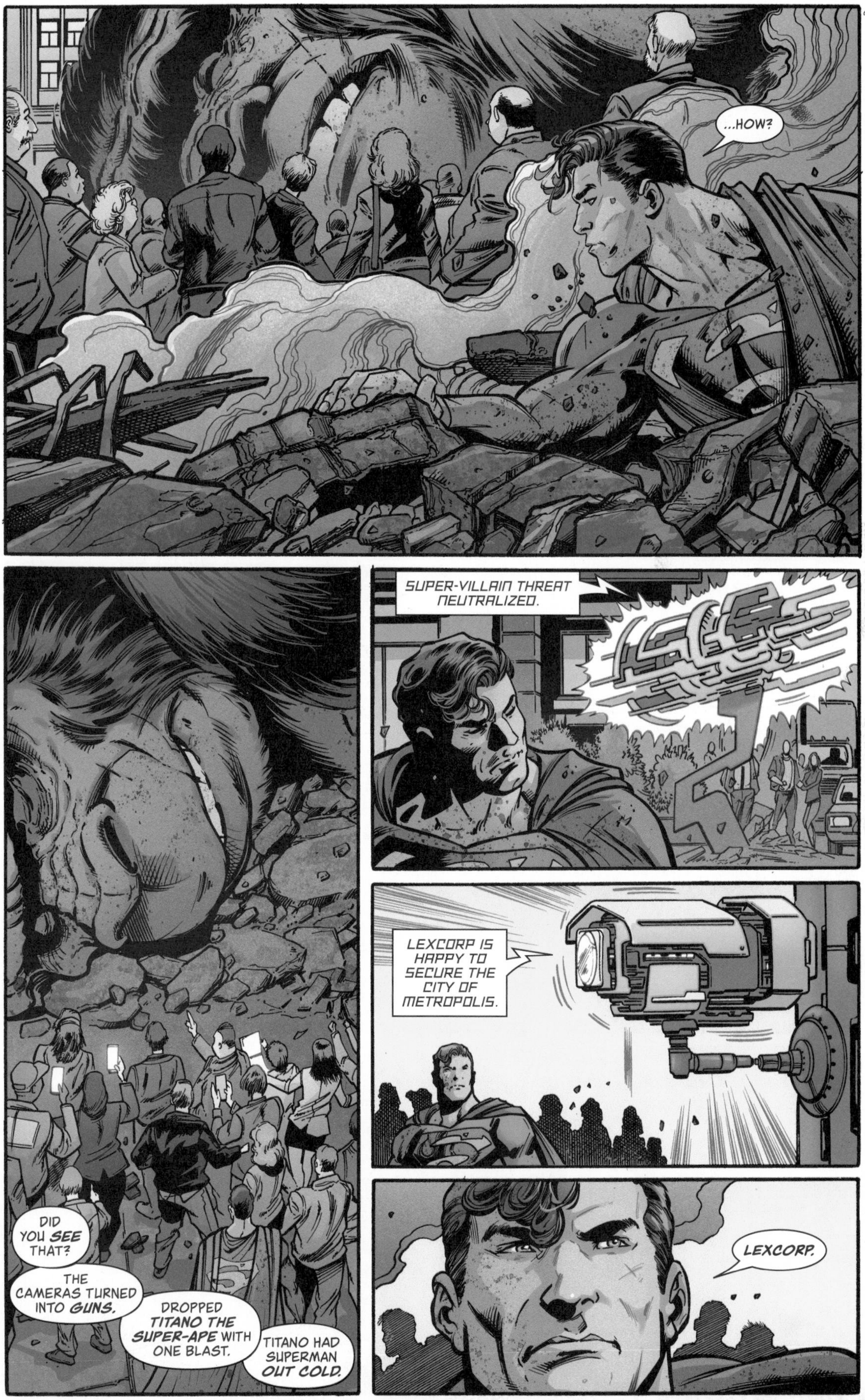
...HOW?
DID YOU SEE THAT?
THE CAMERAS TURNED INTO GUNS.
DROPPED TITANO THE SUPER-APE WITH ONE BLAST.
TITANO HAD SUPERMAN OUT COLD.
SUPER-VILLAIN THREAT NEUTRALIZED.
LEXCORP IS HAPPY TO SECURE THE CITY OF METROPOLIS.
LEXCORP.

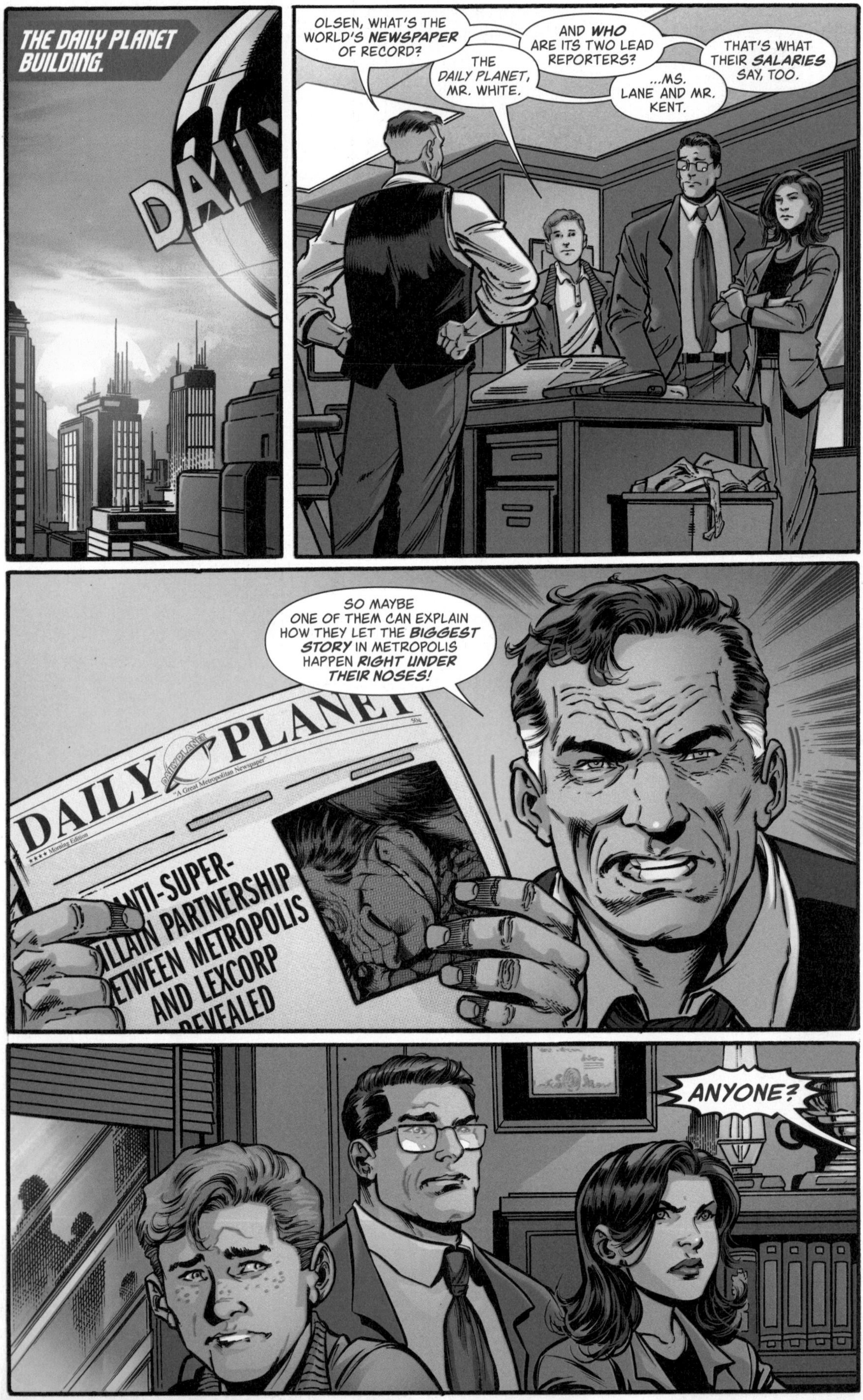
THE DAILY PLANET BUILDING.
DAILY
OLSEN, WHAT'S THE WORLD'S NEWSPAPER OF RECORD?
THE DAILY PLANET, MR. WHITE.
AND WHO ARE ITS TWO LEAD REPORTERS?
...MS. LANE AND MR. KENT.
THAT'S WHAT THEIR SALARIES SAY, TOO.
SO MAYBE ONE OF THEM CAN EXPLAIN HOW THEY LET THE BIGGEST STORY IN METROPOLIS HAPPEN RIGHT UNDER THEIR NOSES!
DAILY PLANET
"A Great Metropolitan Newspaper"
Morning Edition
ANTI-SUPER-
ILLAIN PARTNERSHIP
ETWEEN METROPOLIS
AND LEXCORP
REVEALED
ANYONE?

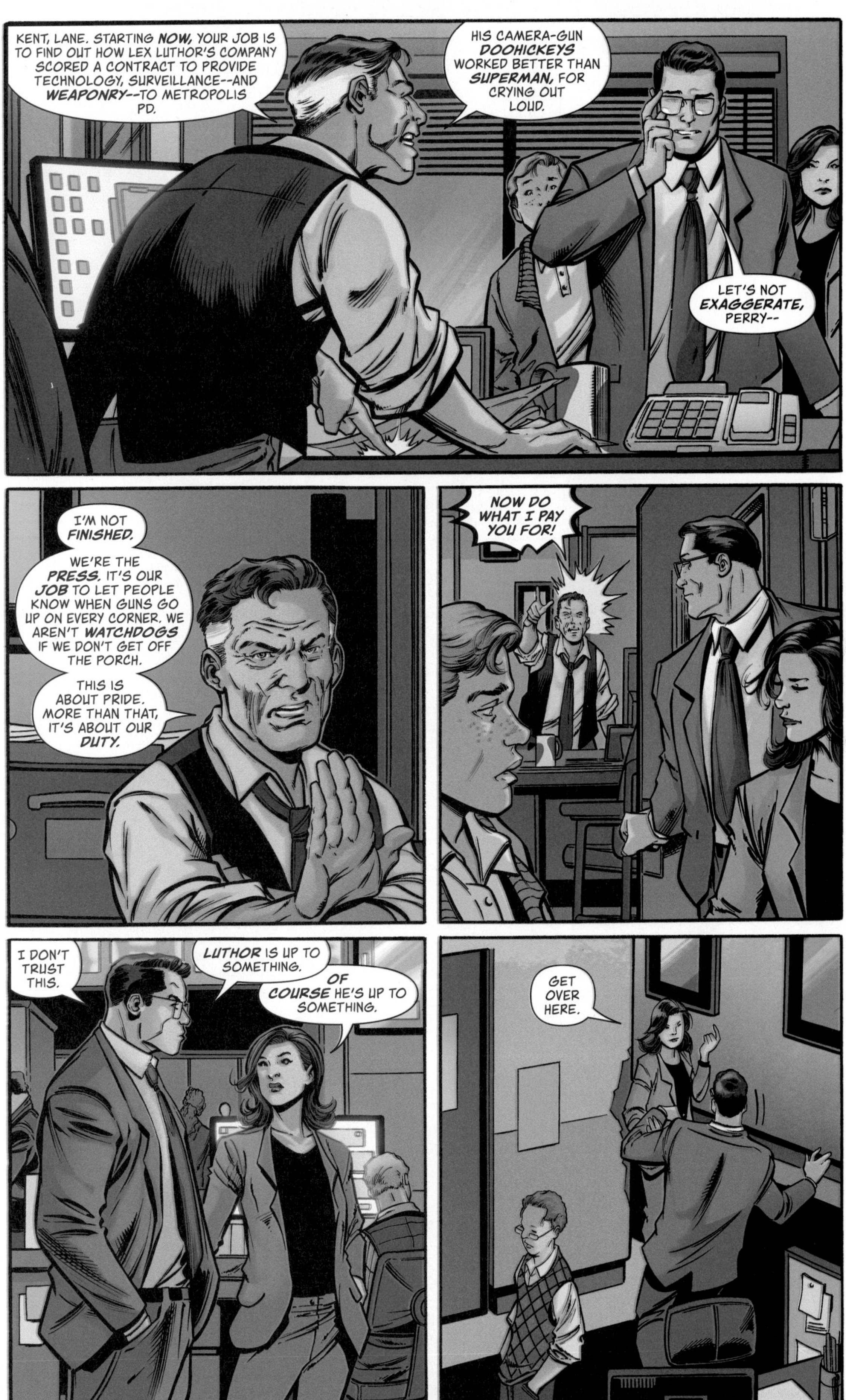
KENT, LANE. STARTING NOW, YOUR JOB IS TO FIND OUT HOW LEX LUTHOR'S COMPANY SCORED A CONTRACT TO PROVIDE TECHNOLOGY, SURVEILLANCE--AND WEAPONRY--TO METROPOLIS PD.
HIS CAMERA-GUN DOOHICKEYS WORKED BETTER THAN SUPERMAN, FOR CRYING OUT LOUD.
LET'S NOT EXAGGERATE, PERRY--
I'M NOT FINISHED.
WE'RE THE PRESS. IT'S OUR JOB TO LET PEOPLE KNOW WHEN GUNS GO UP ON EVERY CORNER. WE AREN'T WATCHDOGS IF WE DON'T GET OFF THE PORCH.
THIS IS ABOUT PRIDE. MORE THAN THAT, IT'S ABOUT OUR DUTY.
NOW DO WHAT I PAY YOU FOR!
I DON'T TRUST THIS.
LUTHOR IS UP TO SOMETHING.
OF COURSE HE'S UP TO SOMETHING.
GET OVER HERE.

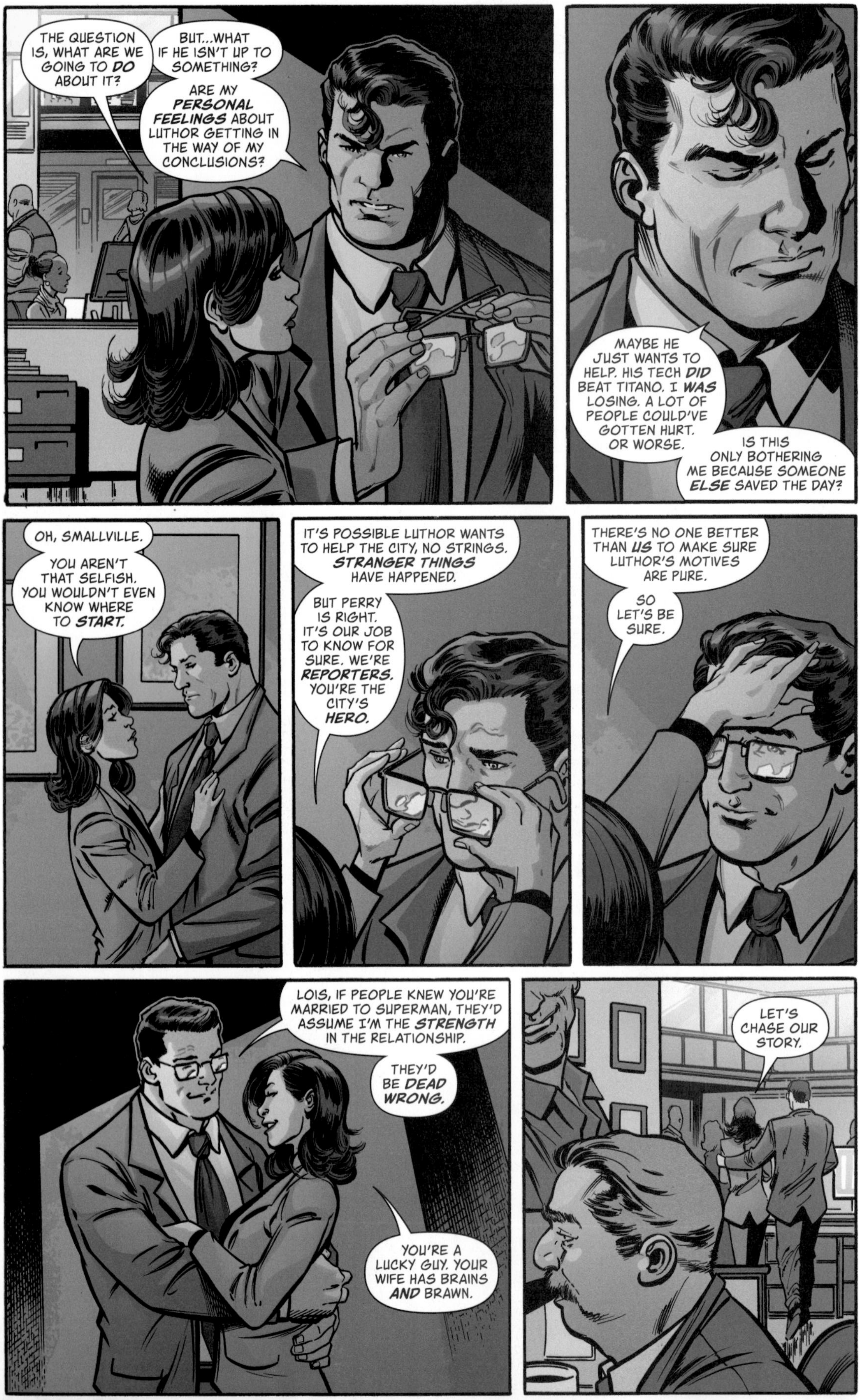
THE QUESTION IS, WHAT ARE WE GOING TO *DO* ABOUT IT?
BUT...WHAT IF HE ISN'T UP TO SOMETHING?
ARE MY *PERSONAL FEELINGS* ABOUT LUTHOR GETTING IN THE WAY OF MY CONCLUSIONS?
MAYBE HE JUST WANTS TO HELP. HIS TECH *DID* BEAT TITANO. I *WAS* LOSING. A LOT OF PEOPLE COULD'VE GOTTEN HURT. OR WORSE.
IS THIS ONLY BOTHERING ME BECAUSE SOMEONE *ELSE* SAVED THE DAY?
OH, SMALLVILLE.
YOU AREN'T THAT SELFISH. YOU WOULDN'T EVEN KNOW WHERE TO *START.*
IT'S POSSIBLE LUTHOR WANTS TO HELP THE CITY, NO STRINGS. *STRANGER THINGS* HAVE HAPPENED.
BUT PERRY IS RIGHT. IT'S OUR JOB TO KNOW FOR SURE. WE'RE *REPORTERS.* YOU'RE THE CITY'S *HERO.*
THERE'S NO ONE BETTER THAN *US* TO MAKE SURE LUTHOR'S MOTIVES ARE PURE.
SO LET'S BE SURE.
LOIS, IF PEOPLE KNEW YOU'RE MARRIED TO SUPERMAN, THEY'D ASSUME I'M THE *STRENGTH* IN THE RELATIONSHIP.
THEY'D BE *DEAD WRONG.*
YOU'RE A LUCKY GUY. YOUR WIFE HAS BRAINS *AND* BRAWN.
LET'S CHASE OUR STORY.

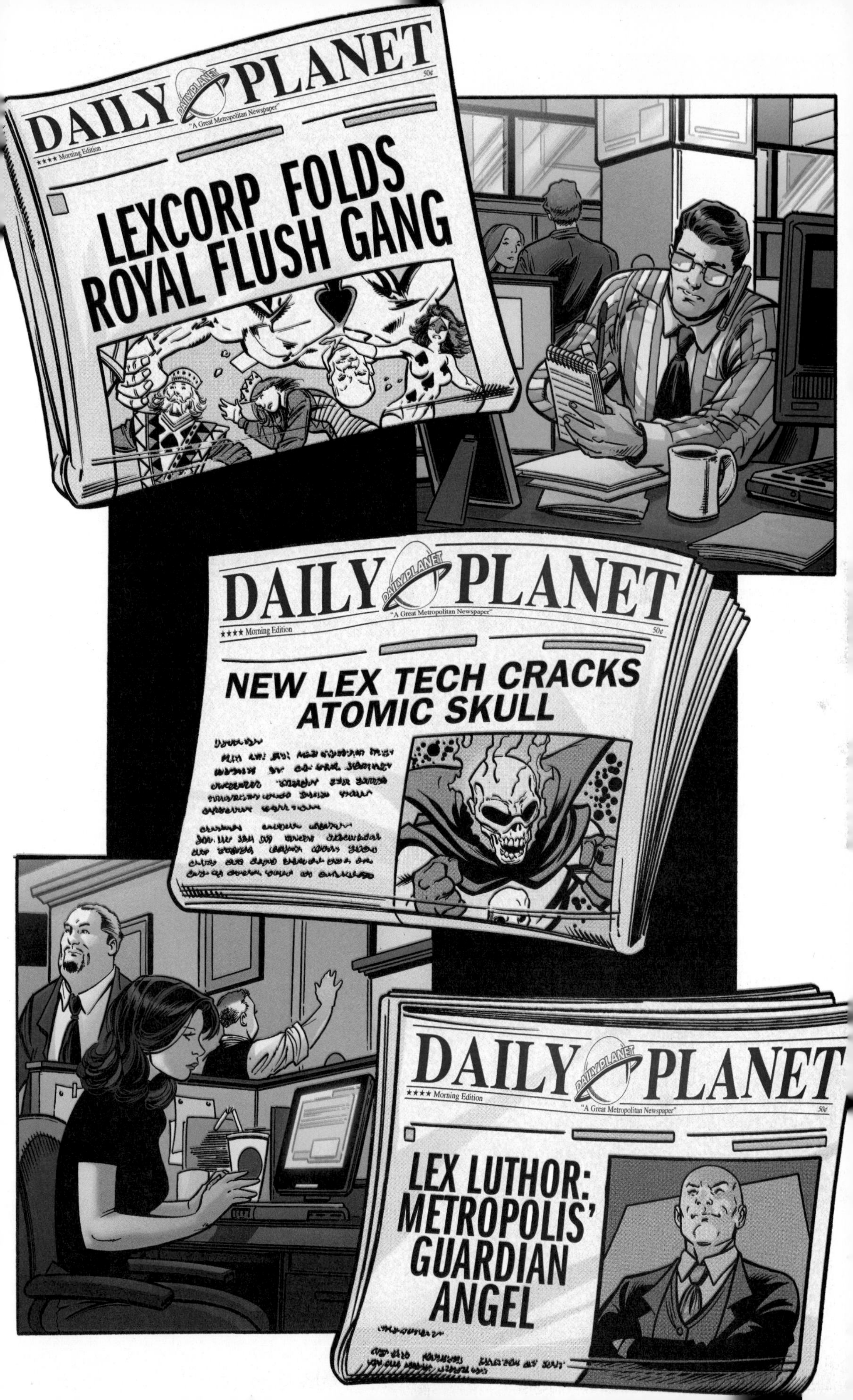
DAILY PLANET
"A Great Metropolitan Newspaper"
★★★★ Morning Edition
50¢
LEXCORP FOLDS ROYAL FLUSH GANG
DAILY PLANET
"A Great Metropolitan Newspaper"
★★★★ Morning Edition
50¢
NEW LEX TECH CRACKS ATOMIC SKULL
DAILY PLANET
★★★★ Morning Edition
"A Great Metropolitan Newspaper"
50¢
LEX LUTHOR: METROPOLIS' GUARDIAN ANGEL

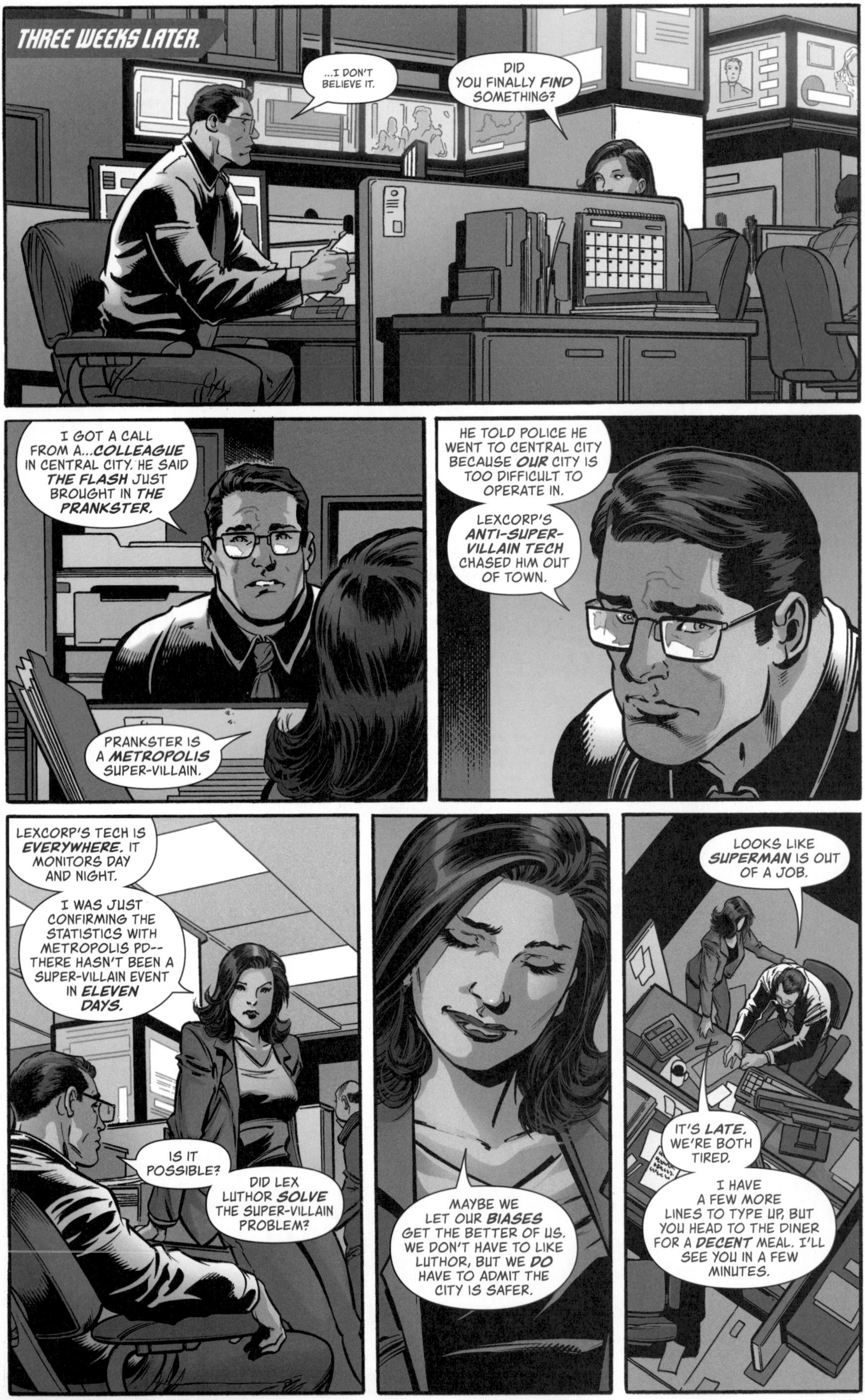
THREE WEEKS LATER.
...I DON'T BELIEVE IT.
DID YOU FINALLY *FIND* SOMETHING?
I GOT A CALL FROM A...*COLLEAGUE* IN CENTRAL CITY. HE SAID *THE FLASH* JUST BROUGHT IN *THE PRANKSTER.*
PRANKSTER IS A *METROPOLIS* SUPER-VILLAIN.
HE TOLD POLICE HE WENT TO CENTRAL CITY BECAUSE *OUR* CITY IS TOO DIFFICULT TO OPERATE IN.
LEXCORP'S *ANTI-SUPER-VILLAIN TECH* CHASED HIM OUT OF TOWN.
LEXCORP'S TECH IS *EVERYWHERE.* IT MONITORS DAY AND NIGHT.
I WAS JUST CONFIRMING THE STATISTICS WITH METROPOLIS PD-- THERE HASN'T BEEN A SUPER-VILLAIN EVENT IN *ELEVEN DAYS.*
IS IT POSSIBLE?
DID LEX LUTHOR *SOLVE* THE SUPER-VILLAIN PROBLEM?
MAYBE WE LET OUR *BIASES* GET THE BETTER OF US. WE DON'T HAVE TO LIKE LUTHOR, BUT WE *DO* HAVE TO ADMIT THE CITY IS SAFER.
LOOKS LIKE *SUPERMAN* IS OUT OF A JOB.
IT'S *LATE.* WE'RE BOTH TIRED.
I HAVE A FEW MORE LINES TO TYPE UP, BUT YOU HEAD TO THE DINER FOR A *DECENT* MEAL. I'LL SEE YOU IN A FEW MINUTES.

"THINK ABOUT SOMETHING *ELSE* FOR A CHANGE."

HELP!

THIEF!

SUPER-VILLAIN THREAT DETECTED.

WHAT--?

NO!

CRIME: ROBBERY.

I-I JUST SKIPPED OUT ON MY CHECK, THAT'S ALL!

IT'S ONLY A COUPLE BUCKS!

STOP! YOU CAN'T *HURT* THIS MAN OVER A FEW DOLLARS. HE MADE A *MISTAKE.*

...

NEW SUPER-VILLAIN THREAT DETECTED.

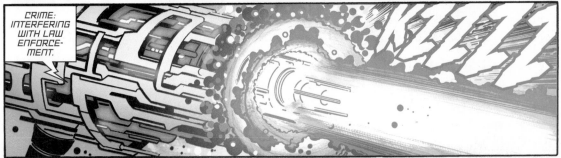

CRIME: INTERFERING WITH LAW ENFORCEMENT.

KZZZZ

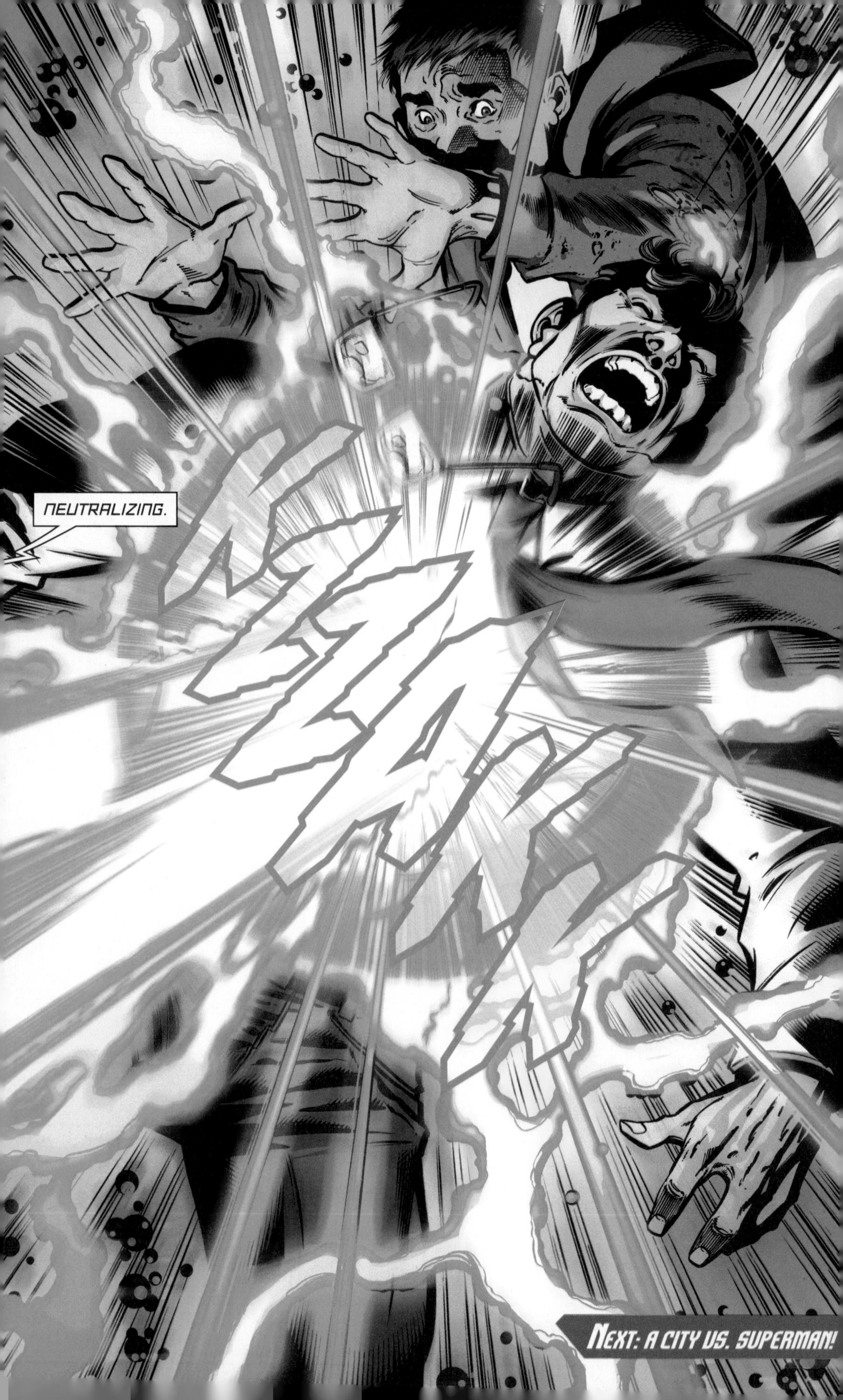
NEUTRALIZING.
NEXT: A CITY VS. SUPERMAN!

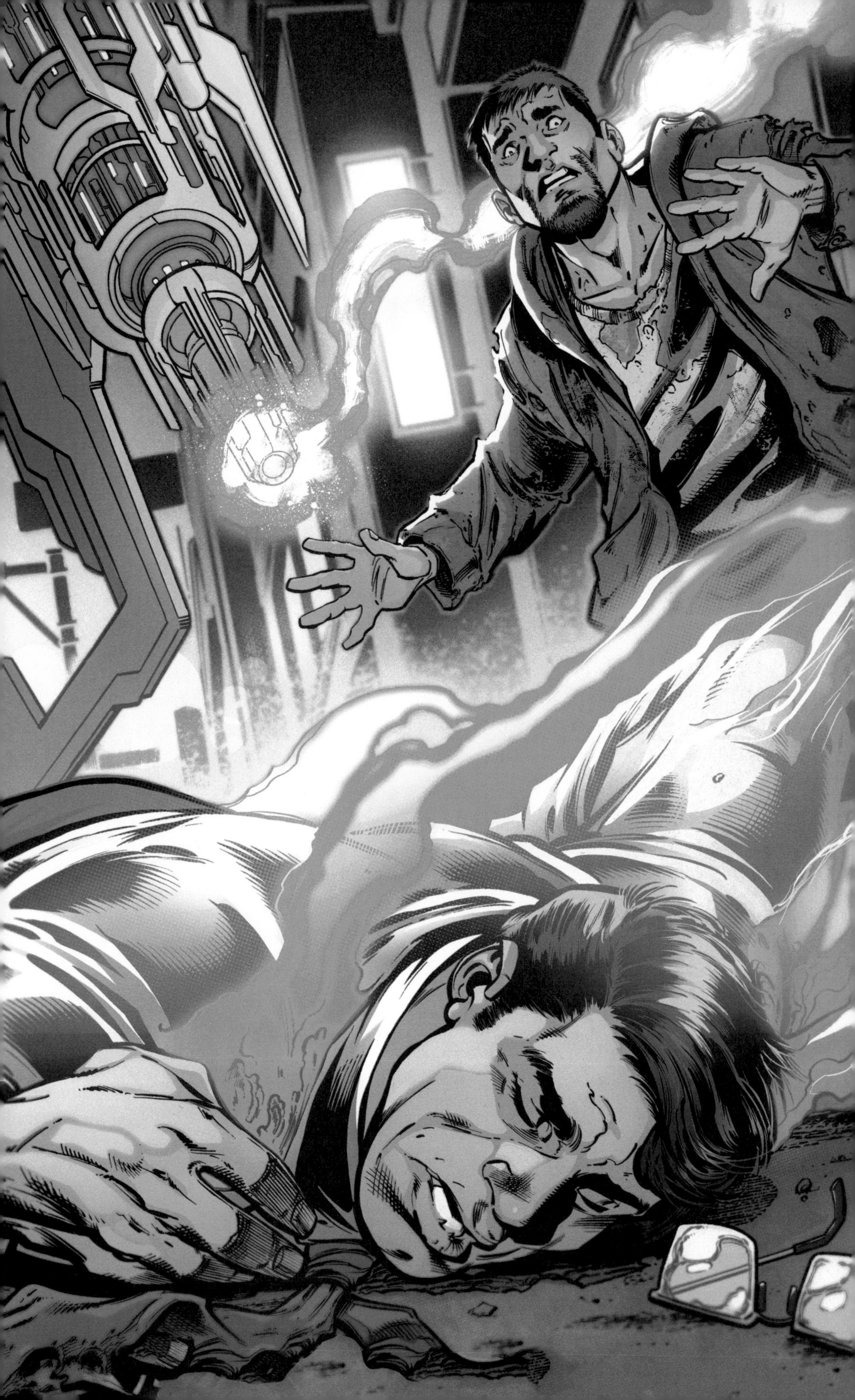

COVER ART BY
PAUL PELLETIER, DREW HENNESSY,
AND **ADRIANO LUCAS**

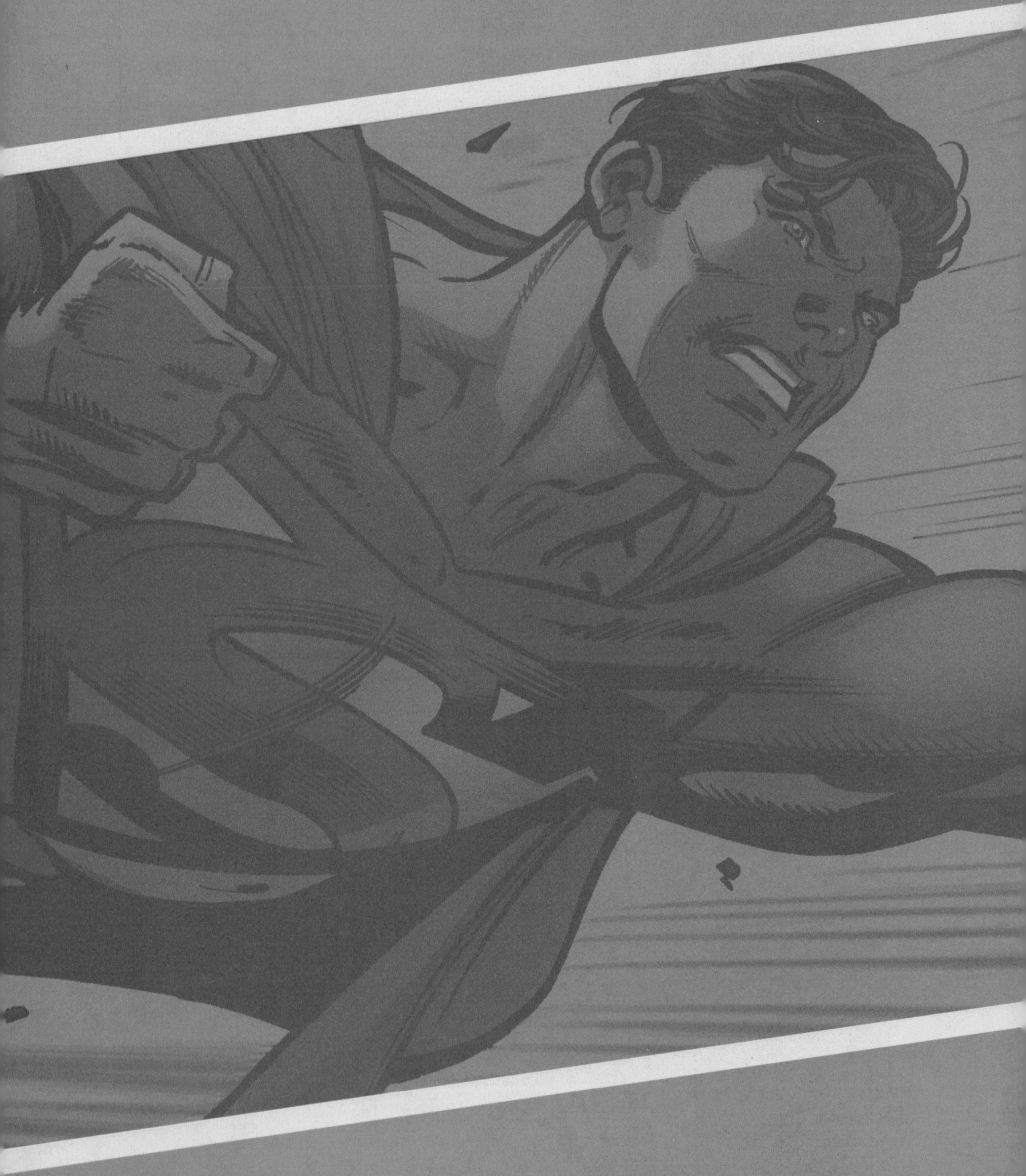

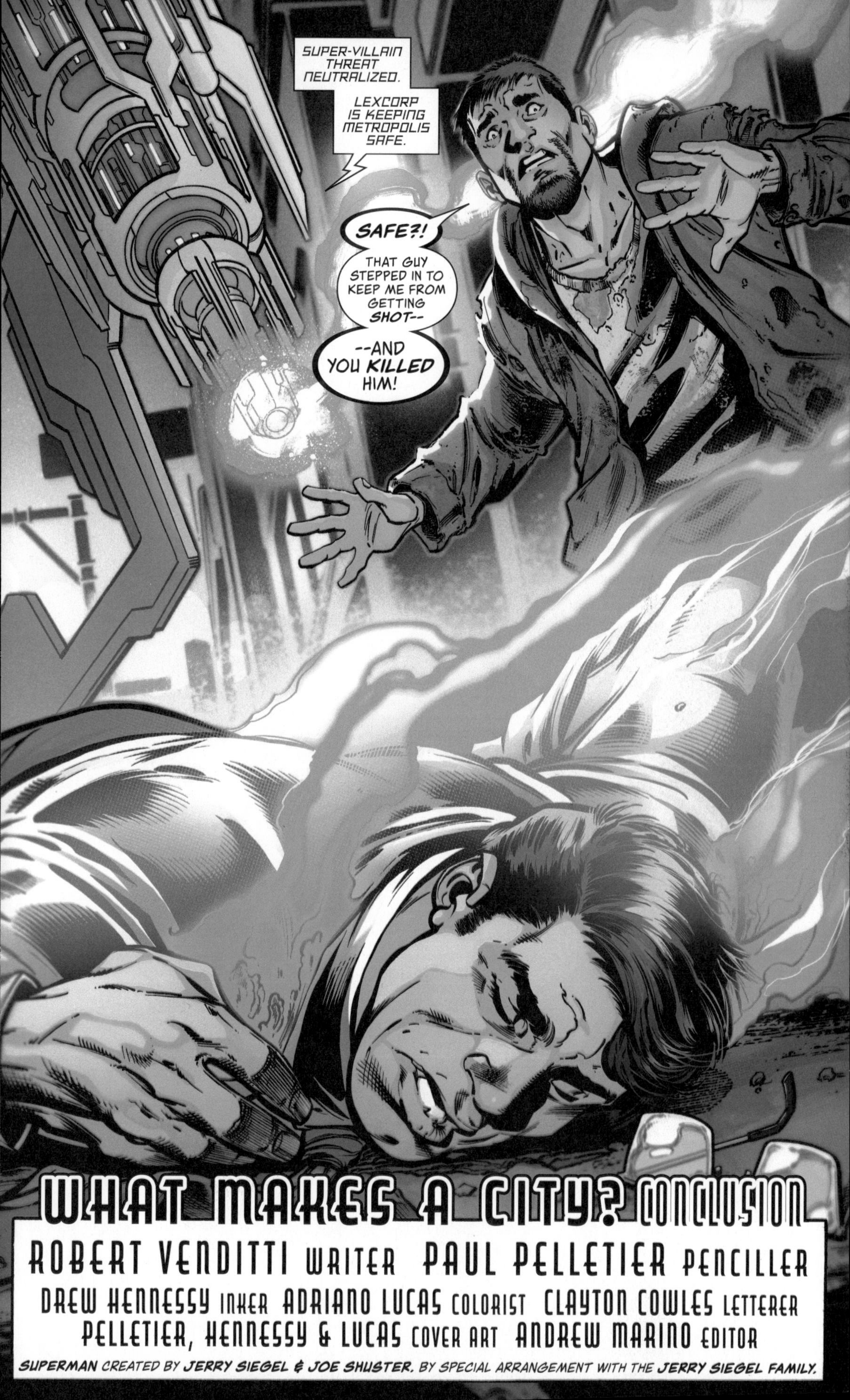
SUPER-VILLAIN THREAT NEUTRALIZED.
LEXCORP IS KEEPING METROPOLIS SAFE.
SAFE?!
THAT GUY STEPPED IN TO KEEP ME FROM GETTING SHOT--
--AND YOU KILLED HIM!
WHAT MAKES A CITY? CONCLUSION
ROBERT VENDITTI WRITER PAUL PELLETIER PENCILLER
DREW HENNESSY INKER ADRIANO LUCAS COLORIST CLAYTON COWLES LETTERER
PELLETIER, HENNESSY & LUCAS COVER ART ANDREW MARINO EDITOR
SUPERMAN CREATED BY JERRY SIEGEL & JOE SHUSTER. BY SPECIAL ARRANGEMENT WITH THE JERRY SIEGEL FAMILY.

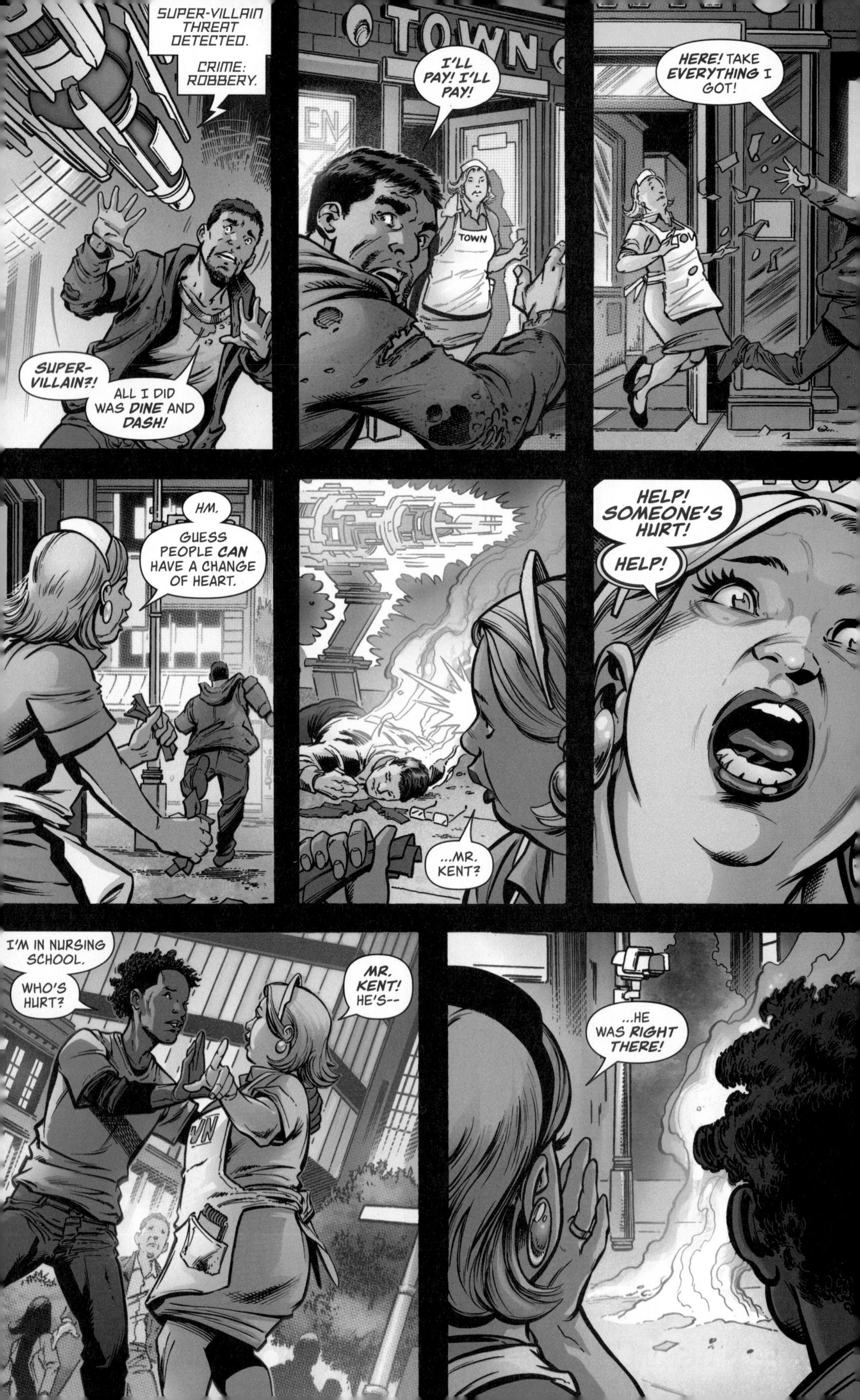
SUPER-VILLAIN THREAT DETECTED.
CRIME: ROBBERY.
SUPER-VILLAIN?!
ALL I DID WAS DINE AND DASH!
TOWN
I'LL PAY! I'LL PAY!
TOWN
HERE! TAKE EVERYTHING I GOT!
HM.
GUESS PEOPLE CAN HAVE A CHANGE OF HEART.
...MR. KENT?
HELP! SOMEONE'S HURT!
HELP!
I'M IN NURSING SCHOOL.
WHO'S HURT?
MR. KENT! HE'S--
...HE WAS RIGHT THERE!

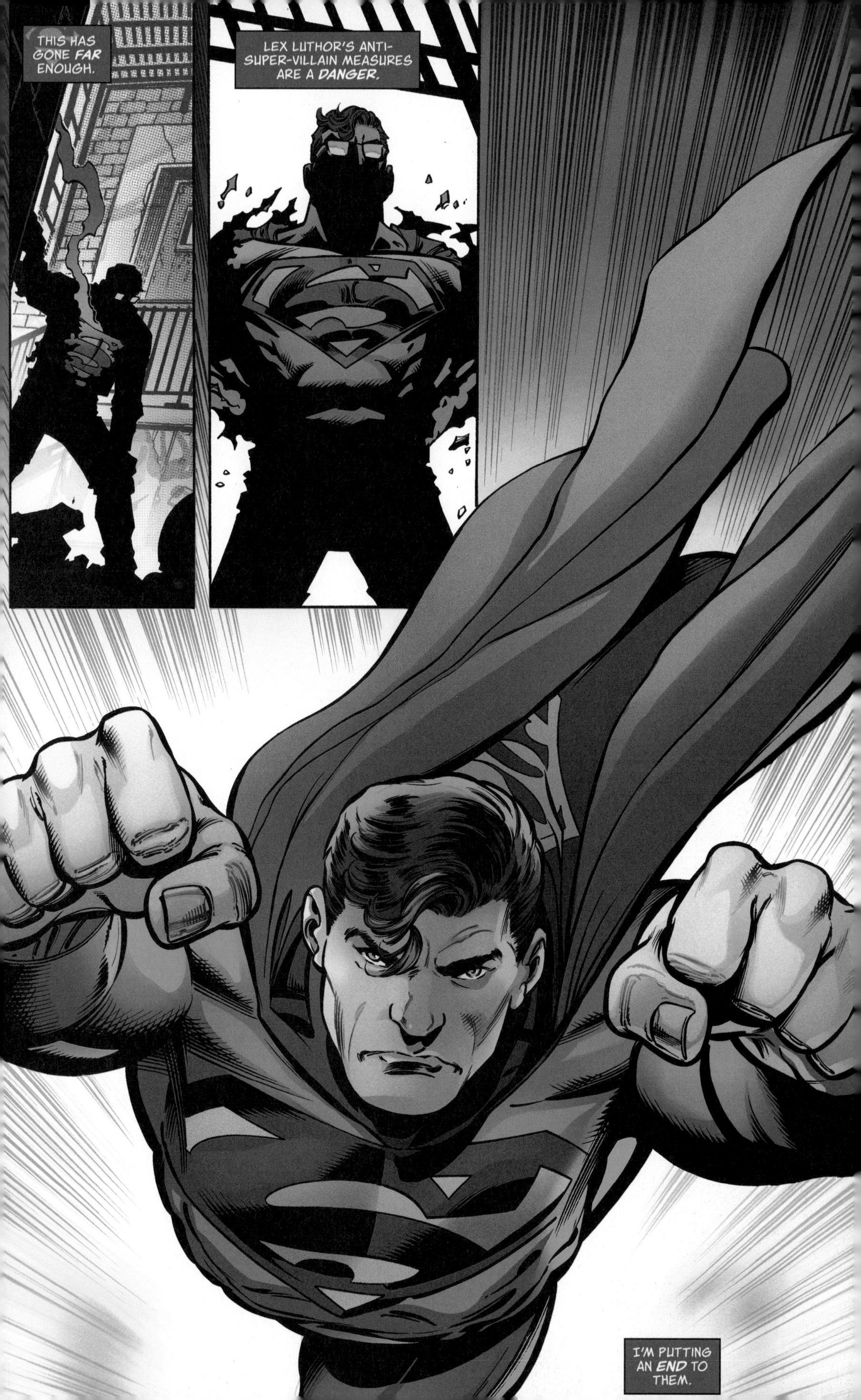
THIS HAS GONE FAR ENOUGH.
LEX LUTHOR'S ANTI-SUPER-VILLAIN MEASURES ARE A DANGER.
I'M PUTTING AN END TO THEM.

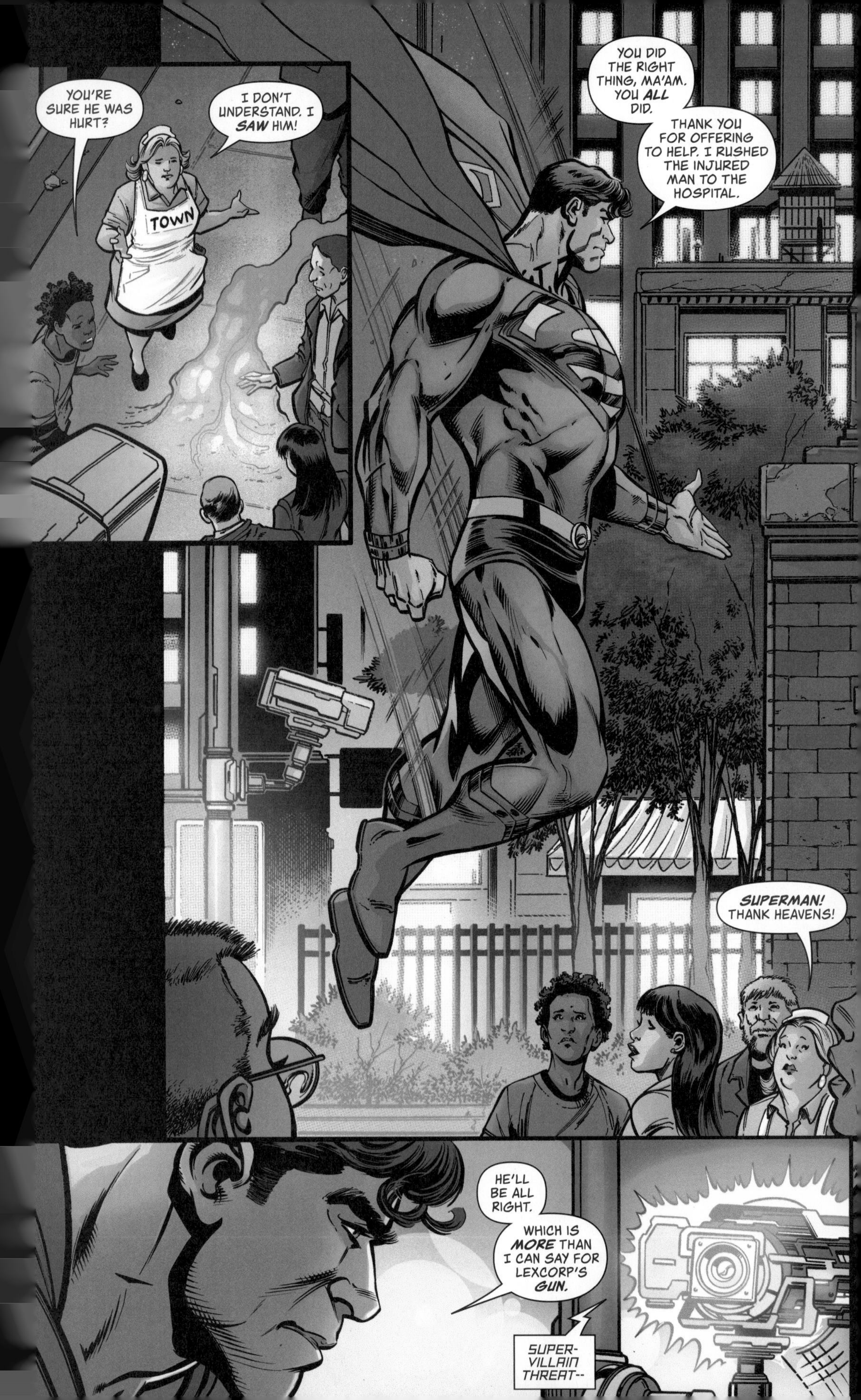
YOU'RE SURE HE WAS HURT?
I DON'T UNDERSTAND. I SAW HIM!
YOU DID THE RIGHT THING, MA'AM. YOU ALL DID.
THANK YOU FOR OFFERING TO HELP. I RUSHED THE INJURED MAN TO THE HOSPITAL.
SUPERMAN! THANK HEAVENS!
HE'LL BE ALL RIGHT.
WHICH IS MORE THAN I CAN SAY FOR LEXCORP'S GUN.
TOWN
SUPER-VILLAIN THREAT--

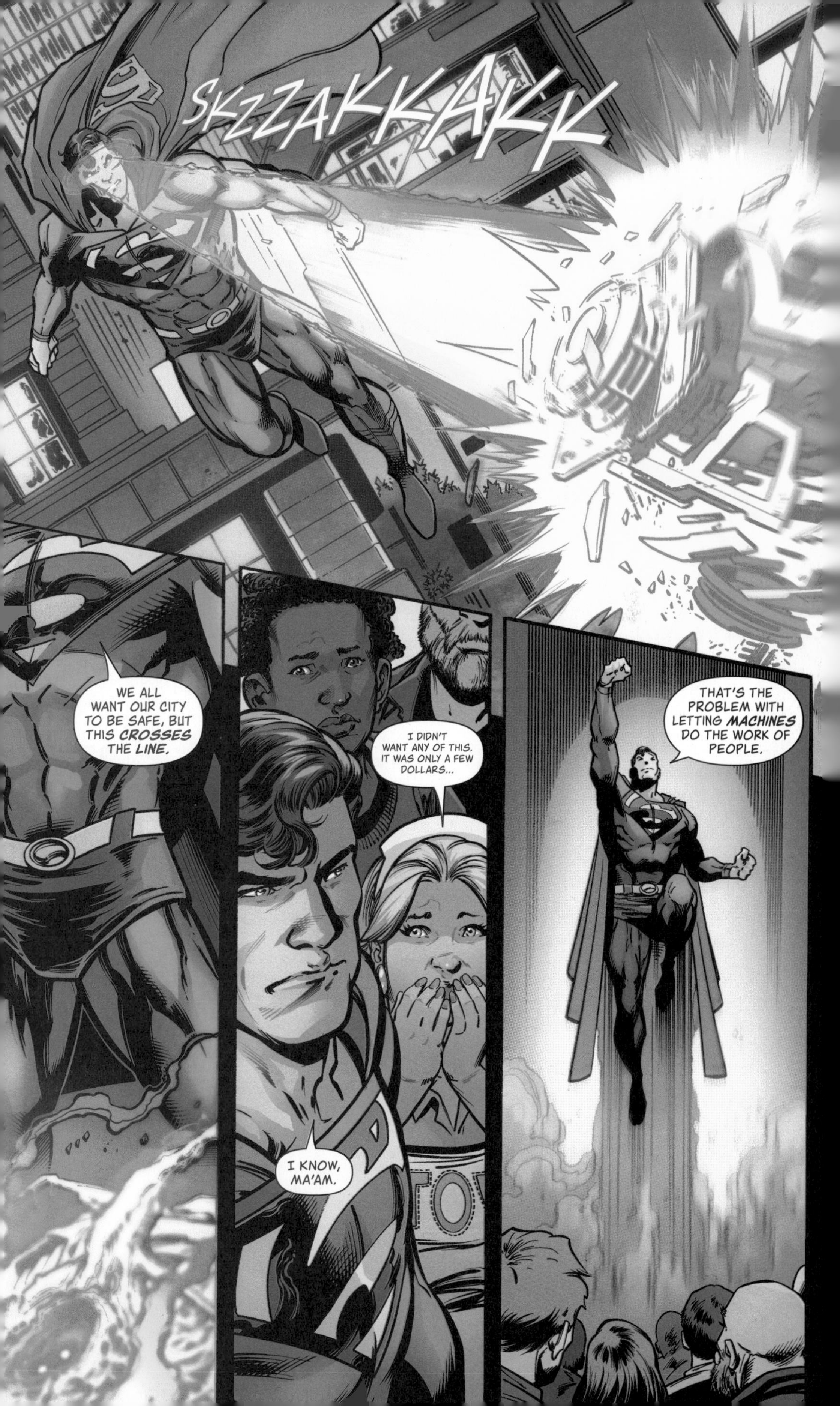
SKZZAKKKAKK
WE ALL WANT OUR CITY TO BE SAFE, BUT THIS CROSSES THE LINE.
I DIDN'T WANT ANY OF THIS. IT WAS ONLY A FEW DOLLARS...
I KNOW, MA'AM.
THAT'S THE PROBLEM WITH LETTING MACHINES DO THE WORK OF PEOPLE.

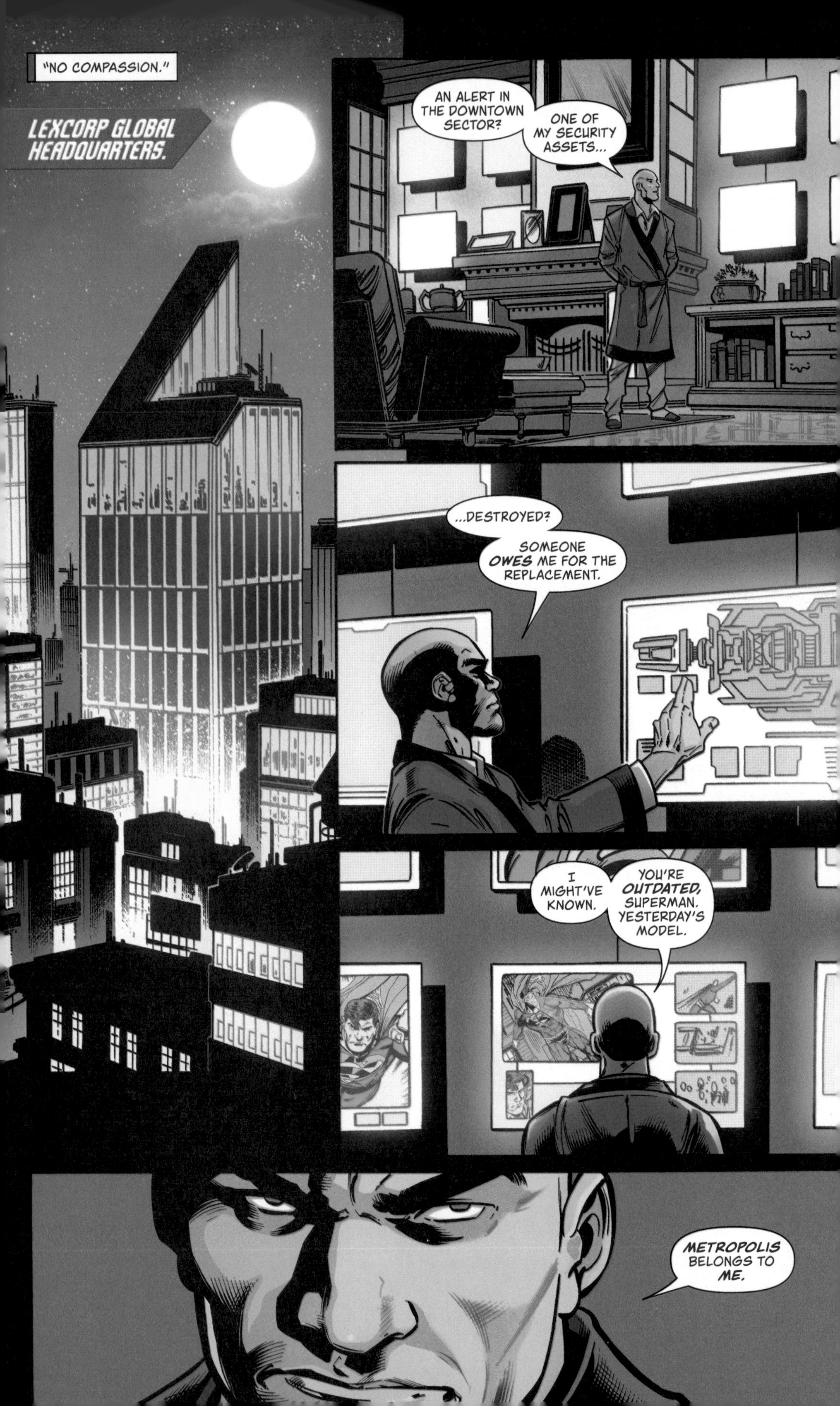
"NO COMPASSION."
LEXCORP GLOBAL HEADQUARTERS.
AN ALERT IN THE DOWNTOWN SECTOR?
ONE OF MY SECURITY ASSETS...
...DESTROYED?
SOMEONE OWES ME FOR THE REPLACEMENT.
I MIGHT'VE KNOWN.
YOU'RE OUTDATED, SUPERMAN. YESTERDAY'S MODEL.
METROPOLIS BELONGS TO ME.

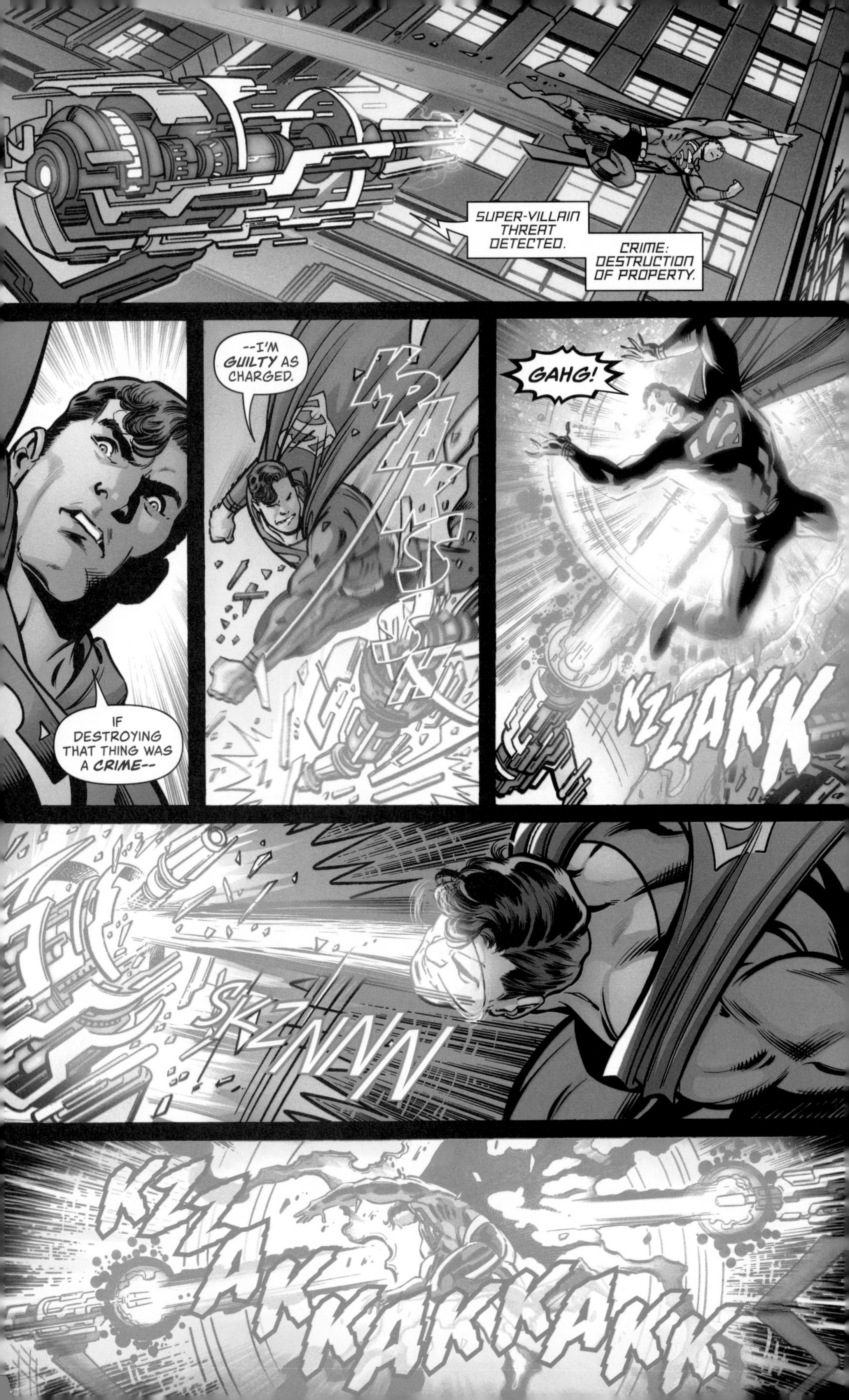

SUPER-VILLAIN THREAT DETECTED.
CRIME: DESTRUCTION OF PROPERTY.
IF DESTROYING THAT THING WAS A CRIME--
--I'M GUILTY AS CHARGED.
GAHG!
KZZAKK
SKZNNN

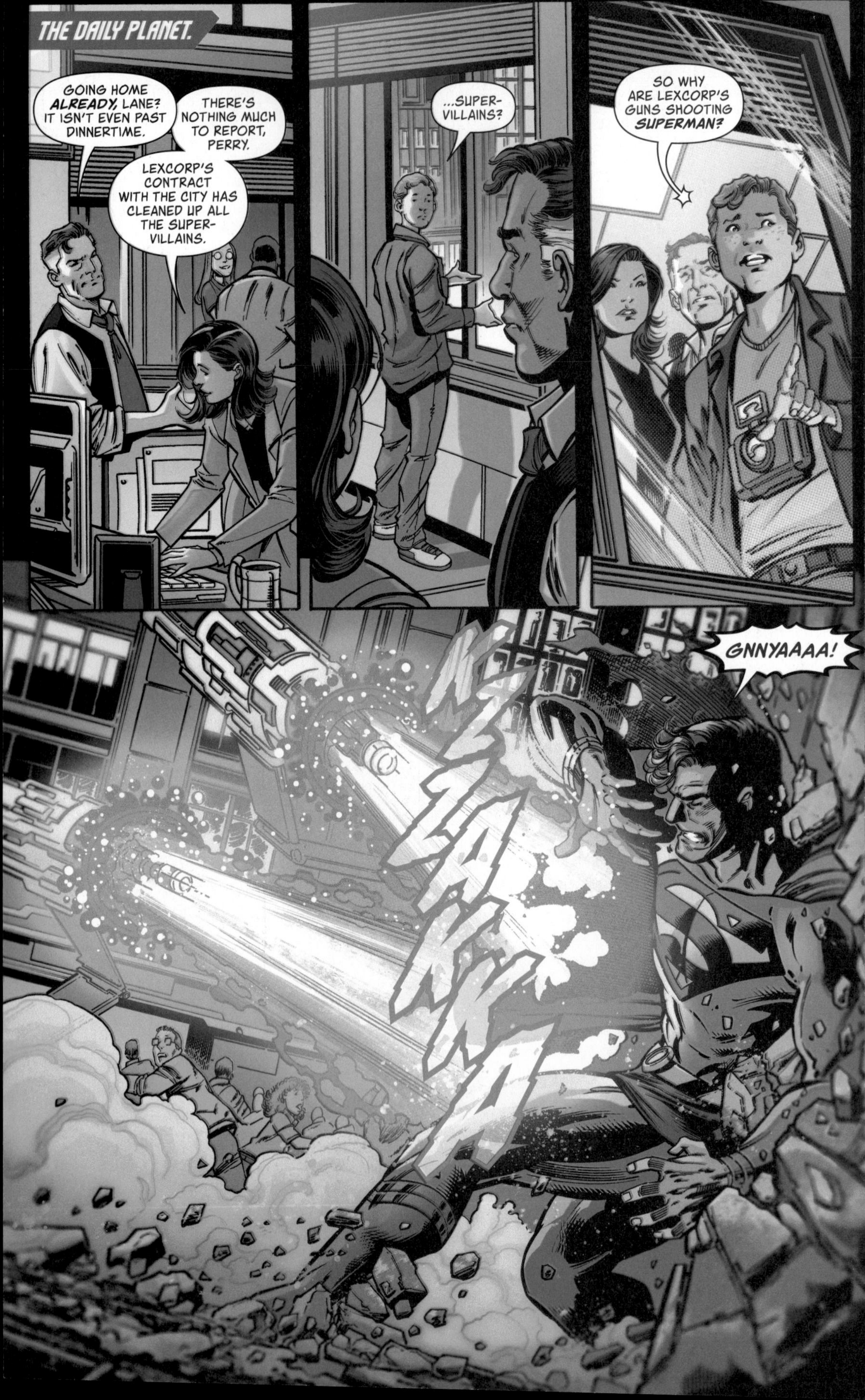

THE DAILY PLANET.
GOING HOME ALREADY, LANE? IT ISN'T EVEN PAST DINNERTIME.
THERE'S NOTHING MUCH TO REPORT, PERRY.
LEXCORP'S CONTRACT WITH THE CITY HAS CLEANED UP ALL THE SUPER-VILLAINS.
...SUPER-VILLAINS?
SO WHY ARE LEXCORP'S GUNS SHOOTING SUPERMAN?
GNNYAAAA!

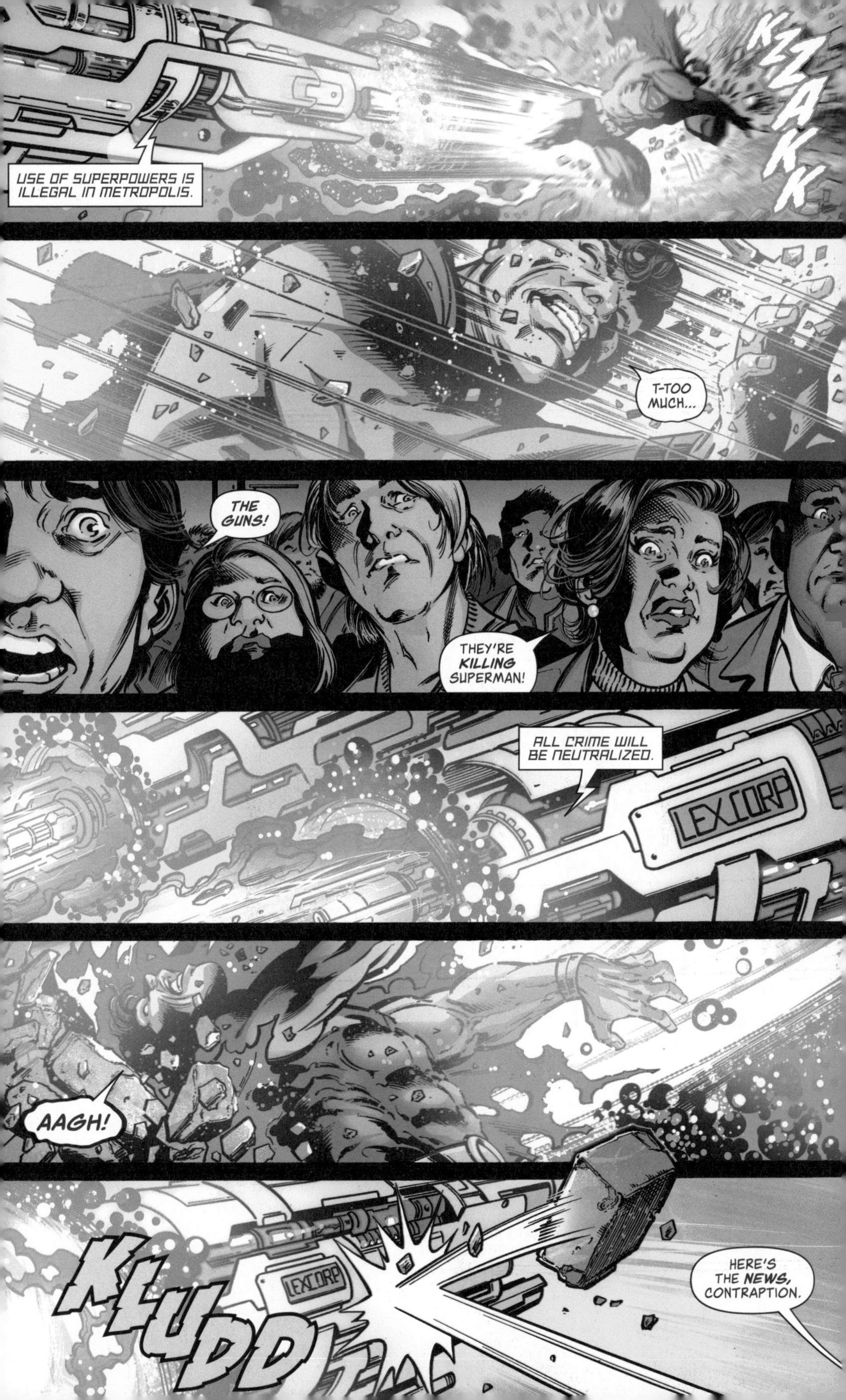
KZZAKK
USE OF SUPERPOWERS IS ILLEGAL IN METROPOLIS.
T-TOO MUCH...
THE GUNS!
THEY'RE KILLING SUPERMAN!
ALL CRIME WILL BE NEUTRALIZED.
LEXCORP
AAGH!
KLUDD
LEXCORP
HERE'S THE NEWS, CONTRAPTION.

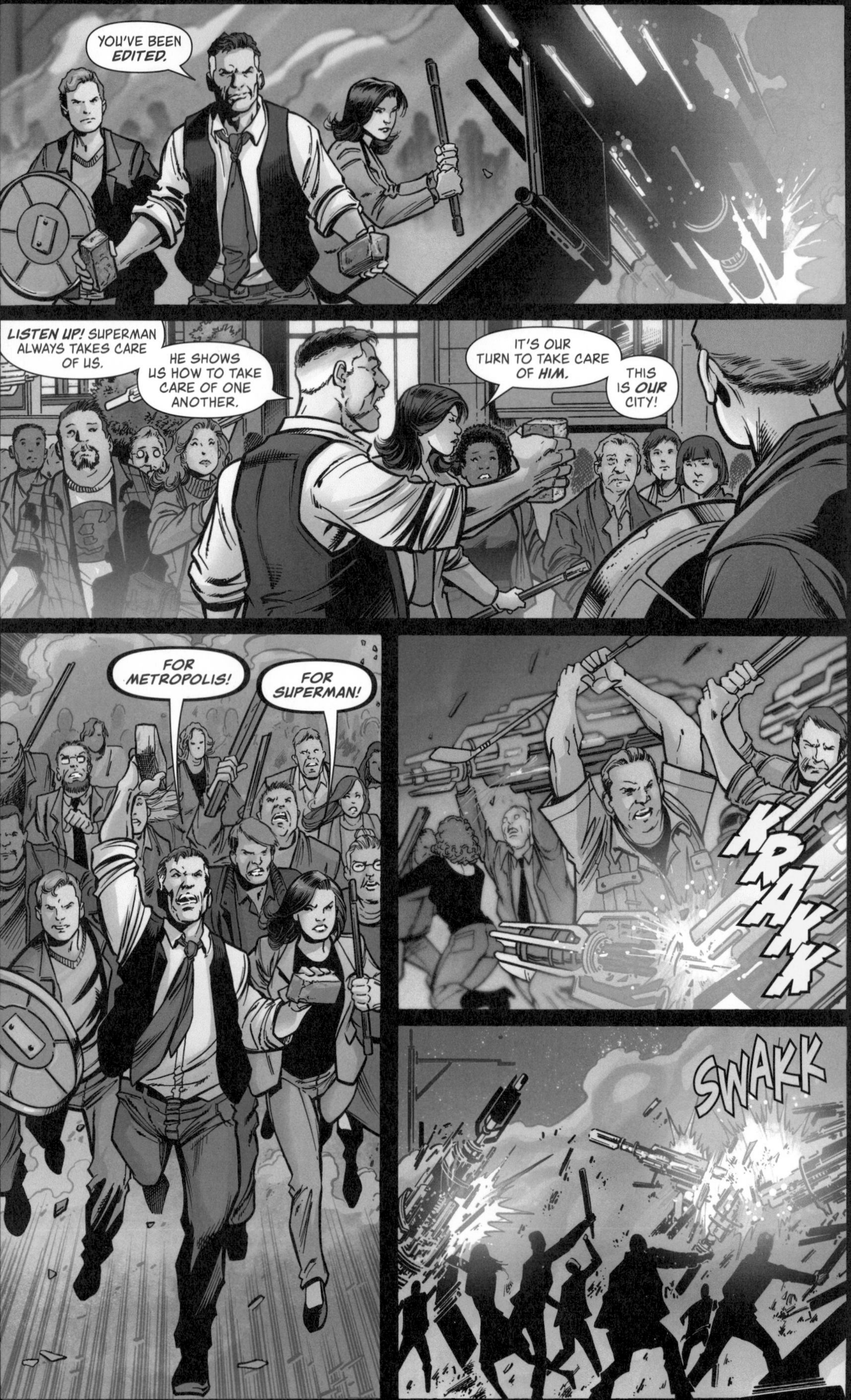
YOU'VE BEEN EDITED.
LISTEN UP! SUPERMAN ALWAYS TAKES CARE OF US.
HE SHOWS US HOW TO TAKE CARE OF ONE ANOTHER.
IT'S OUR TURN TO TAKE CARE OF HIM.
THIS IS OUR CITY!
FOR METROPOLIS!
FOR SUPERMAN!
KRAKKK
SWAKK

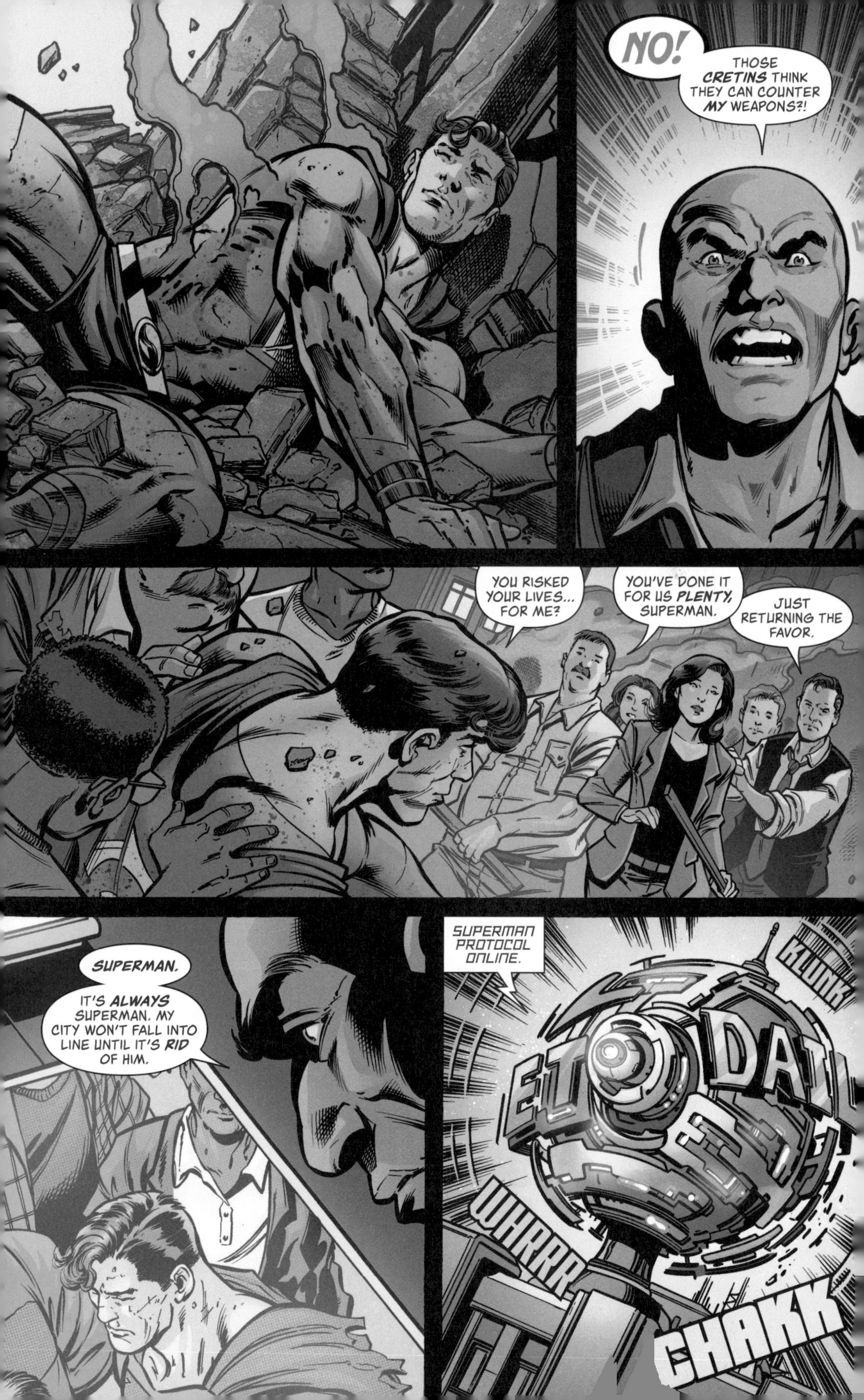
NO!
THOSE CRETINS THINK THEY CAN COUNTER MY WEAPONS?!
YOU RISKED YOUR LIVES... FOR ME?
YOU'VE DONE IT FOR US PLENTY, SUPERMAN.
JUST RETURNING THE FAVOR.
SUPERMAN.
IT'S ALWAYS SUPERMAN. MY CITY WON'T FALL INTO LINE UNTIL IT'S RID OF HIM.
SUPERMAN PROTOCOL ONLINE.
KLUNK
WHRRR
CHAKK

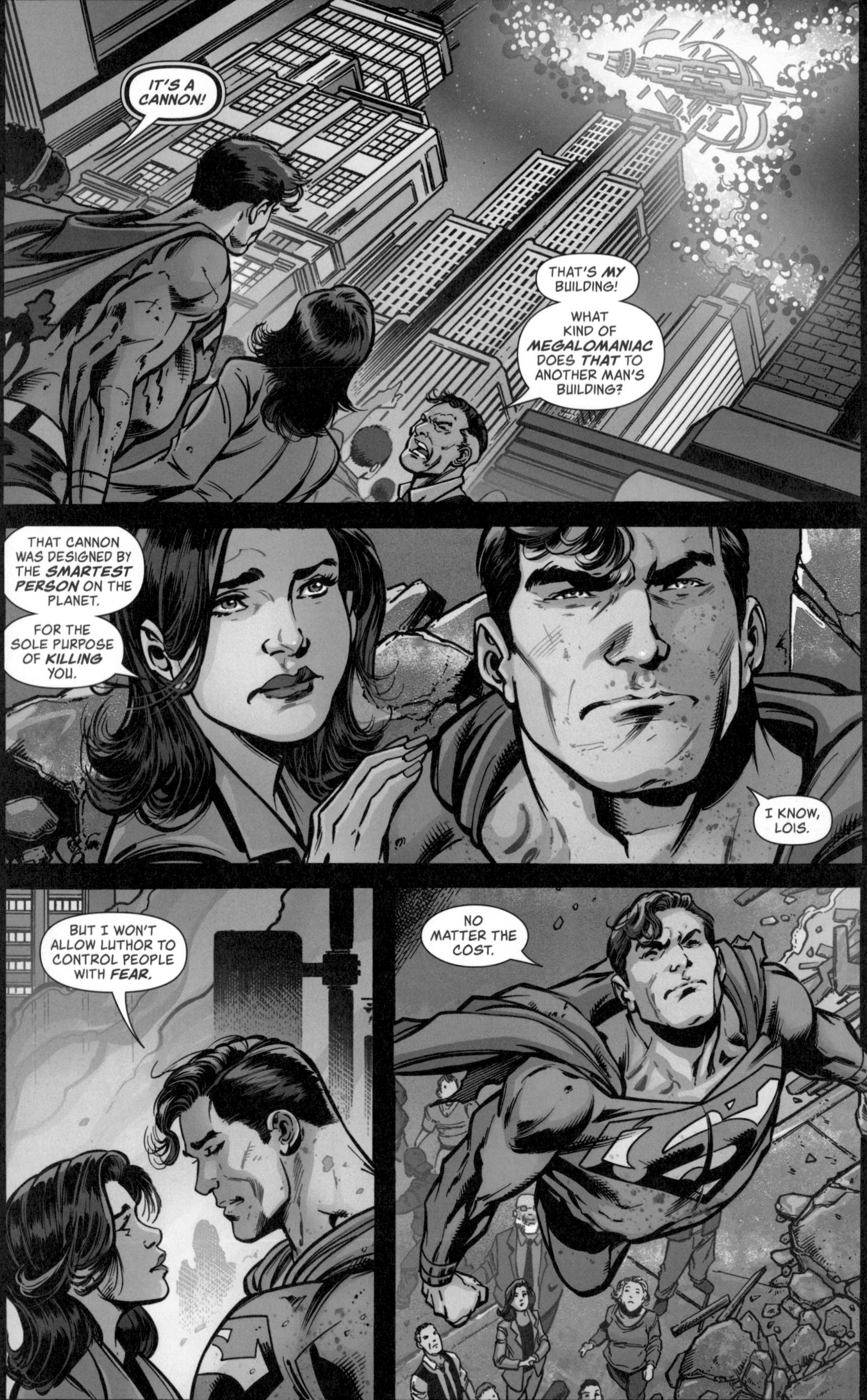
IT'S A CANNON!
THAT'S MY BUILDING!
WHAT KIND OF MEGALOMANIAC DOES THAT TO ANOTHER MAN'S BUILDING?
THAT CANNON WAS DESIGNED BY THE SMARTEST PERSON ON THE PLANET.
FOR THE SOLE PURPOSE OF KILLING YOU.
I KNOW, LOIS.
BUT I WON'T ALLOW LUTHOR TO CONTROL PEOPLE WITH FEAR.
NO MATTER THE COST.

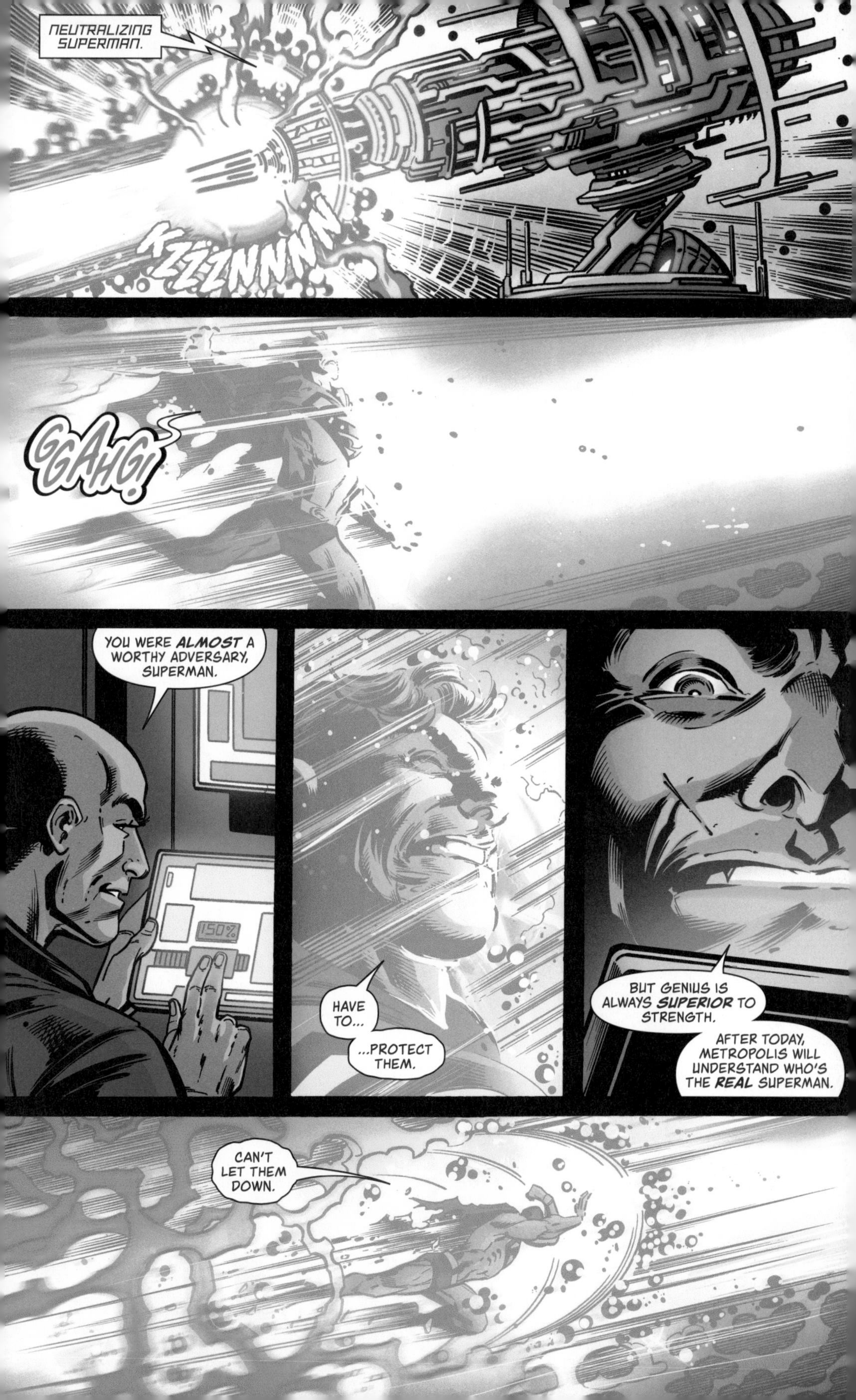
NEUTRALIZING SUPERMAN.
KZZZNNNNN
GGAHG!
YOU WERE ALMOST A WORTHY ADVERSARY, SUPERMAN.
150%
HAVE TO...
...PROTECT THEM.
BUT GENIUS IS ALWAYS SUPERIOR TO STRENGTH.
AFTER TODAY, METROPOLIS WILL UNDERSTAND WHO'S THE REAL SUPERMAN.
CAN'T LET THEM DOWN.

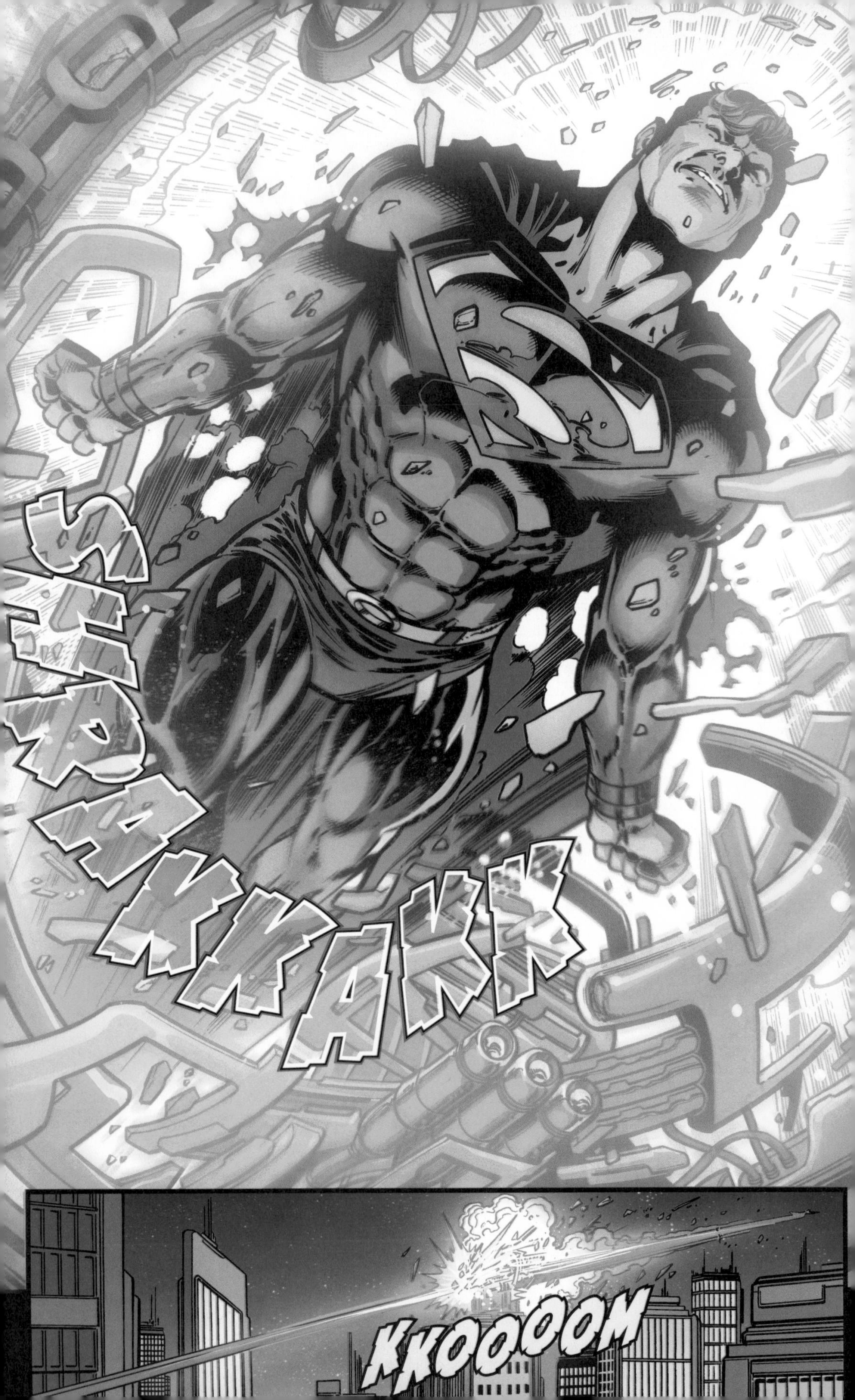
SHRAKKAKK
KKOOOOM

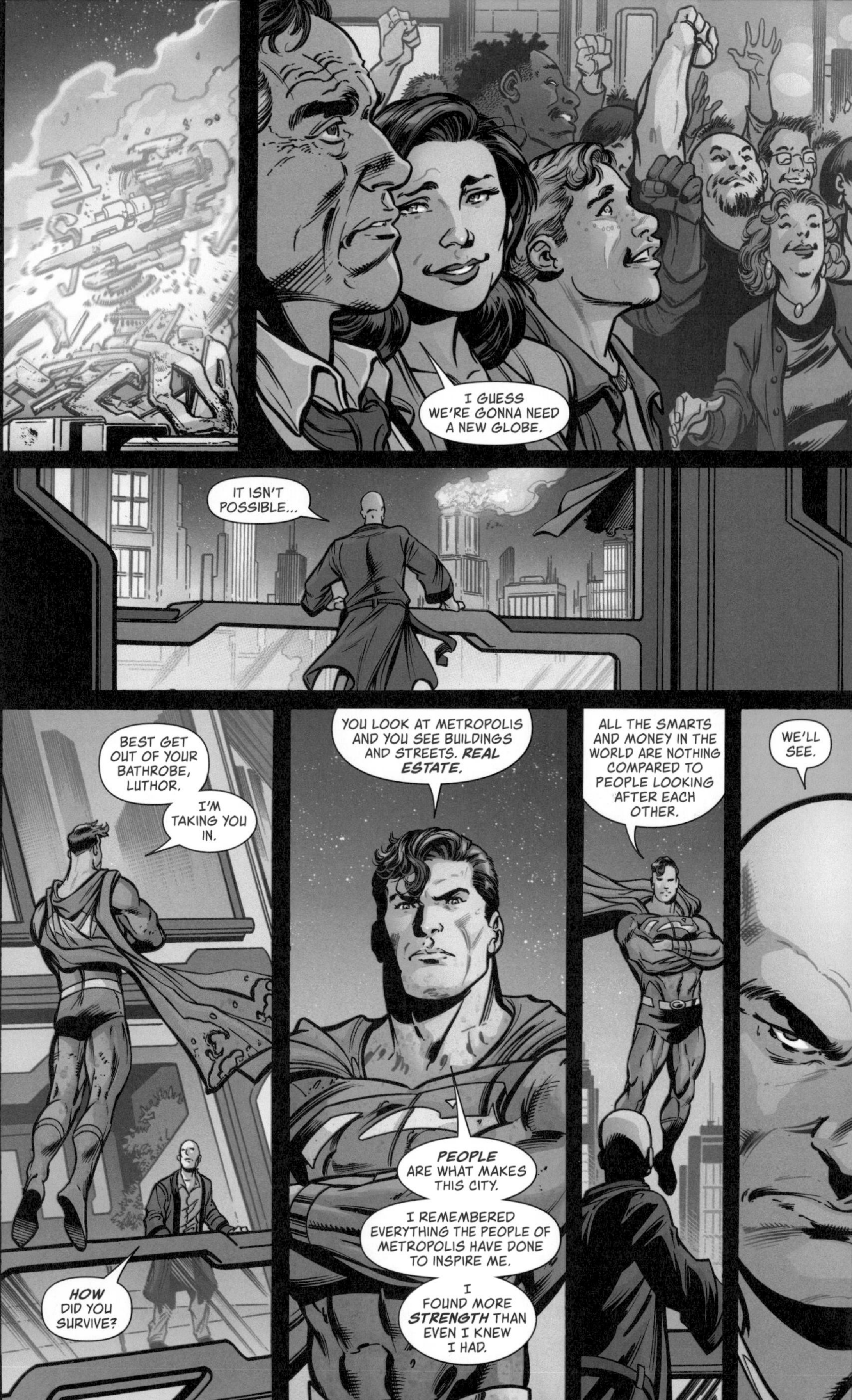
I GUESS WE'RE GONNA NEED A NEW GLOBE.
IT ISN'T POSSIBLE...
BEST GET OUT OF YOUR BATHROBE, LUTHOR.
I'M TAKING YOU IN.
HOW DID YOU SURVIVE?
YOU LOOK AT METROPOLIS AND YOU SEE BUILDINGS AND STREETS. REAL ESTATE.
PEOPLE ARE WHAT MAKES THIS CITY.
I REMEMBERED EVERYTHING THE PEOPLE OF METROPOLIS HAVE DONE TO INSPIRE ME.
I FOUND MORE STRENGTH THAN EVEN I KNEW I HAD.
ALL THE SMARTS AND MONEY IN THE WORLD ARE NOTHING COMPARED TO PEOPLE LOOKING AFTER EACH OTHER.
WE'LL SEE.

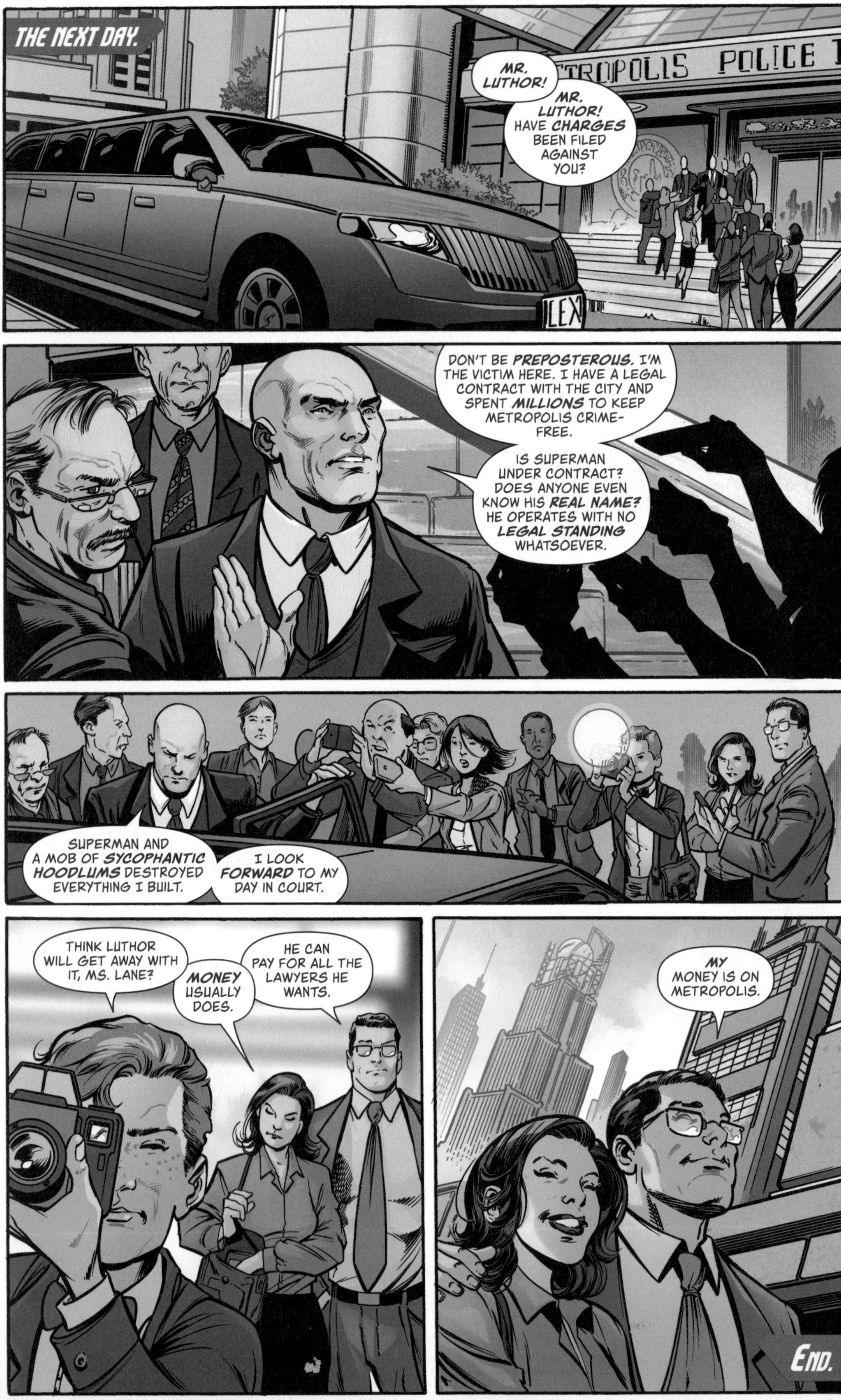
THE NEXT DAY.
TROPOLIS POLICE
MR. LUTHOR!
MR. LUTHOR! HAVE CHARGES BEEN FILED AGAINST YOU?
LEX
DON'T BE PREPOSTEROUS. I'M THE VICTIM HERE. I HAVE A LEGAL CONTRACT WITH THE CITY AND SPENT MILLIONS TO KEEP METROPOLIS CRIME-FREE.
IS SUPERMAN UNDER CONTRACT? DOES ANYONE EVEN KNOW HIS REAL NAME? HE OPERATES WITH NO LEGAL STANDING WHATSOEVER.
SUPERMAN AND A MOB OF SYCOPHANTIC HOODLUMS DESTROYED EVERYTHING I BUILT.
I LOOK FORWARD TO MY DAY IN COURT.
THINK LUTHOR WILL GET AWAY WITH IT, MS. LANE?
MONEY USUALLY DOES.
HE CAN PAY FOR ALL THE LAWYERS HE WANTS.
MY MONEY IS ON METROPOLIS.
END.

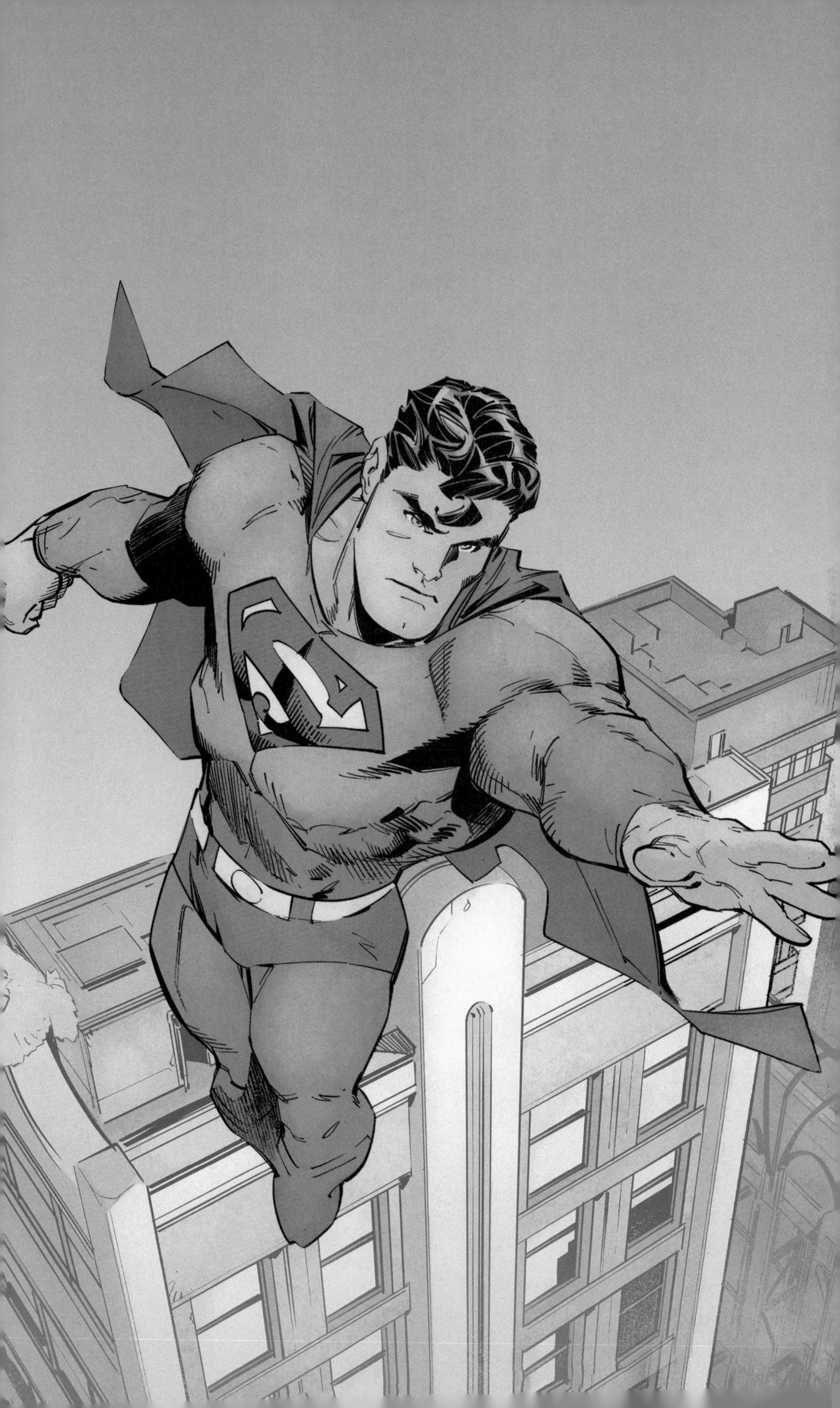

COVER ART BY
GLEB MELNIKOV AND **JORDIE BELLAIRE**

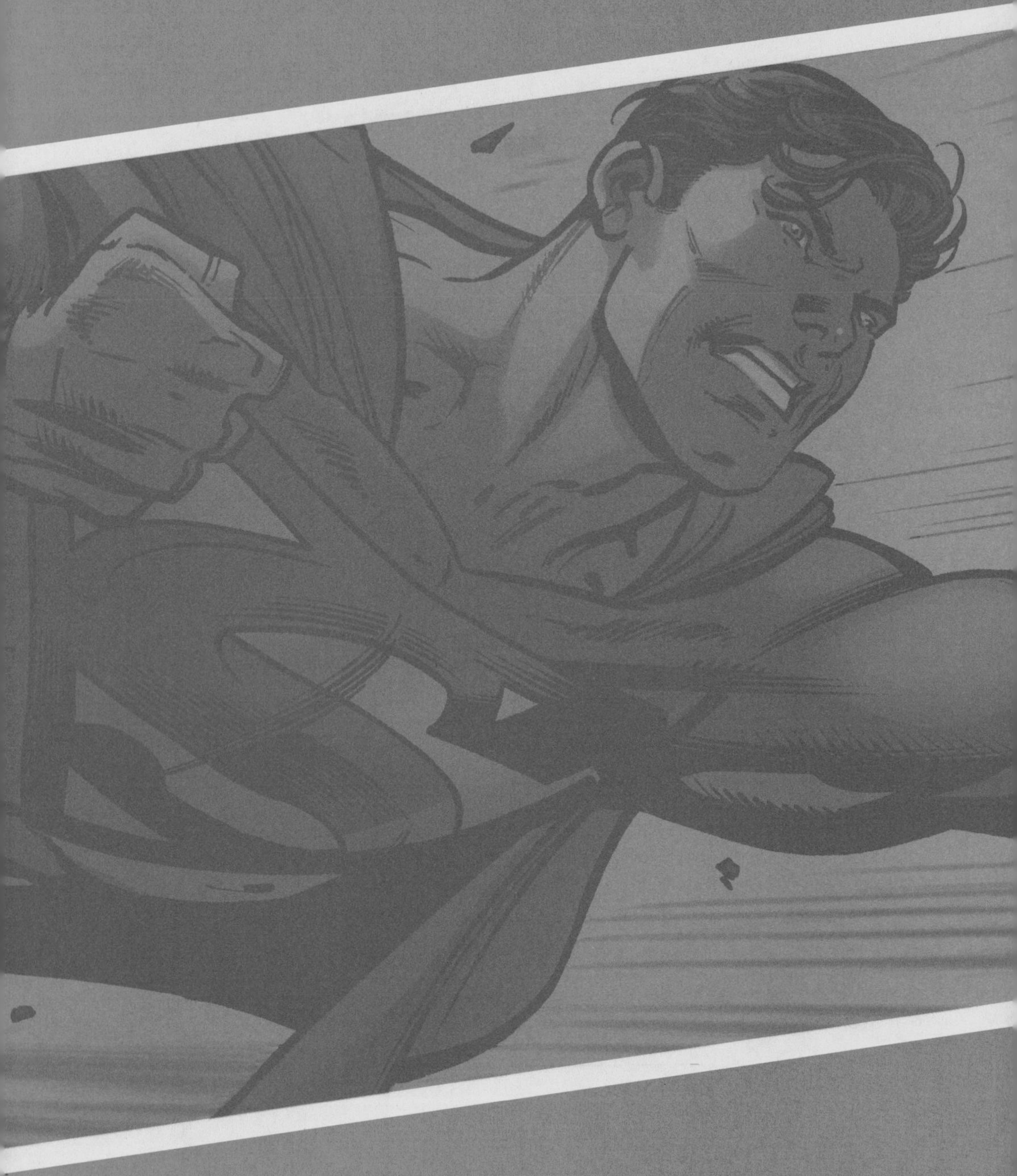

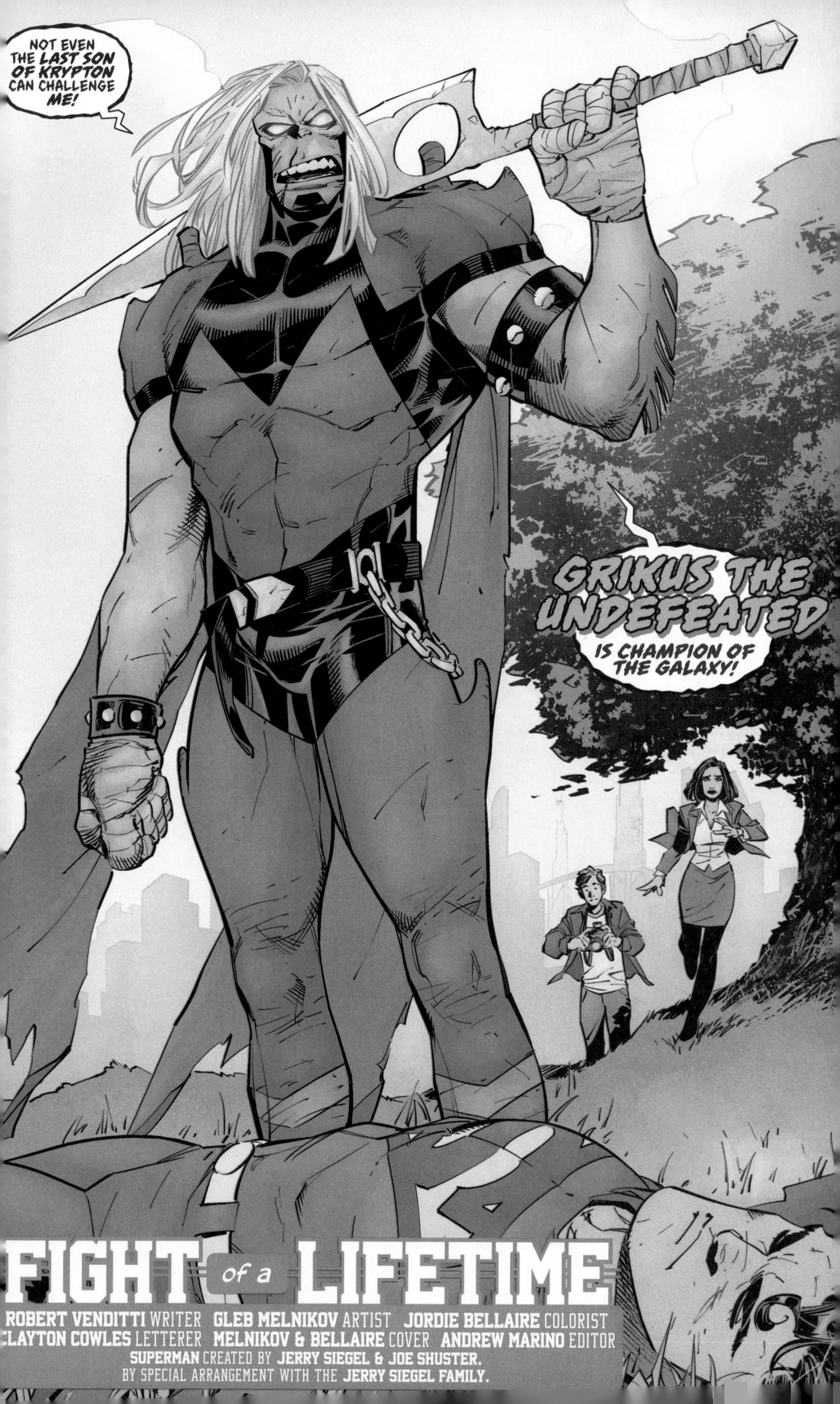
NOT EVEN THE LAST SON OF KRYPTON CAN CHALLENGE ME!
GRIKUS THE UNDEFEATED IS CHAMPION OF THE GALAXY!
FIGHT of a LIFETIME
ROBERT VENDITTI WRITER GLEB MELNIKOV ARTIST JORDIE BELLAIRE COLORIST
CLAYTON COWLES LETTERER MELNIKOV & BELLAIRE COVER ANDREW MARINO EDITOR
SUPERMAN CREATED BY JERRY SIEGEL & JOE SHUSTER.
BY SPECIAL ARRANGEMENT WITH THE JERRY SIEGEL FAMILY.

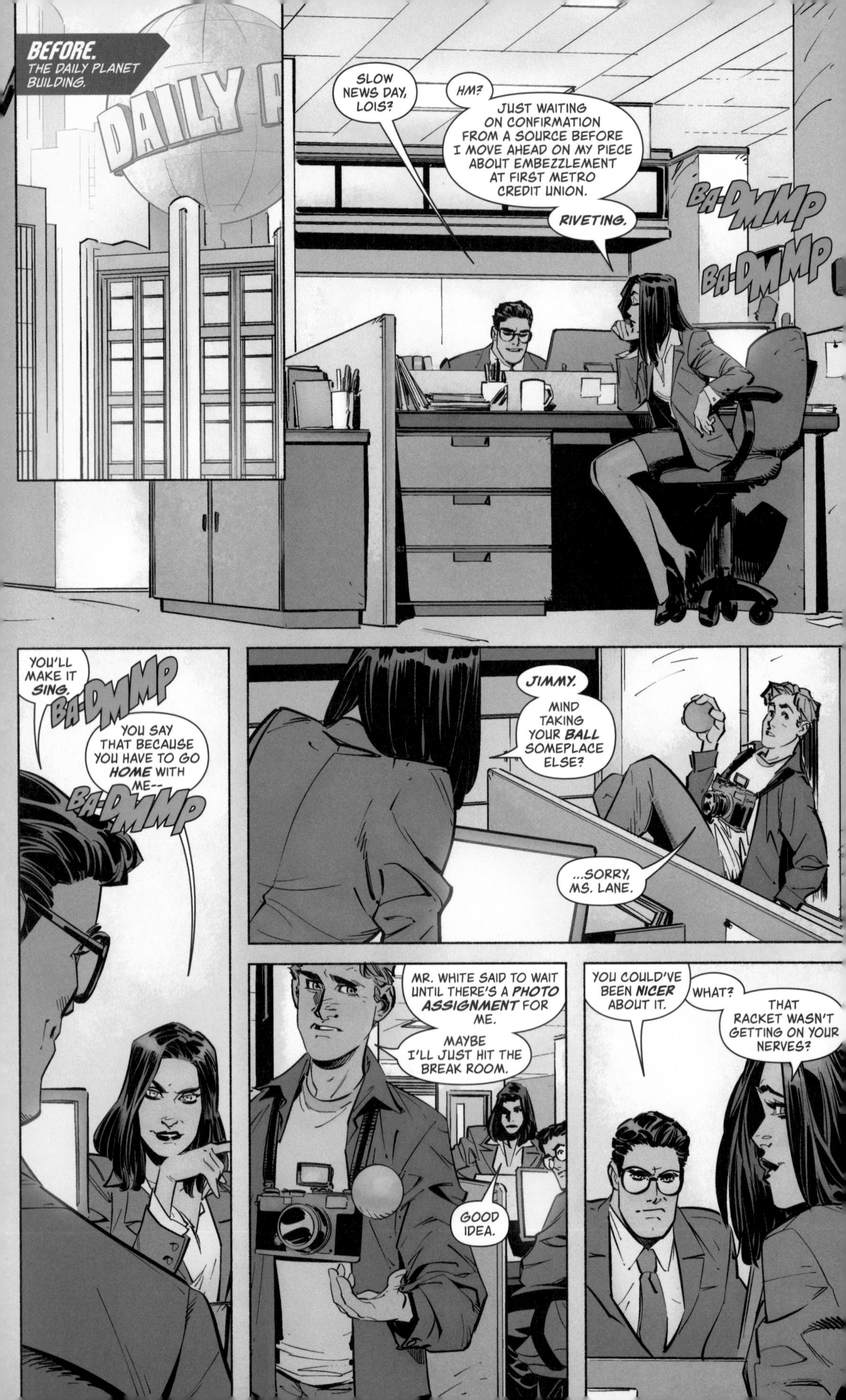
BEFORE.
THE DAILY PLANET BUILDING.
DAILY P
SLOW NEWS DAY, LOIS?
HM?
JUST WAITING ON CONFIRMATION FROM A SOURCE BEFORE I MOVE AHEAD ON MY PIECE ABOUT EMBEZZLEMENT AT FIRST METRO CREDIT UNION.
RIVETING.
BA-DMMP
BA-DMMP
YOU'LL MAKE IT SING.
BA-DMMP
YOU SAY THAT BECAUSE YOU HAVE TO GO HOME WITH ME--
BA-DMMP
JIMMY.
MIND TAKING YOUR BALL SOMEPLACE ELSE?
...SORRY, MS. LANE.
MR. WHITE SAID TO WAIT UNTIL THERE'S A PHOTO ASSIGNMENT FOR ME.
MAYBE I'LL JUST HIT THE BREAK ROOM.
GOOD IDEA.
YOU COULD'VE BEEN NICER ABOUT IT.
WHAT?
THAT RACKET WASN'T GETTING ON YOUR NERVES?

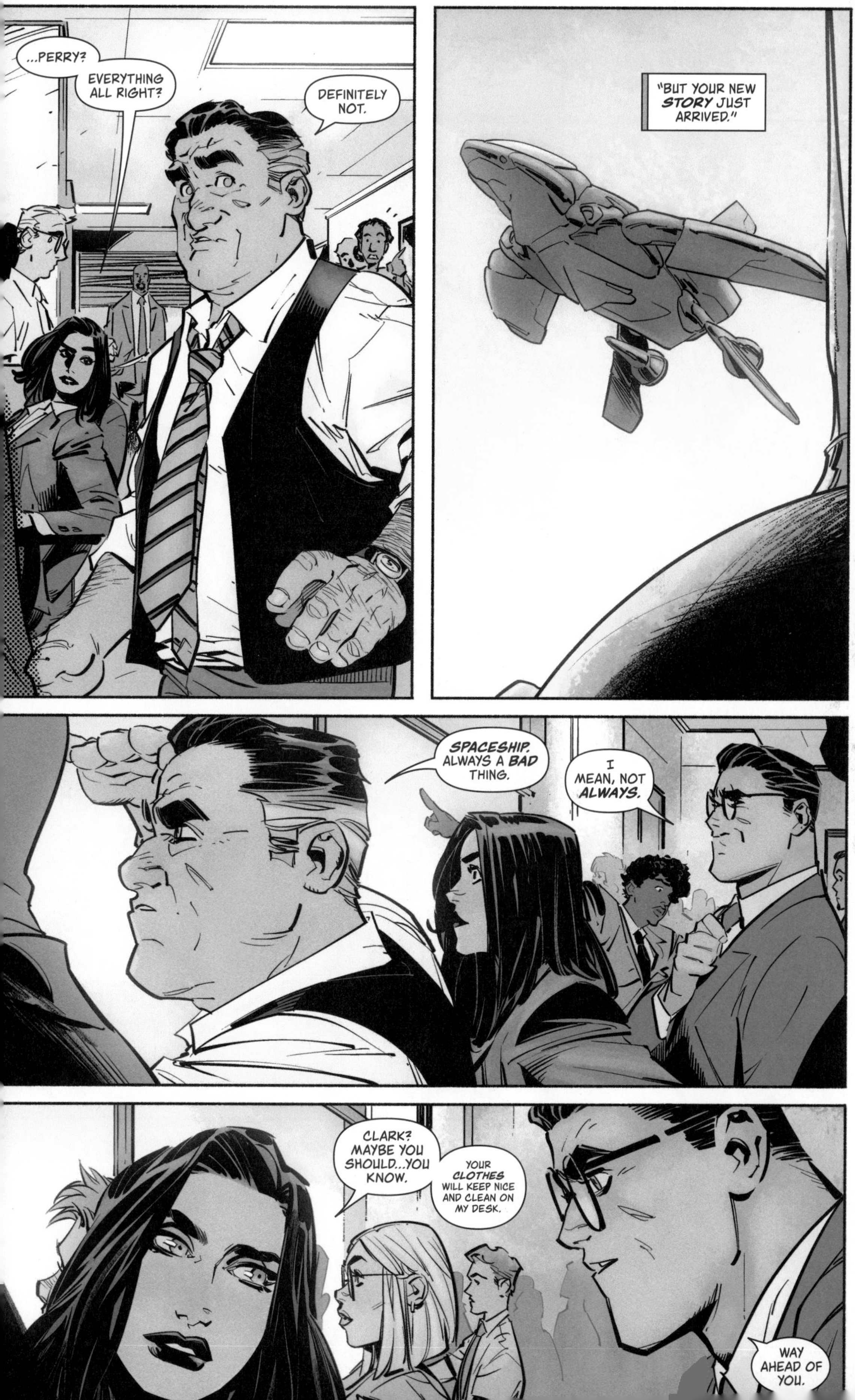
...PERRY?
EVERYTHING ALL RIGHT?
DEFINITELY NOT.
"BUT YOUR NEW STORY JUST ARRIVED."
SPACESHIP. ALWAYS A BAD THING.
I MEAN, NOT ALWAYS.
CLARK? MAYBE YOU SHOULD...YOU KNOW.
YOUR CLOTHES WILL KEEP NICE AND CLEAN ON MY DESK.
WAY AHEAD OF YOU.

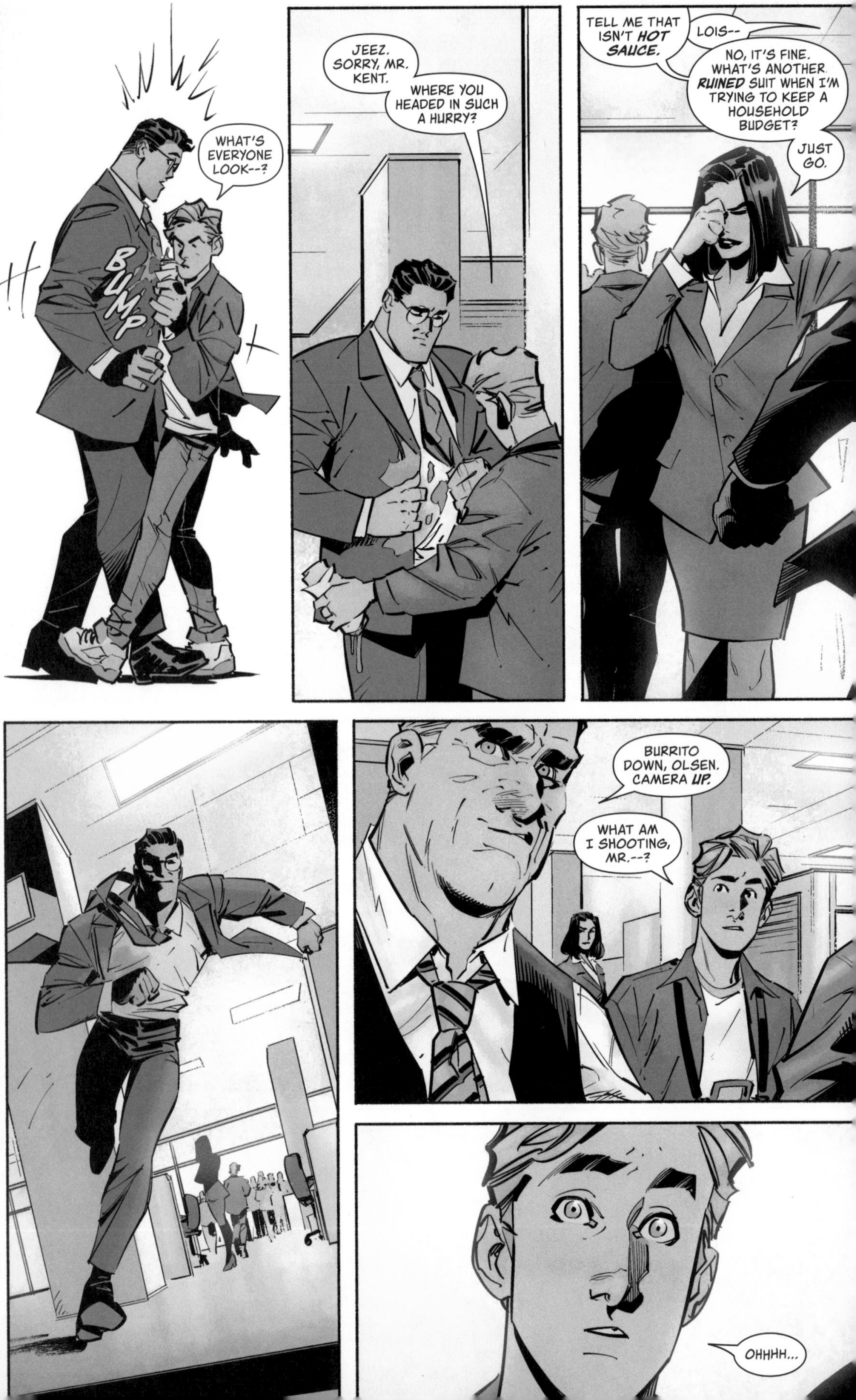
WHAT'S EVERYONE LOOK--?
BUMP
JEEZ. SORRY, MR. KENT.
WHERE YOU HEADED IN SUCH A HURRY?
TELL ME THAT ISN'T HOT SAUCE.
LOIS--
NO, IT'S FINE. WHAT'S ANOTHER RUINED SUIT WHEN I'M TRYING TO KEEP A HOUSEHOLD BUDGET?
JUST GO.
BURRITO DOWN, OLSEN. CAMERA UP.
WHAT AM I SHOOTING, MR.--?
OHHHH...

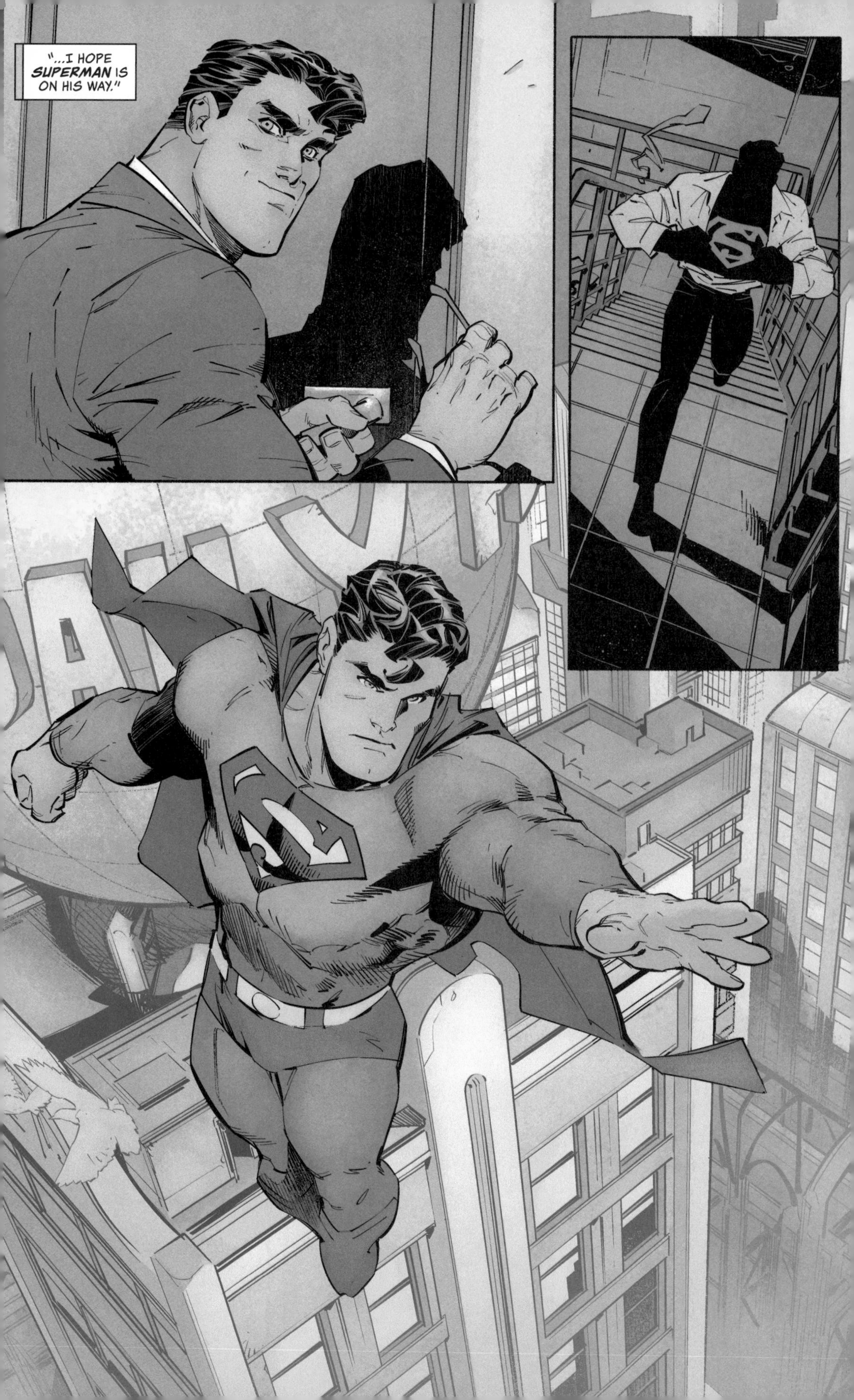
"...I HOPE SUPERMAN IS ON HIS WAY."

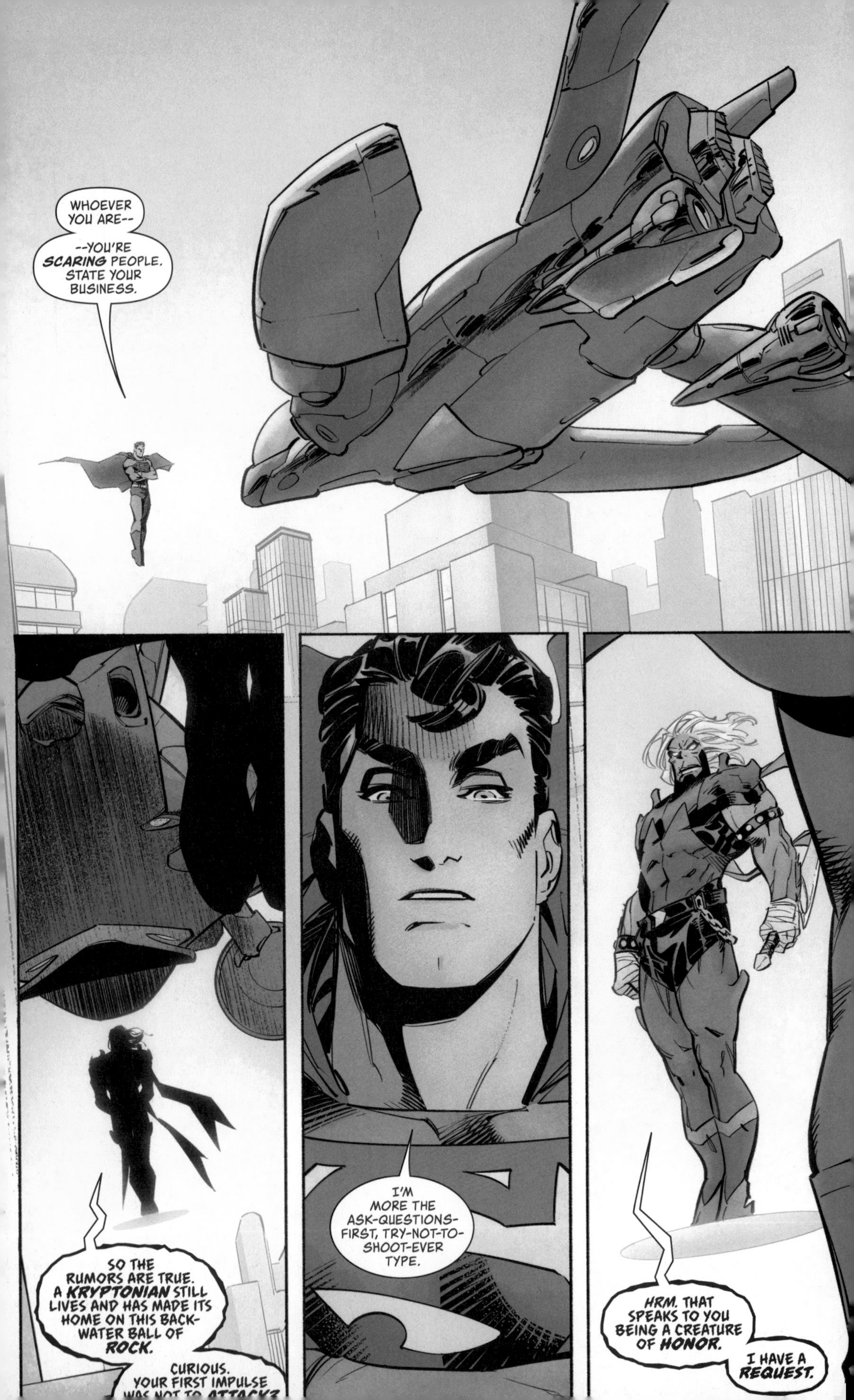
WHOEVER YOU ARE--
--YOU'RE *SCARING* PEOPLE. STATE YOUR BUSINESS.
SO THE RUMORS ARE TRUE. A *KRYPTONIAN* STILL LIVES AND HAS MADE ITS HOME ON THIS BACK-WATER BALL OF *ROCK.*
CURIOUS. YOUR FIRST IMPULSE
I'M MORE THE ASK-QUESTIONS-FIRST, TRY-NOT-TO-SHOOT-EVER TYPE.
HRM. THAT SPEAKS TO YOU BEING A CREATURE OF *HONOR.*
I HAVE A *REQUEST.*

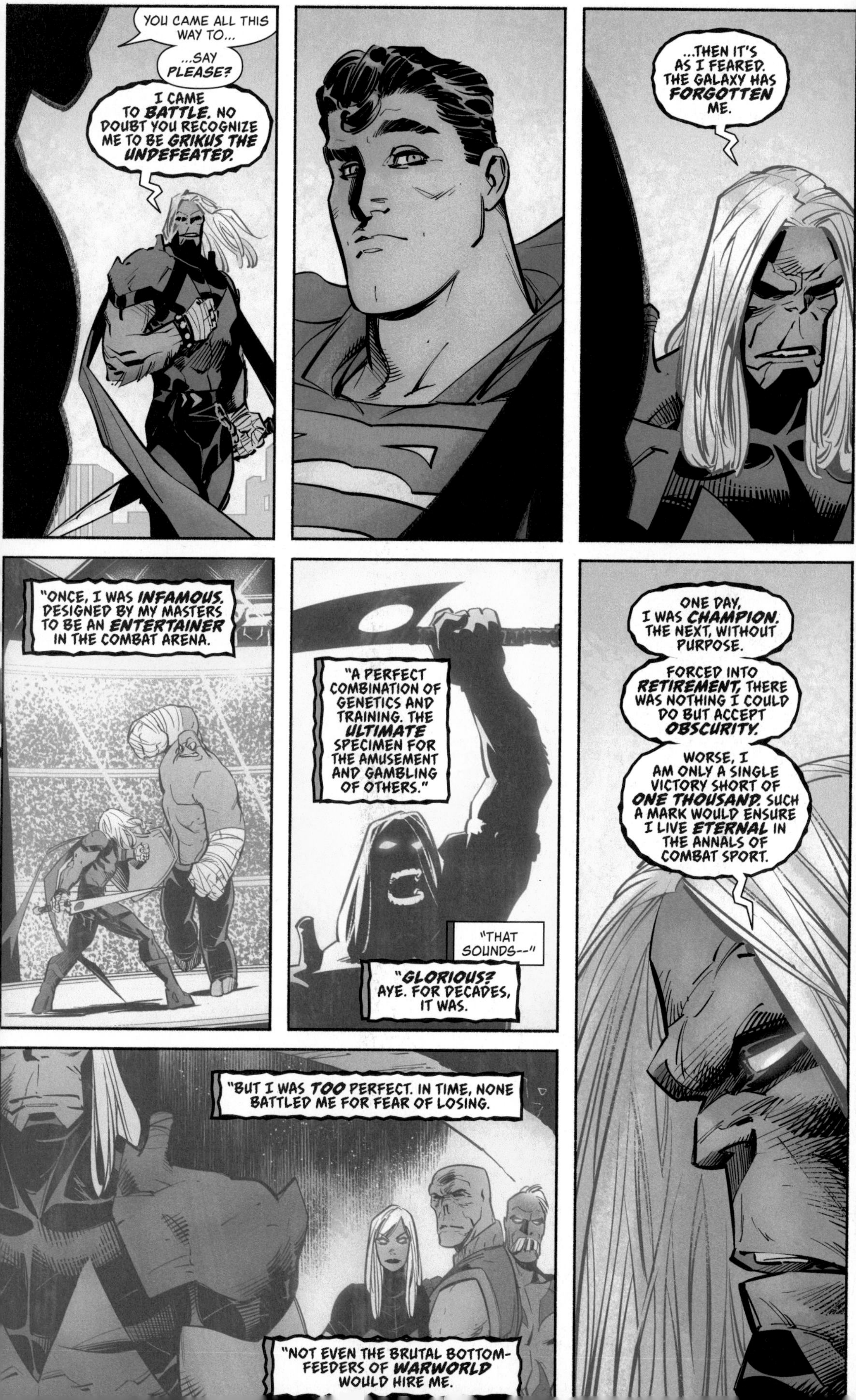

YOU CAME ALL THIS WAY TO...
...SAY PLEASE?
I CAME TO BATTLE. NO DOUBT YOU RECOGNIZE ME TO BE GRIKUS THE UNDEFEATED.
...THEN IT'S AS I FEARED. THE GALAXY HAS FORGOTTEN ME.
"ONCE, I WAS INFAMOUS. DESIGNED BY MY MASTERS TO BE AN ENTERTAINER IN THE COMBAT ARENA.
"A PERFECT COMBINATION OF GENETICS AND TRAINING. THE ULTIMATE SPECIMEN FOR THE AMUSEMENT AND GAMBLING OF OTHERS."
"THAT SOUNDS--"
"GLORIOUS? AYE. FOR DECADES, IT WAS.
"BUT I WAS TOO PERFECT. IN TIME, NONE BATTLED ME FOR FEAR OF LOSING.
"NOT EVEN THE BRUTAL BOTTOM-FEEDERS OF WARWORLD WOULD HIRE ME.
ONE DAY, I WAS CHAMPION. THE NEXT, WITHOUT PURPOSE.
FORCED INTO RETIREMENT, THERE WAS NOTHING I COULD DO BUT ACCEPT OBSCURITY.
WORSE, I AM ONLY A SINGLE VICTORY SHORT OF ONE THOUSAND. SUCH A MARK WOULD ENSURE I LIVE ETERNAL IN THE ANNALS OF COMBAT SPORT.

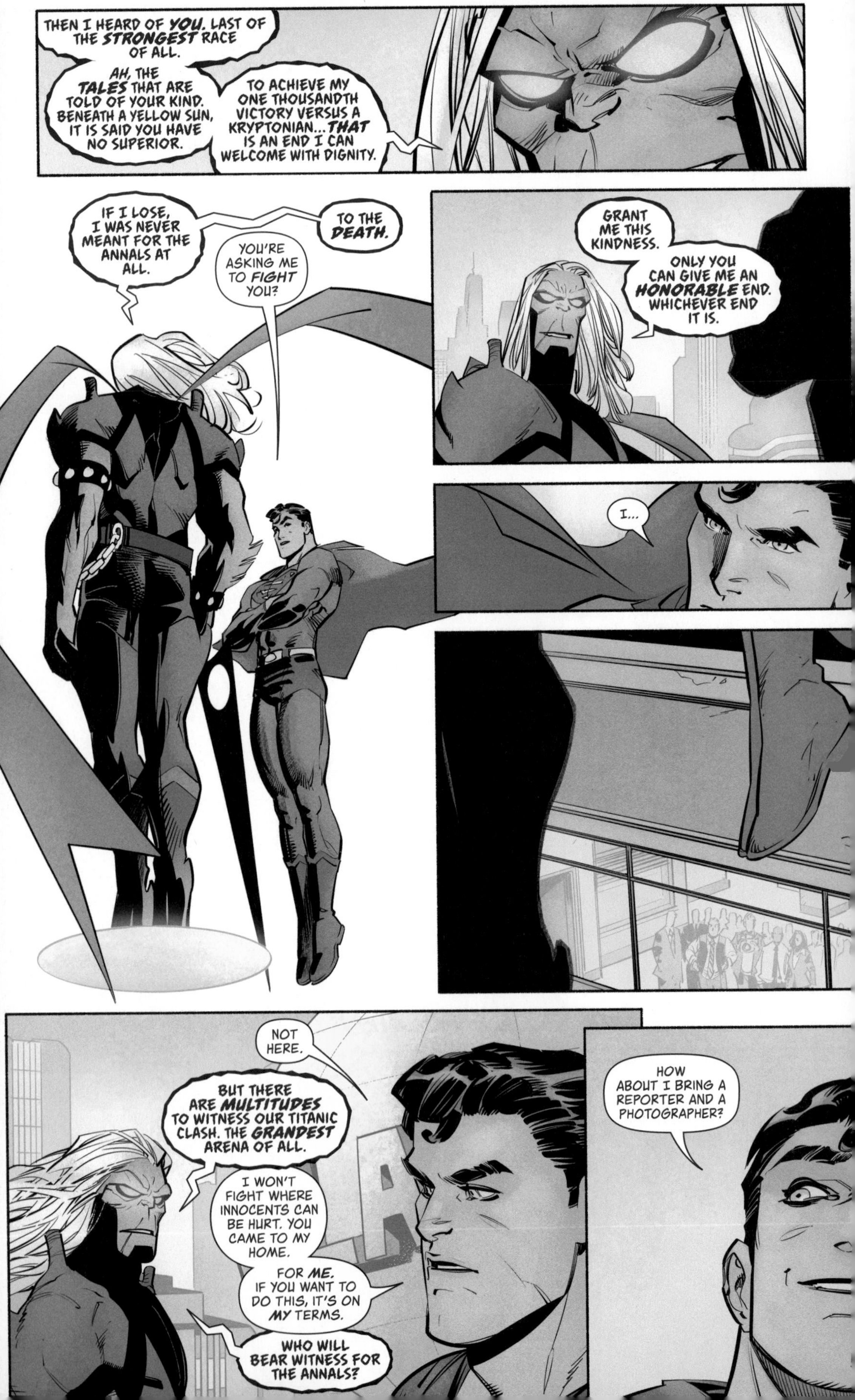
THEN I HEARD OF YOU. LAST OF THE STRONGEST RACE OF ALL.
AH, THE TALES THAT ARE TOLD OF YOUR KIND. BENEATH A YELLOW SUN, IT IS SAID YOU HAVE NO SUPERIOR.
TO ACHIEVE MY ONE THOUSANDTH VICTORY VERSUS A KRYPTONIAN... THAT IS AN END I CAN WELCOME WITH DIGNITY.
IF I LOSE, I WAS NEVER MEANT FOR THE ANNALS AT ALL.
TO THE DEATH.
YOU'RE ASKING ME TO FIGHT YOU?
GRANT ME THIS KINDNESS.
ONLY YOU CAN GIVE ME AN HONORABLE END. WHICHEVER END IT IS.
I...
NOT HERE.
BUT THERE ARE MULTITUDES TO WITNESS OUR TITANIC CLASH. THE GRANDEST ARENA OF ALL.
I WON'T FIGHT WHERE INNOCENTS CAN BE HURT. YOU CAME TO MY HOME.
FOR ME. IF YOU WANT TO DO THIS, IT'S ON MY TERMS.
WHO WILL BEAR WITNESS FOR THE ANNALS?
HOW ABOUT I BRING A REPORTER AND A PHOTOGRAPHER?

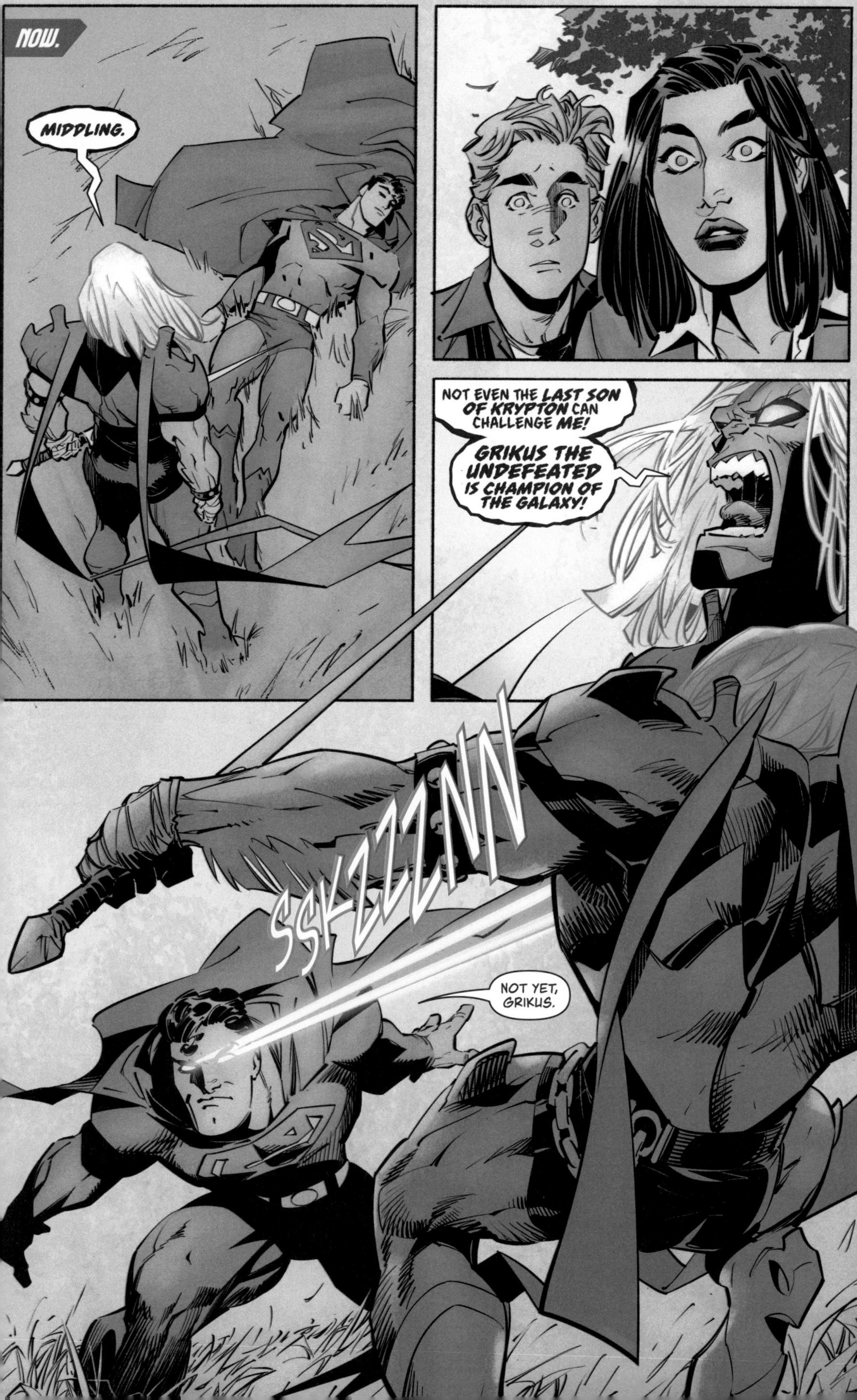
NOW.
MIDDLING.
NOT EVEN THE LAST SON OF KRYPTON CAN CHALLENGE ME!
GRIKUS THE UNDEFEATED IS CHAMPION OF THE GALAXY!
SSKZZZNN
NOT YET, GRIKUS.

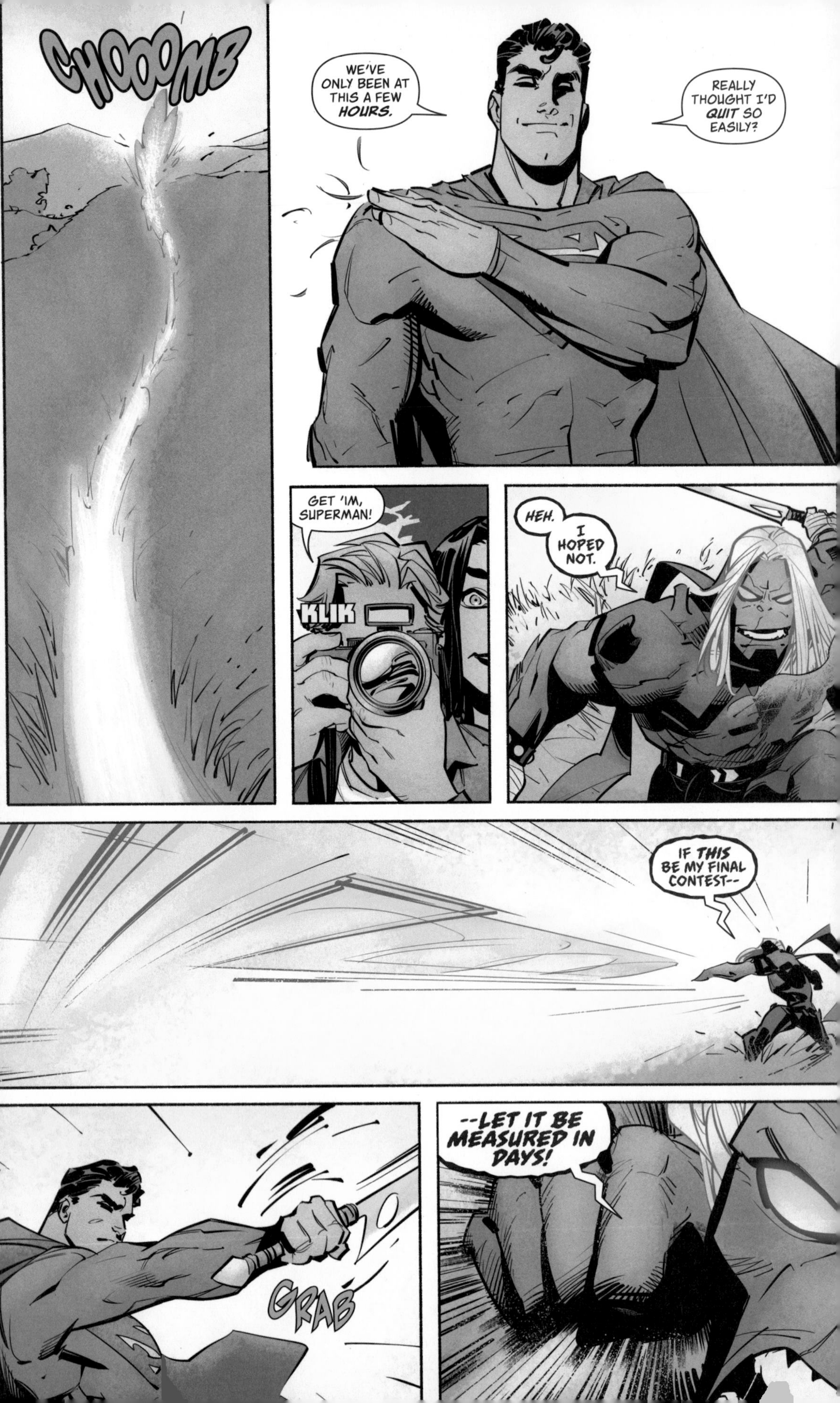
CHOOOMB
WE'VE ONLY BEEN AT THIS A FEW HOURS.
REALLY THOUGHT I'D QUIT SO EASILY?
GET 'IM, SUPERMAN!
KLIK
HEH.
I HOPED NOT.
IF THIS BE MY FINAL CONTEST--
GRAB
--LET IT BE MEASURED IN DAYS!

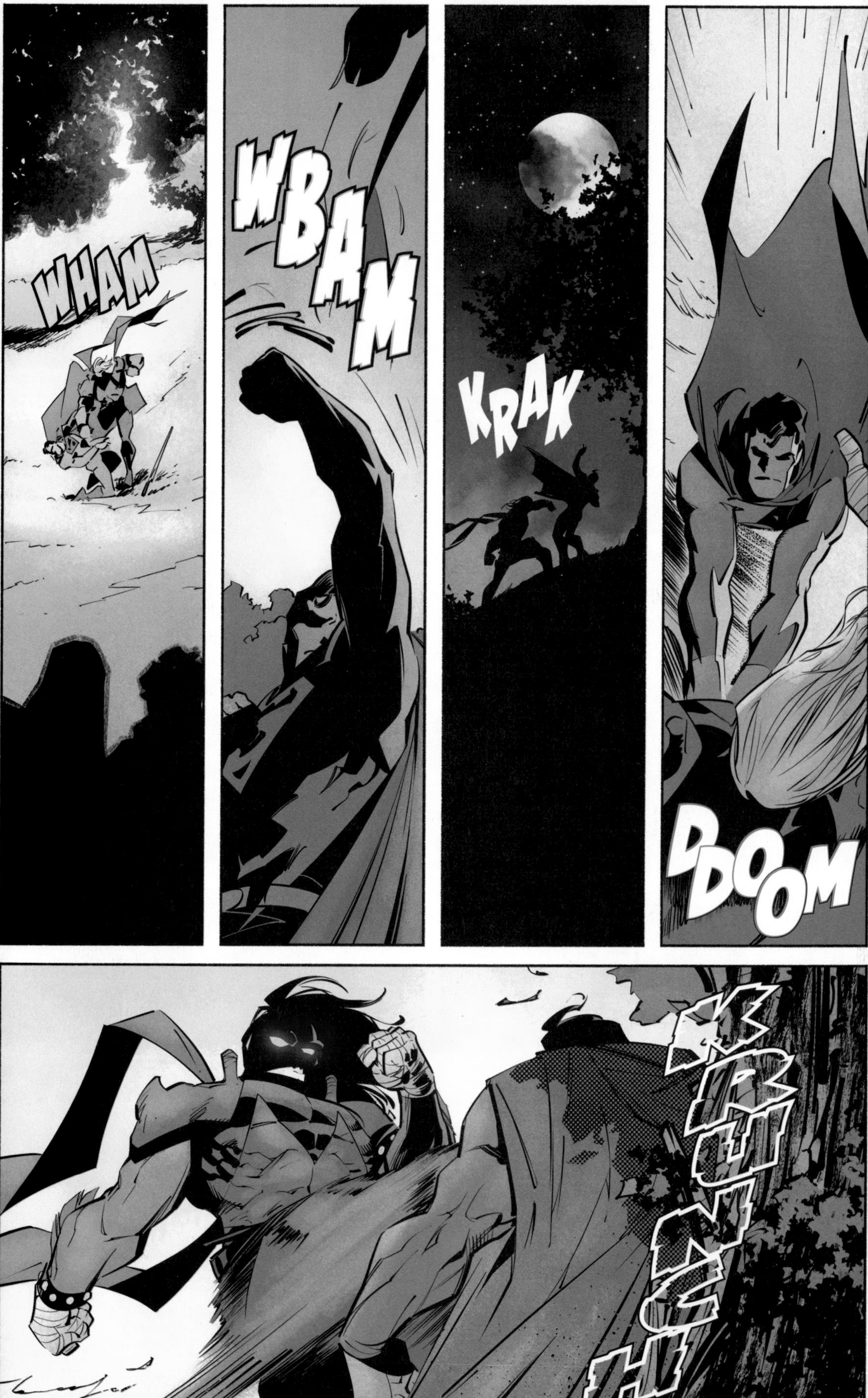
WHAM
WBAM
KRAK
DDOOM
KRUNCH

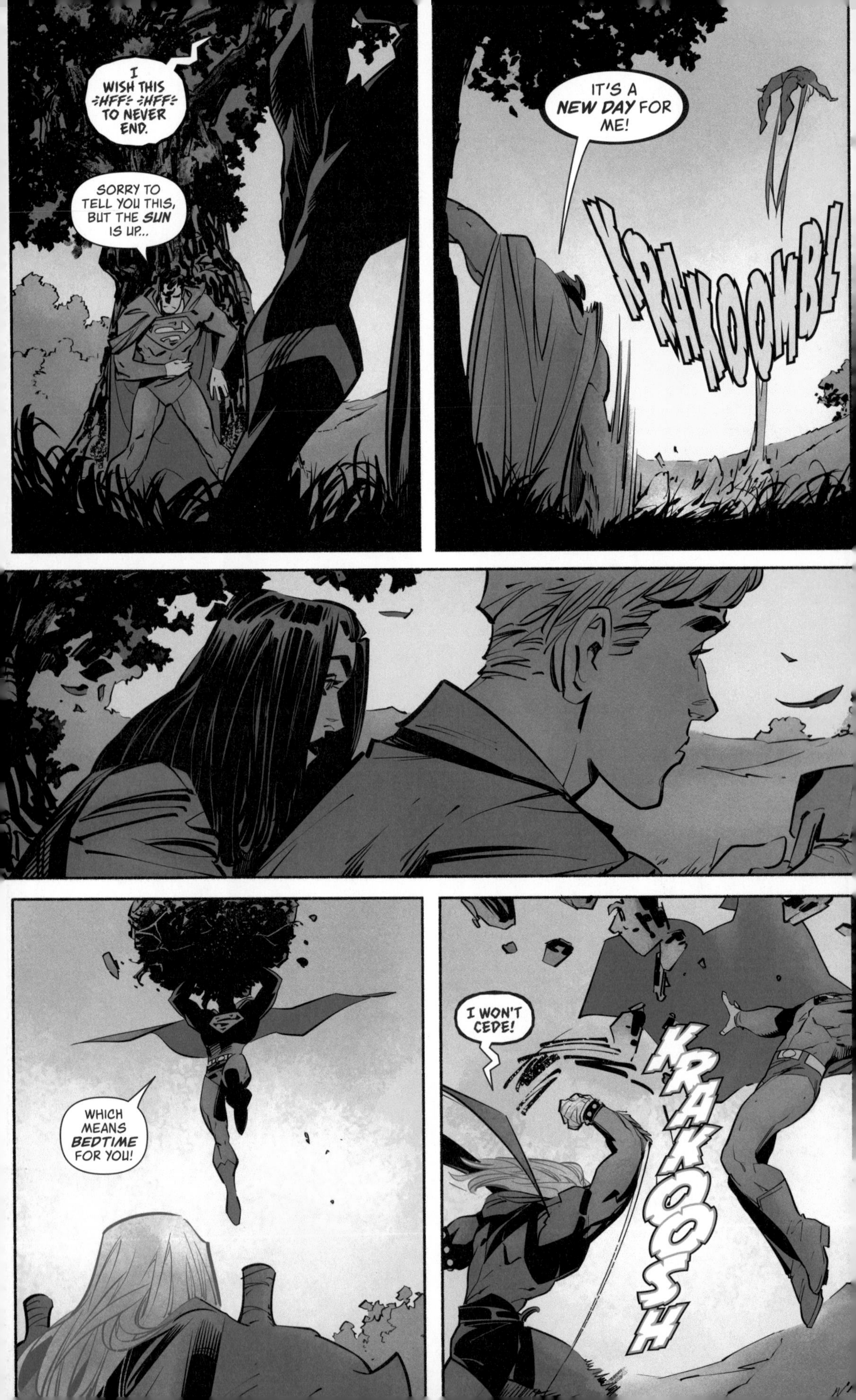
I WISH THIS -HFF- -HFF- TO NEVER END.
SORRY TO TELL YOU THIS, BUT THE SUN IS UP...
IT'S A NEW DAY FOR ME!
KRAKOOMBL
WHICH MEANS BEDTIME FOR YOU!
I WON'T CEDE!
KRAKOOSH

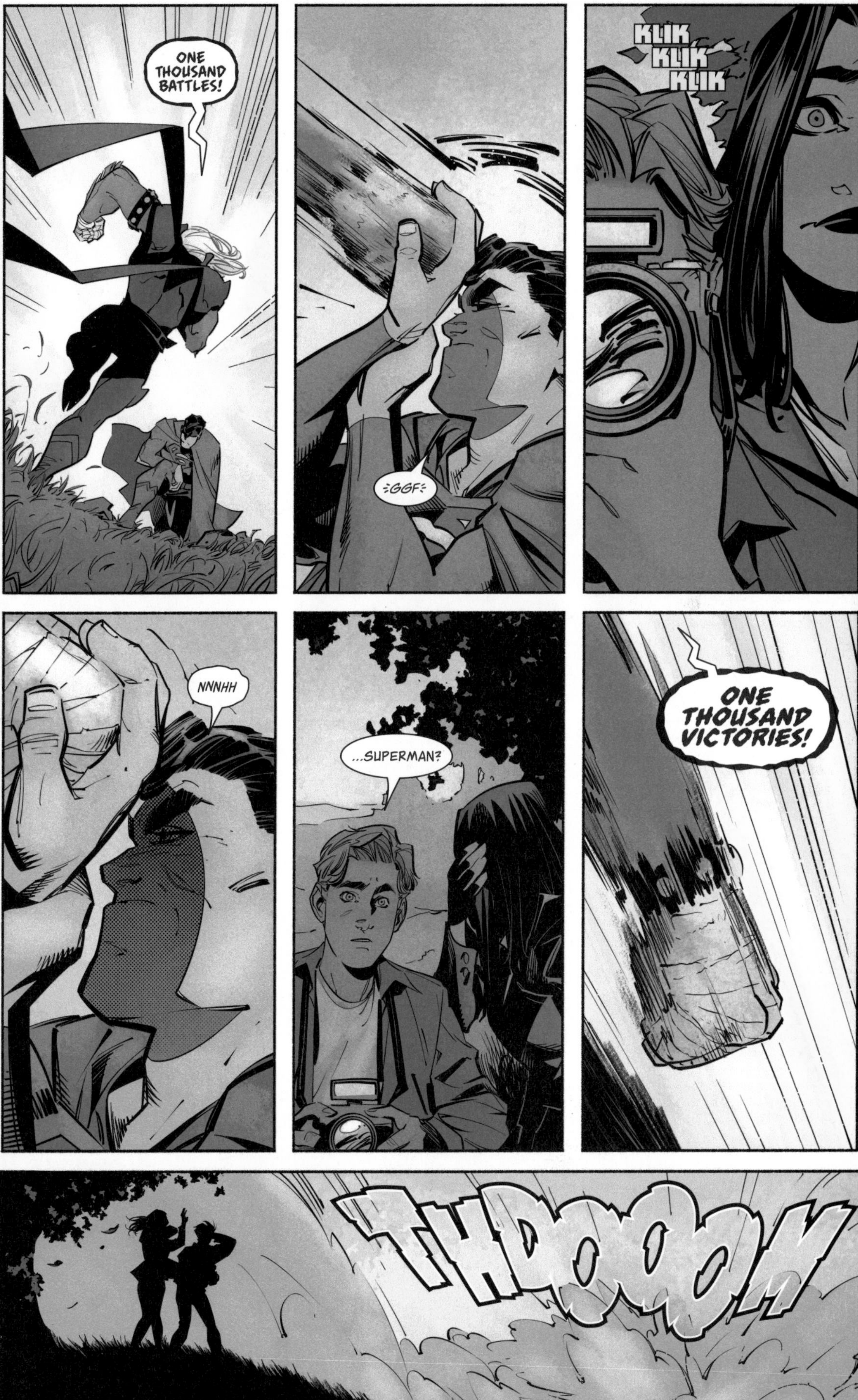
ONE THOUSAND BATTLES!
GGF
KLIK KLIK KLIK
NNNHH
...SUPERMAN?
ONE THOUSAND VICTORIES!
THOOOOM

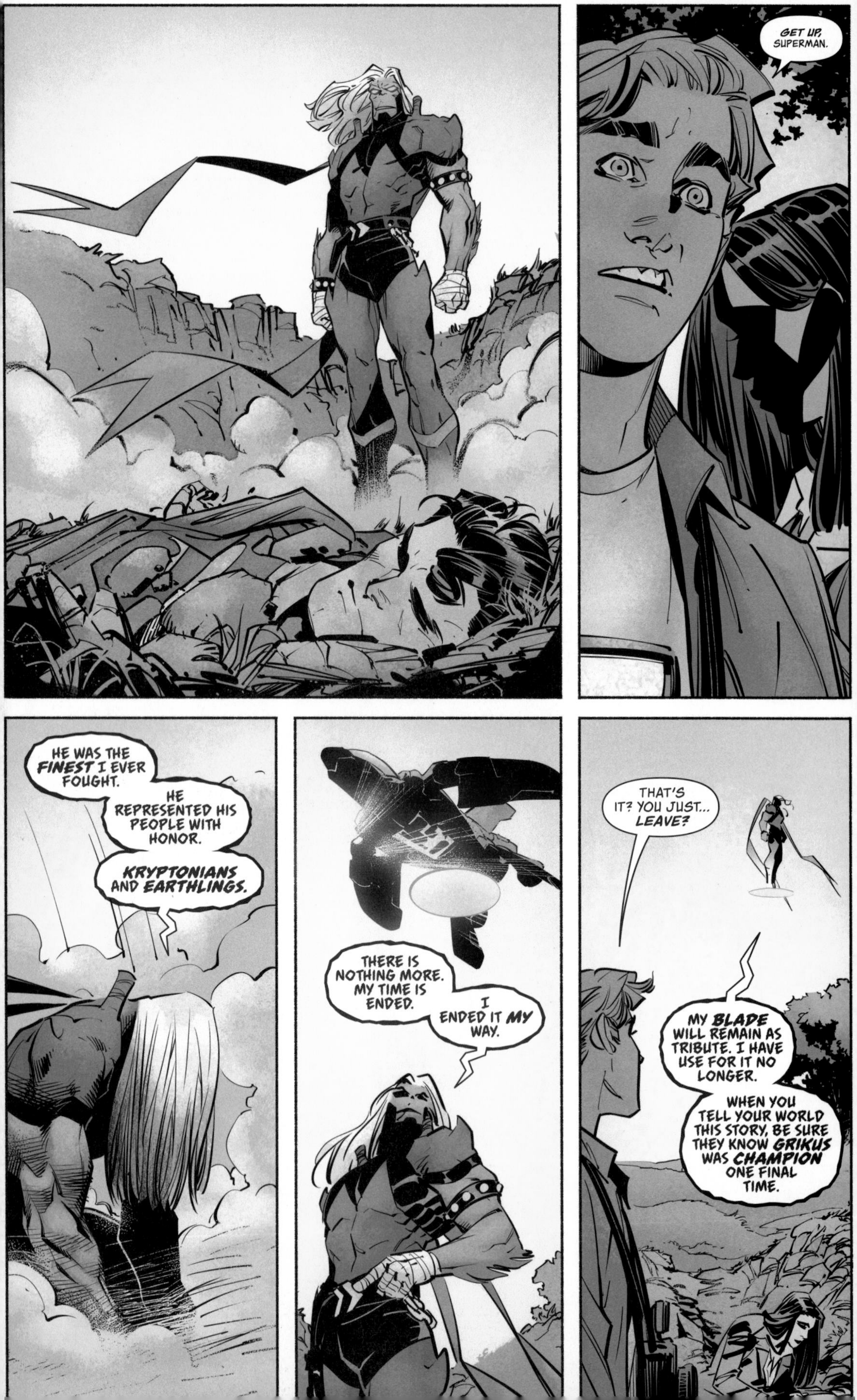
GET UP, SUPERMAN.
HE WAS THE FINEST I EVER FOUGHT.
HE REPRESENTED HIS PEOPLE WITH HONOR.
KRYPTONIANS AND EARTHLINGS.
THERE IS NOTHING MORE. MY TIME IS ENDED.
I ENDED IT MY WAY.
THAT'S IT? YOU JUST... LEAVE?
MY BLADE WILL REMAIN AS TRIBUTE. I HAVE USE FOR IT NO LONGER.
WHEN YOU TELL YOUR WORLD THIS STORY, BE SURE THEY KNOW GRIKUS WAS CHAMPION ONE FINAL TIME.

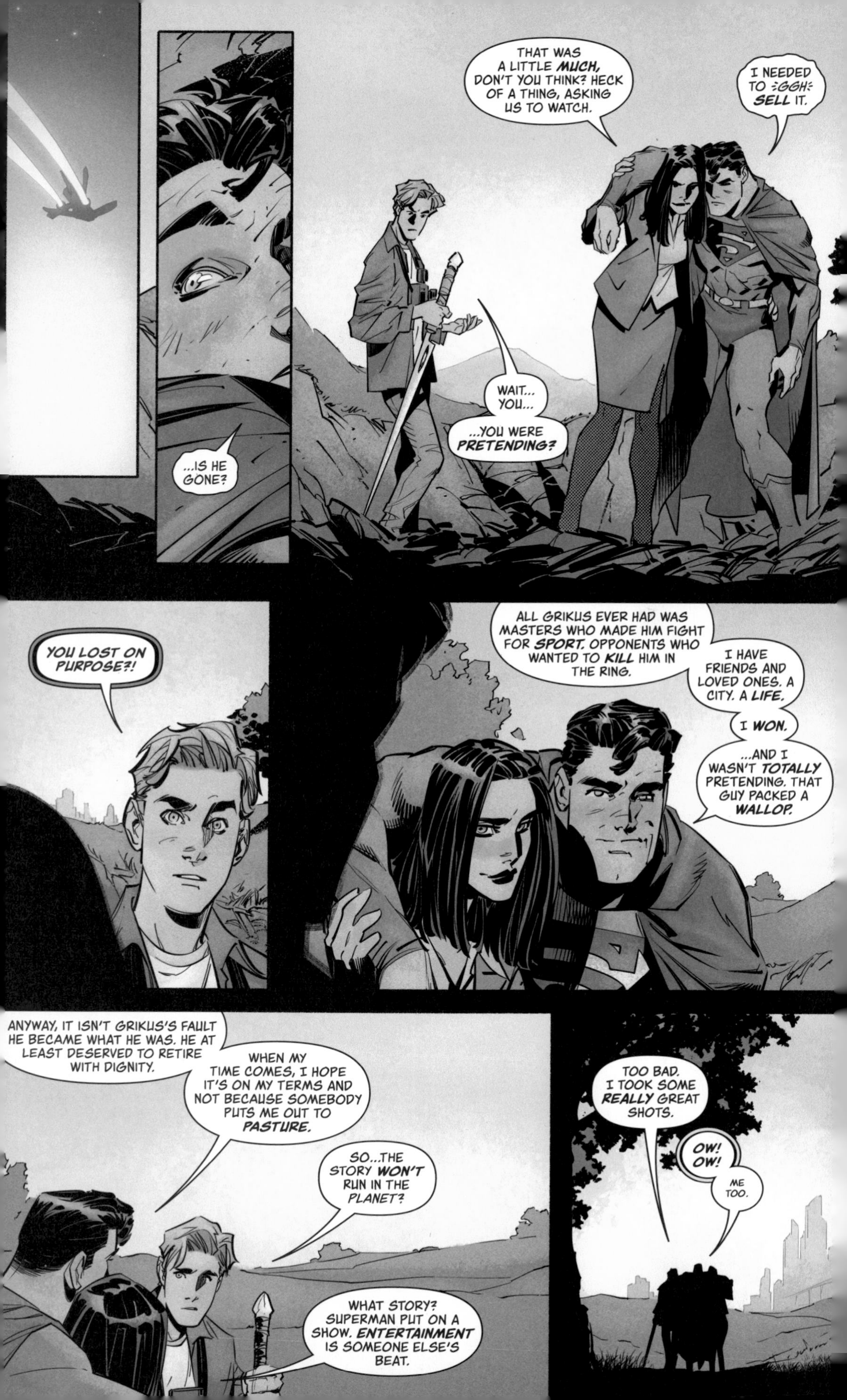
...IS HE GONE?
WAIT... YOU...
...YOU WERE **PRETENDING?**
THAT WAS A LITTLE **MUCH,** DON'T YOU THINK? HECK OF A THING, ASKING US TO WATCH.
I NEEDED TO -GGH- **SELL** IT.
YOU LOST ON PURPOSE?!
ALL GRIKUS EVER HAD WAS MASTERS WHO MADE HIM FIGHT FOR **SPORT.** OPPONENTS WHO WANTED TO **KILL** HIM IN THE RING.
I HAVE FRIENDS AND LOVED ONES. A CITY. A **LIFE.**
I **WON.**
...AND I WASN'T **TOTALLY** PRETENDING. THAT GUY PACKED A **WALLOP.**
ANYWAY, IT ISN'T GRIKUS'S FAULT HE BECAME WHAT HE WAS. HE AT LEAST DESERVED TO RETIRE WITH DIGNITY.
WHEN MY TIME COMES, I HOPE IT'S ON MY TERMS AND NOT BECAUSE SOMEBODY PUTS ME OUT TO **PASTURE.**
SO...THE STORY **WON'T** RUN IN THE **PLANET?**
WHAT STORY? SUPERMAN PUT ON A SHOW. **ENTERTAINMENT** IS SOMEONE ELSE'S BEAT.
TOO BAD. I TOOK SOME **REALLY** GREAT SHOTS.
OW! OW!
ME TOO.

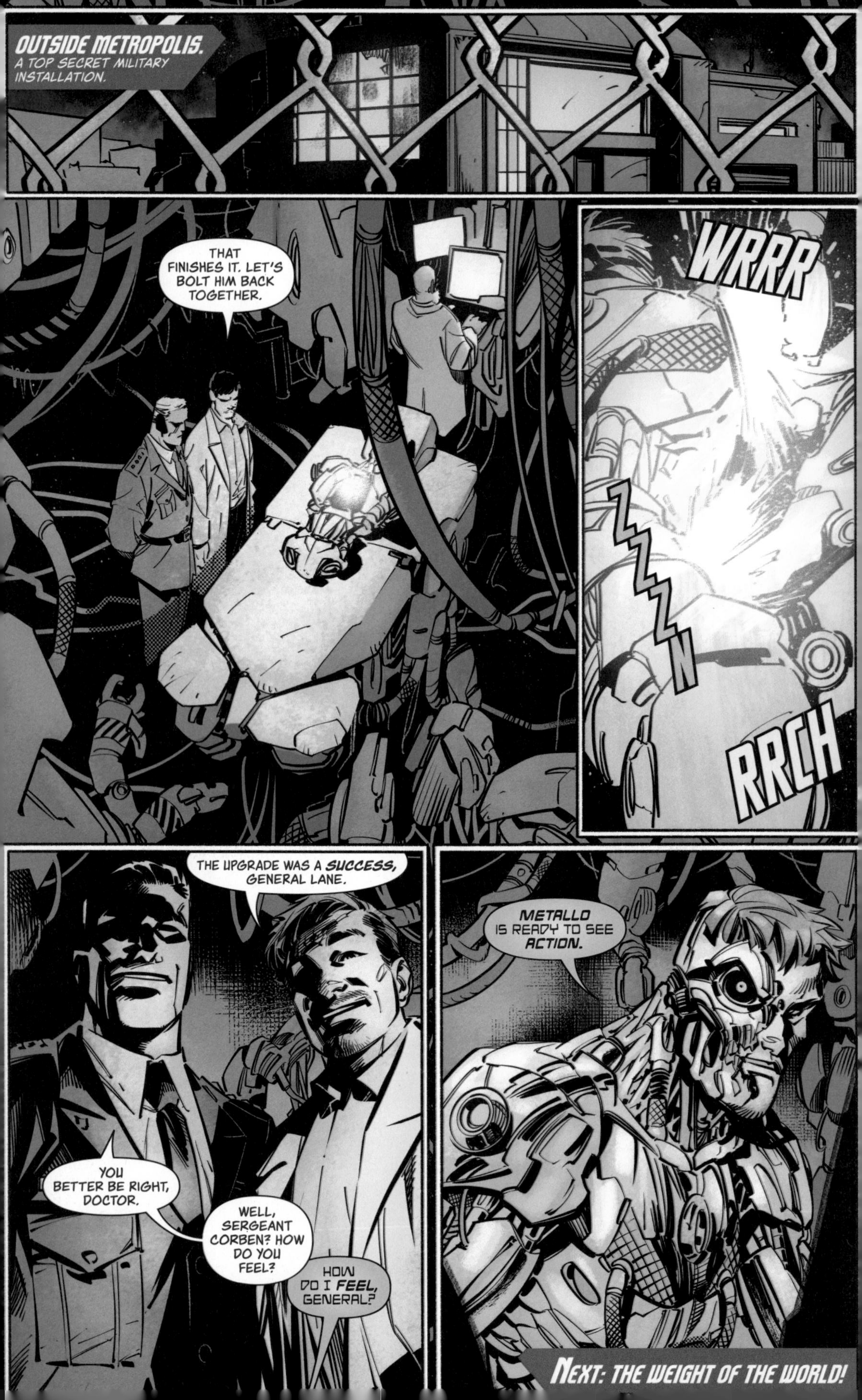
OUTSIDE METROPOLIS.
A TOP SECRET MILITARY INSTALLATION.
THAT FINISHES IT. LET'S BOLT HIM BACK TOGETHER.
WRRR
ZZZZN
RRCH
THE UPGRADE WAS A *SUCCESS*, GENERAL LANE.
YOU BETTER BE RIGHT, DOCTOR.
WELL, SERGEANT CORBEN? HOW DO YOU FEEL?
HOW DO I *FEEL*, GENERAL?
METALLO IS READY TO SEE *ACTION*.
NEXT: THE WEIGHT OF THE WORLD!

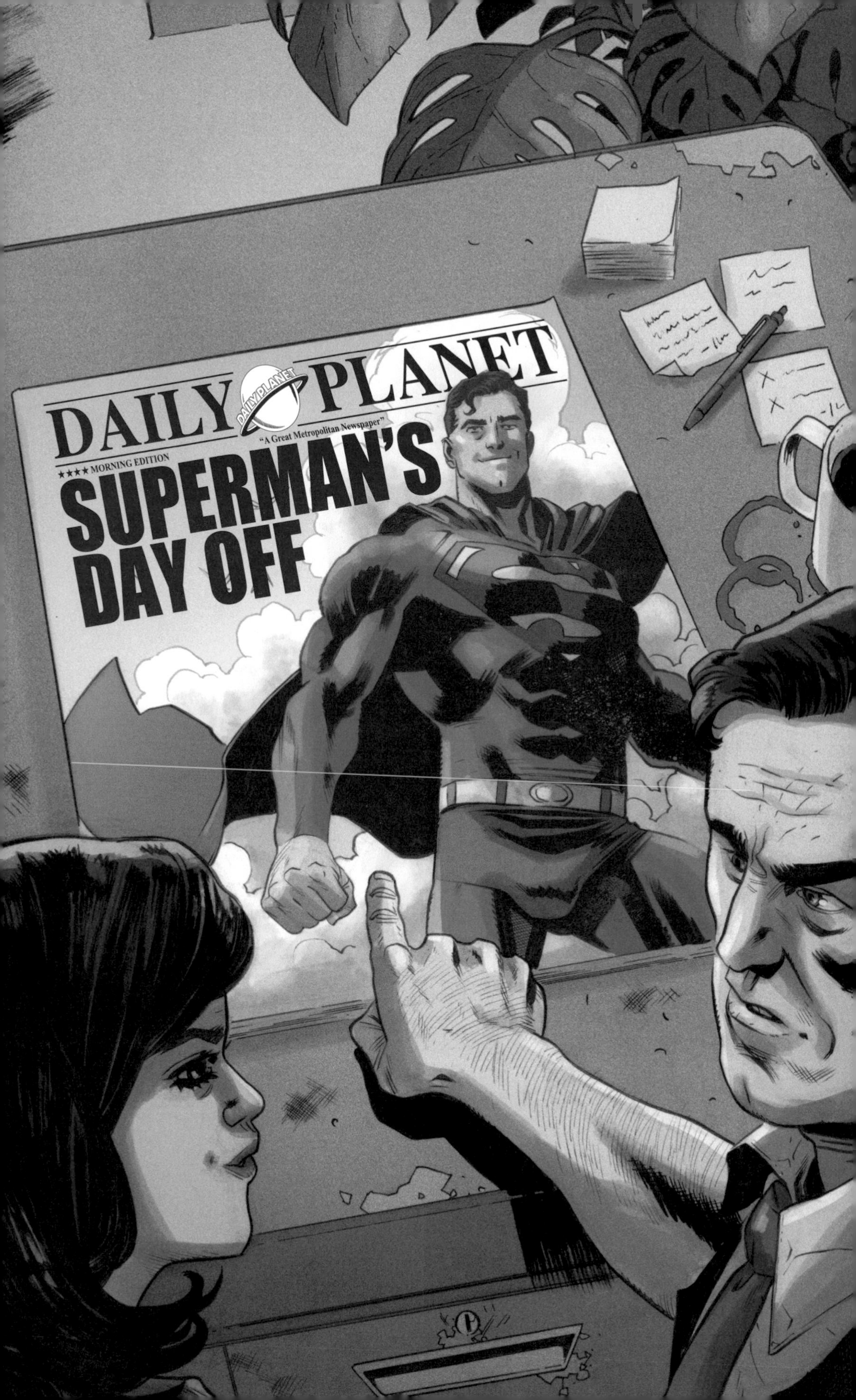

DAILY PLANET
"A Great Metropolitan Newspaper"
★★★★ MORNING EDITION
SUPERMAN'S DAY OFF

COVER ART BY
SCOTT HEPBURN AND **IAN HERRING**

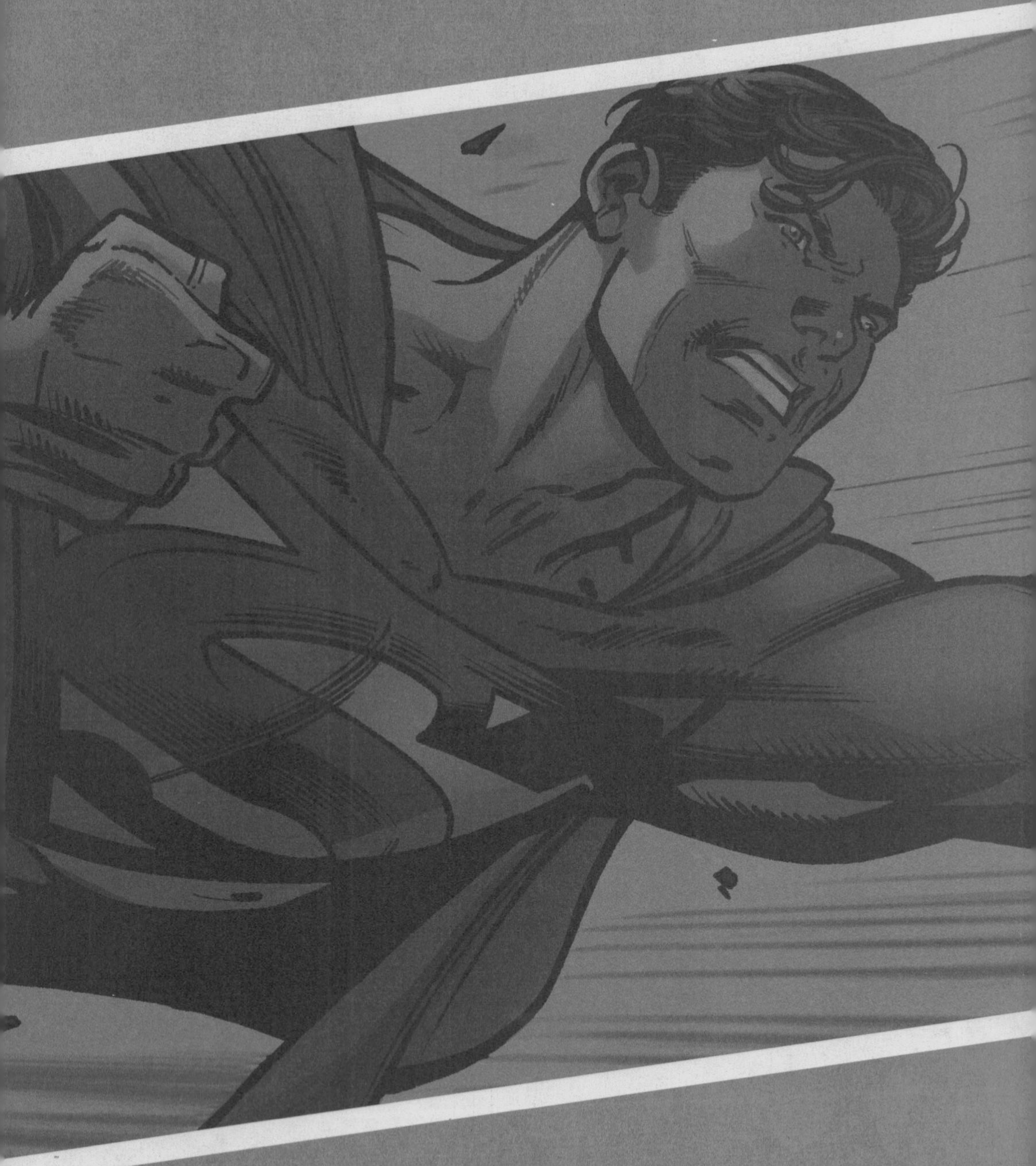

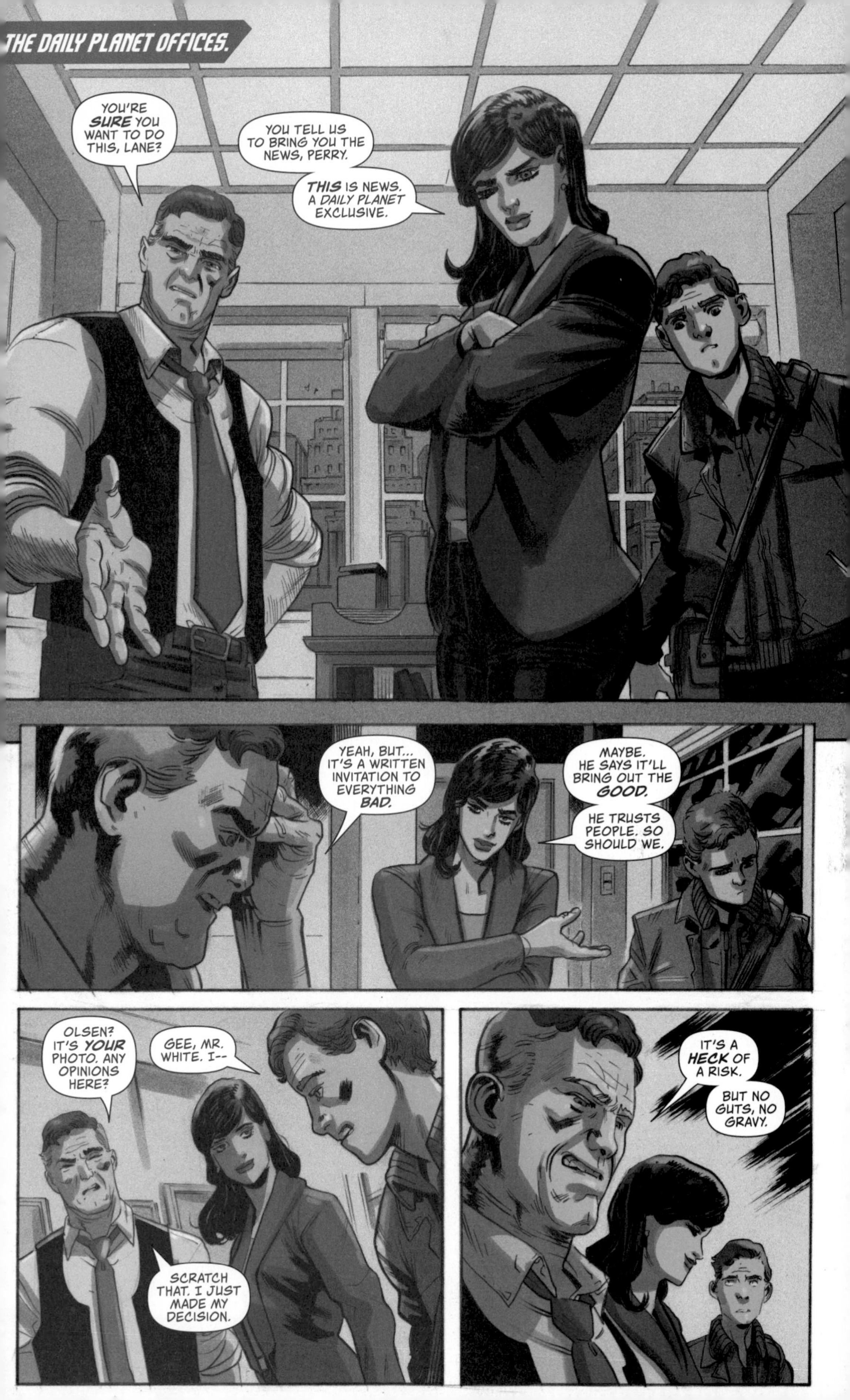
THE DAILY PLANET OFFICES.
YOU'RE SURE YOU WANT TO DO THIS, LANE?
YOU TELL US TO BRING YOU THE NEWS, PERRY.
THIS IS NEWS. A DAILY PLANET EXCLUSIVE.
YEAH, BUT... IT'S A WRITTEN INVITATION TO EVERYTHING BAD.
MAYBE. HE SAYS IT'LL BRING OUT THE GOOD.
HE TRUSTS PEOPLE. SO SHOULD WE.
OLSEN? IT'S YOUR PHOTO. ANY OPINIONS HERE?
GEE, MR. WHITE. I--
SCRATCH THAT. I JUST MADE MY DECISION.
IT'S A HECK OF A RISK.
BUT NO GUTS, NO GRAVY.

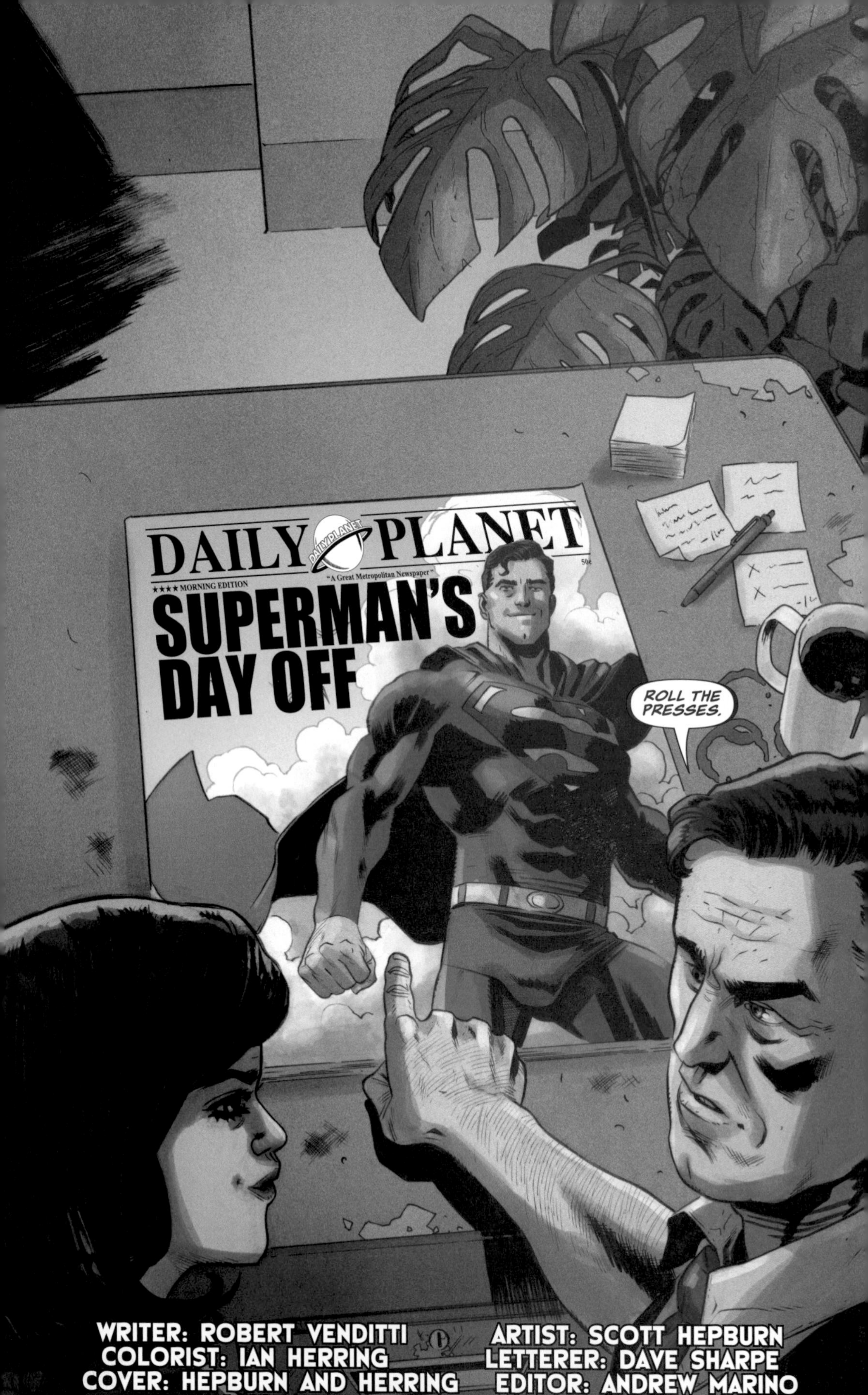
DAILY PLANET PLANET
DAILY PLANET
"A Great Metropolitan Newspaper"
50¢
★★★★ MORNING EDITION
SUPERMAN'S DAY OFF
ROLL THE PRESSES.

WRITER: ROBERT VENDITTI ARTIST: SCOTT HEPBURN
COLORIST: IAN HERRING LETTERER: DAVE SHARPE
COVER: HEPBURN AND HERRING EDITOR: ANDREW MARINO
SUPERMAN CREATED BY JERRY SIEGEL & JOE SHUSTER.

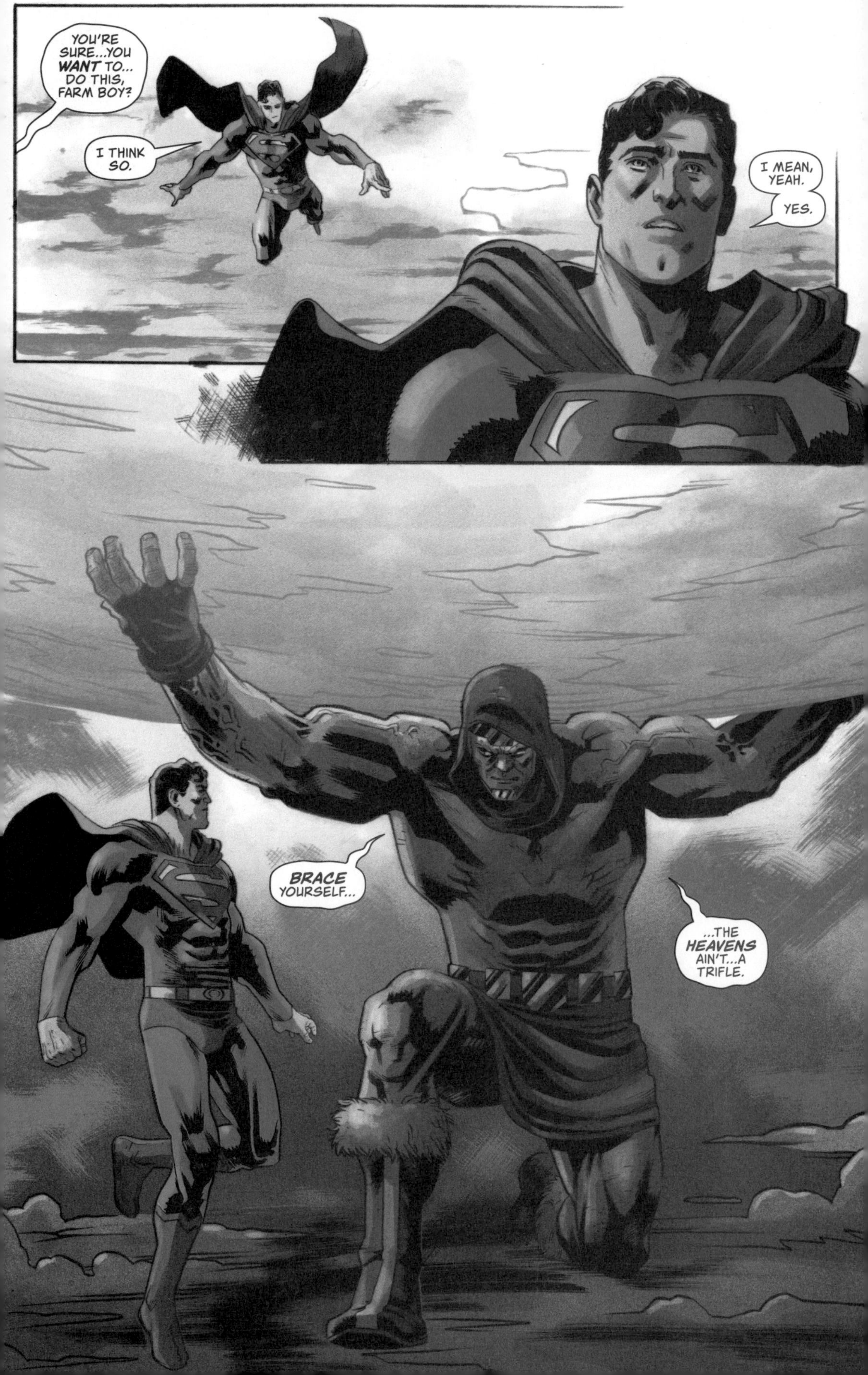
YOU'RE SURE...YOU WANT TO... DO THIS, FARM BOY?
I THINK SO.
I MEAN, YEAH.
YES.
BRACE YOURSELF...
...THE HEAVENS AIN'T...A TRIFLE.

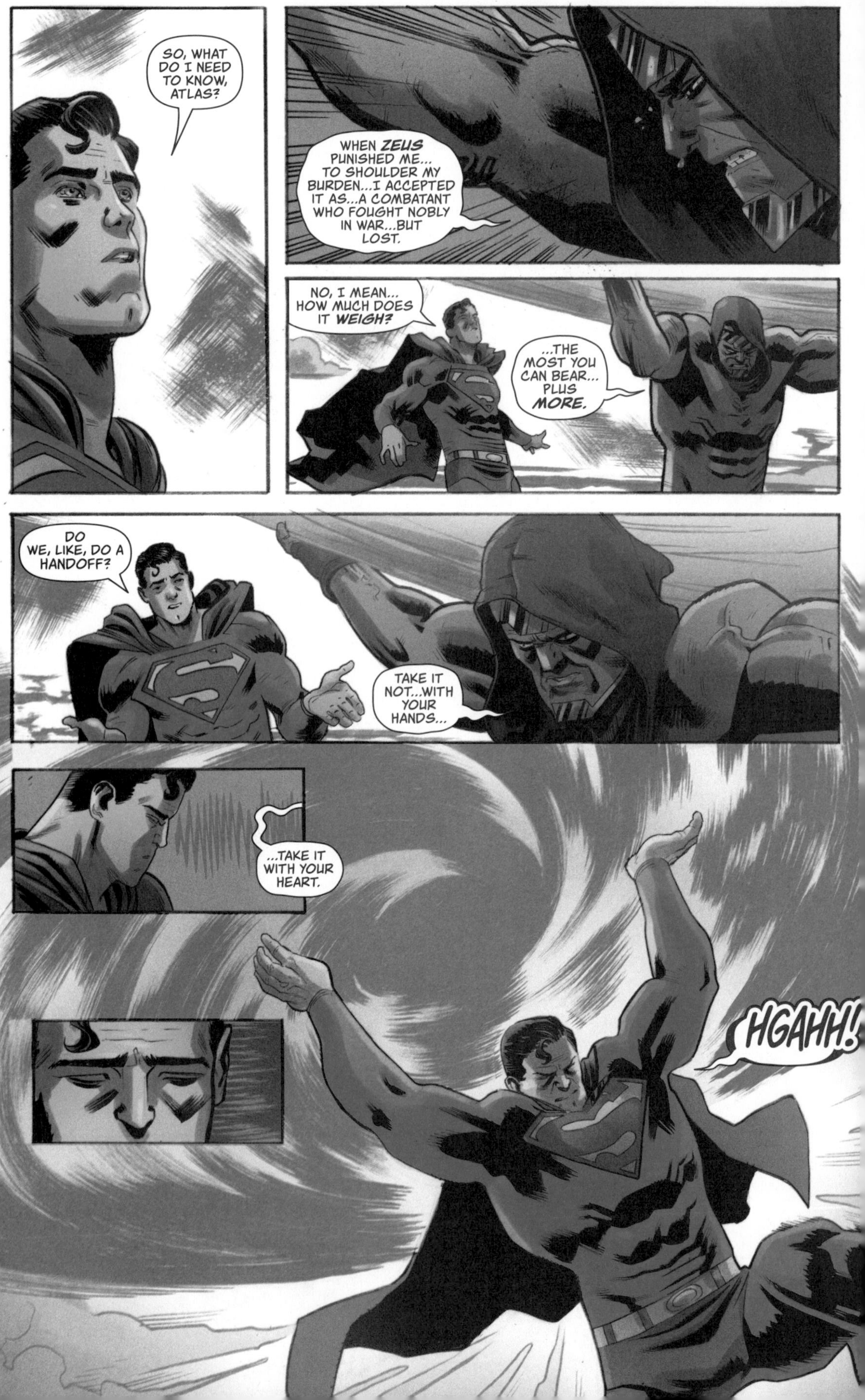
SO, WHAT DO I NEED TO KNOW, ATLAS?
WHEN ZEUS PUNISHED ME... TO SHOULDER MY BURDEN...I ACCEPTED IT AS...A COMBATANT WHO FOUGHT NOBLY IN WAR...BUT LOST.
NO, I MEAN... HOW MUCH DOES IT WEIGH?
...THE MOST YOU CAN BEAR... PLUS MORE.
DO WE, LIKE, DO A HANDOFF?
TAKE IT NOT...WITH YOUR HANDS...
...TAKE IT WITH YOUR HEART.
HGAHH!

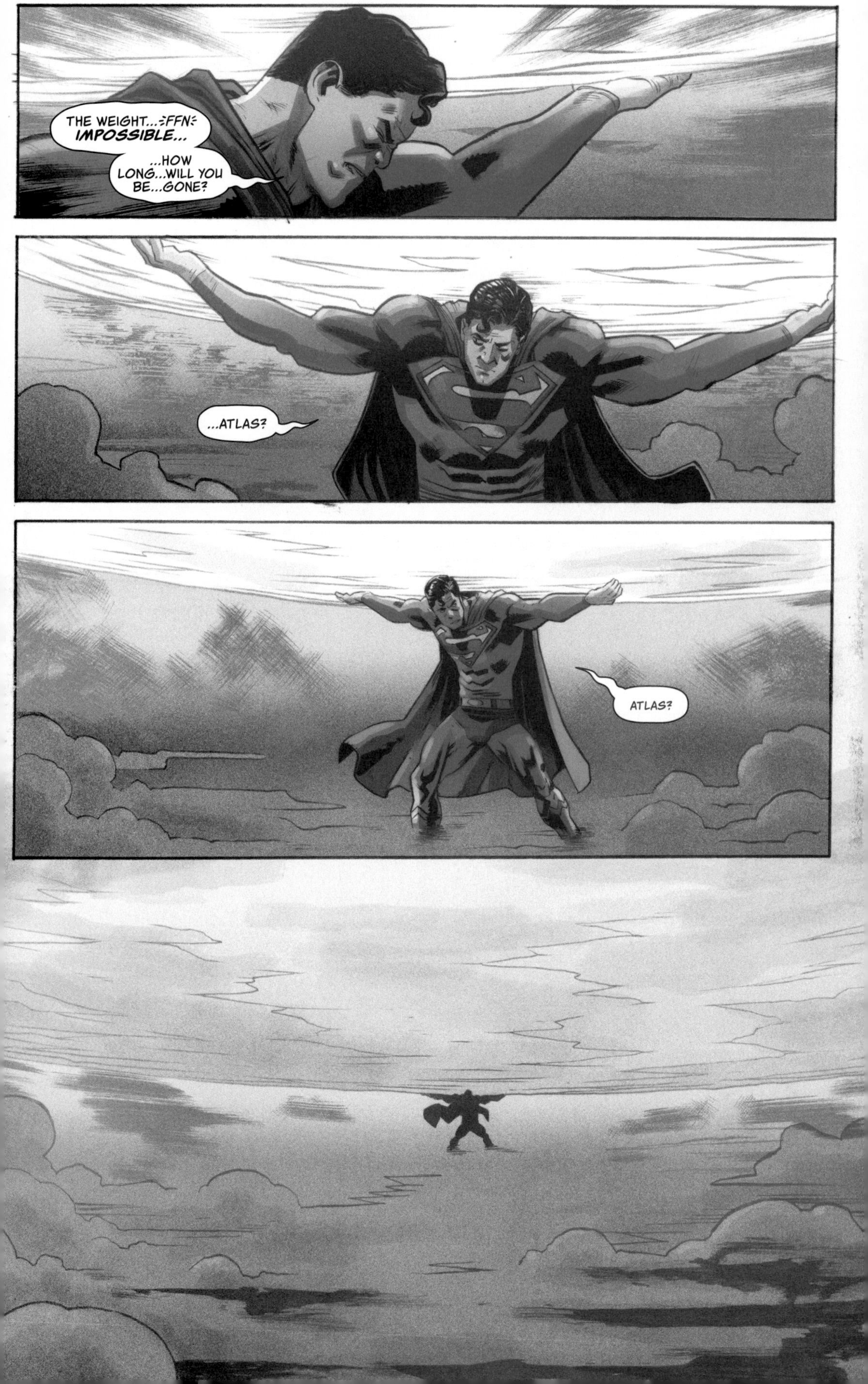
THE WEIGHT...:FFN: IMPOSSIBLE...
...HOW LONG...WILL YOU BE...GONE?
...ATLAS?
ATLAS?

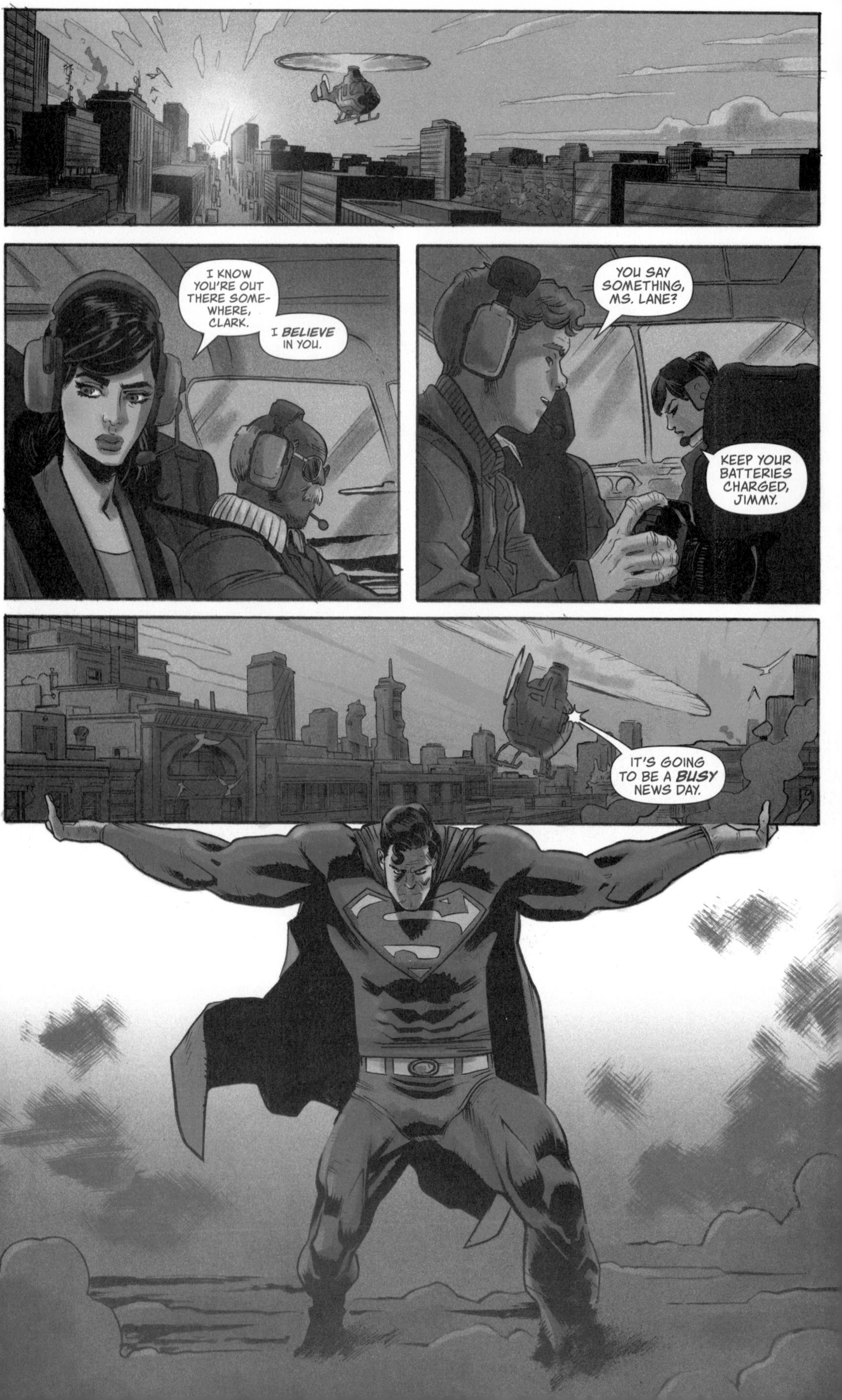
I KNOW YOU'RE OUT THERE SOME-WHERE, CLARK.
I BELIEVE IN YOU.
YOU SAY SOMETHING, MS. LANE?
KEEP YOUR BATTERIES CHARGED, JIMMY.
IT'S GOING TO BE A BUSY NEWS DAY.

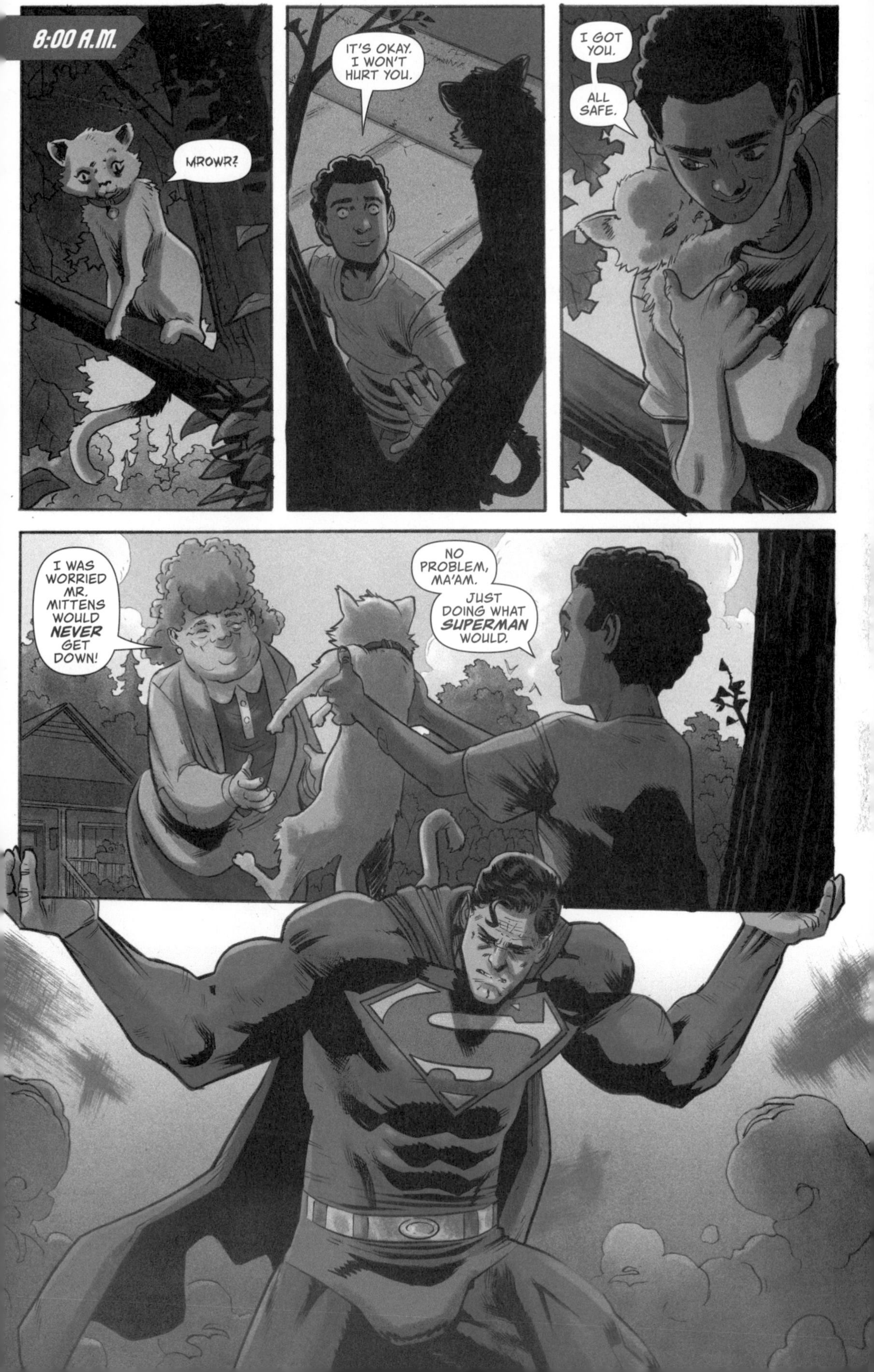
8:00 A.M.
MROWR?
IT'S OKAY. I WON'T HURT YOU.
I GOT YOU.
ALL SAFE.
I WAS WORRIED MR. MITTENS WOULD NEVER GET DOWN!
NO PROBLEM, MA'AM.
JUST DOING WHAT SUPERMAN WOULD.

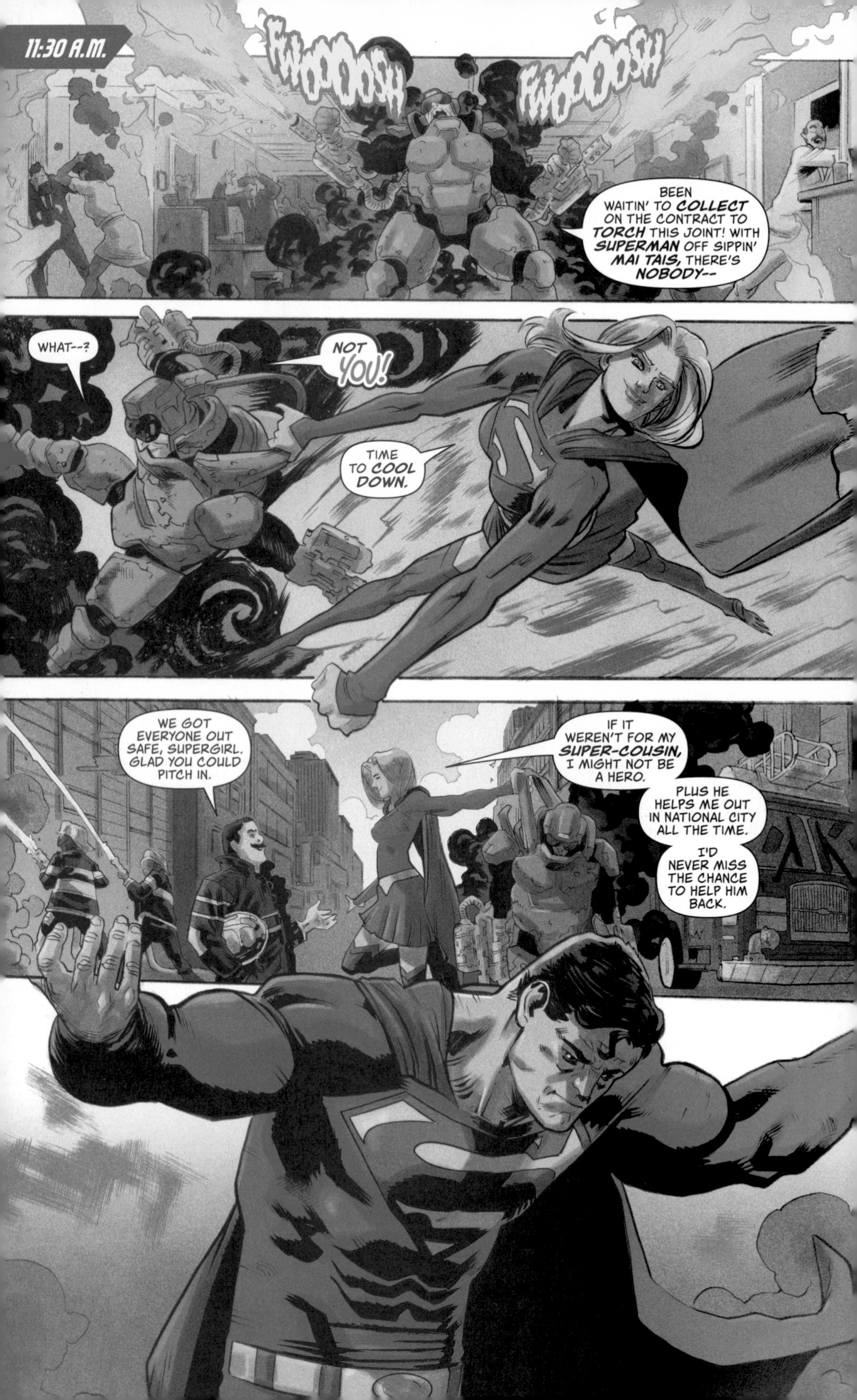
11:30 A.M.
FWOOOOSH
FWOOOOSH
BEEN WAITIN' TO COLLECT ON THE CONTRACT TO TORCH THIS JOINT! WITH SUPERMAN OFF SIPPIN' MAI TAIS, THERE'S NOBODY--
WHAT--?
NOT YOU!
TIME TO COOL DOWN.
WE GOT EVERYONE OUT SAFE, SUPERGIRL. GLAD YOU COULD PITCH IN.
IF IT WEREN'T FOR MY SUPER-COUSIN, I MIGHT NOT BE A HERO.
PLUS HE HELPS ME OUT IN NATIONAL CITY ALL THE TIME.
I'D NEVER MISS THE CHANCE TO HELP HIM BACK.

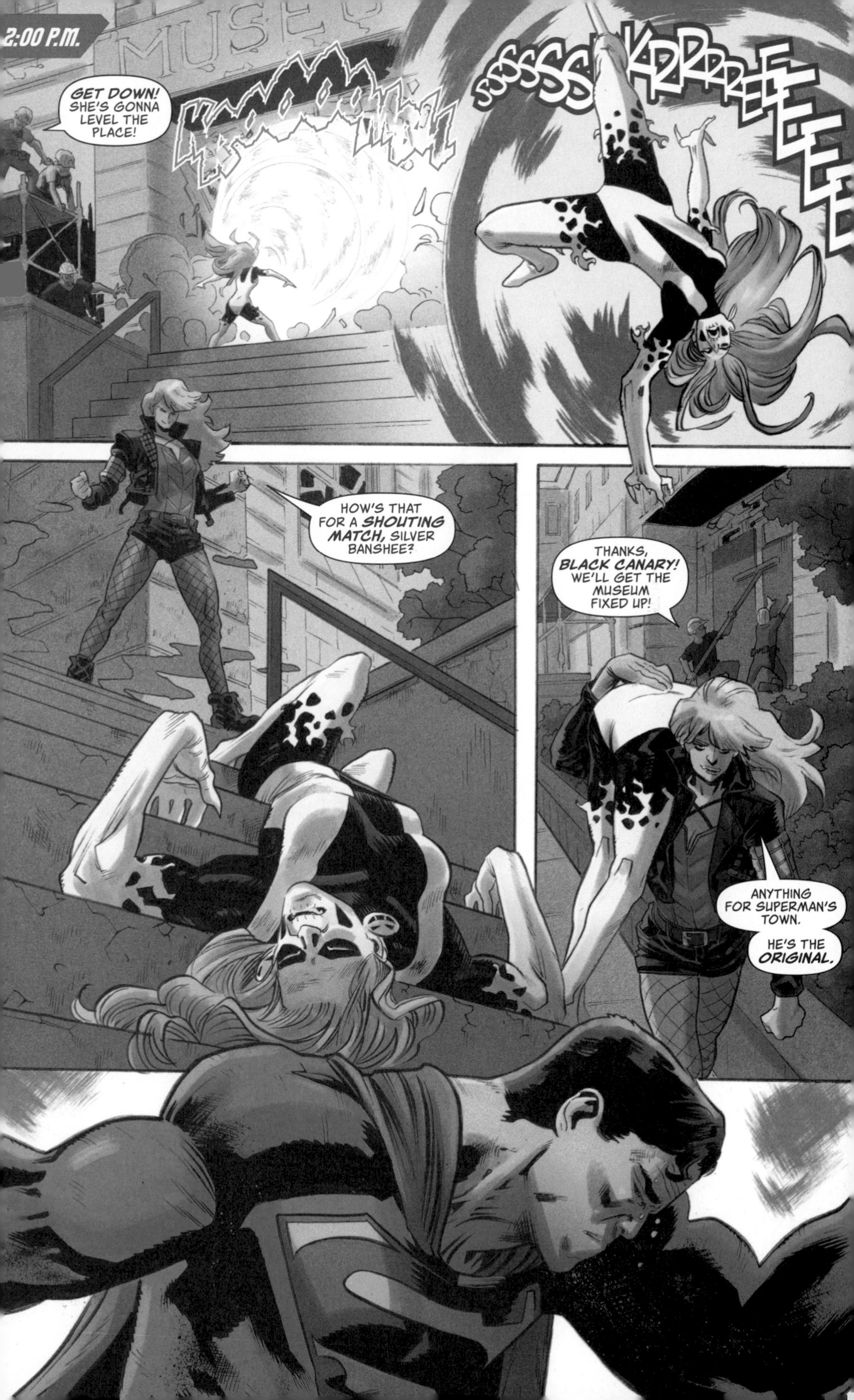
2:00 P.M.
GET DOWN! SHE'S GONNA LEVEL THE PLACE!
HOW'S THAT FOR A SHOUTING MATCH, SILVER BANSHEE?
THANKS, BLACK CANARY! WE'LL GET THE MUSEUM FIXED UP!
ANYTHING FOR SUPERMAN'S TOWN.
HE'S THE ORIGINAL.

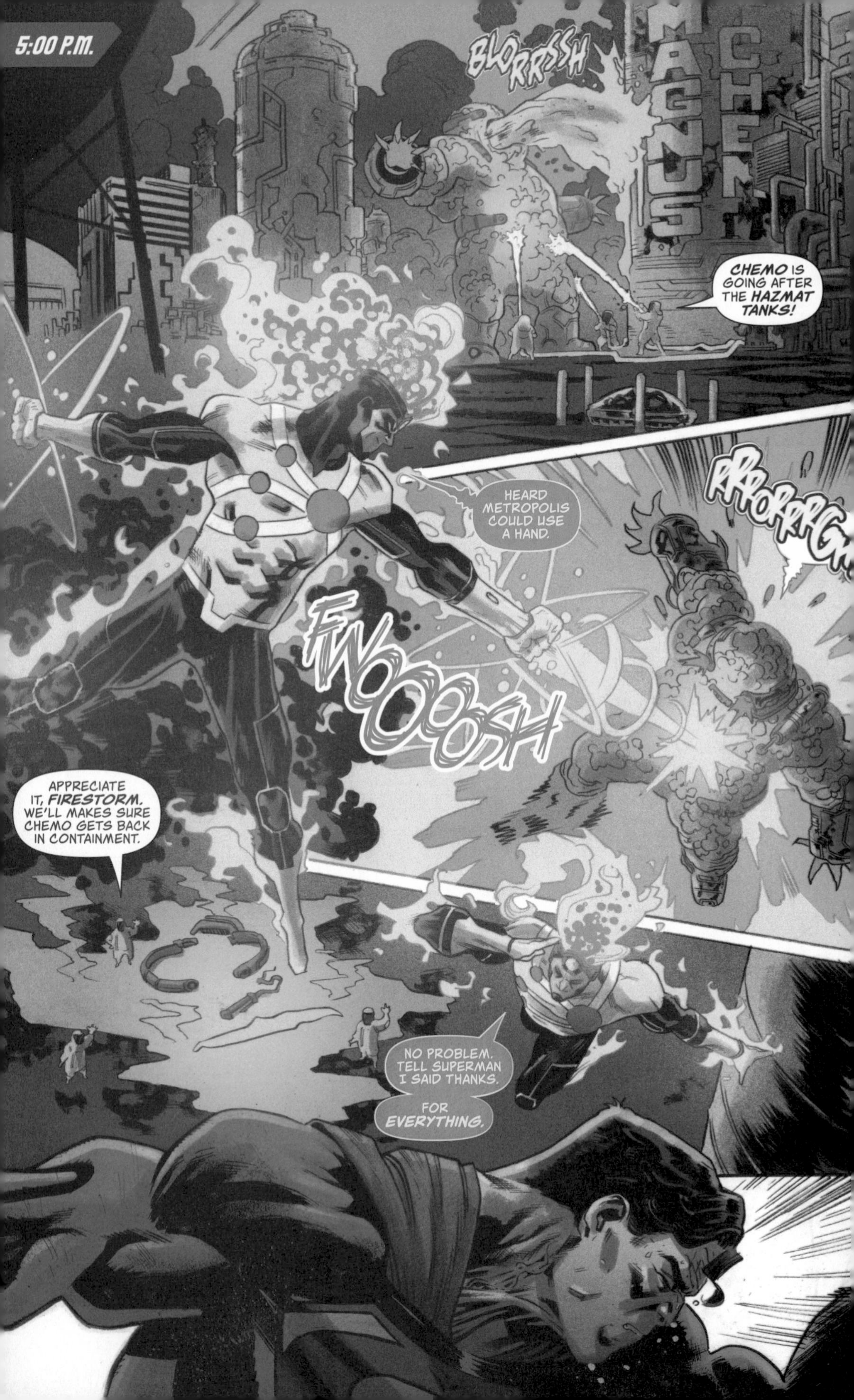

5:00 P.M.
BLORRRSSH
MAGNUS
CHEM
CHEMO IS GOING AFTER THE HAZMAT TANKS!
HEARD METROPOLIS COULD USE A HAND.
RRROORRRGH
FWOOOOSH
APPRECIATE IT, FIRESTORM. WE'LL MAKES SURE CHEMO GETS BACK IN CONTAINMENT.
NO PROBLEM. TELL SUPERMAN I SAID THANKS.
FOR EVERYTHING.

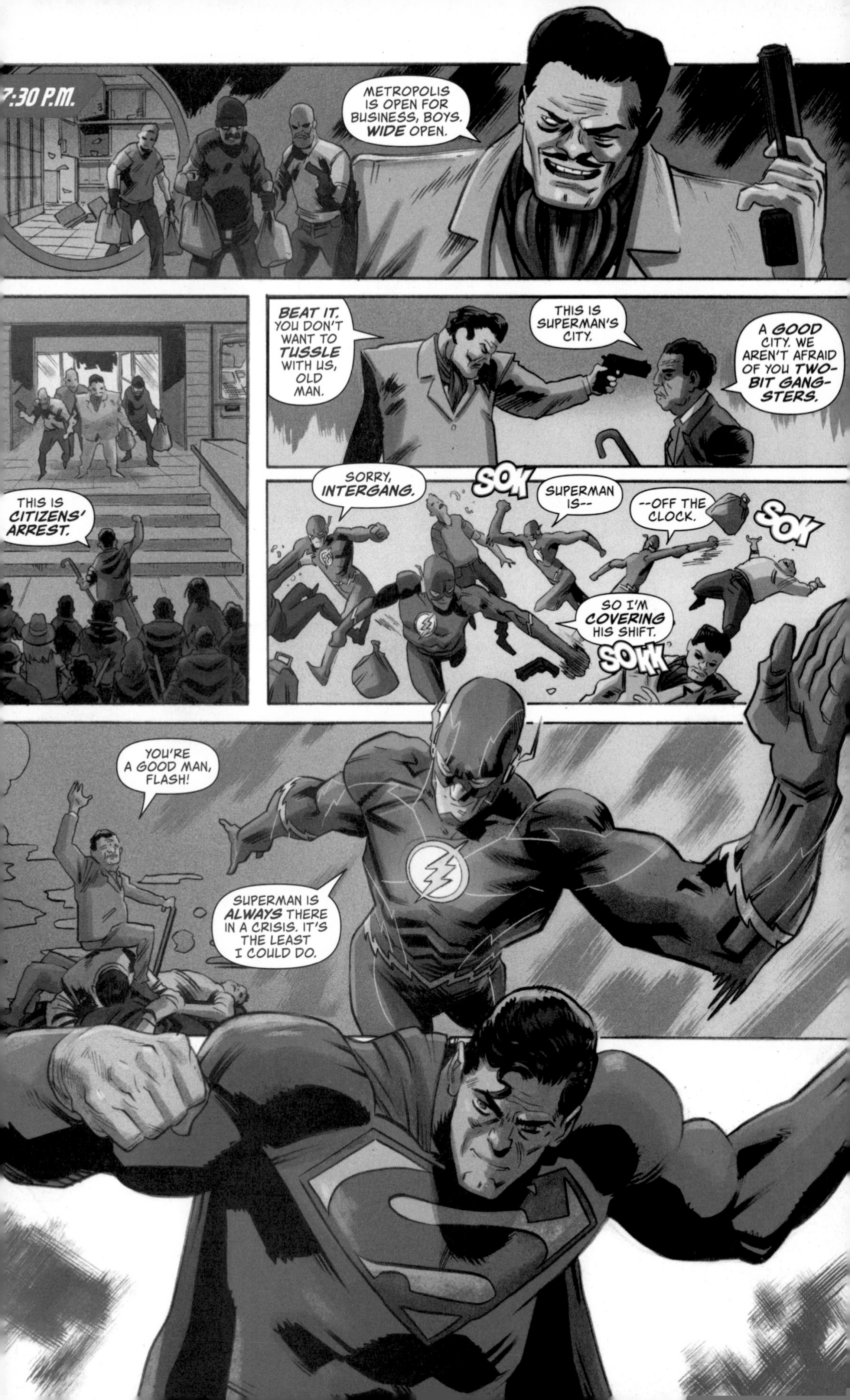
7:30 P.M.
METROPOLIS IS OPEN FOR BUSINESS, BOYS. WIDE OPEN.
BEAT IT. YOU DON'T WANT TO TUSSLE WITH US, OLD MAN.
THIS IS SUPERMAN'S CITY.
A GOOD CITY. WE AREN'T AFRAID OF YOU TWO-BIT GANGSTERS.
THIS IS CITIZENS' ARREST.
SORRY, INTERGANG.
SOK
SUPERMAN IS--
--OFF THE CLOCK.
SOK
SO I'M COVERING HIS SHIFT.
SOKK
YOU'RE A GOOD MAN, FLASH!
SUPERMAN IS ALWAYS THERE IN A CRISIS. IT'S THE LEAST I COULD DO.

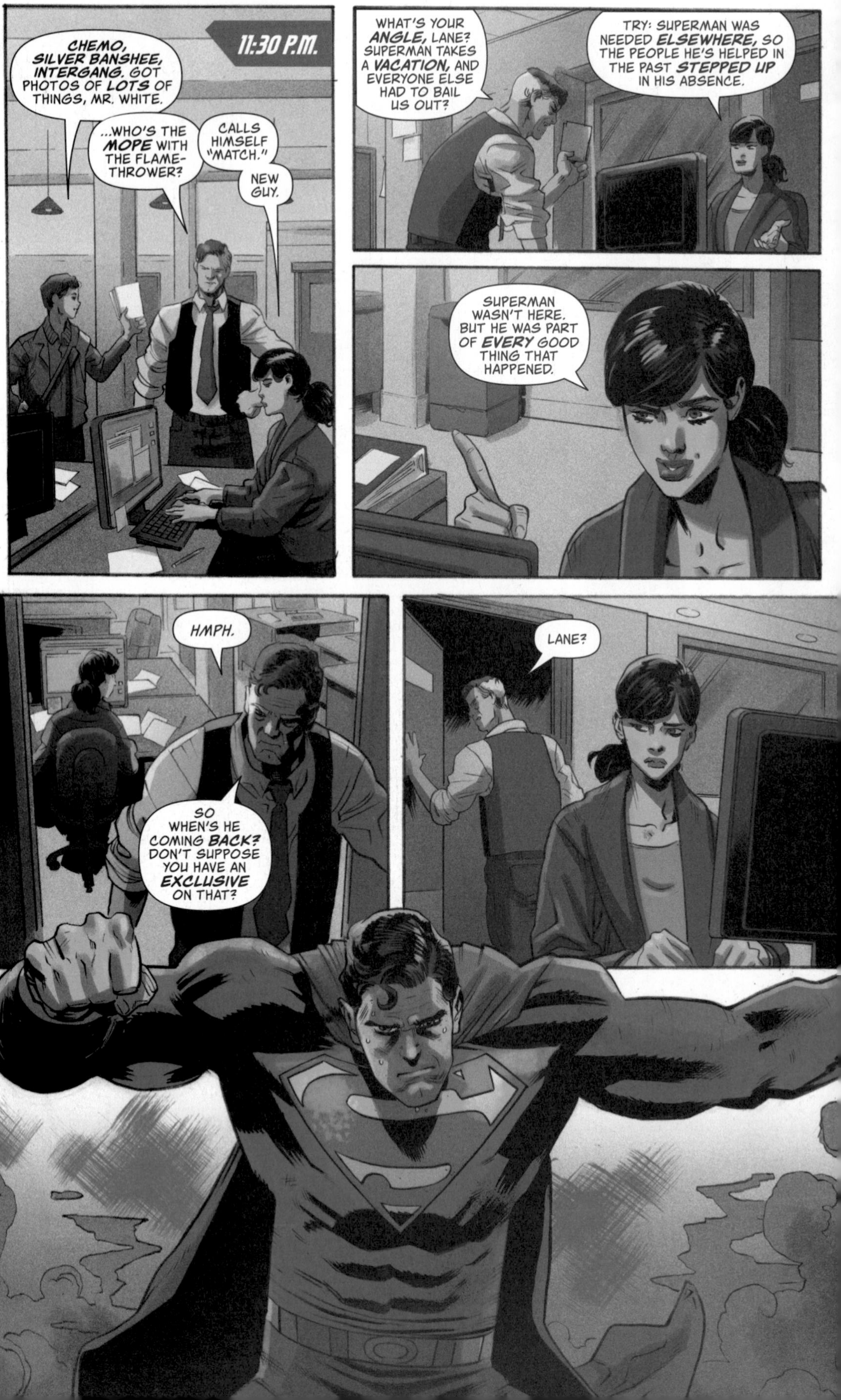
11:30 P.M.
CHEMO, SILVER BANSHEE, INTERGANG. GOT PHOTOS OF LOTS OF THINGS, MR. WHITE.
...WHO'S THE MOPE WITH THE FLAME-THROWER?
CALLS HIMSELF "MATCH."
NEW GUY.
WHAT'S YOUR ANGLE, LANE? SUPERMAN TAKES A VACATION, AND EVERYONE ELSE HAD TO BAIL US OUT?
TRY: SUPERMAN WAS NEEDED ELSEWHERE, SO THE PEOPLE HE'S HELPED IN THE PAST STEPPED UP IN HIS ABSENCE.
SUPERMAN WASN'T HERE. BUT HE WAS PART OF EVERY GOOD THING THAT HAPPENED.
HMPH.
SO WHEN'S HE COMING BACK? DON'T SUPPOSE YOU HAVE AN EXCLUSIVE ON THAT?
LANE?

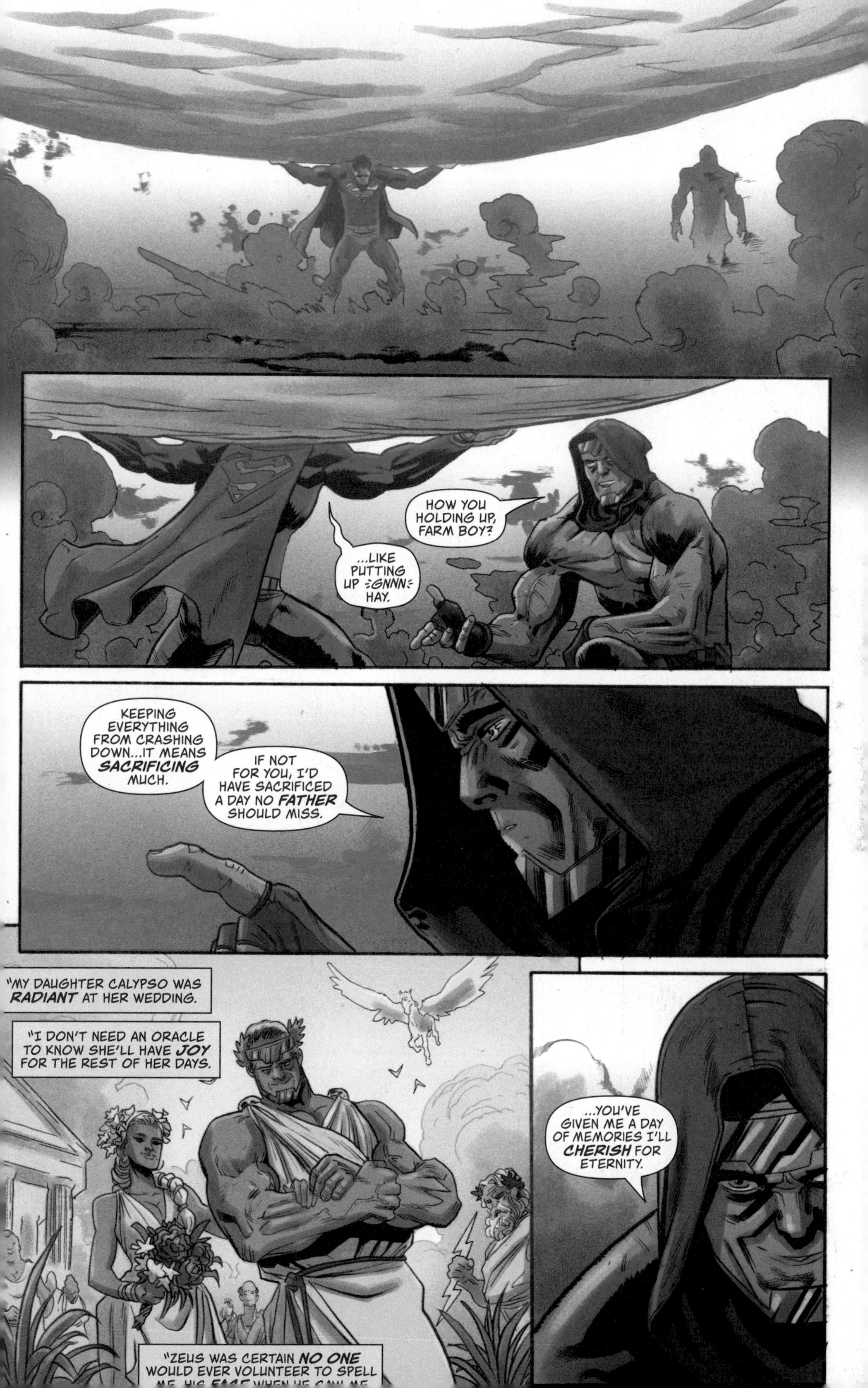

HOW YOU HOLDING UP, FARM BOY?
...LIKE PUTTING UP =GNNN= HAY.
KEEPING EVERYTHING FROM CRASHING DOWN...IT MEANS **SACRIFICING** MUCH.
IF NOT FOR YOU, I'D HAVE SACRIFICED A DAY NO **FATHER** SHOULD MISS.
"MY DAUGHTER CALYPSO WAS **RADIANT** AT HER WEDDING.
"I DON'T NEED AN ORACLE TO KNOW SHE'LL HAVE **JOY** FOR THE REST OF HER DAYS.
...YOU'VE GIVEN ME A DAY OF MEMORIES I'LL **CHERISH** FOR ETERNITY.
"ZEUS WAS CERTAIN **NO ONE** WOULD EVER VOLUNTEER TO SPELL

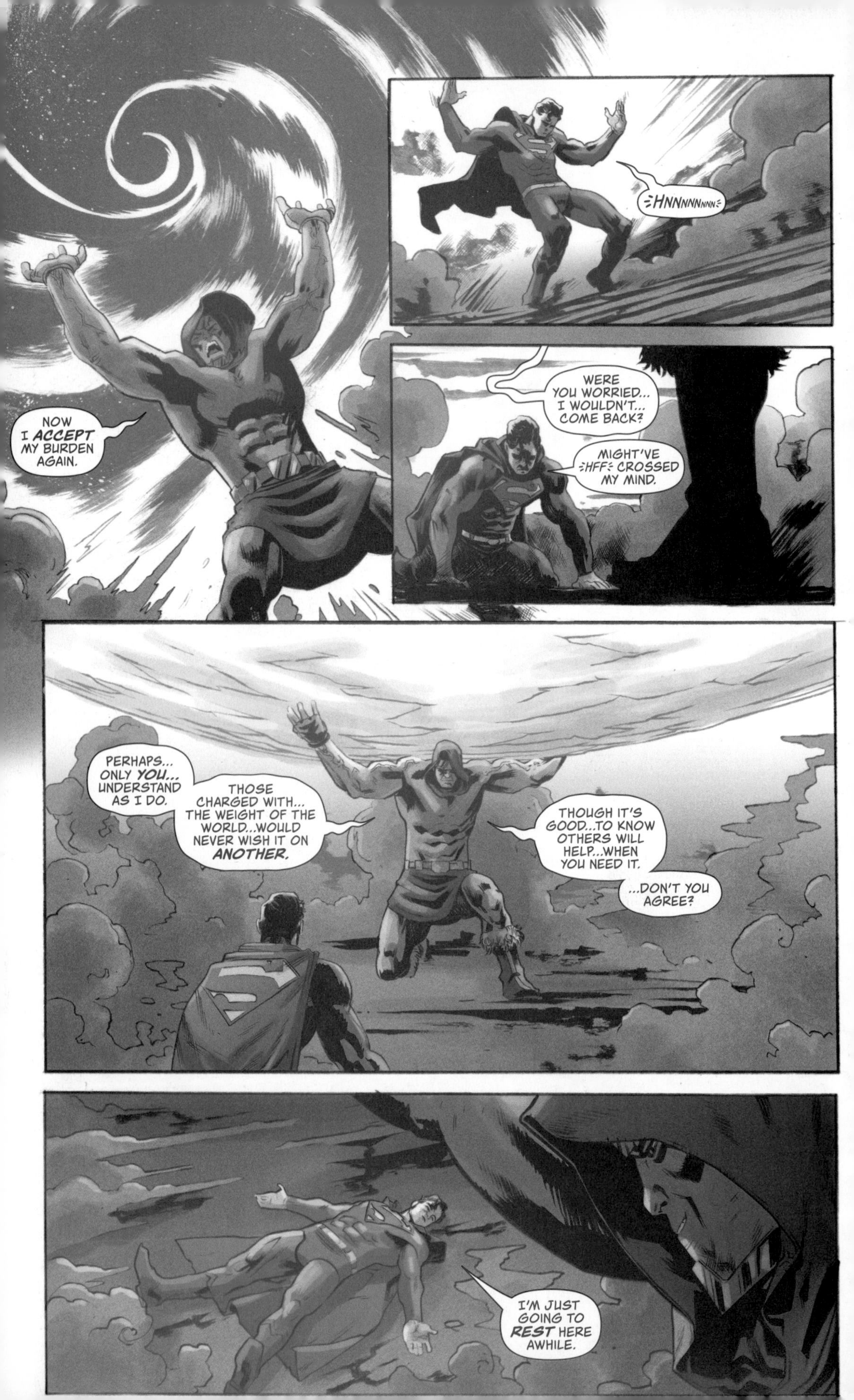
NOW I ACCEPT MY BURDEN AGAIN.
HNNNNNNNN
WERE YOU WORRIED... I WOULDN'T... COME BACK?
MIGHT'VE HFF CROSSED MY MIND.
PERHAPS... ONLY YOU... UNDERSTAND AS I DO.
THOSE CHARGED WITH... THE WEIGHT OF THE WORLD...WOULD NEVER WISH IT ON ANOTHER.
THOUGH IT'S GOOD...TO KNOW OTHERS WILL HELP...WHEN YOU NEED IT.
...DON'T YOU AGREE?
I'M JUST GOING TO REST HERE AWHILE.

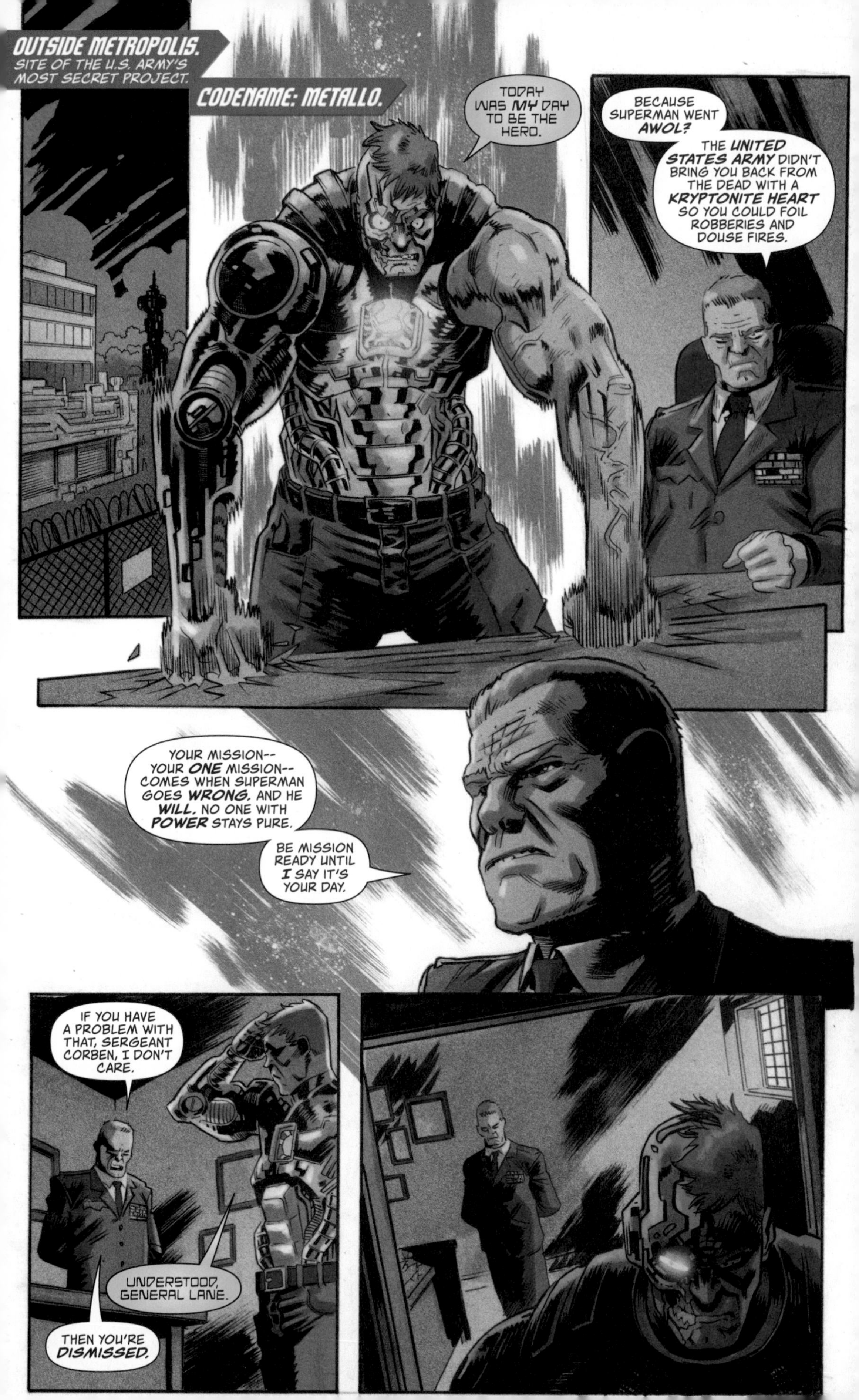
OUTSIDE METROPOLIS.
SITE OF THE U.S. ARMY'S MOST SECRET PROJECT.
CODENAME: METALLO.
TODAY WAS MY DAY TO BE THE HERO.
BECAUSE SUPERMAN WENT AWOL?
THE UNITED STATES ARMY DIDN'T BRING YOU BACK FROM THE DEAD WITH A KRYPTONITE HEART SO YOU COULD FOIL ROBBERIES AND DOUSE FIRES.
YOUR MISSION-- YOUR ONE MISSION-- COMES WHEN SUPERMAN GOES WRONG. AND HE WILL. NO ONE WITH POWER STAYS PURE.
BE MISSION READY UNTIL I SAY IT'S YOUR DAY.
IF YOU HAVE A PROBLEM WITH THAT, SERGEANT CORBEN, I DON'T CARE.
UNDERSTOOD, GENERAL LANE.
THEN YOU'RE DISMISSED.

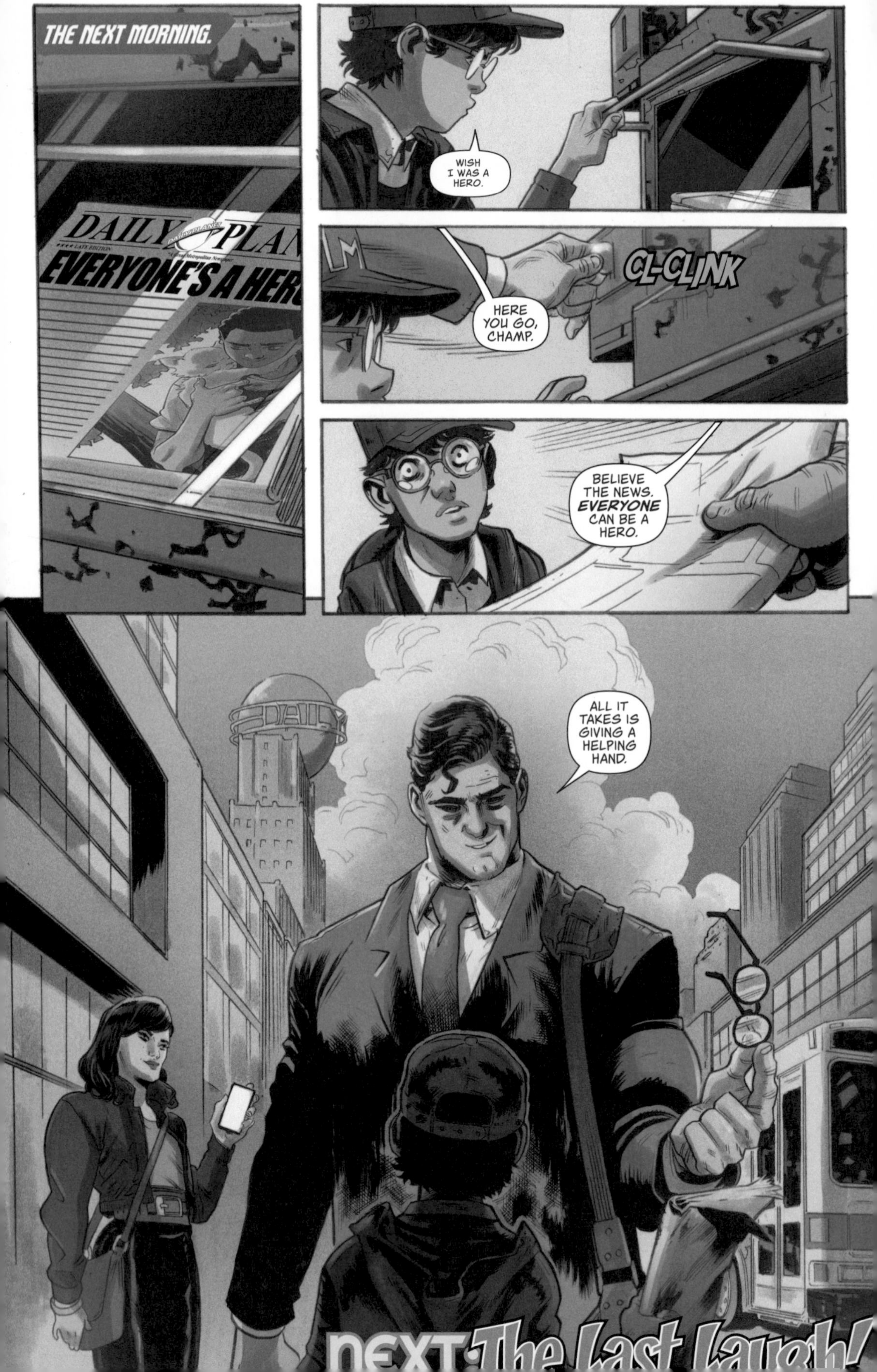
THE NEXT MORNING.
DAILY PLANET
LATE EDITION
EVERYONE'S A HERO
WISH I WAS A HERO.
CL-CLINK
HERE YOU GO, CHAMP.
BELIEVE THE NEWS. *EVERYONE* CAN BE A HERO.
ALL IT TAKES IS GIVING A HELPING HAND.
NEXT: The Last Laugh!

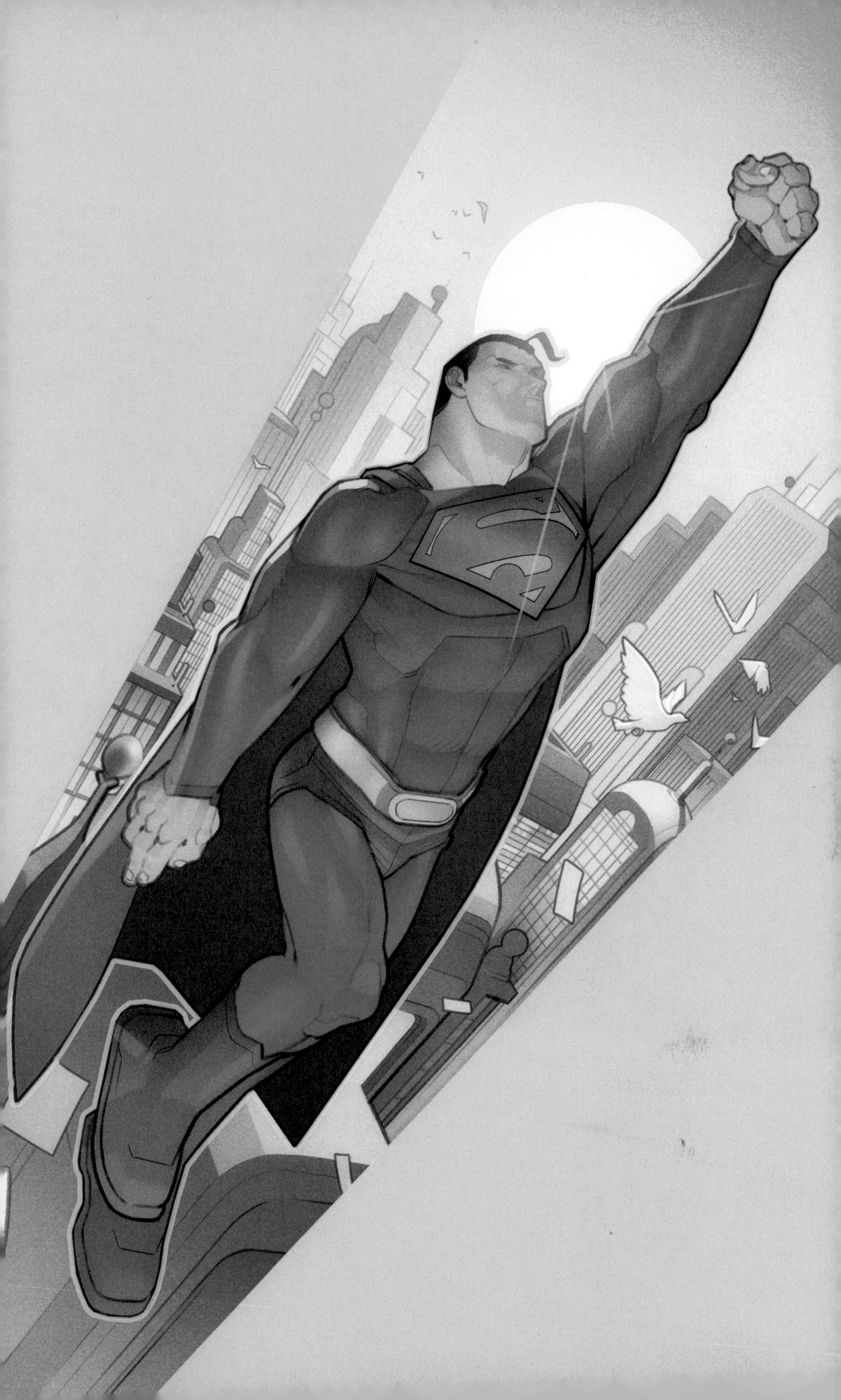

COVER ART BY
DAVID LAFUENTE AND LUIS GUERRERO

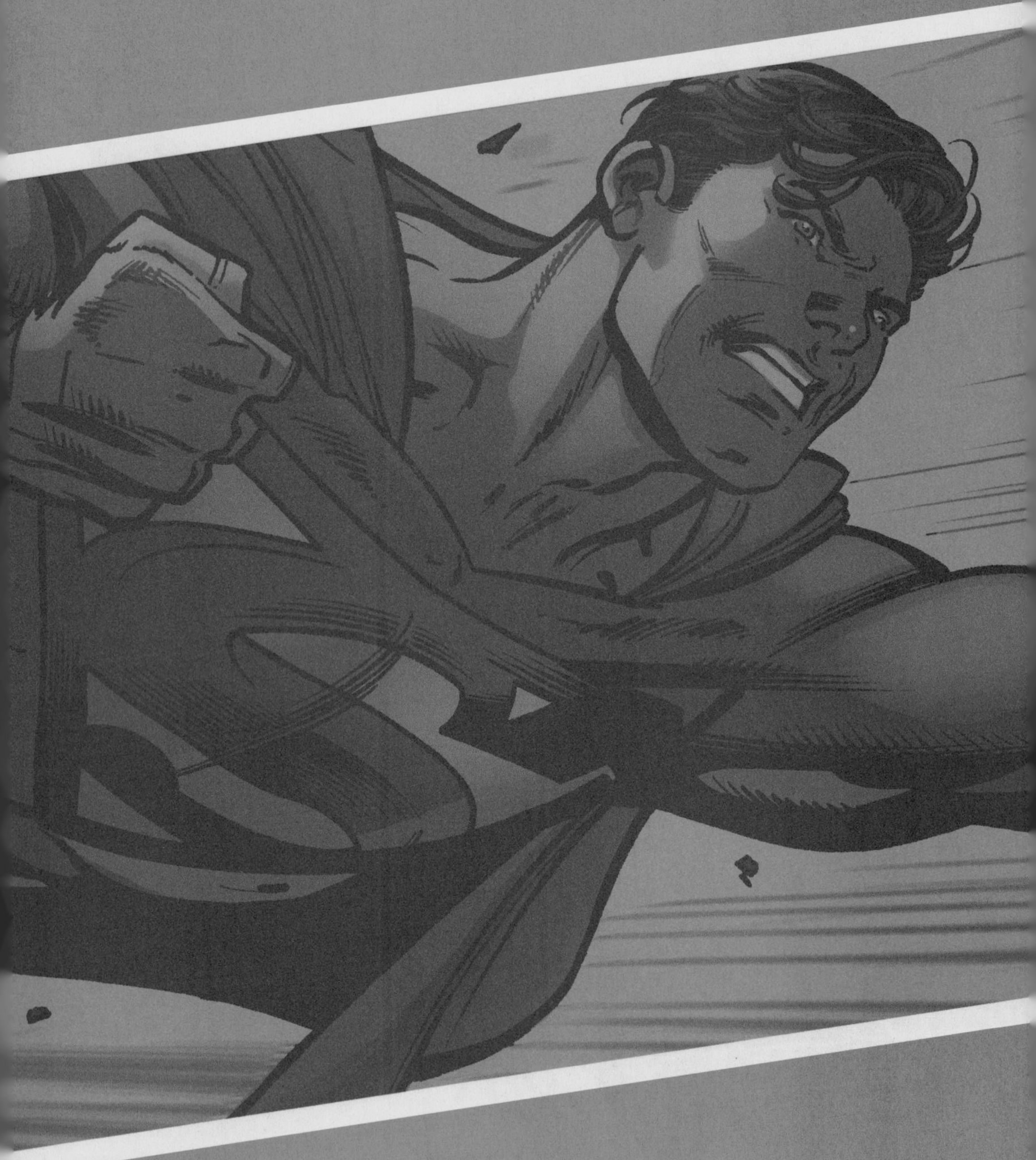

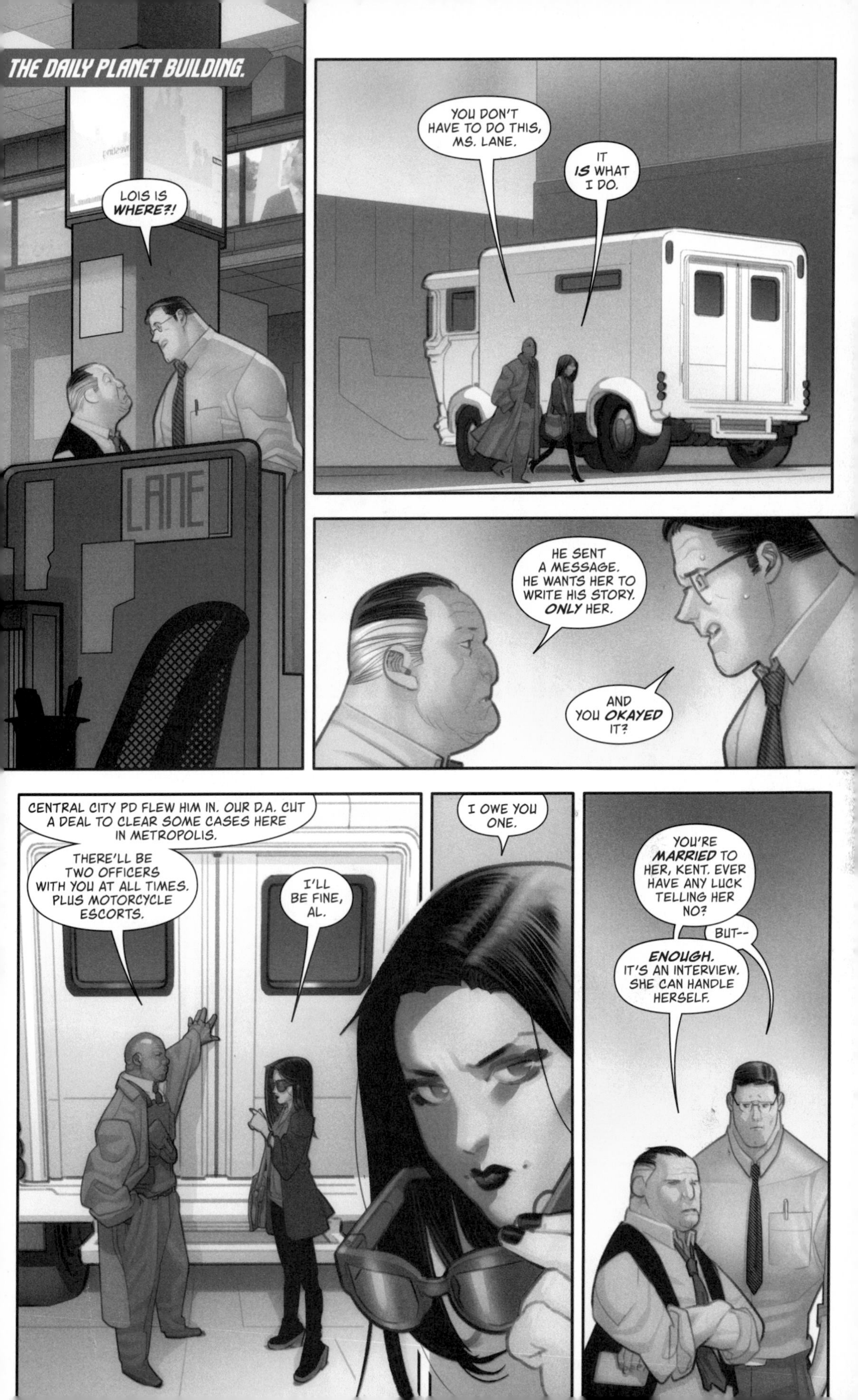
THE DAILY PLANET BUILDING.
LOIS IS WHERE?!
LANE
YOU DON'T HAVE TO DO THIS, MS. LANE.
IT IS WHAT I DO.
HE SENT A MESSAGE. HE WANTS HER TO WRITE HIS STORY. ONLY HER.
AND YOU OKAYED IT?
CENTRAL CITY PD FLEW HIM IN. OUR D.A. CUT A DEAL TO CLEAR SOME CASES HERE IN METROPOLIS.
THERE'LL BE TWO OFFICERS WITH YOU AT ALL TIMES. PLUS MOTORCYCLE ESCORTS.
I'LL BE FINE, AL.
I OWE YOU ONE.
YOU'RE MARRIED TO HER, KENT. EVER HAVE ANY LUCK TELLING HER NO?
BUT--
ENOUGH. IT'S AN INTERVIEW. SHE CAN HANDLE HERSELF.

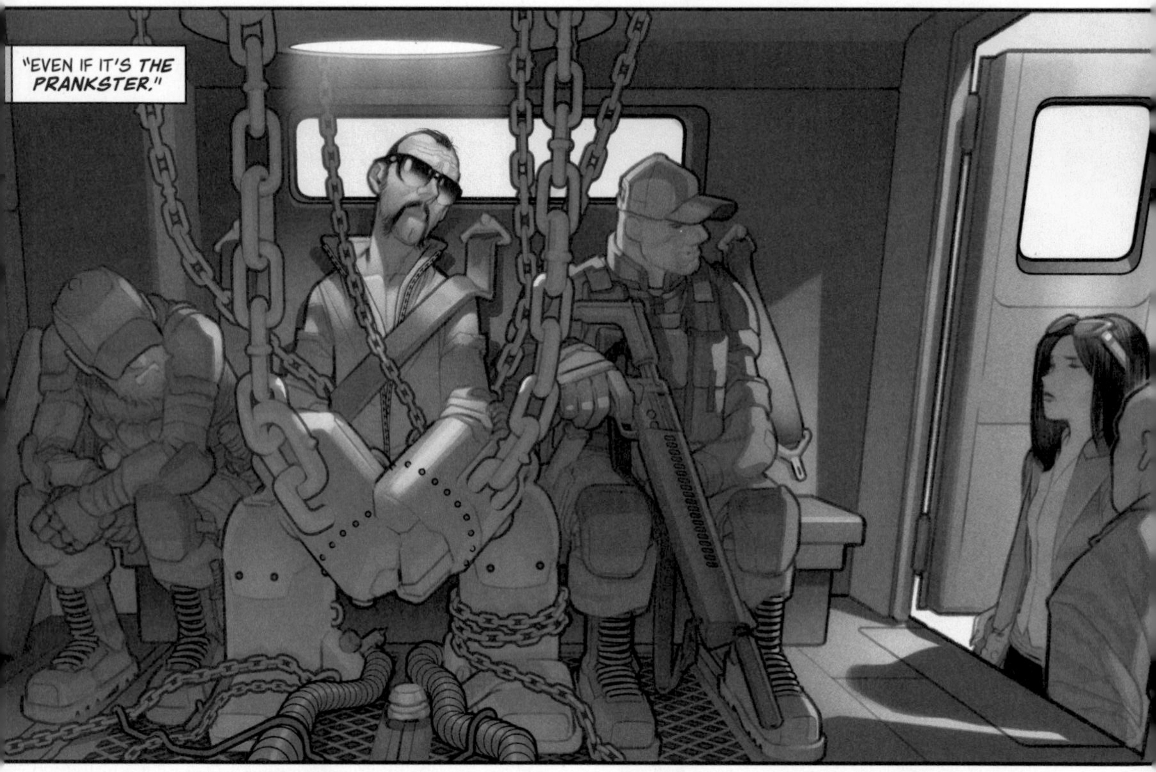
"EVEN IF IT'S *THE PRANKSTER.*"

WHO PRANKS THE PRANKSTER?

ROBERT VENDITTI WRITER
DAVID LAFUENTE ARTIST
LUIS GUERRERO COLORIST
CLAYTON COWLES LETTERER
LAFUENTE & GUERRERO COVER
ANDREW MARINO EDITOR

SUPERMAN CREATED BY **JERRY SIEGEL & JOE SHUSTER.**
BY SPECIAL ARRANGEMENT WITH THE **JERRY SIEGEL FAMILY.**

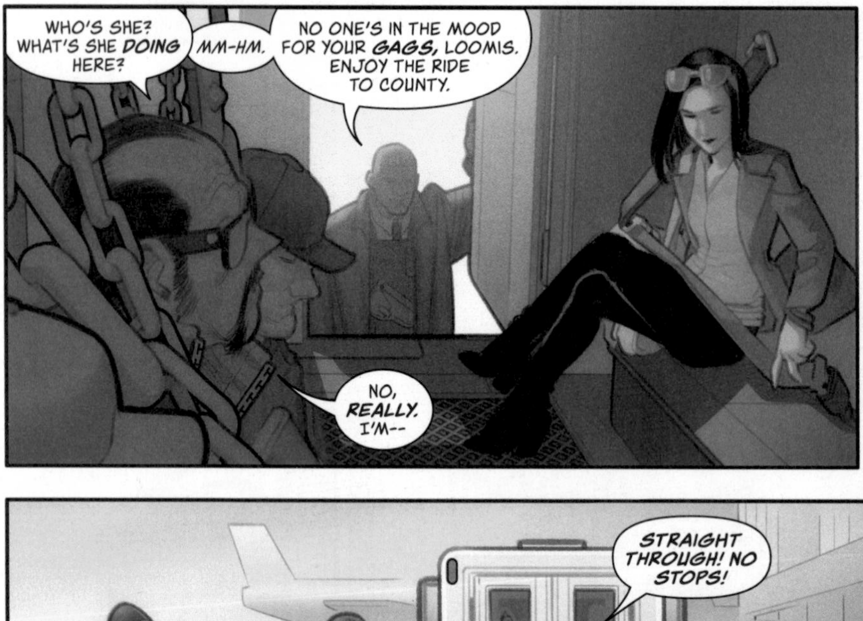
WHO'S SHE? WHAT'S SHE *DOING* HERE?
MM-HM.
NO ONE'S IN THE MOOD FOR YOUR *GAGS,* LOOMIS. ENJOY THE RIDE TO COUNTY.
NO, *REALLY.* I'M--

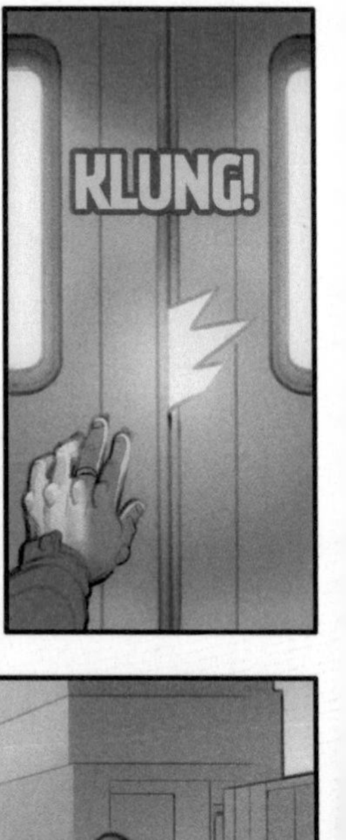
KLUNG!

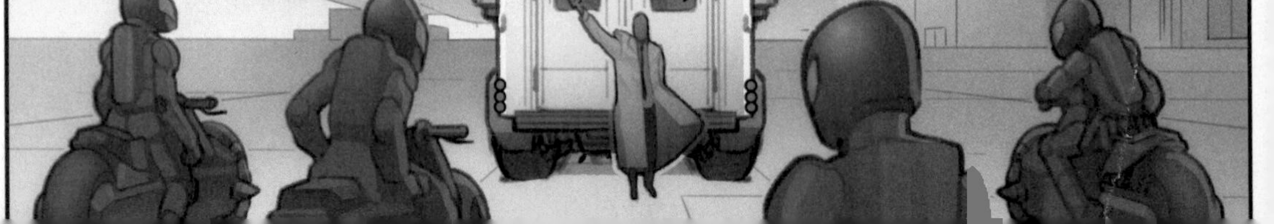
STRAIGHT THROUGH! NO STOPS!

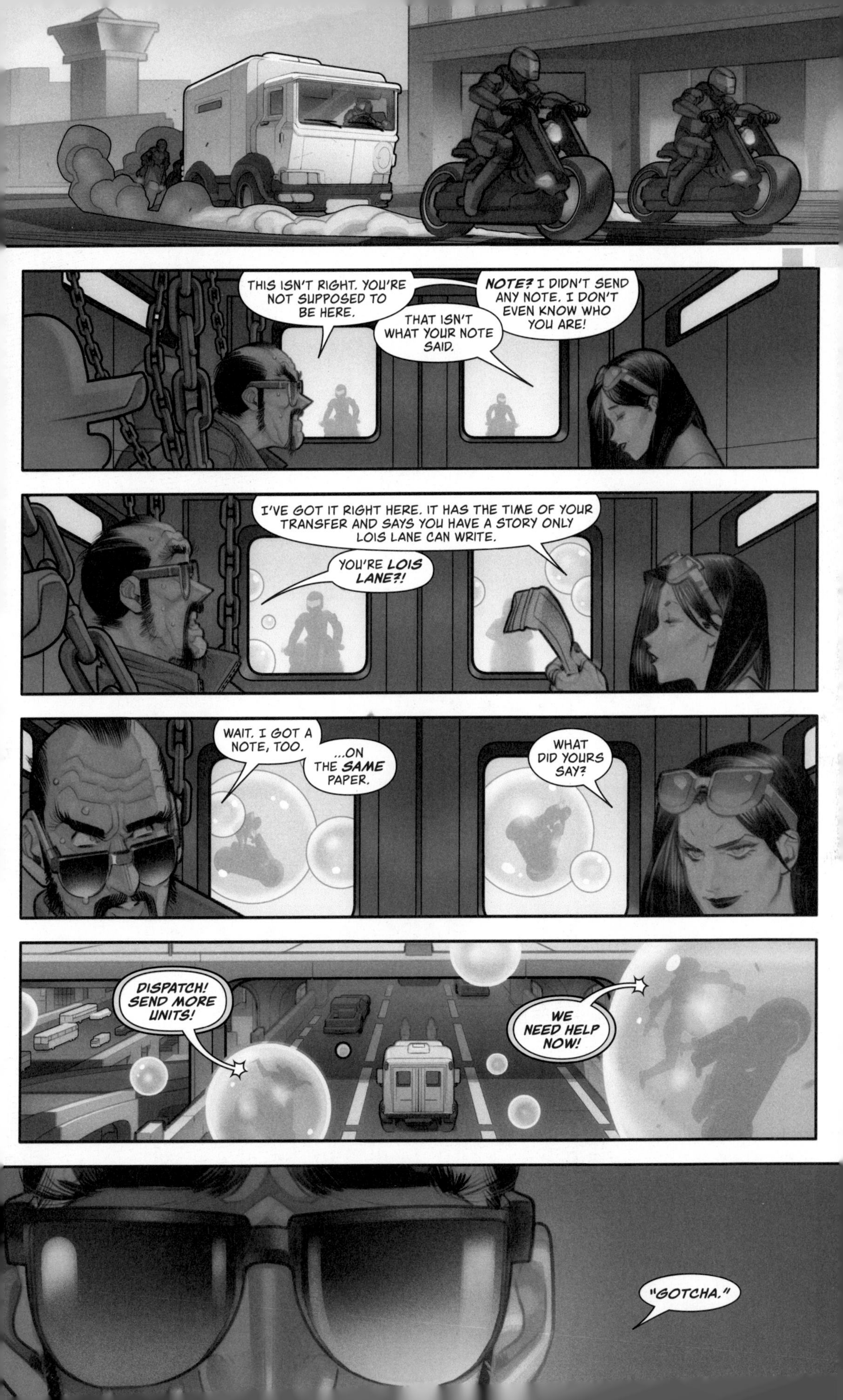
THIS ISN'T RIGHT. YOU'RE NOT SUPPOSED TO BE HERE.
THAT ISN'T WHAT YOUR NOTE SAID.
NOTE?! I DIDN'T SEND ANY NOTE. I DON'T EVEN KNOW WHO YOU ARE!
I'VE GOT IT RIGHT HERE. IT HAS THE TIME OF YOUR TRANSFER AND SAYS YOU HAVE A STORY ONLY LOIS LANE CAN WRITE.
YOU'RE LOIS LANE?!
WAIT. I GOT A NOTE, TOO.
...ON THE SAME PAPER.
WHAT DID YOURS SAY?
DISPATCH! SEND MORE UNITS!
WE NEED HELP NOW!
"GOTCHA."

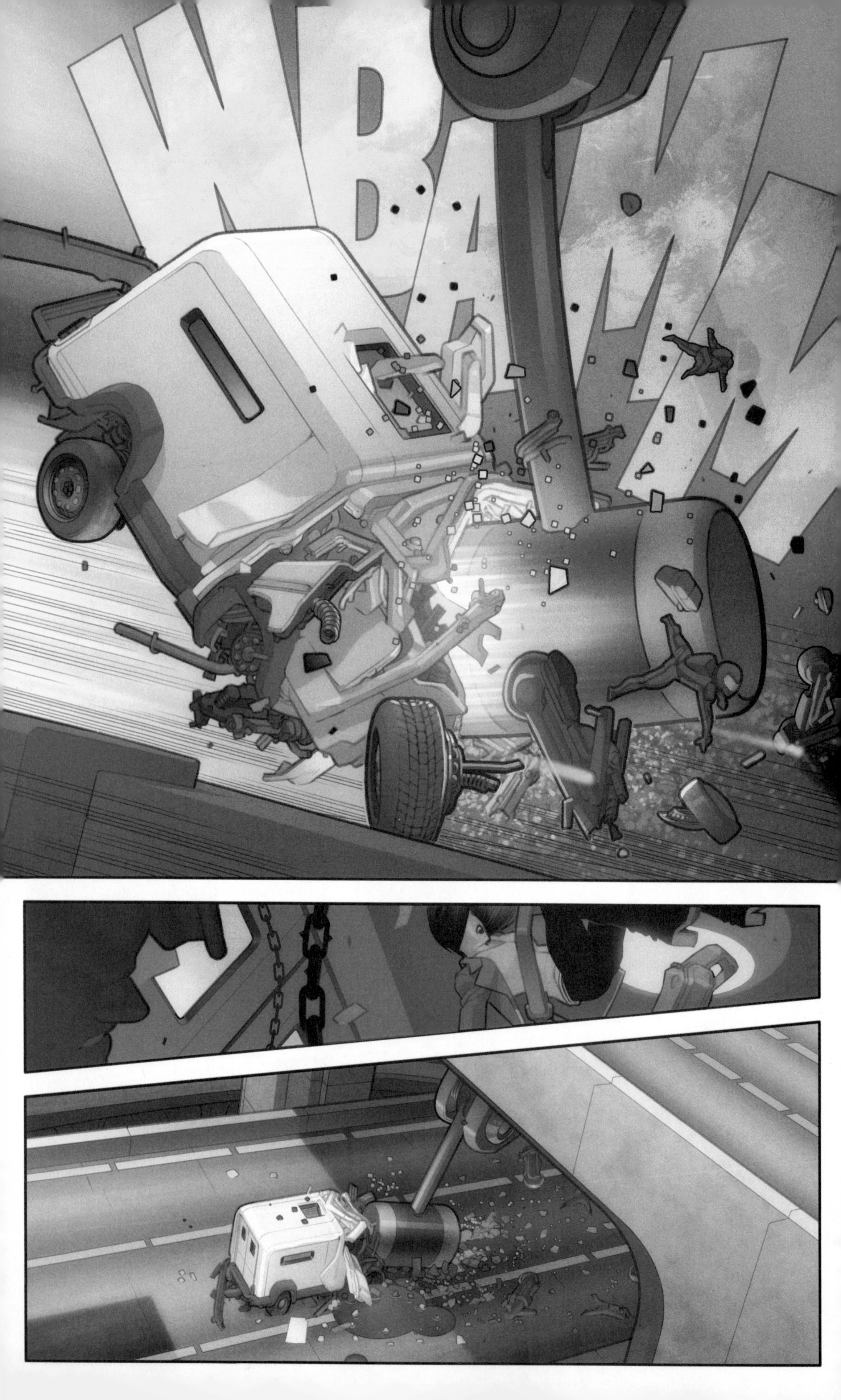
WBAMM

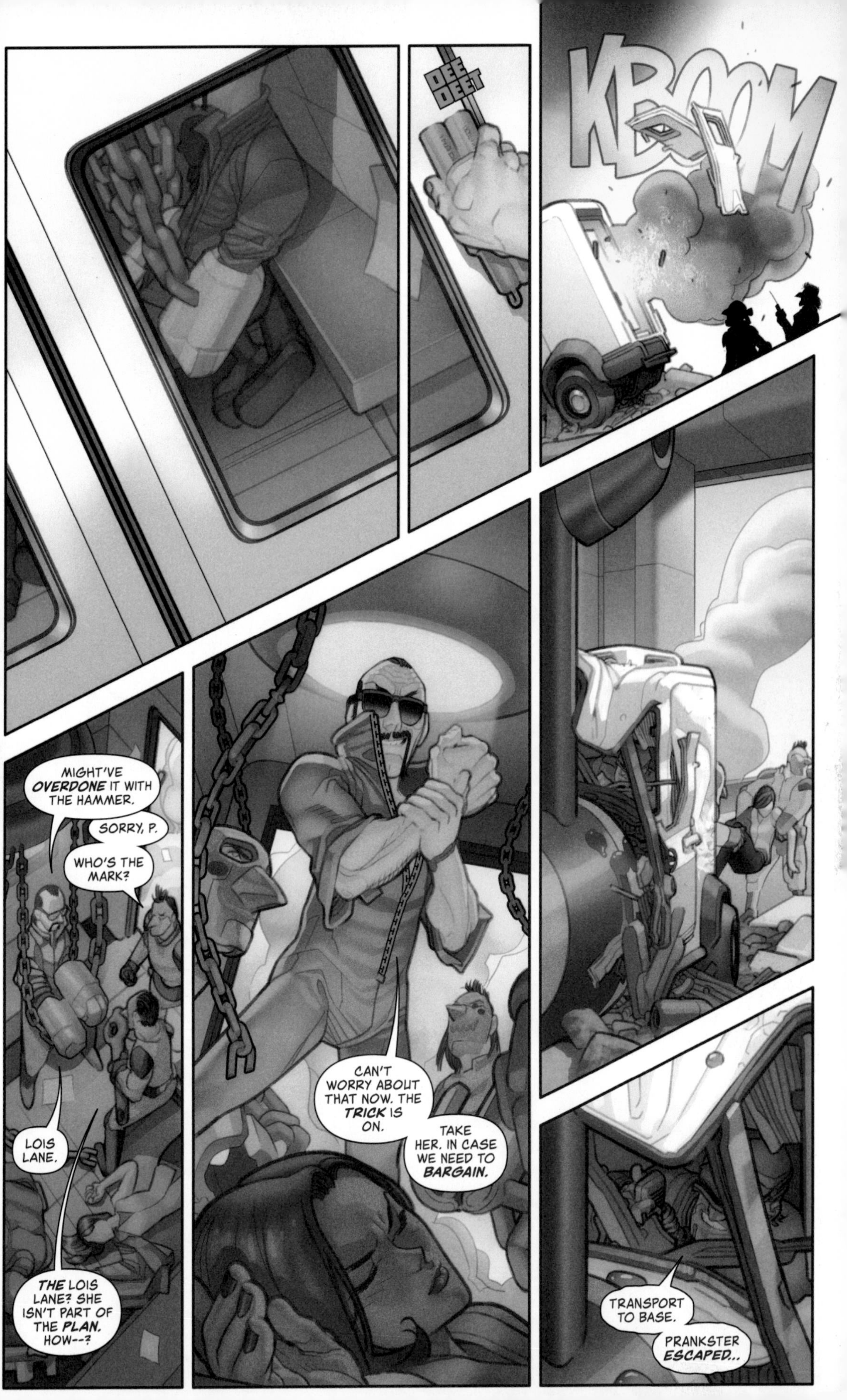
DEE DEET
KBOOM
MIGHT'VE OVERDONE IT WITH THE HAMMER.
SORRY, P.
WHO'S THE MARK?
LOIS LANE.
THE LOIS LANE? SHE ISN'T PART OF THE PLAN. HOW--?
CAN'T WORRY ABOUT THAT NOW. THE TRICK IS ON.
TAKE HER. IN CASE WE NEED TO BARGAIN.
TRANSPORT TO BASE.
PRANKSTER ESCAPED...

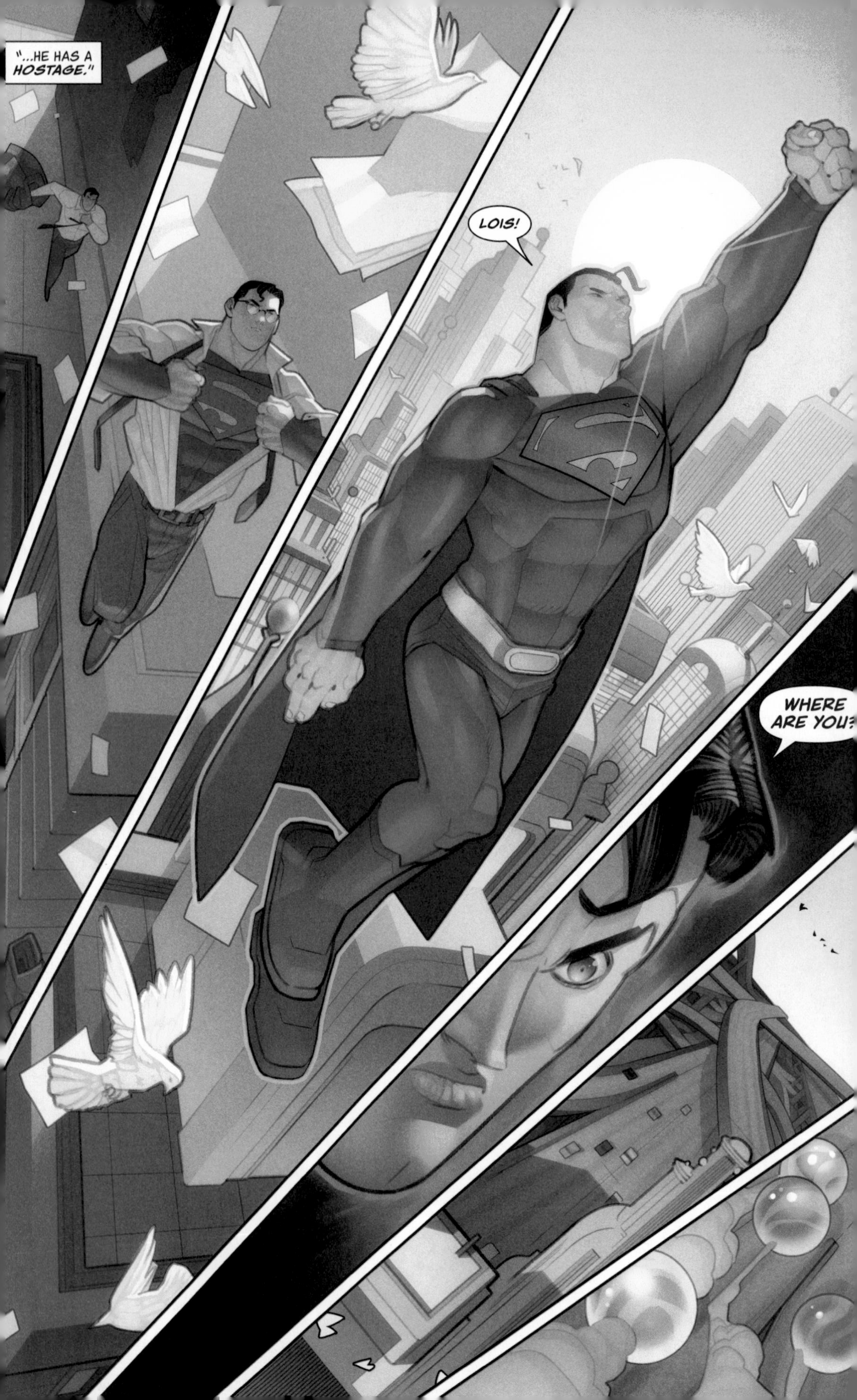
"...HE HAS A HOSTAGE."
LOIS!
WHERE ARE YOU?

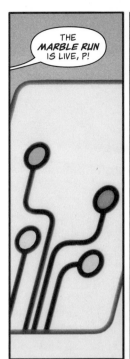

THE *MARBLE RUN* IS LIVE, P!

WHAT A *GAG!*

JUST KEEP YOUR EYES ON *LANE.*

AW, SHE'S *OUT* LIKE AN EXPLODING CIGAR.

YOU WANT I SHOULD POP HER?

NOT YET!

SOMEBODY IS TRYING TO *SPOIL* MY BIT. KILLING HER MIGHT BE WHAT THEY *WANT.*

WHOEVER *"THEY"* IS.

"WAIT UNTIL *AFTER* WE MAKE OUR GETAWAY."

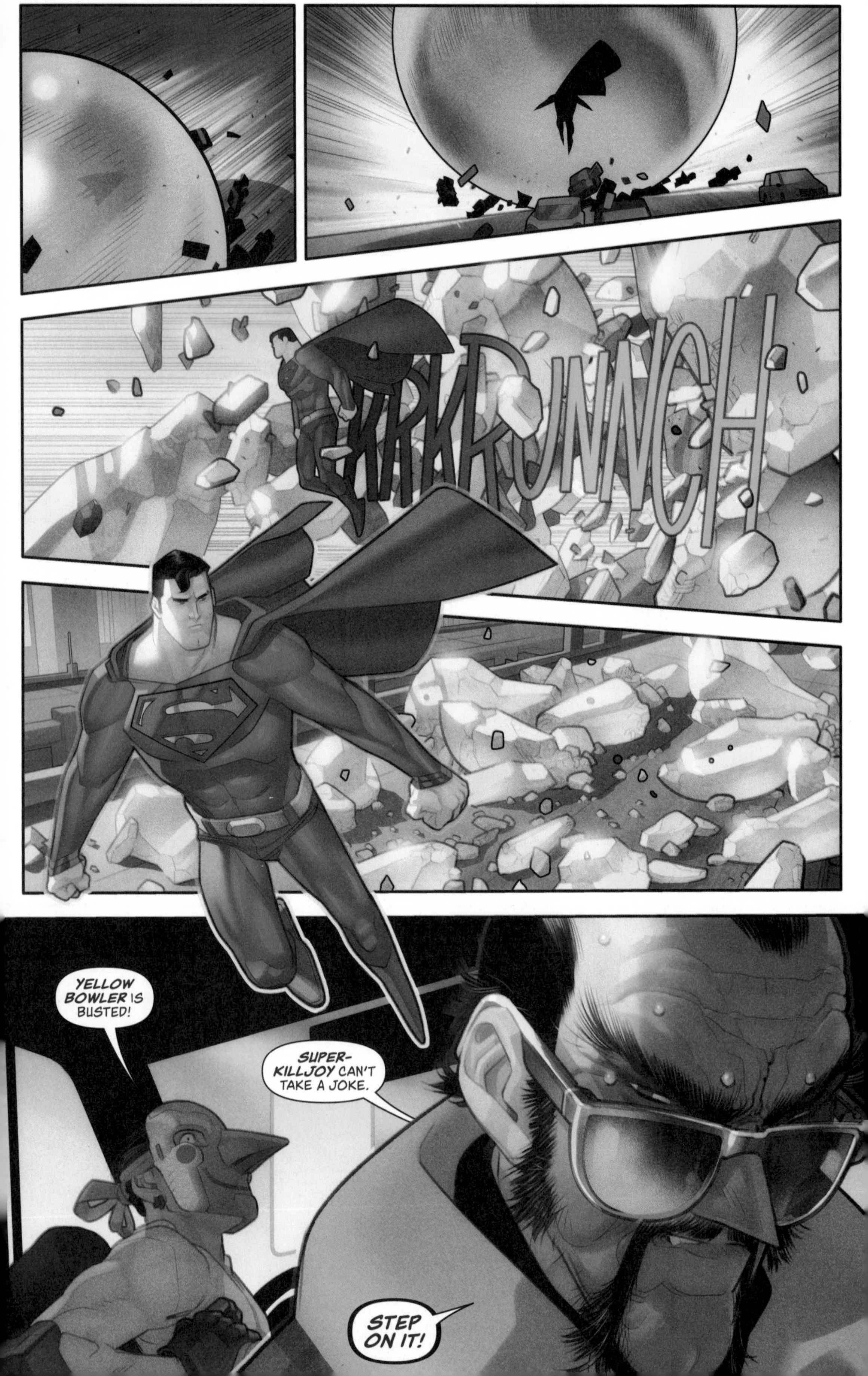
KRKKRUNNCH!
YELLOW BOWLER IS BUSTED!
SUPER-KILLJOY CAN'T TAKE A JOKE.
STEP ON IT!

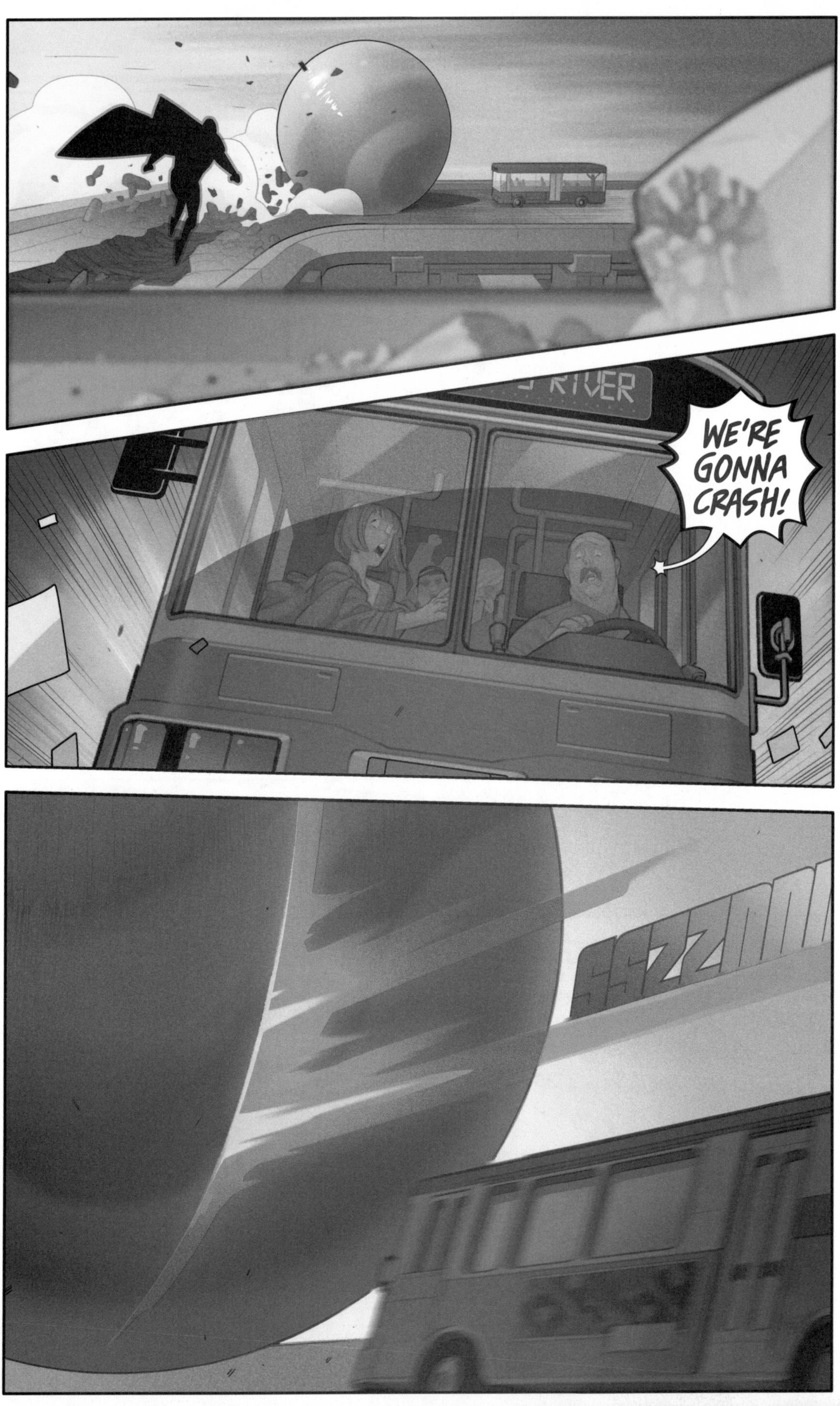

RIVER
WE'RE GONNA CRASH!

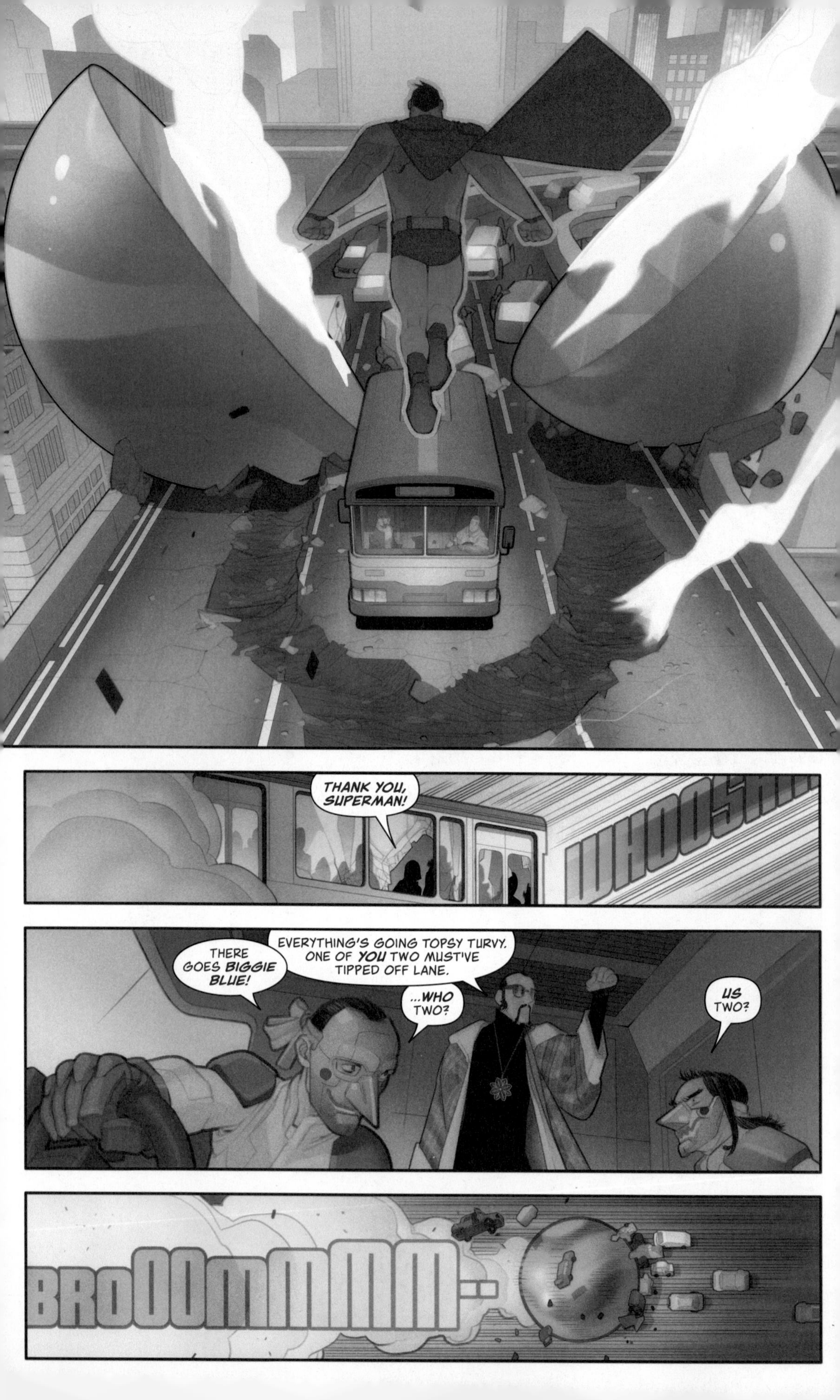

THANK YOU, SUPERMAN!
WHOOSH
THERE GOES BIGGIE BLUE!
EVERYTHING'S GOING TOPSY TURVY. ONE OF YOU TWO MUST'VE TIPPED OFF LANE.
...WHO TWO?
US TWO?
BROOOmmMMM--

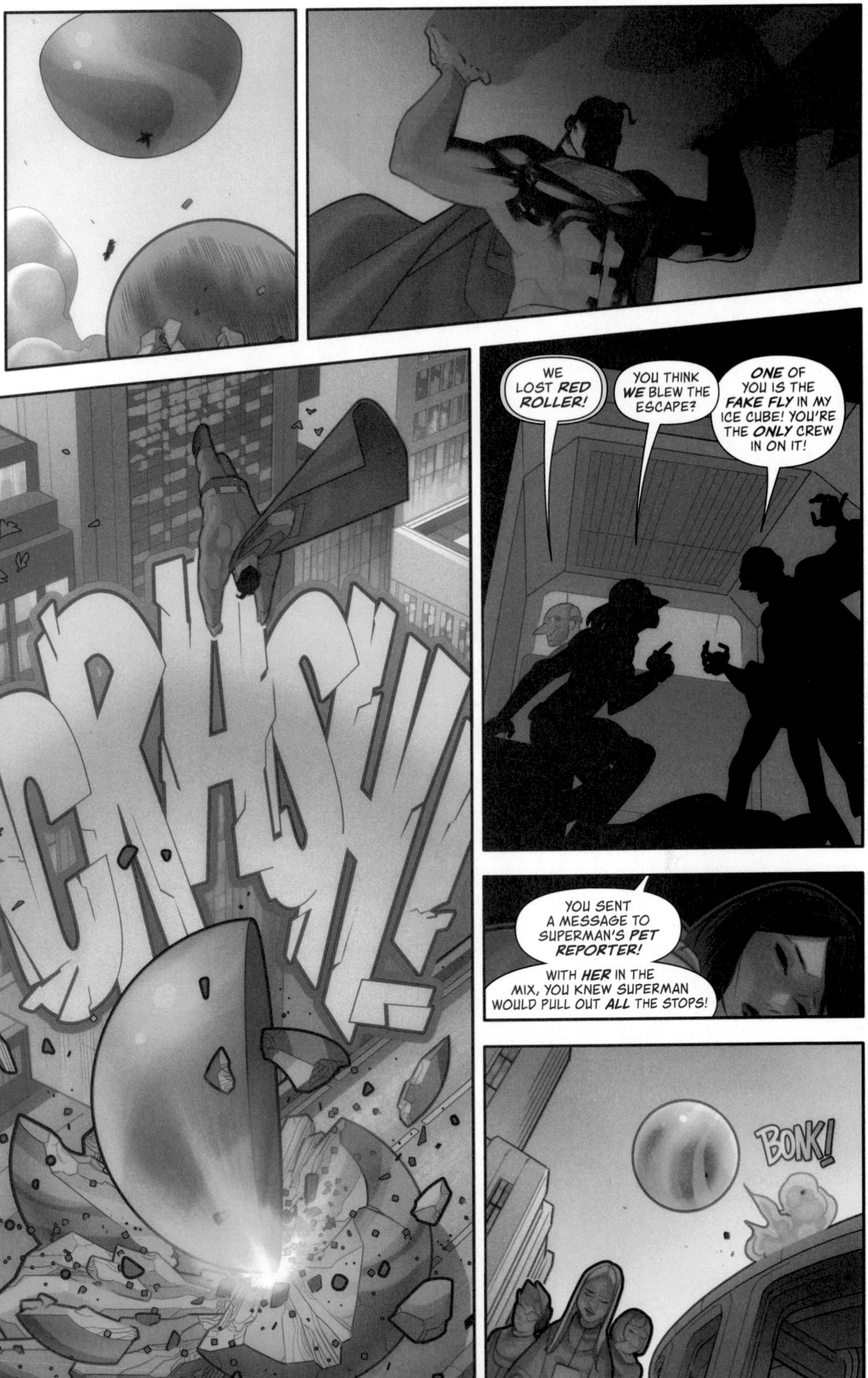
WE LOST RED ROLLER!
YOU THINK WE BLEW THE ESCAPE?
ONE OF YOU IS THE FAKE FLY IN MY ICE CUBE! YOU'RE THE ONLY CREW IN ON IT!
YOU SENT A MESSAGE TO SUPERMAN'S PET REPORTER!
WITH HER IN THE MIX, YOU KNEW SUPERMAN WOULD PULL OUT ALL THE STOPS!
BONK!

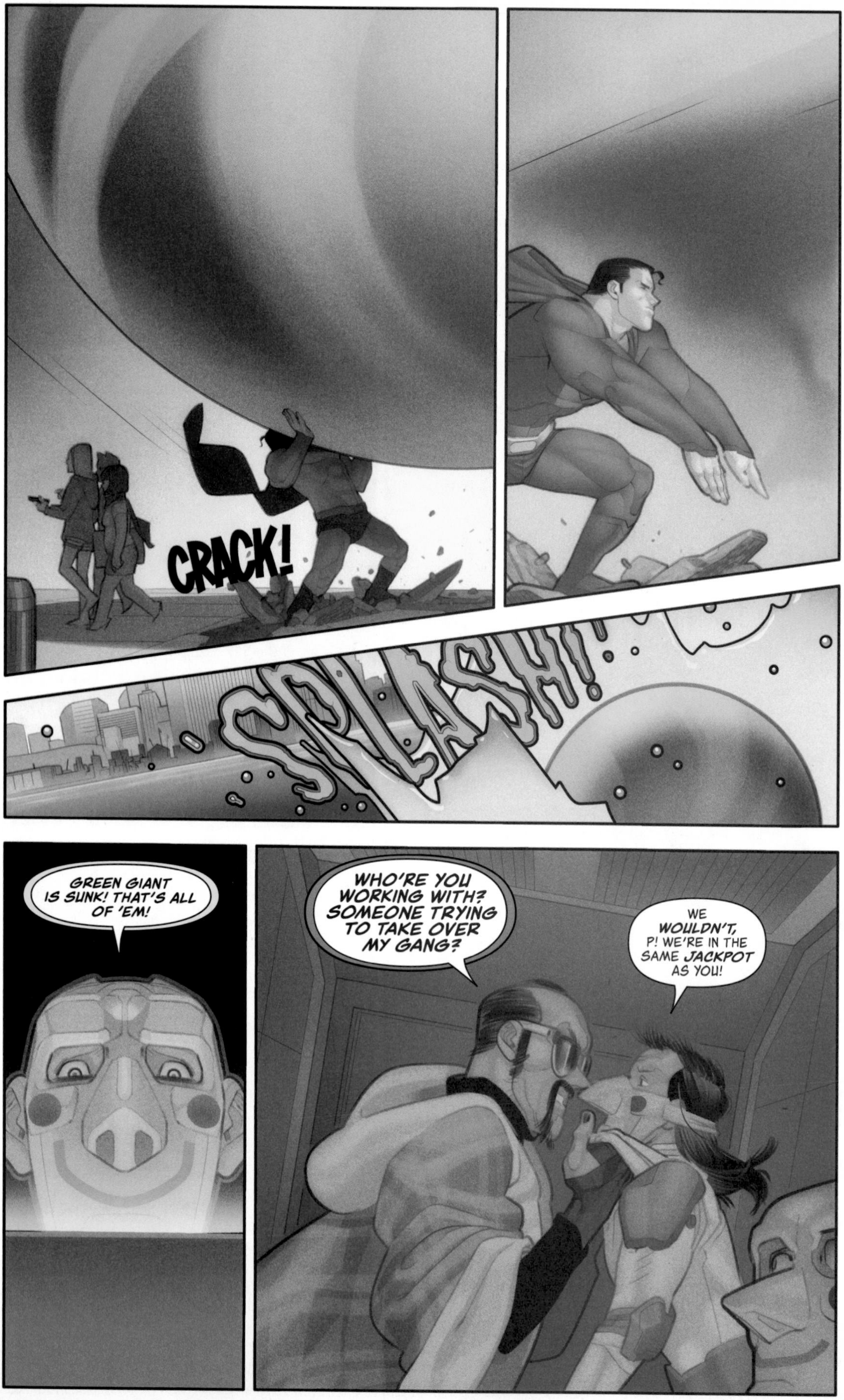
CRACK!
SPLASH!
GREEN GIANT IS SUNK! THAT'S ALL OF 'EM!
WHO'RE YOU WORKING WITH? SOMEONE TRYING TO TAKE OVER MY GANG?
WE WOULDN'T, P! WE'RE IN THE SAME JACKPOT AS YOU!

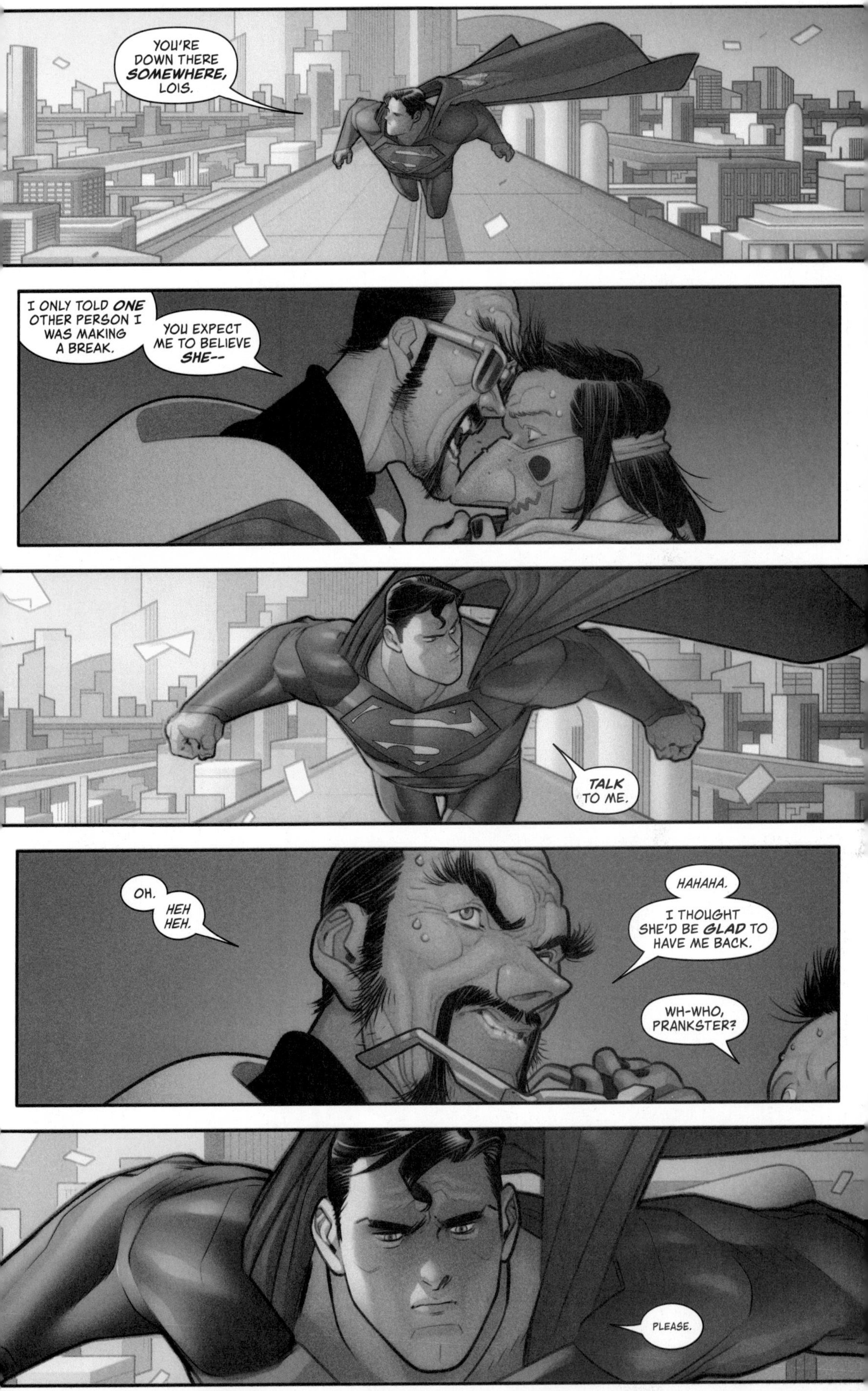

YOU'RE DOWN THERE SOMEWHERE, LOIS.
I ONLY TOLD ONE OTHER PERSON I WAS MAKING A BREAK.
YOU EXPECT ME TO BELIEVE SHE--
TALK TO ME.
OH.
HEH HEH.
HAHAHA.
I THOUGHT SHE'D BE GLAD TO HAVE ME BACK.
WH-WHO, PRANKSTER?
PLEASE.

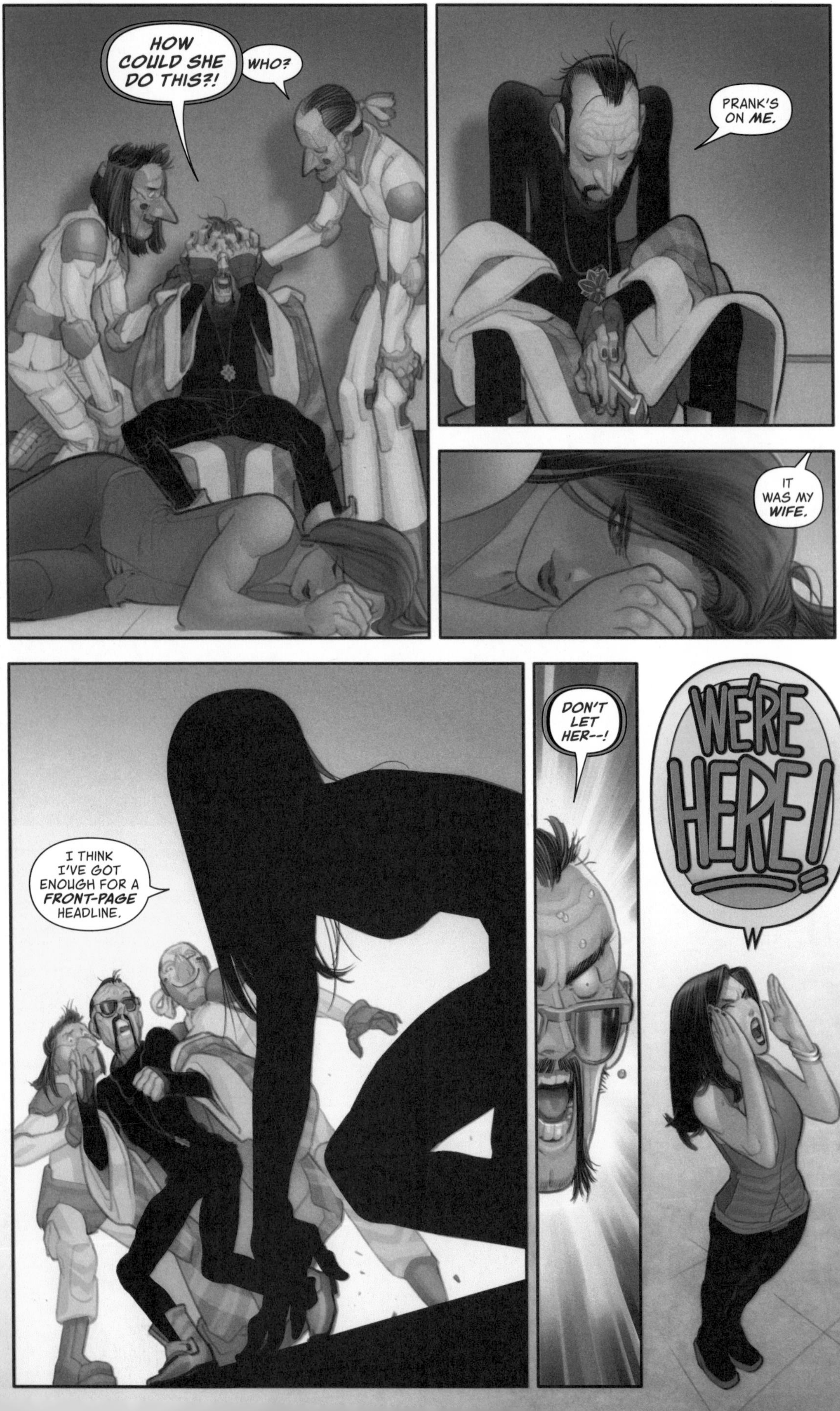
HOW COULD SHE DO THIS?!
WHO?
PRANK'S ON *ME*.
IT WAS MY *WIFE*.
I THINK I'VE GOT ENOUGH FOR A *FRONT-PAGE* HEADLINE.
DON'T LET HER--!
WE'RE HERE!

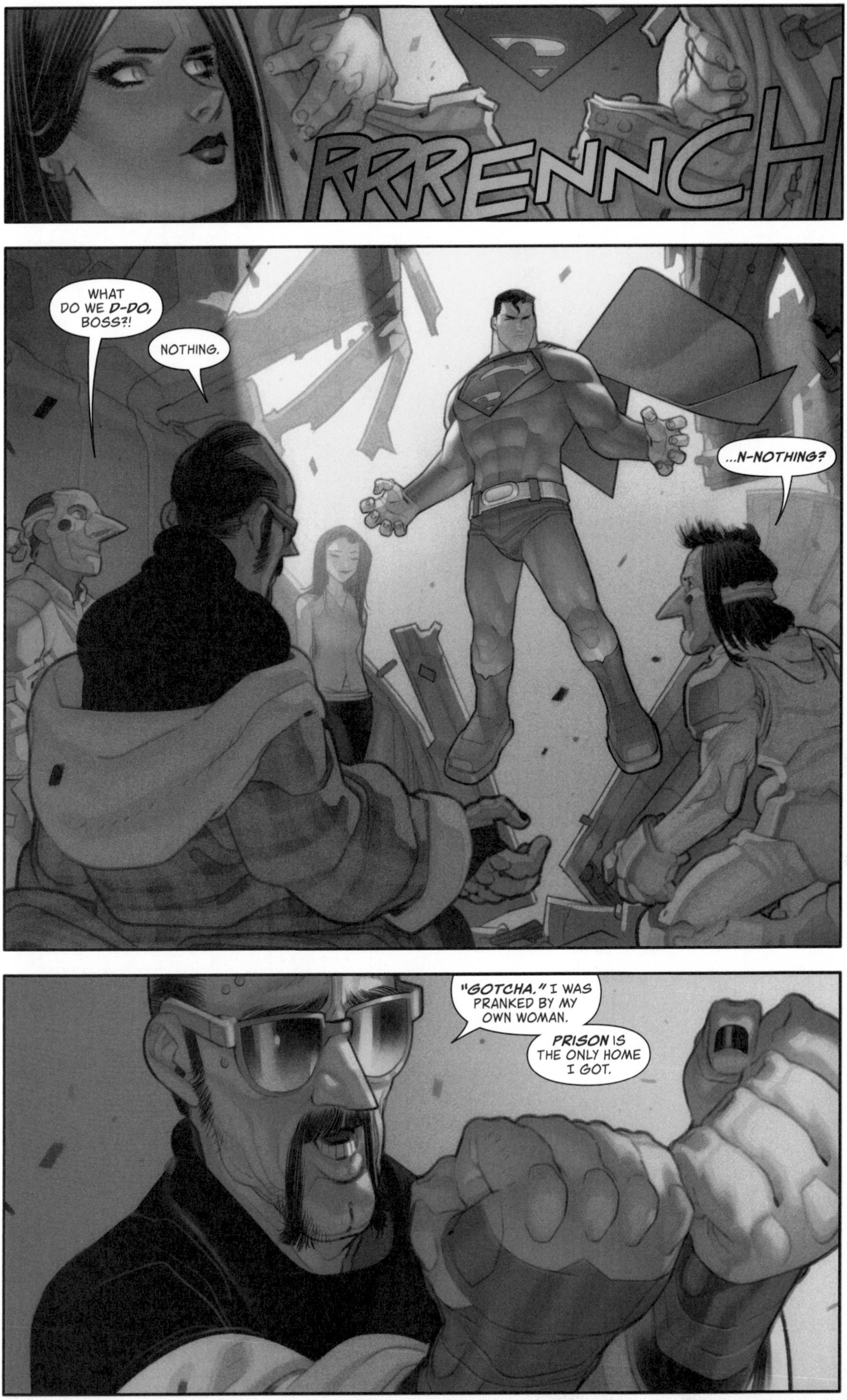
RRRENNCH
WHAT DO WE D-DO, BOSS?!
NOTHING.
...N-NOTHING?
"GOTCHA." I WAS PRANKED BY MY OWN WOMAN.
PRISON IS THE ONLY HOME I GOT.

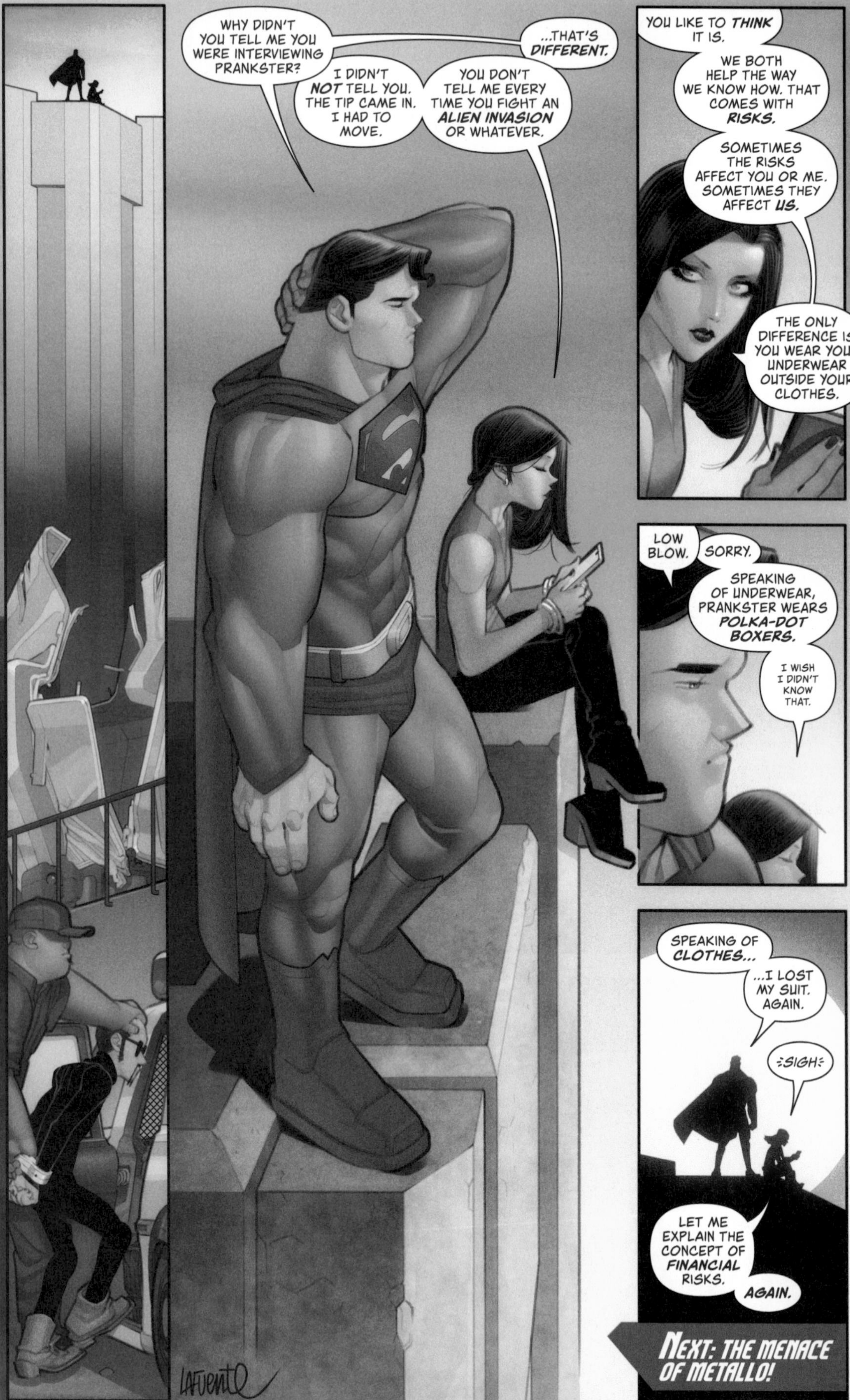

WHY DIDN'T YOU TELL ME YOU WERE INTERVIEWING PRANKSTER?
I DIDN'T NOT TELL YOU. THE TIP CAME IN. I HAD TO MOVE.
...THAT'S DIFFERENT.
YOU DON'T TELL ME EVERY TIME YOU FIGHT AN ALIEN INVASION OR WHATEVER.
LAFUENTE
YOU LIKE TO THINK IT IS.
WE BOTH HELP THE WAY WE KNOW HOW. THAT COMES WITH RISKS.
SOMETIMES THE RISKS AFFECT YOU OR ME. SOMETIMES THEY AFFECT US.
THE ONLY DIFFERENCE IS YOU WEAR YOUR UNDERWEAR OUTSIDE YOUR CLOTHES.
LOW BLOW.
SORRY.
SPEAKING OF UNDERWEAR, PRANKSTER WEARS POLKA-DOT BOXERS.
I WISH I DIDN'T KNOW THAT.
SPEAKING OF CLOTHES...
...I LOST MY SUIT. AGAIN.
SIGH
LET ME EXPLAIN THE CONCEPT OF FINANCIAL RISKS.
AGAIN.
NEXT: THE MENACE OF METALLO!

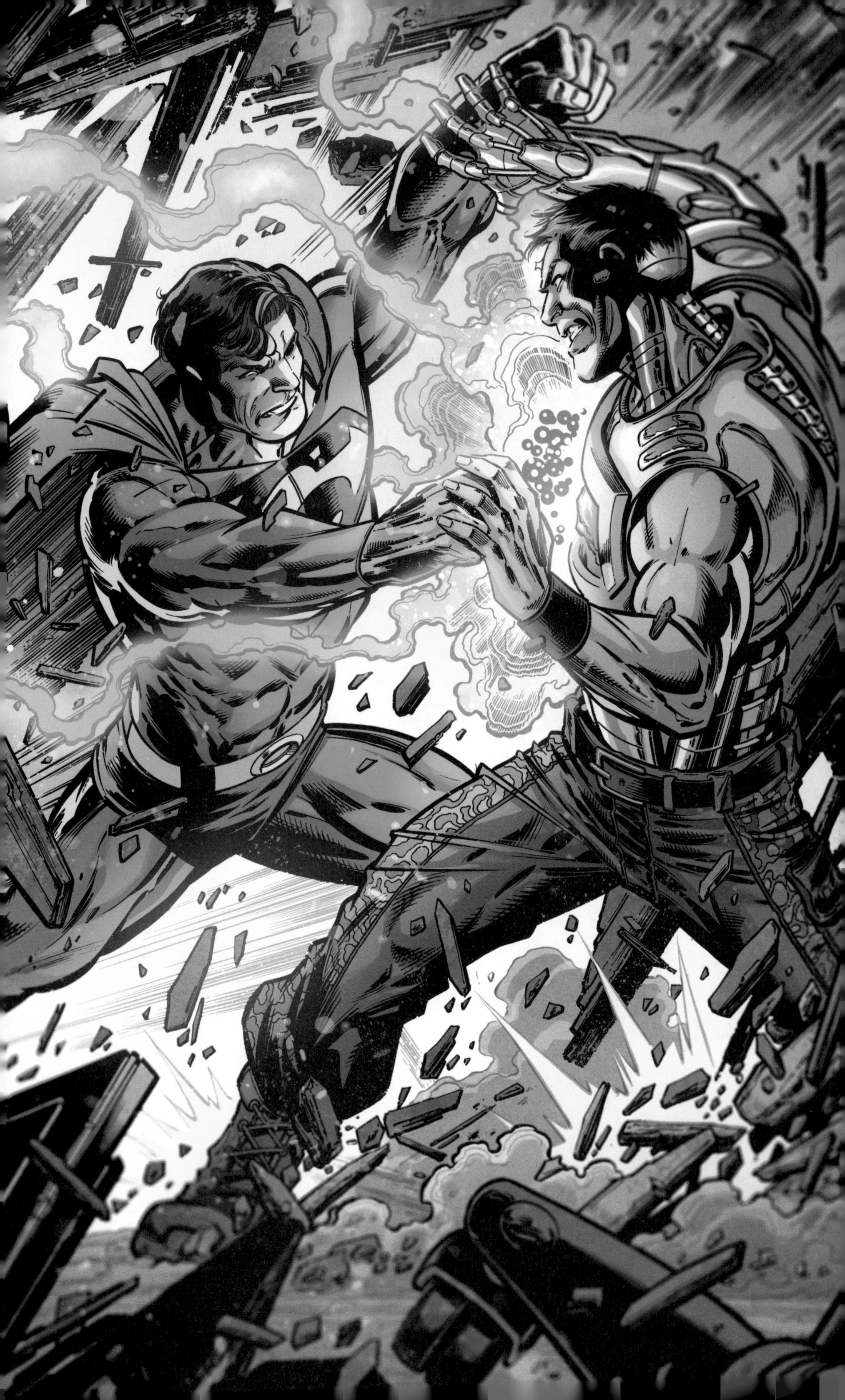

COVER ART BY
PAUL PELLETIER, DREW HENNESSY,
AND **ADRIANO LUCAS**

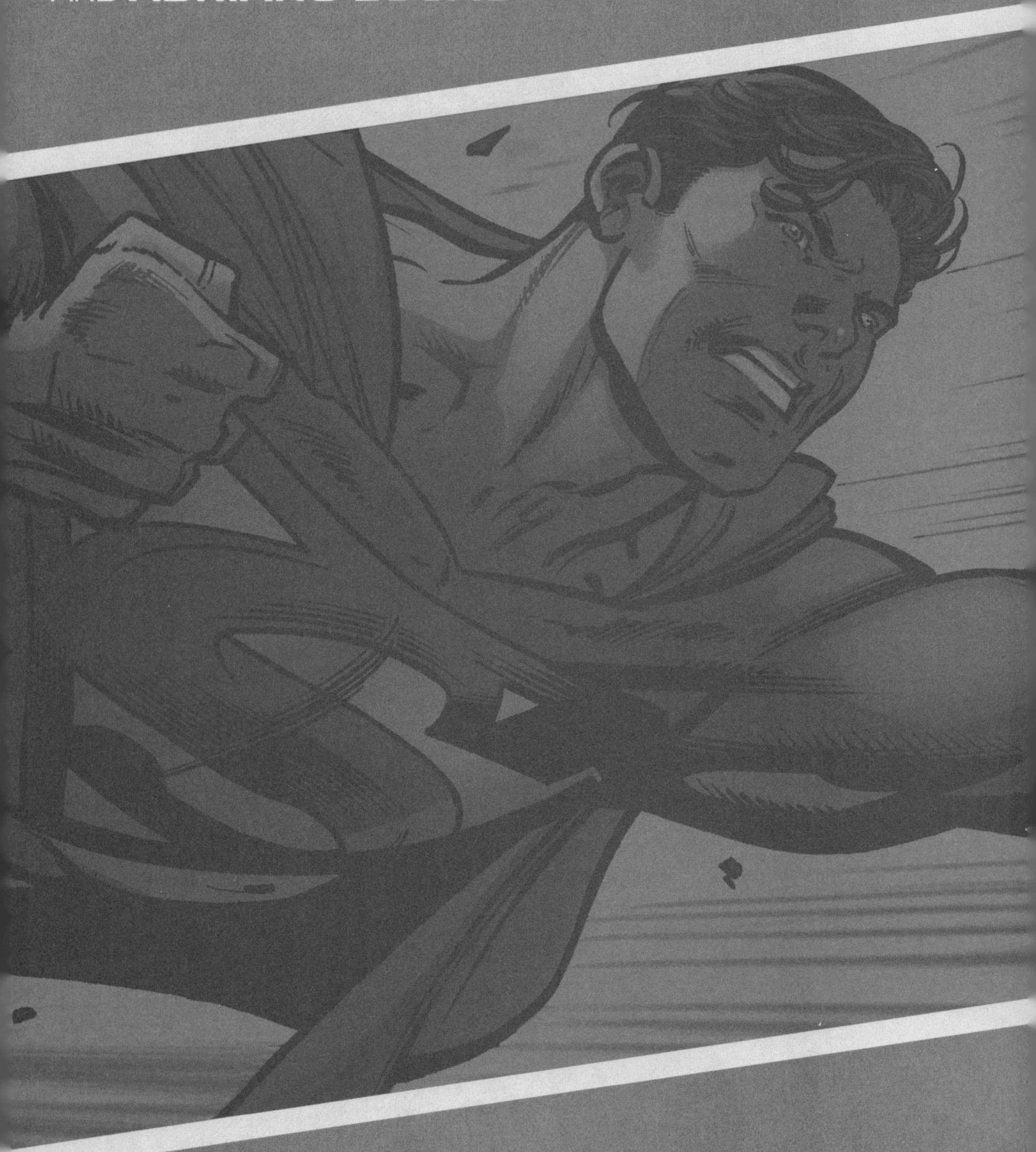

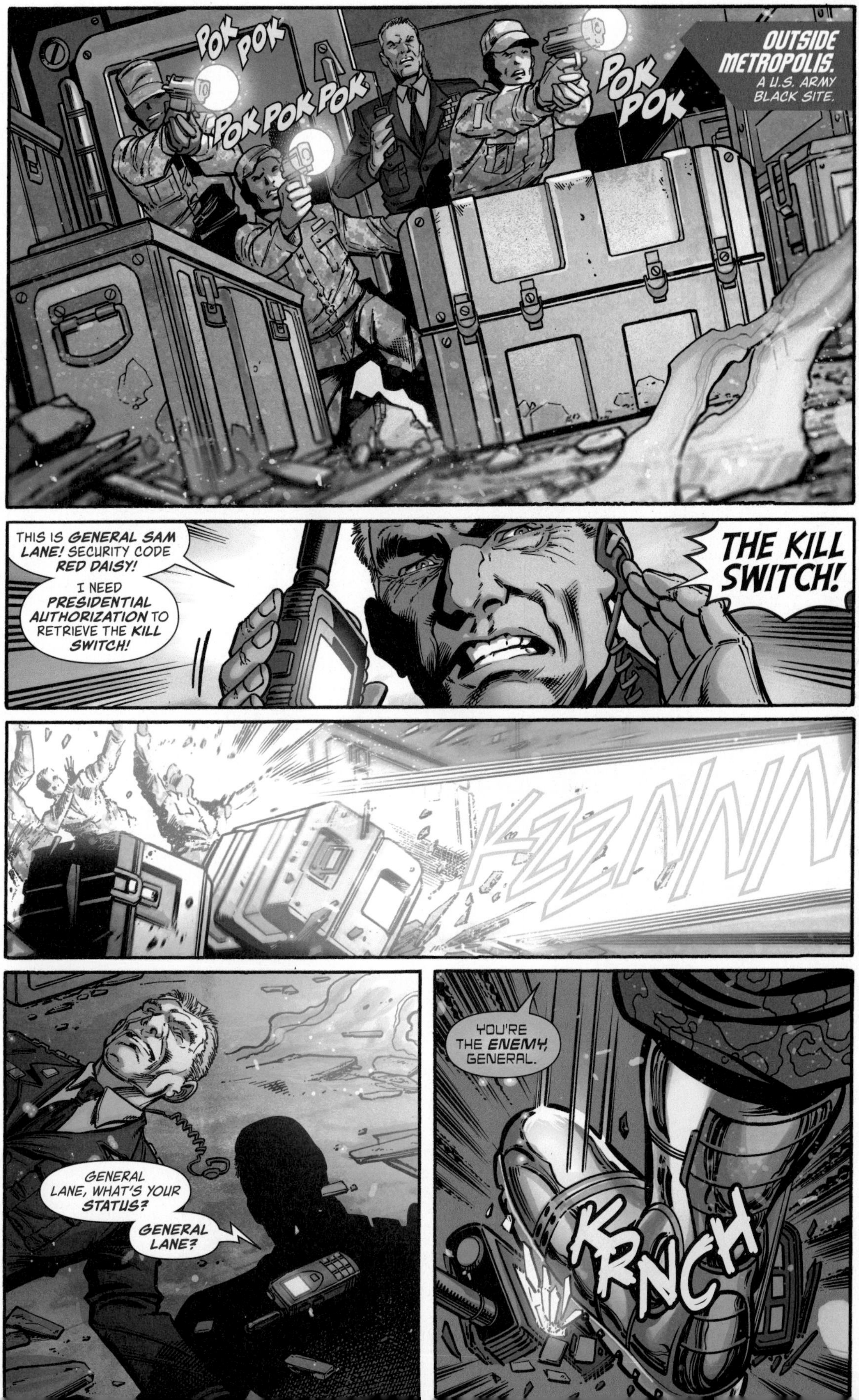
POK POK
POK POK POK
POK POK
OUTSIDE METROPOLIS.
A U.S. ARMY BLACK SITE.
THIS IS GENERAL SAM LANE! SECURITY CODE RED DAISY!
I NEED PRESIDENTIAL AUTHORIZATION TO RETRIEVE THE KILL SWITCH!
THE KILL SWITCH!
KZZNNN
GENERAL LANE, WHAT'S YOUR STATUS?
GENERAL LANE?
YOU'RE THE ENEMY, GENERAL.
KRNCH

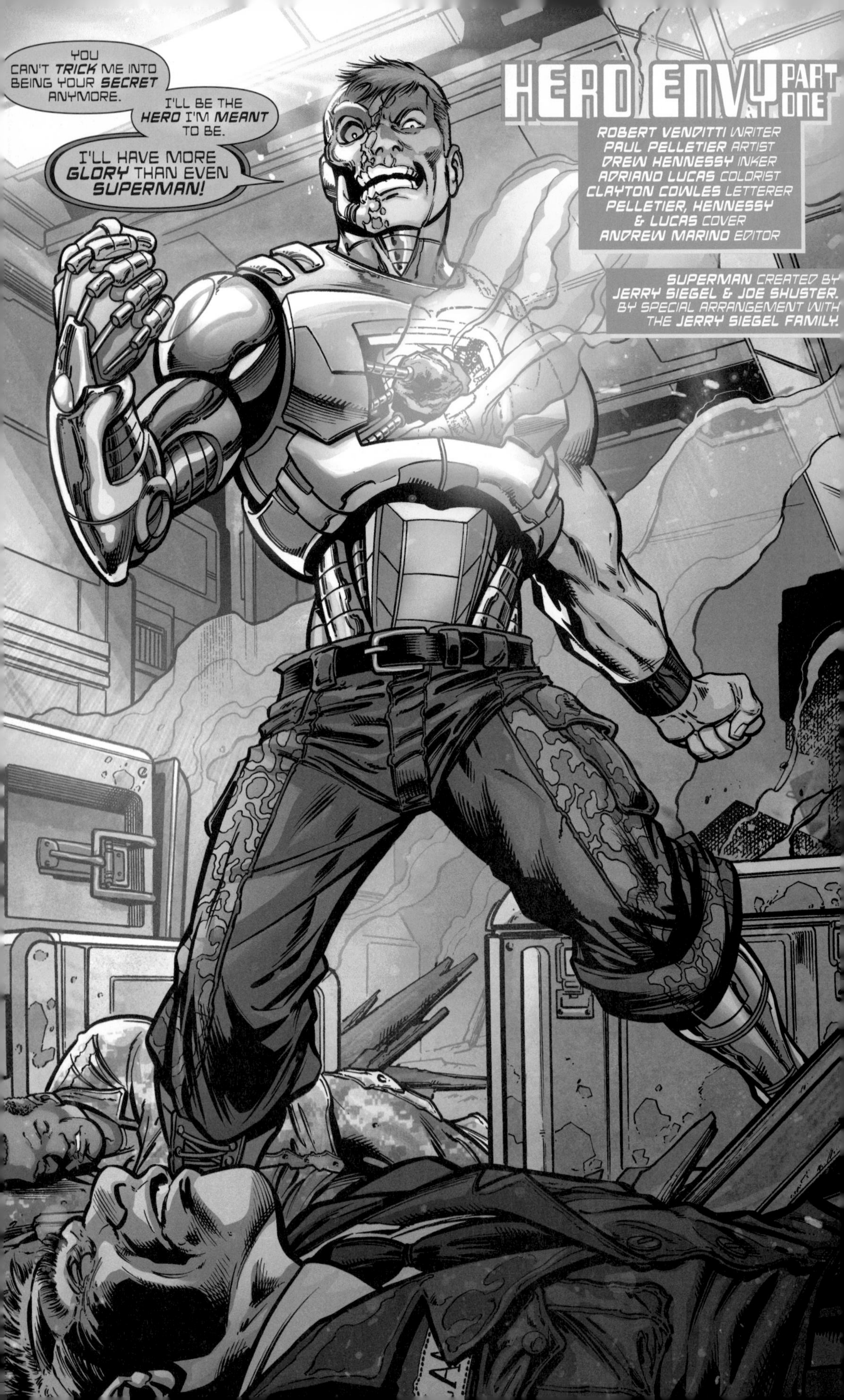
YOU CAN'T TRICK ME INTO BEING YOUR SECRET ANYMORE.
I'LL BE THE HERO I'M MEANT TO BE.
I'LL HAVE MORE GLORY THAN EVEN SUPERMAN!
HERO ENVY PART ONE
ROBERT VENDITTI WRITER
PAUL PELLETIER ARTIST
DREW HENNESSY INKER
ADRIANO LUCAS COLORIST
CLAYTON COWLES LETTERER
PELLETIER, HENNESSY & LUCAS COVER
ANDREW MARINO EDITOR
SUPERMAN CREATED BY JERRY SIEGEL & JOE SHUSTER. BY SPECIAL ARRANGEMENT WITH THE JERRY SIEGEL FAMILY.

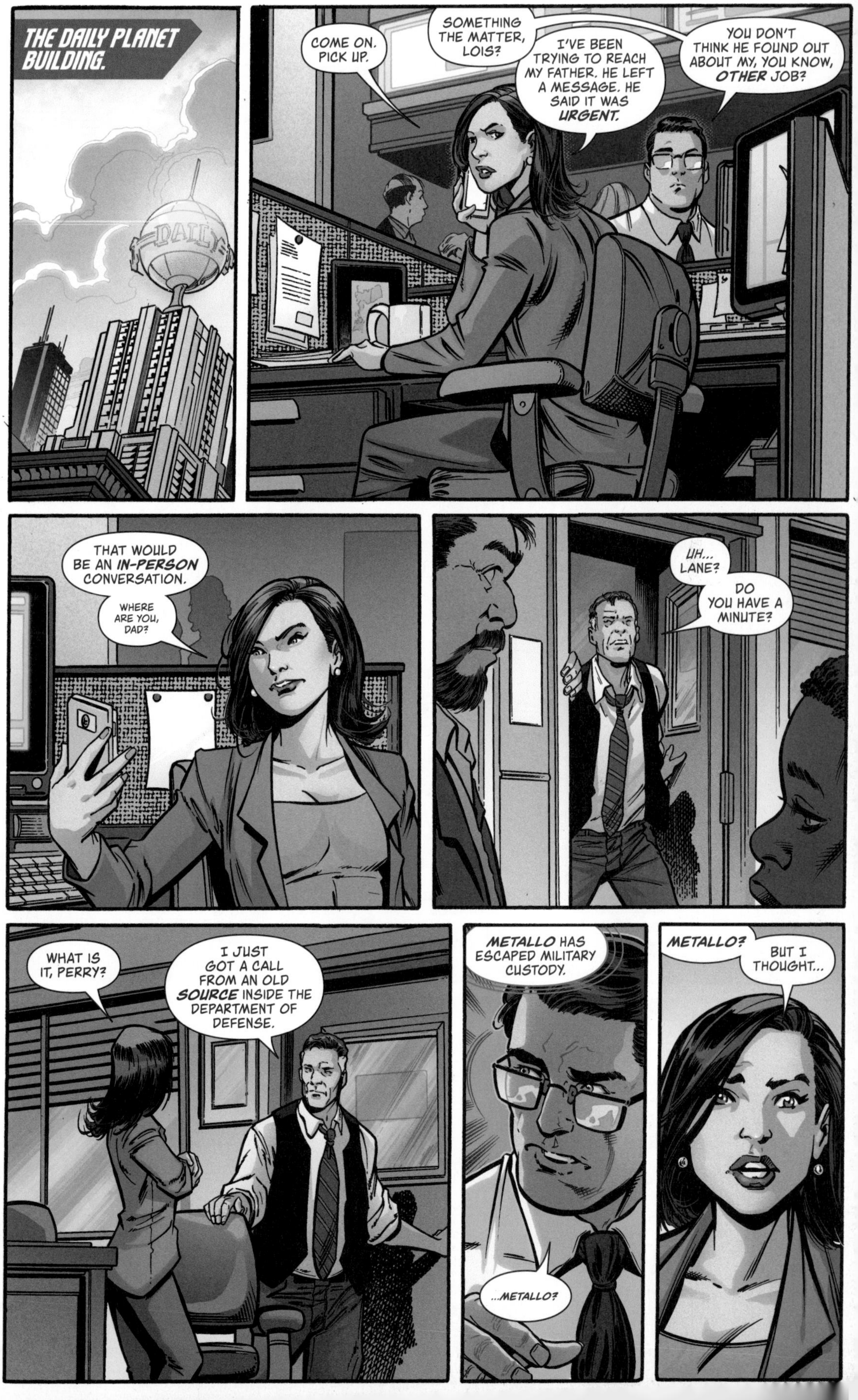
THE DAILY PLANET BUILDING.
DAILY
COME ON. PICK UP.
SOMETHING THE MATTER, LOIS?
I'VE BEEN TRYING TO REACH MY FATHER. HE LEFT A MESSAGE. HE SAID IT WAS URGENT.
YOU DON'T THINK HE FOUND OUT ABOUT MY, YOU KNOW, OTHER JOB?
THAT WOULD BE AN IN-PERSON CONVERSATION.
WHERE ARE YOU, DAD?
UH... LANE?
DO YOU HAVE A MINUTE?
WHAT IS IT, PERRY?
I JUST GOT A CALL FROM AN OLD SOURCE INSIDE THE DEPARTMENT OF DEFENSE.
METALLO HAS ESCAPED MILITARY CUSTODY.
...METALLO?
METALLO?
BUT I THOUGHT...

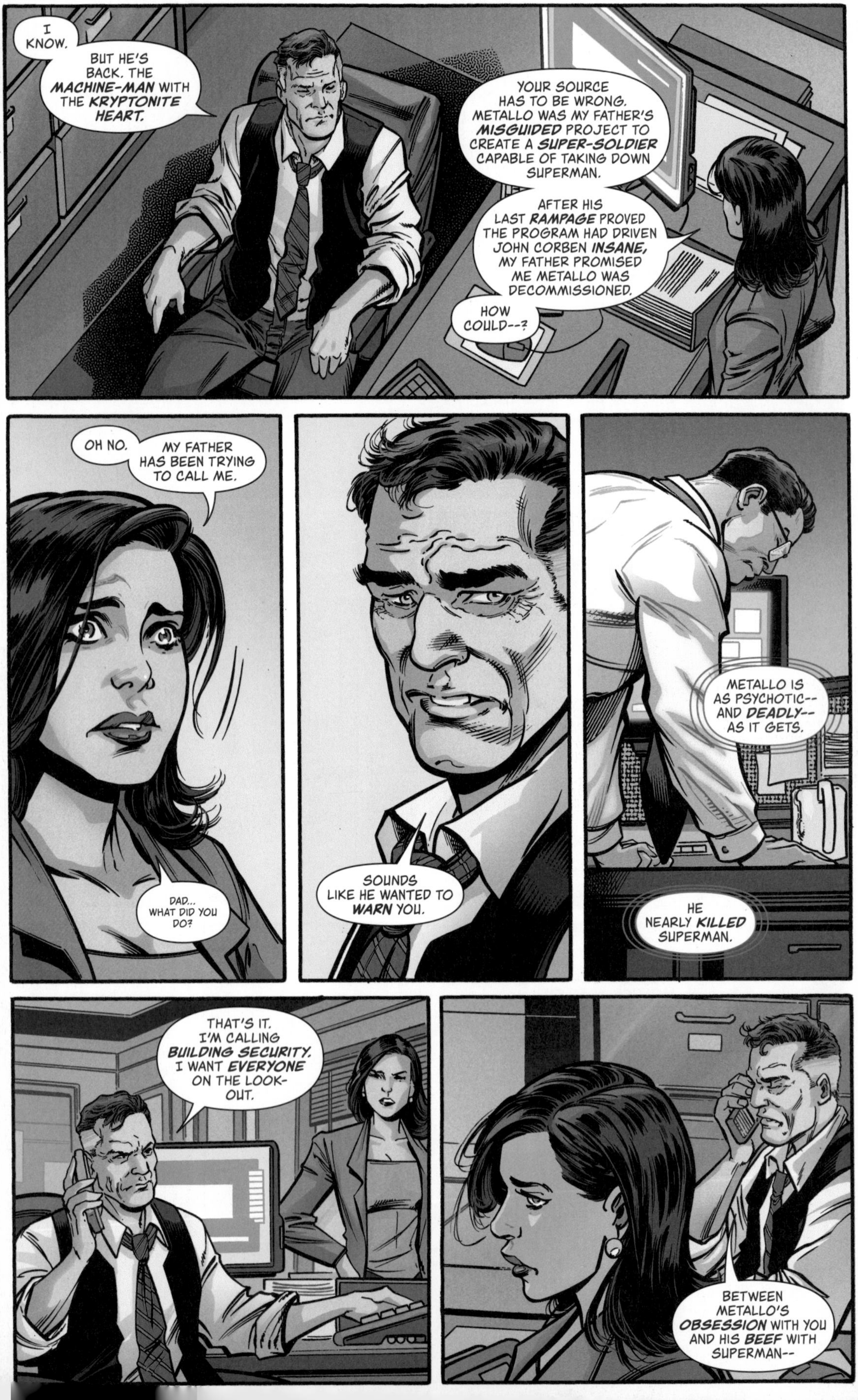
I KNOW.
BUT HE'S BACK. THE MACHINE-MAN WITH THE KRYPTONITE HEART.
YOUR SOURCE HAS TO BE WRONG. METALLO WAS MY FATHER'S MISGUIDED PROJECT TO CREATE A SUPER-SOLDIER CAPABLE OF TAKING DOWN SUPERMAN.
AFTER HIS LAST RAMPAGE PROVED THE PROGRAM HAD DRIVEN JOHN CORBEN INSANE, MY FATHER PROMISED ME METALLO WAS DECOMMISSIONED.
HOW COULD--?
OH NO.
MY FATHER HAS BEEN TRYING TO CALL ME.
DAD... WHAT DID YOU DO?
SOUNDS LIKE HE WANTED TO WARN YOU.
METALLO IS AS PSYCHOTIC-- AND DEADLY-- AS IT GETS.
HE NEARLY KILLED SUPERMAN.
THAT'S IT. I'M CALLING BUILDING SECURITY. I WANT EVERYONE ON THE LOOK-OUT.
BETWEEN METALLO'S OBSESSION WITH YOU AND HIS BEEF WITH SUPERMAN--

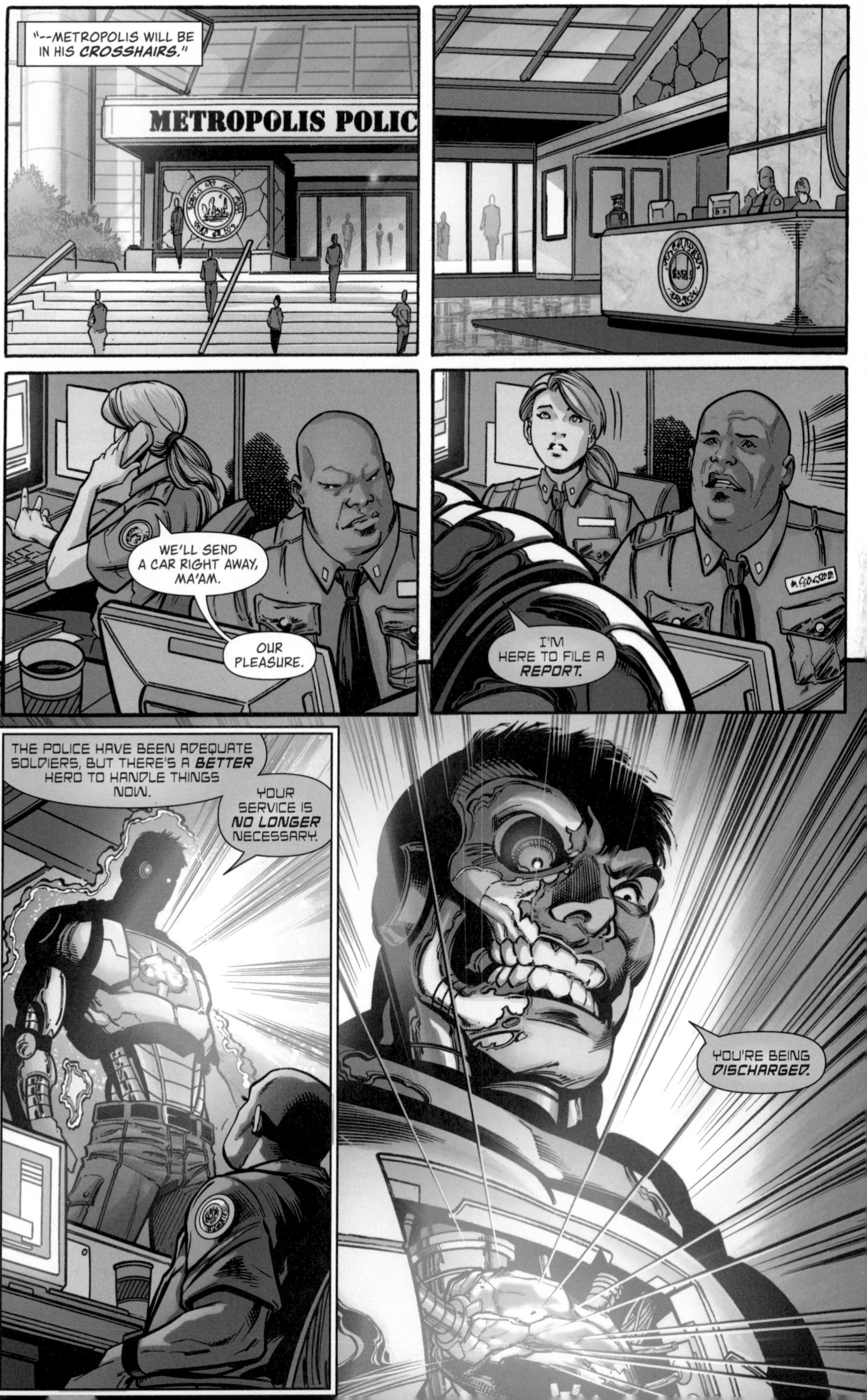
"--METROPOLIS WILL BE IN HIS CROSSHAIRS."
METROPOLIS POLIC
WE'LL SEND A CAR RIGHT AWAY, MA'AM.
OUR PLEASURE.
I'M HERE TO FILE A REPORT.
THE POLICE HAVE BEEN ADEQUATE SOLDIERS, BUT THERE'S A BETTER HERO TO HANDLE THINGS NOW.
YOUR SERVICE IS NO LONGER NECESSARY.
YOU'RE BEING DISCHARGED.

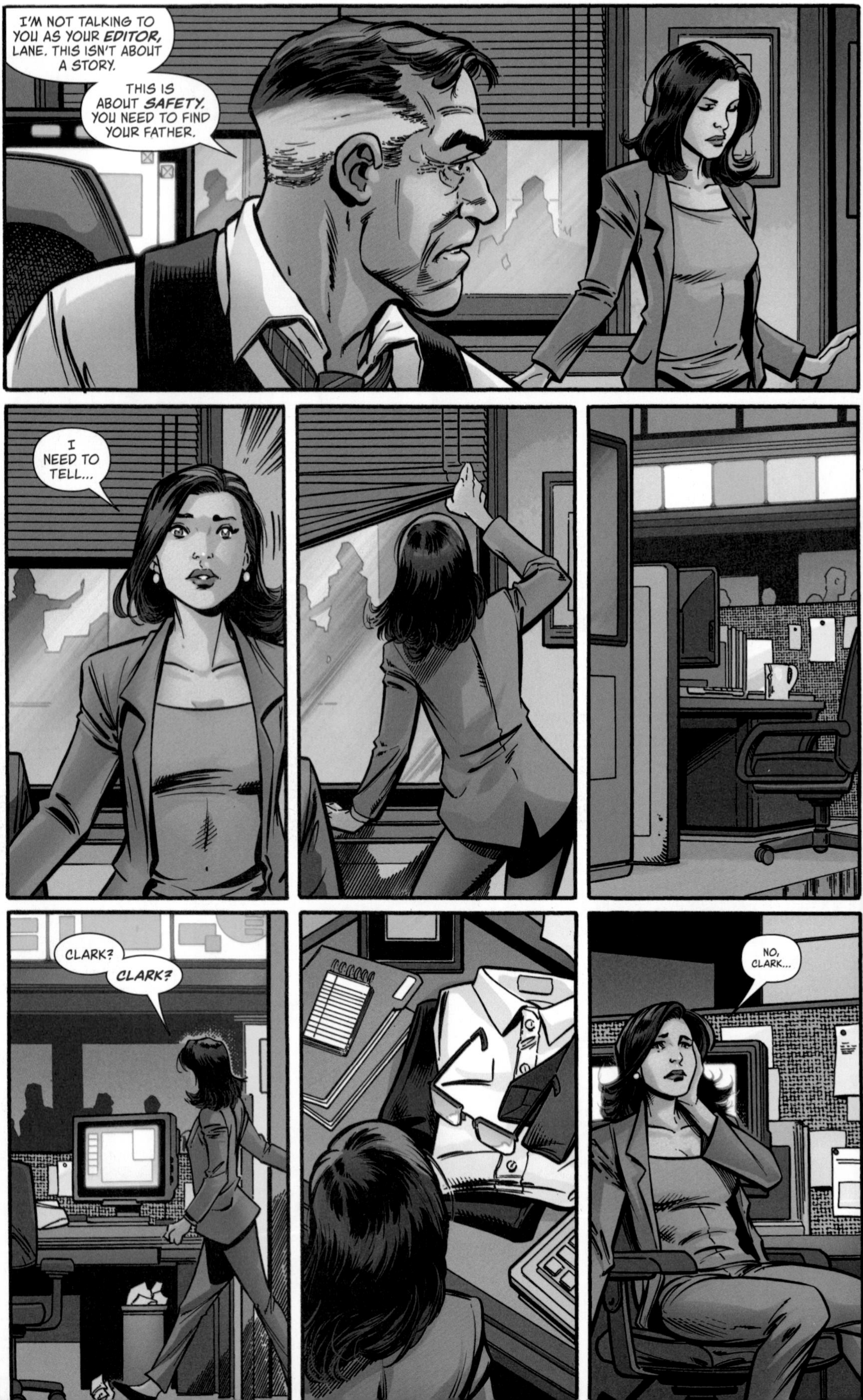
I'M NOT TALKING TO YOU AS YOUR EDITOR, LANE. THIS ISN'T ABOUT A STORY.
THIS IS ABOUT SAFETY. YOU NEED TO FIND YOUR FATHER.
I NEED TO TELL...
CLARK?
CLARK?
NO, CLARK...

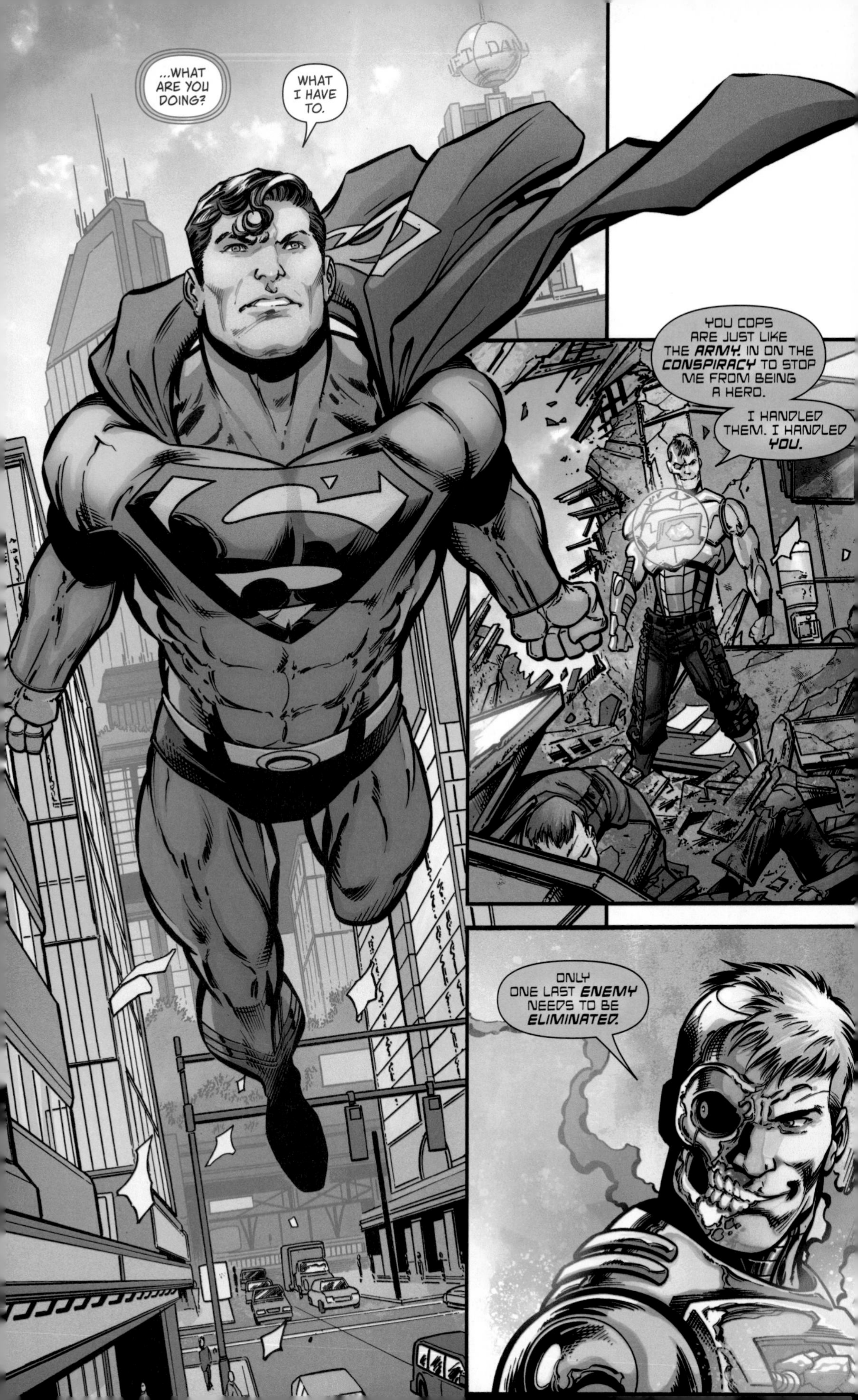
...WHAT ARE YOU DOING?
WHAT I HAVE TO.
YOU COPS ARE JUST LIKE THE ARMY. IN ON THE CONSPIRACY TO STOP ME FROM BEING A HERO.
I HANDLED THEM. I HANDLED YOU.
ONLY ONE LAST ENEMY NEEDS TO BE ELIMINATED.

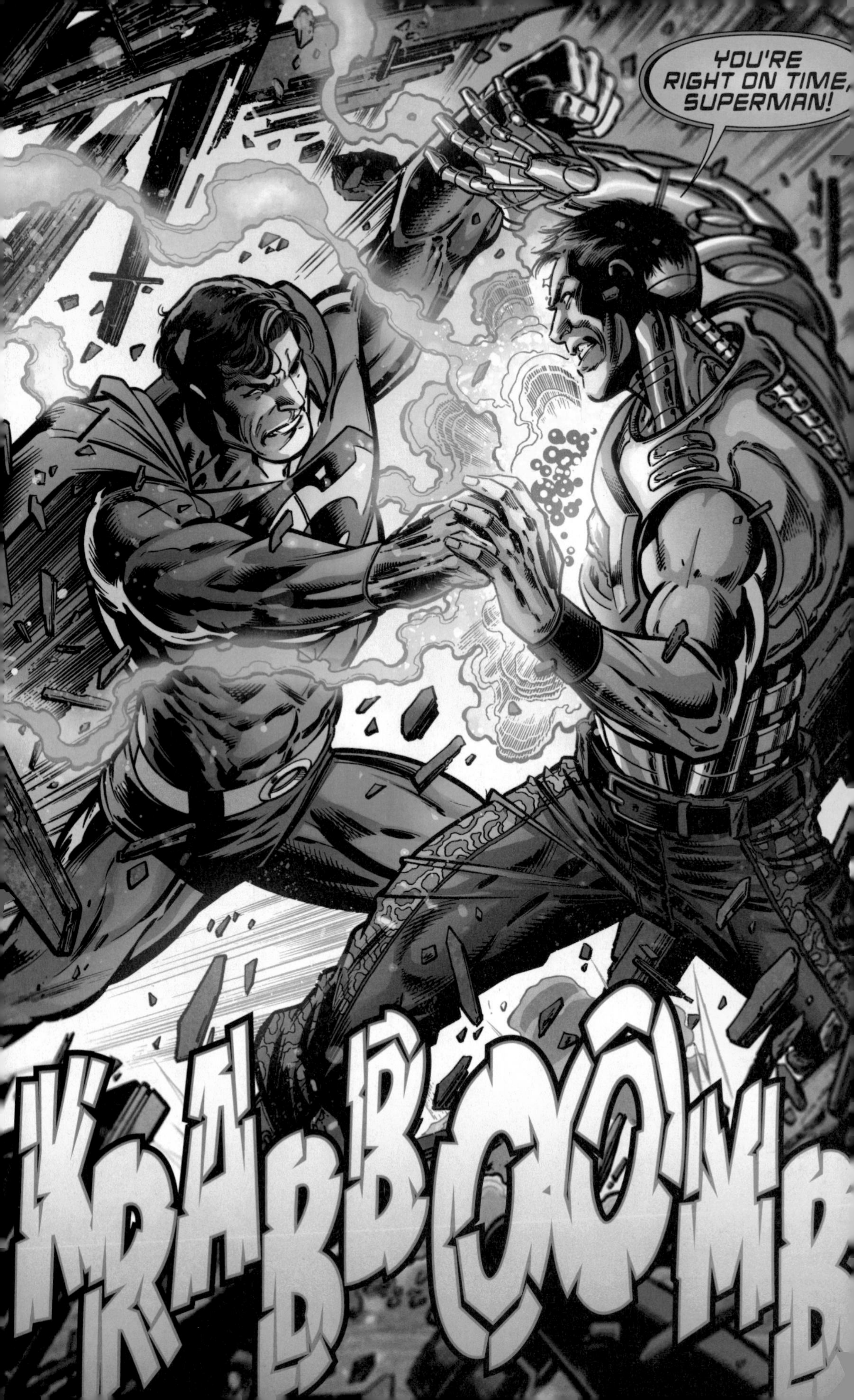
YOU'RE RIGHT ON TIME, SUPERMAN!
KRABBOOM

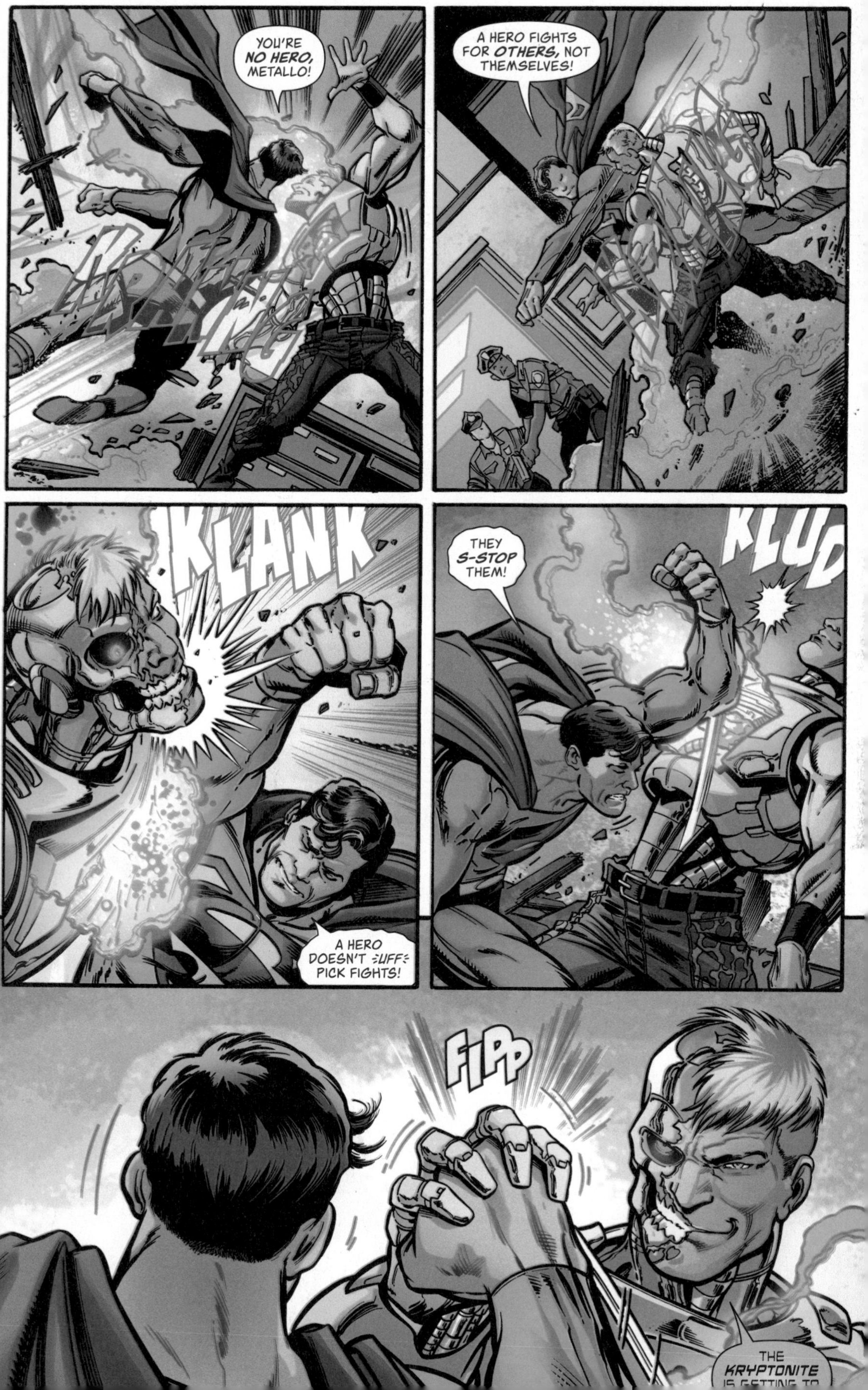
YOU'RE NO HERO, METALLO!
A HERO FIGHTS FOR OTHERS, NOT THEMSELVES!
KLANK
A HERO DOESN'T =UFF= PICK FIGHTS!
THEY S-STOP THEM!
FIPP
THE KRYPTONITE

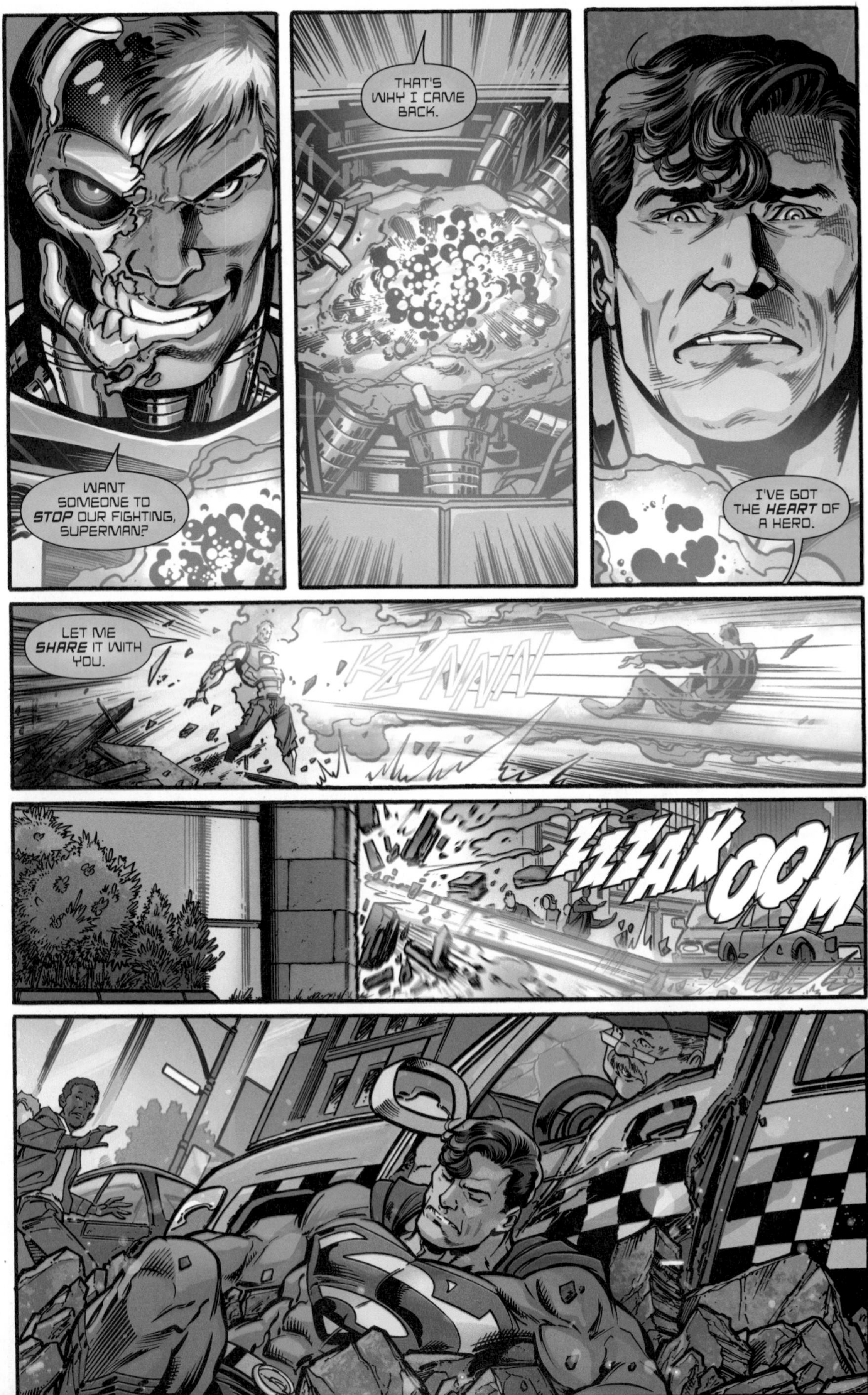
WANT SOMEONE TO STOP OUR FIGHTING, SUPERMAN?
THAT'S WHY I CAME BACK.
I'VE GOT THE HEART OF A HERO.
LET ME SHARE IT WITH YOU.
KZZNNNN
ZZZAKOOOM

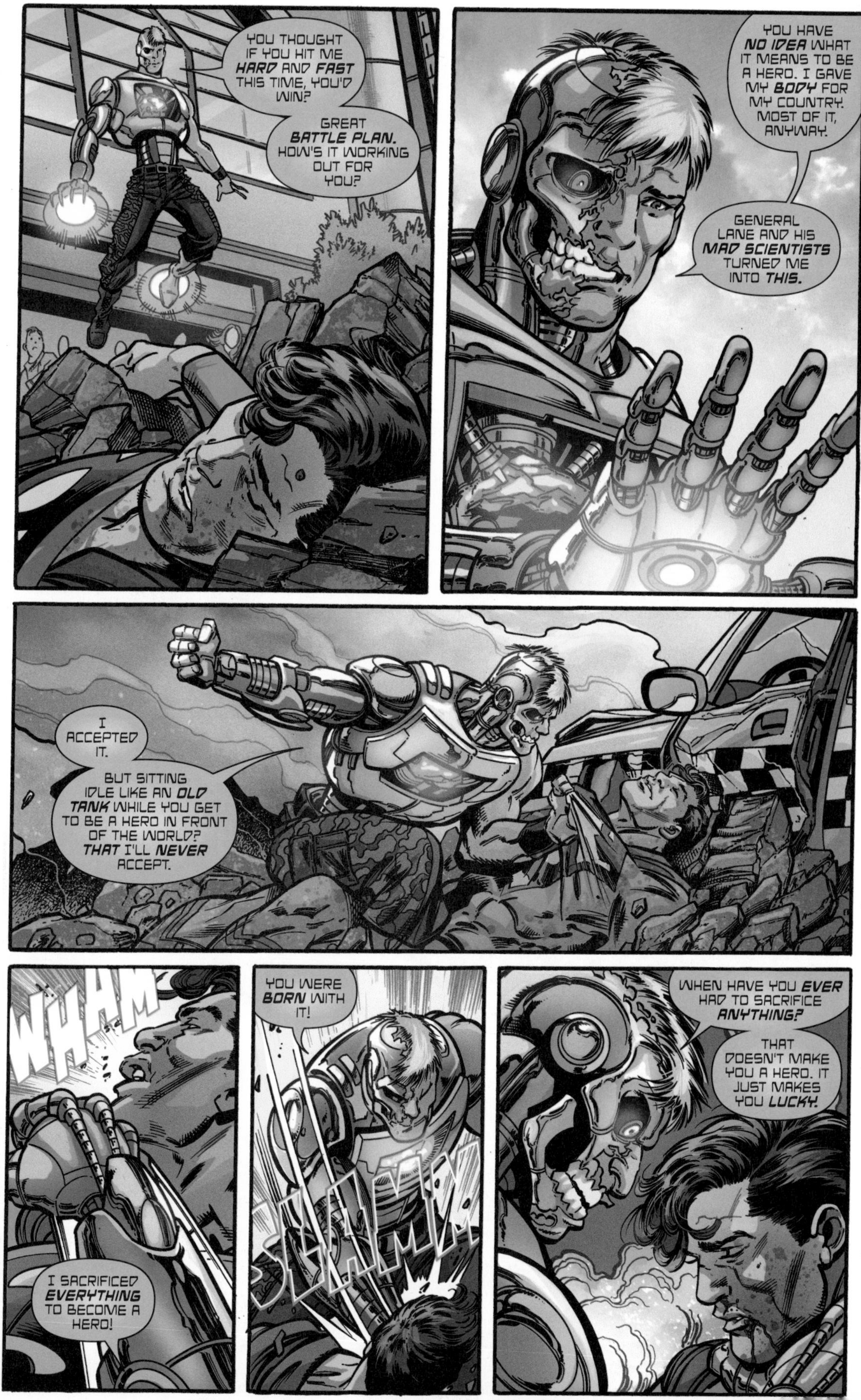

YOU THOUGHT IF YOU HIT ME HARD AND FAST THIS TIME, YOU'D WIN?
GREAT BATTLE PLAN. HOW'S IT WORKING OUT FOR YOU?
YOU HAVE NO IDEA WHAT IT MEANS TO BE A HERO. I GAVE MY BODY FOR MY COUNTRY. MOST OF IT, ANYWAY.
GENERAL LANE AND HIS MAD SCIENTISTS TURNED ME INTO THIS.
I ACCEPTED IT.
BUT SITTING IDLE LIKE AN OLD TANK WHILE YOU GET TO BE A HERO IN FRONT OF THE WORLD? THAT I'LL NEVER ACCEPT.
WHAM
I SACRIFICED EVERYTHING TO BECOME A HERO!
YOU WERE BORN WITH IT!
SLAMM
WHEN HAVE YOU EVER HAD TO SACRIFICE ANYTHING?
THAT DOESN'T MAKE YOU A HERO. IT JUST MAKES YOU LUCKY.

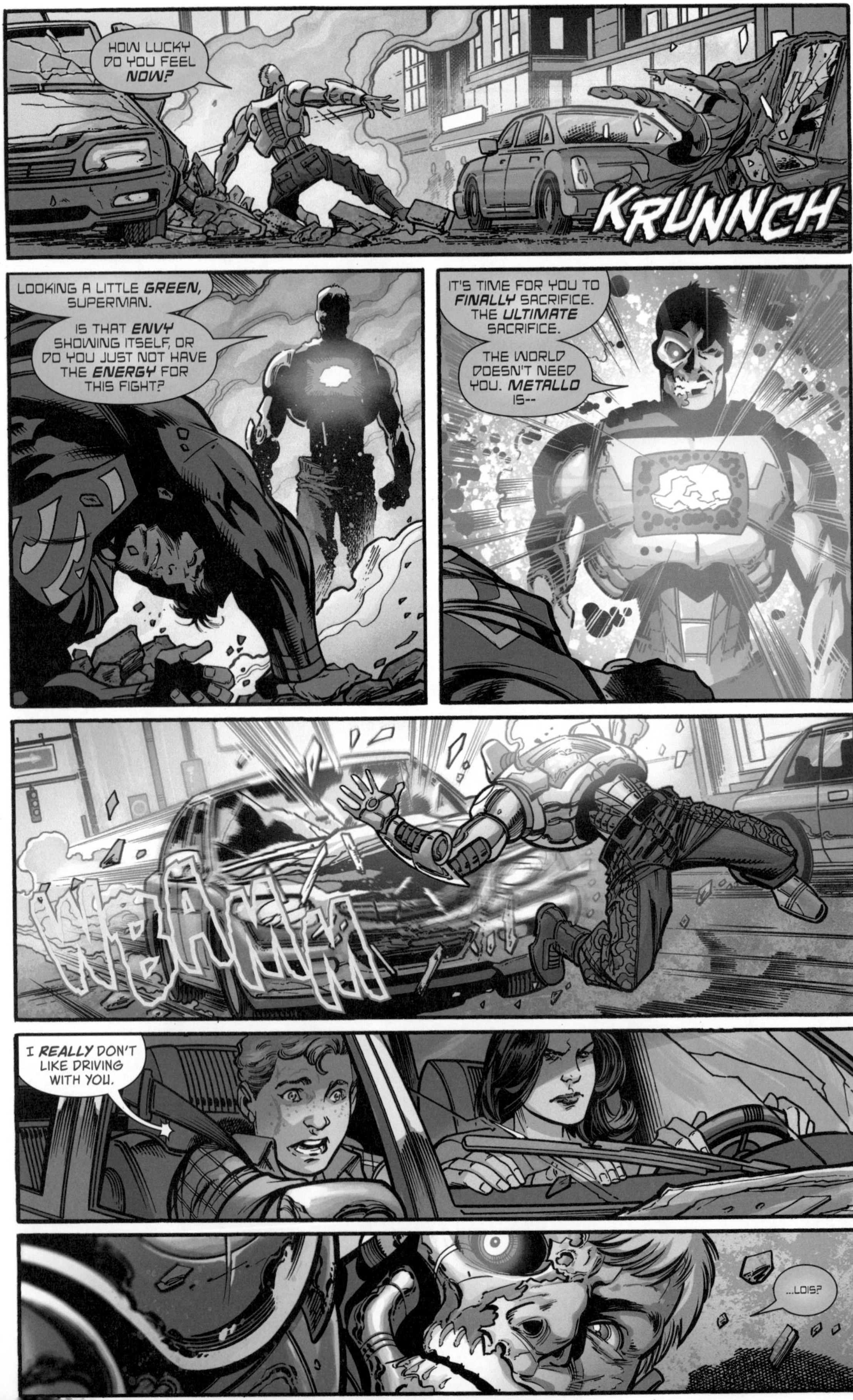
HOW LUCKY DO YOU FEEL NOW?
KRUNNCH
LOOKING A LITTLE GREEN, SUPERMAN.
IS THAT ENVY SHOWING ITSELF, OR DO YOU JUST NOT HAVE THE ENERGY FOR THIS FIGHT?
IT'S TIME FOR YOU TO FINALLY SACRIFICE. THE ULTIMATE SACRIFICE.
THE WORLD DOESN'T NEED YOU. METALLO IS--
I REALLY DON'T LIKE DRIVING WITH YOU.
...LOIS?

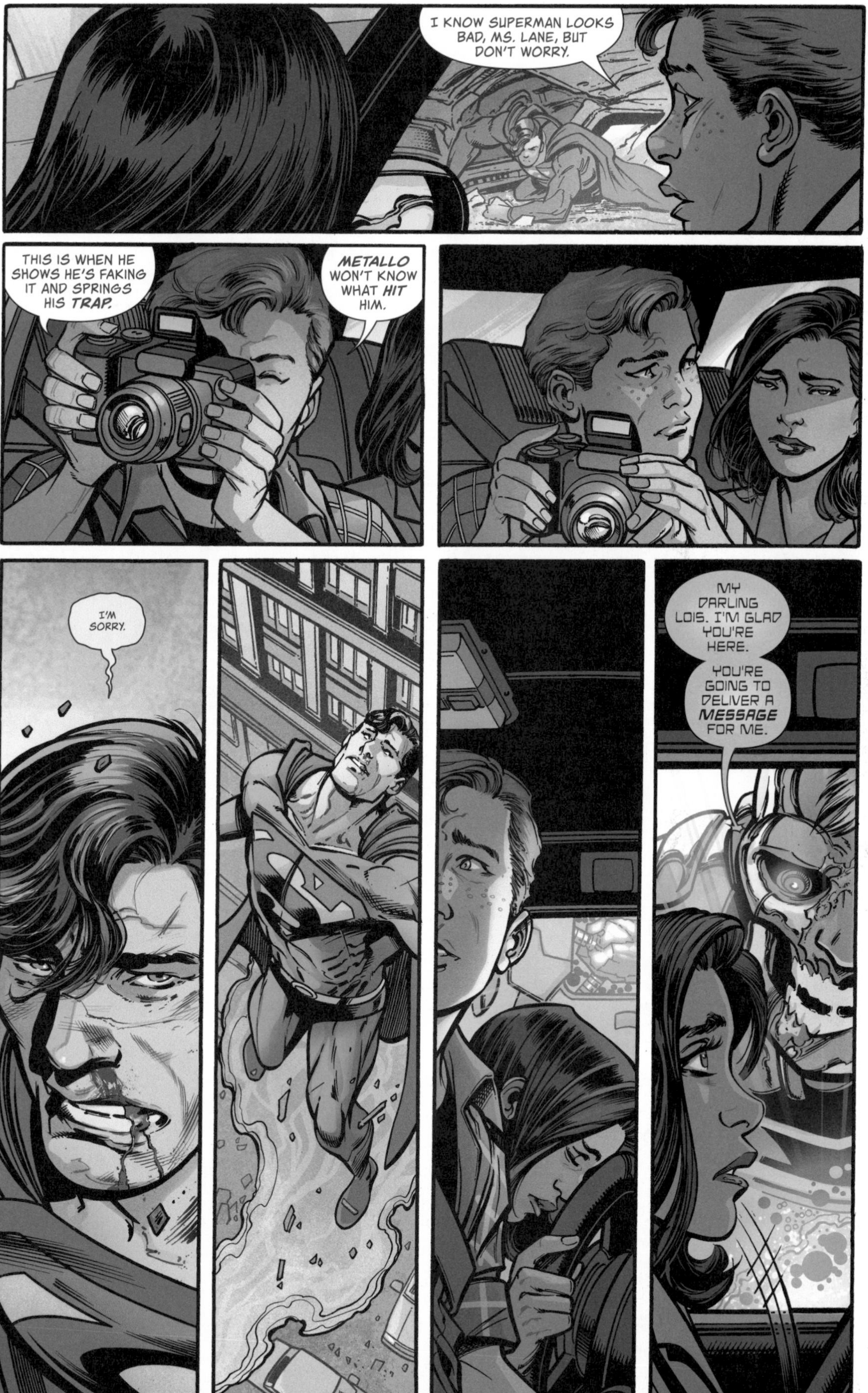
I KNOW SUPERMAN LOOKS BAD, MS. LANE, BUT DON'T WORRY.
THIS IS WHEN HE SHOWS HE'S FAKING IT AND SPRINGS HIS **TRAP.**
METALLO WON'T KNOW WHAT **HIT** HIM.
I'M SORRY.
MY DARLING LOIS. I'M GLAD YOU'RE HERE.
YOU'RE GOING TO DELIVER A **MESSAGE** FOR ME.

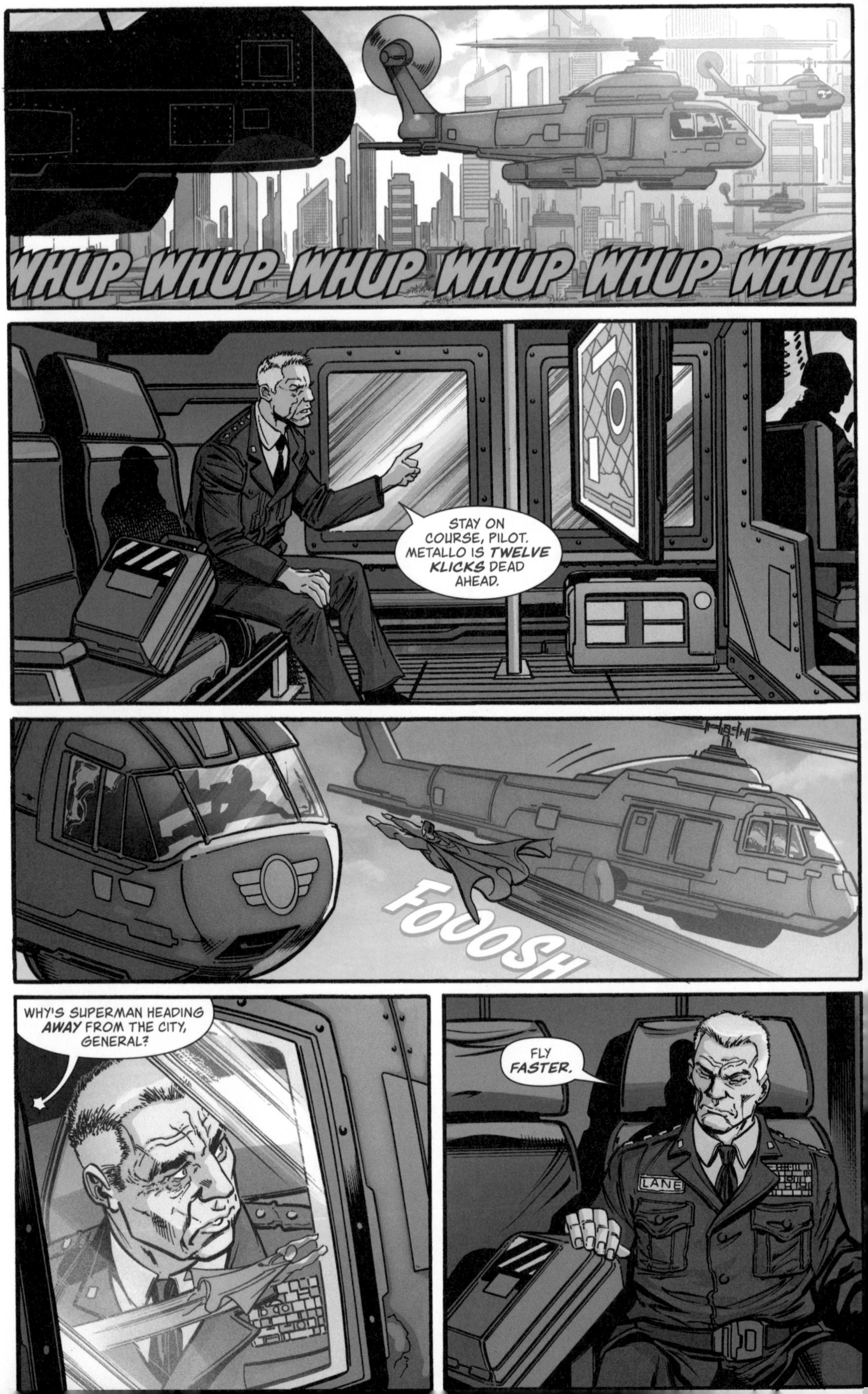
WHUP WHUP WHUP WHUP WHUP WHUP
STAY ON COURSE, PILOT. METALLO IS TWELVE KLICKS DEAD AHEAD.
FOOOSH
WHY'S SUPERMAN HEADING AWAY FROM THE CITY, GENERAL?
FLY FASTER.
LANE

S.T.A.R. LABS.

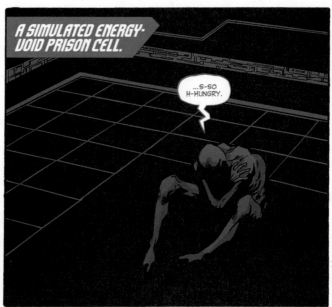

A SIMULATED ENERGY-VOID PRISON CELL.

...S-SO H-HUNGRY.

KRAKOOM!

WHAT DO YOU WANT WITH ME?

WHO--?

YOU!

YOU LEFT ME HERE TO STARVE!

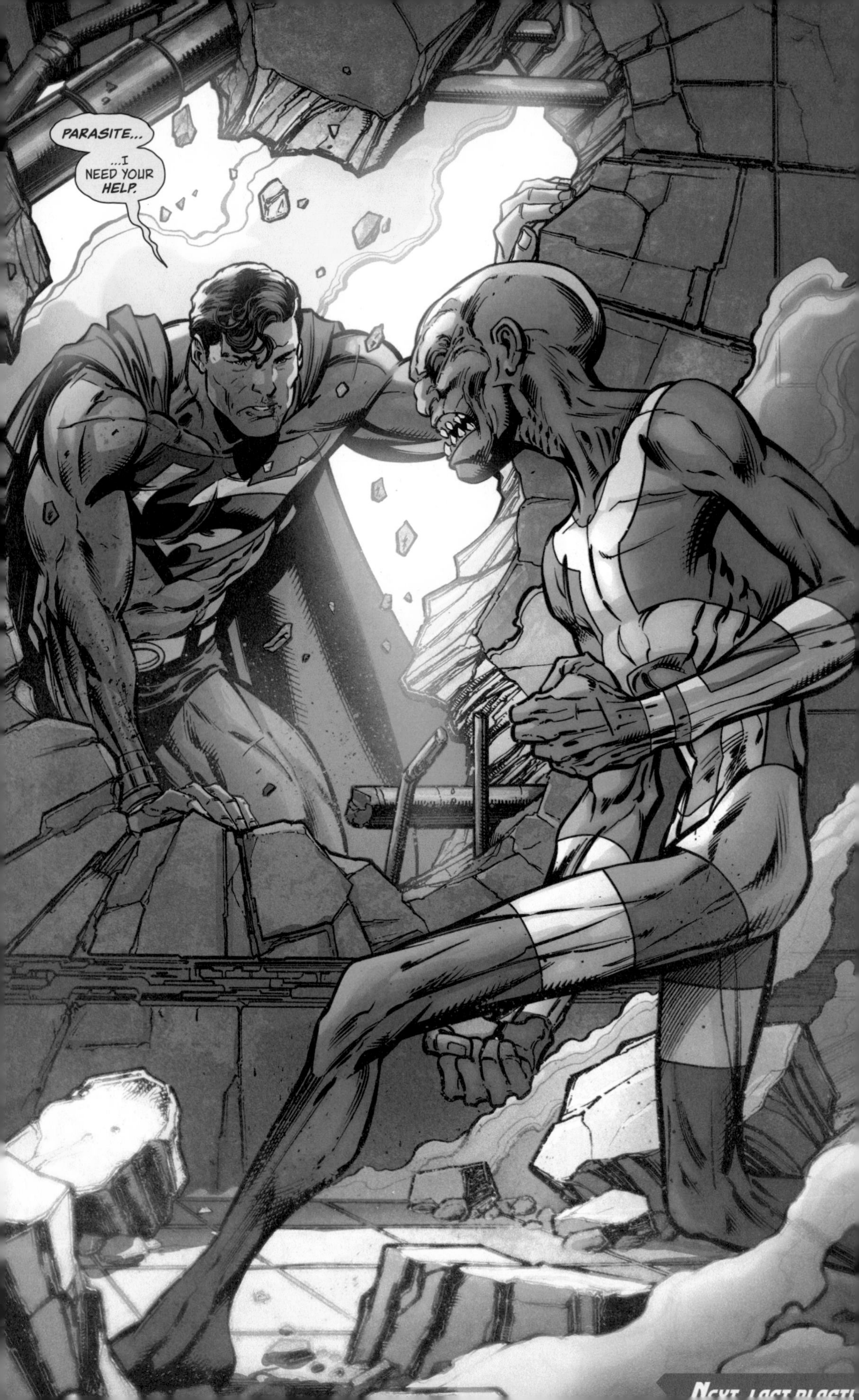
PARASITE...
...I NEED YOUR HELP.

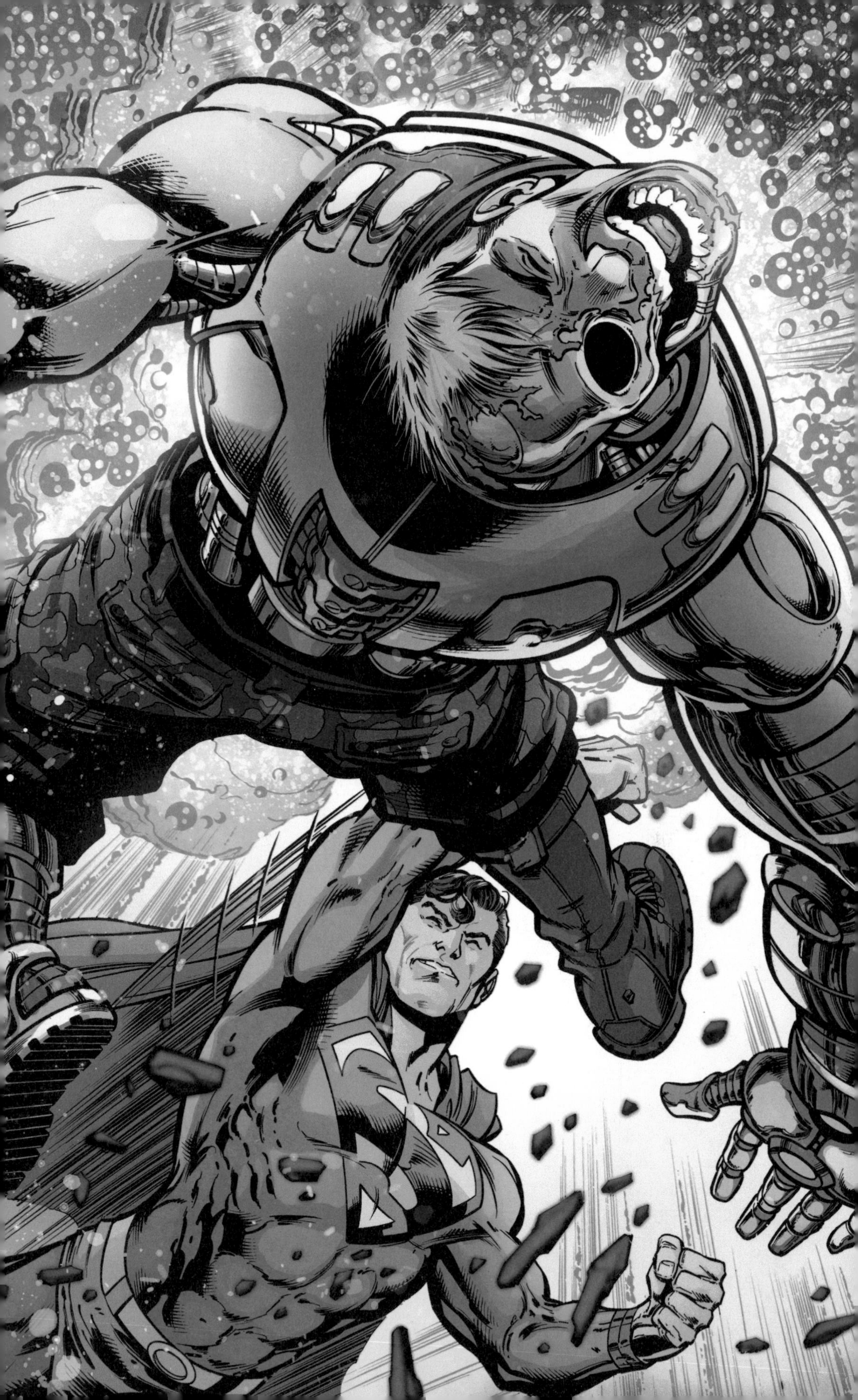

COVER ART BY
PAUL PELLETIER, DREW HENNESSY,
AND **ADRIANO LUCAS**

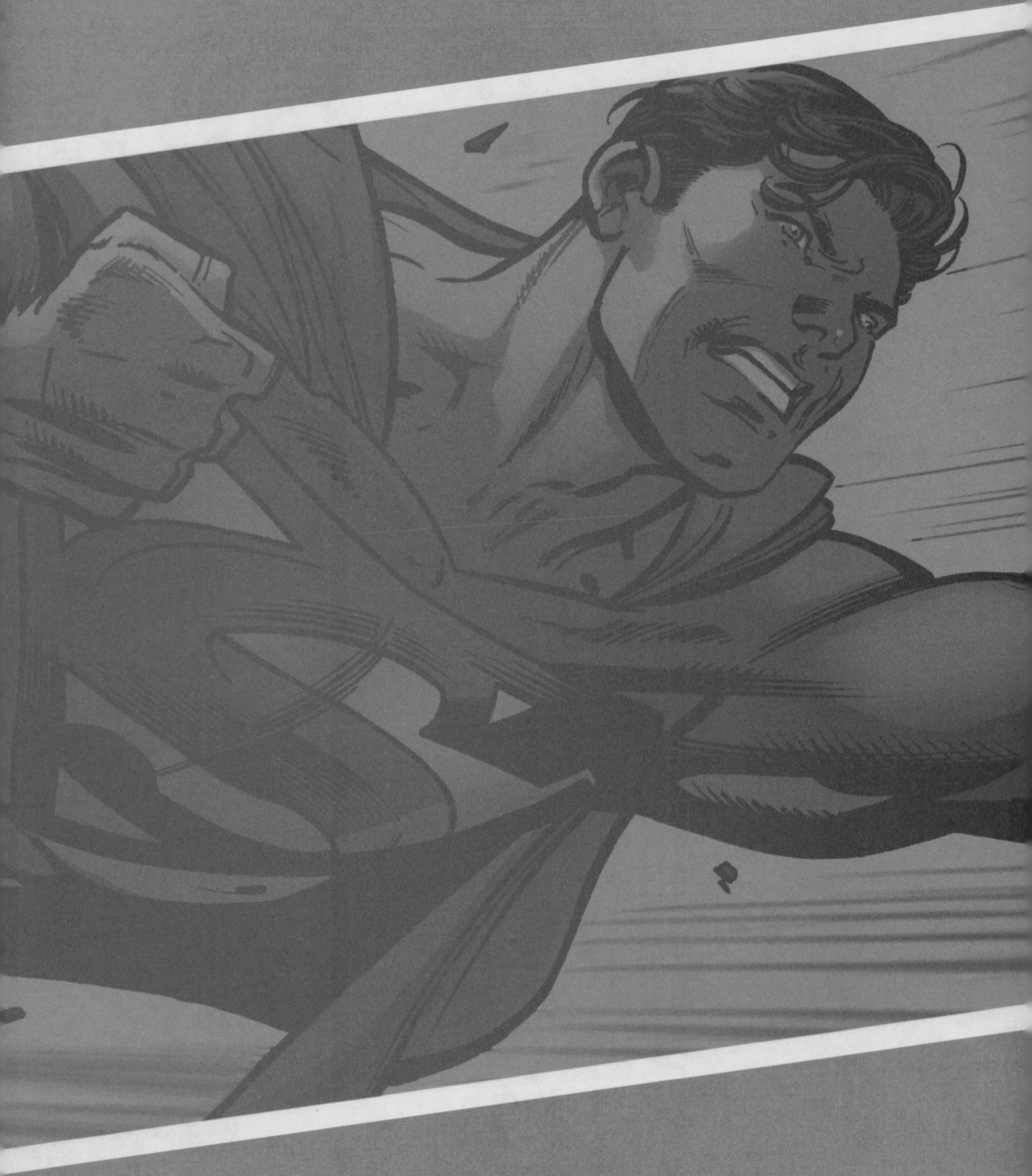

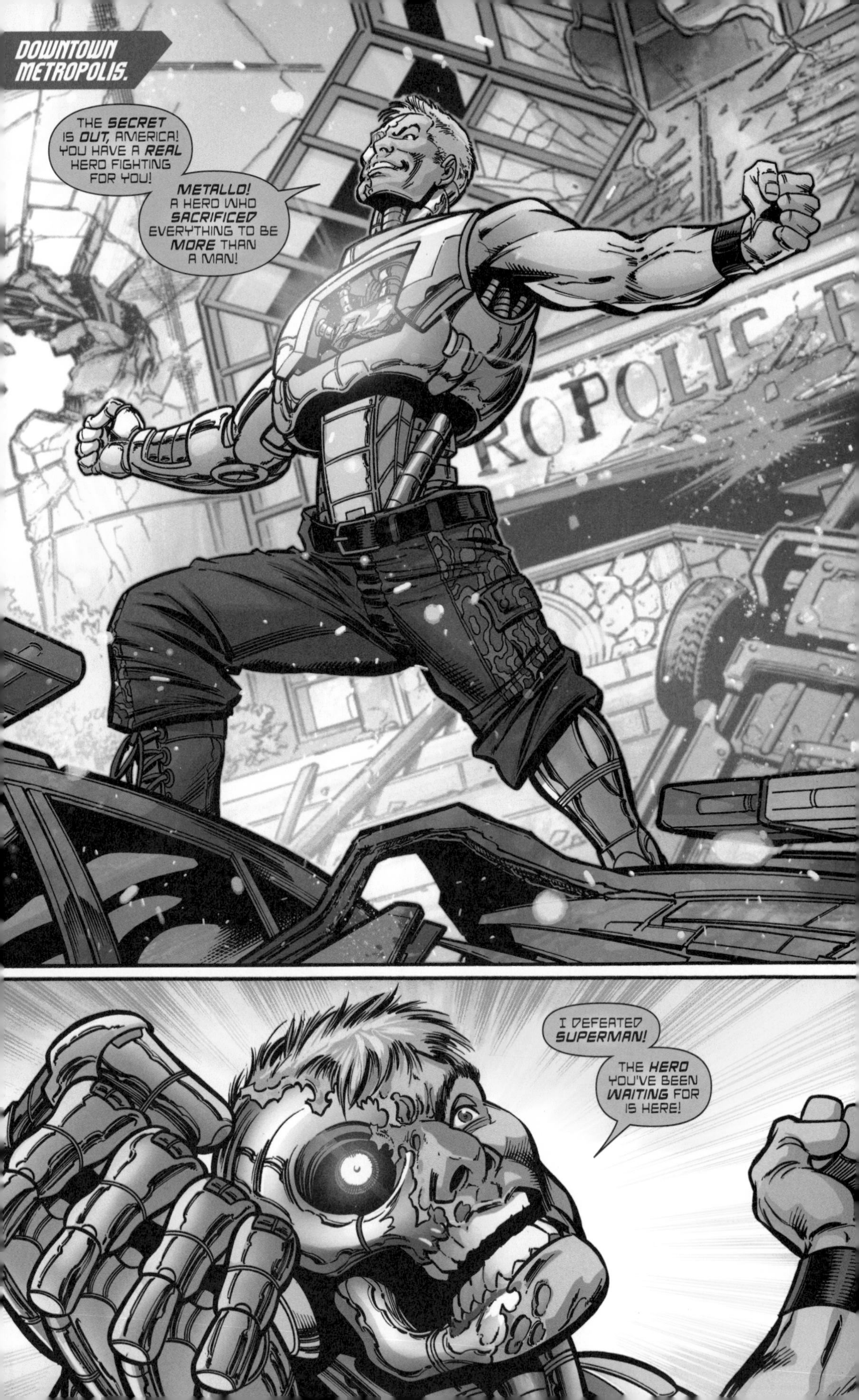
DOWNTOWN METROPOLIS.
THE SECRET IS OUT, AMERICA! YOU HAVE A REAL HERO FIGHTING FOR YOU!
METALLO! A HERO WHO SACRIFICED EVERYTHING TO BE MORE THAN A MAN!
ROPOLIS
I DEFEATED SUPERMAN!
THE HERO YOU'VE BEEN WAITING FOR IS HERE!

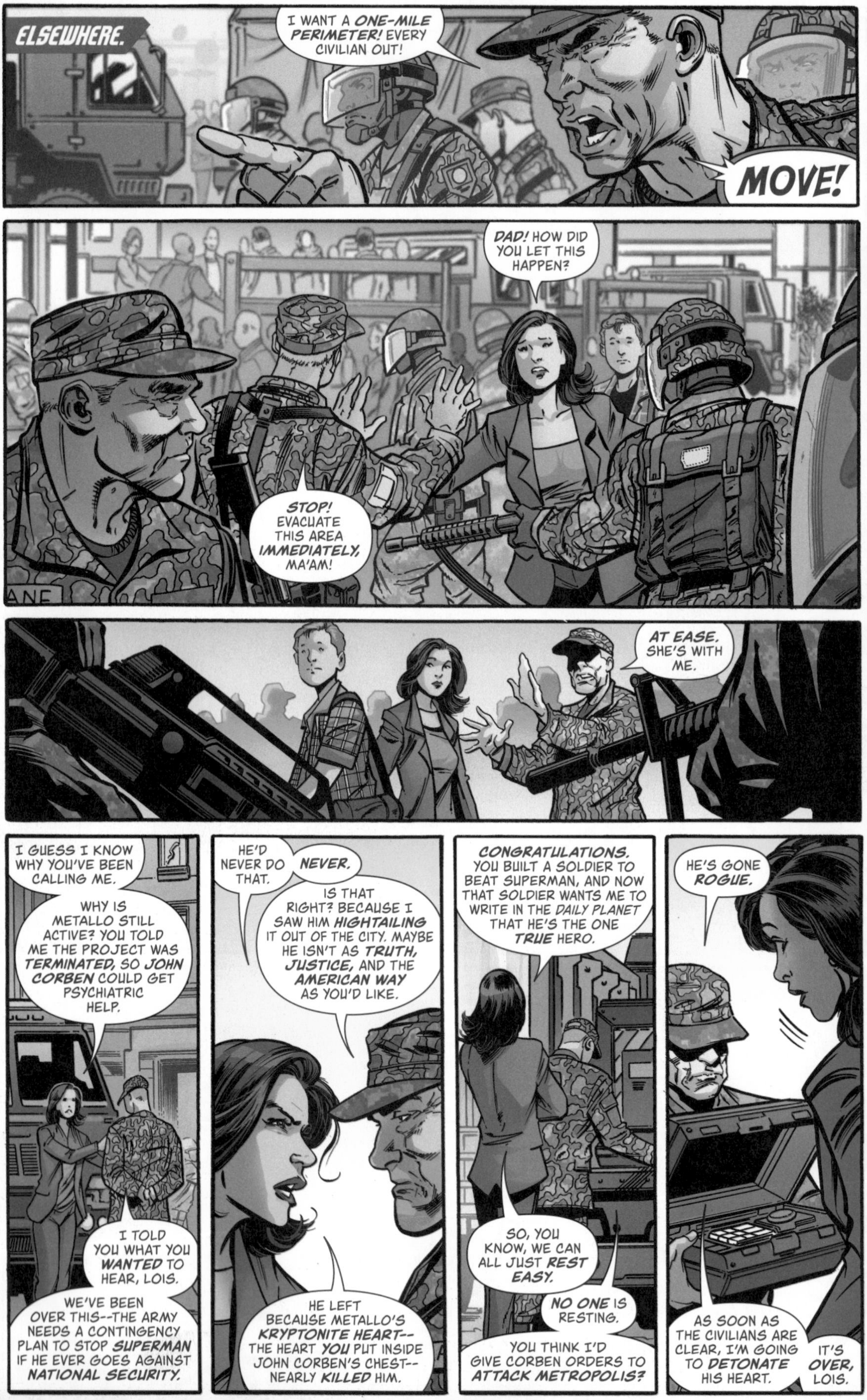

ELSEWHERE.
I WANT A ONE-MILE PERIMETER! EVERY CIVILIAN OUT!
MOVE!
DAD! HOW DID YOU LET THIS HAPPEN?
STOP! EVACUATE THIS AREA IMMEDIATELY, MA'AM!
AT EASE. SHE'S WITH ME.
I GUESS I KNOW WHY YOU'VE BEEN CALLING ME.
WHY IS METALLO STILL ACTIVE? YOU TOLD ME THE PROJECT WAS TERMINATED, SO JOHN CORBEN COULD GET PSYCHIATRIC HELP.
I TOLD YOU WHAT YOU WANTED TO HEAR, LOIS.
WE'VE BEEN OVER THIS--THE ARMY NEEDS A CONTINGENCY PLAN TO STOP SUPERMAN IF HE EVER GOES AGAINST NATIONAL SECURITY.
HE'D NEVER DO THAT.
NEVER.
IS THAT RIGHT? BECAUSE I SAW HIM HIGHTAILING IT OUT OF THE CITY. MAYBE HE ISN'T AS TRUTH, JUSTICE, AND THE AMERICAN WAY AS YOU'D LIKE.
HE LEFT BECAUSE METALLO'S KRYPTONITE HEART--THE HEART YOU PUT INSIDE JOHN CORBEN'S CHEST--NEARLY KILLED HIM.
CONGRATULATIONS. YOU BUILT A SOLDIER TO BEAT SUPERMAN, AND NOW THAT SOLDIER WANTS ME TO WRITE IN THE DAILY PLANET THAT HE'S THE ONE TRUE HERO.
SO, YOU KNOW, WE CAN ALL JUST REST EASY.
NO ONE IS RESTING.
YOU THINK I'D GIVE CORBEN ORDERS TO ATTACK METROPOLIS?
HE'S GONE ROGUE.
AS SOON AS THE CIVILIANS ARE CLEAR, I'M GOING TO DETONATE HIS HEART.
IT'S OVER, LOIS.

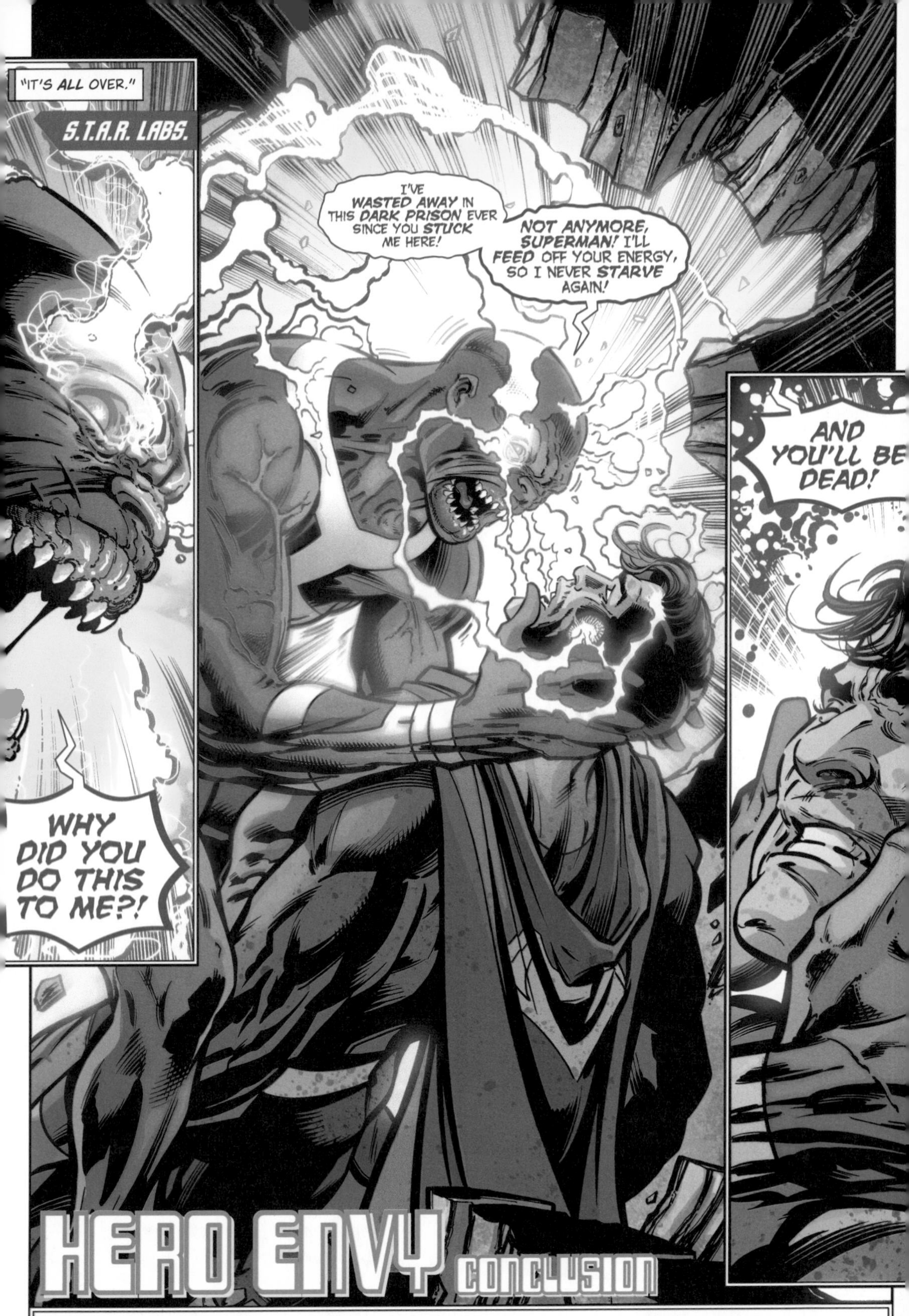
"IT'S ALL OVER."
S.T.A.R. LABS.
WHY DID YOU DO THIS TO ME?!
I'VE WASTED AWAY IN THIS DARK PRISON EVER SINCE YOU STUCK ME HERE!
NOT ANYMORE, SUPERMAN! I'LL FEED OFF YOUR ENERGY, SO I NEVER STARVE AGAIN!
AND YOU'LL BE DEAD!
HERO ENVY
CONCLUSION

ROBERT VENDITTI WRITER PAUL PELLETIER ARTIST DREW HENNESSY INKER
ADRIANO LUCAS COLORIST CLAYTON COWLES LETTERER
PELLETIER, HENNESSY & LUCAS COVER ANDREW MARINO EDITOR

SUPERMAN CREATED BY JERRY SIEGEL & JOE SHUSTER.
BY SPECIAL ARRANGEMENT WITH THE JERRY SIEGEL FAMILY.

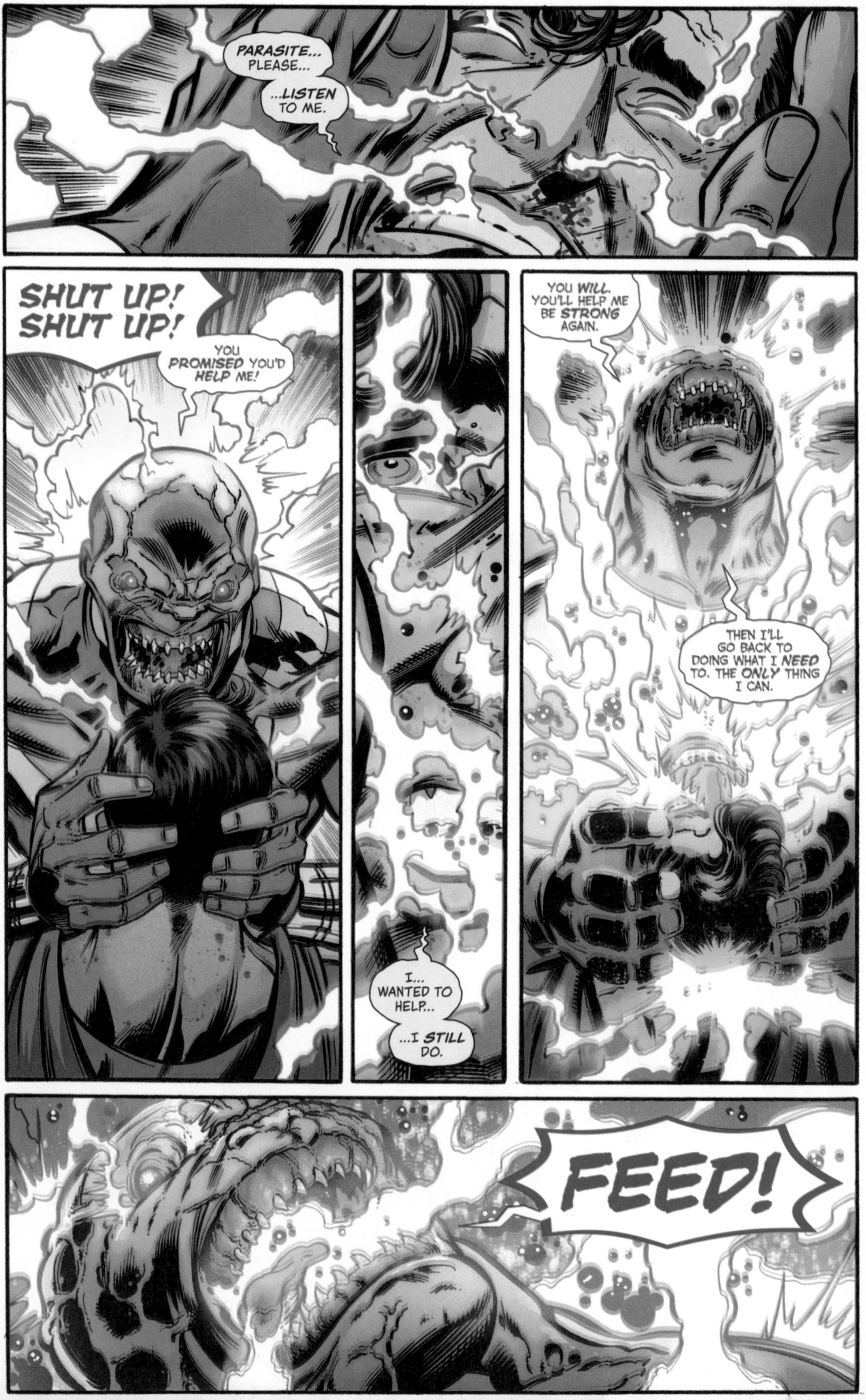
PARASITE... PLEASE...
...LISTEN TO ME.
SHUT UP! SHUT UP!
YOU PROMISED YOU'D HELP ME!
I... WANTED TO HELP...
...I STILL DO.
YOU WILL. YOU'LL HELP ME BE STRONG AGAIN.
THEN I'LL GO BACK TO DOING WHAT I NEED TO. THE ONLY THING I CAN.
FEED!

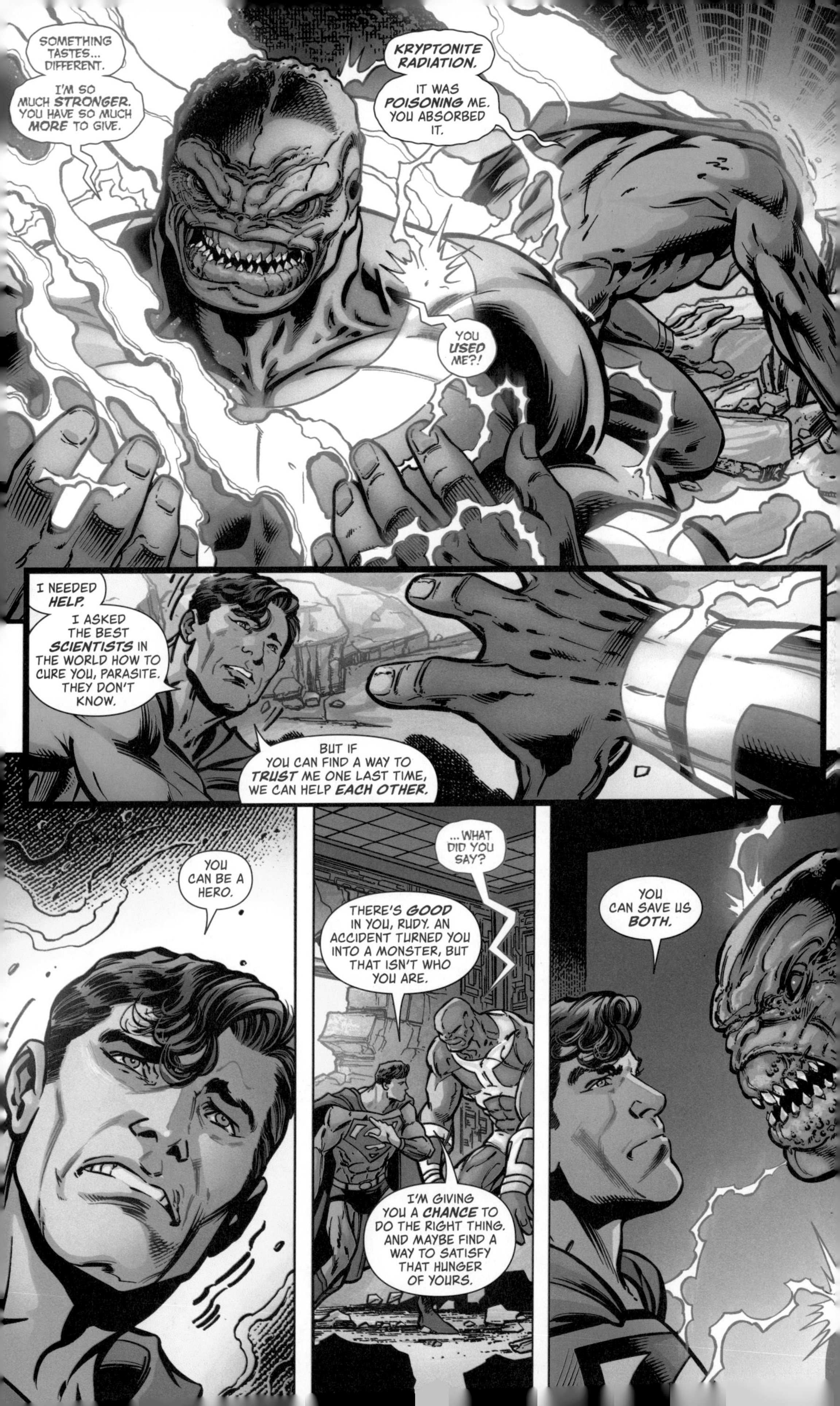

SOMETHING TASTES... DIFFERENT.
I'M SO MUCH STRONGER. YOU HAVE SO MUCH MORE TO GIVE.
KRYPTONITE RADIATION.
IT WAS POISONING ME. YOU ABSORBED IT.
YOU USED ME?!
I NEEDED HELP.
I ASKED THE BEST SCIENTISTS IN THE WORLD HOW TO CURE YOU, PARASITE. THEY DON'T KNOW.
BUT IF YOU CAN FIND A WAY TO TRUST ME ONE LAST TIME, WE CAN HELP EACH OTHER.
YOU CAN BE A HERO.
...WHAT DID YOU SAY?
THERE'S GOOD IN YOU, RUDY. AN ACCIDENT TURNED YOU INTO A MONSTER, BUT THAT ISN'T WHO YOU ARE.
I'M GIVING YOU A CHANCE TO DO THE RIGHT THING. AND MAYBE FIND A WAY TO SATISFY THAT HUNGER OF YOURS.
YOU CAN SAVE US BOTH.

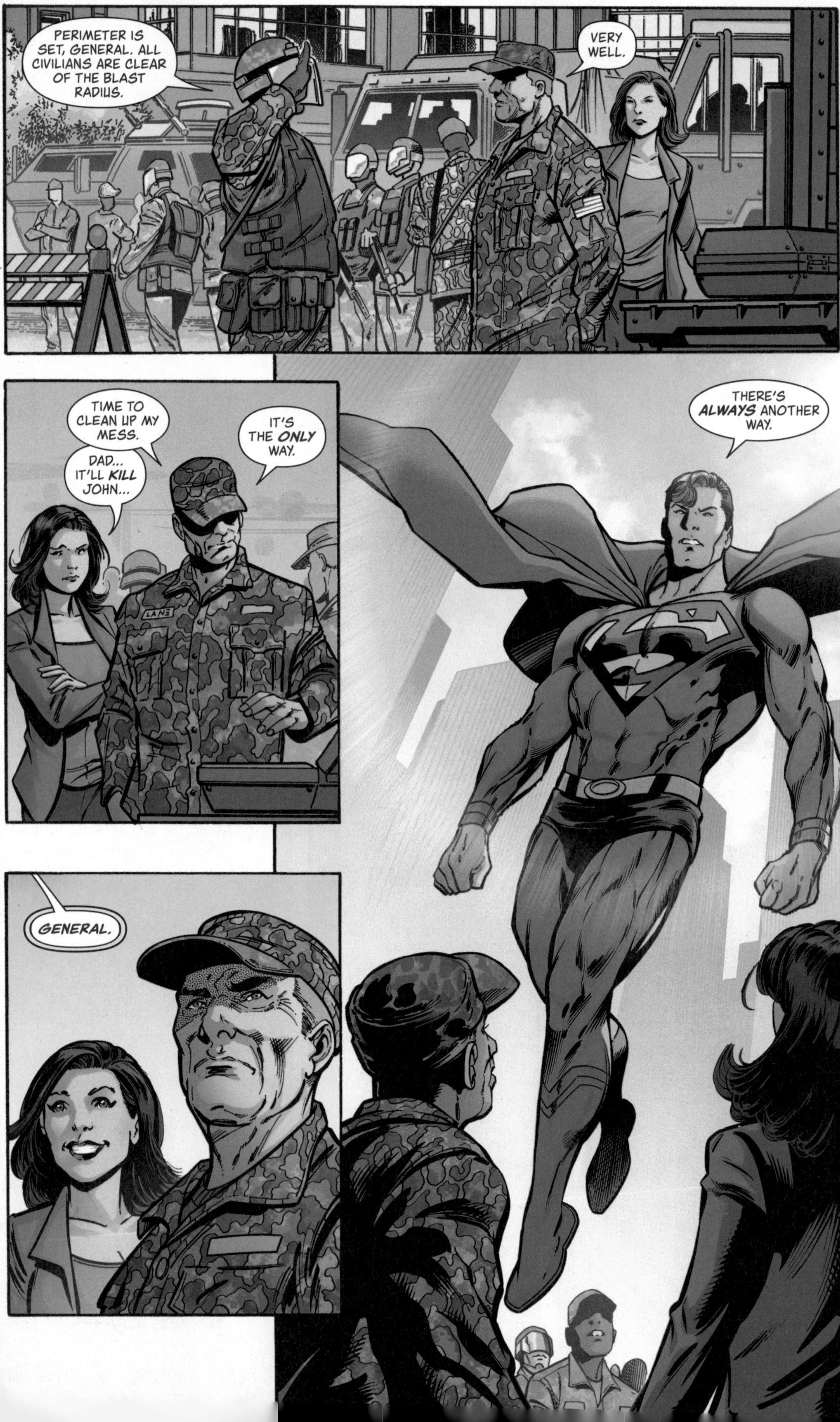

PERIMETER IS SET, GENERAL. ALL CIVILIANS ARE CLEAR OF THE BLAST RADIUS.
VERY WELL.
TIME TO CLEAN UP MY MESS.
DAD... IT'LL KILL JOHN...
IT'S THE ONLY WAY.
THERE'S ALWAYS ANOTHER WAY.
GENERAL.
LANE

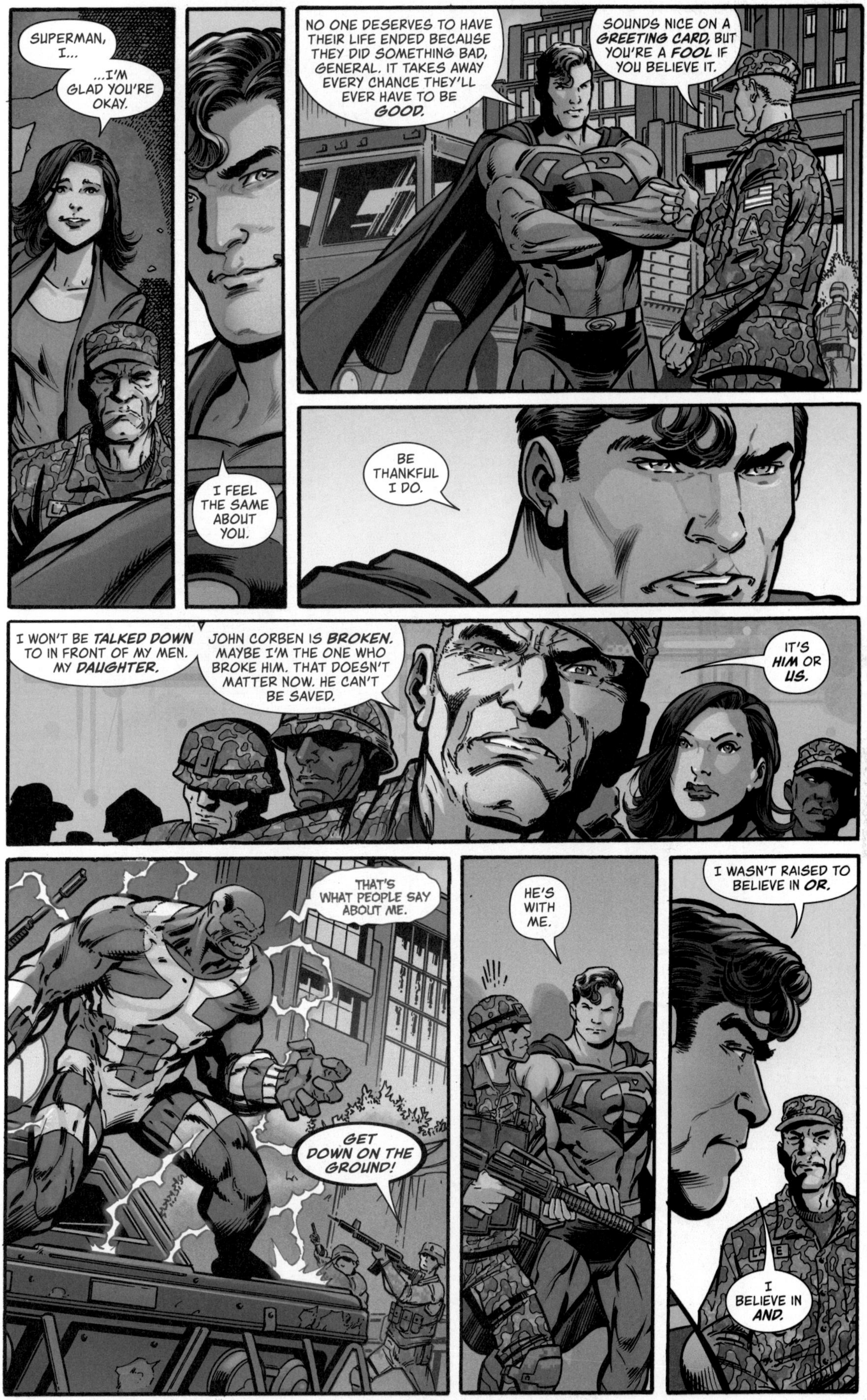
SUPERMAN, I...
...I'M GLAD YOU'RE OKAY.
I FEEL THE SAME ABOUT YOU.
NO ONE DESERVES TO HAVE THEIR LIFE ENDED BECAUSE THEY DID SOMETHING BAD, GENERAL. IT TAKES AWAY EVERY CHANCE THEY'LL EVER HAVE TO BE GOOD.
SOUNDS NICE ON A GREETING CARD, BUT YOU'RE A FOOL IF YOU BELIEVE IT.
BE THANKFUL I DO.
I WON'T BE TALKED DOWN TO IN FRONT OF MY MEN. MY DAUGHTER.
JOHN CORBEN IS BROKEN. MAYBE I'M THE ONE WHO BROKE HIM. THAT DOESN'T MATTER NOW. HE CAN'T BE SAVED.
IT'S HIM OR US.
THAT'S WHAT PEOPLE SAY ABOUT ME.
GET DOWN ON THE GROUND!
HE'S WITH ME.
I WASN'T RAISED TO BELIEVE IN OR.
I BELIEVE IN AND.

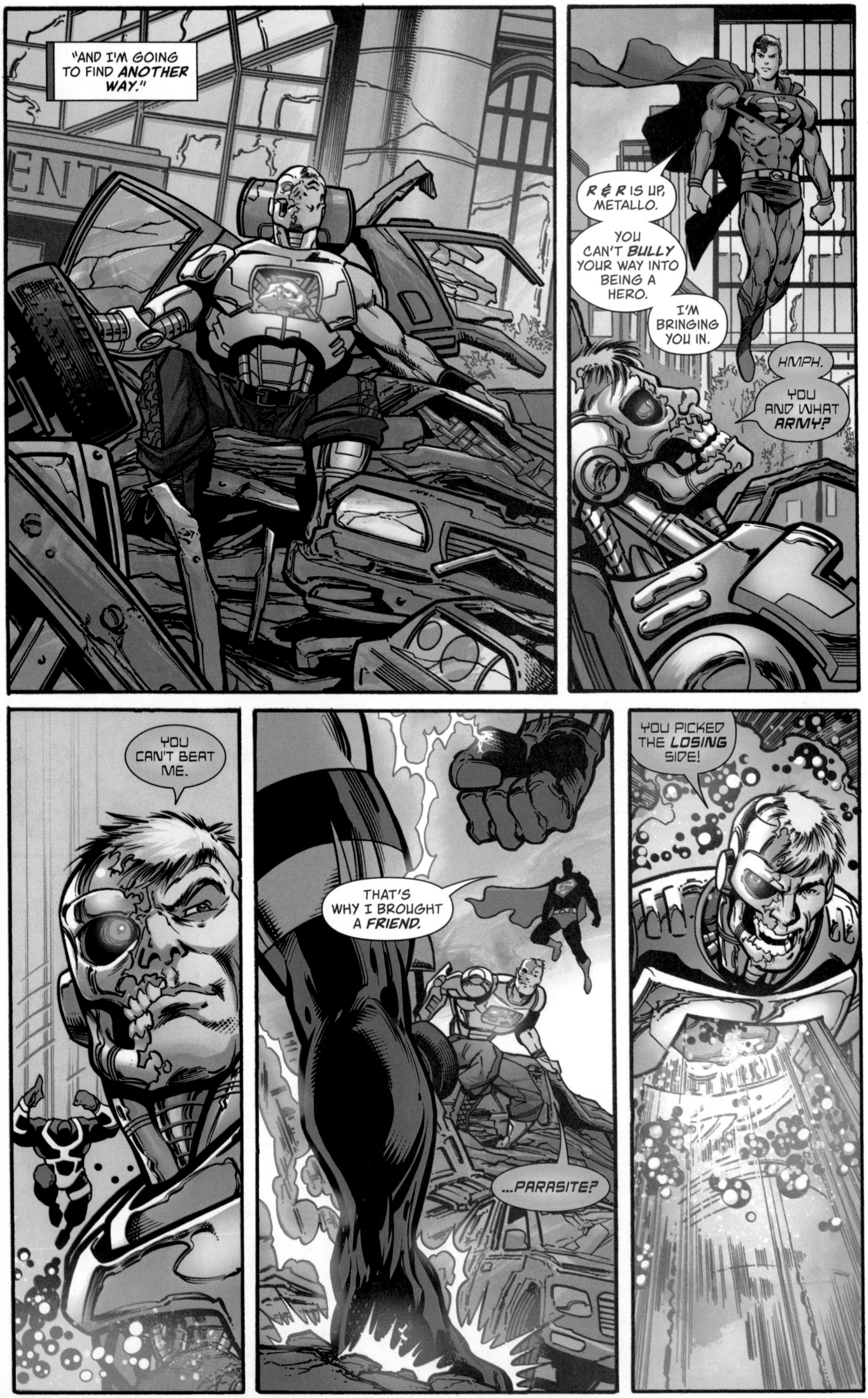
"AND I'M GOING TO FIND ANOTHER WAY."
R & R IS UP, METALLO.
YOU CAN'T BULLY YOUR WAY INTO BEING A HERO.
I'M BRINGING YOU IN.
HMPH.
YOU AND WHAT ARMY?
YOU CAN'T BEAT ME.
THAT'S WHY I BROUGHT A FRIEND.
...PARASITE?
YOU PICKED THE LOSING SIDE!

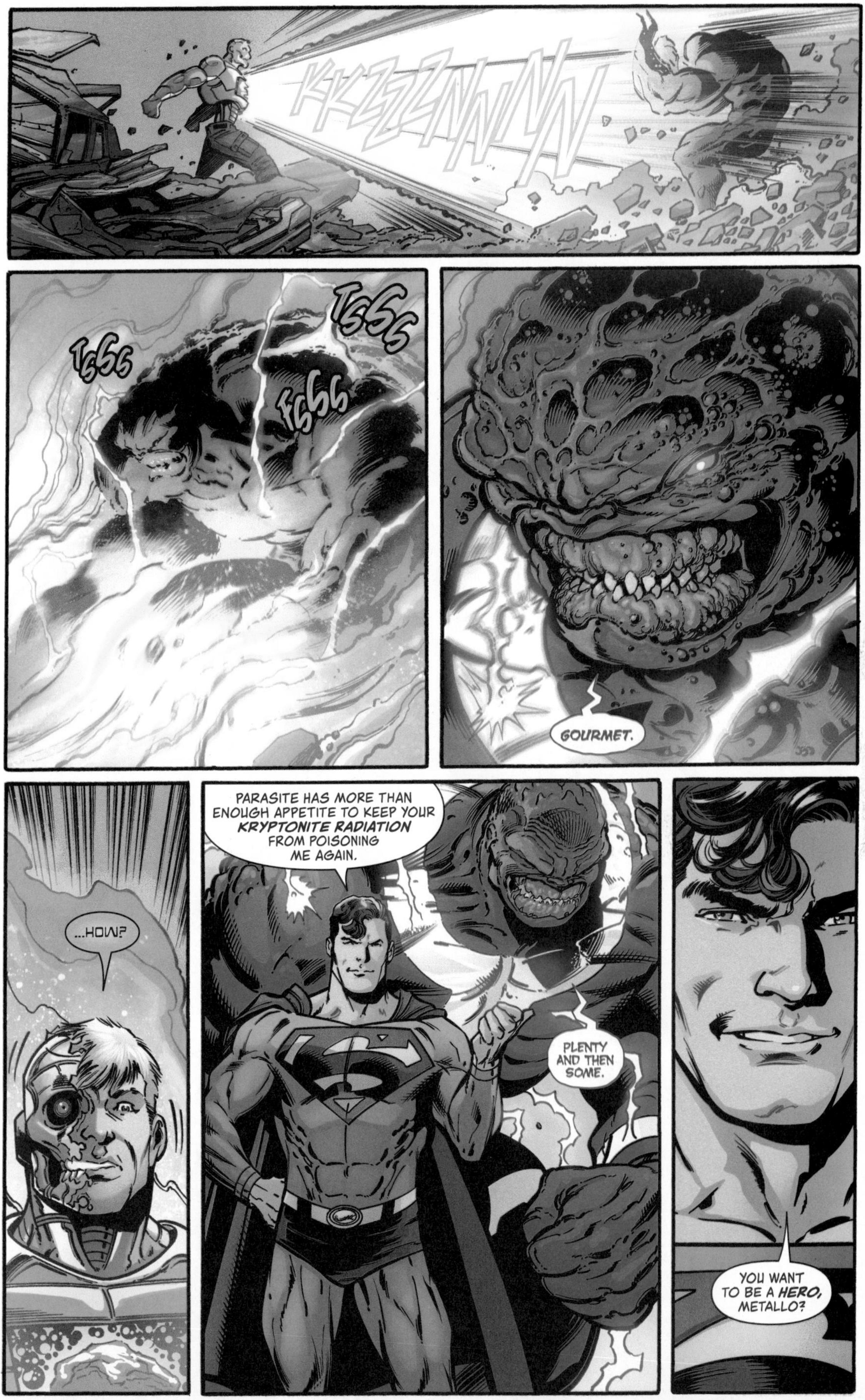
KKZZZNNNNN
TSSS
TSSS
TSSS
GOURMET.
...HOW?
PARASITE HAS MORE THAN ENOUGH APPETITE TO KEEP YOUR ***KRYPTONITE RADIATION*** FROM POISONING ME AGAIN.
PLENTY AND THEN SOME.
YOU WANT TO BE A ***HERO,*** METALLO?

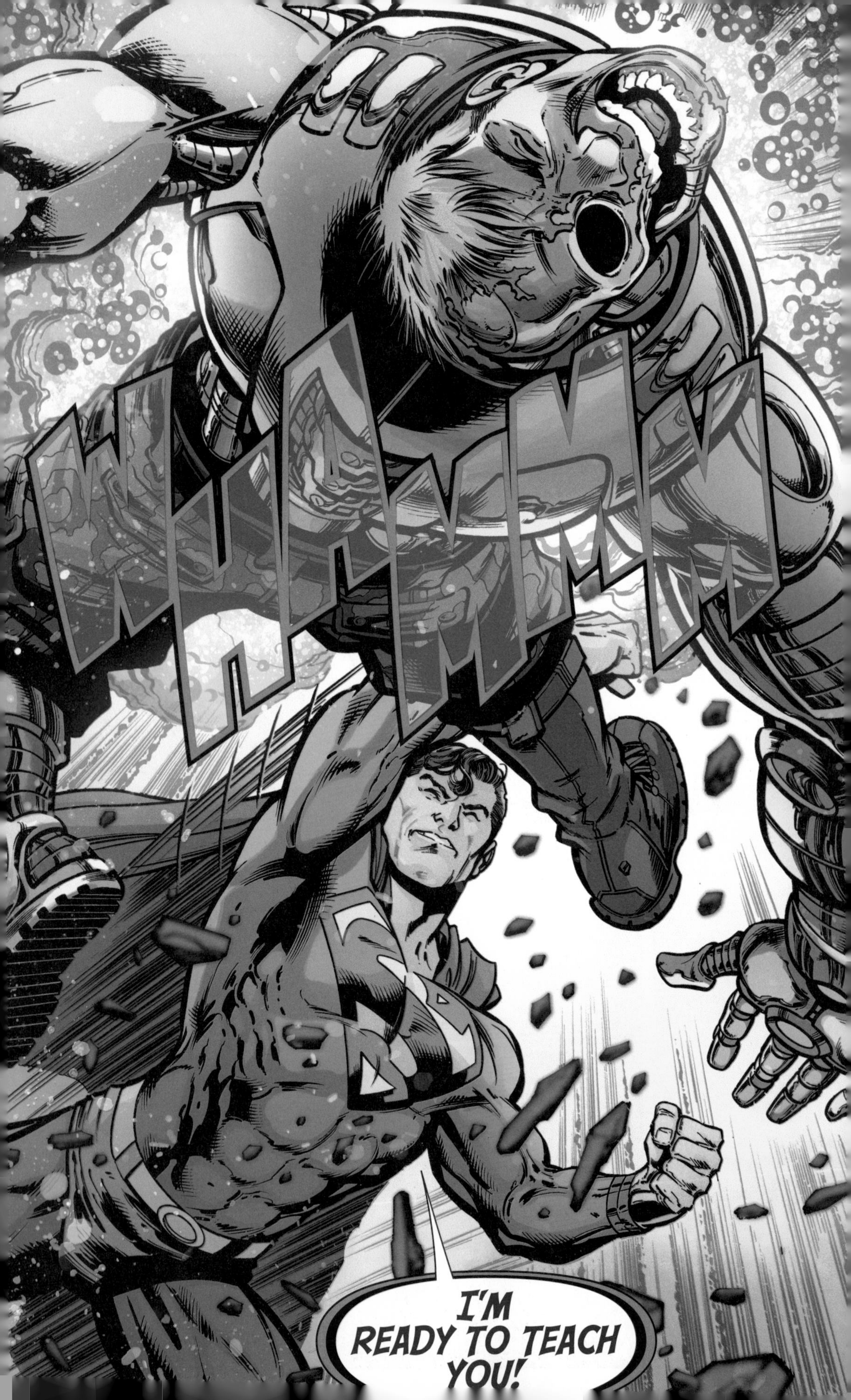
WHAMMM
I'M READY TO TEACH YOU!

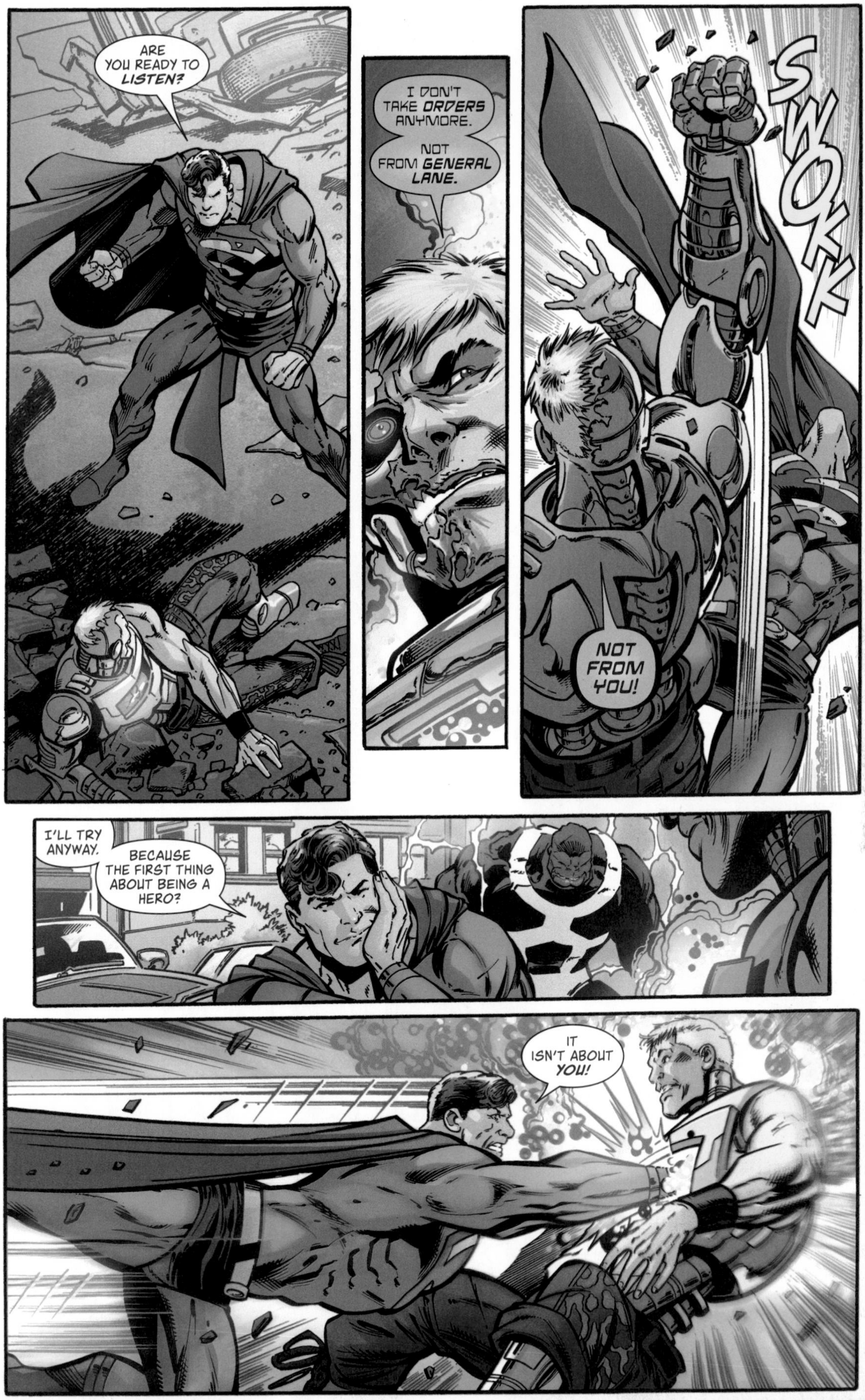
ARE YOU READY TO LISTEN?
I DON'T TAKE ORDERS ANYMORE.
NOT FROM GENERAL LANE.
SWOKK
NOT FROM YOU!
I'LL TRY ANYWAY.
BECAUSE THE FIRST THING ABOUT BEING A HERO?
IT ISN'T ABOUT YOU!

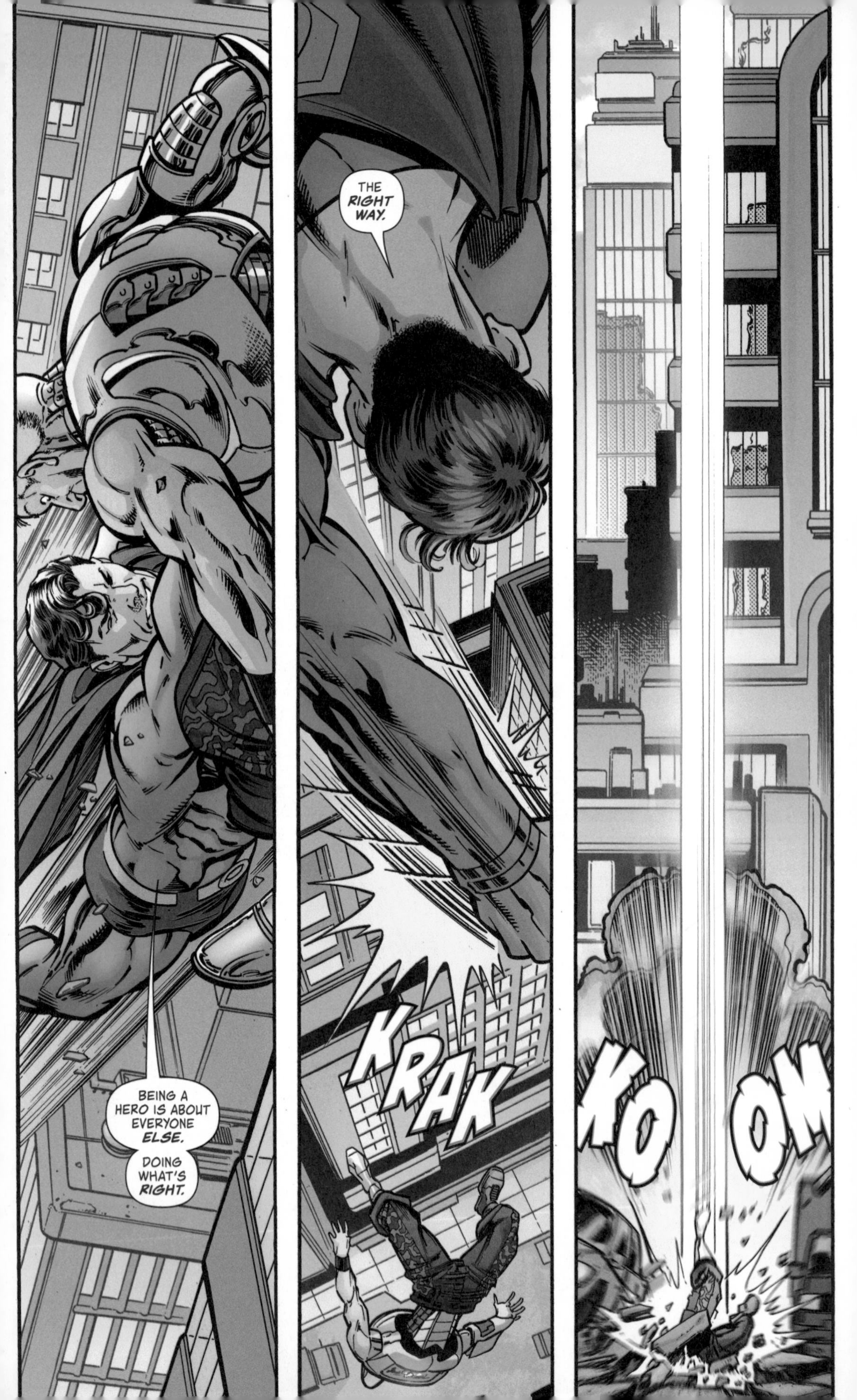
BEING A HERO IS ABOUT EVERYONE ELSE.
DOING WHAT'S RIGHT.
THE RIGHT WAY.
KRAK
KO OM

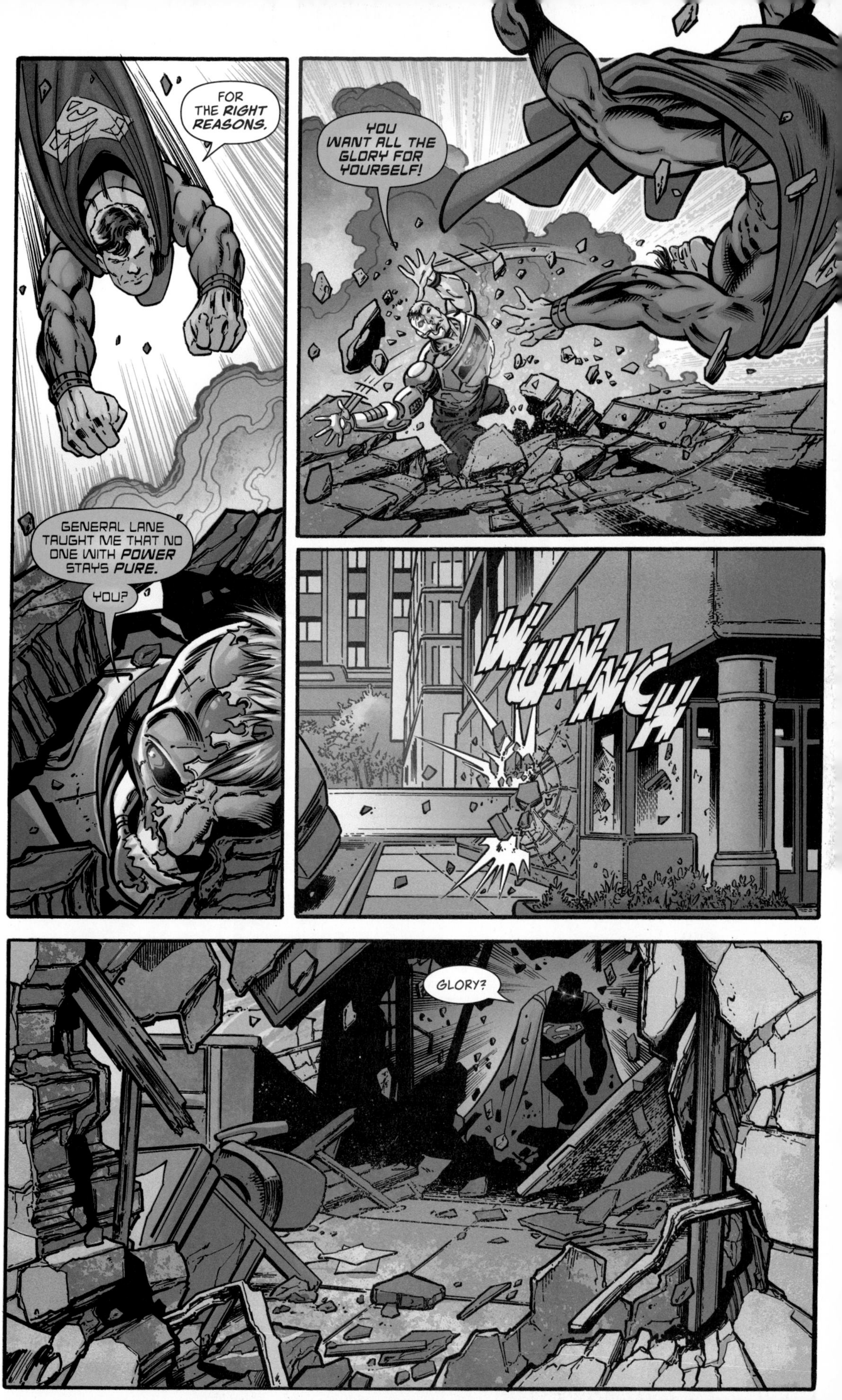
FOR THE RIGHT REASONS.
YOU WANT ALL THE GLORY FOR YOURSELF!
GENERAL LANE TAUGHT ME THAT NO ONE WITH POWER STAYS PURE.
YOU?
WUNNCH
GLORY?

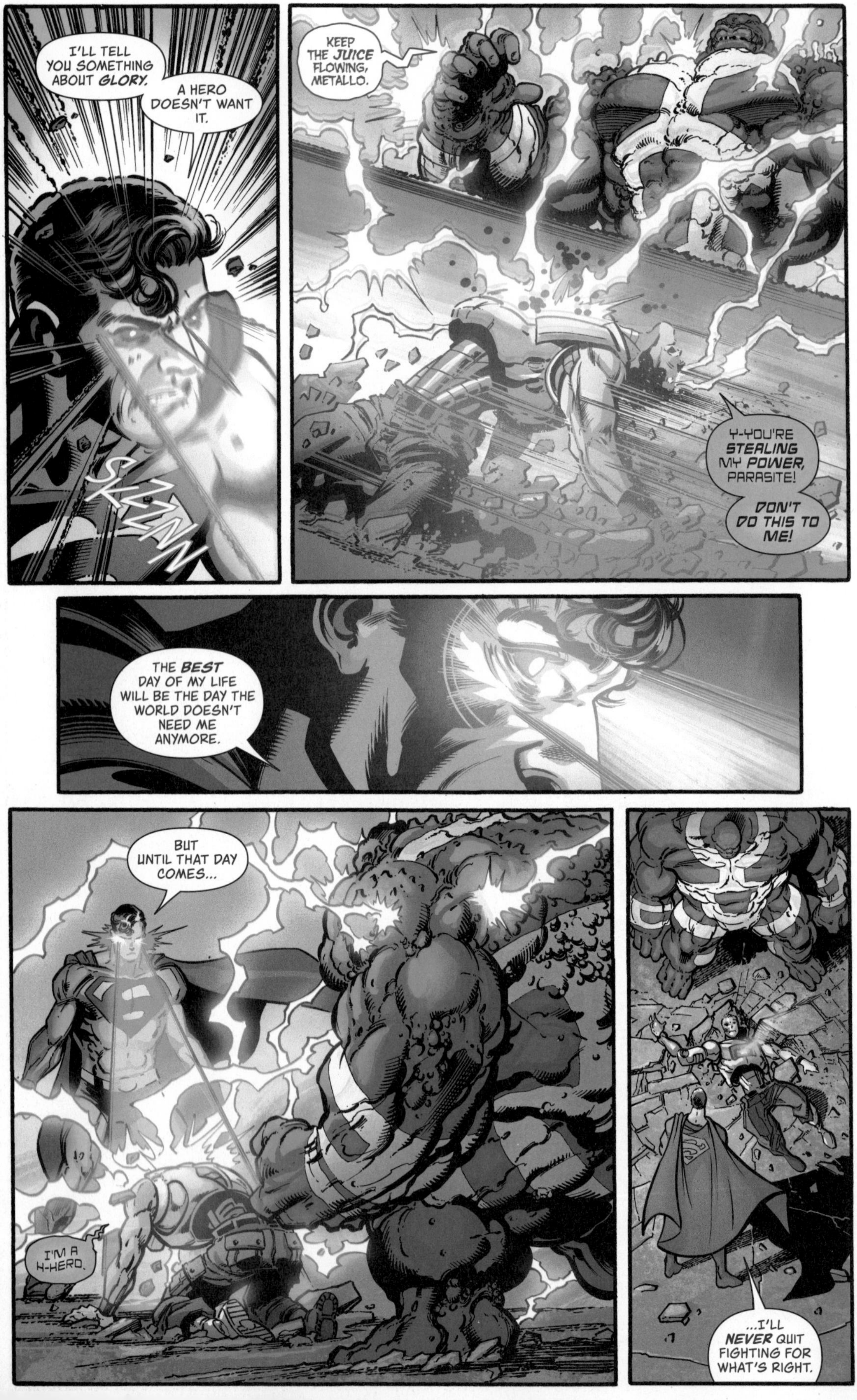
I'LL TELL YOU SOMETHING ABOUT GLORY.
A HERO DOESN'T WANT IT.
SKZZNN
KEEP THE JUICE FLOWING, METALLO.
Y-YOU'RE STEALING MY POWER, PARASITE!
DON'T DO THIS TO ME!
THE BEST DAY OF MY LIFE WILL BE THE DAY THE WORLD DOESN'T NEED ME ANYMORE.
BUT UNTIL THAT DAY COMES...
I'M A H-HERO.
...I'LL NEVER QUIT FIGHTING FOR WHAT'S RIGHT.

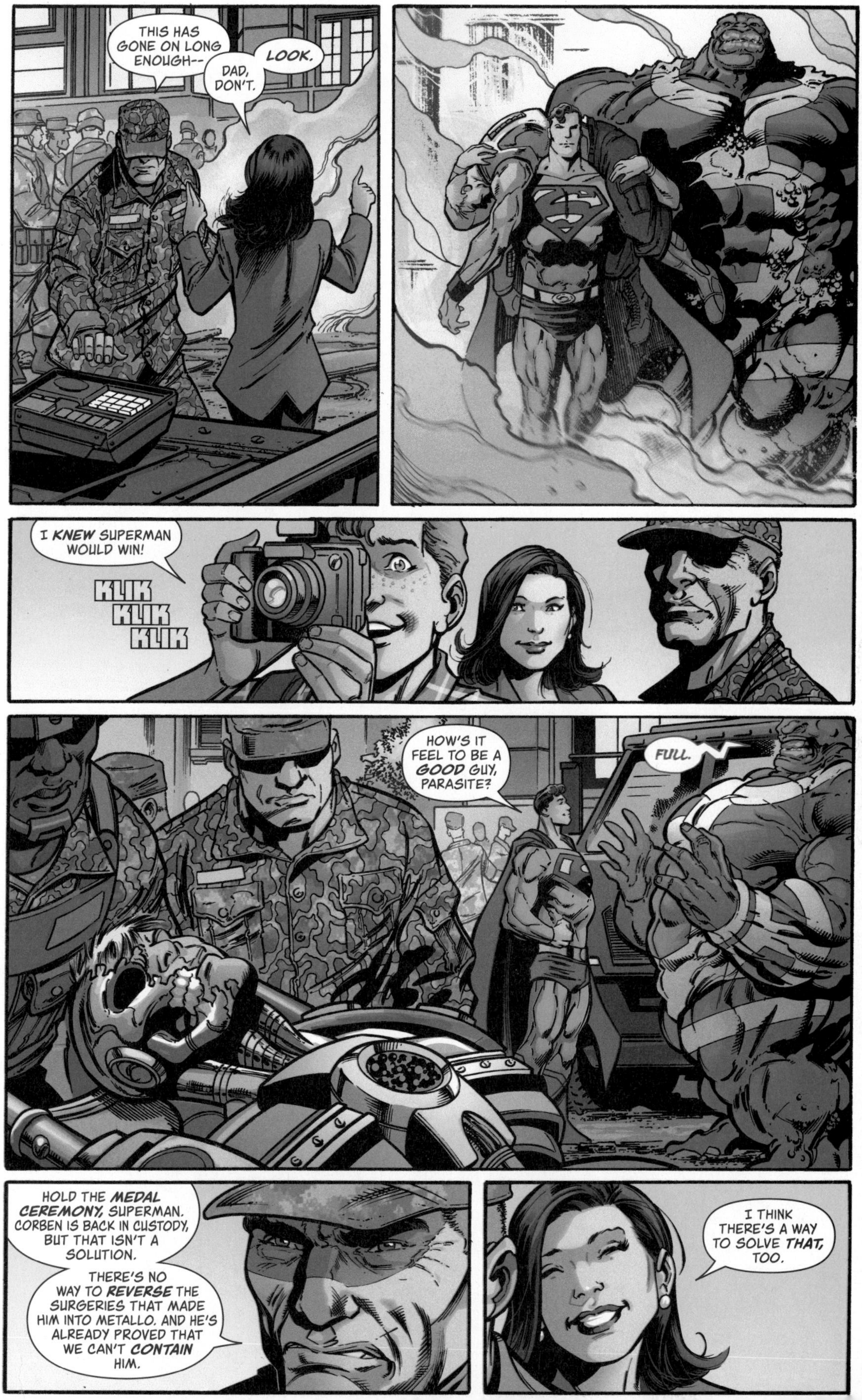
THIS HAS GONE ON LONG ENOUGH--
LOOK.
DAD, DON'T.
I KNEW SUPERMAN WOULD WIN!
KLIK KLIK KLIK
HOW'S IT FEEL TO BE A GOOD GUY, PARASITE?
FULL.
HOLD THE MEDAL CEREMONY, SUPERMAN. CORBEN IS BACK IN CUSTODY, BUT THAT ISN'T A SOLUTION.
THERE'S NO WAY TO REVERSE THE SURGERIES THAT MADE HIM INTO METALLO. AND HE'S ALREADY PROVED THAT WE CAN'T CONTAIN HIM.
I THINK THERE'S A WAY TO SOLVE THAT, TOO.

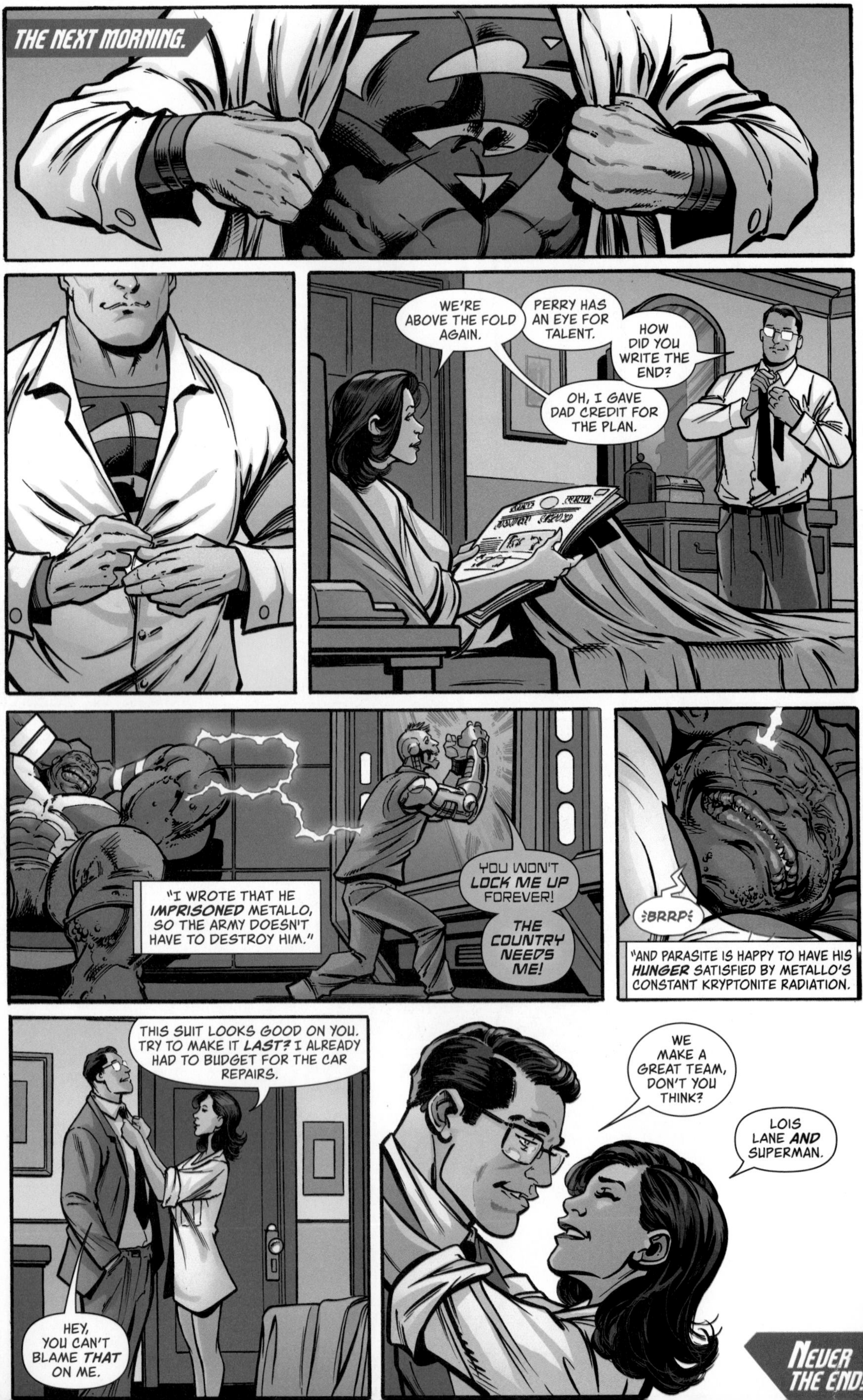
THE NEXT MORNING.
WE'RE ABOVE THE FOLD AGAIN.
PERRY HAS AN EYE FOR TALENT.
HOW DID YOU WRITE THE END?
OH, I GAVE DAD CREDIT FOR THE PLAN.
"I WROTE THAT HE IMPRISONED METALLO, SO THE ARMY DOESN'T HAVE TO DESTROY HIM."
YOU WON'T LOCK ME UP FOREVER!
THE COUNTRY NEEDS ME!
BRRP
"AND PARASITE IS HAPPY TO HAVE HIS HUNGER SATISFIED BY METALLO'S CONSTANT KRYPTONITE RADIATION.
THIS SUIT LOOKS GOOD ON YOU. TRY TO MAKE IT LAST? I ALREADY HAD TO BUDGET FOR THE CAR REPAIRS.
HEY, YOU CAN'T BLAME THAT ON ME.
WE MAKE A GREAT TEAM, DON'T YOU THINK?
LOIS LANE AND SUPERMAN.
NEVER THE END!

THE *MAN OF TOMORROW* SKETCHBOOK

Take a peek behind the curtain at the designs and process of the amazing artists who brought *Superman: Man of Tomorrow* to life!

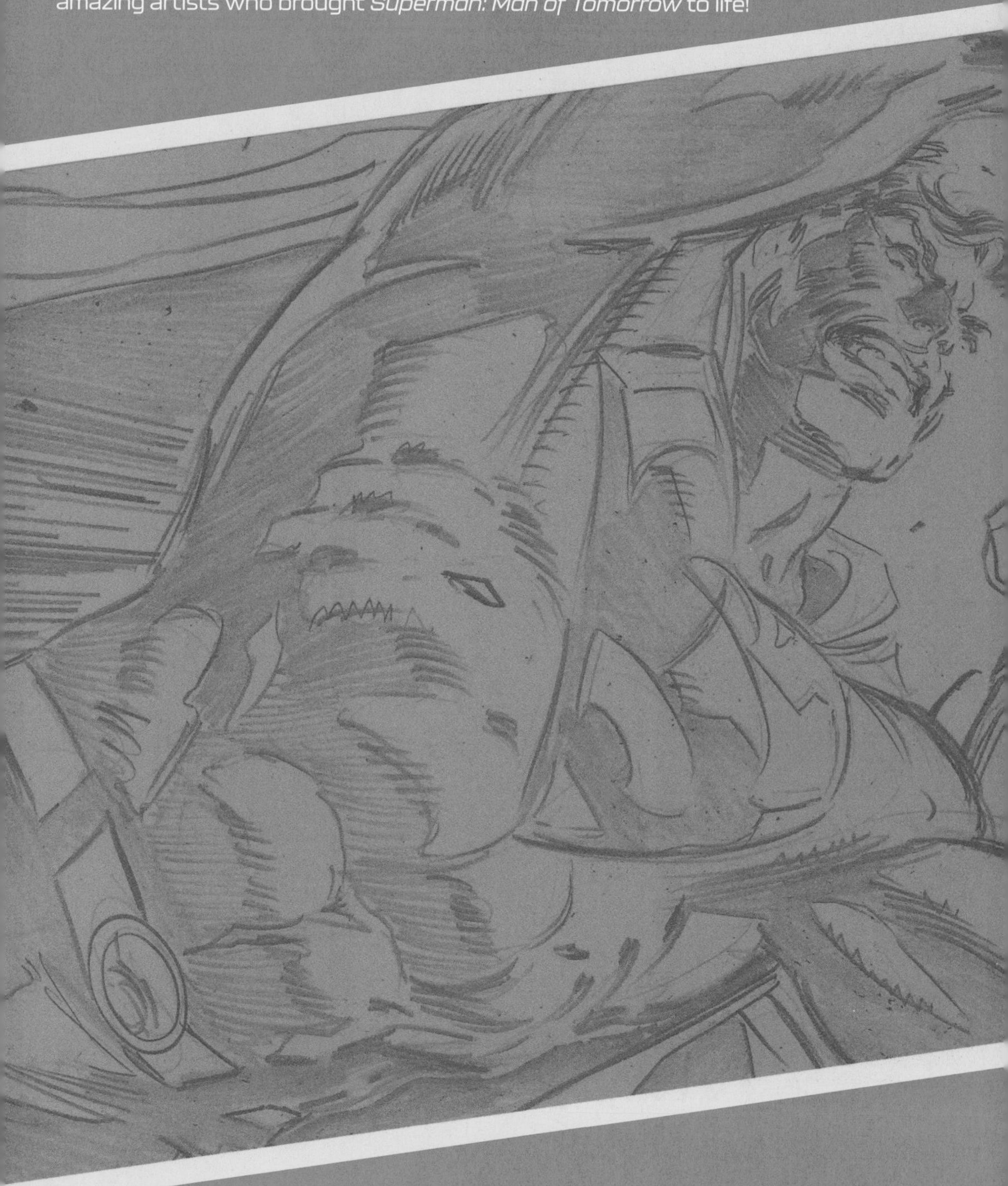

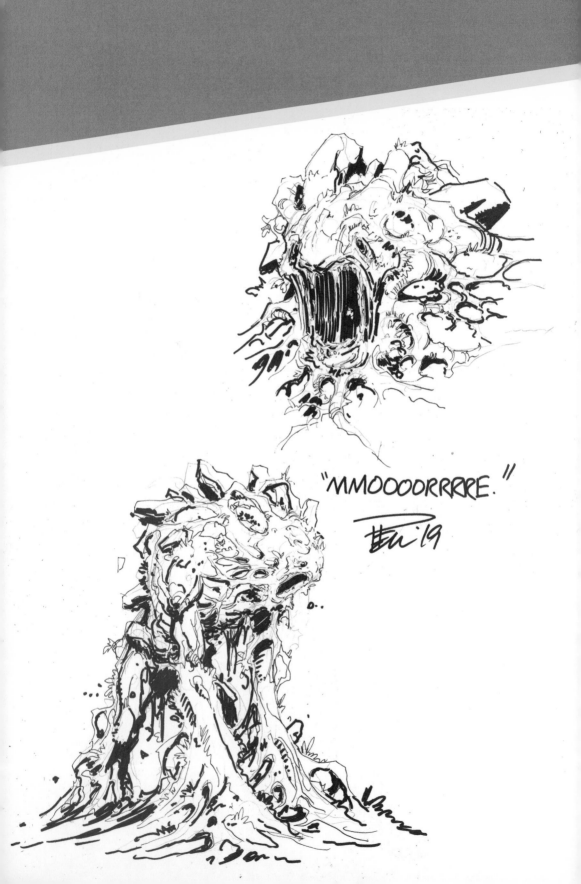

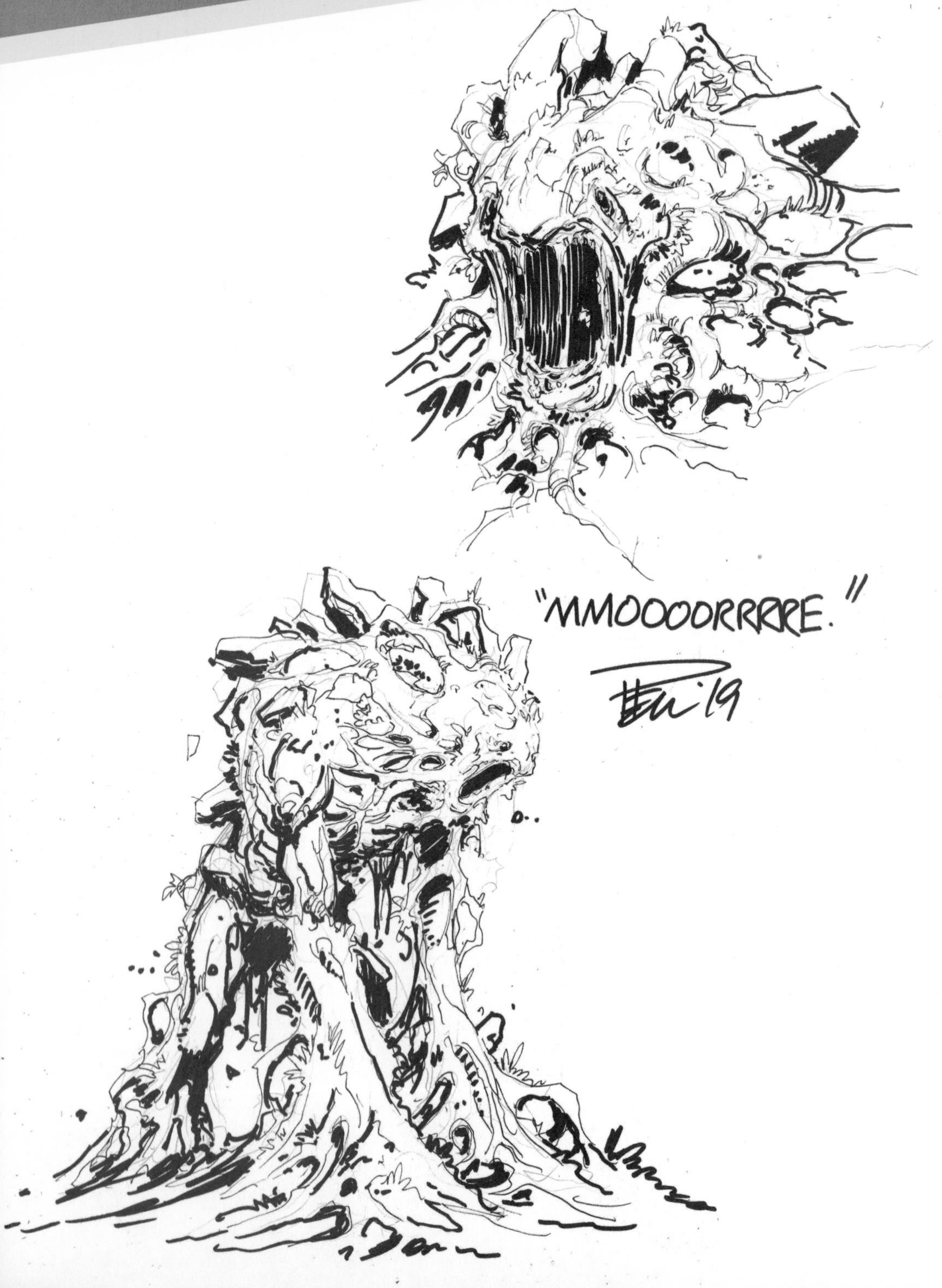
"MMOOOORRRRE."

Grikus Design by **GLEB MELNIKOV**

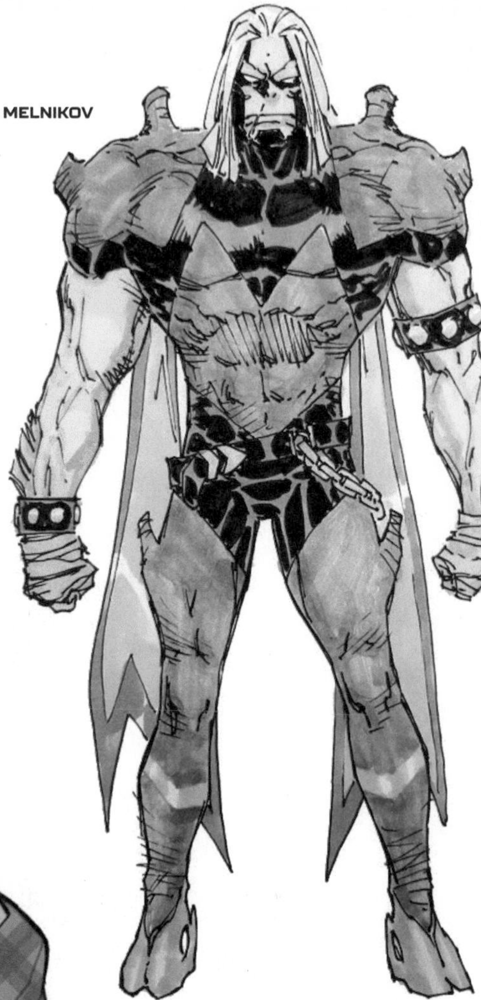

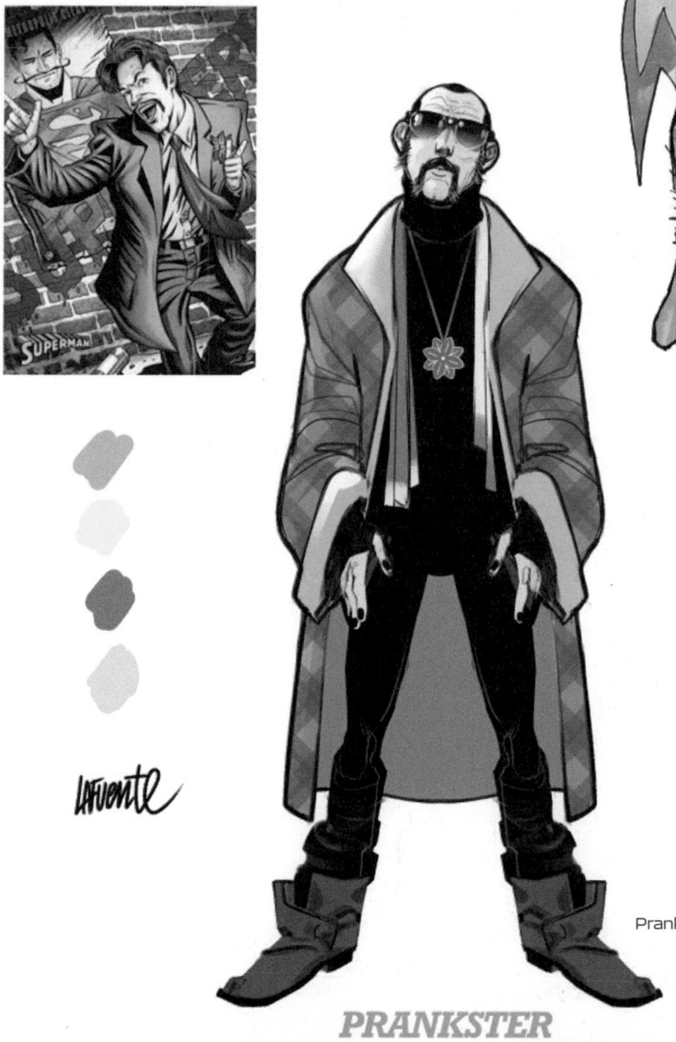
SUPERMAN
LAFUENTE
PRANKSTER

Prankster Design by **DAVID LAFUENTE**

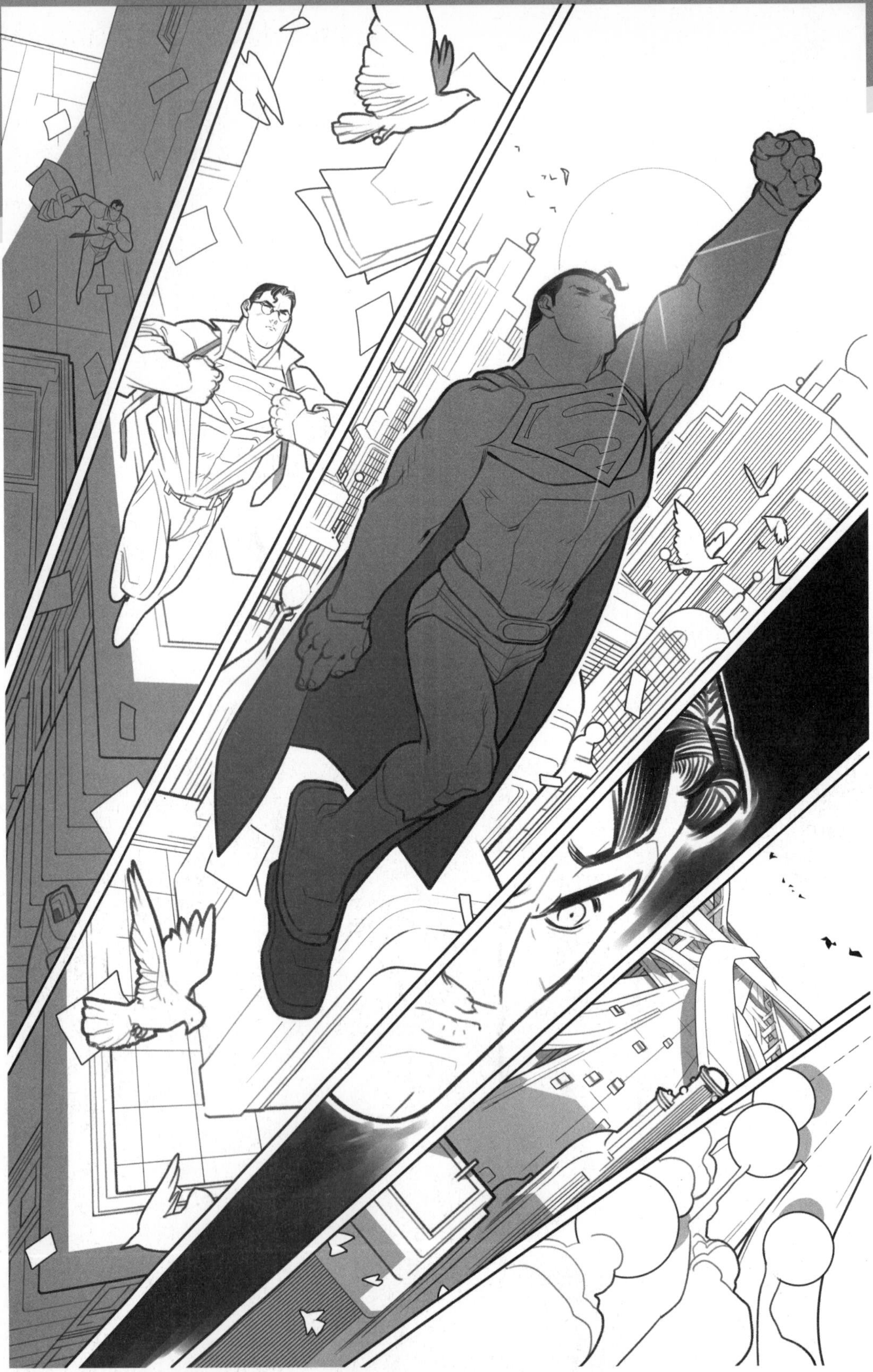

Page 6 from *Superman: Man of Tomorrow* #13 by **DAVID LAFUENTE**

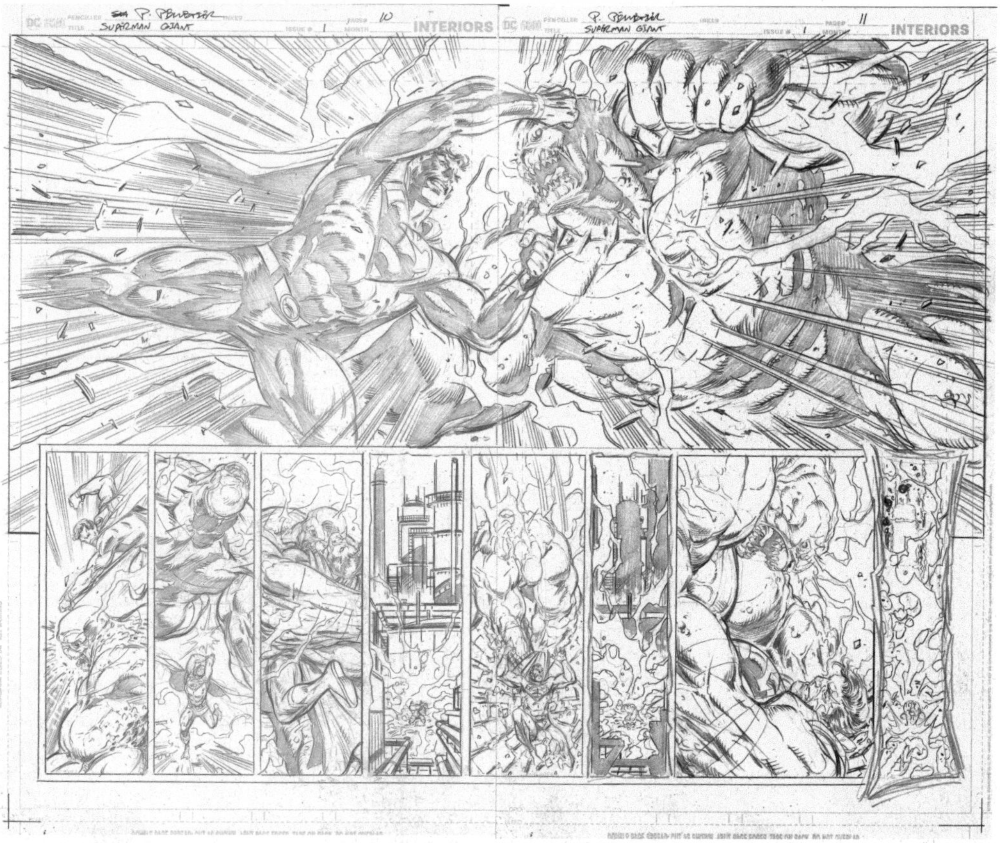
INTERIORS
INTERIORS

Pages 10-11 Pencils from *Superman: Man of Tomorrow* #13 by **PAUL PELLETIER**

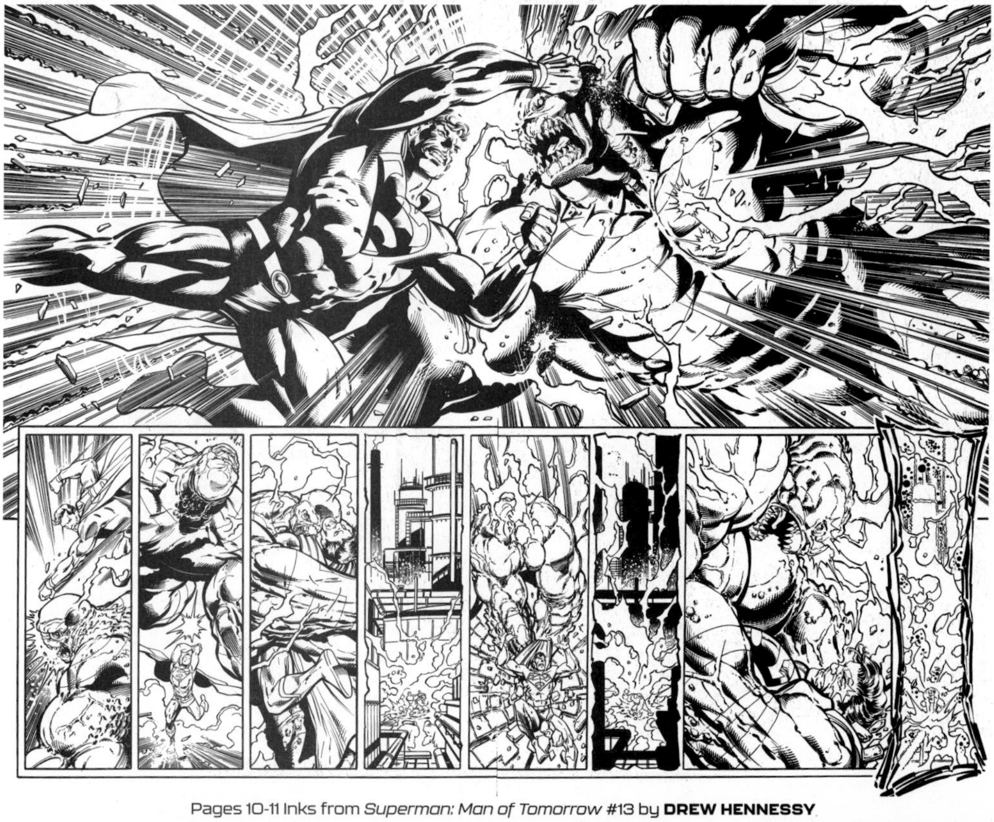

Pages 10-11 Inks from *Superman: Man of Tomorrow* #13 by **DREW HENNESSY**

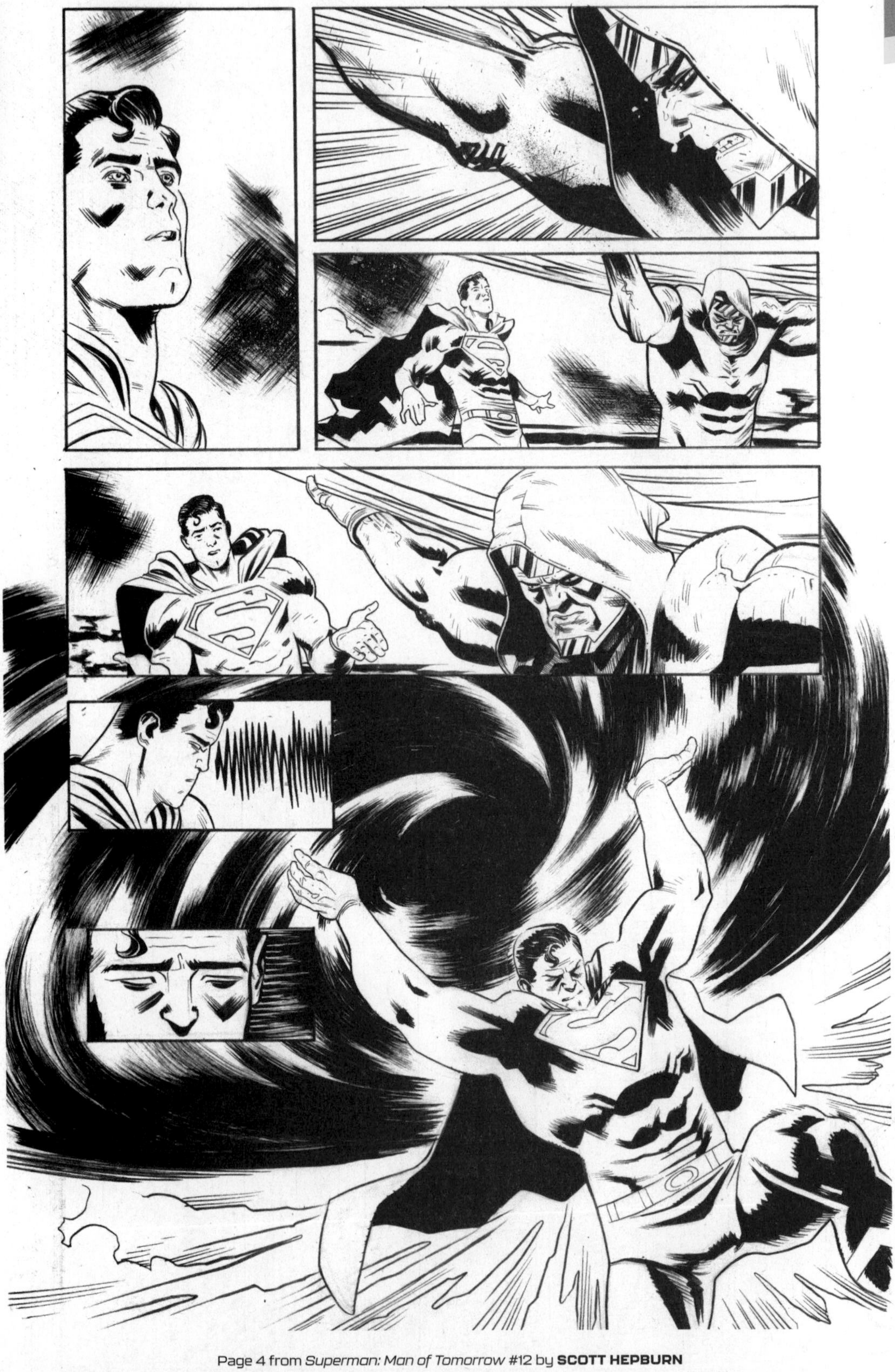

Page 4 from *Superman: Man of Tomorrow* #12 by **SCOTT HEPBURN**